A Companion to Digital Humanitie

C000177790

Blackwell Companions to Literature and Culture

This series offers comprehensive, newly written surveys of key periods and movements and certain major authors, in English literary culture and history. Extensive volumes provide new perspectives and positions on contexts and on canonical and post-canonical texts, orientating the beginning student in new fields of study and providing the experienced undergraduate and new graduate with current and new directions, as pioneered and developed by leading scholars in the field.

Published

A COMPANION TO

$\mathcal{D}$IGITAL $\mathcal{H}$UMANITIES

EDITED BY **SUSAN SCHREIBMAN**,
RAY SIEMENS AND **JOHN UNSWORTH**

Blackwell
Publishing

BLACKWELL PUBLISHING
350 Main Street, Malden, MA 02148-5020, USA
108 Cowley Road, Oxford OX4 1JF, UK
550 Swanston Street, Carlton, Victoria 3053, Australia

First published 2004 by Blackwell Publishing Ltd

Library of Congress Cataloging-in-Publication Data

A companion to digital humanities/edited by Susan Schreibman, Ray Siemens,
and John Unsworth.
    p. cm. – (Blackwell companions to literature and culture; 26)
  Includes bibliographical references and index.
   ISBN 1-4051-0321-3 (hardcover : alk. paper)
  1. Humanities–Data processing. 2. Humanities–Research–Data processing.
3. Information storage and retrieval systems–Humanities. I. Schreibman, Susan. II. Siemens, Raymond
George, 1966- (John M.) IV. Series III. Unsworth, John.

AZ105.C588 2004
001.3'0285–dc22

                                     2004004337

A catalogue record for this title is available from the British Library.

Set in 10.5/12.5pt Garamond 3
by Kolam Information Services Pvt. Ltd, Pondicherry, India
Printed and bound in the United Kingdom
by TJ International, Padstow, Cornwall

For further information on
Blackwell Publishing, visit our website:
http://www.blackwellpublishing.com

Contents

Notes on Contributors

Howard Besser is Director of the Moving Image Archive and Preservation Program at New York University's Tisch School of the Arts. He has been extensively involved in the movement to construct digital libraries and museums, and has taught, researched, and published extensively in the areas of technological change, and the social and cultural impact of new information environments.

John Bradley was the original author and designer of TACT from 1985 until 1992. He now works within the Centre for Computing in the Humanities at King's College London, where he is involved in both teaching and research. His research interests focus on alternative approaches to computer-assisted textual analysis, and on issues that arise from the modeling of historical data in computing systems. He has played an important role in the design and implementation of systems behind the Prosopographies of the Byzantine Empire/World and of Anglo-Saxon England, of the Clergy of the Church of England, of the Corpus Vitrearum Medii Aevi and the Corpus of Romanesque Sculpture in Britain and Ireland, of the Stellenbibliographie zum "Parzival" Wolframs von Eschenbach, of the Modern Poetry in Translation website, and a number of other research projects.

John Burrows is Emeritus Professor of English at the University of Newcastle, NSW, Australia, and was the Foundation Director of the Centre for Literary and Linguistic Computing in that university. His many publications in the field of computational stylistics include *Computation into Criticism* (1987). In 2001 he became the second recipient of the Roberto Busa Award for Humanities Computing. The lecture he gave on that occasion appeared in *Computers and the Humanities* (February 2003).

Roberto A. Busa entered the Jesuit order in 1933, and was ordained priest on May 20, 1940. He is Professor of Philosophy at Aloisianum's Department of Philosophy in

Gallarate, at Gregorian Pontifical University in Rome, and at the Catholic University in Milan. He is internationally recognized as the pioneer of computational linguistics.

Hugh Craig is Director of the Centre for Literary and Linguistic Computing at the University of Newcastle, NSW, Australia. He also teaches English in the School of Language and Media where he is currently Head of School. His research in recent years has been in computational stylistics, applying evidence from the frequencies of very common words to authorial and stylistic problems in Early Modern English literature.

Greg Crane is Winnick Family Chair of Technology and Entrepreneurship, Professor of Classics and Director of the Perseus Project at Tufts University. Originally trained as a classicist, his current interests focus more generally on the application of information technology to the humanities.

Marilyn Deegan has a PhD in medieval studies: her specialism is Anglo-Saxon medical texts and herbals and she has published and lectured widely in medieval studies, digital library research, and humanities computing. She is Director of Research Development, Centre for Computing in the Humanities, King's College London, and was formerly Director of Forced Migration Online at the Refugee Studies Centre at Oxford University, a major digital library and portal for materials concerned with all aspects of refugee studies. She is Editor-in-Chief of *Literary and Linguistic Computing*, the Journal of the Association for Literary and Linguistic Computing, and Director of Publications for the Office for Humanities Communication based at King's College London. Dr. Deegan has recently published a book, *Digital Futures: Strategies for the Information Age*, with Simon Tanner.

Johanna Drucker is currently the Robertson Professor of Media Studies at the University of Virginia, where she is Professor in the Department of English and Director of Media Studies. She helped establish the Speculative Computing Laboratory in 2000 to explore experimental projects in humanities computing. She is well known for her work in the history of written forms, typography, design, and visual poetics. Her scholarly books include: *Theorizing Modernism* (1994), *The Visible Word: Experimental Typography and Modern Art* (1994); *The Alphabetic Labyrinth* (1995), and *The Century of Artists' Books* (1995). Her most recent collection, *Figuring the Word*, was published in November 1998.

Harrison Eiteljorg, II, is a classical archaeologist who specializes in the architecture of classical Greece. He has worked to use computer technology in his own work and to explore how that technology can best be applied to the work of archaeologists generally.

Charles Ess is Distinguished Research Professor, Interdisciplinary Studies, Drury University, Springfield, Missouri. He researches, lectures, and publishes on Internet research ethics and, with Fay Sudweeks, organizes conferences and edits publications on cultural attitudes toward technology and computer-mediated communication.

Ichiro Fujinaga is an Assistant Professor at the Faculty of Music at McGill University and the Chair of the Music Technology Area. He has degrees in music/percussion and mathematics from the University of Alberta, and a Master's degree in music theory, and a PhD in music technology from McGill University.

Michael Greenhalgh has been interested in computing applications in the humanities since playing with a Commodore PET-2001 in 1977 at Leicester University, England.

Graduating to large Cyber machines, PDP 11s and then VAXes, and writing books on them, he started teaching humanities computing courses in 1980. Elected to the Sir William Dobell Foundation Chair in Art History at the Australian National University in 1987, he introduced similar courses there and, using powerful graphics machines, was ready with over 300 digitized images to start his web-server "ArtServe" (<http://rubens.anu.edu.au>) in January 1994. This server now offers over 190,000 images, and receives about 1.3 million hits per week. Since 1997, his lecturing and seminar work has been done exclusively over the network from servers, via a video projector.

Jan Hajič is an Associate Professor of Computational Linguistics at Charles University, Prague, Czech Republic. His interests range from morphology of inflective languages to syntax and treebanking to machine translation, using extensively statistical methods in natural language processing. He has previously worked at Johns Hopkins University (Maryland), and at IBM Research (New York).

Susan Hockey was Professor of Library and Information Studies and Director of the School of Library, Archive, and Information Studies at University College London until July 31, 2004. She was Chair of the Association for Literary and Linguistic Computing (1984–97) and a member, twice Chair, of the Steering Committee for the Text Encoding Initiative. Her current interests are markup technologies for the humanities and the history of humanities computing.

Nancy Ide is Professor and Chair of Computer Science at Vassar College in Poughkeepsie, New York. She has been involved in humanities computing and computational linguistics for 20 years. She was president of the Association for Computers and the Humanities from 1985 to 1995, and is currently co-editor of the journal *Computers and the Humanities*. She is also co-editor of the Kluwer book series Text, Speech, and Language Technology, and has co-directed the past four EUROLAN summer schools on various topics in computational linguistics. In 1987 she spearheaded the Text Encoding Initiative and served on its steering committee until 1997. She has published numerous papers on the application of statistical methods to language analysis, including computational lexicography, word sense disambiguation, and discourse analysis. Most recently she has been involved in developing standards for the representation of linguistically annotated resources, the creation of the American National Corpus, the development of an "intelligently searchable" corpus for historical research comprising materials from the Franklin D. Roosevelt Library, and adapting language processing practices to the Semantic Web.

Michael Jensen was recently appointed Director of Web Communications for the National Academies: the National Academy of Sciences, the National Research Council, the Institute of Medicine, and the National Academy of Engineering. He remains Director of Publishing Technologies at the National Academies Press, which makes more than 2,800 books (more than 500,000 pages) fully searchable and browsable online for free. In the mid-1990s, he helped establish Project Muse, the pioneering online journals project of Johns Hopkins University Press. For the University of Nebraska Press, he produced the first searchable publisher's catalogue available on the Internet, via Telnet, in 1990.

Matthew G. Kirschenbaum is Assistant Professor of English and Digital Studies at the University of Maryland, College Park. He does both theoretical and applied work in the digital humanities, participating in projects from the William Blake Archive to the

Electronic Literature Organization. He has long-standing interests in images, interface, and visualization, and is co-developer of a software tool called the Virtual Lightbox. His book-in-progress, entitled *Mechanisms: New Media and the New Textuality*, is forthcoming from the MIT Press.

Robert Kolker is the author of a number of books in cinema studies, including the third edition of *A Cinema of Loneliness: Penn, Stone, Kubrick, Scorsese, and Altman* (2000). His textbook, *Film, Form, and Culture* (2nd edn., 2002) is an introduction to film with an accompanying interactive CD-ROM, containing moving image clips. Kolker was one of the first film scholars to put moving images on the Web, in a *Postmodern Culture* essay, "The Moving Image Reclaimed." He will soon publish a Casebook of essays on Hitchcock's *Psycho* and a critical work, *Dreadful Landscapes in the Spaces of Modernity: Welles, Kubrick and the Imagination of the Visible*. He has been Professor of English at the University of Maryland, and Chair of the School of Literature, Communication, and Culture at Georgia Tech.

Ian Lancashire, Professor of English at the University of Toronto, founded the Center for Computing in the Humanities there in 1986 and co-developed TACT (Text Analysis Computing Tools), with which he does research on Chaucer and Shakespeare. He now edits *Representative Poetry Online*, teaches a fully online course in reading poetry, develops the Early Modern English Dictionaries (LEME) database, and is a member of the Inter-PARES2 project. From 1992 to 2003 he presided over a Canadian learned society, the Consortium for Computers in the Humanities/Consortium pour ordinateurs en sciences humaines (COCH/COSH).

Andrea Laue is a PhD candidate at the University of Virginia. She is a technical editor for the William Blake Archive, a researcher in the Speculative Computing Lab, and a graduate instructor in the media studies program. Her research interests include narratology, cognitive poetics, textual studies, digital media, and information visualization. In her dissertation, she investigates narrative structuring as manifested in the emergent text, the nexus produced by the interactions of an interpreter and a literary artifact.

Andrew Mactavish is an Assistant Professor of Multimedia in the School of the Arts at McMaster University. He has published and presented papers in the areas of computer games, humanities computing, and multimedia. He currently holds a research grant from the Social Sciences and Humanities Research Council of Canada (SSHRC) to study the cultural politics of computer game play. He is also a member of collaborative research projects, including Globalization and Autonomy (SSHRC-MCRI) and two projects funded by the Canada Foundation for Innovation: TAPoR (Text Analysis Portal for Research) and IRIS (Infrastructure for Research on Internet Streaming).

Willard McCarty is Senior Lecturer in Humanities Computing, King's College London, and editor of *Humanist*. Recently his research has centered on modeling and more broadly explored the intellectual integrity of humanities computing by probing and interrelating its disciplinary kinships. He is currently finishing a book on the field, for which the chapter included here is a preview. His primary research on modeling has drawn heavily on his *Analytical Onomasticon to the Metamorphoses of Ovid*, forthcoming when a sufficiently adventurous publisher can be found. Details at <www.kcl.ac.uk/cch/wlm>.

Jerome McGann is the John Stewart Bryan University Professor, University of Virginia and Adjunct Professor at Royal Holloway, University of London. His recent book *Radiant*

Textuality: Literature after the World Wide Web, was awarded the Modern Language Association's James Russell Lowell Award (2002). He is currently developing digital resources for the interpretation of literary works. These include the collaborative environment IVANHOE and the 'Patacritical Demon.

Bethany Nowviskie is a doctoral candidate at the University of Virginia. She serves as design editor for the Rossetti Archive, and is the lead designer and manager of the Temporal Modeling Project. Her other SpecLab projects include Biblioludica, the Ivanhoe Game, and the 'Patacritical Demon. Nowviskie's dissertation theorizes and describes the production of digital environments that both promote humanistic interpretation and emerge from the interpretative acts of their users.

Carole L. Palmer is an Associate Professor at the Graduate School of Library and Information Science at the University of Illinois at Urbana–Champaign. Her research explores how information systems and services can best support the work of researchers. She is engaged in projects to develop information technologies that support interdisciplinary inquiry, discovery, and collaboration in the humanities and the sciences. Her recent publications include *Scholarly Work in the Humanities and the Evolving Information Environment* and *Work at the Boundaries of Science: Information and the Interdisciplinary Research Process*.

Daniel V. Pitti is project director at the Institute for Advanced Technology in the Humanities (IATH) at the University of Virginia. As project director, he is responsible for project design in general, and Extensible Markup Language (XML) and object-relational databases design and development in particular. Before coming to IATH in 1997, he was Librarian for Advanced Technologies Projects at the University of California at Berkeley Library.

Stephen Ramsay worked as a programmer and software engineer for the Institute for Advanced Technology in the Humanities at the University of Virginia before becoming an Assistant Professor of English at the University of Georgia. He edits the online version of the journal *TEXT Technology*, and has lectured widely on subjects related to humanities computing, public policy, and software design.

Allen H. Renear is an Associate Professor in the Graduate School of Library and Information Science (GSLIS) at the University of Illinois, Urbana–Champaign, where he teaches courses in knowledge representation and document modeling, and, as head of the Electronic Publishing Research Group, leads research on XML semantics and document ontology. He has been involved in humanities-oriented electronic publishing, standards development, and research for over twenty years. Currently Chair of the Open eBook Publication Structure Working Group, he has served as President of the Association for Computers and the Humanities, on the Advisory Board of the Text Encoding Initiative, and prior to joining GSLIS, was Director of the Scholarly Technology Group at Brown University.

Geoffrey Rockwell is an Associate Professor of Humanities Computing and Multimedia in the School of the Arts at McMaster University. He received a BA in philosophy from Haverford College, an MA and PhD in philosophy from the University of Toronto and worked at the University of Toronto as a Senior Instructional Technology Specialist. He has published and presented papers in the area of textual visualization and analysis, humanities computing, instructional technology, computer games, and multimedia. With colleagues at McMaster University he set up an honors Multimedia program. He is currently the project leader for the CFI (Canada Foundation for Innovation) funded project TAPoR, a Text Analysis Portal for Research, which is developing a text tool portal for researchers who work with electronic texts. He recently published a book, *Defining Dialogue: From Socrates to the Internet* (2003).

Thomas Rommel is Professor of English at International University Bremen (IUB). He is a member of the executive committee of the Association for Literary and Linguistic Computing (ALLC). His publications include a book on Byron's poetry (1995), *Anglistik im Internet* (1996), a study of Adam Smith (1999), and an edition of essays on literary hypertexts (forthcoming). He is co-editor of *Prolepsis, The Heidelberg Review of English Studies*. His research interests include theories of electronic text and the methodological implications of computer-assisted studies of literature.

Marie-Laure Ryan is a native of Geneva, Switzerland, and is currently an independent scholar based in Colorado. She is the author of *Possible Worlds, Artificial Intelligence and Narrative Theory* (1991), and of *Narrative as Virtual Reality: Immersion and Interactivity in Literature and Electronic Media* (2001), which received the Jeanne and Aldo Scaglione Prize for Comparative Literature from the Modern Language Association. She is also the editor of two collections of essays, *Cyberspace Textuality* (1999) and *Narrative Across Media* (2004).

David Z. Saltz is Associate Professor of Drama at the University of Georgia. He is Principal Investigator of Virtual Vaudeville: A Live Performance Simulation System, funded by the NSF, and has published essays about performance theory and interactive media in scholarly books and journals including *Theatre Research International, Performance Research*, and the *Journal of Aesthetics and Art Criticism*. He is also a practicing director and installation artist whose work focuses on the interaction between digital media and live performance.

Susan Schreibman is General Editor and Project Manager of the MacGreevy Archive, and editor of *Collected Poems of Thomas MacGreevy: An Annotated Edition* (1991). She is the founder and editor of the web-based *Irish Resources in the Humanities*. She is currently serving a two-year term on the TEI Council. Dr. Schreibman is Assistant Director of the Maryland Institute for Technology in the Humanities (MITH), and an Affiliate Faculty member in the Department of English. Previously she was an Assistant Professor of Professional and Technical Communication at New Jersey Institute of Technology (2000–1), and the Semester in Irish Studies Newman Fellow at University College Dublin (1997–2000).

Ray Siemens is Canada Research Chair in Humanities Computing and Associate Professor of English at the University of Victoria; formerly, he was Professor of English at Malaspina University-College (1999–2004). He is President (English) of the *Consortium for Computers in the Humanities/Consortium pour ordinateurs en sciences humaines* and, in 2003, was Visiting Senior Research Fellow at the Centre for Computing in the Humanities at King's College London. Director of the Digital Humanities/Humanities Computing Summer Institute, founder of Malaspina University-College's Center for Digital Humanities Innovation, and founding editor of the electronic scholarly journal *Early Modern Literary Studies*, he is also author of works chiefly focusing on areas where literary studies and computational methods intersect, is editor of several Renaissance texts, and is co-editor of several book collections on humanities computing topics.

Abby Smith is Director of Programs at the Council on Library and Information Resources, where her work focuses on the development and preservation of research collections in all formats and genres. She worked as program specialist at the Library of Congress, and taught intellectual and Russian history at Harvard and Johns Hopkins. Her recent publications include: *New-Model Scholarship: How Will It Survive?* (2003); *The Evidence in Hand: Report of the Task Force on the Artifact in Library Collections* (2001); *Strategies for Building Digitized Collections* (2001); *Building and Sustaining Digital Collections: Models for Libraries and Museums* (2001); and *Collections, Content, and the Web* (2000).

Martha Nell Smith is Professor of English and Director of the Maryland Institute for Technology in the Humanities (MITH) at the University of Maryland. Her numerous publications include three award-winning books – *Open Me Carefully: Emily Dickinson's Intimate Letters to Susan Dickinson*, co-authored with Ellen Louise Hart (1998), *Comic Power in Emily Dickinson*, co-authored with Cristanne Miller and Suzanne Juhasz (1993), *Rowing in Eden: Rereading Emily Dickinson* (1992) – and more than thirty articles in such journals as *American Literature*, *Studies in the Literary Imagination*, *South Atlantic Quarterly*, *Women's Studies Quarterly*, *Profils Américains*, *San Jose Studies*, and *The Emily Dickinson Journal*. With Mary Loeffelholz, she is editing the *Blackwell Companion to Emily Dickinson* (forthcoming in 2005). The recipient of numerous awards from the National Endowment for the Humanities (NEH), the American Council of Learned Societies (ACLS), and the Fund for the Improvement of Postsecondary Education (FIPSE) for her work on Dickinson and in new media, Smith is also Coordinator and General Editor of the Dickinson Electronic Archives projects at the Institute for Advanced Technology in the Humanities (IATH) at the University of Virginia. With Lara Vetter, Smith is a general editor of *Emily Dickinson's Correspondences*, forthcoming from the Mellon-sponsored University of Virginia Press Electronic Imprint.

C. M. Sperberg-McQueen is a member of the technical staff of the World Wide Web Consortium, an international membership organization responsible for developing Web standards. He co-edited the XML 1.0 specification and the Guidelines of the Text Encoding Initiative.

Simon Tanner is the Director of Digital Consultancy Services at King's College London (KDCS). He has an international reputation as a consultant and has consulted for prestigious digitization projects in Europe and America. Tanner has a library and information science background and prior to KDCS was Senior Consultant with HEDS Digitization Services and held librarian and systems posts at Loughborough University, Rolls Royce, and IBM. He recently authored a book, *Digital Futures: Strategies for the Information Age*, with Marilyn Deegan; he co-edits the Digital Futures series of books from Facet Publishing and is a guest editor for the *Journal of Digital Information*.

William G. Thomas, III, is an Assistant Professor of History and Director of the Virginia Center for Digital History at the University of Virginia. He is the co-author with Edward L. Ayers of "The Difference Slavery Made: A Close Analysis of Two American Communities," a fully electronic journal article for the *American Historical Review*. He is the author of *Lawyering for the Railroad: Business Law and Power in the New South* (1999) and co-author of the Emmy nominee documentary film *Massive Resistance*. He is currently researching and producing a digital project on the environmental and social history of the Chesapeake Bay.

John Unsworth served from 1993 to 2003 as the first Director of the Institute for Advanced Technology in the Humanities and as faculty in the Department of English at the University of Virginia. As the Institute's Director, he oversaw research projects across the disciplines in the humanities and published widely on electronic scholarship, humanities computing, and other topics. In 2003, he was appointed Dean of the Graduate School of Library and Information Science (GSLIS) at the University of Illinois, Urbana–Champaign, with appointments as Professor in GSLIS, in the Department of English, and on the Library faculty.

Claire Warwick is a lecturer at the School of Library Archive and Information Studies, University College London, where she is programme director of the MA in Electronic Communication and Publishing. She is also a research supervisor for Cambridge University's MSt in International Relations. She has previously worked at Sheffield University, Department of Information Studies, and Oxford University English Faculty and Humanities Computing Unit, and at Chadwyck-Healey Ltd. Her research interests center on the study of the use and impact of computing on humanities scholarship, and on the societal effects of electronic publishing. She is a member of the advisory panel for the Portsmouth Historical Records Series, e-press and the Digital Egypt for Universities project and is a visiting lecturer at City College Thessaloniki, Greece.

Susan Forscher Weiss holds a joint appointment in the Departments of Musicology and Romance Languages and Literature at the Johns Hopkins University. Her numerous publications include *Bologna Q 18: I-Bologna, Civico Museo Bibliografico Musicale, Ms.BolC Q 18 (olim 143)*, Introduction and Facsimile Edition (1998), chapters, articles, reviews, and entries in numerous scholarly publications. She has collaborated in web-based programming, exhibits, CD-ROMs, and audio tours. She has also been the recipient of numerous awards and fellowships for teaching and research including grants from the National Endowment for the Humanities, the American Council of Learned Societies, Harvard University, the Johns Hopkins University, and the Folger Shakespeare Library.

Perry Willett was appointed the Head of the Digital Library Production Service at the University of Michigan in 2004. He served as the Assistant Director of the Digital Library Program at Indiana University from 2001, and was a bibliographer at the Main Library of Indiana University from 1992 to 2001. He is the general editor of the Wright American Fiction project and the Victorian Women Writers Project, and is a member of the Text Encoding Initiative Consortium Council. He has written on electronic text and digital libraries.

William Winder is Assistant Professor of French at the University of British Columbia's French, Hispanic, and Italian Studies Department. He is on the board of directors of the Consortium for Computers in the Humanities and the editorial board of TEXT Technology, and he co-edits Computing in the Humanities Working Papers. His interests lie in computational and formalist approaches to the semantics of language and literature. See his website (http://www.fhis.ubc.ca/winder) for recent publications and research.

Russon Wooldridge is Professor in the Department of French, University of Toronto. He is a teacher/researcher in French language, French lexicography, translation, and corpus linguistics of the Web. Research details and content at: <http://www.chass.utoronto.ca/~wulfric>.

Foreword: Perspectives on the Digital Humanities

Roberto A. Busa

During World War II, between 1941 and 1946, I began to look for machines for the automation of the linguistic analysis of written texts. I found them, in 1949, at IBM in New York City. Today, as an agèd patriarch (born in 1913) I am full of amazement at the developments since then; they are enormously greater and better than I could then imagine. *Digitus Dei est hic*! The finger of God is here!

I consider it a great honor to be asked to write the Foreword to this fine book. It continues, underlines, completes, and recalls the previous *Survey* of Antonio Zampolli (produced in Pisa, 1997), who died before his time on August 22, 2003. In fact, the book gives a panoramic vision of the *status artis*. It is just like a satellite map of the points to which the wind of the ingenuity of the sons of God moves and develops the contents of computational linguistics, i.e., the computer in the humanities.

Humanities computing is precisely the automation of every possible analysis of human expression (therefore, it is exquisitely a "humanistic" activity), in the widest sense of the word, from music to the theater, from design and painting to phonetics, but whose nucleus remains the discourse of written texts.

In the course of the past sixty years I have added to the teaching of scholastic philosophy, the processing of more than 22 million words in 23 languages and 9 alphabets, registering and classifying them with my teams of assistants. Half of those words, the main work, are in Latin. I will summarize the three different perspectives that I have seen and experienced in these sixty years.

Technological "Miniaturization"

According to the perspective of technological miniaturization, the first perspective I will treat, the *Index Thomisticus* went through three phases. The first one lasted less than 10 years. I began, in 1949, with only electro-countable machines with punched cards. My goal was to have a file of 13 million of these cards, one for each word, with a context of 12 lines stamped on the back. The file would have been 90 meters long, 1.20 m in height, 1 m in depth, and would have weighed 500 tonnes.

In His mercy, around 1955, God led men to invent magnetic tapes. The first were the steel ones by Remington, closely followed by the plastic ones of IBM. Until 1980, I was working on 1,800 tapes, each one 2,400 feet long, and their combined length was 1,500 km, the distance from Paris to Lisbon, or from Milan to Palermo. I used all the generations of the dinosaur computers of IBM at that time. I finished in 1980 (before personal computers came in) with 20 final and conclusive tapes, and with these and the automatic photocompositor of IBM, I prepared for offset the 20 million lines which filled the 65,000 pages of the 56 volumes in encyclopedia format which make up the *Index Thomisticus* on paper.

The third phase began in 1987 with the preparations to transfer the data onto CD-ROM. The first edition came out in 1992, and now we are on the threshold of the third. The work now consists of 1.36 GB of data, compressed with the Hufmann method, on one single disk.

Textual Informatics

The second perspective is textual informatics, and it has branched into three different currents. Today the two greater and richer ones must be clearly distinguished from the third, the smallest and poorest. I must say that many people still do not realize this.

I call the first current "documentaristic" or "documentary," in memory of the American Documentation Society, and of the Deutsche Gesellschaft für Dokumentation in the 1950s. It includes databanks, the Internet, and the World Wide Web, which today are the infrastructures of telecommunications and are in continuous ferment. The second current I call "editorial." This is represented by CDs and their successors, including the multimedia ones, a new form of reproduction of a book, with audio-visual additions. Both these, albeit in different ways, provide for the multiplication, distribution, and swift traceability of both information and of a text. Both are recognizable by the fact that they substantially transfer and present, on an electronic support system, words and punctuation plus some operative commands. Because they provide a service and so have a quick return on investment, both have grown abundantly – the first, despite significant obstacles, more solidly and with fewer disappointments than the second.

I call the third current "hermeneutic" or interpretative, that informatics most associated with linguistic analysis and which I would describe as follows. In the electronic *Index Thomisticus* each of the 11 million words is encapsulated in a record of 152 bytes. Some 22 are reserved for the word, and 130 contain 300 alternating "internal hypertexts," which specify the values within the levels of the morphology.

At the moment, I am trying to get another project under way, which will obviously be posthumous, the first steps of which will consist in adding to the morphological encoding of each single separate word of the Thomistic lexicon (in all there are 150,000, including all the particles, such as *et*, *non*, etc.), the codes that express its syntax (i.e., its direct elementary syntactic correlations) within each single phrase in which it occurs. This project is called *Lessico Tomistico Biculturale* (LTB). Only a computer census of the syntactic correlations can document what concepts the author wanted to express with that word. Of a list of syntactic correlations, the "conceptual" translation can thus be given in modern languages. I have already published, mainly in the series of the Lessico Intellectuale Europeo (directed by T. Gregory of the University of Rome), the results of such syntactical analysis of a dozen words in their more than 500,000 context lines. To give one example, in the mind of St Thomas *ratio seminalis* meant then what today we call *genetic programme*. Obviously, St Thomas did not know of either DNA or genes, because at the time microscopes did not exist, but he had well understood that something had to perform their functions.

Hermeneutic Informatics

This third sort of informatics was the first to come into being, with the *Index Thomisticus* project, in 1949. It brought the following facts to my attention. First, everyone knows how to use his own mother tongue, but no one can know "how," i.e., no one can explain the rules and no one can list all the words of the lexicon that he uses (the active lexicon) nor of that which he understands but never uses (the passive lexicon).

What scholar could answer the following questions? How many verbs does he know at least passively? Which and how many of them are always and only transitive? Which and how many of them are always and only intransitive? Which and how many of them are sometimes the one, and sometimes the other, and what is the percentage of each? Lastly, which contextual situations characteristically mark the transitive or intransitive use of the latter?

Second, there is still no scientific grammar of any language that gives, in a systematized form, all the information necessary to program a computer for operations of artificial intelligence that may be currently used on vast quantities of natural texts, at least, e.g., for indexing the key words under which to archive or summarize these texts to achieve "*automatic indexing – automatic abstracting.*"

Third, it is thus necessary for the use of informatics to reformulate the traditional morphology, syntax, and lexicon of every language. In fact all grammars have been formed over the centuries by nothing more than sampling. They are not to be revolutionized, abandoned, or destroyed, but subjected to a re-elaboration that is progressive in extent and depth.

Schematically, this implies that, with integral censuses of a great mass of natural texts in every language, in synchrony with the discovered data, methods of observation used in the natural sciences should be applied together with the apparatus of the exact and statistical sciences, so as to extract categories and types and, thus, to organize texts in a general lexicological system, each and all with their probability index, whether great or small.

Hermeneutic informatics hinges on the Alpac Report (Washington, DC, 1966) and, now, this perspective is perhaps awaiting its own globalization. I have already said that hermeneutic informatics was the first to come into existence. Shortly afterwards, in the early 1950s, if I am correct, the move toward automatic translation started. The magazine *MT – Mechanical Translation* was started at MIT, launched, I think, by Professor

Billy Locke and others. The Pentagon financed various centers. I was involved in this. I connected the Anglo-Russian project of Léon Dostert and Peter Toma (of Georgetown University, Washington, DC) with the Computing Center of the Euratom of Ispra, which is on Lake Maggiore in Lombardy. My contributions were on an exchange basis. I supplied them, from my laboratory at Gallarate, with Russian abstracts of biochemistry and biophysics in Cyrillic script on punched cards, a million words. These were translated with the Georgetown programs. The translation was sufficient for an expert on the subject to be able to evaluate the merits of a more accurate translation done by hand, i.e., by a person's brain.

Unfortunately, in 1966, as a result of the Alpac Report, the Pentagon cut off all funding. This was not because computers at that time did not have sufficient memory capability or speed of access, but precisely because the information on the categories and their linguistic correspondences furnished by the various branches of philology were not sufficient for the purpose. The "machine" required greater depth and more complex information about our ways of thinking and modes of expression!

Future Perspectives

In certain respects this was a boon. In fact, as this volume, too, documents, the number and devotion of those few volunteers, who in almost every part of the world have a passion for computational informatics, increased. They are not an organized army, but hunters who range freely, and this produces some obvious side effects.

It also provokes a valuable consideration. Namely, it makes us realize that no single research center ever seems to have been able to answer, alone and completely, the linguistic challenge of globalized telematics. It seems that the answer to globalization, at least in principle, should be global as well, i.e., collective, or rather undertaken by one or more supranational organizations, this for the obvious reason of the commitments required. Speaking is an interface between infinity and the cosmos, between time and eternity, and is evidence of the thirst for knowledge, understanding, possession, and manipulation of everything, according to one's own personal freedom, but on track with a common ballast of logic and beauty. Speaking must thus be taken seriously; it is sacred, as is every human person. We are far from having exhausted the precept inscribed on Apollo's temple at Delphi, "Know thyself." It seems, therefore, that the problem must be attacked: in its totality – with comprehensive, i.e., global, research; collectively – by exploiting informatics with its enormous intrinsic possibilities, and not by rushing, just to save a few hours, into doing the same things which had been done before, more or less in the same way as they were done before.

It seems that the attack on the Twin Towers of New York City on September 11, 2001, has brought in an unforeseen season of *lean kine*. In Italy, as everywhere else, this has meant reductions in public funds for research. This period will pass, as surely as all the others we have experienced. Such reductions were also in evidence at the Exploratory Workshop on Computer Texts, which the European Science Foundation of the European Union held at Strasburg on June 14 and 15, 2002. On the one hand, these cutbacks in finance are certainly worrying for the many operators of computational linguistics, which today is fragmented, but on the other hand, it could also lead to the according of priority to a

definitive solution of the linguistic problem, like that which could facilitate the fulfill-
ment of the globalization of economic exchange.

A Proposal

I should like to summarize the formula of a global solution to the linguistic challenge that
I presented at the above-mentioned conference at Strasburg, much as if it were my
spiritual testament, although I am uncertain whether to call it prophecy or utopia.

   I suggest that – care of, for example, the European Union – for every principal language
A, B, C, D, etc., from each of the principal university textbooks in present use in the
various disciplines (for these represent the present state of what is knowable) there should
be extracted its integral "lexicological system" (with the help of the instruments tested in
the *Index Thomisticus*). In it, two "hemispheres" of each lexicon should be distinguished,
the few words of very high frequency present in every argument which express the logic,
and which are sometimes called "grammatical," and the very many words of relatively
minor frequency that specify messages and arguments. The systems of each text of each
discipline in each language should be integrally compared with each other by isolating
and specifying both the coincidences and divergences with their quantities and percentages, including those of hapax, extracting from them, i.e., mixing them, in one single
system of the same language, a system which totals statistically and with percentages both
how much they have in common and their co-respective divergences.

   Then these statistical summaries of the various languages A, B, C, D, etc., should be
compared with each other, with the same method of reporting their convergences and
divergences, with quantity and percentage in a single system. (One has only to think of
how much data could be published *a latere* as valid and useful documents, although to be
constantly updated, for example for contrastive grammars, etc.)

   Thus there would be on the computer a common interlingual system consisting solely
of strings of bits and bytes with correspondence links both between convergences and
divergences in themselves and between each other. It would be a sort of universal
language, in binary alphabet, "antiBabel," still in virtual reality. From this, going in
the reverse direction, there could be extracted in the respective alphabets of the individual
languages A, B, C, D, etc., the number of words and expressions, situations of morphology and syntax, of each language which have found correspondence in other languages,
and the number of those which have not. The number of such correspondences thus
extracted (lexicon and grammar) would be a set of "disciplined" basic languages, to be
adopted for the telematic use of the computer, to be also printed and then updated
according to experience.

   In input, therefore, everybody could use their own native disciplined language and have
the desired translations in output. The addressee could even receive the message both in
their own language, in that of the sender, and in others.

   In addition, the problems of keys and privacy will have to be solved, as (one step at a
time!) will those of the phonetic version of both input and output.

   These thoughts have formed gradually in my mind over the years, starting from the
realization that my programs for Latin, which I always wanted broken up for monofunc-
tional use, could be applied with the same operative philosophy to more than twenty

other languages (all in a phonetic script), even those that do not descend from Latin, such as Arabic and Hebrew, which are written from right to left. I had only to transfer elements from one table to another, changing the length of fields, or adding a field. (However, I cannot say anything about languages written in ideograms or pictograms.)

Conclusion

In conclusion, I will therefore summarize the third perspective, that of textual hermeneutic informatics, as follows. The first period began with my *Index Thomisticus* and ended, though not for me, with the Alpac Report. The second, after the Alpac Report, is the parcelization in progress of free research. The third would begin if and when comparative global informatics begins in the principal languages, more or less in the sense I have tried to sketch here. Those who live long enough will see whether these roses (and thorns), which today are merely thoughts, will come to flower, and so will be able to tell whether they were prophecy or dream.

The Digital Humanities and Humanities Computing: An Introduction

Susan Schreibman, Ray Siemens, and John Unsworth

History

This collection marks a turning point in the field of digital humanities: for the first time, a wide range of theorists and practitioners, those who have been active in the field for decades, and those recently involved, disciplinary experts, computer scientists, and library and information studies specialists, have been brought together to consider digital humanities as a discipline in its own right, as well as to reflect on how it relates to areas of traditional humanities scholarship.

This collection has its origins in the research carried out over the past half a century in textually focused computing in the humanities, as Susan Hockey notes in this volume, found in Father Roberto Busa's adaptation of early computing to textual location, comparison, and counting as part of his work in creating the *Index Thomisticus*, a concordance to the works of St Thomas Aquinas. Yet even a cursory glance at this *Companion*'s table of contents reveals how broadly the field now defines itself. It remains deeply interested in text, but as advances in technology have made it first possible, then trivial to capture, manipulate, and process other media, the field has redefined itself to embrace the full range of multimedia. Especially since the 1990s, with the advent of the World Wide Web, digital humanities has broadened its reach, yet it has remained in touch with the goals that have animated it from the outset: using information technology to illuminate the human record, and bringing an understanding of the human record to bear on the development and use of information technology.

The first section of the *Companion* addresses the field of digital humanities from disciplinary perspectives. Although the breadth of fields covered is wide, what is revealed is how computing has cut across disciplines to provide not only tools, but methodological focal points. There is, for example, a shared focus on preserving physical artifacts (written, painted, carved, or otherwise created), that which is left to us by chance (ruin, and other debris of human activity), or that which has been near-impossible to capture in its intended form (music, performance, and event). Yet many disciplines have gone beyond simply wishing to preserve these artifacts, what we might now call early forms of data management, to re-represent and manipulate them to reveal properties and traits not evident when the artifact was in its native form. Moreover, digital humanities now also concerns itself with the creation of new artifacts which are born digital and require rigorous study and understanding in their own right.

Eiteljorg notes that archaeologists, like most other early adopters in the arts and humanities, first used the computer for record making and record keeping, in the knowledge that data in this form would see more flexible utilization, particularly in computer-assisted statistical analysis. More recent applications derive from the introduction of global data-recording standards, allowing large corpora of archaeological data to be navigated, as well as the integration of global information systems (GIS)-derived data to represent standard locational information across these corpora. Art historians, as described by Greenhalgh, use computers to image, order, sort, interrogate, and analyze data about artworks, and increasingly use the Internet as the carrier for multimedia research or teaching/learning projects. Classical studies has always been a data-intensive enterprise, Crane demonstrates, and has seen the development of lexica, encyclopedias, commentaries, critical editions, and other elements of scholarly infrastructure that are well suited to an electronic environment which, ultimately, reflects a natural impulse toward systematic knowledge management and engineering within the field. So, too, is this impulse essential to the understanding of computing's role in literary studies (as noted by Rommel), linguistics (as discussed by Hajič), and lexicography (as charted by Wooldridge). In discussing the discipline of musicology, Fujinaga and Weiss note that the Internet has revolutionized not only the distribution potential for the artifacts that lie at the heart of their consideration but, also, other more analytical applications pertinent to the future of the field. Thomas documents the intense methodological debates sparked by the introduction of computing in history, debates which computing ultimately lost (in the United States, at least), after which it took a generation for historians to reconsider the usefulness of the computer to their discipline. The rhetoric of revolution proved more predictive in other disciplines, though – for example, in philosophy and religion. Today, one hears less and less of it, perhaps because (as Ess notes) the revolution has succeeded: in almost all disciplines, the power of computers, and even their potential, no longer seem revolutionary at all. While this may be true of a number of disciplines, in fields such as the performing arts, as discussed by Saltz, and new media studies, by Rockwell and Mactavish, there is an inherent kinship between the ever-evolving developments in computing and their performative and analytical potentials.

Principles, Applications, and Dissemination

The digital humanities, then, and their interdisciplinary core found in the field of humanities computing, have a long and dynamic history best illustrated by examination of the locations at which specific disciplinary practices intersect with computation. Even so, just as the various fields that make up the humanities share a focus on the examination of artifactual evidence of that which makes us human, so, too, do these fields share a number of commonly held assumptions about the way in which such examination is carried out, both with and without the assistance of the computer. Widely spread through the digital humanities community is the notion that there is a clear and direct relationship between the interpretative strategies that humanists employ and the tools that facilitate exploration of original artifacts based on those interpretative strategies; or, more simply put, those working in the digital humanities have long held the view that application is as important as theory. Thus, exemplary tasks traditionally associated with humanities computing hold the digital representation of archival materials on a par with analysis or critical inquiry, as well as theories of analysis or critical inquiry originating in the study of those materials. The field also places great importance on the means of disseminating the results of these activities and, as Pitti discusses, recognizes that project conception and management can be as important pragmatic concerns as others which are more traditionally associated with disciplinary pursuits.

The representation of archival material involves the use of computer-assisted means to describe and express print-, visual-, and audio-based material in tagged and searchable electronic form, as discussed by Deegan and Tanner. This representation is a critical and self-conscious activity, from the choice of what to represent to the reproduction of primary materials, for example, in the preparation of an electronic edition or digital facsimile (as discussed by Smith) and the exploration of the relationship between digital surrogates to legacy data (Warwick). Related to the process of representation is the necessity of understanding the tools being used, as Laue outlines, and the implications of decisions that we make in the use of those tools and the impact they have on analytical processes (McGann). The growing field of knowledge representation, which draws on the field of artificial intelligence and seeks to "produce models of human understanding that are tractable to computation" (Unsworth 2001), provides a lens through which we might understand such implications. This is especially true in issues related to archival representation and textual editing, high-level interpretative theory and criticism, and protocols of knowledge transfer – as modeled with computational techniques (discussed by McCarty), and captured via encoding and classification systems (Renear; Sperberg-McQueen) and represented in data structures (Ramsay), some of which have great impact on the ways in which we associate human information (Ryan) and interpret the ways in which it has influence upon us (Drucker).

In the digital humanities, critical inquiry involves the application of algorithmically facilitated search, retrieval, and critical processes that, originating in humanities-based work, have been demonstrated to have application far beyond. Associated with critical theory, this area is typified by interpretative studies that assist in our intellectual and aesthetic understanding of humanistic works. It also involves the application (and applicability) of critical and interpretative tools and analytic algorithms, as discussed by Bradley, on those artifacts produced through processes associated with archival representation made available via resources associated with processes of publishing and the communication of results. Manifested in the analysis techniques that Burrows and Ide each discuss – and seeing utility in a wide-ranging array of applications, from authorship attribution (Craig) to cognitive stylistics (Lancashire) – the basis of such analysis is the encoded and digitally stored corpora governed by strategies of knowledge representation that, themselves, are capable of possessing what we might term a "poetics" (Winder). So, too, with digital media such as film (Kolker), and with issues of interface and usability that are, as Kirschenbaum discusses, integral to all materials in electronic form and our interaction with them. Further, efforts toward dissemination have their roots, ultimately, in issues related to re-presentation but are themselves manifested in concerns pertinent to the nature of computer-facilitated communities (Willett): preservation in the electronic medium (discussed by Abby Smith), professional electronic publication (treated by Jensen's chapter, and addressed further by Palmer), and the unique array of challenges and opportunities that arise with the emergence of digital libraries, as outlined by Besser.

Conclusion

The editors intended this collection to serve as a historical record of the field, capturing a sense of the digital humanities as they have evolved over the past half century, and as they exist at the moment. Yet, if one looks at the issues that lie at the heart of nearly all contributions to this volume, one will see that these contributions reflect a relatively clear view of the future of the digital humanities. In addition to charting areas in which past advances have been made, and in which innovation is currently taking place, this volume reveals that digital humanities is addressing many of the most basic research paradigms and methods in the disciplines, to focus our attention on important questions to be asked and answered, in addition to important new ways of asking and answering that are enabled by our interaction with the computer.

What this collection also reveals is that there are central concerns among digital humanists which cross disciplinary boundaries. This is nowhere more evident than in the representation of knowledge-bearing artifacts. The process of such representation – especially so when done with the attention to detail and the consistency demanded by the computing environment – requires humanists to make explicit what they know about their material and to understand the ways in which that material exceeds or escapes representation. Ultimately, in computer-assisted analysis of large amounts of material that has been encoded and processed according to a rigorous, well thought-out system of knowledge representation, one is afforded opportunities for perceiving and analyzing patterns, conjunctions, connections, and absences that a human being, unaided by the computer, would not be likely to find.

The process that one goes through in order to develop, apply, and compute these knowledge representations is unlike anything that humanities scholars, outside of philosophy, have ever been required to do. This method, or perhaps we should call it a heuristic, discovers a new horizon for humanities scholarship, a paradigm as powerful as any that has arisen in any humanities discipline in the past – and, indeed, maybe more powerful, because the rigor it requires will bring to our attention undocumented features of our own ideation. Coupled with enormous storage capacity and computational power, this heuristic presents us with patterns and connections in the human record that we would never otherwise have found or examined.

ACKNOWLEDGMENTS

The editors would like to thank Emma Bennett, Andrew McNeillie, and Karen Wilson at Blackwell for their assistance, encouragement, and support. Ray Siemens would also like to acknowledge the assistance of Karin Armstrong and Barbara Bond with some materials present in this volume, and the Malaspina Research and Scholarly Activity Committee, for their support.

BIBLIOGRAPHY

McCarty, Willard. What is Humanities Computing? Toward a Definition of the Field. URL: <http://ilex.cc.kcl.ac.uk/wlm/essays/what/>.

Schreibman, Susan (2002). Computer-mediated Discourse: Reception Theory and Versioning. *Computers and the Humanities* 36,3: 283–93.

Siemens, R. G. (2002). A New Computer-assisted Literary Criticism? Introduction to *A New Computer-assisted Literary Criticism?*, ed. R. G. Siemens. [A special issue of] *Computers and the Humanities* 36,3: 259–67.

Unsworth, John (2001). Knowledge Representation in Humanities Computing. Inaugural E-humanities Lecture at the National Endowment for the Humanities (April 3). URL: <http://www.iath.virginia.edu/~jmu2m/KR/>.

PART I
History

1

The History of Humanities Computing

Susan Hockey

Introduction

Tracing the history of any interdisciplinary academic area of activity raises a number of basic questions. What should be the scope of the area? Is there overlap with related areas, which has impacted on the development of the activity? What has been the impact on other, perhaps more traditional, disciplines? Does a straightforward chronological account do justice to the development of the activity? Might there be digressions from this, which could lead us into hitherto unexplored avenues? Each of these questions could form the basis of an essay in itself but within the space and context available here, the approach taken is to present a chronological account which traces the development of humanities computing. Within this, the emphasis is on highlighting landmarks where significant intellectual progress has been made or where work done within humanities computing has been adopted, developed or drawn on substantially within other disciplines.

It is not the place of this essay to define what is meant by humanities computing. The range of topics within this *Companion* indeed sends plenty of signals about this. Suffice it to say that we are concerned with the applications of computing to research and teaching within subjects that are loosely defined as "the humanities," or in British English "the arts." Applications involving textual sources have taken center stage within the development of humanities computing as defined by its major publications and thus it is inevitable that this essay concentrates on this area. Nor is it the place here to attempt to define "interdisciplinarity," but by its very nature, humanities computing has had to embrace "the two cultures," to bring the rigor and systematic unambiguous procedural methodologies characteristic of the sciences to address problems within the humanities that had hitherto been most often treated in a serendipitous fashion.

Beginnings: 1949 to early 1970s

Unlike many other interdisciplinary experiments, humanities computing has a very well-known beginning. In 1949, an Italian Jesuit priest, Father Roberto Busa, began what even to this day is a monumental task: to make an *index verborum* of all the words in the works of St Thomas Aquinas and related authors, totaling some 11 million words of medieval Latin. Father Busa imagined that a machine might be able to help him, and, having heard of computers, went to visit Thomas J. Watson at IBM in the United States in search of support (Busa 1980). Some assistance was forthcoming and Busa began his work. The entire texts were gradually transferred to punched cards and a concordance program written for the project. The intention was to produce printed volumes, of which the first was published in 1974 (Busa 1974).

A purely mechanical concordance program, where words are alphabetized according to their graphic forms (sequences of letters), could have produced a result in much less time, but Busa would not be satisfied with this. He wanted to produce a "lemmatized" concordance where words are listed under their dictionary headings, not under their simple forms. His team attempted to write some computer software to deal with this and, eventually, the lemmatization of all 11 million words was completed in a semi-automatic way with human beings dealing with word forms that the program could not handle. Busa set very high standards for his work. His volumes are elegantly typeset and he would not compromise on any levels of scholarship in order to get the work done faster. He has continued to have a profound influence on humanities computing, with a vision and imagination that reach beyond the horizons of many of the current generation of practitioners who have been brought up with the Internet. A CD-ROM of the Aquinas material appeared in 1992 that incorporated some hypertextual features ("*cum hypertextibus*") (Busa 1992) and was accompanied by a user guide in Latin, English, and Italian. Father Busa himself was the first recipient of the Busa award in recognition of outstanding achievements in the application of information technology to humanistic research, and in his award lecture in Debrecen, Hungary, in 1998 he reflected on the potential of the World Wide Web to deliver multimedia scholarly material accompanied by sophisticated analysis tools (Busa 1999).

By the 1960s, other researchers had begun to see the benefits of working with concordances. A series of four articles by Dolores Burton in the journal *Computers and the Humanities* in 1981–2 attempted to bring these together, beginning with a discussion of the 1950s (Burton 1981a, 1981b, 1981c, 1982). Some of these researchers were individual scholars whose interests concentrated on one set of texts or authors. In the UK, Roy Wisbey produced a series of indexes to Early Middle High German texts (Wisbey 1963). In the USA Stephen Parrish's concordances to the poems of Matthew Arnold and W. B. Yeats introduced the series of concordances published by Cornell University Press (Parrish 1962). This period also saw the establishment of computing facilities in some major language academies in Europe, principally to assist with the compilation of dictionaries. Examples include the Trésor de la Langue Française (Gorcy 1983), which was established in Nancy to build up an archive of French literary material, and the Institute of Dutch Lexicology in Leiden (De Tollenaere 1973).

Although much activity at this time was concentrated on the production of concord-ances as ends in themselves, one application of these tools began to take on a life of its own. The use of quantitative approaches to style and authorship studies predates comput-ing. For example, Augustus de Morgan in a letter written in 1851 proposed a quantitative study of vocabulary as a means of investigating the authorship of the Pauline Epistles (Lord 1958) and T. C. Mendenhall, writing at the end of the nineteenth century, described his counting machine, whereby two ladies computed the number of words of two letters, three, and so on in Shakespeare, Marlowe, Bacon, and many other authors in an attempt to determine who wrote Shakespeare (Mendenhall 1901). But the advent of computers made it possible to record word frequencies in much greater numbers and much more accurately than any human being can. In 1963, a Scottish clergyman, Andrew Morton, published an article in a British newspaper claiming that, according to the computer, St Paul only wrote four of his epistles. Morton based his claim on word counts of common words in the Greek text, plus some elementary statistics. He continued to examine a variety of Greek texts producing more papers and books concentrating on an examination of the frequen-cies of common words (usually particles) and also on sentence lengths, although it can be argued that the punctuation which identifies sentences was added to the Greek texts by modern editors (Morton 1965; Morton and Winspear 1971).

It is believed that the first use of computers in a disputed authorship study was carried out on the Junius Letters by Alvar Ellegård. Published in 1962, this study did not use a computer to make the word counts, but did use machine calculations which helped Ellegård get an overall picture of the vocabulary from hand counts (Ellegård 1962). What is probably the most influential computer-based authorship investigation was also carried out in the early 1960s. This was the study by Mosteller and Wallace of the *Federalist Papers* in an attempt to identify the authorship of the twelve disputed papers (Mosteller and Wallace 1964). With so much material by both authorship candidates on the same subject matter as the disputed papers, this study presented an ideal situation for comparative work. Mosteller and Wallace were primarily interested in the statistical methods they employed, but they were able to show that Madison was very likely to have been the author of the disputed papers. Their conclusions generally have been accepted, to the extent that the *Federalist Papers* have been used as a test for new methods of authorship discrimination (Holmes and Forsyth 1995; Tweedie et al. 1996).

At this time much attention was paid to the limitations of the technology. Data to be analyzed were either texts or numbers. They were input laboriously by hand either on punched cards, with each card holding up to eighty characters or one line of text (upper-case letters only), or on paper tape, where lower-case letters were perhaps possible but which could not be read in any way at all by a human being. Father Busa has stories of truckloads of punched cards being transported from one center to another in Italy. All computing was carried out as batch processing, where the user could not see the results at all until printout appeared when the job had run. Character-set representation was soon recognized as a substantial problem and one that has only just begun to be solved now with the advent of Unicode, although not for every kind of humanities material. Various methods were devised to represent upper- and lower-case letters on punched cards, most often by inserting an asterisk or similar character before a true upper-case letter. Accents and other non-standard characters had to be treated in a similar way and non-Roman alphabets were represented entirely in transliteration.

Most large-scale datasets were stored on magnetic tape, which can only be processed serially. It took about four minutes for a full-size tape to wind from one end to the other and so software was designed to minimize the amount of tape movement. Random access to data such as happens on a disk was not possible. Data had therefore to be stored in a serial fashion. This was not so problematic for textual data, but for historical material it could mean the simplification of data, which represented several aspects of one object (forming several tables in relational database technology), into a single linear stream. This in itself was enough to deter historians from embarking on computer-based projects.

Representation problems extended far beyond specific characters. For concordance and retrieval programs there was a need to identify citations by their location within the text. The methods used by conventional document retrieval systems were inadequate because they tended to assume document structures similar to those of journal articles and were unable to cope with the structures found in poetry or drama, or in manuscript sources where the lineation is important. Various methods of defining document structures were proposed, but the most sophisticated one developed at this time was that used by the COCOA concordance program (Russell 1967). Modeled on a format developed by Paul Bratley for an Archive of Older Scottish texts (Hamilton-Smith 1971), COCOA enables the user to define a specification for the document structure which matches the particular set of documents. It also enables the markup of overlapping structures, making it possible, for example, to encode a citation system for a printed version in parallel with that for the manuscript source of the material. COCOA is also economical of file space, but is perhaps less readable for the human.

The other widely used citation scheme was more dependent on punched card format. In this scheme, often called "fixed format," every line began with a coded sequence of characters giving citation information. Each unit within the citation was positioned in specific columns across the line, for example the title in columns 1–3, verse number in columns 5–6, and line number in columns 7–9. The entry of this information was speeded up by functions on the punched card machine, but the information also occupied more space within the computer file.

The legacy of these citation schemes can still be found in electronic texts created some time ago. COCOA, particularly, was very influential and other schemes were derived from it. COCOA cannot easily handle the markup of small features within the content such as names, dates, and abbreviations, but its ability to deal with overlapping structures outstrips that of almost all modern markup schemes.

This period also saw the first opportunities for those interested in humanities computing to get together to share ideas and problems. In 1964, IBM organized a conference at Yorktown Heights. The subsequent publication, *Literary Data Processing Conference Proceedings*, edited by Jess Bessinger and Stephen Parrish (1965), almost reads like something from twenty or so years later, except for the reliance on punched cards for input. Papers discuss complex questions in encoding manuscript material and also in automated sorting for concordances where both variant spellings and the lack of lemmatization are noted as serious impediments.

As far as can be ascertained, the Yorktown Heights conference was a one-off event. The first of a regular series of conferences on literary and linguistic computing and the precursor of what became the Association for Literary and Linguistic Computing/ Association for Computers and the Humanities (ALLC/ACH) conferences was organized by Roy Wisbey and Michael Farringdon at the University of Cambridge in March, 1970. This was a truly international event with good representation from both sides of the Atlantic as well as from Australia. The proceedings, meticulously edited by Wisbey (1971), set the standard for subsequent publications. A glance through them indicates the emphasis of interest on input, output, and programming as well as lexicography, textual editing, language teaching, and stylistics. Even at this time the need for a methodology for archiving and maintaining electronic texts was fully recognized.

Another indication of an embryonic subject area is the founding of a new journal. *Computers and the Humanities* began publication in 1966 under the editorship of Joseph Raben. With characteristic energy, Raben nurtured the new journal and during its first years, at least until the regular series of conferences and associations that developed from them got going, it became the main vehicle for dissemination of information about humanities computing. Raben recognized the need just to know what is going on and the journal's Directory of Scholars Active was the first point of call for people who were thinking about starting a project. Other informal newsletters also served specific communities, notably *Calculi* for computers and classics, edited by Stephen Waite.

The 1960s also saw the establishment of some centers dedicated to the use of computers in the humanities. Wisbey founded the Centre for Literary and Linguistic Computing in Cambridge in 1963 as support for his work with Early Middle High German Texts. In Tübingen, Wilhelm Ott established a group which began to develop the suite of programs for text analysis, particularly for the production of critical editions. The TuStep software modules are in use to this day and set very high standards of scholarship in dealing with all phases from data entry and collation to the production of complex print volumes.

Work in this early period is often characterized as being hampered by technology, where technology is taken to mean character sets, input/output devices and the slow turnaround of batch processing systems. However, researchers did find ways of dealing with some of these problems, albeit in a cumbersome way. What is more characteristic is that key problems which they identified are still with us, notably the need to look at "words" beyond the level of the graphic string, and to deal effectively with variant spellings, multiple manuscripts, and lemmatization.

Consolidation: 1970s to mid-1980s

If any single-word term can be used to describe this period, it would almost certainly be "consolidation." More people were using methodologies developed during the early period. More electronic texts were being created and more projects using the same applications were started. Knowledge of what is possible had gradually spread through normal scholarly channels of communication, and more and more people had come across computers in their everyday life and had begun to think about what computers might do for their research and teaching.

The diffusion of knowledge was helped not only by *Computers and the Humanities* but also by a regular series of conferences. The 1970 symposium in Cambridge was the start of a biennial series of conferences in the UK, which became a major focal point for computing in the humanities. Meetings in Edinburgh (1972), Cardiff (1974), Oxford

(1976), Birmingham (1978), and Cambridge (1980) all produced high-quality papers. The Association for Literary and Linguistic Computing was founded at a meeting in King's College London in 1973. Initially it produced its own *Bulletin* three times per year. It also began to organize an annual meeting with some invited presentations and by 1986 had a journal, *Literary and Linguistic Computing*. By the mid-1970s, another series of conferences began in North America, called the International Conference on Computing in the Humanities (ICCH), and were held in odd-numbered years to alternate with the British meetings. The British conference and the ALLC annual meetings gradually began to coalesce. They continued to concentrate on literary and linguistic computing with some emphasis on "linguistic," where they offered a forum for the growing number of European researchers in what became known as corpus linguistics. ICCH attracted a broader range of papers, for example on the use of computers in teaching writing, and on music, art, and archaeology. The Association for Computers and the Humanities (ACH) grew out of this conference and was founded in 1978.

The requirements of humanities computing also began to be recognized within academic computing centers. Still in the days of mainframe computing, it was necessary to register to use any computing facilities and that registration provided an opportunity for academic computing staff to find out what users wanted and to consider providing some standard software that could be used by many different people. The second version of the COCOA concordance program in Britain was designed to be run on different mainframe computers for exactly this purpose (Berry-Rogghe and Crawford 1973). It was distributed to different computing centers in the mid-1970s and many of these centers designated one person to act as support. Dissatisfaction with its user interface coupled with the termination of support by the Atlas Laboratory, where it was written, led the British funding bodies to sponsor the development of a new program at Oxford University. Called the Oxford Concordance Program (OCP), this software was ready for distribution in 1982 and attracted interest around the world with users in many different countries (Hockey and Marriott 1979a, 1979b, 1979c, 1980). Other packaged or generic software also appeared at this time and significantly reduced the cost of a project in terms of programming support.

The need to avoid duplication of effort also led to consolidation in the area of text archiving and maintenance. With the advent of packaged software and the removal of the need for much programming, preparing the electronic text began to take up a large proportion of time in any project. The key driver behind the establishment of the Oxford Text Archive (OTA) in 1976 was the need simply to ensure that a text that a researcher had finished with was not lost. The OTA undertook to maintain electronic texts and, subject to the permission of the depositor and with appropriate copyright permissions, to make these texts available to anyone else who wanted to use them for academic purposes. It was the beginnings of a digital library, although nobody called it this initially, and its staff had to devise their own method of describing and documenting the material (Proud 1989). The amount of undocumented material highlighted the need for recognized procedures for describing electronic texts.

The OTA's approach was to offer a service for maintenance of anything that was deposited. It managed to do this for some considerable time on very little budget, but was not able to promote the creation of specific texts. Groups of scholars in some discipline areas made more concerted attempts to create an archive of texts to be used as a source for research. Notable among these was the *Thesaurus Linguae Graecae* (*TLG*) begun at the University of California Irvine and directed for many years by Theodore Brunner. Brunner raised millions of dollars to support the creation of a "databank" of Ancient Greek texts, covering all authors from Homer to about AD 600, some 70 million words (Brunner 1993). A complementary collection of Classical Latin was later produced by the Packard Humanities Institute, and together with the *TLG* gave scholars in classical studies a research resource that was unrivaled in other disciplines for many years. Only Old English scholars had access to a similar comprehensive, but smaller corpus with the completion of the Old English Corpus for the Dictionary of Old English (Healey 1989).

More centers for humanities computing were also established during this period. Some, for example the Norwegian Computing Center for the Humanities (now HIT) at Bergen, with substantial government support, incorporated a wide range of applications and projects. Others such as the Center for Computer Analysis of Texts (CCAT) at the University of Pennsylvania were more narrowly focused on the interests of the academics who had initially promoted them. Pockets of interest had become established around the world and scholars in those institutions on the whole enjoyed a good deal of support.

This period also saw the introduction of courses on various aspects of humanities computing. Some courses were given by staff within academic computing centers and concentrated mostly on the mechanics of using specific software programs. Others looked more broadly at application areas. Those given by academics tended to concentrate on their own interests giving rise to student projects in the same application areas. A debate about whether or not students should learn computer programming was ongoing. Some felt that it replaced Latin as a "mental discipline" (Hockey 1986). Others thought that it was too difficult and took too much time away from the core work in the humanities. The string handling language SNOBOL was in vogue for some time as it was easier for humanities students than other computer languages, of which the major one was still Fortran.

There were some developments in processing tools, mostly through the shift from tape to disk storage. Files no longer had to be searched sequentially. For a time there were various technologies for organizing material in databases, some of which were very effective for humanities material (Burnard 1987b), but gradually the relational model prevailed. In mainframe implementations this presented a better structure within which historians and others working with material drawn from sources (rather than the sources themselves) could work. However, relational technologies still presented some problems for the representation of information that needed to be fitted into tables. At least two hardware devices were invented in the 1970s for assisting searching. One was implemented in David Packard's Ibycus computer, which was built to work with the *TLG* and some other classics material (Lancashire 1991: 204–5). The other was the Content Addressing File Store (CAFS), which worked on the British ICL computers (Burnard 1987a). The idea of transferring processing into the hardware was very attractive to humanities researchers who had to deal with large amounts of material, but it did not catch on in a big way, possibly because it was overtaken by advances in the speed of conventional hardware.

A glance through the various publications of this period shows a preponderance of papers based on vocabulary studies generated initially by concordance programs. The results were of interest either for some kinds of stylistic analyses or for linguistic applications. Increasingly complex mathematics were brought to bear on vocabulary counts, leaving some more humanities-oriented conference participants out in the cold. Apart from these, there was little really new or exciting in terms of methodology and there was perhaps less critical appraisal of methodologies than might be desirable. The important developments during this period lay more in support systems generated by the presence of more outlets for dissemination (conferences and journals) and the recognition of the need for standard software and for archiving and maintaining texts. Dissemination was concentrated in outlets for humanities computing and much less in mainstream humanities publications. It seems that we were still at a stage where academic respectability for computer-based work in the humanities was questionable and scholars preferred to publish in outlets where they were more likely to be accepted.

New Developments: Mid-1980s to Early 1990s

This period saw some significant developments in humanities computing. Some of these can be attributed to two new technologies, the personal computer and electronic mail. Others happened simply because of the increase of usage and the need to reduce duplication of effort.

At first there were several different and competing brands of personal computers. Some were developed for games, some were standalone word processors and could not be used for anything else, and others were specifically aimed at the educational market rather than for general use. Gradually IBM PCs and models based on the IBM architecture began to dominate, with Apple Macintoshes also attracting plenty of use, especially for graphics.

The personal computer is now a necessity of scholarly life, but in its early days it was considerably more expensive in relation to now and early purchasers were enthusiasts and those in the know about computing. The initial impact in humanities computing was that it was no longer necessary to register at the computer center in order to use a computer. Users of personal computers could do whatever they wanted and did not necessarily benefit from expertise that already existed. This encouraged duplication of effort, but it also fostered innovation where users were not conditioned by what was already available.

By the end of the 1980s, there were three DOS-based text analysis programs: Word-Cruncher, TACT, and MicroOCP, all of which had very good functionality. Owners of personal computers would work with these at home and, in the case of WordCruncher and TACT, obtain instantaneous results from searches. MicroOCP was developed from the mainframe program using a batch concordance technique rather than interactive searching. However, the main application of personal computers was that shared with all other disciplines, namely word processing. This attracted many more users who knew very little about other applications and tended to assume that the functions within word processing programs might be all that computers could do for them.

The Apple Macintosh was attractive for humanities users for two reasons. Firstly, it had a graphical user interface long before Windows on PCs. This meant that it was much better at displaying non-standard characters. At last it was possible to see Old English characters, Greek, Cyrillic, and almost any other alphabet, on the screen and to manipulate text containing these characters easily. Secondly, the Macintosh also came with a program that made it possible to build some primitive hypertexts easily. HyperCard provided a model of file cards with ways of linking between them. It also incorporated a simple programming tool making it possible for the first time for humanities scholars to write computer programs easily. The benefits of hypertext for teaching were soon recognized and various examples soon appeared. A good example of these was the Beowulf Workstation created by Patrick Conner (Conner 1991). This presents a text to the user with links to a modern English version and linguistic and contextual annotations of various kinds. The first version of the Perseus Project was also delivered to the end user in HyperCard.

Networking, at least for electronic mail, was previously confined to groups of computer scientists and research institutes. By the mid-1980s, facilities for sending and receiving electronic mail across international boundaries were provided by most academic computing services. At the 1985 ALLC conference in Nice, electronic mail addresses were exchanged avidly and a new era of immediate communication began. Soon e-mail was being sent to groups of users and the ListServ software for electronic discussion lists was established. Ansaxnet, the oldest electronic discussion list for the humanities, was founded by Patrick Conner in 1986 (Conner 1992).

At the ICCH conference in Columbia, South Carolina, in spring 1987 a group of people mostly working in support roles in humanities computing got together and agreed that they needed to find a way of keeping in touch on a regular basis. Willard McCarty, who was then at the University of Toronto, agreed to look into how they might do this. On his return from the conference he discovered the existence of ListServ, and *Humanist* was born (McCarty 1992). The first message was sent out on May 7, 1987. McCarty launched himself into the role of editing what he prefers to call an "electronic seminar" and, except for a hiatus in the early 1990s when *Humanist* was edited from Brown University, has continued in this role ever since.

Humanist has become something of a model for electronic discussion lists. McCarty has maintained excellent standards of editing and the level of discussion is generally high. For those of us in Europe the regular early morning diet of three to six *Humanist* digests is a welcome start to the day. *Humanist* has become central to the maintenance and development of a community and it has made a significant contribution to the definition of humanities computing. Its archives going back to 1987 are a vast source of information on developments and concerns during this period and it was taken as an exemplar by the founders of the Linguist List, the key electronic forum for linguistics.

This period also saw the publication in print form of the only large-scale attempt to produce a bibliography of projects, software, and publications. Two volumes of the *Humanities Computing Yearbook* (*HCY*) were published. The first, edited by Ian Lancashire and Willard McCarty appeared in 1988 with some 400 pages. The second volume, for 1989–90, has almost 700 pages with a much better index. For several years, until it began to get out of date, the *HCY* was an extremely valuable resource, fulfilling the role originally taken by the *Computers and the Humanities* Directory of Scholars Active, which had ceased to appear by the early 1970s. Preparing the *HCY* was a truly enormous undertaking and no further volumes appeared. By the early 1990s, the general consensus was that in future an online database would be a more effective resource. Although there have been various attempts to start something similar, nothing on a serious scale has emerged, and the picture of overall activity in terms of projects and publications is once again incomplete.

In terms of intellectual development, one activity stands out over all others during this period. In November 1987 Nancy Ide, assisted by colleagues in ACH, organized an invitational meeting at Vassar College, Poughkeepsie, to examine the possibility of creating a standard encoding scheme for humanities electronic texts (Burnard 1988). There had been various previous attempts to address the problem of many different and conflicting encoding schemes, a situation that was described as "chaos" by one of the participants at the Vassar meeting. Now, the time was ripe to proceed. Scholars were increasingly tired of wasting time reformatting texts to suit particular software and had become more frustrated with the inadequacies of existing schemes. In 1986, a new encoding method had appeared on the scene. The Standard Generalized Markup Language (SGML), published by ISO, offered a mechanism for defining a markup scheme that could handle many different types of text, could deal with metadata as well as data, and could represent complex scholarly interpretation as well as the basic structural features of documents.

Participants at the meeting agreed on a set of principles ("the Poughkeepsie Principles") as a basis for building a new encoding scheme and entrusted the management of the project to a Steering Committee with representatives from ACH, ALLC, and the Association for Computational Linguistics (Text Encoding Initiative 2001). Subsequently, this group raised over a million dollars in North America and oversaw the development of the Text Encoding Initiative (TEI) *Guidelines for Electronic Text Encoding and Interchange*. The work was initially organized into four areas, each served by a committee. Output from the committees was put together by two editors into a first draft version, which was distributed for public comment in 1990. A further cycle of work involved a number of work groups that looked at specific application areas in detail. The first full version of the TEI *Guidelines* was published in May 1994 and distributed in print form and electronically.

The size, scope, and influence of the TEI far exceeded what anyone at the Vassar meeting envisaged. It was the first systematic attempt to categorize and define all the features within humanities texts that might interest scholars. In all, some 400 encoding tags were specified in a structure that was easily extensible for new application areas. The specification of the tags within the *Guidelines* illustrates some of the issues involved, but many deeper intellectual challenges emerged as the work progressed. Work in the TEI led to an interest in markup theory and the representation of humanities knowledge as a topic in itself. The publication of the TEI *Guidelines* coincided with full-text digital library developments and it was natural for digital library projects, which had not previously come into contact with humanities computing, to base their work on the TEI rather than inventing a markup scheme from scratch.

Much of the TEI work was done by e-mail using private and public discussion lists, together with a fileserver where drafts of documents were posted. From the outset anyone who served on a TEI group was required to use e-mail regularly and the project became an interesting example of this method of working. However, participants soon realized that it is not easy to reach closure in an e-mail discussion and it was fortunate that funding was available for a regular series of face-to-face technical meetings to ensure that decisions were made and that the markup proposals from the different working groups were rationalized effectively.

Apart from major developments in personal computing, networking, and the TEI, the kind of humanities computing activities which were ongoing in the 1970s continued to develop, with more users and more projects. Gradually, certain application areas spun off from humanities computing and developed their own culture and dissemination routes. "Computers and writing" was one topic that disappeared fairly rapidly. More important for humanities computing was the loss of some aspects of linguistic computing, particularly corpus linguistics, to conferences and meetings of its own. Computational linguistics had always developed independently of humanities computing and, despite the efforts of Don Walker on the TEI Steering Committee, continued to be a separate discipline. Walker and Antonio Zampolli of the Institute for Computational Linguistics in Pisa worked hard to bring the two communities of humanities computing and computational linguistics together but with perhaps only limited success. Just at the time when humanities computing scholars were beginning seriously to need the kinds of tools developed in computational linguistics (morphological analysis, syntactic analysis, and lexical databases), there was an expansion of work in computational and corpus linguistics to meet the needs of the defense and speech analysis community. In spite of a landmark paper on the convergence between computational linguistics and literary and linguistic computing given by Zampolli and his colleague Nicoletta Calzolari at the first joint ACH/ALLC conference in Toronto in June 1989 (Calzolari and Zampolli 1991), there was little communication between these communities, and humanities computing did not benefit as it could have done from computational linguistics techniques.

The Era of the Internet: Early 1990s to the Present

One development far outstripped the impact of any other during the 1990s. This was the arrival of the Internet, but more especially the World Wide Web. The first graphical browser, Mosaic, appeared on the scene in 1993. Now the use of the Internet is a vital part of any academic activity. A generation of students has grown up with it and naturally looks to it as the first source of any information.

Initially, some long-term humanities computing practitioners had problems in grasping the likely impact of the Web in much the same way as Microsoft did. Those involved with the TEI felt very much that HyperText Markup Language (HTML) was a weak markup system that perpetuated all the problems with word processors and appearance-based markup. The Web was viewed with curiosity but this tended to be rather from the outside. It was a means of finding some kinds of information but not really as a serious tool for humanities research. This presented an opportunity for those institutions and organizations that were contemplating getting into humanities computing for the first time. They saw that the Web was a superb means of publication, not only for the results of their scholarly work, but also for promoting their activities among a much larger community of users. A new group of users had emerged.

Anyone can be a publisher on the Web and within a rather short time the focus of a broader base of interest in humanities computing became the delivery of scholarly material over the Internet. The advantages of this are enormous from the producer's point of view. The format is no longer constrained by that of a printed book. Theoretically there is almost no limit on size, and hypertext links provide a useful way of dealing with annotations, etc. The publication can be built up incrementally as and when bits of it are ready for publication. It can be made available to its audience immediately and it can easily be amended and updated.

In the early to mid-1990s, many new projects were announced, some of which actually succeeded in raising money and getting started. Particularly in the area of electronic scholarly editions, there were several meetings and publications devoted to discussion about what an electronic edition might look like (Finneran 1996; Bornstein and Tinkle 1998). This was just at the time when editorial theorists were focusing on the text as a physical object, which they could represent by digital images. With the notable exception of work carried out by Peter Robinson (Robinson 1996, 1997, 1999) and possibly one or two others, few of these publications saw the light of day except as prototypes or small samples, and by the second half of the decade interest in this had waned somewhat. A good many imaginative ideas had been put forward, but once these reached the stage where theory had to be put into practice and projects were faced with the laborious work of entering and marking up text and developing software, attention began to turn elsewhere.

Debates were held on what to call these collections of electronic resources. The term "archive" was favored by many, notably the Blake Archive and other projects based in the Institute for Advanced Technology in the Humanities at the University of Virginia. "Archive" meant a collection of material where the user would normally have to choose a navigation route. "Edition" implies a good deal of scholarly added value, reflecting the views of one or more editors, which could be implemented by privileging specific navigation routes. SGML (Standard Generalized Markup Language), mostly in applications based on the TEI, was accepted as a way of providing the hooks on which navigation routes could be built, but significant challenges remained in designing and building an effective user interface. The emphasis was, however, very much on navigation rather than on the analysis tools and techniques that had formed the major application areas within humanities computing in the past. In the early days of the Web, the technology for delivery of SGML-encoded texts was clunky and in many ways presented a less satisfying user interface than what can be delivered with raw HTML. Nevertheless, because of the easy way of viewing them, the impact of many of these publishing projects was substantial. Many more people became familiar with the idea of technology in the humanities, but in a more limited sense of putting material onto the Web.

Although at first most of these publishing projects had been started by groups of academics, it was not long before libraries began to consider putting the content of their collections on the Internet. Several institutions in the United States set up electronic text or digital library collections for humanities primary source material, most usually using the OpenText SGML search engine (Price-Wilkin 1994). While this provides good and fast facilities for searching for words (strings), it really provides little more than a reference tool to look up words. Other projects used the DynaText SGML electronic book system for the delivery of their material. This offered a more structured search but with an interface that is not particularly intuitive.

A completely new idea for an electronic publication was developed by the Orlando Project, which is creating a History of British Women's Writing at the Universities of Alberta and Guelph. With substantial research funding, new material in the form of short biographies of authors, histories of their writing, and general world events was created as a set of SGML documents (Brown et al. 1997). It was then possible to consider extracting portions of these documents and reconstituting them into new material, for example to generate chronologies for specific periods or topics. This project introduced the idea of a completely new form of scholarly writing and one that is fundamentally different from anything that has been done in the past. It remains to be seen whether it will really be usable on a large scale.

The Internet also made it possible to carry out collaborative projects in a way that was never possible before. The simple ability for people in different places to contribute to the same document collections was a great advance on earlier methods of working. In the Orlando Project, researchers at both institutions add to a document archive developed as a web-based document management system, which makes use of some of the SGML markup for administrative purposes. Ideas have also been floated about collaborative editing of manuscript sources where people in different locations could add layers of annotation, for example for the Peirce Project (Neuman et al. 1992) and the Codex Leningradensis (Leningrad Codex Markup Project 2000). The technical aspects of this are fairly clear. Perhaps less clear is the management of the project, who controls or vets the annotations, and how it might all be maintained for the future.

The TEI's adoption as a model in digital library projects raised some interesting issues about the whole philosophy of the TEI, which had been designed mostly by scholars who wanted to be as flexible as possible. Any TEI tag can be redefined and tags can be added where appropriate. A rather different philosophy prevails in library and information science where standards are defined and then followed closely – this to ensure that readers can find books easily. It was a pity that there was not more input from library and information science at the time that the TEI was being created, but the TEI project was started long before the term "digital library" came into use. A few people made good contributions, but in the library community there was not the widespread range of many years' experience of working with electronic texts as in the scholarly community. The TEI was, however, used as a model by the developers of the Encoded Archival Description (EAD), which has had a very wide impact as a standard for finding aids in archives and special collections.

An additional dimension was added to humanities electronic resources in the early 1990s, when it became possible to provide multimedia information in the form of images, audio, and video. In the early days of digital imaging there was much discussion about file formats, pixel depth, and other technical aspects of the imaging process and much less about what people can actually do with these images other than view them. There are of course many advantages in having access to images of source material over the Web, but humanities computing practitioners, having grown used to the flexibility offered by searchable text, again tended to regard imaging projects as not really their thing, unless, like the Beowulf Project (Kiernan 1991), the images could be manipulated and enhanced in some way. Interesting research has been carried out on linking images to text, down to the level of the word (Zweig 1998). When most of this can be done automatically we will be in a position to reconceptualize some aspects of manuscript studies. The potential of other forms of multimedia is now well recognized, but the use of this is only really feasible with high-speed access and the future may well lie in a gradual convergence with television.

The expansion of access to electronic resources fostered by the Web led to other areas of theoretical interest in humanities computing. Electronic resources became objects of study in themselves and were subjected to analysis by a new group of scholars, some of whom had little experience of the technical aspects of the resources. Hypertext in particular attracted a good many theorists. This helped to broaden the range of interest in, and discussion about, humanities computing but it also perhaps contributed to misapprehensions about what is actually involved in building and using such a resource. Problems with the two cultures emerged again, with one that was actually doing it and another that preferred talking about doing it.

The introduction of academic programs is another indication of the acceptance of a subject area by the larger academic community. For humanities computing this began to happen by the later 1990s although it is perhaps interesting to note that very few of these include the words "Humanities Computing" in the program title. King's College London offers a BA Minor in Applied Computing with a number of humanities disciplines, and its new MA, based in the Centre for Humanities Computing, is also called MA in Applied Computing. McMaster University in Canada offers a BA in Multimedia. The MA that the University of Virginia is soon to start is called Digital Humanities and is under the auspices of the Media Studies Program. The University of Alberta is, as far as I am aware, the first to start a program with Humanities Computing in its title, although the University of Glasgow has had an MPhil in History and Computing for many years.

As the Internet fostered the more widespread use of computers for humanities applications, other organizations began to get involved. This led to some further attempts to define the field or at least to define a research agenda for it. The then Getty Art History Information Program published what is in my view a very interesting Research Agenda for Networked Cultural Heritage in 1996 (Bearman 1996). It contains eight papers tackling specific areas that cover topics which really bridge across digital libraries, and humanities research and teaching. Each of these areas could form a research program in its own right, but the initiative was not taken further. Meanwhile the ALLC and ACH continued to organize a conference every year with a predominance of papers on markup and other technical issues. An attempt to produce a roadmap and new directions for humanities computing for the 2002 conference in Germany produced a useful survey (Robey 2002), but little new, and would perhaps have benefited from more input from a broader community. But how to involve other communities was becoming more of a problem in an era when many more electronic resources for the humanities were being developed outside the humanities computing community.

Conclusion

If one humanities computing activity is to be highlighted above all others, in my view it must be the TEI. It represents the most significant intellectual advances that have been made in our area, and has influenced the markup community as a whole. The TEI attracted the attention of leading practitioners in the SGML community at the time when XML (Extensible Markup Language) was being developed and Michael Sperberg-McQueen, one of the TEI editors, was invited to be co-editor of the new XML markup standard. The work done on hyperlinking within the TEI formed the basis of the linking mechanisms within XML. In many ways the TEI was ahead of its time, as only with the rapid adoption of XML in the last two to three years has the need for descriptive markup been recognized by a wider community. Meanwhile, the community of markup theorists that has developed from the TEI continues to ask challenging questions on the representation of knowledge.

There are still other areas to be researched in depth. Humanities computing can contribute substantially to the growing interest in putting the cultural heritage on the Internet, not only for academic users, but also for lifelong learners and the general public. Tools and techniques developed in humanities computing will facilitate the study of this material and, as the Perseus Project is showing (Rydberg-Cox 2000), the incorporation of computational linguistics techniques can add a new dimension. Our tools and techniques can also assist research in facilitating the digitization and encoding processes, where we need to find ways of reducing the costs of data creation without loss of scholarly value or of functionality. Through the Internet, humanities computing is reaching a much wider audience, and students graduating from the new programs being offered will be in a position to work not only in academia, but also in electronic publishing, educational technologies, and multimedia development. Throughout its history, humanities computing has shown a healthy appetite for imagination and innovation while continuing to maintain high scholarly standards. Now that the Internet is such a dominant feature of everyday life, the opportunity exists for humanities computing to reach out much further than has hitherto been possible.

REFERENCES FOR FURTHER READING

Bearman, D. (ed.) (1996). *Research Agenda for Networked Cultural Heritage*. Santa Monica, CA: Getty Art History Information Program.

Berry-Rogghe, G. L. M. and T. D. Crawford (1973). Developing a Machine-independent Concordance Program for a Variety of Languages. In A. J. Aitken, R. W. Bailey, and N. Hamilton-Smith (eds.), *The Computer and Literary Studies* (pp. 309–16). Edinburgh: Edinburgh University Press.

Bessinger, J. B. and S. M. Parrish (1965). *Literary Data Processing Conference Proceedings*. White Plains, NY: IBM.

Bornstein, G. and T. Tinkle (1998). *The Iconic Page in Manuscript, Print, and Digital Culture*. Ann Arbor: University of Michigan Press.

Brown, S., S. Fisher, P. Clements, K. Binhammer, T. Butler, K. Carter, I. Grundy, and S. Hockey (1997). SGML and the Orlando Project: Descriptive Markup for an Electronic History of Women's Writing. *Computers and the Humanities* 31: 271–84.

Brunner, T. F. (1993). Classics and the Computer: The History of a Relationship. In J. Solomon (ed.), *Accessing Antiquity: The Computerization of Classical Studies* (pp. 10–33). Tucson: University of Arizona Press.

Burnard, L. (1987a). CAFS: A New Solution to an Old Problem. *Literary and Linguistic Computing* 2: 7–12.

——(1987b). Principles of Database Design. In S. Rahtz (ed.), *Information Technology in the Humanities* (pp. 54–68). Chichester: Ellis Horwood.

——(1988). Report of Workshop on Text Encoding Guidelines. *Literary and Linguistic Computing* 3: 131–3.

Burton, D. M. (1981a). Automated Concordances and Word Indexes: The Fifties. *Computers and the Humanities* 15: 1–14.

——(1981b). Automated Concordances and Word Indexes: The Early Sixties and the Early Centers. *Computers and the Humanities* 15: 83–100.

——(1981c). Automated Concordances and Word Indexes: The Process, the Programs, and the Products. *Computers and the Humanities* 15: 139–54.

——(1982). Automated Concordances and Word Indexes: Machine Decisions and Editorial Revisions. *Computers and the Humanities* 16: 195–218.

Busa, R. (1974–). *Index Thomisticus*. Stuttgart: Frommann-Holzboog.

——(1980). The Annals of Humanities Computing: The Index Thomisticus. *Computers and the Humanities* 14: 83–90.

——(ed.) (1992). *Thomae Aquinatis Opera Omnia Cum Hypertextibus in CD-ROM*. Milano: Editoria Elettronica Editel.

——(1999). Picture a Man. . . . Busa Award Lecture, Debrecen, Hungary, July 6, 1998. *Literary and Linguistic Computing* 14: 5–9.

Calzolari, N. and A. Zampolli (1991). Lexical Databases and Textual Corpora: A Trend of Convergence between Computational Linguistics and Literary and Linguistic Computing. In S. Hockey, N. Ide, and I. Lancashire (eds.), *Research in Humanities Computing 1: Selected Papers from the ALLC/ACH Conference, Toronto, June 1989* (pp. 272–307). Oxford: Clarendon Press.

Conner, P. W. (1991). The Beowulf Workstation: One Model of Computer-assisted Literary Pedagogy. *Literary and Linguistic Computing* 6: 50–8.

——(1992). Networking in the Humanities: Lessons from Ansaxnet. *Computers and the Humanities* 26: 195–204.

De Tollenaere, F. (1973). The Problem of the Context in Computer-aided Lexicography. In A. J. Aitken, R. W. Bailey, and N. Hamilton-Smith (eds.), *The Computer and Literary Studies* (pp. 25–35). Edinburgh: Edinburgh University Press.

Ellegård, A. (1962). *A Statistical Method for Determining Authorship: The Junius Letters 1769–1772*. Gothenburg: Gothenburg Studies in English.

Finneran, R. J. (1996). *The Literary Text in the Digital Age*. Ann Arbor: University of Michigan Press.

Gorcy, G. (1983). L'informatique et la mise en oeuvre du trésor de la langue française (TLF), dictionnaire de la langue du 19e et du 20e siècle (1789–1960). In A. Cappelli and A. Zampolli (eds.), *The Possibilities and Limits of the Computer in Producing and Publishing Dictionaries: Proceedings of the European Science Foundation Workshop, Pisa 1981*. Linguistica Computazionale III (pp. 119–44). Pisa: Giardini.

Hamilton-Smith, N. (1971). A Versatile Concordance Program for a Textual Archive. In R. A. Wisbey (ed.), *The Computer in Literary and Linguistic Research* (pp. 235–44). Cambridge: Cambridge University Press.

Healey, A. (1989). The Corpus of the Dictionary of Old English: Its Delimitation, Compilation and Application. Paper presented at the Fifth Annual Conference of the UW Centre for the New Oxford English Dictionary. Oxford, September, 1989.

Hockey, S. (1986). Workshop on Teaching Computers and the Humanities Courses. *Literary and Linguistic Computing* 1: 228–9.

Hockey, S. and I. Marriott (1979a). The Oxford Concordance Project (OCP) – Part 1. *ALLC Bulletin* 7: 35–43.

——(1979b). The Oxford Concordance Project (OCP) – Part 2. *ALLC Bulletin* 7: 155–64.

——(1979c). The Oxford Concordance Project (OCP) – Part 3. *ALLC Bulletin* 7: 268–75.

——(1980). The Oxford Concordance Project (OCP) – Part 4. *ALLC Bulletin* 8: 28–35.

Holmes, D. I. and R. S. Forsyth (1995). The *Federalist* Revisited: New Directions in Authorship Attribution. *Literary and Linguistic Computing* 10: 111–27.

Kiernan, K. S. (1991). Digital Image Processing and the Beowulf Manuscript. *Literary and Linguistic Computing* 6: 20–7.

Lancashire, I. (ed.) (1991). *The Humanities Computing Yearbook 1989–90: A Comprehensive Guide to Software and Other Resources*. Oxford: Clarendon Press.

Lancashire, I. and W. McCarty (eds.) (1988). *The Humanities Computing Yearbook 1988*. Oxford: Clarendon Press.

Leningrad Codex Markup Project (2000). Project "EL": The XML Leningrad Codex. Available at: <http://www.leningradensis.org>, accessed May 15, 2003.

Lord, R. D. (1958). Studies in the History of Probability and Statistics: viii. de Morgan and the Statistical Study of Literary Style. *Biometrika* 45: 282.

McCarty, W. (1992). Humanist: Lessons from a Global Electronic Seminar. *Computers and the Humanities* 26: 205–22.

Mendenhall, T. C. (1901). A Mechanical Solution of a Literary Problem. *The Popular Science Monthly* 60: 97–105.

Morton, A. Q. (1965). *The Authorship of the Pauline Epistles: A Scientific Solution*. Saskatoon: University of Saskatchewan.

Morton, A. Q. and Winspear, A. D. (1971). *It's Greek to the Computer*. Montreal: Harvest House.

Mosteller, F. and D. L. Wallace (1964). *Inference and Disputed Authorship: The Federalist*. Reading, MA: Addison-Wesley.

Neuman, M., M. Keeler, C. Kloesel, J. Ransdell, and A. Renear (1992). The Pilot Project of the Electronic Peirce Consortium (abstract). *ALLC-ACH92 Conference Abstracts and Program* (pp. 25-7). Oxford.

Parrish, S. M. (1962). Problems in the Making of Computer Concordances. *Studies in Bibliography* 15: 1–14.

Price-Wilkin, J. (1994). Using the World Wide Web to Deliver Complex Electronic Documents: Implications for Libraries. *The Public-Access Computer Systems Review* 5: 5-21. <http://jpw.umdl.umich.edu/pubs/yale.html>, accessed July 21, 2004.

Proud, J. K. (1989). *The Oxford Text Archive*. London: British Library Research and Development Report.

Robey, D. (2002). New Directions in Humanities Computing. <http://www.uni-tuebingen.de/zdv/zrkinfo/pics/aca4.htm>, accessed May 15, 2003.

Robinson, P. (ed.) (1996). *Geoffrey Chaucer: The Wife of Bath's Prologue on CD-ROM*. Cambridge: Cambridge University Press.

Robinson, P. M. W. (1997). New Directions in Critical Editing. In K. Sutherland (ed.), *Electronic Text: Investigations in Method and Theory* (pp. 145–71). Oxford: Clarendon Press.

——(1999). New Methods of Editing, Exploring and Reading The Canterbury Tales. <http://www.cta.dmu.ac.uk/projects/ctp/desc2.html>, accessed May 14, 2003.

Russell, D. B. (1967). *COCOA – A Word Count and Concordance Generator for Atlas*. Chilton: Atlas Computer Laboratory.

Rydberg-Cox, J. A. (2000). Co-occurrence Patterns and Lexical Acquisition in Ancient Greek Texts. *Literary and Linguistic Computing* 15: 121–30.

Text Encoding Initiative (2001). Text Encoding Initiative. <http://www.tei-c.org>, accessed May 15, 2003.

Tweedie, F. J., S. Singh, and D. I. Holmes (1996). Neural Network Applications in Stylometry: The Federalist Papers. *Computers and the Humanities* 30: 1–10.

Wisbey, R. (1963). The Analysis of Middle High German Texts by Computer: Some Lexicographical Aspects. *Transactions of the Philological Society*, 28–48.

Wisbey, R. A. (ed.) (1971). *The Computer in Literary and Linguistic Research*. Cambridge: Cambridge University Press.

Zweig, R. W. (1998). Lessons from the Palestine Post Project. *Literary and Linguistic Computing* 13: 89–97.

2

Computing for Archaeologists

Harrison Eiteljorg, II

Archaeology[1] is the study of history as written not with ink on paper but with the debris of human activity found where it fell. Whereas historians read the written records of our ancestors, archaeologists read the material record, either to augment the historic one or to reconstruct prehistory when there is no written record. As with the historic record, the archaeological record is often prejudiced by accidental survival, biased sources, and skewed representations of certain materials. Of course, both historic and material records from the past may carry inadvertent meaning. When Shelley's Ozymandias cried out, "My name is Ozymandias, king of kings, / Look on my works, ye Mighty, and despair!" he, as have many figures from the past, sent an ironic and unintended message.

The archaeologist's work is, first, to find the material remains of our ancestors, second, to unearth those remains in ways that maximize the information they can convey, and, finally, to interpret the evidence. Finding those remains may be done by excavation or surface survey, but both processes require the destruction of the very evidence that is the first fruit of the work. In some cases, the destruction is literal and complete, as when an archaeologist must dig through one level of a site to find another; often the destruction is not so complete but involves the removal of objects from their physical contexts. Since contexts provide crucial clues to both physical and temporal relationships, evidence is lost even by removing objects. The destructive nature of the work demands extraordinarily careful record keeping to avoid accidental information loss. Indeed, it can be argued that record keeping is the real occupation of the field archaeologist.

The interpretative process requires careful examination of the records of excavation or survey; the contexts of the objects are as important to a full understanding as the objects themselves. For instance, a figurine found in the remains of a tomb later covered by a house must have been deposited before the construction of the house and before the deposit of anything in that house. On the other hand, a potsherd found in the bottom of a trash pit must have been deposited at roughly the time the pit was dug, which may have been long after the deposit of flint tools located near the potsherd but not in the trash pit.

The importance of context to the archaeologist highlights the importance of good records. Records of both the archaeological contexts and the artifacts, not to mention a great many other aspects of an excavation or survey, provide the keys to analyses. Those records are truly crucial, and the potential utility of the computer for that record keeping is obvious today. Less obvious is the fact that, if computers are used to record the basic information on which archaeologists build their understanding of the past, *all* practitioners must ultimately be able to use computers to retrieve that information. That is, computers and computer skills will be needed by all archaeologists if a substantial portion of the archaeological record is maintained in computer form.

It is now obvious that computers are ideal for record keeping, but when archaeologists first started using computers, in the late 1950s, computers were arcane and foreign. Their record-keeping potential could not then be utilized by academics because of costs and access limits; affordable microcomputers lay well in the future. Data entry required punchcards or tape, and results were only available on paper. As a natural result, computers were used for tasks that required considerable processing power, not routine data storage. Early uses therefore tended to be for statistical processing, and, though statistics had been used in archaeology for decades, more statistical procedures and more mathematically complex statistical procedures could be performed with computers.

During these early years of computer usage in archaeology, archaeologists had to learn computer languages in order to prepare data for processing and then to carry out the statistical processes. That made the use of computers less likely to penetrate deeply into the field. Nevertheless, some saw even in the late 1960s the enormous potential for computers to store large quantities of information for retrieval from what were then called databanks.

By the early 1970s, there had already been some conferences on archaeological computing, and the microcomputer revolution began later in that decade, though the first microcomputers did not have the advantage of the IBM name. One of the most important things the early microcomputers did have was the database management system, dBase. That program and its many offspring have had an enormous impact on archaeology because of their record-keeping potential. Database management programs make it possible to manage large datasets without first learning to write long and complex computer programs (though the need to write routines for specific operations remains).

The database software of the mid-1970s and after brought the promise of efficient record keeping, and the new capabilities were desperately needed as excavators were then expanding the quantity of material collected. For instance, studies of plant and animal remains in the archaeological record (to understand food sources and the surrounding ecosystem) required sifting through large quantities of earth to find seeds and bones that could only be interpreted with statistical analyses; such work cried out for sophisticated data-handling techniques. Similarly, more careful and conscientious attention to small finds and fragmentary evidence could only become common with the advent of better recording techniques. It goes without saying that the recording of all these data would have been of little use had the programs not also made the retrieval of information – in an incredibly wide variety of forms – more efficient and flexible.

Microcomputers – with relatively easy-to-use software – arrived just as those needs for more sophisticated data handling were being felt. As a result, database technology seemed to many a godsend. That is not to say that all archaeologists immediately began using computers and databases, or even that all have adopted them today, but the need for assistance with ever-more-voluminous records and the availability of sophisticated computer programs fed on one another. Archaeologists who were eager to deal with seeds, shells, bones, and small, fragmentary finds could do so, and the fact that they could record so much information with the aid of computers encouraged them to treat that level of record keeping as standard. That pushed others to attend to similar levels of detail and, of necessity, to turn to computers to help. The process is continuing, with new technologies being regularly added to the tool kit.

The acceleration of computer use is ongoing, and the extent to which the quantity of recorded data may overwhelm the scholar's ability to synthesize is a matter of some debate. Until archaeologists can dispassionately evaluate the utility of different approaches to data collection, there is a natural tendency to record more, whether or not all the information is useful.

The growth of computer use spawned the organization called Computer Applications and Quantitative Methods in Archaeology (CAA). It began with a small meeting at the University of Birmingham (England) in 1973 and has grown to an international organization with annual meetings in various cities in Europe. In December 1984 the *Archaeological Computing Newsletter* was launched to report on information about archaeological computing, and by the mid-1980s established professional archaeology organizations featured regular sessions about one or another aspect of computing at their annual meetings.

The early and lasting interest in databases stemmed not only from the need to control huge quantities of excavation data but also from the hope that data storehouses could be used by scholars to retrieve and analyze information from related excavations, thus permitting broader syntheses. Indeed, many archaeologists still hope for such aggregations of data. While that giant data warehouse has been seen by many as the pot at the end of the rainbow, those most intimately familiar with the technology have, from the beginning, seen aggregated databases as a far more distant goal at best. Even archaeologists working in the same cultural and geographic areas do not – and cannot – excavate, survey, record their results, or use terms in precisely the same ways. As a result, combining data from multiple projects remains an illusive goal. Efforts to impose standardization have met with little success, and even such a carefully crafted and unthreatening potential aid as the Getty *Art and Architecture Thesaurus* has not been noticeably helpful in bringing the scholars in the field into terminological uniformity for a single language, much less across languages.

The difficulties with common terms and data structures have been exacerbated by the divergence between the needs of the archaeological community and those of museum professionals. Archaeologists and the museum curators who ultimately receive the excavated artifacts record their information about those artifacts in strikingly different arrangements, the one beginning with excavation context and the other with either a cultural classification or an object-based classification system. As a result, the databases of the two groups are organized differently, making large-scale cooperation problematic.

Large-scale constructed datasets such as the collection of information about archaeological sites in Turkey (*The Archaeological Settlements of Turkey* website online at <http://

tayproject.org/>) are less ambitious than the enormous, automatic aggregations once anticipated, but they are now becoming more common and often prove to be remarkably useful. Another good example of such constructed databases is the National Archeological Database of US public archaeological sites (online at <http://www.cast.uark.edu/other/nps/nadb/>) developed by the National Park Service and the Center for Advanced Spatial Technologies at the University of Arkansas (CAST, <http://www.cast.uark.edu/index_main.html>). Websites that serve as gateways to information, for instance, ARGE, the Archaeological Guide to Europe (<http://odur.let.rug.nl/arge/>), have also proved to be very valuable, and a recent project, called OASIS (<http://ads.ahds.ac.uk/project/oasis/>), which makes possible timely access to information about archaeological projects throughout Britain, is an excellent example of real benefits for scholars by providing access to disparate data through a common central point but without imposing unrealistic new standards.

Combining disparate datasets may not be a realistic near-term goal, but preserving datasets for future access is a necessity now. There are active digital repositories now available to archaeologists for the long-term preservation of their data files, and preservation of digital data is a major responsibility. The recovered artifacts and the data about them are the only surviving evidence of fieldwork. Neither is fully meaningful without the other. It may also be argued that economic development will result in fewer possibilities for excavation and field survey, making excavations in museum basements and old records the archaeology of the future.

There is a serious problem with the expansion of data quantity and the consequently increasing use of databases. When archaeologists use computers to view data rather than spending time with the objects themselves, they risk losing the familiarity with the objects that can only come from sustained, intimate, physical contact.

Databases were recognized as valuable tools quickly; so were graphical applications. Early graphics programs could only generate printed output – and slowly, very slowly. Nevertheless, maps and drawings have been so integral to the record keeping of the discipline that the development of graphics aids was an obvious necessity. The earliest graphics products were maps, but there were also programs developed before the end of the 1970s for drawing plans and sections. The early programs, often written by scholars, replicated many of the hand-drawing processes, and the drawings – the physical products – were the desired results; the underlying computer data simply represented a means to an end.

Programs were written by scholars to create maps, and even digital terrain models (draped grids illustrating the undulations of terrain) could be created from survey data before the advent of the personal computer. Maps were simply drawings, but powerful mapping software providing other sophisticated features was developed for other disciplines; that software, called geographic information system (GIS) programs, has been eagerly used by archaeologists, starting in the mid-1980s. For these programs the underlying data are far more important than any particular drawing.

GIS programs combine maps and data about maps in ways that bring significant benefits to archaeology. The data about the maps are of two kinds, standard relational data tables (with information about artifacts, flora, fauna, etc.) linked to areas or points on maps, and information derived from map data, such as the steepness of the grade in a given area (from contour lines or point-source elevation data). The crucial benefit of GIS is the connection between bounded portions or individual points on a map and data about them – and the ability to analyze the data according to any of the available criteria. The resulting ability to analyze material remains in concert with the physical environment is extremely powerful.

Vector-based maps rely upon stored data points and are only scaled when output to a screen or paper; as a result the precision of coordinates available from a vector-based map is limited only by the survey technology that produced the data points. On the other hand, raster-based maps are scaled drawings, and a given map may be at virtually any scale. Issues of scale and precision may thus become very complex, and using together maps with differing scales, precision, and levels of generalization (e.g., how many survey points define a river course or a coastline?) can yield very misleading results. These issues of scale, precision, and generalization with GIS make it necessary that users of GIS data be sophisticated and self-conscious in their use of maps and the data connected to them.

The use of GIS has been aided in archaeology, as in other disciplines, by the fact that GIS data – maps and data files – can be created for one use/user and re-used by many others. Archaeologists may use GIS maps created by and for others, e.g., digital elevation maps made for the military, in addition to maps and data tables of their own. This is not an unmixed blessing, however, since available data – whether maps or data tables – may determine the questions asked or, more worrisome, the ones not asked.

GIS software is the graphics road taken for mapping. The other graphics road, taken for plans and other record drawings, is computer-assisted design (CAD) software. The advent of CAD programs for personal computers brought significant and almost imme-diate change to record keeping for many archaeologists. Although CAD programs were created to assist with design processes, it was a short step to see their utility for modeling the existing world and existing structures; archaeologists began to use them in the mid-1980s.

Many archaeologists initially used CAD programs as drafting aids only, treating the computer-generated drawing as the final product. Plans and elevations can be generated at various scales and with differing emphases without time-consuming redrafting.[2] How-ever, dimensional information can be retrieved from the CAD file at original measurement precision, unaffected by drawing scale, and the computer data can be segmented so that specific phases or other selections from the entire digital file can be included or excluded in any specific drawing. As a result, CAD data eventually came to be recognized as more full and complex than any individual drawing.

The larger promise of CAD lay in its ability to record three-dimensionally and to generate drawings based on the full 3-D geometry of a site or structure. As database technology made it possible to record the added information that archaeologists were unearthing in the 1960s and 1970s, CAD made it possible for archaeologists to record 3-D information easily and with the precision of the original field measurements. Fortunately, advanced surveying equipment, particularly the total station and, to a lesser extent, desktop photogrammetry, made the gathering of 3-D data far easier. The 3-D capabilities of CAD and advanced surveying instruments have led to very complex 3-D models as archaeological records. The models record the full geometry, and all dimensions can be retrieved at surveyed precision. The 3-D models can also be segmented to permit any on-screen view or paper drawing to include or exclude parts of the whole according to the needs of the moment.

Scholars conceive of CAD models of structures in two quite different ways. For some, the CAD model is the kind of record that a drawing once was – containing all the dimensional and geometric information known from surveying. For others the model is the starting point for reconstructing missing parts or phases, for making realistic images, or for envisioning larger ensembles, cityscapes, or landscapes. Those intending to reconstruct, illustrate, or envision the past may not need an exact record of existing conditions. As a result, two approaches to CAD modeling – one based on record-keeping practices and the other less concerned with precise dimensions – have been common. In general, archaeologists have been more likely to use CAD as a record-keeping technology, since their approach to data gathering emphasizes such recording. Archaeologists and architectural historians dealing with older and less complete structures have often used CAD for precise records as well.

Archaeologists using CAD models principally for reconstructing, illustrating, or envisioning the past have worried less about precise dimensions and more about appearances. Buildings or larger ensembles imagined with the aid of the computer and with simpler, idealized dimensions are much easier and less expensive to make and can be presented in ways that are extremely compelling. However, using CAD as an aid to illustrate reconstructed realities nearly always involves subsidiary technologies, usually rendering programs or virtual reality programs that use CAD models as their starting points.

Reconstructions based on CAD data – even idealized and simplified CAD data – have one very important benefit over hand-drawn reconstructions: they must be based on fitting geometric shapes to one another. Therefore, CAD models are limited by the rules of geometry. A CAD program will only generate a reconstructed view based on the rules of geometry, not the hopes or dreams of a scholar.

Computer reconstructions can be truly photorealistic, providing believably real images. That has drawbacks as well as obvious benefits. The photorealistic views generally omit the inevitable irregularities of real structures, dirt and grime, marks of age and deterioration, nearby vegetation, and so on. The surrounding structures must often be omitted as well – or be included as if they were fully known when they are not – or be shown only as featureless blocks. Standing alone or in a generalized context, an ancient structure looks unnatural; placed in a hypothetical context it provides a sense of reality that exceeds our knowledge. The root problem here is not with the computer but with the necessarily partial state of our knowledge.

Virtual reality (VR) systems based on CAD models promise realistic visions of computer worlds through which users may navigate. However, they face similar problems of inadequate data. A new hybrid system provides reconstructions that are visible in glasses through which the actual remains can be seen at the same time. This promises a better marriage of the real and the reconstructed, but the technology has yet to be proved in actual use.

VR and generalized models permit serious examination of larger settings. Both VR worlds and very generalized models can provide information about landscapes, urban scale, open spaces, communication arteries, and other aspects of both the natural and the constructed world.

Archaeologists have used CAD, GIS, and databases primarily for data recording. In fact, that is the most important benefit the computer has brought to archaeology – the ability to manage more data more effectively. Of course, managing the data effectively implies accessing the data effectively as well. Databases, CAD models, and GIS programs all provide many ways to retrieve information, to analyze, to ask questions of the data, and to understand better what has been found and the relationships between and among those finds. That retrieval, of course, requires some computer skill.

There are concerns unique to archaeology that complicate the use of all these technologies. For example, terminology issues greatly complicate the potential to share data with all these technologies, as already mentioned regarding databases. In addition, the ways archaeologists apply CAD and GIS technologies to data recording are quite different from the ways the software developers expected. Standards designed by the developers do not generally suffice for scholarly users, and the development of scholarly standards has been slow and ill-focused. The Archaeology Data Service in England has been especially helpful in this area, producing guides to good practice for scholars.

Much early archaeological computing required scholars to write their own programs, but that is no longer necessary. Most now use commercial software, although special archaeological problems such as certain statistical procedures and seriation routines continue to inspire programming by archaeologists. Another area in which programming has remained a necessity is that of simulation. Using computers to simulate development in relatively simple societies was considered a very promising technique as early as the 1960s, but, as the popularity of the "new archaeology" waned, so did the enthusiasm for simulation. Those interested in simulation today are more likely to use GIS, CAD, or statistics and to compare various predefined scenarios to test possible explanations of development, than to use simulation algorithms or artificial intelligence algorithms, which have seen little use in archaeology.

The use of commercial software has made it easier for scholars to work cooperatively on data, since many can access the same data files – whether data tables, CAD models, or GIS datasets – for data entry, examination, or analysis. The potential to share digital files over the Internet, of course, has made collaboration even easier and more common. In some cases, excavators have entered data into on-site database systems connected to the Internet so that the data can be accessed almost immediately after being entered.

The value of the Internet for communications is easily missed in a discussion of technology; it seems too obvious and pervasive to need mentioning. In archaeology, however, colleagues are routinely working together on projects while living on different continents. Simple e-mail can be crucial in such cases. For communicating to a wider audience, of course, use of the Web has already changed the extent to which scholars can and will offer their information to the public.

Computers have also aided archaeologists' use of photographs. Photographs of buildings, sites, features, and objects are central to the practice of archaeology, and digital imagery has not changed that. However, it has made possible the use of color for a much greater portion of the photographs – not in printed publications but over the Internet where the cost of a color photo is not noticeably different from the cost of a black-and-white photo. (In printed publications the problem remains. Small print runs make color prohibitively expensive.) The value of color is greater than one might imagine; scholars need to see colors accurately if they are fully to grasp the appearance of a structure or object. In particular, ceramic analysis demands careful attention to colors, but it is much too expensive to print color photos of the sherds that make up such a large portion of the recovered material from an archaeological project.

Digital imagery has also brought better, less time-consuming, and less expensive enhancements of photographs. Such enhancements aid in interpreting satellite images or the stratigraphy represented in a trench wall by subtly changing colors. In at least one instance, photographs of faded and damaged fragments of frescoes were digitally enhanced to aid the restoration work, and satellite photographs of the Near East have been used to locate ancient roadways that seemed to have left no evidence on the landscape.

Only recently coming into use has been photography/digitizing that includes a 3-D modeling component so that photographs and 3-D digitizers can be used to provide 3-D geometry of objects as well as color and tone. Objects can be modeled with these techniques so that scholars can see – and rotate and measure – fully 3-D representations of objects on a computer. While still too expensive for general use, these processes provide unprecedented access to objects without risk of damage, although they also remove the scholars from the objects themselves.

Sharing digital data over the Internet may be important for archaeologists, but scholarly electronic publication – over the Internet or on CDs – has not met the predictions of its early supporters. Some web-based monographs have appeared, as have some publications on CDs, and *Internet Archaeology* has been extraordinarily innovative in putting complex digital data on the Web as journal "articles." Sadly, very few of the electronic monographs seem to offer real permanence. CDs have a lifespan that can probably be measured in years, not decades, and too many websites are ephemeral. Thus, too few electronic publications provide the permanence required. Probably more important, electronic publication still does not normally carry the value of paper publication when advancement or promotion is considered.

Although electronic monographs may not become common, web-delivered journals such as *Internet Archaeology* and supplements to printed articles, as pioneered by the *American Journal of Archaeology*, promise to bring more digital information to more archaeologists. That is not sufficient, however, because archaeology desperately needs the potential offered by electronic publication. The volume of material collected in the course of a project simply cannot be presented in a book or even a multi-volume series. Indeed, the use of databases, CAD models, and GIS programs creates a concomitant need to "publish" databases, CAD models, and GIS datasets – which can only be done digitally. Since electronic publication in the sense of a single, unified item that can be called *the* publication of a project now seems unlikely, and since there must be ways for archaeologists to obtain the electronic data along with the analyses, syntheses, and other expository texts that combine to make the record of a project, the future seems to lie in hybrid publications involving either printed or web-served text coupled with permanent access to the digital files that are the basic record of the project. Archival repositories for those files are required as part of this approach, and they are necessary anyway, as mentioned previously, to preserve the original data. There have been some successful repositories, most notably the Archaeology Data Service in the United Kingdom. At the same time, however, there is not a universally understood responsibility on the part of all archaeologists to prepare digital material for such repositories – not a trivial task – and then to make the actual deposit; nor have funding agencies generally recognized the importance of the long-term preservation of digital data.[3] Therefore, hybrid publications – text plus access to digital files – remain uncommon.

Should the day come when hybrid publications are common, a major obstacle remains. Despite the importance of computers and computing to archaeology, too few scholars are being trained in the use of computers. Scholars have bemoaned the problem for more than 15 years (see Richards 1985; Eiteljorg 2001), but there remains a divide between those who understand the computer technologies required for the discipline and those who do not. The divide is not a matter of age but of education; young scholars are not required to learn computer skills in graduate programs. In addition, young scholars who seem computer-savvy often lack precisely the skills most needed for archaeological computing – skills with database design, CAD programs, and GIS. Although it is now a given that any archaeology project will involve the use of computers, it is not a given that the project directors will know how to use them well or have the requisite skills to find helpers who do. Nor is it a given that the archaeologists of the future will be able to use the digital data created in the field today. Unfortunately, those who are adept with the technologies must often be self-taught, although these technologies are better learned from experts who understand the problems and pitfalls that are likely to be encountered. This problem of untrained or self-taught users of computer technology is not widely recognized or acknowledged in the field of archaeology at large, at least in part because archaeologists have not realized that *all* archaeologists need at least to be able to retrieve digital data from computer databases, CAD models, or GIS datasets. The absence of formal training represents a serious impediment both to effective application of computer technology and to the reuse of the digital data already gathered in computer form.

Despite the many changes computers have brought to archaeology, the transformation from paper-based to digital recording is still incomplete. The discipline at large has not fully absorbed the need to preserve access to digital data for future scholars. It has not yet found an effective and relatively standard way to present digital data as part of a final publication. Its educational institutions have not accepted the need to prepare all archaeologists in the use of those computer technologies necessary in the field and the laboratory. In part, these problems reflect the nature of the discipline, a uniquely fragmented one consisting of practitioners who may have begun as historians, art historians, students of ancient languages, or anthropologists – but not as scientists dependent upon a tradition of prompt and full data sharing. The problems also reflect the unique independence of archaeologists, who must have a strong entrepreneurial spirit in order to fund and operate complex projects. To the extent that these problems will be solved, as they surely will, it is likely that centralized initiatives such as the Archaeology Data Service in England will be crucial to the process. Other countries are pursuing similar avenues, but the more decentralized United States may find a voice in the process only through individual institutions seeking practical standards as a matter of sheer necessity.

See also CHAPTER 15: Databases.

Notes

1   Archaeology as a discipline may be seen as monolithic, and archaeologists may be expected to know about the archaeology of any cultural or geographic area. In fact, however, archaeologists specialize very early in their educational careers, and areas of specialization can be remarkably narrow.

Consequently, readers should be forewarned that the author may not be aware of developments far from his archaeological ken.

2   Other programs can produce drawings at various scales and may seem to have the necessary virtues of CAD, but the use of 3-D Cartesian grid systems as the core for data storage makes CAD more than a drafting aid.

3   Despite the obvious need for archiving archaeological information, archival preservation of paper records has not been routine. Thus, the situation with digital data can be seen as a continuation of sadly normal archaeological practices.

REFERENCES FOR FURTHER READING

Allen, Kathleen M. S., W. Green Standton, and Ezra B. W. Zubrow (eds.) (1990). *Interpreting Space: GIS and Archaeology*. London, New York, Philadelphia: Taylor and Francis.

Badler, Norman and Virginia R. Badler (1977). *SITE: A Color Computer Graphics System for the Display of Archaeological Sites and Artifacts*. Philadelphia: University of Pennsylvania, Moore School of Electrical Engineering, Department of Computer and Information Science.

Binford, Sally R. and Binford, Lewis R. (eds.) (1968). *New Perspectives in Archeology*. Chicago: Aldine.

Duncan, J. M. and P. L. Main (1977). The Drawing of Archaeological Sections and Plans by Computer. *Science and Archaeology* 20: 17–26.

Eiteljorg, H., II (2001). Computing in the Archaeological Curriculum. *CSA Newsletter* 14,2. Available at: <http://csan.org/newsletter/fall01/nlf0104.html>.

Richards, J. D. (1985). Training Archaeologists to Use Computers. *Archaeological Computing Newsletter* 2: 2–5.

Richards, J. D. and N. S. Ryan (eds.) (1985). *Data Processing in Archaeology* (from the series Cambridge Manuals in Archaeology). Cambridge: Cambridge University Press.

Sabloff, Jeremy A. (ed.) (1981). *Simulations in Archaeology*. Albuquerque: University of New Mexico Press.

Upham, Steadman (ed.) (1979). Computer Graphics in Archaeology: Statistical Cartographic Applications to Spatial Analysis in Archaeological Contexts (Anthropological Research Papers no. 15). Tempe: Arizona State University.

The following contain numerous articles concerning archaeological computing and should be consulted broadly:

Annual proceedings of the meetings on Computer Applications and Quantitative Methods in Archaeology beginning in 1973 (published for that one year only as *Science in Archaeology*, 9).

Archaeological Computing Newsletter (tables of contents from number 45 (Spring 1996) onward may be found at <http://www.gla.ac.uk/Acad/Archaeology/acn/index.html>. The *Archaeological Computing Newsletter* will be published by *Archeologia & Calcolatone* from the end of 2004.

CSA Newsletter (All issues beginning with volume 8 are available on the Web, <http://csanet.org/newsletter/>; volumes 13 and following are only available on the Web.)

Selected Websites

<http://catal.arch.cam.ac.uk/catal/catal.html> – the website for the excavations at Çatalhöyük, Turkey, where modern technology has not only been extensively used but discussed and debated.

<http://archaeology.la.asu.edu/teo/> – information about the site Teotihuacan, a site that has benefited from extensive use of computer technology and at which computers have been used for a very long time.

<http://www.getty.edu/artsednet/Exhibitions/Trajan> – should be used in concert with the publication by James Packer (1997), *The Forum of Trajan in Rome* (Berkeley: University of California Press), for an example of an architectural historian using both traditional and computer methods.

<http://ads.ahds.ac.uk/> – the Archaeology Data Service in England (and <http://ads.ahds.ac.uk/project/goodguides/g2gp.html> for the ADS Guides to Good Practice and <http://csanet.org/inftech/cadgd/cadgd.html> for a different version of the CAD Guide to Good Practice).

<http://intarch.ac.uk/> – online journal, *Internet Archaeology.*

<http://propylaea.org/> – CSA Propylaea Project, still in early stages, to construct a stone-by-stone CAD model of the Propylaea. Discussions of methods, but only the CAD model of the predecessor is available.

<http://www.cobb.msstate.edu/dig/LRP-1999-01/> – excavations at Lahav, Israel, with discussion of data collection methods and computer use in the field.

<http://www.arch.columbia.edu/DDL/projects/amiens/> – Amiens cathedral project at Columbia University, with extensive imagery showing the illustrative power of CAD and rendering tools.

<http://vsav.scad.edu> – Savannah urban design/history/development project of the Savannah College of Art and Design, still in early stages. Only Windows users need apply, alas.

<http://www.informatics.org/france/gis.html> – a study of hill forts in France with effective use of GIS technology.

<http://corinth.sas.upenn.edu/corinth.html> – the Corinth Computer Project at the University of Pennsylvania.

<http://atl.ndsu.edu/archive/> – the Digital Archive Network for Anthropology at North Dakota State University, a project involving the use of 3-D models of archaeological objects that may be examined on the Web.

3

Art History

Michael Greenhalgh

Introduction

The discipline itself in this context should be understood to include not only lecturers and students who impart and acquire knowledge, and curators who look after resources such as slides, but also the staff of museums and galleries, with the oversight and care of large quantities of works, usually many more than can be displayed. And we should remember that other historians need and use images from the past,[1] a fact reflected in the broad church of participants included in conferences.[2] In large collections especially, computers were early recognized as an essential tool in regimenting what was often incomplete paper documentation for the use of curators, conservators, registrars, and, eventually, the general public.

Art historians use computers to order, sort, interrogate, and analyze data about artworks, preferably with images; increasingly they wish to use the Web as the carrier for multimedia research or teaching/learning projects. The fact that primary data for art historians are visual – images, still and perhaps moving – did not prevent an early interest in the ordering and interrogation of text data arranged into databases (following the development of automation in libraries) or studying how to deal with the quantitative data churned out by a counting machine (Floud 1979).

This chapter charts such developing use, from the development of text databases through the introduction of digital imaging and then to the use of the Web in teaching and learning. It does not consider the use of computers in art,[3] nor yet text bibliographies of art historical material, such as the *Bibliographie d'Histoire de l'Art*, which are library-based activities. It illustrates how disciplinary innovation in this area is inevitably dependent upon and triggered by technical innovation, and how the introduction and popularization of the Web with its consistent interface has brought new possibilities for computer use in learning. Each section introduces and explains the various problems, and then charts with relevant links how various people and organizations tried to solve them. Far from hymning today's computing world as a nirvana, the theme throughout is of difficulties with expertise, communication, and finance – that is, with people rather than technology. These are problems that intensify as the technologies and the potential applications become more sophisticated (cf. the Virtual Museum of Computing: see http://vmoc.museophile.org/).

Text Databases

Early computers were unsuitable for humanities use: large, slow, expensive, and with software designed by and therefore for scientists, they were jealously guarded. Using one to write a book (with the attraction of supposed "automated indexing") was seen as near-blasphemy and, in any case, was difficult given the restricted software and the way such machines dealt with text. The construction of databases was no easier, because interface programs, which softened and simplified data entry and retrieval, were rare. And the discipline had two problems, which did not confront run-of-the-mill author-title-date databases: the *part–whole problem* (i.e., how to catalogue a multipart altarpiece, let alone a Gothic portal or a complete cathedral), and the element of imprecision, which is often part of historical data.

What is more, the interchangeability and communication we take for granted (and demand) today did not exist: operating system did not necessarily talk unto operating system; input was usually via a text terminal if not via punchcards or paper tape (certainly not a VDU); interfaces hovered between the obscure and the feral; output was to line printer or daisy-wheel or, with some difficulty, to phototypesetter; and inter-computer communication was tricky because of the myriad of physical and logical formats in use. Nevertheless, some institutions (such as the Detroit Institute of Arts: cf. today's Visual Resources Art Image Database) used computers to develop catalogues of their collection, perforce using specially commissioned software, or adapting mainframe programs (such as IBM's STAIRS) to their needs. By the early 1980s, art historians began to develop database projects that grappled with the problem of describing images (see Corti 1984). As in other areas (such as theater history: cf. *The London Stage*; see Donahue, website) the road was often rocky and long, with memory and storage restrictions of early systems demanding laconic descriptors (Villard 1984); and funding for staff, machinery, and programming difficult to find. The Università degli Studi in Siena was early in the field, with a how-to-do-it manual (Bisogni and Corti 1980) followed by one on method-ology describing projects (Bisogni 1980), two giving exemplary applications (di Bari et al. 1981) and yet another tackling the problem of dealing with images (Bisogni 1981).

The first problem in establishing art historical databases was terminology. Even well after the penetration of the microcomputer, the gap between the attitudes of visual resources (VR) curators and academics was clear: few of the latter would take an interest in computerization until machine and network could demonstrably help with teaching or research; and all who had done battle with different slide rooms were quite used to a flexible (read: vague) use of terminology. In any case, most departments had "legacy" collections of slides, and few intended to relabel them all to fit some grand scheme. The VR curators were more precise, reasoning that chaos would result unless the same terminology was employed. Several conferences concentrated on this important matter (see Roberts 1990). Standards are fine, but is it the researchers who want them or the librarians? When somebody at such a conference opined that *For every simple problem, there is a complicated solution*, perhaps she was thinking of the Art History Information Program[4] at the Getty, and its Art and Architecture Thesaurus: begun pre-computers, it offers an excellent set of standards, but these are expensive to implement and far from universally applicable.[5] The fears and expectations of museum professionals are well reflected in the journals of the period.[6]

In any case, how to catalogue an artwork? One possibility was by meaning; and a fruitful project which began without any connection with a computer is ICONCLASS, the origins of which go back to 1954, and which provides an iconographical classification system, and now a CD-ROM, and web browser software.

In these days before effective and cheap graphics, the discipline's associations and journals naturally concentrated on database matters. Thus, *Computers and the History of Art* publishes since 1991 a journal (*CHArt*, a development of a Newsletter begun in 1985), holds annual conferences, usually themed, and now publishes them on the Web. The Visual Resources Association, initially curators meeting annually since 1968 at College Art Association conferences, was founded formally in 1982: it now has some 600 members and a quarterly *Bulletin*, and correctly titles itself "The international organization of image media professionals" with members working in "educational and cultural heritage environments." The range of the membership indicates just how broadly "Art History" images are used and the problems and possibilities they entail are recognized: they include information specialists; digital image specialists; art, architecture, film, and video librarians; museum curators; slide, photograph, microfilm, and digital archivists; architectural firms; galleries; publishers; image system vendors; rights and reproductions officials; photographers; art historians; artists; and scientists.

The Lure of "Intelligent" Software

But surely computers are "thinking" machines, or so it was too often assumed. Much was made in the 1980s of computers as "intelligent," and able to learn and therefore respond just like a teacher. It should be difficult today to conceive of the computer as any more than a speedy idiot obeying a set of precise instructions; but many in the humanities do indeed continue to regard it as a black and magical (or black-magical) box – throw the data at it, and somehow the computer will make sense of them.

Such a continuing substitute for idol-worship has had many adverse consequences, which continue to this day. The first was in the early 1980s, when the heralded "Fifth Generation," to be developed by the Japanese (the very mention of MITI struck apprehension into the Western heart), was to produce new levels of software. Second, this was the age, not coincidentally, when Artificial Intelligence programs – AI – would supposedly take over medical diagnosis, mineral exploration, and, of course, education. Intelligent systems were also proposed for art historians, because computer databases were seen as able to provide intelligent answers to researchers' questions, such as Cerri's expert system for archaeologists and art historians. Characteristically, Cerri was from the Computer Department at the Scuola Normale Superiore (SNS) at Pisa. The SNS provided conferences, examples, and publications to drive along the application of computer processing to art history.[7]

Graphics

The breakthrough for art historians and other humanists came not with the introduction of microcomputers in the later 1970s (usually tricky to program and to use, with strange storage possibilities and nil communication, and intended for aficionados) but with the IBM PC in 1981 and then the Macintosh. I borrowed one from a computer laboratory at a large American University in late 1981: perhaps not recognizing the cuckoo in their superior mainframe nest, they hadn't played with it and didn't want to do so (just as many IBM engineers considered it a toy). As is well known, that machine with its open (i.e., easily and freely imitable) architecture led to an explosion of cheap machines with increasingly user-friendly and sometimes useful software, a cheap storage medium (the floppy disk) and, eventually, a hard disk and then CD-ROM. In 1984 arrived the Apple Macintosh, the first PC with a graphical user interface. The cheapness and apparent utility of micros set many people pondering how they might organize, access, and disseminate the mountains of text and graphics data used in art historical research and teaching (see Heusser 1987).

Pictures on a computer were now theoretically possible for every art historian, even if only in greyscale. Given the puny power of such machines, however, they were not yet feasible – but that would change in the following decade. If the first programs that ensured the popularity of micros were spreadsheets, the second were database packages, for the first time enabling art historians and museum personnel to construct at minimal cost databases of artifacts. Until the late 1980s, these were text-only, and sometimes relational. Only with the more powerful hard-disk machines of the late 1980s did image databases come along, and then the users faced a perennial dilemma: should they purchase a commercial product, paying for the privilege of testing it as version follows version, and lock themselves into a proprietary setup? Or should they go for open roll-your-own software? Luckily, with the development of the freeware/shareware ethos, good open programs could be had for little money; while the development of avowedly non-proprietary operating systems such as Linux not only made people look at the PC with greater fondness, but also encouraged the development of freely distributable software in all application areas.

So was it immediately "goodbye 35 mm slides, hello digital images"? If all successful computers have been digital machines from the start, the last twenty years have high-lighted the problem of how to deal with analogue materials in an increasingly digital age. For the art historians, this means principally slides and photographs. The 1960s had seen the move from 6 × 6 lantern slides (usually greyscale) to 35 mm slides (usually color), and most university departments built up large collections which had to be bought, labeled, catalogued, perhaps mounted, and sometimes repaired. With strong light projected through them, slides fade: a prize exhibit in one collection was six slides of the selfsame Monet *Haystack*, all with different coloration, and none that of the actual painting. Every collection had much the same basic set of slides, curated by expensive personnel: might money not be saved by collecting such images onto a more cheaply reproducible medium?

The late 1980s also saw the introduction of powerful workstations with sufficient memory and screen resolution to manipulate graphics. These were still too expensive for most people, but pioneering projects such as Marilyn Aronberg Lavin's Piero Project and the English VASARI Project were funded, and demonstrated the possibilities of high-power computer graphics (including VRML models [Lavin 1992]: see below) to explore Piero della Francesca's monumental chapel in Arezzo.

Examples

1 Princeton Index of Christian Art, founded 1917. By 1990 it had some 800,000 file cards documenting over 25,000 different subjects, plus a cross-referenced photo file with nearly a quarter of a million images. Copies also in the Vatican, UCLA, Utrecht and Dumbarton Oaks. In 1990, with Mellon Foundation and Princeton funding, a computerized database was begun.
2 The Marburger Index Inventory of Art in Germany is another long-lived venture,[8] which as Foto Marburg goes back to 1913, and collected photographs of art in Germany. Placed on microfiche in the 1980s, the Web version[9] currently offers access to some 220,000 images. It offers a variety of iconographic catalogues ordered by ICONCLASS, as well as orderings according to function, form, material, techniques, and so on.
3 The Witt Computer Index at the Courtauld Institute in London: controlled vocabulary, authority files, ICONCLASS for subject matter.
4 The Census of Antique Works of Art Known to the Renaissance: beginning in 1946 in the photographic collection of the Warburg Institute, funding from the Getty Art History Information Program allowed a start to be made on its computerization; from 1981 housed at both the Warburg and the Biblioteca Hertziana, Rome, a demonstration videodisk was pressed in 1988. Its home from 1995 has been the Kunstgeschichtlichen Seminar of the Humboldt University in Berlin. Cf. the conference *Inaugurating a Scholarly Database: the Census of Antique Works of Art and Architecture Known to the Renaissance*, Warburg Institute, March 19–21, 1992.

Laserdisks

One viable technology, which lost the race for watch-at-home films to the VCR, was the laserdisk or videodisk, which could hold about 40,000 still frames, was cheap to copy, and played to an ordinary TV monitor. What is more, it was a random-access device (simply punch in the desired frame number), and the images thereon did not fade. The images could be enregistered professionally, or a recorder (e.g., by Sony) bought and used. Although it could be operated standalone, the laserdisk player was easily linked to a computer, with the latter holding the text data controlling the display of images.

The 1980s therefore saw the production of several very ambitious laserdisk projects. Some of these were by Art History departments who laserdisked their holdings; little information is now available about these copyright-precarious ventures, and the results certainly did not get much circulated, so that economies of scale were unavailable.

However, several museums and galleries also produced laserdisks of some of their holdings. High-quality projects included the Vatican Library videodisks, on sale from 1993: the first three disks offered a total of 75,000 images, and it was estimated that the Latin MSS alone would occupy 400,000 images.[10] But the relatively high cost of the playing equipment, and their specialized market, meant that few such ventures were a financial (as opposed to a scholarly) success. Where laserdisks were useful was in supplementing the speed and storage deficiencies of computers; thus the first edition of Perseus had the software and text on a CD-ROM, with the images displayed on the linked laserdisk player.

However, although laid down in digital format on the platter, the laserdisk is an analogue technology, and is really video, so that only one dimension of image is possible (NTSC and PAL being slightly different but neither offering more in modern digital parlance than a 300,000-pixel image). By comparing such images with what is possible today (up to about 5,000,000 pixels, or over 16 times that resolution), it is easy to see why the laserdisk has died. But it poses the dilemma: if laserdisks had a ten-year life, and even assuming today's support media will remain readable, will today's digital images soon seem puny, and need redigitizing?

The decade 1984–94 therefore saw much activity as text databases began to be populated with images, at first by scanner or video. This was to be a long and difficult journey because of the huge number of records involved, the cost of digitizing, and worries about image resolution and longevity of the support (tapes, hard disks).

3-D graphics

Interest in graphics was not circumscribed by still images, because it seemed that the new power of computers and speedy networks could deliver much more interesting scenarios in the form of virtual reality. The construction in a computer of a graphical representation of the real world or an imaginary one was seen by some visionaries as offering much more attractive and educationally rich presentations. Why display St Peter's Square or the inside of the Louvre in flat images? Why not build them in the machine, and allow the user to zoom in, out, and around, accessing other resources (text, sound, video) with the click of a mouse? Was this not an effective way of allowing students to experience real environments it was impractical to visit? Package the presentations for the Web, using the Virtual Reality Modeling Language (VRML), and use them for teaching – although the flaw in the argument is that technologies developed for gaming do not necessarily meet exacting standards either of detail or of accuracy – of "realism."

VRML models are difficult to prepare and expensive to construct; so that even if one convincing model were to be constructed, this would not help much in art history courses dealing with tens of monuments. Nor are there any signs that more "intelligent" software will rescue what looks increasingly like a dead end (but not before many art historians, architects, and archaeologists had spent time on ambitious plans for a computer-generated version of the world). Of course, a continuing problem in anything to do with computers is hype versus reality; so that while we can all agree that three dimensions should be an improvement on two (cf. human sight), computer reconstructions of the real world (I exclude drawn reconstructions of archaeological sites – cf. titles such as *Rediscovering*

Ancient Sites through New Technology – where such technologies probably do have a future) remain the triumph of hope over experience. Even if for the devotees of virtual reality we are "virtually there" (Lanier 2001), it is sensible to recognize the scale of the problem from data acquisition to processing and display.[11] Nevertheless, computer graphics, both raster and bitmapped, have a very large part to play in the study of art and architecture (cf. Stenvert 1991).[12] We may even hope for the further development of autostereoscopic 3-D displays, which will allow the user to view the displayed scene without using stereo glasses.[13]

CD-ROM *and digital camera*

In the late 1980s and early 1990s, the generation of digital images for manipulation on standalone computers was done by the end user with a video camera, or by Kodak putting images onto their multi-resolution Photo-CD format. Two technologies that between 1993 and 1998 moved from the high-price, low-volume specialist to the low-price, high-volume consumer category were the CD-ROM burner and the digital camera. CD-ROMs could be professionally pressed in the 1980s, but at high cost; and the first expensive and tricky "end user" burners appeared in 1994. For art history the burner and the camera go together (with their cousin the scanner), because the output of the latter is conveniently stored on the former; as images get larger, so more CD-ROM blanks are needed – hence the recent introduction of its child, the DVD burner, one version of which holds 4.2 GB, rather than the 700 MB of the conventional CD-ROM.

By 1999, prices were reasonable for both items (about a tenfold drop in six years), and light and cheap portable cameras and burners helped scholars on research trips. Only now did the old argument of the art-historical computer-deniers that digital images were inferior to 35 mm slides come to grief. At last it became feasible and cheap to digitize sets of images for class use, although difficulties in the provision of such material to the students remained, as we shall see below.

Examples

1   To encourage involvement, the CIHA Conference in 2000 organized a competition for "the best digital productions in Art History."
2   The Deutsche Forschungsgemeinschaft supports an initiative of the Art History Department of the Humboldt University intended to build up an international archive of Virtual Art (see Grau website).

The Internet, Web, and Communication

In the mid-1980s, micros communicated little better than mainframes. For museums and galleries with data, how to interchange them? By tape, certainly; but would the tape from machine A fit machine B and, if so, could the data thereon be read with or without the program with which they were written? Were two sets of data compatible to the extent that they could be merged, and thereby fulfill a main reason for communication? In general, dog-in-the-manger attitudes have kept data discrete; and it is ironic that the development of the Web has meant that anyone's data can be read in a web browser, thereby negating any urgency in actually sharing them. Idealists, who expected that the Internet and then the Web would mean access to artifacts beyond gallery boundaries, after the manner of the librarians' union catalogue,[14] have been largely disappointed.

If the PC and graphical user interface held the promise of the easy manipulation of images and concomitant text by art historians, their communication across the Internet (Naughton 1999) in universally readable formats was lacking. The enthusiasm and effort in humanities computing may be measured by the 701 pages of the 1989–90 *Humanities Computing Yearbook: A Comprehensive Guide to Software and Other Resources.*[15] Although digitizing images was in hand by 1990 (see Durran 1992–3, for examples), the Web and its protocols and software, a European invention from CERN (Naughton 1999: 230–9), was the breakthrough (in 1993/4), offering a consistent way of viewing data in various formats, and hyperlinking between them. The data could be served from the local machine or, more normally, pulled down from a server Out There somewhere on the Web. Text and still images would write to the browser quickly; sound and video would continue to be problematical on slower networks. For the first time, communication looked easy, in that any connected machine that could run the browser could get the data – no need to bother about incompatible operating systems any more. This cheap, easy, and attractively multimedia protocol saw the designers of earlier teaching and learning packages (most of which began with the penetration of the micro) eager to upgrade their work and reach a larger audience.

Education

Suddenly, with the Web, computing in an education context also looked practicable at a reasonable price. Some departments offered course images on the Web using Mosaic as early as 1994. Although useful websites grew only slowly, and access around the world also (spreading from the G8 outwards), educators could now contemplate the use of these learning materials, with teacher and students being in different locations, and the data being accessed asynchronously, even if they stipulated the survival of the campus-based university.

The minutiae and problems of communication and cooperation bypassed many administrators, in government as well as in education, who since its introduction had seen the microcomputer as a cost-effective way of teaching without teachers. Typical of this period (and our own!) was an increasing demand for education and a reluctance to fund personnel: machines are cheaper, do not get sick or sue, and can be written down for tax purposes. So computers came into education, sometimes as a requirement based on faith rather than need, but more often as cost-cutters, not as education-enhancers or facilitators. The consequences are with us today – usually as much hardware as anyone can use, but an inadequate level of personnel, and no understanding of the need for programmers to write humanities-specific programs. The current hope is to have computers search visual databases by subject, and have the software recognize and retrieve – *all images containing a tree and a river.* Such content-based retrieval might be realized: it is logical to wish for software be able to "recognize" real-world objects, and it would be interesting to see such a process demonstrated on a wide range of art historical data.[16]

Examples

1   Journals promoted education via computer.[17]
2   In the museum world, the Museum Computer Network played an important role, with its archives online since March 1999 (eSpectra website).
3   The Computers in Teaching Initiative (CTI) project was begun in 1984 by the British Computer Board for Universities and Research Councils to help staff use computers in support of teaching. In 1989, 24 specialist centers were established, including a CTI Center for History, Archaeology, and Art History. This offered workshops, and published a Newsletter welcoming "reports on the use of computers for teaching or research... announcements of new courses, reports on running courses, news about projects, software, datasets and conferences, and letters." The mission of the CTI (<http://www.cti.ac.uk>), according to its publicity, was "to maintain and enhance the quality of learning and increase the effectiveness of teaching through the application of appropriate learning technologies." The aim was to "enable change in higher education, because with computers teachers and learners can determine the place, time and pace for learning." Their refereed journal, *Active Learning*, emphasizes "learning outcomes rather than enabling technologies." In 1991, 314 packages for historians were listed (Spaeth 1991).

Art History and Computing Today

The discipline continues to be a minnow in the humanities pond, and a relatively expensive one (all those slides and photographs, and glossy books), but books which in years past targeted a very broad audience now focus on art historians.[18] There are many projects and ventures in the area (cf. CNI and Düsseldorf), and several ventures (to add to the pioneering Marburg Index – see above) which offer an overview of national holdings, such as the Joconde database of works in 75 French museums, which joins a series of other French initiatives (see, for example, the Ministère de la culture website). These are important undertakings: the architecture database called Mérimée, for instance, has over 150,000 records. It also derives from a base prepared in the 1980s: as early as 1985, the Ministère de la culture committed in hardware alone FF18.2 million to archaeology, FF10.8 million for laboratories, and FF10.3 million for the digitization of images and sound (Ministère de la culture 1985). Why are not the governments or cultural organizations of other first-world, computer-rich countries doing likewise?

But as in many other disciplines, moves toward the use of computers and the Web in teaching and learning have been left to the initiative of individual academics; some of these have been told sententiously that academics should leave such technical matters to programmers; others have seen their enterprise met by lack of interest, help, or adequate financing from the administration. On the other hand, institutions in Germany and Switzerland promote computers in research and conferences (see Hamburg

University website), and in courses on computing in the discipline (see Universität Trier website). A collaborative venture – *Schule des Sehens* – offers web-based seminars, using Web-CT. And although the connectivity of computers should also mean the enthusiastic cooperation of academics across institutions, and a willingness to share data, in no country has any such organizational initiative been taken nationally, and international initiatives tend to address narrow research issues rather than to aim to facilitate teaching. "No man is an island," wrote John Donne; but then he had no experience of our supposedly connected world, and of the fears throughout the system. If I develop a web-based course, who owns it, the institution or me? If it works, am I still needed? If ArtA1 exists as such a course, how many young lecturers will be needed, except to keep it updated?

So although the technologies (including Web software) are clever and advanced, it is the human element that restricts obvious developments in the discipline. These (some of which are valid across other disciplines) include: acknowledgment that computer literacy is essential for all staff and students; rethinking of traditional modes of course delivery (which doesn't mean their complete replacement by the Web); gradual replacement of analogue slide collections by digital ones retrieved from some international database-in-the-sky; insistence that web-based learning should improve the quality of education, rather than lower the unit of resource for the administrators; planning for classrooms which encompass existing web-based technologies, including videoconferencing.

Conclusion: The Future

Although computing for art historians is considerably simpler now than it was ten or twenty years ago, many problems remain, and they still revolve around communication, expertise, and finance.

Ease of communication, and a relative freedom from hackers as from the 90 percent or more of idiocy which overloads the net, requires the development of private or restricted networks which will allow the easy transmission and viewing of visual material of spectacularly high resolution. In many ways it is a pity that the Internet and the Web, both developed in universities or university-like institutions on public money, did not tie all the technologies up with patents (against the ideology, I know), and then recoup funds by making commerce pay hugely for their use. This would certainly have softened the funding crisis in higher education.

A growing desire of art historians to teach using the Web requires either the upgrading of useful but general-purpose course-construction programs such as Blackboard or WebCT, or the development of suitable programs usable by newly computer-savvy staff.

Yet financial problems in a small discipline are certain to remain. If there are more than 1,999 museums online worldwide (MCN website), funding prevents many teaching institutions from presenting their materials on the Web. This will happen gradually, as 35 mm slides degrade and as digital cameras take over from analogue ones. Then the day will soon come when VR curators must be as computer-literate as staff in university libraries (now usually part of something like a Division of Scholarly Information), as the Visual Resources Association (VRA) (see above) has recognized for years. In other words, such personnel must capture the high ground of indispensability just as librarians have so successfully presented themselves as the natural high priests for the curating of digital as well as of paper-based information. So how will such a small discipline keep its head above water if it goes thoroughly digital? We already have a system where numbers count instead of quality (5 students taking *Poussin*: bad; 200 students taking *Desire and the Body*: good). In the nineteenth century academics were sometimes paid according to the number of students they attracted (*plus ça change...*); so can we envisage those academics who develop expensive web-based courses recouping the outlay by some kind of pay-per-use micro-money, since computers are good at such calculations? Since tourism is a crucial element in the economy, and since universities are increasingly commercial organizations, should art historians relocate themselves (as many museums have done) as part of the heritage industry (see <http://www.archimuse.com/consulting/bearman.html>), and produce cultural tourism courses for paying customers as spin-offs from their student-directed university work?

The wind of commerce hit museums harder than many universities. In some instances necessity occasioned the creation of good websites as the public face of the institution (interest logged via hits per week); in others it provoked a rethink of the mission of museums and a dumbing down to a lower common denominator, in displays, special exhibitions, and websites. Museums are in a state of flux because of computers and the Web: can/should technology be applied to these dusty mausolea of out-of-context artifacts to provide a learned, multimedia, immersive context – the nearest thing now possible to reintegrating the works with the context from which they were removed? Or is the museum of the future to be a theme park, lacking any truly educational mission, with Web displays as part of the fun? Believers in culture should hope for the former; but, as the inscription on Wren's tomb nearly has it, *Si monumentum requiris, circumclicke*.

Indeed, should we extrapolate from the existence of the Web to the decline of campus-based universities and physical museums and galleries? If galleries can only display a small proportion of their collection at any one time, should not funding go into web-based image databases? And if seminars and tutorials should remain because everyone recognizes the human and pedagogic value of face-to-face sessions, the fixed-term, fixed-place lecture might disappear in the face of the twin pressures of web-based profusely illustrated "lectures," and the increasing inability of students working to pay for their education to attend them. The challenge is to ensure that web-based "lectures" are of a quality equivalent to or higher than traditional ones. We might hope that the digital image, available well-catalogued and in profusion in a discipline for the development of which the photograph was partly responsible, will enhance art history's popularity and underline the worldwide importance of culture in an age where networks reach around the world.

Notes

1 Thus the Institut de Recherche et d'Histoire des Textes published *Le Médiéviste et l'Ordinateur*, issues 26/7 of which (Autumn 1992–Spring 1993) were devoted to digitized images, "*source essentielle pour l'historien et la plupart du temps difficile à consulter.*"

2 Cf. Peter Denley and Deian Hopkin's *History and Computing* (1987): the result of a conference in 1986 to inaugurate an association for historians who used or wished to use computers in their work, whether that work was research or teaching; or Jean-Philippe Genet's *L'Ordinateur et le Métier d'Historien* (1990), from the conference at Talence, September 1989.

3   See <http://www.mediaartnet.org/Texteud.html> for a *tour d'horizon*.

4   Earlier, <http://www.ahip.getty.edu/>.

5   Online at <http://www.getty.edu/research/tools/vocabulary/>. Other Getty projects have included
     the Union List of Artist Names; Guide for the Description of Architectural Drawings and Archives;
     Anthology of Museum Automation; Bibliography of the History of Art (BHA); The Provenance
     Index; The Avery Index to Architectural Periodicals; Witt Computer Index; Census of Antique Art
     and Architecture Known to the Renaissance.

6   *The International Journal of Museum Management and Curatorship* 8,1 (March 1989), is largely devoted
     to computerization; the *False Gods* of the Editorial's title refers to the process of intellectual
     cheapening, not computers.

7   The SNS Centro di Elaborazione Automatica di Dati e Documenti Storico-Artistici produced a
     Bollettino d'Informazioni. Vol. 2 for 1981, for example, offered papers on computerization of a lexicon
     of goldsmiths' work; a report on a seminar to discuss digitization at the Bargello and Museo Stibbert
     in Florence, a catalogue of reused antique sarcophagi, and a report on the computerization of a
     Corpus dell'Arte Senese. For the later history of this organization, cf. <http://www.cribecu.sns.it/
     info/storia.html>.

8   See <http://www.fotomarburg.de>.

9   See <http://www.bildindex.de>.

10   Details in Baryla (1992–3: 23–4). NB: these were accompanied by a database.

11   See Debevec's notes for SIGGRAPH 99 Course no. 28, and cf. <http://www.debevec.org/Research/>;
     a course at SIGGRAPH 2002 was devoted to *Recreating the Past*: <http://www.siggraph.org/s2002/
     conference/courses/crs27.html>; also Polleyes et al., *Reconstruction Techniques with Applications in
     Archeology*, at <http://www.esat.kuleuven.ac.be/sagalassos/3-Dreconstruction/3-D.html>.

12   Cf. Stenvert (1991), with its excellent bibliography.

13   For example, <http://www.seereal.com/default.en.htm> or the list at <http://www.mrl.nyu.edu/
     ~perlin/courses/fall98/projects/autostereo.html>.

14   Cf. virtual library catalogues of art history, such as that at <http://www.ubka.unikarlsruhe.de/kvk/
     vkk/vk_kunst_engl.html> with the interface available in English, French, German, and Italian.

15   See Lancashire (1991: 9–17). These pages are devoted to art history. This gives an indication of the
     relatively slow start of this image-based discipline *vis-à-vis* text-based ones.

16   Romer, who had previously published a paper entitled *A Keyword is Worth 1,000 Images*, correctly
     concluded that "image and multimedia databases are heavily dependent on the quality of their
     stored descriptions" (1996: 55).

17   Such as the *Journal of Educational Multimedia and Hypermedia,* or the CTI's *Active Learning*, no. 2, for
     July 1995, having the theme *Using the Internet for Teaching*.

18   See also Andrews and Greenhalgh (1987) and Richard and Tiedemann's *Internet für Kunsthistoriker:
     Eine praxisorientierte Einführung* (1999).

REFERENCES FOR FURTHER READING

AHWA-AWHA:CIHA London 2000. Section 23: Digital Art History Time. Accessed: September 28,
    2003. At <http://www.unites.uqam.ca/AHWA/Meetings/2000.CIHA/>.
Andrews, Derek and Michael Greenhalgh (1987). *Computing for Non-Scientific Applications*. Leicester:
    Leicester University Press.
Autostereoscopic display project plan. Accessed September 28, 2003. At <http://www.mrl.nyu.edu/
    ~perlin/courses/fall98/projects.autostereo.html>.
Baryla, C. (1992–93). Les vidéodisques de la Bibliothèque Vaticane [The videodisks of the Vatican
    Library]. *Le Médiéviste et l'Ordinateur* 26-7: 23–4.

Bisogni, Fabio (ed.) (1980). *Metodologie di Analisi e di Catalogazione dei beni Culturali* [Methodologies for the analysis and cataloguing of cultural property]. In the series Quaderni di Informatica e Beni Culturali, 2. Siena: Università degli Studi di Siena/Regione Toscana.

——(ed.) (1981). *Sistemi di Trattamento di Dati e Immagini* [The processing of data and images]. In the series Quaderni di Informatica e Beni Culturali, 4. Siena: Università degli Studi di Siena/Regione Toscana.

Bisogni, Fabio and Laura Corti (1980). *Manuale Tecnico per l'Elaborazione Automatica di Dati Storico-Artistici* [Technical manual for the automatic processing of art-historical data]. In the series Quaderni di Informatica e Beni Culturali, 1. Siena: Università degli Studi di Siena/Regione Toscana.

Bowen, Jonathan (2003). *Virtual Museum of Computing. The Virtual Library Museums Pages.* Accessed September 28, 2003. Available at: <http://vmoc.museophile.com/>.

CENSUS: Census of Antique Works of Art and Architecture Known in the Renaissance. Accessed September 28, 2003. At <http://bak-information.ub.tu-berlin.de/fachinfo/DBANKEN/CENSUS. html>.

Cerri, Stefano A. (1983). Sistema esperto di elaborazione elettronica sui beni archeologici di Roma: Come un calculatore può usare competenze archeologica per rispondere a domande ingenue e complesse [Expert system for the processing of Roman archaeological artifacts: how a computer can exploit archaeological information to respond to subtle and complex questions]. In the Conference Roma: Archeologia e Projetto, Campidoglio, Rome, pp. 23–28, 20.

CHArt: Computers and the History of Art. Accessed September 28, 2003. At <http://www.chart.ac.uk/>.

Coalition for Networked Information (CNI). *Humanities and Arts Report: Appendices.* Last updated July 3, 2002. Accessed September 28, 2003. At <http://www.cni.org/projects.humartiway/humartiway-rpt. append.html>.

Corti, Laura (1984). *Census: Computerization in the History of Art, I*, Pisa and Los Angeles: Scuola Normale Superiore Pisa / J. Paul Getty Trust Los Angeles.

Courtauld Institute of Art. University of London. Accessed September 28, 2003. At <http://www. courtauld.ac.uk/>.

Crane, Gregory (ed.) *The Perseus Digital Library.* Accessed September 28, 2003. At: <http://www. perseus.tufts.edu/>.

Cribecu Online. Centro Ricerche Informatiche per i Beni Culturali. Accessed September 28, 2003. At <http://www.cribecu.sns.it/info/storia.html>.

Daniels, Dieter. *Medien Kunst Netz* [Strategies of Interactivity], tr. Tom Morrison. At <http://www. mediaartnet.org/Texteud.html>.

Debevec, Paul. Modelling and Rendering Architecture from Photographs. Notes for SIGGRAPH 99 Course no. 28. Accessed September 28, 2003. At <http://www.debevec.org/Research/>.

Denley, Peter, and Deian Hopkin (eds.) (1987). *History and Computing.* Manchester: Manchester University Press.

Detroit Institute of Arts. *DIA Visual Resource Home Page.* Accessed September 28, 2003. At <http:// www.diamondial.org/>.

di Bari, Vittoria Carla et al. (1981). *Elaborazione Automatica dei Dati relativi alle Monete Romane dello Scavo di Campo all'Oro (Siena)* [Computer processing of Roman coin data from the excavation at Campo all'Oro (Siena)]. In the series Quaderni di Informatica e Beni Culturali, 3. Siena: Università degli Studi di Siena/Regione Toscana.

Direction des Musées de France base Joconde. Accessed September 28, 2003. At <http://www.culture.fr/ documentation/joconde/pres.htm>.

Donahue, Joseph. *The London Stage 1800–1900: A Documentary Record and Calendar of Performances.* Accessed September 28, 2003. At <http://www-unix.oit.umass.edu/~a0fs000/lsp.html>.

Dota, Michele and Franco Niccolucci (1981). *Elaborazione Automatica dei Dati relativi ai Conventi del Centro Storico di Firenze, Siena.* [Computer processing of data concerning the convents of the historical centers of Florence and Siena]. In the series Quaderni di Informatica e Beni Culturali, 5. Siena: Università degli Studi di Siena/Regione Toscana.

Durran, Jennifer. *Developments in Electronic Image Databases for Art History* [1992–3]. Last updated April 14, 2000. First published in: *Drinking From A Fire Hose: Managing Networked Information Conference Preprints* (pp. 86–96). Victorian Association for Library Automation 7th Biennial Conference and Exhibition, November 9–11, 1993. Accessed September 28, 2003. At <http://www.arts.monash.edu.au/visual_culture/about/staff/jdurran/vala_report.html>.

——(1994). *EVA: Electronic Imaging and the Visual Arts Conference, Tutorials and Exhibition: A Review.* Last updated April 14, 2000. First published: *ARLIS/ANZ News* 39, November 1994: 71–5. Accessed September 28, 2003. At <http://www.arts.monash.edu.au/visual_culture/about/staff.jdurran/eva93.html>.

Düsseldorf. Die Düsseldorfer Virtuelle Bibliothek: Kunstwissenschaft. Last updated September 18, 2003. Accessed September 28, 2003. At <http://www.rz.uni-duesseldorf.de/WWW/ulb.kun.html>.

eSpectra Features: March 1999. Accessed September 28, 2003. At <http://www.mcn.edu/eSpectra/03_1999.html>.

Floud, Roderick (1979). *An Introduction to Quantitative Methods for Historians*, 2nd edn. London: Methuen.

Genet, Jean-Philippe (1990). *L'Ordinateur et le métier d'historien*. From the conference at Talence, September 1989. Bordeaux: Maison des Pays Ibériques.

Getty Vocabulary Program. The J. Paul Getty Trust. Accessed September 28, 2003. At <http://www.getty.edu/research/tools/vocabulary/>.

Grau, Oliver. *Ancestors of the Virtual, Historical Aspects of Virtual Reality and its Contemporary Impact*. CIHA London, 2000. Section 23: Digital Art History Time. Accessed September 28, 2003. At <http://www.unites.uqam.ca/AHWA/Meetings/2000.CIHA/Grau.html>.

Hamber, Anthony (1991). The VASARI Project. *Computers and the History of Art* 1,2: 3–19.

Hamburg University. Schule des Sehens – Neue Medien der Kunstgeschichte. Accessed September 28, 2003. At <http://www.uni-hamburg.de/Wiss/FB/09/KunstgeS/schulesehen.html>.

Heusser, Hans-Jörg (ed.) (1987). Computers and the Future of Research: Visions, Problems, Projects. *AICARC: Bulletin of the Archives and Documentation Centers for Modern and Contemporary Art* 14,2/15,1.

ICONCLASS. Accessed September 28, 2003. At <http://www.iconclass.nl/>.

INIST-CNRS. *Bibliographie de l'Histoire de l'Art* [Bibliography of the History of Art]. Accessed September 28, 2003. At <http://www.inist.fr/BHA/>.

Institut de Recherche et d'Histoire des Textes (1992–3). *Le Médiéviste et l'Ordinateur* 26/7.

International Journal of Museum Management and Curatorship (1989). 8,1.

Lancashire, Ian (ed.) (1991). *The Humanities Computing Yearbook, 1989–90*. Oxford: Clarendon Press.

Lanier, Jaron (2001). Virtually There. *Scientific American*. Available at <http://www.scientificamerican.com/2001/0401issue/9401lanier.html>.

Lavin, Marilyn Aronberg (1992). Researching Visual Images with Computer Graphics. *Computers and the History of Art* 2,2: 1–5.

Lavin, Marilyn Aronberg and Kirk Alexander. *Piero Project: ECIT/Electronic Compendium of Images and Text*. Accessed September 28, 2003. At <http://etc.princeton.edu/art430/art430.html>.

MCN (Museum Computer Network). *Museum Sites Online*. Accessed September 28, 2003. At <http://www.mcn.edu/resources/sitesonline/htm>.

Ministère de la culture. Documentation: Bases de données patrimoniales. [Documentation: national heritage databases]. Accessed September 28, 2003. At <http://www.culture.fr/documentation/docum.htm>.

Ministère de la culture (1985). *Mission de la Recherche* [brochure]. Paris: Ministère de la culture.

Naughton, John (1999). *A Brief History of the Future: The Origins of the Internet*. London: Weidenfeld and Nicolson.

Otey, Astrid. *Visual Resources Association*. Last updated September 9, 2003. Accessed September 28, 2003. At <http://www.vraweb.org/>.

Polleyes, M., et al. *Reconstruction Techniques with Applications in Archeology*. Accessed September 28, 2003. At <http://www.esat.kuleuven/ac.be/sagalassos/3-Dreconstruction/3-D.html>.

Richard, Birgit and Tiedemann, Paul (1999). *Internet für Künsthistoriker: Eine praxisorientierte Einführung*. Darmstadt.

Roberts, D. Andrew (ed.) (1990). *Terminology for Museums. Proceedings of the International Conference*, Cambridge, England, September 21–4, 1988.

Romer, Donna M. (1996). Image and Multimedia Retrieval. In David Bearman et al., *Research Agenda for Networked Cultural Heritage* (pp. 49–56). Santa Monica, CA: Getty AHIP.

SIGGRAPH (2002). *Course 27: Recreating the Past*. Accessed September 28, 2003. At <http://www.siggraph.org/s2002/conference/courses/crs27.html>.

Spaeth, Donald (1991). *A Guide to Software for Historians*. Glasgow: CTI.

Stenvert, Ronald (1991). *Constructing the Past: Computer-assisted Architectural-Historical Research: The Application of Image-processing using the Computer and Computer-Aided Design for the Study of the Urban Environment, Illustrated by the Use of Treatises in Seventeenth-century Architecture*. The Hague: self-published in association with the Dutch Government Service for the Preservation of Monuments and Historic Buildings.

Universität Trier. D. W. Dörrbecker: *Veranstaltungsangebote im Wintersemester 2002–2003*. Accessed September 28, 2003. At <http://www.uni-trier.de/uni/fb3/kunstgeschichte/2002/WS/dwd.html>.

Villard, Laurence (1984). *Système descriptif des antiquités classiques*. Paris: Réunion des Musées Nationaux.

VRND: *A Real-Time Virtual Reconstruction, Notre Dame Cathedral*. Accessed September 28, 2003. At <http://www.vrndproject.com/>.

4

Classics and the Computer: An End of the History

Greg Crane

Many non-classicists from academia and beyond still express surprise that classicists have been aggressively integrating computerized tools into their field for a generation. The study of Greco-Roman antiquity is, however, a data-intensive enterprise. Classicists have for thousands of years been developing lexica, encyclopedias, commentaries, critical editions, and other elements of scholarly infrastructure that are best suited to an electronic environment. Classicists have placed great emphasis on systematic knowledge management and engineering. The adoption of electronic methods thus reflects a very old impulse within the field of classics. The paper knowledge base on Greco-Roman antiquity is immense and well organized; classicists, for example, established standard, persistent citations schemes for most major authors, thus allowing us to convert nineteenth-century reference tools into useful electronic databases. Classicists are thus well prepared to exploit emerging digital systems. For many classicists, electronic media are interesting not (only) because they are new and exciting but because they allow us to pursue more effectively intellectual avenues than had been feasible with paper. While many of us compare the impact of print and of new electronic media, classicists can see the impact of both revolutions upon the 2,500-year history of their field. Electronic media thus allow us to pursue both our deepest and most firmly established scholarly values and challenge us to rethink every aspect of our field.

The title of this chapter alludes to a 1993 article, "Classics and the Computer: the History," in which Theodore Brunner, the founder of the *Thesaurus Linguae Graecae* (*TLG*), described the development of computing in the classics up to the end of the 1980s. Those wishing an account of the first generation of computer-based work in classics will find the story well documented in Brunner's work. This chapter takes a broader, more schematic, and more tendentious approach. To some extent, this approach is reactive: the rise of the personal computer and, more recently, of the World Wide Web has diffused computation throughout the daily life of scholars, and especially of students. A Foucauldian scholar might compare the shift from a few very specialized projects and extremely expensive hardware to the ubiquitous e-mail viewers, web browsers, word processing systems, bibliographic database systems, etc., to the shift from the spectacle of the sovereign to the diffused microphysics of modern power. New computer-based projects continue to emerge; the December 2002 *Ancient Studies – New Technology* conference at Rutgers hosted presentations on roughly thirty computer-based projects about the ancient world. Perhaps more significant, even superficially traditional publications distributed even now in traditional format (whether paper-only publication or as electronic files that mimic paper presentation) depend upon an infrastructure that is almost entirely electronic. Digital systems have quietly become the norm. A follow-on to Brunner's history would lead far beyond the growing but much more tractable body of work that Brunner confronted more than a decade ago.

The title of this chapter reflects an argument as well as a defensive strategy. There should not be a history of classics and the computer, for the needs of classicists are simply not so distinctive as to warrant a separate "classical informatics." Disciplinary specialists learning the strengths and weaknesses have, in the author's experience, a strong tendency to exaggerate the extent to which their problems are unique and to call for a specialized, domain-specific infrastructure and approach. Our colleagues in the biological sciences have been able to establish bioinformatics as a vigorous new field – but the biologists can bring to bear thousands of times more resources than can classicists. A tiny field such as classics, operating at the margins of the humanities, cannot afford a distinctive and autonomous history of its own. For classicists to make successful use of information technology, they must insinuate themselves within larger groups, making allies of other disciplines and sharing infrastructure. For classicists, the question is not whether they can create a classical informatics but whether such broad rubrics as computational humanities, computing in the humanities, cultural informatics, and so on, are sufficient or whether they should more aggressively strive to situate themselves within an informatics that covers the academy as a whole. Even academic technology, strictly defined, may be too limiting, since the most revolutionary information technology for twenty-first-century philologists may well emerge from programs such as TIDES (Translingual Information Detection Extraction Summarization), supported by the US military.

But much as some of us may struggle to minimize the future history of classical computing as a separate movement, classicists have had to forge their own history. Even in the best of futures, where classicists customize general tools and share a rich infrastructure with larger disciplines, classicists will have to struggle mightily for their voices to be heard so that emerging systems and standards meet their needs. This chapter seeks to explain why classicists needed to create this separate history in the past and to ground current trends in a larger historical context. It is relatively easy to pass judgments on the past, but in using the past to argue for trends in the future this chapter justifies any unfairness in its own perfect hindsight by exposing its own predictions for the future.

The following broad movements – which overlap with one another and all continue to the present – provide one way of looking at the history of classical computing. First, beginning with Father Roberto Busa's concordance of Aquinas's Latin writing in the late 1940s, standard machines were used to produce particular projects (especially concordances such as Packard's *Livy Concordance*). Second, beginning at roughly 1970, large, fairly centralized efforts took shape that sought to address major issues of classical computing infrastructure. These projects included David Packard's Ibycus system, the *TLG*, the *Database of Classical Bibliography*, the *Bryn Mawr Classical Review*, the Duke Databank of Documentary Papyri, and the Perseus Project. Third, beginning in the mid-1980s, the rise of the personal computer distributed computing throughout classics and, indeed, the humanities. Fourth, beginning in the mid-1990s, the rise of the Web spurred a vast outpouring of smaller projects in classics as in other fields.

The following section takes one particular point in time twenty years ago (1982–3). The selection reflects the situation that existed when the author of this piece began his own work, but focusing on this point in time provides a brief case study with the particular illustrating more general conditions. The subsequent section provides a schematic view of classical computing. The conclusion briefly suggests how trends rooted in the past may carry us forward into the future.

Cincinnati 1983: Retrospectives and Prospectives

In the American Philological Association convention in 1983, held at Cincinnati, a crowded session considered the merits of two very different approaches to classical computing. I was part of a group describing a Unix-based approach that we had begun developing at the Harvard Classics Department in the summer of 1982. David Packard, who was then, and remains today, arguably the most significant figure in classical computing, was prepared to explain the rationale for his own Ibycus system, which he had spent years developing from the ground up to serve the needs of classicists. Then a graduate student and very conscious of my junior position, I was very nervous – if there was a tradition of young entrepreneurial leadership in technology, I had certainly not encountered it as a classicist. The underlying issues remain interesting topics of debate: how far do we follow generic standards, and at what point do the benefits of specialization justify departures from broader practice?

Looking back after twenty years, we could argue that the positions we espoused had prevailed. The Ibycus minicomputer system is long gone and its successor, the Ibycus Scholarly Computer (SC) PC system, is no longer under development (although a few venerable Ibycus SCs continue to serve dedicated users to this day). The benefits which my colleagues and I placed on standards have, to some extent, proven themselves: the 10,000 lines of source code, written in the C programming language under Unix, which provided an efficient searching environment for Greek and other languages, still compiles and can run on any Unix system (including Linux and OS X) – it would not be possible to buy today a computer that was less powerful than the fastest systems to which we had access twenty years ago. The *Thesaurus Linguae Graecae* itself now uses a Unix server to provide the core string-searching operations on which both Packard and my group were working twenty years ago.

Such a triumphalist retrospective upon the past would, however, be unjust and inaccurate. First, systems are only a means to an end. David Packard opened his presentation in December 1983 with an observation that put our discussions into perspective and that has shaped my own decision making ever since. He observed that software and systems were ephemeral but that primary sources such as well structured, cleanly entered source texts were objects of enduring value. In fact, the *TLG* had released a core set of Greek authors in machine-readable form and our work concentrated above all on providing text-searching facilities for this collection. Word processing and typesetting were major advantages of the new technology and the decrease in per page typesetting costs helped justify the considerable expense of any systems – Unix, Ibycus, or other – at the time.

The *TLG* had begun work more than a decade before in 1972. The *TLG* began creating its digital library of classical Greek source texts by using the standard tools available from the UC Irvine computer center, but the problems of entering, formatting, and verifying Greek texts were very different from those of the number-crunching experiments and administrative databases for which those tools were developed. Packard's Ibycus system provided an environment far more suited to their needs than anything else available. Packard had gone so far as to modify the microcode of the Hewlett Packard minicomputer to enhance the speed of text searching. He created an entire environment, from the operating system up through a high-level programming language, aimed initially at serving the needs of classicists. Decades later, the boldness and achievement of creating this system seems only greater to this observer. It would have been immensely more difficult for the *TLG* – and many other smaller projects (such as the Duke Databank of Documentary Papyri and Robert Kraft's Septuagint Project) – to have been as successful. Without the Ibycus environment, few departments would have been able to justify the use of computers in the 1970s or early 1980s. Nor might the field have been able to provide the National Endowment to the Humanities funders with the same level of support for the *TLG*.

The early 1980s represented a tipping point, for at that time new systems were emerging that would provide inexpensive and, even more important, relatively stable platforms for long-term development. The Unix operating system, C programming language, and similar resources provided tools that were independent of any one commercial vendor and that have continued to evolve ever since. MS DOS and the IBM PC appeared in 1981 – before most of our current undergraduates were born. The Macintosh (which has now built its current operating system on a Berkeley Unix base) appeared in 1984 – at the same time as many students who entered American universities as freshmen in 2002. New languages such as Java and Perl have emerged, and web browsers have provoked a substantially new model of cross-platform interaction, but tools developed under Unix twenty years ago can still run. They may be abandoned, but only if better tools have emerged – not because the systems in which they were created are gone and they need to be, at the least, reconstituted.

But even if the early 1980s represented the beginning of a new phase in the evolution of digital technology, the gap between our needs as classicists and the infrastructure at hand remained immense. The labor needed to adapt existing infrastructure to our needs was not so daunting as that which faced David Packard in building the Ibycus, but it was substantial.

Two classes of problems faced us, and they continue to face us even now. The first, to which I will return, consisted of tangible problems that we needed to solve. The second, however, arose from the gap in understanding between those of us who were new to the technology and our technological colleagues who were innocent of classics. Because we were unable to communicate our real needs, we made serious initial errors, investing heavily in tools that seemed suitable but proved, on closer examination, to be fundamentally unable to do what we needed. While many of the problems that we faced then have resolved themselves, the general problem remains: the biggest government funders of academic technology are the National Institutes of Health and the National Science Foundation whose aggregate funding ($20 billion and $5 billion respectively) exceeds that of the National Endowment for the Humanities ($135 million requested for 2003) by a factor of 185. The academic technology specialists in higher education surely devote at least 1 percent of their time to the humanities, but the staggering disparity in support – governmental and private – for science, technology, and medicine means that the humanities are trapped at the margins of decision making. If our needs require substantial added investment beyond those of our colleagues outside the humanities (not to mention classics in particular), we will have great difficulties. We must be proactive and influence the shape of information technology as early as possible, tirelessly exploring common ground with larger disciplines and taking responsibility for pointing out where our challenges do, in fact, overlap with those of our colleagues from beyond the humanities.

Our lack of sophistication, which became clear when Harvard began its own computing project in the summer of 1982, had one advantage. If we had been more knowledgeable, the department probably would not have moved forward but would have waited for technology to advance further. Instead, the department invested so many resources that we could not easily pull back. In the end, our work on the specialized problems of classical typesetting helped lower the publication costs of Harvard Studies in Classical Philology and the Loeb Classical Library, thus providing a justification for the initial investment. But if the results were ultimately satisfactory, the process was deeply flawed, and we were profoundly lucky to enjoy as much success as we did. Many other projects in classics and throughout the academy have faced similar problems and not been so fortunate.

Several months of intensive work gave us a clearer idea of the challenges that we faced in 1982. I offer the following as a representative survey to document the state of the art at the time.

Computer power and storage

In 1965, Gordon E. Moore observed that the number of transistors that could be stored per unit area had been doubling since the transistor was invented and he argued that the trend would continue for the foreseeable future. The pace has slowed a bit – density has doubled every year and a half – but the exponential change has continued. Thus, twenty years ago we felt ourselves able to control staggering computational resources and looked upon the previous years with satisfaction. Now, of course, the subsequent twenty years have made our initial systems appear primitive. The Psychology Department's Digital Equipment Corporation PDB 11/44 on which we did our work had far less computational power than the smallest desktop machine now available, but served dozens of users typing in manuscripts or conducting experiments. For us as classicists, disk storage was a crucial issue. Modern disks allowed us to imagine keeping vast libraries – dozens of megabytes – of text online for casual searching and analysis. The Psychology lab at the time had two 80-megabyte hard drives, each the size of a small washing machine. The Harvard Classics Department needed more storage to mount the *TLG* and purchased the largest machine then generally available. The Control Data Corporation disk held 660 megabytes – four times the storage of both disks already installed. It cost $34,000 (including our educational discount) and had a service contract of $4,000 per year. The disk arrived in a crate that we had to pry open. We needed a special-purpose disk controller ($2,000). Worst of all, we had to write a software driver to mount this disk, hacking the source code to the Berkeley Unix system. It took months before we could exploit more than a tiny fraction of the disk storage on this heavy, loud, expensive device. Our colleagues in the Ibycus world chose different hardware (at the time, the largest Ibycus systems had, if I recall correctly, 400-megabyte drives) but the basic parameters were the same for all of us. Disk storage was cumbersome and expensive. As I write this, the smallest disk that I can find contains 20 gigabytes (30 times as much as our CDC behemoth) and costs $200 (150 times less). The price/performance ratio has thus increased by a factor of *c*.45,000. This does not even consider the fact that this 20-gigabyte drive plugs directly into a computer without modification and that it fits in a notebook.

Machines have grown so fast and inexpensive that it is perhaps difficult for most of us to imagine the extent to which hardware constrained the way we designed systems and thus the questions that we could pursue. The extraordinarily high cost of disk storage meant that Packard chose not to create indices for the *TLG*. All searches read through the texts from start to finish. Packard modified the microcode of the HP minicomputer to increase the search speed, thus providing another reason to build an entirely new operating system. Limitations on storage meant that digital images of any kind were impractical. The first *TLG* texts that we received at Harvard were in a compressed format that reduced storage by *c*.20 percent. We had to write a program to decompress the files – the program was short but we had to write one ourselves as none existed, and this simply added to the overhead of working with the *TLG* documents.

Greek display

The graphical displays which we now take for granted were not in standard circulation. Displays were monochrome terminals that could cope with letters but not drawings, much less color. Even displaying textual data posed major technical barriers. The *TLG* had already developed an excellent ASCII encoding scheme for classical Greek and we had no scientific reason to use anything other than BETA Code, but our colleagues insisted that they needed to see fully accented classical Greek. We thus had to devote substantial energy to the font problem – some of us who worked on Greek fonts in the period still view "font" as the one most disturbing four-letter word in English.

To display Greek, we needed to use special terminals that could display customized character sets. We designed Greek fonts on graph paper, converted the dot patterns into hexadecimal codes, programmed the data on to chips and then physically inserted these chips into the displays. The monitors that we used cost $1,700 each and provided users with shared access to the overtaxed minicomputers in the psychology department.

Networks

The Internet was still tiny, connecting a few key research institutions over a relatively slow network. When we first began work in 1982, we had access to no machine-to-machine networking other than log-ins via dial-up modems. To provide our colleagues access to the machine in the William James building, we purchased massive spools with thousands of feet of twisted pair cable and then ran this cable through a network of steam tunnels and conduits to Widener Library and other buildings. We did have e-mail within our single machine but we only gained access to inter-machine e-mail when we joined a network called UUCP. At the time, the machine would effectively grind to a halt every time it processed mail. Nor was mail a very effective tool, since we knew very few people outside of our own group who had e-mail accounts. Simple file transfers were beyond us and the current Internet would have seemed outlandish: experience near the bleeding of technology tends to generate a schizophrenic attitude, alternating between the visionary and the cynical.

Multilingual text editing

David Packard developed an editor for the Ibycus that could manage Greek and English. When we first considered working with Unix our best consultant suggested that it would take twenty minutes to modify the source code for the standard Unix text editor (Vi) to handle Greek. In fact, the Unix text editor assumed an ASCII character set and would have required a complete rewrite to manage any other character sets. We spent a good deal of time trying to develop a multilingual text editor. We had made good progress when the Macintosh arrived. The Macintosh knew nothing about languages at the time, but it understood fonts, and multiple fonts were enough to serve the basic needs of classicists. We abandoned our editor and resolved never to address a general problem that the marketplace would solve for us.

Text retrieval

Pioneers such as Gerald Salton had laid the foundation for the science of information retrieval in the 1950s and 1960s. Techniques already existed to provide efficient searching of textual databases. The tools at our disposal were also powerful and flexible. Unix provided a superb scripting language and development environment within which to reuse existing programs. Unix provided several text-searching programs (the infamously non-mnemonic grep, egrep and fgrep). We had the source code for everything and could thus modify any existing Unix program. Searching the *TLG* and other scholarly textual databases should have been easy.

In fact, it proved quite difficult to build services that our colleagues would actually use on the generic tools of Unix. Three issues confronted us. First, we needed a reasonable interface. Few classicists even today have proven willing to learn how to use a Unix environment directly. Since we were working more than a decade before web browsers radically reduced the labor needed to create simple interfaces, this task required both programming and design work.

Second, we needed to generate standard citations for the search results. The Unix search utilities returned lines that had a particular pattern. The *TLG* files had a complex scheme for encoding changes in book, chapter, section, or line numbers. The search program had to examine each line in a file and update the various registers, as well as deal with the exceptions (e.g., line 178a, line 38 appearing before line 34, etc.) that have found their way into our texts. Adding such routines to the fine-tuned text-scanning modules of the Unix search routines proved non-trivial and would have required virtual rewrites.

Third, speed was an issue. The systems to which we had access were too slow. We learned quickly why David Packard had modified the microcode of this HP computer to increase linear search speeds. Ultimately, we were able to match the linear search speeds on the Ibycus on DEC VAX computers by rewriting the core search loop in VAX assembly language so that we could utilize a special pattern-matching language. Of course, the VAX computers were more expensive (and more powerful) than the HP computers. Also, while classics departments owned Ibycus computers, we shared all of our machines with many other users – and others did not appreciate our clogging the system with searches that slowed down the disks and the CPU alike.

Fourth, searching classical Greek raises two problems. First, classical Greek has a complex system of accentuation, with the accent shifting around the word as inflections vary. Thus, searches need to be able to ignore accents and scan for underlying stems: e.g., searching for forms of the verb πέμπω ("to send"), we need to match "ἔπεμπον" and "πέμπεις." We can write regular expressions to accommodate this or simply search for "πεμπ" or "πέμπ" but such permutations can become complex and require knowledge of vowel length and other features of the language. More significantly, Greek is a highly inflected language. The search tools developed under Unix implicitly assumed English – with its minimal system of inflections – as its model. The tools at our disposal simply were not designed for a language in which a single verb can have a thousand different forms.

Ultimately, we developed a multilingual full text retrieval system from scratch. The system used a set of inverted indices, added 50 percent to the storage needs of the *TLG* (a significant factor then), but provided almost instantaneous lookups. The system comprised more than 15,000 lines of code when completed and provided a reasonable *TLG* solution for a decade, finally yielding to personal computer-based programs to search the subsequent *TLG* CDs.

From 1983 to 2003: Past Trends and Prospects

The details listed in the section above provide an insight into one particular point in time. The problems described above warrant documentation in part precisely because it is hard to remember now what barriers they posed. Looking back over the past twenty years, the following broad themes stand out.

Increasingly powerful hardware

Moore's law continues to hold. Even if technology were to freeze at 2003 levels, we would still need a generation to digest its implications. The cost of storing textual databases such as the *TLG* is almost zero. We can store hundreds of thousands of images, vast geographic datasets and anything that was published in print.

Visualizations

These include not only virtual reality displays and geographic information systems but also automatically generated timelines and other data visualization techniques.

The result will be possibilities for more holistic analysis of the Greco-Roman world, with philologists making much more effective use of art and archaeological materials than before.

Language technologies

I single out the broad class of "language technologies," a rubric that includes machine translation, cross-lingual information retrieval (e.g., type in "guest friend" and locate passages in Greek, Latin, Arabic, Sanskrit, etc.), summarization, clustering, syntactic analysis (and the possibility of generating large syntactic databases for Greco-Roman source texts), etc. The US defense establishment is investing heavily in rapidly deployable tools for "low-density languages" (e.g., languages for which few if any computational resources exist) – intelligence analysts have found themselves compelled to develop capabilities in languages such as Albanian and Pashtun. The underlying resources for these techniques are bilingual text corpora, morphological analyzers, online lexica, grammars and other knowledge sources. Classicists already have these resources online, and other languages promise to follow suit. The next twenty years promise to introduce a golden age of philology, in which classicists not only explore new questions about Greek and Latin but also explore corpora in many languages which they will never have the opportunity to master.

Annotation managers

Classicists have a long tradition of standalone commentaries and small notes on individual words and passages. All major literary classical Greek source texts are available from the *TLG* and many from Perseus. Authors can already publish annotations directly linked to the passages that readers see (rather than buried in separate publications). The hypertextual nature of web reading is stimulating new tools and new opportunities with classicists, who can bring online a rich tradition of annotations.

Rise of library repositories

The World Wide Web spurred a generation of pseudo-publication: documents more broadly available than any print publication in history could at any given time reach millions of machines. The same documents often ran, however, under individual accounts, with many URLs being changed or pointing to documents that were no longer online or, arguably worse, that had been substantively changed since the original link had been added. A variety of library repositories are now coming into use.[1] Their features differ but all are dedicated to providing long-term storage of core documents and to separating authors from preservation. In the world of publication, alienation is a virtue, because in alienating publications, the author can entrust them to libraries that are designed to provide stable access beyond the lifespan of any one individual. Unless we transfer stewardship – and control – of our work at some point, then our work will not outlive us.

Convergence of needs

The examples listed above reflect a common theme: as our computing infrastructure grows in power, the generality of the tools developed increases and the degree to which classicists (and other humanists) need to customize general tools becomes more defined. Where Packard had to create a whole operating system, we were, twenty years ago, able to build on Unix. Where we needed to work on our own multilingual text editor, Unicode provides multilingual support now at the system level. The set of problems particular to classicists is shrinking. We are better able now than ever before to share infrastructure with our colleagues not only in the humanities but in the rest of the academy as well. The rising NSF-sponsored National Science Digital Library (NSDL) will, if it is successful, probably establish a foundation for the integration of academic resources across the curriculum. Nevertheless, classicists need to reach out to their colleagues and to begin influencing projects such as the NSDL if these science-based efforts are to serve our needs in the future. Otherwise, we may find that simple steps that could radically improve our ability to work in the future will have been overlooked at crucial points in the coming years. Our history now lies with the larger story of computing and academia in the twenty-first century.

Note

1   Among the best known are D-Space (at <http://www.dspace.org>) and FEDORA (at <http://www.fedora.info/>).

REFERENCES FOR FURTHER READING

Ancient Studies – New Technology, conference held at Rutgers University, December 2002. At <http://tabula.rutgers.edu/conferences/ancient_studies2002/>. Accessed April 5, 2004.

Brunner, T. F. (1993). Classics and the Computer: The History. In J. Solomon (ed.), *Accessing Antiquity: The Computerization of Classical Databases* (pp. 10–33). Tucson: University of Arizona Press.

The Bryn Mawr Classical Review. Accessed April 5, 2004. At <http://ccat.sas.upenn.edu/bmcr/>.

Busa, R. (1949). *La terminologia tomistica dell'interiorità; saggi di metodo per un'interpretazione della metafisica della presenza* (p. 279). Milano: Fratelli Bocca.

The Database of Classical Bibliography. Accessed April 5, 2004. At <http://www.library.usyd.edu.au/databases/dcb.html>.

The Duke Databank of Documentary Papyri. Accessed April 5, 2004. At <http://scriptorium.lib.duke.edu/papyrus/texts/DDBDP.html>.

Packard, D. W. (1968). *A Concordance to Livy.* Cambridge, MA: Harvard University Press.

The Perseus Project. Accessed April 5, 2004. At <http://www.perseus.tufts.edu>.

Thesaurus Linguae Graecae Project. Accessed April 5, 2004. At <http://www.tlg.uci.edu/>.

TIDES (Translingual Information Detection Extraction Summarization). Accessed April 5, 2004. At <http://tides.nist.gov/>.

5

Computing and the Historical Imagination

William G. Thomas, III

In the late 1960s and early 1970s historians seemed to think that their profession, the craft and art of history itself, was on the brink of change. Everywhere one looked the signs were unmistakable. A kind of culture war broke out in the profession and a flurry of tense conference panels, public arguments, and roundtables took place with subtitles, such as "The Muse and Her Doctors" and "The New and the Old History." This culture war pitted the "new" history, largely influenced by social science theory and methodology, against the more traditional practices of narrative historians. The "new" historians used computers to make calculations and connections never before undertaken, and their results were, at times, breathtaking. Giddy with success, perhaps simply enthusiastic to the point of overconfidence, these historians saw little purpose in anyone offering resistance to their findings or their techniques. When challenged at a conference, more than one historian responded with nothing more than a mathematical equation as the answer. Computers and the techniques they made possible have over the years altered how many historians have understood their craft. To some they have opened the historical imagination to new questions and forms of presentation, while to others they have instead shuttered the historical imagination, at best limiting and channeling historical thinking and at worst confining it to procedural, binary steps. This chapter traces where the historical profession has come in the years since these professional debates and tries to assess how computing technologies have affected the discipline and how they will shape its future scholarship.

Not all historians in the 1960s and 1970s considered the computer the future of the profession. One railed against worshiping "at the shrine of that bitch goddess QUANTI-FICATION." Another, Arthur Schlesinger, Jr., one of America's foremost historians, wrote in reply to the rising confidence in cliometrics and quantitative history, "Almost all important questions are important precisely because they are not susceptible to quantitative answers" (Swierenga 1970: 33). Other critics of quantitative methods took aim not at the methods these historians used but instead questioned whether the "armies" of graduate students needed to develop large-scale projects and the technicians to maintain them were worth the cost. One prominent British social historian, Lawrence Stone, disparaged the contributions of the new history and the costs it entailed: "It is just those projects that have been the most lavishly funded, the most ambitious in the assembly of vast quantities of data by armies of paid researchers, the most scientifically processed by the very latest in computer technology, the most mathematically sophisticated in presentation, which have so far turned out to be the most disappointing." These sentiments are still widely held in the discipline and at the heart of them lay fundamental disagreements over the practice and method of history.

In the United States the greatest fight in the contest over computational methods in history took place in 1974 with the publication of Robert Fogel and Stanley Engerman's *Time on the Cross: The Economics of American Negro Slavery.* The book was a magisterial work of quantitative methodology and historical analysis, and it came in two volumes, one of which was dedicated entirely to quantitative methods and data. Fogel and Engerman admitted in their prologue that the book "will be a disturbing one to read." They also admitted that cliometrics, or quantitative history, had limitations and that "there is no such thing as errorless data" (Fogel and Engerman 1974: 8, 10). Fogel and Engerman concentrated their study on some very hotly contested issues: the economic profitability of slavery, the economic success of the South in the years before the Civil War, and the relative productivity of slave and free agriculture.

Time on the Cross received extensive criticism for two main reasons. First, the book rested so much of its key findings and interpretations on purely quantitative analysis and addressed purely economic questions, largely ignoring the textual and qualitative analysis of other historians as well as the social and political context of slavery. Second, the book addressed one of the most explosive and challenging subjects in American history – slavery. It seemed everyone was interested in the subject. Fogel and Engerman appeared on national television and in *Time* magazine, and were reviewed in nearly every newspaper and magazine. The publication of the methods and evidence volume alone was enough to intimidate many scholars.

C. Vann Woodward, a distinguished historian of the American South, in an early review of the book was understanding of the authors but clearly concerned about where their computers had led (or misled) them. He noted that "the rattle of electronic equipment is heard off stage, and the reader is coerced by references to 'vast research effort involving thousands of man and computer hours' and inconceivable mountains of statistical data." Woodward let it be known what the stakes were: "The object of the attack is the entire 'traditional' interpretation of the slave economy." Woodward could hardly believe the line of reasoning that led Fogel and Engerman to assert that on average only " '2 percent of the value of income produced by slaves was expropriated by their masters,' and that this falls well within modern rates of expropriation." It was one of many disturbingly cold and skeptically received findings that the cliometricians put forward. Still, Woodward concluded that "it would be a great pity" if the controversy enflamed by Fogel and Engerman's conclusions were to "discredit their approach and obscure the genuine merits of their contribution" (Woodward 1974).

Other reviewers were unwilling to concede any ground to the cliometricians. Withering criticism began shortly after the book was published, and it was led by Herbert Gutman, whose *Slavery and the Numbers Game* (1975) put forward the most devastating attack. As if to mock the cliometricians' elaborate reliance on numerical analysis and technical jargon, Gutman consistently referred to the book as "T/C" and to the authors as "F + E." Gutman's blood boiled when Fogel and Engerman icily concluded about the frequency of slave sales that "most slave sales were either of whole families or of individuals who were at an age when it would have been normal for them to have left the family." Gutman focused not on the statistical accuracy or the techniques of the cliometricians, but on the implications of their assumptions, the quality of their evidence, and how they used evidence. "Computers are helpful," Gutman pointed out, but not necessary for understanding the assumptions behind the statistical evidence (Gutman 1975: 3). Much of his critique faulted Fogel and Engerman's model of analysis for making almost no room for enslaved persons' agency, and instead making consistent and deeply embedded assumptions that everything in the enslaved person's life was directly subject to control and action by the slave holder. Gutman suggested that Fogel and Engerman's methodological, statistical, and interpretative errors all consistently aligned to produce a deeply flawed book, one that depicted the plantation South and slavery in a benign, even successful, light. In the end, the Fogel and Engerman finding that the typical enslaved person received less than one whipping per year (0.7, to be exact) helped drive home Gutman's critique. The number was presented as relatively minimal, as if such a thing could be counted and its effect established through quantification. Gutman pointed out that the really important measure was to account for the whip as an instrument of "social and economic discipline." The whipping data for *Time on the Cross* came from one plantation, and when Gutman re-examined the data he found that "a slave – 'on average' – was whipped every 4.56 days" (1975: 19).

After *Time on the Cross*, advocates of numerical analysis and computing technology found themselves on the defensive. But this was not always the case. At the end of World War II in 1945 Vannevar Bush, the Director of the Office of Scientific Research and Development and one of the United States' leading scientists, tried to envision how the advances in science during the war might be most usefully directed. In an *Atlantic Monthly* essay, titled "As We May Think," Bush turned to examples from historical inquiry to make his key point – technology might be turned to the possibilities for handling the growing mass of scientific and humanistic data. The problem Bush described seems only more pressing now: "The investigator is staggered by the findings and conclusions of thousands of other workers – conclusions which he cannot find the time to grasp, much less remember, as they appear. Yet specialization becomes increasingly necessary for progress, and the effort to bridge between disciplines is correspondingly superficial" (Bush 1945).

Bush's vision was for a machine he called "the memex," a strikingly prescient description of a networked desktop computer. The machine would enable a scholar to map what Bush called a "trail" through the massive and growing scholarly record of evidence, data, interpretation, and narrative. He wanted machines to make the same kinds of connections, indeed to emulate the human mind with its fantastic power of association and linkage. Bush's principal examples for the memex's applications were spun out of history – a research investigating the origins of the Turkish longbow – and he considered historians strong candidates to become "a new profession of trail blazers, those who find delight in the task of establishing useful trails through the enormous mass of the common record." As historians went about their noble work, Bush thought, they would leave nothing hidden from view, instead producing scholarship that was intricately connected in ways that could be accessed, replicated, and extended: "The inheritance from the master becomes, not only his additions to the world's record, but for his disciples the entire scaffolding by which they were erected."

Some American historians were already working in the ways Bush described. They were using Hollerith (IBM) punchcards and undertaking large-scale analysis of a wide array of records. Frank Owsley and Harriet Owsley in their landmark 1949 study of the Old South used statistical methods to make linkages across disparate federal census records and to create new quantitative datasets to analyze the class structure of the region. Frank Owsley and a large number of his graduate students worked on thousands of manuscript census returns for several counties from Alabama, Mississippi, Georgia, and Tennessee, and linked record-by-record the individuals and households in the population, slave owners, and agricultural schedules. Owsley's work challenged the idea that the planter elite dominated the South and instead suggested that a plain folk democracy characterized the region. The questions Owsley asked demanded methods of computational linking and quantitative analysis. Other historians in the 1940s and 1950s also worked on large statistical projects, including Merl Curti's analysis of the American frontier and William O. Aydelotte's study of the British Parliament in the 1840s.

In retrospect, we can see three distinct phases in the ways historians have used computing technologies. Owsley, Curti, Aydelotte, and a few others in the 1940s were part of the first phase of quantitative history. These historians used mathematical techniques and built large datasets. A second phase began in the early 1960s and was associated with an emerging field of social science history. The "new" social, economic, and political history concentrated on mobility, political affiliation, urbanization, patterns of assimilation, and legislative behavior. It included historians using a range of statistical techniques, such as Lee Benson and Allan Bogue of the so-called "Iowa school" of quantification, as well as Olivier Zunz, Michael F. Holt, Steven Thernstrom, J. Morgan Kousser, and many others. Many "new" social, political, and economic historians drew on the massive data collected in the Inter-University Consortium for Political and Social Research (ICPSR) which was founded at the University of Michigan in 1962 with support from the American Historical Association and the American Political Science Association to collect and make available historical data on county elections, census data, congressional roll call votes, and other miscellaneous political files. The computer made possible, or at least more practical and compelling, the study of history "from the bottom up." Political historians examined the influences at play in voting, not just the rhetoric of a few leaders; social historians found patterns to describe the world of average people; and economic historians developed models to account for multiple variables of causation.

The technology was alluring, but historians worried about the costs of the research and the time and training it took. Robert P. Swierenga, a historian with considerable experience in quantitative methods, confessed in a 1974 article that "to compute the Yules Q coefficient statistic for congressional roll call analysis" might require five hours of mainframe computer time to run the analysis, not to mention the time and cost of coding the 100,000 data cards needed for the computation. Swierenga was skeptical that "desk consoles" would solve the problem because historians' data were simply too large for the machines of the foreseeable future (Swierenga 1974: 1068).

The PC revolution and the rise of the Internet, along with the Moore's law exponential increase in speed and disk capacity of computing technology, led to the third phase. In this current phase, the networking capacity of the Internet offers the greatest opportunities and the most challenges for historians. At the same time as the Internet has created a vast network of systems and data, personal computers and software have advanced so far that nearly every historian uses information technologies in their daily work.

Some significant methodological issues have emerged with the rise of PCs and "off the shelf" software. Manfred Thaller, an experienced quantitative historian, argued in 1987 that database programs suited for businesses simply did not work for historians, who continually face "fuzzy" or incomplete data. The most obvious limitation that historians encounter with commercial database programs is the date function, since most programs cannot interpret or query nineteenth-century or earlier dates and a nest of problems in date functionality accompany any attempt to use historical dating in these programs. The nature of historical sources and the complexity of historical relationships led Thaller and others to challenge the easy comfort historians have with these programs. Thaller has been a voice crying in the wilderness, as historians in the 1980s and 1990s snapped up commercial database and spreadsheet programs with little hesitation and bent them to their needs. Meanwhile, Thaller and other historians at Göttingen developed a software system, KLEIO, for the needs of historical researchers and scholars. KLEIO's data processing system differs from standard packages because of its data structure. The software allows for three forms of related information: documents, groups, and elements. KLEIO handles a wide range of "fuzzy" data, historical dating systems, and types of documents (see Denley and Hopkin 1987: 149; Harvey and Press 1996: 190–3).

Throughout the 1980s historians, especially in Europe, refined the use of databases for historical computing. In the process they questioned how these tools affected their interpretations and whether the relational database models simply could not account for non-tabular data such as long texts, sound, images, and maps. Manfred Thaller's system tried to separate what he called the "knowledge environment" from the system environment or software, so that ideally the meaning of the records in a database remained independent of its source information. Database design for historical computing led Thaller and other quantitative historians to make distinctions between designs that build around the method of analysis or model from those which build around the source. In the former, historians extract information out of sources from the data's original context into a set of well-defined tables arranged to allow for predetermined queries. In the latter, historians concentrate on capturing the original text or data and its entire source context, only later making decisions about analysis and organization of the data. Thaller's purist position on the use of databases in historical computing has gained attention in the field and sharpened the debate, but it has not slowed down the widespread use of commercial software for historical analysis. Most historians have taken a far more pragmatic approach.

Despite the fundamental changes in information technologies and in historians' use of them, the recovery from the "battle royale" over *Time on the Cross* has been slow for those American historians working with computers. Manfred Thaller and the debates over database methodology and theory remained well out of the mainstream of American history in the 1980s. Twenty years after *Time on the Cross*, when Daniel Greenstein published *A Historian's Guide to Computing* (1994), he felt compelled to convince his readers that computers should not be "tarred with the same brush as the social science historians" (1994: 1). His treatment of regression analysis amounted to less than a page, while e-mail, bibliographic software, and note-capturing programs took up more than a chapter. Similarly, Evan Mawdsley and Thomas Munck, in their *Computing for Historians: An Introductory Guide* (1993), cautioned that they were "not champions of 'cliometrics', 'quantification', the 'new' history, 'scientific history', or even what is called 'social science history'." The idea that some historians pushed the profession to use computers and quantification techniques struck these authors as "the tail wagging the dog" (Mawdsley and Munck 1993: xiii). J. Morgan Kousser, in his review of social science history in the 1980s, admitted that most historians were moving abruptly away from quantitative methods. Time and distance tempered some critics, and by 1998 Joyce Appleby in her presidential address to the American Historical Association remarked that the quantifying social historians had "immediate, substantive, conceptual, and ideological effects" on the profession. Appleby considered them responsible for an important shift in the practice of history from unexplained to "explicit" assumptions about research methodology and from descriptive to analytical narrative (Appleby 1998: 4).

British historians, however, have established a long and comparatively polite respect for historical computing. The Association for History and Computing (AHC) was founded at Westfield College, University of London, in 1986, and has sponsored several large conferences and published proceedings. At the 1988 meeting, Charles Harvey speculated on the reasons for the strong interest in AHC among British historians. Chief among them, according to Harvey, is the "strength of support for empirical, scientific, developmental history in Britain" (Mawdsley et al. 1990: 206). Harvey described the British historical profession as focused on process not outcomes, rooted in scientific inquiry and only marginally concerned with theoretical debates. British historical scholarship was characterized by a focus on the importance of primary sources, the application of scientific notions in historical analysis, an emphasis on the specialized skills of the profession, the wide gulf between historians and social scientists, and the emphasis on applied skills and research methods in teaching students. Few of these characteristics describe the American historical profession and this may explain the thriving interest in "history and computing" in England.

Despite the success of and interest in AHC, some British historians have viewed computing technology variously as the handmaiden of postmodernism, as a witless accomplice in the collapse of narrative, and as the silent killer of history's obligation to truth and objectivity. One recent British historian argued: "The declining importance of the so-called grand narratives of national and class histories, and the fragmentation and loss of cultural authority of scholarly history in the face of increasingly diffuse popular and political uses of 'history,' cannot be separated from the impact of the new technologies" (Morris 1995: 503). Another suggested that when a historian "embarks on a statistical analysis he crosses a kind of personal Rubicon" (Swierenga 1974: 1062). Across that divide, in this view, the historian finds restrictions imposed by the software that defy the historian's allegiance to basic craft and adherence to evidence.

If *Time on the Cross* soured many American historians on computational methods, the Philadelphia Social History Project helped sustain them for a time. The project began in the 1970s under the leadership of Theodore Hershberg and took over a decade to complete. At first, skeptical critics considered it a painful example of the tail wagging the dog, long on money, time, and detail and short on results. Hershberg and his colleagues at the University of Pennsylvania used the computer to make linkages between a vast array of historical data and set out to establish guidelines for large-scale historical relational databases. The project took in nearly $2 million in grants and, in the process, offered historians a model for large-scale research and interdisciplinary activity. Numerous dissertations and theses drew on its data collection, and great expectations for the project were widely claimed. Still, the project ended with what many considered a thud – the publication in 1981 of a book of essays by sixteen historians working with the Phila-delphia Social History Project that offered no larger synthesis for urban history. Critics faulted the project and its authors for over-quantification, for paying too much attention to cultivating an interdisciplinary "research culture," and for allowing federal dollars to push a research agenda about "public policy" matters removed from history.

While historians continued to ponder the pros and cons of quantitative methods and while the profession increasingly turned to cultural studies, or took the "linguistic turn," as some have called the move toward the textual and French theory, computer scientists were hammering out a common language for shared files over the Internet. The World Wide Web's opening in 1993 with the creation of HTML and browser technologies offered historians a new medium in which to present their work. One of the first historians to understand the implications of the Web for scholarship, teaching, and historical study generally was Edward L. Ayers at the University of Virginia. He was already embarking on a computer-aided analysis of two communities in the American Civil War when he first saw the Mosaic® browser and the Web in operation at the Institute for Advanced Technology in the Humanities at the University of Virginia. Ayers immediately discarded his initial plans to distribute his research project on tape to libraries and instead shifted the direction entirely to the World Wide Web. As a result, Ayers's Valley of the Shadow Project was one of the earliest sites on the World Wide Web and perhaps the first work of historical scholarship on it.

From its inception the Valley of the Shadow Project was more than met the eye. The general public understood it as a set of Civil War letters, records, and other accounts. Students and teachers praised it for opening up the past to them and allowing everyone "to be their own historian." Scholars stood initially aloof, wondering what could possibly be so exciting about an electronic archive. Gradually historians began to pay attention to the Web and to the Valley of the Shadow Project in particular. Some historians saw the Project as perhaps a potentially troublesome upstart that threatened to change the narrative guideposts laid down in other media. James M. McPherson, one of the leading historians of the Civil War period whose work had done so much to influence Ken Burns's *The Civil War*, considered the Project potentially too narrow and argued in a major conference panel on the Valley Project that the communities Ayers had chosen were not representative of the North and South. McPherson, and other critics as well, were beginning to recognize that the digital medium allowed Ayers to create a thoroughly captivating, technically savvy, and wholly unexpected comparative approach to the Civil War, one so complex and interconnected that such a thing seemed impossible in more linear media such as film and books.

While Ayers was getting started on the Valley of the Shadow Project, another group of historians was already producing an electronic textbook for the American history survey course. The American Social History Project, based at City University of New York, included Roy Rosenzweig, Steve Brier, and Joshua Brown. Their *Who Built America?*, a

CD-ROM of film, text, audio, images, and maps, aggressively and successfully placed social history, especially labor history, at the center of the national story. The CD-ROM won a major prize from the American Historical Association in 1994 and one reviewer called it a "massive tour-de-force, setting the standard for historians who aim to make their work accessible to broad audiences via multimedia" (Darien 1998). Other reviewers, for N-Net, speculated that *Who Built America?* was part of a larger trend toward CD-ROMs and multimedia history, an "experiment" that would undoubtedly inspire others and lead to new forms of scholarship and teaching (Frost and Saillant 1994). These reviewers, though, also listed the daunting system requirements to run the CD-ROM: "Macintosh computer running system 6.0.7 or higher; 4 megabytes of installed RAM in System 6 or 5 megabytes in System 7, with a minimum of 3.5 megabytes to allocate to HyperCard; hard disk with 7 megabytes of free space, or 8 if QuickTime and HyperCard must be installed; 13-inch color monitor; QuickTime-ready CD-ROM drive."

It turns out that Edward Ayers's early decision to produce the Valley of the Shadow Project for the World Wide Web was one of the keys to that Project's long-term success. While the team at the University of Virginia working with Ayers has produced CD-ROMs and Ayers himself is publishing a narrative book out of the electronic archive, it is the website that has reached millions of users and to which all of the other scholarly objects point. The CD-ROMs of the *Valley of the Shadow* and *Who Built America?* contain remarkable materials, but their self-contained systems and off-the-network approach hobbled them, and by the late 1990s the CD-ROM seemed a relic in the fast-moving technology marketplace. The World Wide Web offered connectivity and hypertext on a scale that the public demanded and that scholars were beginning to see as immensely advantageous. "Historians might begin to take advantage of the new media," Ayers wrote, "by trying to imagine forms of narrative on paper that convey the complexity we see in the digital archives." In his call for a "hypertext history," Ayers admitted that while the technology offers grand possibilities, even with the crude tools presently in use, there are significant barriers for historians. Ayers called hypertext history potentially a "culmination of a long-held desire to present a more multidimensional history and a threat to standard practice" (Ayers 1999).

All of the connectivity and digitization has opened up history and historical sources in unprecedented ways, yet the technology has not come without tensions, costs, and unexpected sets of alliances and demands for historians, educators, administrators, and the public. The opportunities of digital technology for history notwithstanding, Roy Rosenzweig, one of the leading scholars of the *Who Built America?* CD-ROM, and Michael O'Malley questioned whether professional historians can "compete with commercial operations" (Rosenzweig and O'Malley 1997: 152). Permission to pay for copyright, the costs of design and graphical layout, maintaining programming technologies and software all conspire to favor commercial publishing companies rather than professional historians. More recently, Rosenzweig has cautioned historians about the prospects of writing history in a world of information overload. "Historians, in fact, may be facing a fundamental paradigm shift from a culture of scarcity to a culture of abundance," Rosenzweig observed, while at the same time archivists and librarians warn that vast electronic records are being lost every day in government, business, and academic institutions, not to mention in homes, churches, schools, and nonprofits. Problems of "authenticity," Rosenzweig pointed out, plague digital preservation, and libraries and archives face skyrocketing costs and difficult choices. But the historians face equally demanding problems. "The historical narratives that future historians write may not actually look much different from those that are crafted today," according to Rosenzweig, "but the methodologies they use may need to change radically" (Rosenzweig 2003). The vast size of born digital electronic data collections and the interrelationships among these data present historians with a fundamental methodological issue, according to Rosenzweig. They will need tools and methods, perhaps borrowed from the tradition of social science history, to make sense of these records.

If historians face an unprecedented scale of information, they also encounter in the digital medium an unexpectedly versatile mode of presenting their work. Many historians are beginning to ask what can we expect historical scholarship to look like in the networked electronic medium of the Internet and what forms of historical narrative might be enhanced or enabled. Robert Darnton, past president of the American Historical Association, National Book Award finalist, and innovator in historical forms of scholarship, sketched out his ideas for the future of electronic publishing in a 1999 *New York Review of Books* essay, titled "The New Age of the Book." He was concerned in large part with the future of the book, especially the academic monograph, and the university presses that produce and publish them. Darnton considered history to be "a discipline where the crisis in scholarly publishing is particularly acute" (Darnton 1999). Books won prizes and sold fewer than 200 copies; academic presses struggled to stay out of the red, and authors, especially young scholars before tenure, frantically tried to publish their work. Darnton used Middle East Studies as his example of "an endangered field of scholarship" about which the public cared and thought little. Only a few years after Darnton's review article, the importance of Middle East Studies could hardly be argued, as the events of September 11, 2001, brought the field to the immediate attention of the American public. Darnton observed that the unpredictability of the market and the pressures on presses, tenure committees, and scholars seemed to conspire against the future of the academic book.

Darnton asked whether electronic publishing "could provide a solution." He outlined significant advantages for the field of history where connections among evidence were so eye-opening during research in the archive and often so difficult to reproduce in narrative. Darnton wished for a new form for historical scholarship: "If only I could show how themes crisscross outside my narrative and extend far beyond the boundaries of my book . . . instead of using an argument to close a case, they could open up new ways of making sense of the evidence, new possibilities of making available the raw material embedded in the story, a new consciousness of the complexities involved in construing the past" (Darnton 1999). Darnton cautioned against "bloating" the book and piling on appendages to narrative. Instead, he called for a trim pyramid of layers: summary at the top and documentation, evidence, commentary, and other materials below.

It is not yet clear how digital technology will affect the practice of history or whether historians will heed Darnton's call to consider the advantages of electronic publication. In a show of leadership Darnton offered historians an example of what new electronic scholarship might look like, publishing a dynamic essay in the *American Historical Review* (Darnton 2000). In recent years several historians are working toward common ends. Philip Ethington has written an electronic essay and presentation for the Web on the urban history of Los Angeles. Ethington "explores the hypothesis that the key concept in the search for historical certainty should be 'mapping' in a literal, not a metaphoric, sense" (Ethington 2000). His work includes a wide range of media and sources to create, or rather recreate, the "panorama" of the city. Ethington suggests that the website can be read like a newspaper, inviting readers to wander through it, skipping from section to section, and focusing on what strikes their interest. Motivated "simultaneously by two ongoing debates: one among historians about 'objective knowledge,' and another among urbanists about the depthless postmodern condition," Ethington's electronic scholarship grasps the "archetype of 'hyperspace'" to address these concerns.

Finally, Ayers and this author are working on an *American Historical Review* electronic article, titled "The Differences Slavery Made: A Close Analysis of Two American Communities." This piece of electronic scholarship operates on several levels to connect form and analysis. First, it allows one to reconstruct the process by which our argument was arrived at, to "follow the logic" of our thinking, in effect to reconstruct the kind of "trails" that Vannevar Bush expected the technology to allow historians. This electronic scholarship also uses spatial analysis and spatial presentation to locate its subjects and its readers within the context of the historical evidence and interpretation. And it presents itself in a form that allows for unforeseen connections with future scholarship.

Historians will increasingly use and rely on "born digital" objects for evidence, analysis, and reference, as libraries and other government agencies increasingly digitize, catalogue, and make accessible historical materials (see Rosenzweig 2003). Some of these materials are hypertextual maps, others are annotated letters, edited video, oral histories, or relational databases. These digital objects vary widely according to their origin, format, and purpose. A born digital object is one created expressly for and in the digital medium, and therefore is more than a digital replication of an analogue object. For these objects, such as a reply to an email message, there is no complete analogue surrogate and as a consequence historians will need to understand not only what these objects explain but also how they were created. The electronic text, for example, marked up in Text Encoding Initiative (TEI) language becomes transformed in the process of both digitization and markup. Its unique markup scheme, as well as the software and hardware at both the server and client ends, affect how the text behaves and how its readers encounter it. Literary scholars, such as Espen Aarseth for example, have widely discussed the nature of narrative in cyberspace, and Aarseth calls cybertexts "ergotic" to distinguish them as non-linear, dynamic, explorative, configurative narratives (Aarseth 1997: 62). For historians the first stage in such textual developments for narrative have already been expressed in a wide range of digital archives. While these archives might appear for many users as undifferentiated collections of evidence, they represent something much more interpreted. Digital archives are often themselves an interpretative model open for reading and inquiry, and the objects within them, whether marked-up texts or hypermedia maps, derive from a complex series of authored stages. What Jerome McGann called "radiant textuality," the dynamic multi-layered expressions that digital technologies enable, applies to huge edited digital texts as well as to discrete objects within larger electronic archives (see McGann 2001: for example 151–2, 206–7).

The step from these archives to second-order historical interpretation necessarily involves the incorporation and explication of born digital objects, and "The Differences Slavery Made" offers an example of scholarship that emerges from and in relationship to born digital scholarly objects. The work fuses interpretative argument with the digital resources of the Valley of the Shadow Project, and it is designed for a future of networked scholarship in which interpretation, narrative, evidence, commentary, and other scholarly activities will interconnect. The resulting piece is intended to fuse form and argument in the digital medium. The authors propose a prismatic model as an alternative to Darnton's pyramid structure, one that allows readers to explore angles of interpretation on the same evidentiary and historiographical background. The prismatic functionality of the article offers to open the process of historical interpretation to the reader, providing sequential and interrelated nodes of analysis, evidence, and their relationship to previous scholarship. As important, the article tries to use its form as an explication of its argument and subject. Slavery, in other words, must be understood as having no single determinative value, no one experience or effect; instead, its refractive powers touched every aspect of society. The article's form – its modules of refracted analysis, evidence, and historiography – is meant to instruct and carry forward the argument.

Given the sweeping changes within the field of history and computing, we might ask what digital history scholarship might tackle in the future. A range of opportunities present themselves. The most anticipation and attention currently surround what is loosely called "historical GIS." Historical GIS (geographic information systems) refers to a methodology and an emergent interdisciplinary field in which computer-aided spatial analysis is applied to archaeology, history, law, demography, geography, environmental science, and other areas (see Knowles 2002). Historians are building large-scale systems for rendering historical data in geographic form for places across the world from Great Britain to Tibet, and they are finding new answers to old questions from Salem, Massachusetts, to Tokyo, Japan. Legal scholars have begun to examine "legal geographies" and to theorize about the implications of spatial understandings and approaches to legal questions (see Blomley 1994). These scholars seem only a step away from adopting historical GIS approaches to their studies of segregation, slavery, race relations, labor relations, and worker safety. Environmental historians and scientists, too, have developed new approaches to human and ecological change, examining subjects ranging from salt marsh economies and cultures in North America to the character and culture of Native American Indian societies in the river basins of the Chesapeake. Taken together these efforts represent remarkable possibilities for an integrated and networked spatial and temporal collection.

But historians might dream up even more highly interpretive and imaginative digital creations. Extending historical GIS, they might attempt to recreate "lost landscapes" in ways that fully allow readers to move and navigate through them. These four-dimensional models might restore buildings, roads, and dwellings to historic landscapes as well as the legal, economic, social, and religious geographies within them. Networks of information, finance, trade, and culture might also find expression in these models. Readers might do more than query these datasets; they might interact within them too, taking on roles and following paths they could not predict but cannot ignore. Readers of these interpretations will have some of the same questions that the critics of earlier computer-aided history had. The goal for historians working in the new digital medium needs to be to make the computer technology transparent and to allow the reader to focus his or her whole attention on the "world" that the historian has opened up for investigation, interpretation, inquiry, and analysis. Creating these worlds, developing the sequences of evidence and interpretation and balancing the demands and opportunities of the technology will take imagination and perseverance.

References for Further Reading

Aarseth, Espen (1997). *Cybertext: Perspectives on Ergotic Literature.* Baltimore and London: Johns Hopkins University Press.

Appleby, Joyce (1998). The Power of History, *American Historical Review* 103,1 (February): 1–14.

Ayers, Edward L. (1999). History in Hypertext. Accessed April 5, 2004. At <http://www.vcdh.virginia.edu/Ayers.OAH.html>.

Barzun, J. (1972). History: The Muse and Her Doctors. *American Historical Review* 77: 36–64.

——(1974). *Clio and the Doctors: Psycho-History, Quanto-History and History.* Chicago: University of Chicago Press.

Blomley, Nicholas K. (1994). *Law, Space, and the Geographies of Power.* New York: Guilford Press.

Bogue, A. G. (1983). *Clio and the Bitch Goddess: Quantification in American Political History.* Beverly Hills, CA: Sage Publications.

——(1987). Great Expectations and Secular Depreciation: The First 10 Years of the Social Science History Association. *Social Science History* 11.

Burton, Orville (ed.) (2002). *Computing in the Social Sciences and Humanities.* Urbana and Chicago: University of Illinois Press.

Bush, Vannevar (1945). As We May Think. *Atlantic Monthly* (July).

Clubb, J. M. and H. Allen (1967). Computers and Historical Studies. *Journal of American History* 54: 599–607.

Darien, Andrew (1998). Review of *Who Built America? From the Centennial Celebration of 1876 to the Great War of 1914. Journal of Multimedia History* 1,1 (Fall). At <http://www.albany.edu/jmmh>.

Darnton, Robert (1999). The New Age of the Book. *New York Review of Books* (March): 18.

——(2000). An Early Information Society: News and the Media in Eighteenth-century Paris. *American Historical Review* 105,1 (February). Accessed April 5, 2004. At <http://www.historycooperative.org/journals/ahr/105.1/ah000001.html>.

David, Paul et al. (1976). *Reckoning with Slavery: A Critical Study in the Quantitative History of American Negro Slavery.* New York: Oxford University Press.

Degler, Carl (1980). Remaking American History. *Journal of American History* 67,1: 7–25.

Denley, Peter and Deian Hopkin (1987). *History and Computing.* Manchester: Manchester University Press.

Denley, Peter, Stefan Fogelvik, and Charles Harvey (1989). *History and Computing II.* Manchester: Manchester University Press.

Erikson, C. (1975). Quantitative History. *American Historical Review* 80: 351–65.

Ethington, Philip J. (2000). Los Angeles and the Problem of Urban Historical Knowledge. *American Historical Review* (December). At <http://www.usc.edu/dept/LAS/history/historylab/LAPUHK/>.

Fitch, N. (1984). Statistical Fantasies and Historical Facts: History in Crisis and its Methodological Implications. *Historical Methods* 17: 239–54.

Fogel, R. W. and G. R. Elton (1983). *Which Road to the Past? Two Views of History.* New Haven, CT: Yale University Press.

Fogel, R. W. and Stanley Engerman (1974). *Time on the Cross: The Economics of American Negro Slavery.* London: Little, Brown.

Frost, Carol J. and John Saillant (1994). Review of *Who Built America? From the Centennial Celebration of 1876 to the Great War of 1914. H-Net Reviews.* Accessed April 5, 2004. At <http://www.h-net.org/mmreviews/showrev.cgi?path = 230>.

Greenstein, Daniel I. (1994). *A Historian's Guide to Computing.* Oxford: Oxford University Press.

Gutman, Herbert (1975). *Slavery and the Numbers Game: A Critique of Time on the Cross.* Urbana: University of Illinois Press.

Harvey, Charles and Jon Press (1996). *Databases in Historical Research: Theory, Methods, and Applications.* London: Macmillan Press.

Himmelfarb, G. (1987). *The New History and the Old.* Cambridge, MA: Harvard University Press.

Jenson, Richard (1974). Quantitative American Studies: The State of the Art. *American Quarterly* 26,3: 225–40.

Knowles, Anne Kelly (ed.) (2002). *Past Time, Past Place: GIS for History.* Redlands, CA: ESRI.

Kousser, J. Morgan (1989). The State of Social Science History in the late 1980s. *Historical Methods* 22: 13–20.

McGann, Jerome (2001). *Radiant Textuality: Literature after the World Wide Web.* New York: Palgrave.

Mawdsley, Evan and Thomas Munck (1993). *Computing for Historians: An Introductory Guide.* Manchester: Manchester University Press.

Mawdsley, Evan, Nicholas Morgan, Lesley Richmond, and Richard Trainor (1990). *History and Computing III: Historians, Computers, and Data, Applications in Research and Teaching.* Manchester and New York: Manchester University Press.

Middleton, Roger and Peter Wardley (1990). Information Technology in Economic and Social History: The Computer as Philosopher's Stone or Pandora's Box? *Economic History Review* (n.s.) 43,4: 667–96.

Morris, R. J. (1995). Computers and the Subversion of British History. *Journal of British Studies* 34: 503–28.

Rosenzweig, Roy (1994). "So What's Next for Clio?" CD-ROM and Historians. *Journal of American Historians* 81,4 (March): 1621–40.

——(2003). Scarcity or Abundance? Preserving the Past in a Digital Era. *American Historical Review* 108,3 (June): 735–62.

Rosenzweig, Roy and Michael O'Malley (1997). Brave New World or Blind Alley? American History on the World Wide Web. *Journal of American History* 84,3 (June): 132–55.

——(2001). The Road to Xanadu: Public and Private Pathways on the History Web. *Journal of American History* 88,2 (September): 548–79.

Shorter, Edward (1971). *The Historian and the Computer: A Practical Guide.* Englewood Cliffs, NJ: Prentice Hall.

Swierenga, Robert P. (ed.) (1970). *Quantification in American History.* New York: Atheneum.

Swierenga, Robert P. (1974). Computers and American History: The Impact of the "New" Generation. *Journal of American History* 60,4: 1045–70.

Woodward, C. Vann (1974). The Jolly Institution. *New York Review of Books*, May 2.

6

Lexicography

Russon Wooldridge

Lexicography is here considered in the literal and concrete sense of the word: the writing of the lexicon, the ordered description of the lexicon of a language in the form of a reference work usually called a dictionary.

The following is intended as a typological and partial account of the use of computers in lexicography, dealing with the essential applications and the main examples, for English and French, of computer-assisted lexicographical products. The dictionaries considered are those intended for the general public; scant mention will be made of those created for specialists.

Nature of the Dictionary Text

A dictionary has fundamentally the same structure as a telephone directory, a hospital's or general practitioner's medical files, or a library catalogue. Each unit of these collections is a record containing a number of fields, potentially the same for each record (some fields are blank) and placed in the same order, the essential characteristic of this relational database being its recursiveness.

- telephone directory entry: name, address, telephone number
- medical record: name, personal coordinates, medical history, progress notes, consultations, lab reports, etc.
- library catalogue record: title, author, place and date of publication, subject, material, ISBN number, holdings, etc.
- dictionary entry: headword, pronunciation, part of speech, definition, examples, etymology, etc.

Example of two dictionary entries (source: *Dictionnaire universel francophone*):

dictionnaire n. m. Ouvrage qui recense et décrit, dans un certain ordre, un ensemble particulier d'éléments du lexique (sens 4). *Dictionnaire médical, étymologique. – Dictionnaire de la langue ou dictionnaire de langue*, qui décrit le sens, les valeurs, les emplois, etc. des mots d'une langue. *Le dictionnaire de l'Académie française. – Dictionnaire bilingue*, qui donne les équivalents des mots et expressions d'une langue dans une autre langue. *Un dictionnaire français – vietnamien. – Dictionnaire encyclopédique*, qui, outre les descriptions de mots, fournit des développements encyclopédiques consacrés aux objets désignés par les mots. **Syn.** *Fam. dico.*

informatique n. f. et adj. Technique du traitement automatique de l'information au moyen des calculateurs et des ordinateurs. *Informatique de gestion.* adj. Relatif à cette technique. *Traitement par des moyens informatiques.*
Encycl. L'informatique est apparue avec le développement des calculateurs électroniques à grande capacité, les ordinateurs (le mot informatique date de 1962). La rapidité d'accès et de traitement de l'information, l'automatisme du fonctionnement des ordinateurs et la systématique des résolutions ont ouvert un très vaste champ d'application à l'informatique: recherche scientifique (ex.: contrôle de la trajectoire d'un satellite); industrie (conception assistée par ordinateur, contrôle et commande des machines, des processus); gestion des entreprises (opérations administratives, simulation, recherche opérationnelle); enseignement programmé; documentation, banques d'informations; informatique individuelle. La liaison de plusieurs ordinateurs accroît la puissance de leur traitement, la télématique assurant la transmission (V. télématique, ordinateur, réseau).

The recursiveness of the informational fields of the above two dictionary entries is indicated by typography, position, and abbreviation: (1) headword in bolded large letters; (2) part of speech conventionally abbreviated; (3) definition; (4) examples of usage in italics. Fields 1, 3, and 4 are given in full because of the idiosyncratic nature of lexical units; field 2 is given in abbreviated form since its values belong to a small finite class. Typography, position, abbreviation, and ellipsis (none of the four fields is explicitly named) are the features of dictionary recursiveness and economy (the dictionary is also a commercial product). Occasional fields tend to be named: "**Syn.**" for synonyms; "**Encycl.**" for encyclopedic information (normal, systematic, unlabeled information is linguistic); "V." for cross-reference to related terms.

Even the simplest dictionary entries, such as the ones quoted above, tend to be structurally complex. Besides the main binary equations – (a) *dictionnaire* = masculine noun; (b) *dictionnaire* [means] "Ouvrage qui recense et décrit, dans un certain ordre, un ensemble particulier d'éléments du lexique"; (c) [the word] *dictionnaire* [typically occurs in expressions such as] *Dictionnaire médical* (domain of experience), [*dictionnaire*] *étymologique* (domain of language) – there are also ternary ones: *dictionnaire* > [exemplified in] *Dictionnaire bilingue* > [which means] "[dictionnaire] qui donne les équivalents des mots et expressions d'une langue dans une autre langue." (The implicit copulas and other terms are here made explicit and enclosed in square brackets.)

Idiosyncrasy is characteristic of lexis and also of the dictionary, which in the vast majority of its realizations is composed by (fallible) human beings. Just as the treatment of lexical units will vary enormously according to part of speech, frequency of usage, monosemy or polysemy, register, and other variables, so will dictionary-writing tend to vary according to time (beginning, middle, or end of the alphabet, or of the writing of the dictionary, even day of the week) and writer (entry-writer A and entry-writer B are individual human beings and not clones or machines).

Setting aside the question of idiosyncrasy and variability of lexical units and dictionary-writing (the latter nevertheless an important obstacle in computerizing the *Trésor de la langue française* – see below), the well-ordered dictionary requires three types of sophisticated competence on the part of the user: (1) linguistic competence obviously; (2) dictionary competence, a particular type of textual competence, enabling one, for example, to find a word beginning with *m* by opening the dictionary more or less in the middle, to know that *adj.* means *adjective/adjectif* (and through linguistic competence to know what an adjective is), etc.; (3) pragmatic competence to make sense of references to the outside world: *Le dictionnaire de l'Académie française*, "calculateurs électroniques", etc.

The requirement of different types of user competence combined with the frequent use of ellipsis can result in cases of ambiguity that tax the analytical faculties of the dictionary reader and render powerless the analytical parser of the computer. The following examples are taken from the entry for GAGNER in *Lexis* (Wooldridge et al. 1992):

(a) *Gagner quelque chose* (moyen de subsistance, récompense), l'acquérir par son travail
(b) *Gagner son biftek* (pop.) [= gagner tout juste sa vie]
(c) *Gagner le Pérou* (= des sommes énormes)
(d) *Gagner le maquis* (syn. PRENDRE)
(e) *C'est toujours ça de gagné* (fam.) [= c'est toujours ça de pris]
(f) *Il ne gagne pas lourd* (= peu)
(g) *Je suis sorti par ce froid, j'ai gagné un bon rhume* (syn. plus usuels: ATTRAPER, PRENDRE, fam. CHIPER)

Each of the seven items contains an equation of synonymy, the equation concerning either the whole or part of the first term: the object of the verb in (a) and (c), the adverbial qualifier in (f), the verb in (d) and (g), the whole expression in (b) and (e). Linguistic competence is necessary to equate *quelque chose* and *l'* (a), *ne...pas lourd* with *peu* (f), the conjugated form *ai gagné* with the infinitives *attraper*, *prendre*, and *chiper* (g). The dictionary user also has to deal with the variability of the synonymy delimiters and indicators (parentheses, brackets, equals sign, *syn.* label, upper case).

In brief, the dictionary, in theory a systematic relational database, with ordered records and recurrent fields, may in human practice be as variable as the lexicon it sets out to describe. Successful applications of the computer to man-made dictionaries are, then, usually modest in their ambitions. Computer-driven dictionaries (machine dictionaries) tend to be procrustean in their treatment of language, or limit themselves to relatively simple areas of lexis such as terminology.

Pre-WWW (World Wide Web)

Modern lexicography did not wait for the invention of the computer, nor even that of the seventeenth-century calculating machines of Leibniz and Pascal, to apply computer methods to dictionaries. In 1539, the father of modern lexicography, Robert Estienne,

King's Printer, bookseller, humanist, and lexicographer, published his *Dictionaire francois-latin* (1539), a "mirror-copy" of his *Dictionarium latinogallicum* of the previous year. Each French word and expression contained in the glosses and equivalents of the Latin–French dictionary had its own headword or sub-headword in the French–Latin; each Latin word or expression contained in the headwords and examples of the Latin–French occurred as an equivalent to the corresponding French in the French–Latin. Example of the words *aboleo* and *abolir*:

1. Dispersion:
   1538: "ABOLEO [...] *Abolir, Mettre a neant.*"
   > 1539: "*Abolir*, Abolere" (s.v. Abolir), "*Mettre a neant* [...] Abolere" (s.v. Mettre).
2. Collection:
   1538: "ABOLEO [...] *Abolir*," "ABROGO [...] *Abolir*," "Antiquo [...] *Abolir*," "Conuellere [...] *abolir.*," "Exterminare [...] *abolir.*," "Inducere [...] *Abolir*," "Interuertere [...] *Abolir*," "OBLITERO [...] *abolir.*," "Resignare, *Abolir*".
   > 1539: "*Abolir*, Abolere, Abrogare, Antiquare, Conuellere, Exterminare, Inducere, Interuertere, Obliterare, Resignare."

Moving forward four centuries and several decades, we find the first applications of the computer to lexicography in the 1960s and 1970s. In the 1960s, the Centre pour un Trésor de la langue française in Nancy started keyboarding representative works of literature and technical treatises to provide source material for its print dictionary, the *Dictionnaire de la langue du XIXe et du XXe siècle*, commonly known as the *Trésor de la langue française*, or *TLF*. In the late 1970s, there appeared in England two machine-readable dictionaries, the *Oxford Advanced Learners' Dictionary* and the *Longman Dictionary of Contemporary English*; the latter used the computer not only to print off the paper dictionary, but also to help in its writing (Meijs 1991: 143–5).

The first early dictionary to be computerized was Jean Nicot's *Thresor de la langue françoyse* of 1606. The text was keyboarded in Nancy and Toronto between 1979 and 1984, indexed at the University of Toronto with the mainframe concordance program COGS, published in microfiche concordance form in 1985, indexed as a standalone interactive database with WordCruncher in 1988, and put on the World Wide Web in 1994 (see sections on the WWW era and on technological change, below). It is not without interest to note that in the early 1980s funding agencies expected concordance projects to undertake lemmatization of text forms. An argument had to be made to demonstrate the absurdity of attempting to lemmatize an already partly lemmatized text: dictionary headwords *are* lemmas. The Nicot project initially had the ambition of labeling information fields (Wooldridge 1982), until it quickly became obvious that such fields, though present and analyzable by the human brain, are impossible to delimit systematically in a complex early dictionary such as Nicot's *Thresor*, where position, typography, and abbreviation are variable, and functional polyvalence is common. The challenge is not negligible in modern dictionaries, where explicit field-labeling is the norm. Other early dictionaries have since been digitally retro-converted, notably Samuel Johnson's *Dictionary of the English Language*, published on CD-ROM in 1996.

The 1980s saw the emergence of large-scale computer-assisted lexicographical enterprises. The COBUILD (Collins and Birmingham University International Language

Database) Project started in 1980, with the intention of creating a corpus of contemporary English for the writing of an entirely new dictionary and grammar. The young discipline of corpus linguistics and the COBUILD Project fed off each other in this innovative lexicographical environment (Sinclair 1987; Renouf 1994). The New Oxford English Dictionary Project was formed to produce the second edition of the *OED* with the aid of computer technology. The project was international in scope: it was conceived and directed in England, the role of the computer was defined and implemented in Canada, the text was keyboarded in the United States of America. The second edition appeared in print in 1989 and on CD-ROM in 1992.

Where early electronic tagging of dictionaries was restricted to typographical codes for printing the finished product, it soon became necessary to add information tags so that not only could the text be correctly displayed on screen or paper, but it could also be searched and referenced by fields. The dictionary was just one of the types of text whose structure was analyzed by the Text Encoding Initiative (TEI) (Ide et al. 1992).

The last decade of the twentieth century witnessed the proliferation of electronic dictionaries distributed on CD-ROM. For example, the 1993 edition of the *Random House Unabridged Dictionary* came both in print and on CD-ROM, the two being sold together for the price of one. As one might expect of a freebie, the functionality of the Random House CD-ROM is rudimentary. On the other hand, the CD-ROM version of the *Petit Robert*, published in 1996, offers many advantages over the print edition: besides basic look-up of words and their entries, the user can search for anagrams (the search term *dome* produces *dome* and *mode*), homophones (*saint* produces *sain, saint, sein, seing*), etymologies by language (families: African, Amerindian, Arabic, etc., or specific idioms: Bantu, Hottentot, Somali, etc.), quotations by author, work, or character, plus full-text searches in either the complete dictionary text (full entries), or the particular fields of examples of usage or synonyms and antonyms.

It is often the case that a number of entries are made more complete through the access to the full text granted by an electronic version of a dictionary. For example, to take the case of the *Petit Robert*, *sabotage*, applied to work, organizations, or machinery, in the entry for the word, is used in an important – and common – figurative sense in a quotation concerning *speaker*: "Sabotage de la prononciation de notre belle langue par les speakers de la radio." Dictionaries tend to be more conservative in their treatment of a word in its own entry than elsewhere.

A brief mention should be made of computer-assisted lexicographical tools for the everyday user, the main ones being word-processor spellcheckers and thesauruses.

A good broad account of the period 1960–early 1990s, that of computer-assisted and computer-driven lexicography resulting in print and CD-ROM dictionaries, is given by Meijs (1992); an in-depth one by Knowles (1990).

Lexicography in the WWW Era

Like many other human practices, lexicography – and particularly lexicography – has been transformed by the World Wide Web. The Web works by virtue of words; to quote from the title of a well-known book by James Murray's granddaughter (Murray 1977), the Web, like the dictionary, is a "web of words." One reads the words in a book, one looks up headwords in a dictionary, one surfs the Web by keywords. The millions of documents published on the Web constitute, through the structuring of search engine keywords, a vast dictionary, an encyclopedic dictionary of concepts and words. Conventional dictionaries, whether paper or electronic, pale by comparison, though many of the latter are caught in the online Web of words.

An early demonstration of the Web as super- or meta-dictionary can be found in Wooldridge et al. (1999). A Web search of the Canadian French word *enfirouaper* (search term : `enfirou*`) collected occurrences of the verb and derivatives both used and commented on; the documents were of all types: political and personal, newspaper report and manifesto, poetry and prose, dialogue and dictionary. The occurrences of the word in use showed that dictionary and glossary treatment is narrow and out-of-date (cf. *sabotage* above). Applying the principles of corpus creation and analysis learned from the COBUILD Project, the WebCorp Project at the University of Liverpool uses standard Web search engines such as Google and AltaVista to collect results from the Web and format them in easily analyzable KWIC concordances (Kehoe and Renouf 2002). For example, expressions such as *one Ave short of a rosary, two leeks short of a harvest supper,* or *two sheets short of a bog roll,* encountered in the novels of Reginald Hill, are individual realizations of the commonly used pattern "one/two/three/a/an/several X short of a Y" (X being constituent parts of the whole Y), which can be expressed in Google or AltaVista by variants of the search term "`one * short of a`". Since WebCorp is, at least at the time of writing, freely available on the Web, corpus linguistics has become a lexicographical tool for the general public.

Meta-sites are a good source of information about online dictionaries. For French, two good ones are Robert Peckham's *Leximagne – l'Empereur des pages dico* and Carole Netter's *ClicNet: Dictionnaires.* The latter gives links for the following categories (I translate): Multilingual dictionaries; French-language dictionaries and encyclopedias; Grammar, morphology, orthography, and linguistics; Historical dictionaries; Dictionaries of Architecture, Visual arts, Slang, Law, Economics and Finance, Gastronomy and Dietetics, History, Humor, Games, Multicultural dictionaries, Literature, Media, Music, Nature and Environment, Science, Political science, Services, Social sciences and Humanities, Sports, Techniques, Tourism, Various vocabularies; Internet glossaries; Discussion lists; Lexical columns; Other servers.

Most online dictionaries are fairly modest in scope and are published as straight text, just like a print dictionary. A few, however, can be queried interactively as relational databases, and may offer other features. It is interesting then to compare those of the two main online dictionaries of English and French, the *OED* and the *TLF.*

- In the late 1990s, a first online version of the second edition of the *OED* became available through the OED Project at the University of Waterloo; a more generally available edition, the *OED Online,* was launched on the main *OED* website in 2000. Both versions are accessible by subscription only and allow the following types of search: "lookup" (as in the print version), "entire entry" = full-text search, "etymology," "label" (= field label). Electronic network technology has also made a significant contribution to the *OED*'s reading program: in place of the parcels of paper slips from around the globe delivered by the Post Office to the Oxford Scriptorium of James Murray's day, readers can now send in words, references, and details via the

Web. The *OED* website gives a detailed history of the dictionary, thus adding to a scholarly value rare on online dictionary sites.

- The complete version of the *TLFI* (*Trésor de la langue française informatisé*), published on the Web in 2002, is both free and, somewhat ambitiously, lets the user limit queries to one or several of 29 fields, including "entrée" (the whole entry), "exemple" (with subcategories of various types of example), "auteur d'exemple" (examples by author), "date d'exemple" (by date), "code grammatical," "définition," "domaine technique," "synonyme/antonyme." The 16-volume print *TLF* suffered from a high degree of writing variation (cf. the first section, above), making field tagging an extremely difficult task and forcing the Institut National de la Langue Française (INaLF) team to adopt in part a probabilistic approach in creating the electronic version (Henry 1996).

A characteristic of the Web is the hyperlink, which facilitates, among other things, the association between text and footnote (intratextual link), that between the bibliographical reference and the library (intertextual link), or that between a word *A* encountered within the dictionary entry for word *B* and the entry for word *A* (e.g. "**anaptyxis**: epenthesis of a vowel" > **epenthesis**). The *Dictionnaire universel francophone en ligne* (*DUF*), an important free language resource for speakers and learners of all varieties of French and the online equivalent of the one-volume general language print dictionary to be found in most homes, has hyperlinks for every word contained within its entries, allowing the user to refer to the entry of any given word with a single click (e.g. "**sabotage** n. m. 1. TECH Action de saboter (un pieu, une traverse, etc.)" > **nom, masculin, technique, technologie, technologique, action, de, saboter, un, pieu, traverse, et caetera**).

Apart from dictionaries of general contemporary language, there are a large number of marked or specialized ones. In the field of early dictionaries, there are several sixteenth- to early twentieth-century ones freely accessible in database form in the section *Dictionnaires d'autrefois* on the site of the ARTFL (American and French Research on the Treasury of the French Language) Project at the University of Chicago: Estienne, Nicot, Bayle, Académie française (also on an INaLF server in Nancy). Interactive databases of several of these and others are on a server of the University of Toronto. Terminology, once the reserve of paying specialists, is now freely available on the Web. For example, a *Glossaire typographique et linguistique* or a *Terminology of Pediatric Mastocytosis*; a pediatric mastocytosis term such as *anaphylaxis* occurs on tens of thousands of Web pages (69,700 hits with Google on September 28, 2002).

Web lexicography offers a number of tools, a significant one being automatic translation (e.g., Babelfish) intended to translate the gist of a Web document into a language understood by the user. A good account of the merits and drawbacks of automatic translation on the Web is given by Austermühl (2001).

Along with the professional team dictionaries, such as the *OED*, the *TLF,* or the *DUF*, and the specialized lexicons accessible on the Web, there are also to be found dictionaries and glossaries compiled by amateurs and individuals. If one wants, for example, to explore the Dublin slang encountered in Roddy Doyle's *Barrytown Trilogy*, the most ready source of online information is the *O'Byrne Files*.

A final word should be reserved for recreational lexicography. The word games of the parlor, radio, television, books, and the press proliferate on the Web. The *OED* site proposes "Word of the Day"; COBUILD has "Idiom of the Day," "The Definitions Game," and "Cobuild Competition." Many sites offer "Hangman" or "Le Jeu du pendu." There are various types of "Crossword" or "Mots croisés," "Anagrams" and "Anagrammes;" Online "Scrabble" has interactive play sites and tool box (dictionary) sites.

A Case Study in Technological Change

This last section takes a single dictionary-computerization project and looks at the various technological stages it has gone through over the years. The project in question is that concerning Jean Nicot's *Thresor de la langue françoyse*.

(a)   Mechanography. When the present writer set out to analyze Nicot's *Thresor* in Besançon, the technology of the time used to manipulate textual data involved a BULL mechanographical computer using IBM cards and only capable of handling small, simple corpora such as the plays of Corneille or the poems of Baudelaire. The idea, which occurred in the 1960s, of putting the *Thresor* into digital, full-text searchable form had to wait for technological advances.

(b)   Keyboarding, tape-perforation, and storing on magnetic tape. In 1979, the manual capture of half of the *Thresor* was begun at the Institut national de la langue française in Nancy, followed in 1980 by the commencement of capture of the other half at the University of Toronto. In Nancy, keyboarded data were captured onto paper tape and then transferred to magnetic tape; Toronto entry was sent directly from a keyboard via a telephone modem to an IBM mainframe computer. Data sent from Nancy to Toronto by mail on magnetic tape were made compatible with the Toronto input through a variety of routines written in various languages including Wylbur.

(c)   Concordancing on microfiches. In 1984, the complete unified text was run through the COGS mainframe concordance program written at the University of Toronto. Practically the entire resources of the central computing service of the University of Toronto were reserved for one night to index and concord the approximately 900,000 words of the text of the *Thresor*. Some of the concordance output was done with Spitbol routines. The thirty magnetic tapes were output commercially to microfiches.

(d)   WordCruncher on a standalone. In 1988, the data were transferred via modem and five-and-a-quarter inch floppy diskettes from the mainframe to a midi-computer and thence to an IBM AT personal computer with a 20 MB hard disk. This time it only took the resources of one small machine to index the full text of the *Thresor* and create an interactive concordance database.

(e)   The World Wide Web. The *Thresor* was first put online in 1994 as an interactive database at the ARTFL Project of the University of Chicago, the ASCII data files being converted to run under the program Philologic. In 2000, ARTFL's *Dictionnaires d'autrefois* were installed on a server at the INaLF in Nancy using the Stella interactive database program. In the same year, the *Thresor* was put up as an interactive database on a Windows server at the University of Toronto running under TACTweb, the data files first of all being indexed by TACT on an IBM-compatible.

The reference fields – entry headword, page, and typeface – derive from the tags entered manually during the first stage of data capture in Nancy and Toronto.

Conclusion

The most radical effect that the computer has had on lexicography – from dictionaries on hard disk or CD-ROM, through to dictionaries on the World Wide Web and to the Web-as-mega-dictionary – has been to supplement the limited number of paths for information retrieval determined in advance by author and publisher with the infinite number of paths chosen by the dictionary-user. It is now normal for the user to feel in charge of information retrieval, whether it be through access to the full text of a dictionary or the entire reachable resources of the Web. Headwords have been supplanted by keywords.

REFERENCES FOR FURTHER READING

Austermühl, Frank (2001). *Electronic Tools for Translators*. Manchester: St Jerome Publishing.
ClicNet: Dictionnaires et lexiques [Dictionaries and lexicons] (2002). Carole Netter, Swarthmore College. At <http://clicnet.swarthmore.edu/dictionnaires.html>.
Collins COBUILD. At <http://titania.cobuild.collins.co.uk/>.
Dictionnaire universel francophone en ligne (since 1997). [Online universal francophone dictionary]. Hachette and AUPELF-UREF. At <http://www.francophonie.hachette-livre.fr/>.
Dictionnaires d'autrefois [Early dictionaries]. ARTFL, University of Chicago. Accessed April 5, 2004. At <http://www.lib.uchicago.edu/efts/ARTFL/projects/dicos/>.
Estienne, Robert (1538). *Dictionarium latinogallicum* [Latin–French dictionary]. Paris: R. Estienne.
Estienne, Robert (1539). Dictionaire francoislatin [French-Latin dictionary]. Paris: R. Estienne.
Glossaire typographique et linguistique (since 1996–7) [Typographical and linguistic dictionary]. Alis Technologies Inc. Accessed April 5, 2004. At <http://babel.alis.com:8080/glossaire/index.fr.html>.
Henry, Françoise (1996). Pour une informatisation du *TLF* [For a computerization of the TLF]. In D. Piotrowski (ed.), *Lexicographie et informatique: autour de l'informatisation du Trésor de la langue française* (pp. 79–139). Paris: Didier Érudition.
Ide, Nancy, Jean Véronis, Susan Warwick-Armstrong, and Nicoletta Calzolari (1992). Principles for Encoding Machine Readable Dictionaries. In H. Tommola, K. Varantola, T. Salmi-Tolonen, and J. Schopp (eds.), *Euralex 1992 Proceedings* (pp. 239–46). Tampere: University of Tampere.
Johnson, Samuel (1996). *A Dictionary of the English Language on CD-ROM*, ed. Anne McDermott. Cambridge and New York: Cambridge University Press.
Kehoe, Andrew and Antoinette Renouf (2002). WebCorp: Applying the Web to Linguistics and Linguistics to the Web. In *WWW 2002: Eleventh International World Wide Web Conference*. Accessed April 5, 2004. At <http://www2002.org/CDROM/poster/67/>.
Knowles, Francis E. (1990). The Computer in Lexicography. In F. J. Hausmann, O. Reichmann, H. E. Wiegand, and L. Zgusta (eds.), *Wörterbucher: Ein Internationales Handbuch zur Lexicographie*, vol. 1 (pp. 1645–72). Berlin and New York: Walter de Gruyter.
Leximagne – l'empereur des pages dico [The emperor of dictionary pages]. TennesseeBob Peckham, University of Tennessee-Martin. Accessed April 5, 2004. At <http://www.utm.edu/departments/french/dico.shtml>.
Meijs, Willem (1992). Computers and Dictionaries. In Christopher S. Butler (ed.), *Computers and Written Texts* (pp. 141–65). Oxford and Cambridge, MA: Blackwell.
Murray, K. M. Elisabeth (1977). *Caught in the Web of Words*. New Haven, CT: Yale University Press.

The O'Byrne Files (since 2000). Accessed April 5, 2004. At <http://homepage.tinet.ie/~nobyrne/slang.html>.

Oxford English Dictionary. Accessed April 5, 2004. At <http://www.oed.com/>.

Renouf, Antoinette (1994). Corpora and Historical Dictionaries. In I. Lancashire and R. Wooldridge (eds.), *Early Dictionary Databases* (pp. 219–35). Toronto: Centre for Computing in the Humanities.

Sinclair, John M. (ed.) (1987). *Looking Up.* London and Glasgow: Collins.

Terminology of Pediatric Mastocytosis. MastoKids.org. Accessed April 5, 2004. At <http://www.mastokids.org/index.php?x = terminology.php>.

Le Trésor de la langue française informatisé [Computerized treasury of the French language] (2002). Accessed April 5, 2004. At <http://atilf.atilf.fr/tlf.htm>.

WebCorp. Accessed April 5, 2004. At <http://www.webcorp.org.uk/>.

Wooldridge, Russon (1982). Projet de traitement informatique des dictionnaires de Robert Estienne et de Jean Nicot. [Project for the computerization of the dictionaries of Robert Estienne and Jean Nicot]. In Manfred Höfler (ed.), *La Lexicographie française du XVIe au XVIIIe siècle* (pp. 21–32). Wolfenbüttel: Herzog August Bibliothek.

Wooldridge, Russon (1985). *Concordance du Thresor de la langue françoyse de Jean Nicot (1606)* [Concordance of Nicot's *Thresor de la langue françoyse* (1606)]. Toronto: Éditions Paratexte.

Wooldridge, Russon (2000). Interactive database of *Dictionnaires de la Renaissance.* Accessed April 5, 2004. At <http://www.chass.utoronto.ca/~wulfric/dico_tactweb/tiden.htm>.

Wooldridge, Russon, Astra Ikse-Vitols, and Terry Nadasdi (1992). Le Projet CopuLex. [The CopuLex project]. In R. Wooldridge (ed.), *Historical Dictionary Databases* (pp. 107–24). Toronto: Centre for Computing in the Humanities; and in CH Working Papers, B.9 (1996). Accessed April 5, 2004. At <http://www.chass.utoronto.ca/epc/chwp/copulex/>.

Wooldridge, Russon, Maryam McCubben, John Planka, and Snejina Sonina (1999). *Enfirouaper* dans le World Wide Web [Enfirouaper on the WWW]. Accessed April 5, 2004. At <http://www.chass.utoronto.ca/~wulfric/lexperimenta/enfirouaper/>.

7

Linguistics Meets Exact Sciences

Jan Hajič

Linguistics is a science that studies human language, both spoken and written. It studies the structure of language and its usage, the function of its elements, and its relation to other bordering sciences (psycholinguistics, sociolinguistics, etc.), of which the most important related field today is computer science. Diachronic linguistics studies language from the perspective of its development over time, whereas synchronic linguistics studies the function and structure of the current live language. General linguistics studies human language as a system, but particular languages (such as English, Mandarin, Tamil, or any other) are studied in detail as well. Due to its complexity, the study of language is often divided into several areas. Phonetics and phonology are related to speech (or more precisely, to the spoken language), whereas orthography deals with the standard written form of a particular language, including capitalization and hyphenation where appropriate. Morphology studies the composition of words by morphemes (prefixes, roots, suffixes, endings, segmentation in general, etc.) and its relation to syntax, which introduces structure into the description of language at the level of phrases, clauses, and sentences. Sentences are typically considered to be very important basic language units. Semantics and pragmatics study the relation of the lower levels to meaning and contents, respectively.

A description of a (correct) behavior of a particular language is typically called a grammar. A grammar usually generalizes: it describes the language structurally and in terms of broad categories, avoiding the listing of all possible words in all possible clauses (it is believed that languages are infinite, making such a listing impossible). An English grammar, for example, states that a sentence consisting of a single clause typically contains a subject, expressed by a noun phrase, and a verb phrase, expressed by a finite verb form as a minimum. A grammar refers to a lexicon (set of lexical units) containing word-specific information such as parts of speech (noun, verb, adjective, particle, etc.) or syntactic subcategorization (e.g., that the verb "to attach" has a subject and an indirect object with the preposition "to").

From the historic perspective, the scientific, economic, and political developments in the world before and during World War II were preparing the field of linguistics for what happened shortly thereafter. Natural language moved into the focus of people working in several scientific fields previously quite distant from linguistics (and other humanities as well): computer science, signal processing, and information theory, supported by mathematics and statistics. Today, we can say that one of the turning points for linguistics was Claude Shannon's work (1948). Shannon was an expert in communication theory, and his work belongs to what is known today as information theory, a probabilistic and statistical description of information contents. However, he was interested not only in the mathematical aspects of technical communication (such as signal transfer over telegraph wires), but he and Warren Weaver also tried to generalize this approach to human language communication. Although forgotten by many, this work was the first attempt to describe the use of natural language by strictly formal (mathematical and statistical, or stochastic) methods. The recent revival of stochastic methods in linguistics only underscores the historical importance of their work.

Developments in theoretical linguistics that led to the use of strictly formal methods for language description were strongly influenced by Ferdinand de Saussure's work (1916). His work turned the focus of linguists to so-called synchronic linguistics (as opposed to diachronic linguistics). Based on this shift in paradigm, the language system as a whole began to be studied. Later, Noam Chomsky (even though his view differs from de Saussure's in many respects) came up with the first systematic formalization of the description of the sentences of natural language (1957). It should be noted, however, that Chomsky himself has always emphasized that his motivation for introducing formal grammar has never been connected with computerization. Moreover, he has renounced probabilistic and statistical approaches. For various reasons, most notably the lack of computer power needed for probabilistic and other computationally intensive approaches, his work stayed dominant in the field of computational linguistics for more than thirty years.

In line with the formal means he proposed, Chomsky also adopted the view (introduced by the descriptivist school of American linguists) that sentence structure in natural language can be represented essentially by recursive bracketing, which puts together smaller, immediately adjacent phrases (or so-called constituents) to form bigger and bigger units, eventually leading to a treelike sentence structure. An alternative theory known in essence from the nineteenth century (Becker 1837) but developed in its modern form by Tesnière (1959) and other European linguists states that the relation between two sentence constituents is not that of closeness but that of dependence. This theory offers some more flexibility in expressing relations among constituents that are not immediately adjacent, and it is also more adequate for a functional view of language structure.

Other formal theories emerged during the 1960s, 1970s, and early 1980s. The generalized phrase structure grammars (Gazdar) are still close to the context-free grammar formalism as proposed by Chomsky. The formalism later developed into so-called head-driven phrase structure grammars, a formalism that has characteristics of both the immediate constituent structure and dependency structure. Similarly, the independently developed lexicalized functional grammar (Kaplan and Bresnan 1983) explicitly separates the surface form, or constituent structure (so-called c-structure) from functional structure (f-structure, which is close to the predicate-argument structure) and uses lexical information heavily.

Chomsky himself proposed a number of modifications of his original theory during the same period, most notably the government and binding theory (1981), later referred to as the principles and parameters theory, and recently the minimalist theory (1993). While substantially different from the previous theories and enthusiastically followed by some, they seem to contribute little to actual computational linguistics goals, such as building wide-coverage parsers of naturally occurring sentences. Chomsky's work is thus more widely used and respected in the field of computer science itself, namely in the area of formal languages, such as syntax of programming or markup languages.

During the 1980s, stochastic methods (based largely on Shannon and Weaver's work, cf. above) re-emerged on a higher level, primarily thanks to the greatly increased power of computers and their widespread availability even for university-based research teams. First, the use of stochastic methods has led to significant advances in the area of speech recognition (Bahl et al. 1983), then it was applied to machine translation (Brown et al. 1990), and in the late 1990s, almost every field of computational linguistics was using stochastic methods for automatic text and speech processing. More complex, more sophisticated ways of using probability and statistics are now available, and formal non-probabilistic means of language descriptions are being merged with the classic information-theoretic methods, even though we are still waiting for a real breakthrough in the way the different methods are combined.

Computational Linguistics

Computational linguistics is a field of science that deals with computational processing of a natural language. On its theoretical side, it draws from modern (formal) linguistics, mathematics (probability, statistics, information theory, algebra, formal language theory, etc.), logic, psychology and cognitive science, and theoretical computer science. On the applied side, it uses mostly the results achieved in modern computer science, user studies, artificial intelligence and knowledge representation, lexicography (see chapter 6), and language corpora (see chapter 21). Conversely, the results of computational linguistics contribute to the development of the same fields, most notably lexicography, electronic publishing (see chapter 35), and access to any kind of textual or spoken material in digital libraries (see chapter 36).

Computational linguistics can be divided (with many overlappings, of course) into several subfields, although there are often projects that deal with several of them at once.

Theoretical computational linguistics deals with formal theories of language description at various levels, such as phonology, morphology, syntax (surface shape and underlying structure), semantics, discourse structure, and lexicology. Accordingly, these subfields are called computational phonology, computational semantics, etc. Definition of formal systems of language description also belongs here, as well as certain research directions combining linguistics with cognitive science and artificial intelligence.

Stochastic methods provide the basis for application of probabilistic and stochastic methods and machine learning to the specifics of natural language processing. They use heavy mathematics from probability theory, statistics, optimization and numerical mathematics, algebra and even calculus – both discrete and continuous mathematical disciplines are used.

Applied computational linguistics (not to be confused with commercial applications) tries to solve well-defined problems in the area of natural language processing. On the analysis side, it deals with phonetics and phonology (sounds and phonological structure of words), morphological analysis (discovering the structure of words and their function), tagging (disambiguation of part-of-speech and/or morphological function in sentential context), and parsing (discovering the structure of sentences; parsing can be purely structure-oriented or deep, trying to discover the linguistic meaning of the sentence in question). Word sense disambiguation tries to solve polysemy in sentential context, and it is closely related to lexicon creation and use by other applications in computational linguistics. In text generation, correct sentence form is created from some formal description of meaning. Language modeling (probabilistic formulation of language correctness) is used primarily in systems based on stochastic methods. Machine translation usually combines most of the above to provide translation from one natural language to another, or even from many to many (see Zarechnak 1979). In information retrieval, the goal is to retrieve complete written or spoken documents from very large collections, possibly across languages, whereas in information extraction, summarization (finding specific information in large text collections) plays a key role. Question answering is even more focused: the system must find an answer to a targeted question not just in one, but possibly in several documents in large as well as small collections of documents. Topic detection and tracking classifies documents into areas of interest, and it follows a story topic in a document collection over time. Keyword spotting (or, flagging a document that might be of interest based on preselected keywords) has obvious uses. Finally, dialogue systems (for man–machine communication) and multi-modal systems (combining language, gestures, images, etc.) complete the spectrum.

Development tools for linguistic research and applications are needed for quick prototyping and implementation of systems, especially in the area of applied computational linguistics as defined in the previous paragraph. Such support consists of lexicons for natural language processing, tools for morphological processing, tagging, parsing and other specific processing steps, creation and maintenance of language corpora (see chapter 21) to be used in systems based on stochastic methods, and annotation schemas and tools.

Despite sharing many of the problems with written language processing, speech (spoken language) processing is usually considered a separate area of research, apart even from the field of computational linguistics. Speech processing uses almost exclusively stochastic methods. It is often referred to as automatic speech recognition (ASR), but the field is wider: it can be subdivided into several subfields, some of them dealing more with technology, some with applications. Acoustic modeling relates the digitized speech signal and phonemes as they occur in words, whereas language modeling for speech recognition shares many common features with language modeling of written language, but it is used essentially to predict what the speaker will utter next based on what she said in the immediate past. Speaker identification is another obvious application, but it is typically only loosely related to the study of language, since it relies more on acoustic features. Small-vocabulary speech recognition systems are the basis for the most successful commercial applications today. For instance, systems for recognizing digits, typically in difficult acoustic conditions such as when speaking over a telephone line, are widely used. Speaker-independent speech recognition systems with large vocabularies (sometimes called dictation) are the focus of the main research direction in automatic speech recognition. Speaker adaptation (where the speech recognizers are adapted to a particular person's voice) is an important subproblem that is believed to move today's systems to a new level of precision. Searching spoken material (information retrieval, topic detection, keyword spotting, etc.) is similar to its text counterpart, but the problems are more difficult due to the lack of perfect automatic transcription systems. A less difficult, but commercially very viable field is text-to-speech synthesis (TTS).

It is clear however that any such subdivision can never be exact; often, a project or research direction draws upon several of the above fields, and sometimes it uses methods and algorithms even from unrelated fields, such as physics or biology, since more often than not their problems share common characteristics.

One very important aspect of research in computational linguistics, as opposed to many other areas in humanities, is its ability to be *evaluated*. Usually, a gold-standard result is prepared in advance, and system results are compared (using a predefined metric) to such a gold-standard (called also a test) dataset. The evaluation metric is usually defined in terms of the number of errors that the system makes; when this is not possible, some other measure (such as test data probability) is used. The complement of error rate is accuracy. If the system produces multiple results, recall (the rate at which the system hits the correct solution by at least one of its outputs) and precision (the complement of false system results) have to be used, usually combined into a single figure (called F-measure). Objective, automatic system evaluation entered computational linguistics with the revival of statistical methods and is considered one of the most important changes in the field since its inception – it is believed that such evaluation was the driving force in the fast pace of advances in the recent past.

The Most Recent Results and Advances

Given the long history of research in computational linguistics, one might wonder what the state-of-the-art systems can do for us today, at the beginning of the twenty-first century. This section summarizes the recent results in some of the subfields of computational linguistics.

The most successful results have been achieved in the speech area. Speech synthesis and recognition systems are now used even commercially (see also the next section). Speech recognizers are evaluated by using so-called word error rate, a relatively simple measure that essentially counts how many words the system missed or confused. The complement of word error rate is the accuracy, as usual. The latest speech recognizers can handle vocabularies of 100,000 or more words (some research systems already contain million-word vocabularies). Depending on recording conditions, they have up to a 95 percent accuracy rate (with a closely mounted microphone, in a quiet room, speaker-adapted). Broadcast news is recognized at about 75–90 percent accuracy. Telephone speech (with specific topic only, smaller vocabulary) gives 30–90 percent accuracy, depending on vocabulary size and domain definition; the smaller the domain, and therefore the more restricted the grammar, the better the results (very tiny grammars and vocabularies are usually used in successful commercial applications). The worst situation today is in the case of multi-speaker spontaneous speech under, for example, standard video recording conditions: only 25–45 percent accuracy can be achieved.

It depends very much on the application whether these accuracy rates are sufficient or not; for example, for a dictation system even 95 percent accuracy might not be enough, whereas for spoken material information retrieval an accuracy of about 30 to 40 percent is usually sufficient.

In part-of-speech tagging (morphological disambiguation), the accuracy for English (Brants 2000) has reached 97–98 percent (measuring the tag error rate). However, current accuracy is substantially lower (85–90 percent) for other languages that are morphologically more complicated or for which not enough training data for stochastic methods is available. Part-of-speech tagging is often used for experiments when new analytical methods are considered because of its simplicity and test data availability.

In parsing, the number of crossing brackets (i.e., wrongly grouped phrases) is used for measuring the accuracy of parsers producing a constituent sentence structure, and a dependency error rate is used for dependency parsers. Current state-of-the-art English parsers (Collins 1999; Charniak 2001) achieve 92–94 percent combined precision and recall in the crossing-brackets measure (the number would be similar if dependency accuracy is measured). Due to the lack of training data (treebanks) for other languages, there are only a few such parsers; the best-performing published result of a foreign-language parser (on Czech, see Collins et al. 1999) achieves 80 percent dependency accuracy.

Machine translation (or any system that produces free, plain text) is much more difficult (and expensive) to evaluate. Human evaluation is subjective, and it is not even clear what exactly should be evaluated, unless a specific task and environment of the machine translation system being evaluated is known. Machine translation evaluation exercises administered by DARPA (Defense Advanced Research Projects Agency) in the 1990s led to about 60 percent subjective translation quality of both the statistical machine translation (MT) systems as well as the best commercial systems. Great demand for an automatic evaluation of machine translation systems by both researchers and users has led to the development of several automated metrics (most notably, those of Papineni, see Papineni et al. 2001) that try to simulate human judgment by computing a numeric match between the system's output and several reference (i.e., human) translations. These numbers cannot be interpreted directly (current systems do not go over 0.30–0.35 even for short sentences), but only in relation to a similarly computed distance between human translations (for example, that number is about 0.60 with 4 reference translations; the higher the number, the better).

Successful Commercial Applications

The success of commercial applications is determined not so much by the absolute accuracy of the technology itself, but rather by the relative suitability to the task at hand. Speech recognition is currently the most successful among commercial applications of language processing, using almost exclusively stochastic methods. But even if there are several dictation systems on the market with accuracy over 95 percent, we are for the most part still not dictating e-mails to our computers, because there are many other factors that make dictation unsuitable: integration with corrections is poor, noisy environments decrease the accuracy, sometimes dramatically. On the other hand, scanning broadcast news for spotting certain topics is routinely used by intelligence agencies. Call routing in the customer service departments of major telephone companies (mostly in the USA) is another example of a successful application of speech recognition and synthesis: even if the telephone speech recognition is far from perfect, it can direct most of the customer's calls correctly, saving hundreds of frontline telephone operators. Directory inquiries and call switching in some companies are now also handled automatically by speech recognition; and we now have cell phones with ten-number voice dialing – a trivial, but fashionable application of speech recognition technology – not to mention mass-market toys with similar capabilities.

Successful applications of non-speech natural language processing technology are much more rare, if we do not count the ubiquitous spelling and grammar checkers in word processing software. The most obvious example is machine translation. General machine translation systems, an application that has been being developed at many places for almost fifty years now, is still lousy in most instances, even if it sort of works for rough information gathering (on the Web for example); most translation bureaus are using translation memories that include bilingual and multilingual dictionaries and previously translated phrases or sentences as a much more effective tool. Only one system – SYSTRAN – stands out as a general machine translation system, now being used also by the European Commission for translating among many European languages (Wheeler 1984). Targeted, sharply constrained domain-oriented systems are much more successful: an excellent example is the Canadian METEO system (Grimaila and Chandioux 1992), in use since May 24, 1977, for translating weather forecasts between English and French. Research systems using stochastic methods do surpass current general systems, but a successful commercial system using them has yet to be made.

Searching on the Web is an example of a possible application of natural language processing, since most of the Web consists of natural language texts. Yet most of the search engines (with the notable exception of AskJeeves and its products <www.ask.com>, which allows queries to be posted in plain English) still use simple string matching, and even commercial search applications do not usually go beyond simple stemming. This may be sufficient for English, but with the growing proportion of foreign-language web pages the necessity of more language-aware search techniques will soon become apparent.

Future Perspectives

Due to the existence of corpora, to the ascent of stochastic methods and evaluation techniques, computational linguistics has become mostly an experimental science – something that can hardly be said about many other branches of humanities sciences. Research applications are now invariably tested against real-world data, virtually guaranteeing quick progress in all subfields of computational linguistics. However, natural language is neither a physical nor a mathematical system with deterministic (albeit unknown) behavior; it remains a social phenomenon that is very difficult to handle automatically and explicitly (and therefore, by computers), regardless of the methods used. Probability and statistics did not solve the problem in the 1950s (weak computer power), formal computational linguistics did not solve the problem in the 1960s and 1970s (language seems to be too complex to be described by mere introspection), and stochastic methods of the 1980s and 1990s apparently did not solve the problem either (due to the lack of data needed for current data-hungry methods). It is not unreasonable to expect that we are now, at the beginning of the twenty-first century, on the verge of another shift of research paradigm in computational linguistics. Whether it will be more linguistics (a kind of return to the 1960s and 1970s, while certainly not leaving the new experimental character of the field), or more data (i.e., the advances in computation – statistics plus huge amounts of textual data which are now becoming available), or neural networks (a long-term promise and failure at the same time), a combination of all of those, or something completely different, is an open question.

REFERENCES FOR FURTHER READING

There are excellent textbooks now for those interested in learning the latest developments in computational linguistics and natural language processing. For speech processing, Jelinek (2000) is the book of choice; for those interested in (text-oriented) computational linguistics, Charniak (1996), Manning and Schütze (1999), and Jurafsky and Martin (2000) are among the best.

Bahl, L. R., F. Jelinek, and R. L. Mercer (1983). A Maximum Likelihood Approach to Continuous Speech Recognition. *IEEE Transactions on Pattern Analysis and Machine Intelligence* 5,2: 179–90.

Becker, K. F. (1837). *Ausfürliche Deutsche Grammatik als Kommentar der Shulgrammatik. Zweite Abtheilung* [Detailed Grammar of German as Notes to the School Grammar]. Frankfurt am Main: G. F. Kettembeil.

Brants, T. (2000). TnT – A Statistical Part-of-Speech Tagger. In S. Nirenburg, *Proceedings of the 6th ANLP* (pp. 224–31). Seattle, WA: ACL.

Brown, P. F., J. Cocke, S. A. Della Pietra, V. J. Della Pietra, F. Jelinek, J. D. Lafferty, R. L. Mercer, and P. S. Roossin (1990). A Statistical Approach to Machine Translation. *Computational Linguistics* 16,2: 79–85.

Charniak, E. (1996). *Statistical Language Learning*. Cambridge, MA: MIT Press.

——(2001). Immediate-head Parsing for Language Models. In N. Reithinger and G. Satta, *Proceedings of the 39th Annual Meeting of the Association for Computational Linguistics* (pp. 116–23). Toulouse: ACL.

Chomsky, A. N. (1957). *Syntactic Structures*. The Hague: Mouton.

——(1981). *Lectures on Government and Binding* (The Pisa Lectures). Dordrecht and Cinnaminson, NJ: Foris.

——(1993). A Minimalist Program for Linguistic Theory. In K. Hale and S. J. Keyser (eds.), *The View from Building 20: Essays in Linguistics in Honor of Sylvain* (pp. 1–52). Cambridge, MA: Bromberger.

Collins, M. (1999). Head-driven Statistical Models for Natural Language Parsing. PhD dissertation, University of Pennsylvania.

Collins, M., J. Hajič, L. Ramshaw, and C. Tillmann (1999). A Statistical Parser for Czech. In R. Dale and K. Church, *Proceedings of ACL 99* (pp. 505–12). College Park, MD: ACL.

Gazdar, G. et al. (1985). *Generalized Phrase Structure Grammar*. Oxford: Blackwell.

Grimaila, A. and J. Chandioux (1992). Made to Measure Solutions. In J. Newton (ed.), *Computers in Translation, A Practical Appraisal* (pp. 33–45). New York: Routledge.

Jelinek, F. (2000). *Statistical Methods for Speech Recognition*. Cambridge, MA: MIT Press.

Jurafsky, D. and J. H. Martin (2000). *Speech and Language Processing*. New York: Prentice Hall.

Kaplan, R. M., and J. Bresnan (1983). Lexical-functional Grammar: A Formal System for Grammatical Representation. In J. Bresnan, *The Mental Representation of Grammatical Relations* (pp. 173–381). Cambridge, MA: MIT Press.

Manning, C. D. and H. Schütze (1999). *Foundations of Statistical Natural Language Processing.* Cambridge, MA: MIT Press.

Papineni, K., S. Roukos, T. Ward, and Wei-Jing Zhu (2001). *Bleu: A Method for Automatic Evaluation of Machine Translation.* Published as IBM Report RC22176. Yorktown Heights, NY: IBM T. J. Watson Research Center.

Pollard, C. and I. Sag (1992). *Head-driven Phrase Structure Grammar.* Chicago: University of Chicago Press.

Saussure, F. de (1949). *Cours de linguistique générale,* 4th edn. Paris: Libraire Payot.

Shannon, C. (1948). The Mathematical Theory of Communication. *Bell Systems Technical Journal* 27: 398–403.

Tesnière, L. (1959). *Eléments de Syntaxe Structurale.* Paris: Editions Klincksieck.

Wheeler, P. J. (1984). Changes and Improvements to the European Comission's SYSTRAN MT System, 1976–1984. *Terminologie Bulletin* 45: 25–37. European Commission, Luxembourg.

Zarechnak, M. (1979). The History of Machine Translation. In B. Henisz-Dostert, R. Ross Macdonald, and M. Zarechnak (eds.), *Machine Translation.* Trends in Linguistics: Studies and Monographs, vol. 11 (pp. 20–8). The Hague: Mouton.

8

Literary Studies

Thomas Rommel

The systematic study and analysis of literature dates back to the beginnings of literary "text production"; even the earliest forms of oral literature were practiced in a context of descriptive and prescriptive aesthetics. With the rise of written literature emerged a canon of rules that could be applied to text in order to evaluate its adherence to poetic norms and values, and very soon quantitative and qualitative methods of text analysis were applied in textual exegesis. But the analysis of literature is traditionally seen as a subjective procedure. Objectivity, based on empirical evidence, does not seem to figure prominently in studies that elucidate meaning from literary texts. In most studies, however, some kind of exemplary textual sampling does take place, and scholars occasionally arrive at value judgments that are based on the observation of frequent occurrences or the absence of certain textual features. The exact number of occurrences and/or their distribution in long texts is difficult to establish, because literary texts, in particular novels, make a thorough analysis of every single word or sentence almost impossible. Empirical evidence that is truly representative for the whole text is extremely difficult to come by, and mainstream literary scholarship has come to accept this limitation as a given fact:

> A simultaneous possession by the reader of all the words and images of *Middlemarch*, *À la recherche du temps perdu*, or *Ulysses* may be posited as an ideal, but such an ideal manifestly cannot be realized. It is impossible to hold so many details in the mind at once. (Miller 1968: 23)

The first computer-assisted studies of literature of the 1960s and 1970s used the potential of electronic media for precisely these purposes – the identification of strings and patterns in electronic texts. Word lists and concordances, initially printed as books but later made available in electronic format, too, helped scholars come to terms with all occurrences of observable textual features. The "many details," the complete sets of textual data of some few works of literature, suddenly became available to every scholar. It was no longer acceptable, as John Burrows pointed out, to ignore the potential of electronic media and to continue with textual criticism based on small sets of examples only, as was common usage in traditional literary criticism: "It is a truth not generally acknowledged that, in most discussions of works of English fiction, we proceed as if a third, two-fifths, a half of our material were not really there" (Burrows 1987: 1).

Literary computing was seen to remedy this shortcoming, and it has provided substantial insights into some questions of style and literary theory. Most studies on patterns and themes that were published in the last twenty years question concepts of text and method, and by investigating literature with the help of a powerful tool these studies situate themselves in a context of meta-discourse: the question of "method" remains at the heart of most electronic analysis of literature.

Seen as a mere tool without any inherent analytical power of its own, the computer in literary studies enhances the critic's powers of memory electronically, thereby providing a complete database of findings that meet all predefined patterns or search criteria. As error-prone manual sampling becomes obsolete, textual analysis as well as the ensuing interpretation of a text as a whole can be based on a complete survey of all passages that promise results, no matter how long the text is. Comparative approaches spanning large literary corpora have become possible, and the proliferation of primary texts in electronic form has contributed significantly to the corpus of available digital texts. In order to be successful, literary computing needs to use techniques and procedures commonly associated with the natural sciences and fuse them with humanities research, thereby bringing into contact the Two Cultures: "What we need is a principal use of technology and criticism to form a new kind of literary study absolutely comfortable with scientific methods yet completely suffused with the values of the humanities" (Potter 1989: xxix).

The history of literary computing, however, shows that only a limited number of textual phenomena can be analyzed profitably in the context of quantitative and qualitative computer-based analyses of style. These phenomena have to be linked to some surface features that can be identified by electronic means, usually by some form of pattern matching. Computers are exceptionally well suited for this kind of analysis, and only human intuition and insight, in combination with the raw computing power of machines programmed to act as highly specialized electronic tools, can make some texts or textual problems accessible to scholars. As Susan Hockey writes:

> In the most useful studies, researchers have used the computer to find features of interest and then examined these instances individually, discarding those that are not relevant, and perhaps refining the search terms in order to find more instances. They have also situated their project within the broader sphere of criticism on their author or text, and reflected critically on the methodology used to interpret the results. (Hockey 2000: 84)

The methodological implications of such approaches to literary texts accommodate computer-based and computer-assisted studies within the theoretical framework of literary-linguistic stylistics. In this context, texts are seen as aesthetic constructs that achieve a certain effect (on the reader) by stylistic features on the surface structure of the literary text. These features are sometimes minute details that the reader does not normally recognize individually but that nevertheless influence the overall impression of the text. The presence or absence of such features can only be traced efficiently by electronic means, and while the reader may be left with a feeling of having been manipulated by the text without really knowing how, the computer can work out distribution patterns that may help understand how a particular effect is achieved. "[U]nexpectedly high or low frequencies or occurrences of a feature or some atypical tendency of co-occurrence are, in their very unexpectedness or atypicality, noteworthy," Michael Toolan maintains, but then continues that "[e]laborate statistical computations are unlikely to be illuminating in these matters of subtle textual effect" (1990: 71). This view, frequently expounded by scholars who see literary computing more critically, points at one of the central shortcomings of the discipline: in order to be acknowledged by mainstream criticism, computer-based literary studies need to clarify that the computer is a tool used for a specific result in the initial phases of literary analysis. No final result, let alone an "interpretation" of a text, can be obtained by computing power alone; human interpretation is indispensable to arrive at meaningful results. And in particular the aim of the investigation needs to be clarified; every "computation into criticism," to use Burrows's term, has to provide results that transcend the narrow confines of stylo-statistical exercises.

> As for studies of punctuation, sentence length, word length, vocabulary distribution curves, etc., the numbers have been crunched for about twenty years now. It is clearly established that the distribution of such features is not random, or normal in the statistical sense. The extent of such variance from the models has been measured with great precision. But since no one ever claimed that a literary text was a random phenomenon, or a statistically normal distribution, it is difficult to see the point of the exercise. (Fortier 1991: 193)

Statistics, in conjunction with quantifiable data and a (supposedly) positivistic attitude toward textual phenomena, have contributed to the image of computer-based literary analysis as a "difficult" or "marginal" pursuit. And in the context of a shift away from close reading toward a more theory-oriented approach to literary texts, new models of textuality seemed to suggest that literary computing was occupied with fixed meanings that could be elucidated by counting words and phrases. This image was further enhanced by references to this procedure in literature itself, as David Lodge shows in his novel *Small World*:

> "What's the *use*? Let's show him, Josh." And he passed the canister to the other guy, who takes out a spool of tape and fits it on to one of the machines. "Come over here," says Dempsey, and sits me down in front of a kind of typewriter with a TV screen attached. "With that tape," he said, "we can request the computer to supply us with any information we like about your ideolect." "Come again?" I said. "Your own special, distinctive, unique way of using the English language. What's your favourite word?" "My favourite word. I don't have one." "Oh yes you do!" he said. "The word you use most frequently."

The simplistic view of computer-based studies as "counting words" has been a major factor for later studies that were seen in this light. Contrary to received opinion, studies of literature that use electronic means are mostly concerned with questions of theory and method. Especially the notion of what constitutes a "text" and how, therefore, a given theory of text influences the procedures of analysis and interpretation, form the basis of every literary analysis.

A literary text, interpreted as an aesthetic construct that achieves a certain effect through the distribution of words and images, works on various levels. Without highly elaborate thematic — and therefore by definition interpretative — markup, only surface features of texts can be analyzed. These surface features are read as significant in that they influence the reader's understanding and interpretation of the text. This has a number of theoretical implications: if a literary text carries meaning that can be detected by a method of close reading, then computer-assisted studies have to be seen as a practical extension of the theories of text that assume that "a" meaning, trapped in certain words and images and only waiting to be elicited by the informed reader, exists in literature. By focusing primarily on empirical textual data, computer studies of literature tend to treat text in a way that some literary critics see as a reapplication of dated theoretical models:

> One might argue that the computer is simply amplifying the critic's powers of perception and recall in concert with conventional perspectives. This is true, and some applications of the concept can be viewed as a lateral extension of Formalism, New Criticism, Structuralism, and so forth. (Smith 1989: 14)

Most studies, both quantitative and qualitative, published in the context of literary humanities computing after powerful desktop computers became available, tend to prioritize empirical data, either in the form of automatically extracted stylistic features, or as encoded thematic units that are then quantified, mapped, and interpreted.

Most suitable for this kind of literary analysis are studies of repeated structures in texts. These are usually characters, syllables, words, or phrases that reappear throughout a text or a collection of texts. These repetitions are frequently recognized by readers as structural devices that help segment a text, or link passages in texts. Chapters, characters, locations, thematic units, etc., may thus be connected, parallels can be established, and a systematic study of textual properties, such as echoes, contributes substantially to the understanding of the intricate setup of (literary) texts. This type of analysis is closely linked to theoretical models of intertextuality used in non-computer-based literary studies, and here the impact of electronic procedures is felt most acutely. Repetitions and echoes can be traced throughout a text in a consistent fashion; it takes, however, a sound theoretical model that allows one, first to identify, and then to isolate common formal properties of these textual units. The criterion of reliability and verifiability of results and findings is all-important in studies of repeated structures, and maps of distribution and significant presences and absences of textual features are used as the basis for a more detailed analysis. In this area computer-assisted approaches substantially contributed to the understanding of literary texts, and electronic studies of literary texts provided empirical evidence for the analysis of a broad range of intertextual features.

The methodological problems connected with this kind of approach feature prominently in nearly all electronic studies of literary texts: how does traditional criticism deal with formal properties of text, and where do electronic studies deviate from and/or enhance established techniques. Most computer-assisted studies of literature published in the last twenty years examine their own theoretical position and the impact of formal(ized) procedures on literary studies very critically. Nearly all come to the conclusion that rigorous procedures of textual analysis are greatly enhanced by electronic means, and that the basis for scholarly work with literary texts in areas that can be formalized is best provided by studies that compile textual evidence on an empirical basis.

The concept of rigorous testing, ideally unbiased by personal preferences or interpretation by the critic, relies on the assumption that textual properties can be identified and isolated by automatic means. If automatic procedures cannot be applied, stringent procedures for the preparation of texts have to be designed. It has been, and still is, one of the particular strengths of most electronic studies of literature that the criteria used in the process of analysis are situated in a theoretical model of textuality that is based on a critical examination of the role of the critic and the specific properties of the text.

These textual properties often need to be set off against the rest of the text, and here markup as the most obvious form of "external intervention" plays a leading role. The importance of markup for literary studies of electronic texts cannot be overestimated, because the ambiguity of meaning in literature requires at least some interpretative process by the critic even prior to the analysis proper. Words as discrete strings of characters, sentences, lines, and paragraphs serve as "natural" but by no means value-free textual segments. Any other instance of disambiguation in the form of thematic markup is a direct result of a critic's reading of a text, which by definition influences the course of the analysis. As many computer-based studies have shown, laying open one's criteria for encoding certain textual features is of prime importance to any procedure that aspires to produce quantifiable results. The empirical nature of the data extracted from the electronic text and then submitted to further analysis allows for a far more detailed interpretation that is indeed based on procedures of close reading, and this "new critical analyse de texte, as well as the more recent concepts of inter-textuality or Riffaterrian micro-contexts can lead to defensible interpretations only with the addition of the rigour and precision provided by computer analysis" (Fortier 1991: 194).

As the majority of literary critics still seem reluctant to embrace electronic media as a means of scholarly analysis, literary computing has, right from the very beginning, never really made an impact on mainstream scholarship. Electronic scholarly editions, on the contrary, are readily accepted in the academic community and they are rightly seen as indispensable tools for both teaching and research. But even the proliferation of electronic texts, some available with highly elaborate markup, did not lead to an increasing number of computer-based studies.

This can no longer be attributed to the lack of user-friendly, sophisticated software specifically designed for the analysis of literature. If early versions of TACT, Word-Cruncher, OCP, or TuStep required considerable computing expertise, modern versions of these software tools allow for easy-to-use routines that literary scholars without previous exposure to humanities computing can master. In addition, dedicated scholarly software has become very flexible and allows the user to dictate the terms of analysis, rather than superimpose certain routines (word lists, concordances, limited pattern matching) that would prejudice the analysis.

Early computer-based studies suffered greatly from hardware and software constraints, and as a result software tools were developed that addressed the specific requirements of scholarly computing. Although these tools proved remarkably effective and efficient given that the hardware available for humanities computing was rather slow and basic, it still took considerable expertise to prepare electronic texts and convert them into machine-readable form. As no standardized form of encoding existed until the Text Encoding

Initiative (TEI) was formed, most scholars adopted some system of markup that reflected their particular research needs. Initially, these systems were non-standardized, but later the majority of studies used COCOA tags for markup, but these systems for the scholarly encoding of literary texts needed to be adjusted to the specific software requirements of the programs used for the analysis. Accessing the results of computer-assisted studies in the form of printouts was equally cumbersome, and any statistical evaluation that extended the range of predefined options of standard software would have to be designed specifically for every individual application. Visualization, the plotting of graphs, or the formatting of tables required considerable expertise and expensive equipment and was thus mostly unavailable to one-person projects.

In the light of these technical difficulties it seemed that once hardware limitations no longer existed and the computing infrastructure was up to the demands of scholarly computing, the electronic analysis of literature would become a major field of research. Methodological problems addressed in studies that wanted to but could not, for technical reasons, attempt more demanding tasks that required large sets of data, access to a multitude of different texts and enough computing power to scan long texts for strings, for example, seemed a direct result of technical limitations.

But the three basic requirements, seen as imperative for eventually putting literary computing on the map of mainstream scholarship, have been met since the early 1960s and 1970s:

- virtually unlimited access to high-quality electronic texts;
- sophisticated software that lets the user define the terms of analysis rather than vice versa;
- powerful computing equipment that supplies unlimited computing power and storage capacity.

Despite impressive advances in both hardware and software development, and although electronic texts with markup based on the TEI guidelines have become available on the net, literary computing still remains a marginal pursuit. Scholarly results are presented at international conferences organized by the Association for Literary and Linguistic Computing (ALLC) and the Association for Computers and the Humanities (ACH) that are designed to inform humanists with a background in the discipline. The results are published in scholarly journals (*L&LC*, *Literary and Linguistic Computing*; and *CHum*, *Computers and the Humanities*) but rarely make an impact on mainstream scholarship. This dilemma has been commented on repeatedly: Thomas Corns, Rosanne Potter, Mark Olsen, and Paul Fortier show that even the most sophisticated electronic studies of canonical works of literature failed to be seen as contributions to the discourse of literary theory and method. Computer-based literary criticism has not "escaped from the ghetto of specialist periodicals to the mainstream of literary periodicals," Corns writes, and continues that the "tables and graphs and scattergrams and word lists that are so characteristic of computer-based investigation are entirely absent from mainstream periodicals" (Corns 1991: 127).

One reason for this, apart from a general aversion to all things electronic in traditional literary criticism, is described by Jerome McGann as the notion of relevance, because the general field of humanities education and scholarship will not take the use of digital technology seriously until one demonstrates how its tools improve the ways we explore and explain aesthetic works – until, that is, they expand our interpretational procedures. (McGann 2001: xii)

It is important that computer-assisted studies position themselves in the field of recent scholarship, take up the theoretical issues of text and textuality, and convey to the field of non-experts that the results merit closer inspection. Computers are not used for the sake of using new tools, but computers can supplement the critic's work with information that would normally be unavailable to a human reader. Speed, accuracy, unlimited memory, and the instantaneous access to virtually all textual features constitute the strength of the electronic tool. By tapping into the ever-growing pool of knowledge bases and by linking texts in ways that allow them to be used as huge repositories of textual material to draw on, traditional literary criticism can profit substantially from the knowledge and expertise accumulated in the search for a more rigorous analysis of literature as practiced in computer-based studies.

By looking at the history of literary computing, however, one cannot fail to see that most contributions add significant insight in a very narrow spectrum of literary analysis – in the area of stylistic studies that focus on textual features. The input of computing in these studies is limited to the preparation and preparatory analysis of the material under consideration. No immediate result, of course, can be obtained by the computer, but data are collected that allow for and require further analysis and interpretation by the researcher. The results, however, are impressive. Numerous studies of individual, and collections of, texts show that empirical evidence can be used productively for literary analysis. The history of literary computing shows that the field itself is changing. Stylo-statistical studies of isolated textual phenomena have become more common, even if the computing aspect does not always figure prominently. More and more scholars use electronic texts and techniques designed for computing purposes, but the resulting studies are embedded in the respective areas of traditional research. The methods, tools, and techniques have thus begun to influence literary criticism indirectly.

Right from the very beginning, humanities computing has always maintained its multi-dimensional character as far as literary genre, socio-cultural context and historio-geographical provenance of literary texts is concerned. Studies have focused on poetry, drama, and narrative from antiquity to the present day. Although an emphasis on literature in English can be observed, texts in other languages have also been analyzed. The variety of approaches used to come to terms with heterogeneous textual objects, the multitude of theoretical backgrounds and models of literature brought to bear on studies that share as a common denominator neither one single technique nor one "school of thought," but the application of a common tool, are the strong points of studies of literature carried out with the help of the computer. Discussions of literary theory, textuality, and the interdisciplinary nature of computer-assisted literary analysis feature prominently in modern studies. In this respect, mainstream literary criticism is most open to contributions from a field that is, by its very nature, acutely aware of its own theoretical position. In the future, the discourse of meta-criticism, however, may be fused with innovative approaches to literary texts. As Jerome McGann points out:

A new level of computer-assisted textual analysis may be achieved through programs that randomly but systematically deform the texts they search and that submit those deformations to human consideration. Computers are no more able to "decode" rich imaginative texts than human beings are. What they can be made to do, however, is expose textual features that lie outside the usual purview of human readers. (McGann 2001: 190–1)

REFERENCES FOR FURTHER READING

Ball, C. N. (1994). Automated Text Analysis: Cautionary Tales. *Literary and Linguistic Computing* 9: 293–302.

Burrows, J. F. (1987). *A Computation into Criticism. A Study of Jane Austen's Novels and an Experiment in Method*. Oxford: Oxford University Press.

——(1992). Computers and the Study of Literature. In C. S. Butler (ed.), *Computers and Written Texts* (pp. 167–204). Oxford: Blackwell.

Busa, R. (1992). Half a Century of Literary Computing: Towards a "New" Philology. *Literary and Linguistic Computing* 7: 69–73.

Corns, T. N. (1991). Computers in the Humanities: Methods and Applications in the Study of English Literature. *Literary and Linguistic Computing* 6: 127–30.

Feldmann, D., F.-W. Neumann, and T. Rommel (eds.) (1997). *Anglistik im Internet. Proceedings of the 1996 Erfurt Conference on Computing in the Humanities*. Heidelberg: Carl Winter.

Finneran, R. J. (ed.) (1996). *The Literary Text in the Digital Age*. Ann Arbor: University of Michigan Press.

Fortier, P. A. (1991). Theory, Methods and Applications: Some Examples in French Literature. *Literary and Linguistic Computing* 6, 192–6.

——(ed.) (1993–4). *A New Direction for Literary Studies? Computers and the Humanities* 27 (special double issue).

Hockey, S. (1980). *A Guide to Computer Applications in the Humanities*. London: Duckworth.

——(2000). *Electronic Texts in the Humanities. Principles and Practice*. Oxford: Oxford University Press.

Landow, G. P. and P. Delany (eds.) (1993). *The Digital Word: Text-Based Computing in the Humanities*. Cambridge, MA: MIT Press.

McGann, J. (2001). *Radiant Textuality: Literature After the World Wide Web*. New York: Palgrave.

Miall, D. S. (ed.) (1990). *Humanities and the Computer: New Directions*. Oxford: Oxford University Press.

Miller, J. H. (1968). Three Problems of Fictional Form: First-person Narration in *David Copperfield* and *Huckleberry Finn*. In R. H. Pearce (ed.), *Experience in the Novel: Selected Papers from the English Institute* (pp. 21–48). New York: Columbia University Press.

Opas, L. L. and T. Rommel (eds.) (1995). New Approaches to Computer Applications in Literary Studies. *Literary and Linguistic Computing* 10: 4.

Ott, W. (1978). *Metrische Analysen zu Vergil, Bucolica*. Tübingen: Niemeyer.

Potter, R. G. (ed.) (1989). *Literary Computing and Literary Criticism: Theoretical and Practical Essays on Theme and Rhetoric*. Philadelphia: University of Pennsylvania Press.

Renear, A. (1997). Out of Praxis: Three (Meta)Theories of Textuality. In K. Sutherland (ed.), *Electronic Textuality: Investigations in Method and Theory* (pp. 107–26). Oxford: Oxford University Press.

Robey, D. (1999). Counting Syllables in the Divine Comedy: A Computer Analysis. *Modern Language Review* 94: 61–86.

Rommel, T. (1995). *"And Trace It in This Poem Every Line." Methoden und Verfahren computerunterstützter Textanalyse am Beispiel von Lord Byrons Don Juan*. Tübingen: Narr.

Smedt, K. et al. (eds.) (1999). *Computing in Humanities Education: A European Perspective*. ACO*HUM Report. Bergen: University of Bergen HIT Center.

Smith, J. B. (1989). Computer Criticism. In R. G. Potter (ed.), *Literary Computing and Literary Criticism: Theoretical and Practical Essays on Theme and Rhetoric* (pp. 13–44). Philadelphia: University of Pennsylvania Press.

Sutherland, K. (ed.) (1997). *Electronic Textuality: Investigations in Method and Theory*. Oxford: Oxford University Press.

Toolan, M. (1990). *The Stylistics of Fiction: A Literary-Linguistic Approach*. London: Routledge.

9

Music

Ichiro Fujinaga and Susan Forscher Weiss

Introduction

Technological advances are often accompanied by growing pains. Following the advent of printing, texts were produced in an effort to reach wider audiences. Many of these, in a wide variety of subjects, especially music, were based on the most popular source materials. As with many other disciplines, computer applications in music have been dramatically affected by the advent of the Internet. The best-known phenomenon is the proliferation of files – mostly popular music – in compressed format known as MP3. There are also peer-to-peer file sharing programs such as Napster. The availability of sample music through online music stores such as amazon.com and barnesandnoble.com as well as in other specialized sites such as the Classical Music Archives or the web pages of professors at numerous universities around the world has changed the lives of scholars and music listeners in general. In addition, music notation software has revolutionized the music publishing industry. It allows composers to produce professional-quality scores and scholars to prepare critical editions more efficiently and economically. Optical music recognition (OMR) is still in the process of developing adequate techniques. Once accomplished, OMR and other newer technologies will redefine the way musicians are able to analyze musical scores.

Perhaps the technology that had the most profound influence on music scholarship has been the availability of e-mail, discussion lists, and society listservs, providing scholars and lay people with opportunities to exchange ideas and materials without the delay of traditional modes of communication. This trend is documented as late as 1995 (Troutman 1995).

E-mail has provided scholars with opportunities for communication and the sharing of ideas. It also has paved the way for the formation of national and international consortiums. Some professional listservs include the AMS (American Musicological Society) and

SMT (Society of Music Theory) lists and their many offshoots. Hundreds of websites provide information to scholars in various music disciplines. Online versions of important music reference materials include the *New Grove Dictionary of Music and Musicians*, the Répertoire International des Sources Musicales (RISM), the Répertoire International de Littérature Musicale (RILM), the International Index to Music Periodicals (IIMP), the Music Index, Musical America, and Thesaurus Musicarum Latinarum, among countless others.

The following review of computer applications in music scholarship will focus on the last decade, examining developments in a number of areas including notation software, MIDI (Musical Instrument Data Interchange), and MP3, databases, specialized resources, computer applications for music scholars, and music information retrieval (MIR) systems. For previous reviews of the discipline, see Alphonce (1989), Davis (1988), Bent and Morehen (1978), and Hewlett and Selfridge-Field (1991).

Notation Software

Music notation software has been developed over the course of the last two decades of the twentieth century, now allowing composers to prepare their own music without the necessity of hiring professional copyists. Before the advent of this technology, individual parts were manually copied from the score. Large ensemble pieces that require a score for the conductor as well as parts for individual musicians can now be produced in record time and at a fraction of the cost. Once the master score is entered into the computer, the parts can be generated automatically with a minimal amount of manual editing. This software is also widely used in the music publishing industry and allows musicologists to produce scholarly editions of works much more accurately, efficiently, and economically than before.

One drawback, and an explanation for the lack of widespread use, is the absence of standard music representation format, either as *de facto* proprietary (equivalent to Word in the text world) or as an open standard, such as ASCII. Despite numerous efforts since the advent of computer applications in music to create such a format (Hewlett and Selfridge-Field 1991), no such standard has emerged. Some may argue that the proprietary format of the very popular music notation software Finale is becoming a standard, but others contend that another proprietary format of an increasingly popular competitor called Sibelius may become the standard of the future. Even if one or both of these become the standard, without some open formats, equivalent to ASCII or RTF, these files will be too cumbersome for other purposes such as searching and analysis.

Optical Music Recognition

One way to create a computer-readable format of music notation is to use optical music recognition software, similar to optical character recognition technology. A variety of research protocols are being tested and commercial software is becoming available, but the accuracy of the recognition is highly dependent on the type and quality of the original document and on the complexity of the music. Newer techniques are being applied that will enable the recognition of lute tablature, medieval music notation, and music notation systems from other cultures (Selfridge-Field 1994b).

MIDI and MP3

Outside of music notation, there are two open formats for music that have emerged as standards: MIDI and MP3. Musical Instrument Data Interchange (MIDI) was developed by a consortium of music synthesizer manufacturers in the early 1980s. It has become extremely widespread, becoming the *de facto* standard for popular music and the world standard for exchanging information between electronic musical instruments and music software.

Originally designed to capture the gestures of keyboard performers, it does have some limitations. A MIDI file contains data as to when, which, and how fast a key was depressed. It does not contain the timbre of the instrument or much notational information such as the precise pitch of a note (A♯ or B♭) or which notes are grouped together. Nevertheless, a large amount of music is available in MIDI format on the Internet and in commercial classical piano music recordings. (There are also acoustic pianos that can play back MIDI files.)

In general, most traditional music scholars base their research on scores. The majority of analytical methods and theories are dependent on notated music. Thus, the lack of crucial notational information in MIDI files renders this format less useful for scholarly work.

The recent explosion in the proliferation of MP3 files can be explained as a convergence of various factors. Among these is the standardization of audio format, a higher bandwidth access to the Internet, a dramatic increase in computing power on the desktop, and the invention of clever compression methods.

The representation of digital audio (as sound) was firmly established in the 1980s by the invention of compact discs (CDs). The standard requires that the sound is captured (digitized) 44,100 times per second and each sample is stored as a 16-bit integer. Although there are a number of competing file formats for audio, these are not difficult to interchange because they are basically a series of numbers. The storage required for one minute of stereo audio is about 10 MB (megabytes). Even with a relatively high-speed modem (28.8 KB), it takes a couple of hours to download a pop song of three minutes (30 MB). The MP3 compression technology reduces the size of the audio files to up to one-hundredth of its original size. Finally, a computer powerful enough to decompress and play back the downloaded MP3 file was needed. Home computers in the late 1980s could barely play back a CD-quality stereo audio. Thanks to an almost hundredfold increase in the computing power of desktop computers within the last decade, today almost any computer can download, decompress, and play back music while the users perform other tasks.

Databases

General bibliographical databases

The searchable online bibliographical databases are among the best computer tools for all music scholars in the last decade. Two of the most useful and important bibliographical databases for music scholars are RILM (Répertoire International de Littérature Musicale) and Music Index. RILM Abstracts of Music Literature contains over 275,000 entries from over 500 scholarly periodicals from 60 countries with 140 languages and includes original-language titles; title translations in English; full bibliographic information; and abstracts in English. The Music Index: A Subject–Author Guide to Music Periodical Literature covers 650 publications from 1979 and covers a wider range of publications including popular music magazines. Both of these databases are subscription-based, but because of their importance they are available in most music libraries. International Index to Music Periodicals (IIMP) is a relatively new subscription service that indexes more than 370 international music periodicals with over 60 full-text titles. It also includes retrospective coverage from over 185 periodicals dating back as far as 1874.

The most important music reference in English has been the Grove's Dictionaries for generations of music scholars. Now both *The New Grove Dictionary of Music and Musicians* and *The New Grove Dictionary of Opera* are available online and have greatly enhanced the usability of these valuable sources.

Also, *The Concise Oxford Dictionary of Music*, *The Concise Oxford Dictionary of Opera*, and *Who's Who in Opera* are now part of the Oxford Reference Online. The utility of this system is that items can be searched in other Oxford dictionaries. For example, query of "Beethoven" produces a quote by E. M. Forster: "It will be generally admitted that Beethoven's Fifth Symphony is the most sublime noise that has ever penetrated into the ear of man" (*Howards End* [1910], from *The Oxford Dictionary of Twentieth Century Quotations*).

Other major resources include RISM (Répertoire International des Sources Musicales). "Music manuscripts after 1600" is an annotated index and guide to music manuscripts produced between 1600 and 1850 containing more than 380,000 works by over 18,000 composers found in manuscripts over 595 libraries and archives in 31 countries. The music manuscript database contains over 506,000 searchable musical incipits, which can be viewed as musical scores.

RIPM (Répertoire International de la Presse Musicale) contains over 410,000 annotated records from 127 volumes of nineteenth- and twentieth-century music periodicals from over 15 countries. Another important source is Doctoral Dissertations in Musicology (DDM)-Online, which is a database of bibliographic records for completed dissertations and new dissertation topics in the fields of musicology, music theory, and ethnomusicology, as well as in related musical, scientific, and humanistic disciplines. Available since 1996, it contains more than 12,000 records.

IIPA (International Index to the Performing Arts) Full Text contains 182,550 records drawn from over 210 periodicals and 33 full-text titles. It also contains retrospective coverage with citations dating back to 1864.

The Canadian Music Periodical Index, although restricted to Canadian music periodicals, should be mentioned because, unlike other databases mentioned above, it is free. A service provided by the National Library of Canada, it includes nearly 30,000 entries on articles dating from the late nineteenth century to the present day. Some 500 Canadian music journals, newsletters, and magazines are represented here, almost 200 of which are currently active and continue to be indexed. Another free service provided by the National Library of Canada is an online Encyclopedia of Music in Canada, available both in English and French.

Music databases

The Scribe Medieval Music Database (La Trobe University) is a collection of 6,000 musical scores, color images, texts, and bibliographic information on medieval music, searchable by text or melody. This includes the complete annual cycle of liturgical chant taken from original medieval sources, and the complete works of selected composers from the twelfth to the fifteenth centuries (Stinson 1992).

CANTUS database, started at Catholic University in the 1980s and now hosted at the University of Western Ontario, contains indices of Latin ecclesiastical chants in over 70 selected manuscripts and early printed sources of the liturgical Office. It is searchable by first few words, keywords, chant identification number, or liturgical occasion. Further downloadable chant resources can be found at Cantus Planus Archiv at the University of Regensburg.

In development since 1989, Thesaurus Musicarum Latinarum (TML) is a full-text searchable database (with ASCII text and associated image files) containing a large corpus of Latin music theory written during the Middle Ages and the Renaissance. A similar database of texts on Italian music theory and aesthetics is Saggi Musicali Italiani (SMI) and Texts on Music in English from the Medieval and Early Modern Eras (TME). Another source for Italian treatises, from the Renaissance and early Baroque, is Thesaurus Musicarum Italicarum (TMI). One of the features of this collection, not available in others, is that the many terms are hyperlinked. The CD-ROM version of this database contains complete facsimiles and they are being made available online.

Themefinder is a collaborative project of Stanford University and Ohio State University. It consists of three databases: Classical Instrumental Music (10,000 themes), European Folksongs (7,000 folksongs), and Latin Motets from the sixteenth century (18,000 incipits). A web-based searching interface is provided and the matched themes are displayed in graphical notation (Kornstädt 1998).

MELDEX, a music search engine developed at the University of Waikato, New Zealand, forms part of the New Zealand Digital Library. The database consists of 9,400 folk melodies. This is one of the first search engines that allows query-by-humming, where search can be accomplished by providing a sung audio file online (Bainbridge 1998).

MuseData at Stanford University is a collection of full-text databases of music for several composers, including J. S. Bach, Beethoven, Corelli, Handel, Haydn, Mozart, Telemann, and Vivaldi. It currently contains 2,461 complete movements of 634 classical pieces, including 185 Bach chorales (Selfridge-Field 1994a).

For scholars working with popular music there are a variety of large databases available. For MIDI data searchable by title and artist, there are sites that claim to index over

1 million MIDI files and 95,000 lyrics. Within classical music there are sites with over 20,000 MIDI files.

One can also find opera librettos (RISM-US Libretto Database of over 13,000 libretti), old English ballads, or even hip-hop lyrics, where one can use "Rhymerator" to find rhyming words online.

Specialized bibliography

The Online Bach Bibliography was first launched on the Web in May 1997 by Tomita Yo, and ever since it has been updated regularly. At present, it contains over 18,000 records of bibliographical references that are considered useful for the scholarly discussion of Bach's life and works.

The Beethoven Bibliography Database begun in 1990 currently includes 2,700 records for books and scores and is available from the Center for Beethoven Studies at San Jose State University (Elliott 1994).

Other notable databases include:

- OCLC (Online Computer Library Center) Music Library, which is a subset of the OCLC Online Union Catalogue; it provides citations to nearly 800,000 musical sound recordings.
- National Sound Archive at the British Library, whose catalogue includes entries for almost 2.5 million recordings, published and unpublished, in all genres from pop, jazz, classical, and world music, to oral history, drama and literature, dialect, language, and wildlife sounds.
- SONIC of Library of Congress. The Library of Congress Recorded Sound Collection contains some 2.5 million audio recordings including multiple copies. It currently has 350,000 bibliographic records representing roughly 25 percent of the Library's entire sound recording holding of, among others, 78s, 45s, and radio broadcasts.
- Ufficio Ricerca Fondi Musicali di Milano is a national catalogue of music manuscript and printed scores to 1900, containing over 300,000 entries (Gentili-Tedeschi 2001).

Sheet music

There are many large collections of North American sheet music available on the Web. Most of these are scanned images including the cover artwork and the musical score, with varying amount of metadata; for example, some have subjects for the cover art, and some have partial lyrics. For example, see the Library of Congress 1820–1885 (62,500 pieces registered at the Library for copyright), Brown University 1850–1920 (1,305 pieces of African-American sheet music), Duke University 1850–1920 (3,042 pieces), the Lester Levy Collection of Sheet Music at the Johns Hopkins University 1780–1960 (29,000 pieces), Mississippi State University (22,000 pieces), University of California at Berkeley 1852–1900 (2,000 pieces published in California). The next step for these collections is to provide audio, and full-text/music searching capabilities. In order to achieve these goals, automated optical music recognition system would be required.

Computer Applications

Perhaps the most intensive utilization of computers in music is by composers who use them for various functions. The machines may be used to create new sounds, create new instruments and interfaces, imitate existing instruments with fine control, generate new composition, or train computers to listen to music for interaction with human performers. Other research activities in this field include: pitch recognition, tempo/beat induction, and expressive performance, where the computer attempts to imitate musicians. For thorough introduction and history in this area, see the excellent book by Roads (1996). Similar research topics are also investigated by music psychologists and music educators, where computers are used to model human musical cognition and abilities. Educators are also interested in using computers to aid in music teaching. Music theorists have also actively used computers for analysis of notated music. Applications include melodic and harmonic analysis, key-finder, segmentation, and development of interactive graphic analysis tools.

Music historians have used computers for a range of tasks. Samples of published works can be divided by subject area. Medieval and Renaissance applications include examples of computer-assisted examination and analysis of notational signs in twelfth-century manuscripts (Loos 1996), of the oral transmission of Old Roman chant (Haas 1997), and a computer program to compare a number of motets with questionable attributions (Thomas 1999). There are a number of computer analyses of motets by William Byrd and other English composers in an effort to confirm authorship (see Morehen 1992; Wulstan 1992, 1995). There are also systematic studies of vertical sonorities and melodic features of works by Italian Renaissance theorists and composers (Moll 1996). One example took Palestrina's Masses from the Casimiri edition, entered them into a database without text using a MIDI synthesizer, examined by customized programs, and manipulated by spreadsheet software. Areas of investigation included prolations and contexts of note spans and rests, including metric and textural aspects; the distribution of pitch classes, including the effects of mode; and the distribution of individual pitches correlated with voice ranges. Conclusions revealed that Palestrina's pitch-class collection was conservative and common voice ranges were narrower than previously reported (Miller 1992).

Computer applications in Baroque music include a database, music processor, and coding system for analyzing the music of Telemann (Lange 1995); software to analyze modality versus tonality in Bach's four-part chorales (Rasmussen 1996); a dissertation that used statistics and computer routines to resolve conflicting attributions in works by Bach's sons (Knoll 1998); the use of spreadsheets for statistical analysis in text critical study of Bach's *Well-Tempered Clavier* (Tomita 1993); and a computer analysis of the variable role of dissonance and contrapuntal techniques in Corelli Trio Sonatas (Peiper 1996).

Studies of Classical and Romantic era composers include analysis of melodic affinities and identical melodic elements in music by Mozart and Süssmayr to refute claims of the latter's authorship of portions of Mozart's *Requiem* (Leeson 1995); programs to detect melodic patterns and search text in Schubert's lieder (Nettheim 2000; Yi 1990); and an analytical comparison, based on statistics, using relational database and spreadsheet software, of the final movements of Brahms's symphonies nos. 3 and 4 and Bruckner's symphonies nos. 3 and 4, with findings that contradict a number of related previous studies (McArtor 1995).

Musicologists and theorists are applying computer programs to study tonal, atonal, and post-tonal music of the last century. An example is a study of excerpts from Bartók's *Ten Easy Pieces* in which the key is ambiguous. A program was created to determine the key (as recorded in MIDI) on the basis of the relative frequency and duration of pitch classes (Cooper 1998).

In the area of musical images and iconography, work has been done with the superimposition of divergent sixteenth- and seventeenth-century prints, such as those in the William Byrd edition (Brett and Smith 2001). Other studies focusing on images include one that describes some post-processing procedures for scanned images in re-establishing the content of medieval sources for sacred vocal music preserved in the Vatican Library (Planchart 2001).

Another, the Digital Image Archive of Medieval Music (DIAMM), provides a new resource for scholars desiring to digitize, archive, and make available images of primary sources and to develop techniques of digital image enhancement, or "virtual restoration," to retrieve lost data or improve the legibility of materials that cannot at present be read (Wathey et al. 2001).

Another area of research concerns the transcription of tablatures. Software has been developed to facilitate the assignment of voices when transcribing tablature, lute and guitar, into modern notation (Charnassé 1991; Kelly 1995; Derrien-Peden et al. 1991).

Performance practice is an area in need of further investigation. There is one study that automatically assigns proper fingering for English keyboard music (1560–1630), examining sixty surviving manuscripts, half of which contain fingerings. Ten important works with fingerings are stored and analyzed and then applied to those without fingerings (Morehen 1994). Composer sketches is another area just beginning to benefit from the application of digital techniques. A recent study describes photographic techniques used in an electronic facsimile of the sketches for Alban Berg's *Wozzeck*. By showing various stages of sketches for one scene from this opera, one of the most prominent works of the twentieth century, the paper suggests typical uses of an electronic facsimile for a large body of sketches. The archaeological nature of the task involves the capture of pencil drafts and paper paste-overs as well as the penetration of lacquer occlusions (Hall 2001).

Perhaps one of the most exciting of the recent articles in *Computing in Musicology* is a study of watermarks by Dexter Edge. The traditional methods used by music historians for imaging watermarks are problematic. Freehand tracing is inherently prone to inaccuracy, the Dylux method often seems ineffective with musical manuscripts, and beta-radiography has become prohibitively expensive. Using a scanner equipped with a transparency adapter and manipulating the resulting images, Edge is able to create digital images of watermarks with good results.

Folksong is one category that has inspired a number of studies. A paper on the mapping of European folksong discusses issues related to encoding, displaying, and analyzing geographical information pertaining to music (Aarden and Huron 2001). Other studies examine pulse in German folksong, melodic arch in Western folksongs, and contour analysis of Hungarian folk music (Nettheim 1993; Huron 1996; Juhász 2000; Pintér 1999). For further information on application in musicology see Nettheim (1997) and Selfridge-Field (1992).

Music Information Retrieval

As more and more music is becoming available on the Internet, it has become evident that there is a need for a method of searching for the required music information. Although this branch of research is in its initial stage, it is growing rapidly. With increased interest in digital libraries, in general, preservation and retrieval of musical material both new and old is necessary. Although searching for textual information is becoming easier, as with image searching, searching for music, in audio format or in notated format, is still difficult (Byrd and Crawford 2001).

Topics in this field include: query-by-humming, automatic genre and style classification, music indexing, melodic similarity, and automatic transcription. The latter, especially transcribing polyphonic music, remains the "holy grail" of audio engineers.

The copyright issue is still under intense debate (Anthony et al. 2001).

Although most of these issues have been the academic concerns of music scholars, there is also an ever-increasing commercial interest in knowing more about music. Record companies are eager for buyers to find music more easily and for the companies to be able to classify musical styles and genre so that they can match listeners' preferences. To accomplish this, companies are asking questions such as "What is a melody or theme?" and "Where do they occur?" Knowing the answers will aid in discovering new music that a consumer would like. Thus, with funding from the commercial sector, there may now be additional research opportunities for music investigators.

Conclusions

This is a very exciting time for music. Technology is making new sounds and unprecedented access to music. As more and more musical data become readily available, musical research methodology may undergo a fundamental change. As David Huron hints, the discipline will go from a "data-poor" field to a "data-rich" field (Huron 1999). As of now, significant research has been limited to subjects such as composer attributions, image enhancements, determination of provenance based on watermarks, and some notational studies. More needs to be done. Also, with pressure from music information retrieval (MIR) areas, there may be greater need for scholars from different musical disciplines to work together to solve a variety of musical puzzles. Whether it is for musicologists and theorists or members of the business and lay communities, we will need to develop more sophisticated analytical technologies and programs for search and retrieval of an ever-expanding mass of information and sound.

REFERENCES FOR FURTHER READING

Aarden, B. and D. Huron (2001). Mapping European Folksong: Geographical Localization of Musical Features. *Computing in Musicology* 12: 169–83.
Alphonce, B. (1989). Computer Applications in Music Research: A Retrospective. *Computers in Music Research* 1: 1–74.

Anthony, D., C. Cronin, and E. Selfridge-Field (2001). The Electronic Dissemination of Notated Music: An Overview. *Computing in Musicology* 12: 135–66.

Bainbridge, D. (1998). MELDEX: A Web-based Melodic Locator Service. *Computing in Musicology* 11: 223–9.

Bent, I. and J. Morehen (1978). Computers in Analysis of Music. *Proceedings of the Royal Society of Music* 104: 30–46.

Brett, P. and J. Smith (2001). Computer Collation of Divergent Early Prints in the Byrd Edition. *Computing in Musicology* 12: 251–60.

Byrd, D. and T. Crawford (2001). Problems of Music Information Retrieval in the Real World. *Information Processing and Management* 38,2: 249–72.

Charnassé, H. (1991). ERATTO Software for German Lute Tablatures. *Computing in Musicology* 7: 60–2.

Cooper, D. (1998). The Unfolding of Tonality in the Music of Béla Bartók. *Music Analysis* 17,1: 21–38.

Davis, D. S. (1988). *Computer Applications in Music.* Madison, WI: A-R Editions.

Derrien-Peden, D., I. Kanellos, and J.-F. Maheas (1991). French Sixteenth-century Guitar Tablatures: Transcriptions and Analysis. *Computing in Musicology* 7: 62–4.

Edge, D. (2001). The Digital Imaging of Watermarks. *Computing in Musicology* 12: 261–74.

Elliott, P. (1994). Beethoven Bibliography Online. *Computing and Musicology* 9: 51–2.

Gentili-Tedeschi, M. (2001). Il lavoro dell'Ufficio Ricerca Fondi Musicali di Milano. *Libreria Musicale Italiana* 18: 483–7.

Haas, M. (1997). *Mündliche Überlieferung und altrömischer Choral: Historische und analytische computergestützte Untersuchungen.* Bern: Lang.

Hall, P. (2001). The Making of an Electronic Facsimile: Berg's Sketches for Wozzeck. *Computing in Musicology* 12: 275–82.

Hewlett, W. B. and Selfridge-Field, E. (1991). Computing in Musicology, 1966–91. *Computers and the Humanities* 25,6: 381–92.

Huron, D. (1996). The Melodic Arch in Western Folksongs. *Computing in Musicology* 10: 3–23.

——(1999). The New Empiricism: Systematic Musicology in a Postmodern Age. 1999 Ernest Bloch Lecture, University of California, Berkeley.

Juhász, Z. (2000). Contour Analysis of Hungarian Folk Music in a Multidimensional Metric-Space. *Journal of New Music Research* 29,1: 71–83.

Kelly, W. (1995). Calculating Fret Intervals with Spreadsheet Software. *American Lutherie* 43: 46–7.

Knoll, M. W. (1998). Which Bach Wrote What? A Cumulative Approach to Clarification of Three Disputed Works. PhD dissertation, University of Michigan.

Kornstädt, A. (1998). *Themefinder*: A Web-based Melodic Search Tool. *Computing in Musicology* 11: 231–6.

Lange, C. (1995). Die Telemann Datenbank: Aspekte der Datenspeicherung und der Nutzungsmöglichkeiten [The Telemann Database: Aspects of data storage and possible uses]. *Magdeburger Telemann Studien* 13: 128–44.

Leeson, D. N. (1995). Franz Xaver Süssmayr and the Mozart Requiem: A Computer Analysis of Authorship Based on Melodic Affinity. *Mozart-Jahrbuch*: 111–53.

Loos, I. (1996). Ein Beispiel der Computeranalyse mittelalterlicher Neumen: Das Quilisma im Antiphonar U 406 (12. Jh.) [An example of computer analysis of Medieval neumes: the Quilisma in Antiphoner U 406 (12th c.)]. *Musicologica Austriaca* 14–15: 173–81.

McArtor, M. J. (1995). Comparison of Design in the Finales of the Symphonies of Bruckner and Brahms. DMA thesis, Arizona State University.

Miller, E. J. (1992). Aspects of Melodic Construction in the Masses of Palestrina: A Computer-assisted Study. PhD dissertation, Northwestern University.

Moll, K. N. (1996). Vertical Sonorities in Renaissance Polyphony: A Music-analytic Application of Spreadsheet Software. *Computing in Musicology* 10: 59–77.

Morehen, J. (1992). Byrd's Manuscript Motets: A New Perspective. In A. M. Brown and A. Martin (eds.), *Byrd Studies* (pp. 51–62). Cambridge: Cambridge University Press.

——(1994). Aiding Authentic Performance: A Fingering Databank for Elizabethan Keyboard Music. *Computing in Musicology* 9: 81–92.

Nettheim, N. (1993). The Pulse in German Folksong: A Statistical Investigation. *Musikometrika* 5: 69–89.

——(1997). A Bibliography of Statistical Applications in Musicology. *Musicology Australia – Journal of the Musicological Society of Australia* 20: 94–107.

——(2000). Melodic Pattern-detection Using MuSearch in Schubert's *Die schöne Müllerin*. *Computing in Musicology* 11: 159–64.

Peiper, C. E. (1996). Dissonance and Genre in Corelli's Trio Sonatas: A LISP-based Study of Opp. 1 and 2. *Computing in Musicology* 10: 34–8.

Pintér, I. (1999). Computer-aided Transcription of Folk Music. *Studia Musicologica Academiae Scientiarum Hungaricae* 40,1–3: 189–209.

Planchart, A. E. (2001). Image-enhancement Procedures for Medieval Manuscripts. *Computing in Musicology* 12: 241–50.

Rasmussen, S. C. (1996). Modality vs. Tonality in Bach's Chorale Harmonizations. *Computing in Musicology* 10: 49–58.

Roads, C. (1996). *Computer Music Tutorial*. Cambridge, MA: MIT Press.

Selfridge-Field, E. (1992). Music Analysis by Computer. In G. Haus (ed.), *Music Processing* (pp. 3–24). Madison, WI: A-R Editions.

——(1994a). The MuseData Universe: A System of Musical Information. *Computing in Musicology* 9: 9–30.

——(1994b). Optical Recognition of Musical Notation: A Survey of Current Work. *Computing in Musicology* 9: 109–45.

Stinson, J. (1992). The SCRIBE Database. *Computing in Musicology* 8: 65.

Thomas, J. S. (1999). The Sixteenth-century Motet: A Comprehensive Survey of the Repertory and Case Studies of the Core Texts, Composers, and Repertory. PhD dissertation, University of Cincinnati.

Tomita, Y. (1993). The Spreadsheet in Musicology: An Efficient Working Environment for Statistical Analysis in Text Critical Study. *Musicus* 3: 31–7.

Troutman, L. A. (1995). MLA-L: A New Mode of Communication. *Fontes Artis Musicae* 42,3: 271–81.

Wathey, A., M. Bent, and J. Feely-McCraig (2001). The Art of Virtual Restoration: Creating the Digital Image Archive of Medieval Music (DIAMM). *Computing in Musicology* 12: 227–40.

Wulstan, D. (1992). Birdus Tantum Natus Decorare Magistrum. In A. M. Brown and A. Martin (eds.), *Byrd Studies* (pp. 63–82). Cambridge: Cambridge University Press.

——(1995) Byrd, Tallis, and Ferrabosco. In J. Morehen (ed.), *English Choral Practice c.1400–c.1650: A Memorial Volume to Peter Le Huray* (pp. 109–42). Cambridge: Cambridge University Press.

Yi, S. W. (1990). A Theory of Melodic Contour as Pitch–Time Interaction: The Linguistic Modeling and Statistical Analysis of Vocal Melodies in Selected "Lied." PhD dissertation, University of California, Los Angeles.

10

Multimedia

Geoffrey Rockwell and Andrew Mactavish

How do we think through the new types of media created for the computer? Many names have emerged to describe computer-based forms, such as *digital media, new media, hyper-media*, or *multimedia*. In this chapter we will start with *multimedia*, one possible name that captures one of the features of the emerging genre.

What is Multimedia?

Thinking through a definition starts with a name. Definitions help bring into view limits to that about which you think. Here are some definitions of "multimedia":

> A *multimedia* computer system is one that is capable of input or output of more than one medium. Typically, the term is applied to systems that support more than one physical output medium, such as a computer display, video, and audio. (Blattner and Dannenberg 1992: xxiii)

Blattner and Dannenberg further make the observation that "multimedia systems strive to take the best advantage of human senses in order to facilitate communication" (1992: xix). Embedded in their discussion is a view of communication where the communicator chooses to combine the media best suited to her communicative goals; therefore, multi-media, which encompasses other media, provides the greatest breadth of communicative possibilities.

The *Encyclopaedia Britannica Online* defines "Interactive Multimedia" as "any computer-delivered electronic system that allows the user to control, combine, and manipulate different types of media." In this definition the emphasis is placed on interactivity and the computer control over the delivery of information in different media. This control includes the release of control to the reader or viewer so that they can participate in the development of meaning through interaction with a multimedia work.

While similar, what is interesting in these definitions is what they are defining. The first defines a "multimedia system" while the second specifies "interactive multimedia." This chapter proposes a third and shorter definition that combines many of the features in the others with a focus on multimedia as a genre of communicative work.

A multimedia work is a computer-based rhetorical artifact in which multiple media are integrated into an interactive whole.

We can use the parts of this definition to analyze multimedia.

Computer-based

The word "multimedia" originally referred to works of art that combined multiple traditional art media, as in *a multimedia art installation*. By defining multimedia as "computer-based" such mixed-media works are deliberately excluded. In other words, a multimedia work is a digital work that is accessed through the computer even if parts were created in analogue form and then digitized for integration on the computer. This definition also excludes works that might have been created on a computer, like a desktop publishing file, but are accessed by readers through an analogue medium like print.

Rhetorical artifact

A multimedia work is one designed to convince, delight, or instruct in the classical sense of rhetoric. It is not a work designed for administrative purposes or any collection of data in different media. Nor is it solely a technological artifact. This is to distinguish a multimedia work, which is a work of human expression, from those works that may combine media and reside on the computer, but are not designed by humans to communicate to humans.

Multiple media

Central to all definitions of multimedia is the idea that multimedia combines types of information that traditionally have been considered different media and have therefore had different traditions of production and distribution. Digitization makes this possible as the computer stores all information, whatever its original form, as binary digital data. Thus it is possible to combine media, especially media that are incompatible in other means of distribution, like synchronous or time-dependent media (audio and video) and asynchronous media (text and still images).

Integrated . . . artistic whole

A multimedia work is not just a random collection of different media gathered somewhere on the system. By this definition the integration of media is the result of deliberate artistic imagination aimed at producing a work that has artistic unity, which is another way of saying that we treat multimedia as unified works that are intended by their creator to be experienced as a whole. Likewise, consumers of multimedia treat such works as integrated in their consumption. The art of multimedia consists in how you integrate media.

Interactive

One of the features of multimedia is the interactivity or the programming that structures the viewer's experience. Some level of interactivity is assumed in any computer-based work, but by this definition interactivity becomes a defining feature that helps weave the multiplicity into a whole. Interactivity is thus important to the artistic integrity of multimedia. We might go further and say that interactivity, in the sense of the programming that structures the work, is the form that integrates the others.

The names given for multimedia works emphasize different characteristics of these works. "New media" emphasizes the experience of these works as "new" and different from existing forms of entertainment and instruction, but new media can also refer to media new to the twentieth century, including electronic (but not necessarily digital) media like television. "Hypermedia" evolved out of "hypertext" and emphasizes the way these works are multi-linear labyrinths of information that the user navigates. This name, however, suggests that all new media are organized as hypertexts with nodes and links, which is not the case for works like arcade games. While "hypermedia" is a useful term for those works that make use of hypertext features, "multimedia" emphasizes the combination of traditional media into rhetorical unities.

Defining multimedia as a way of thinking about the new medium made possible by the computer runs the risk of fixing a moving target inappropriately. It could turn out that multimedia works are not a new form of expression, but that they are remediated forms of existing genres of expression (Bolter and Grusin 1999). These traditional forms, when represented digitally, are transformed by the limitations and capabilities of the computer. They can be processed by the computer; they can be transmitted instantaneously over the Internet without loss of quality; they can be extended with other media annotations; they can be transcoded from one form to another (a text can be visualized or read out as synthesized audio).

The ways in which traditional media are created, distributed and consumed are also transformed when represented digitally. Multimedia books are not only bought at bookstores and read in bed, they can be distributed over the Internet by an e-text library for your PDA (personal digital assistant) and consumed as concordances with text analysis tools. In short, even if we think of multimedia as a way of digitally re-editing (re-encoding) traditional works, there are common limitations and possibilities to the digital form. Multimedia works, whether born digital or remediated, share common characteristics including emerging modes of electronic production, distribution, and consumption. They can be defined as multimedia for the purposes of thinking through the effects of the merging of multiple media into interactive digital works to be accessed on the computer.

What are the Types of Multimedia?

Classifying is a second way of thinking through multimedia, and one that involves surveying the variety of the phenomena. It is also a common move in any discussion of multimedia to give examples of these types of multimedia, especially to make the point that these types are no longer academic experiments inaccessible to the everyday consumer. The challenge of multimedia to the humanities is thinking through the variety of multimedia artifacts and asking about the clusters of works that can be aggregated into types. Here are some examples:

Web hypermedia

The first multimedia works to be considered seriously in humanities computing circles were hypertexts like *The Dickens Web* by George P. Landow, a work created to explore the possibilities for hypertext and multimedia in education. It was an exemplary educational hypertext that illustrated and informed Landow's theoretical work around hypertext theory. With the evolution of the World Wide Web as a common means for distributing and accessing hypertextual information, we now have thousands of educational and research Web hypertexts, some of which combine multiple media and can be called hypermedia works. The early technologies of the Web, like HTML, have been extended with technologies like XML and the Macromedia Flash file format (SWF for Shockwave-Flash) that make sophisticated interactive graphics and animation possible.

Computer games

By far the most commercially successful multimedia works are computer games, whose short but rich history is interwoven with the development of multimedia technologies. Games like *Myst* (Cyan) introduced consumers of all ages to the effective use of images, animations, and environmental sound to create a fictional world characterized by navigation and puzzle-solving. More recently, advancements in hardware and software technologies for graphics, audio, animation, and video, and sophisticated artificial intelligence and physics models are making game worlds look and act more convincing. Games are normally distributed on CD-ROM or DVD, but the Web is frequently used for distributing software updates and game demos.

Digital art

Artists have been using multimedia to create interactive installations that are controlled by computers and use multiple media. An example would be David Rokeby's *Very Nervous System* (1986–90), an interactive sound installation where the user or a performer generates sound and music through body movement. These playful works are exhibited in galleries and museums as works of art that bring multimedia into the traditions of art exhibition. Other digital artists have created Web works that are submitted to online exhibitions like those mounted by the San Francisco Museum of Modern Art in their E•SPACE, which collects and commissions Web art objects.

Multimedia encyclopedia

Multimedia has been used widely in education and for the presentation of research. A common form of educational and reference multimedia is the multimedia encyclopedia, like the *Encyclopaedia Britannica Online* and Microsoft's *Encarta* (on CD-ROM). Multimedia encyclopedias are the logical extension of the print genre, taking advantage of the computer's capability to play time-dependent media like audio, animation, and video to enhance the accessibility of information.

These are but examples of types of multimedia. A proper topology would be based on criteria. For example, we could classify multimedia works in terms of their perceived use, from entertainment to education. We could look at the means of distribution and the context of consumption of such works, from free websites that require a high-speed Internet connection, to expensive CD-ROM games that require the latest video cards to be playable. We could classify multimedia by the media combined, from remediated works that take a musical work and add synchronized textual commentary, to virtual spaces that are navigated. Other criteria for classification could be the technologies of production, the sensory modalities engaged, the type of organization that created the work, or the type of interactivity.

What is the History of Multimedia?

A traditional way of thinking through something that is new is to recover its histories. The histories of multimedia are still being negotiated and include the histories of different media, the history of computing, and the history of the critical theories applied to multimedia. One history of multimedia is the history of the personal computer as it evolved from an institutional machine designed for numerical processing to a multimedia personal computer that most of us can afford. The modern computer as it emerged after World War II is a general-purpose machine that can be adapted to new purposes through programming and peripherals. The history of the computer since the ENIAC (1946) can be seen as the working out of this idea in different ways, including the techniques for managing different media. While the first computers were designed solely to do scientific and applied numerical calculations, they were eventually extended to handle alpha-numeric strings (text), raster and vector graphics, audio, moving pictures (video and animation), and finally, three-dimensional objects and space. Today's personal computer can handle all these media with the appropriate peripherals, making multimedia development and consumption available to the home user.

Numbers and text

If the first computers were designed for number crunching and data processing for military, scientific, and then business applications, they soon became adapted to text editing or the manipulation of alphanumeric strings. The first commercial word processor was the IBM MT/ST (magnetic tape / Selectric typewriter), which was marketed by IBM as a "word processor" and released in 1964. It stored text on a tape for editing and reprinting through a Selectric typewriter. A word processor, as opposed to a text editor, was meant for producing rhetorical documents while text editors were for programming and interacting with the system. By the late 1970s, personal computers had primitive word processing programs that allowed one to enter, edit, and print documents. MicroPro International's WordStar (1979) was one of the first commercially successful word processing programs for a personal computer, expanding the media that could be handled by a home user from numbers to text.

Images

The next step was access to graphics on a personal computer, a development that came with the release of the Apple Macintosh in 1984. The Macintosh (Mac), which made innovations from the Xerox Palo Alto Research Center accessible on a commercially successful personal computer, was designed from the start to handle graphics. It came bundled with a "paint" program, MacPaint, and a mouse for painting and interacting with the graphical user interface (GUI). While it was not the first computer with graphical capabilities, it was the first widely available computer with standard graphical capabilities built-in so that anyone could paint simple images, edit them, print them or integrate them into other documents like word processing documents created with Mac-Write, a WYSIWIG (what-you-see-is-what-you-get) word processor also bundled with the early Macs.

Desktop publishing

In 1986, the capabilities of the Macintosh were extended with the release of the Mac Plus, Aldus PageMaker and the PostScript capable Apple LaserWriter. The combination of these three technologies made "desktop publishing" accessible on the personal computer where before it had been limited to very expensive specialized systems. While MacPaint was a playful tool that could not compete with commercial graphics systems, a designer outfitted with PageMaker and a LaserWriter could compete with professional designers working on dedicated typesetting systems for low-end, monochrome publishing jobs like manuals and newsletters. It was not long before a color-capable Macintosh was released (the Mac II), which, when combined with image-editing software like Adobe PhotoShop, helped the Mac replace dedicated systems as the industry standard for graphic design and publishing. Now, just about any publication, from newspapers to glossy annual reports, is created, edited, and proofed on personal computer systems. The only components still beyond the budget of the home user are the high-resolution digital cameras, scanners, and printers necessary to produce top-quality publications. But even these components are slowly moving into the reach of everyday computer users.

Desktop publishing is the precursor to multimedia, even though desktop publishing aims at rhetorical artifacts that are not viewed on a computer. Computer-aided graphic design and desktop publishing are arts that use computers instead of traditional technologies to produce rhetorical artifacts that combine media, such as text and images. The challenge of combining two media, each with different creative and interpretative traditions, predates desktop publishing – designers before the computer struggled to design the word and image. What was new, however, was that the personal computer user now had the opportunity to experiment with the design and placement of content in two-dimensional space. The initial result was a proliferation of horrid, over-designed newsletters and posters that frequently exhibited unrestrained use of fonts and visual styles.

Authoring environments

Further, the desktop publishing tools were themselves multimedia environments that provided for the direct manipulation of images and text. Desktop publishing was a precursor to multimedia; desktop publishers typically spent most of their time viewing the for-print documents they manipulated on the interactive screen, not on paper. Graphic designers comfortable with design for print (but on a screen) were ready when the first authoring tools became available for the design of screen-based media. They knew how to work with images and text in the two-dimensional screen space and were competent with the graphics tools needed to lay out and create computer graphics. When Apple released HyperCard in 1987, the graphics community was positioned to take advantage of their new skills in screen-based design. HyperCard, developed by the creator of MacPaint (Andy Hertzfield), was an immediate success, especially since it came free with every Macintosh and allowed multimedia authors to distribute HyperCard stacks without licensing costs to other Macintosh users. Given the high penetration of Macs in schools, it is not surprising that within a year of the release of HyperCard there were thousands of simple educational multimedia works that combined text, images, simple animations, and simple interactivity.

Authoring environments like HyperCard are important to the growth of multimedia as they were easier to learn than the programming languages needed previously to create multimedia, and they were designed specifically for the combination of media into interactive works. HyperCard, as its name suggests, was inspired by hypertext theory. The metaphor of HyperCard was that authors created a stack of cards (nodes of information), which could have text, graphics, and buttons on them. The buttons were the hypertext links to other cards. HyperCard had a scripting language with which one could create more complex behaviors or add extensions to control other media devices like audio CDs and videodisk players. One of the most popular computer games of its time, *Myst* (1993), was first developed on HyperCard. The card stack metaphor was quickly imitated by Asymetrix ToolBook, one of the more popular multimedia authoring environments for the IBM PC. ToolBook's metaphor was a book of pages with text, graphics, and buttons and it added color capability.

Today, the most popular authoring environments other than HTML editors such as Dreamweaver and GoLive are tools like Macromedia Director and Macromedia Flash. Both Director and Flash use a cell and timeline metaphor that evolved out of animation environments. Flash is used extensively to add animations and interactive components to websites while Director is used for more complex projects that are typically delivered on a CD-ROM. The Flash file format (SWF) has been published so that other tools can manipulate SWF.

Sound

The Macintosh also incorporated sound manipulation as a standard feature. The first Macs released in the mid-1980s had built-in sound capabilities beyond a speaker for beeps. The

128K Mac had 8-bit mono sound output capability. By 1990, Apple was bundling microphones with standard Macs. HyperCard could handle audio, though it could not edit it. The standard Macintosh thus had simple audio capabilities suitable for interactive multimedia. With the addition of Musical Instrument Digital Interface (MIDI) controllers and software, Macintoshes became popular in the electronic music community along with the now discontinued Atari ST (1985), which came with a built in MIDI port.

One of the first multimedia works to make extensive use of audio was Robert Winter's interactive Beethoven's *Ninth Symphony*. This 1989 work came with HyperCard stacks on floppy disk, which could control a commercial audio CD of Beethoven's *Ninth Symphony*. The user could navigate the audio and read critical notes that were synchronized to the symphony.

Digital video

The latest media threshold to be overcome in affordable personal computers is digital video. The challenge of multimedia is to combine not just asynchronous media like text and images, neither of which need to be played over time, but also time-dependent media like audio, animation, and video. Video puts the greatest stress on computer systems because of the demands of accessing, processing, and outputting the 29.97 frames-per-second typical of television-quality video. Only recently, with the introduction of computers with FireWire or IEEE-1394 ports, has it become easy to shoot video, download it to the personal computer for editing, and transfer it back to tape, CD, or DVD, or even to stream it over the Internet. Given the challenge of integrating video, there have been some interesting hybrid solutions. One of the first multimedia works, the *Aspen Movie Map* (1978), by Andrew Lippman (and others) from what is now called the MIT Media Lab, combined photographs on a videodisk with computer control so that the user could wander through Aspen, going up and down streets in different seasons. With the release of digital video standards like MPEG (MPEG-1 in 1989, MPEG-2 in 1991) and Apple QuickTime (1991), it became possible to manage video entirely in digital form. An early published work that took advantage of QuickTime was the Voyager CD-ROM of the Beatles' *A Hard Day's Night* (1993). This was built around a digital video version of the innovative Beatles' music movie. It is now common for multimedia works to include low-resolution digital video elements.

Virtual space and beyond

Current multimedia systems present the user with a two-dimensional graphical user interface. While such systems can manipulate three-dimensional information (3-D), they do not typically have the 3-D input and output devices associated with virtual reality (VR) systems. Is VR the next step in the evolution of the multimedia computer and user interface? In the 1990s it seemed that cyberspace, as described by William Gibson in *Neuromancer* (1984), was the next frontier for multimedia computing. Gibson's vision was implemented in systems that combine head-tracking systems, data gloves, and 3-D goggles to provide an immersive experience of a virtual space. The metaphor for computing would no longer be the desktop, but would be virtual spaces filled with avatars representing people and 3-D objects. The relationship between user and computer would go from one of direct manipulation of iconographic representations to immersion in a simulated world. Space and structure were the final frontier of multimedia.

While this projected evolution of the multimedia interface is still the subject of academic research and development, it has been miniaturization and the Internet that have driven the industry instead. The desktop multimedia systems of the 1990s are now being repackaged as portable devices that can play multiple media. The keyboard and the mouse are being replaced by input devices like pen interfaces on personal digital assistants (PDAs). Rather than immersing ourselves in virtual caves, we are bringing multimedia computing out of the office or lab and weaving it in our surroundings. The challenge to multimedia design is how to scale interfaces appropriately for hand-held devices like MP3 players and mobile phones.

What are the Academic Issues in the Study of Multimedia?

How can we study multimedia in the academy? What are the current issues in multi-media theory and design? The following are some of the issues that the community is thinking through.

Best practices in multimedia production

The academic study of multimedia should be distinguished from the craft of multimedia. Learning to create multimedia works is important to the study of multimedia in applied programs, but it is possible to study digital media in theory without learning to make it. That said, a rich area of academic research is in the study of appropriate practices in multimedia design. For example, the field of Human Computer Interface (HCI) design is one area that crosses computer science, information science, psychology, and design. HCI tends to be the scientific study of interface and interactivity. In art and design schools the issue of interface tends to be taken up within the traditions of visual design and the history of commercial design. An important issue for computing humanists building multimedia is digitization – what to digitize, how to digitally represent evidence, and how to digitize evidence accurately.

Game criticism and interactivity

If the practice of digitization creates the media that make up multimedia, it is the practice of combining multiple media into rhetorically effective works that is the play of multi-media. The possibilities of interactivity are what characterize computer-based media. In particular, interactive game designers have created complex systems for interaction with media. For this reason, the emerging field of Digital Game Criticism that attempts to study computer games seriously as popular culture and rhetoric is important to the study of multimedia. What is a game and how can we think of games as forms of human art? What makes an effective or playable game? What are the possibilities for playful inter-action through the computer? The interactive game may be the paradigmatic form of multimedia, or for that matter, the paradigmatic form of expression in the digital age.

Theories and histories of multimedia

The study of multimedia as a form of expression has yet to develop a theoretical tradition of its own. Instead, critical theories from existing disciplines are being applied with increasing ingenuity from film studies to literary theory. The very issue of which existing theoretical traditions can be usefully applied to multimedia is a source of debate and discussion. This essay has taken a philosophical/historical approach, asking questions about how to think through multimedia. Theorists like Brenda Laurel (*Computers as Theatre*, 1991) look at multimedia as dramatic interactions with users. George Landow, in *Hypertext: The Convergence of Contemporary Critical Theory and Technology* (1992), has applied literary theory to computing. Lev Manovich, in *The Language of New Media* (2001), looks at the historical, social, and cultural continuity of film and new media. In *Hamlet on the Holodeck: The Future of Narrative in Cyberspace* (1997), Janet H. Murray considers the new aesthetic possibilities of multimedia within the context of narrative tradition.

The intersection of technology, communication, and culture has also been a topic of wide interest. Marshall McLuhan, in *Understanding Media* (1964), popularized an approach to thinking about the effects of technology and media on content. He and others, like Walter Ong (*Orality and Literacy*, 1982), draw our attention to the profound effects that changes in communications technology can have on what is communicated and how we think through communication. Influential industry magazines like *Wired* take it as a given that we are going through a communications revolution as significant as the development of writing or print. There is no shortage of enthusiastic evangelists, like George Gilder (*Life After Television*, 1992) and critics like Neil Postman (*Technopoly*, 1993). There are also influential popular works on personal computing and media technology – works that have introduced ideas from the research community into popular culture, like those of Stewart Brand (*The Media Lab*, 1987), Howard Rheingold (*Tools for Thought*, 1985, and *Virtual Communities*, 1994), and Nicholas Negroponte (*Being Digital*, 1995).

Conclusion

There are two ways we can think through multimedia. The first is to think about multimedia through definitions, histories, examples, and theoretical problems. The second way is to use multimedia to think and to communicate thought. The academic study of multimedia is a "thinking-about" that is typically communicated through academic venues like textbooks, articles, and lectures. "Thinking-with" is the craft of multimedia that has its own traditions of discourse, forms of organization, tools, and outcomes. To think-with multimedia is to use multimedia to explore ideas and to communicate them. In a field like multimedia, where what we think about is so new, it is important to think-with. Scholars of multimedia should take seriously the challenge of creating multimedia as a way of thinking about multimedia and attempt to create exemplary works of multimedia in the traditions of the humanities.

REFERENCES FOR FURTHER READING

This bibliography is organized along the lines of the chapter to guide readers in further study.

Introductions to Multimedia

Ambron, Sueann and Kristina Hooper (eds.) (1988). *Interactive Multimedia: Visions of Multimedia for Developers, Educators, and Information Providers*. Redmond, WA: Microsoft Press.

Blattner, Meera M. and Roger B. Dannenberg (eds.) (1992). *Multimedia Interface Design*. New York: ACM Press.

Buford, John F. Koegel (ed.) (1994). *Multimedia Systems*. New York: Addison-Wesley.

Cotton, Bob, and Richard Oliver (1994). *The Cyberspace Lexicon: An Illustrated Dictionary of Terms from Multimedia to Virtual Reality*. London: Phaidon.

——(1997). *Understanding Hypermedia 2.000: Multimedia Origins, Internet Futures*. London: Phaidon.

Elliot, John and Tim Worsley (eds.) (1996). *Multimedia: The Complete Guide*. Toronto: Élan Press.

Encyclopaedia Britannica. Interactive multimedia. Encyclopaedia Britannica Online. URL: <http://search.eb.com/bol/topic?eu = 1461&sctn = 1>. Accessed October 1999.

Haykin, Randy (ed.) (1994). *Multimedia Demystified: A Guide to the World of Multimedia from Apple Computer, Inc*. New York: Random House.

Hofstetter, Fred T. (1995). *Multimedia Literacy*. New York: McGraw-Hill.

Keyes, Jessica (ed.) (1994). *The McGraw-Hill Multimedia Handbook*. New York: McGraw-Hill.

Nielsen, Jakob (1995). *Multimedia and Hypertext: The Internet and Beyond*. Boston: AP Professional.

Nyce, J. M. and P. Kahn (eds.) (1991). *From Memex to Hypertext*. Boston: Academic Press. (Includes *As We May Think*, by Vannevar Bush.)

Reisman, Sorel (ed.) (1994). *Multimedia Computing: Preparing for the 21st Century*. Harrisburg and London: Idea Group Publishing.

Tannenbaum, Robert S. (1998). *Theoretical Foundations of Multimedia*. New York: Computer Science Press.

Theories and Multimedia

Barrett, Edward (ed.) (1992). *Sociomedia: Multimedia, Hypermedia, and the Social Construction of Knowledge*. Cambridge, MA: MIT Press.

Benjamin, Walter (1968). The Work of Art in the Age of Mechanical Reproduction, tr. Harry Zohn. In Hannah Arendt (ed.), *Illuminations* (pp. 217–51). New York: Schocken Books.

Bolter, Jay David and Richard Grusin (1999). *Remediation*. Cambridge, MA: MIT Press.

Landow, George P. (1992). *Hypertext: The Convergence of Contemporary Critical Theory and Technology*. Baltimore: Johns Hopkins University Press.

——(ed.) (1994). *Hyper/Text/Theory*. Baltimore: Johns Hopkins University Press.

Laurel, Brenda (1991). *Computers as Theatre*. New York: Addison-Wesley.

Lévy, Pierre (1997). *Cyberculture; Rapport au Conseil de l'Europe*. Paris: Édition Odile Jacob/Éditions du Conseil de l'Europe.

Liestøl, Gunnar, et al. (eds.) (2003). *Digital Media Revisited: Theoretical and Conceptual Innovations in Digital Domains*. Cambridge, MA: MIT Press.

McLuhan, Marshall (1964). *Understanding Media: The Extensions of Man*. London: Routledge.

Manovich, Lev (2001). *The Language of New Media*. Cambridge, MA: MIT Press.

Mitchell, William J. (1992). *The Reconfigured Eye: Visual Truth in the Post-Photographic Era*. Cambridge, MA: MIT Press.

Ong, Walter J. (1982). *Orality and Literacy: The Technologizing of the Word*. New York: Routledge.

Stephens, Mitchell (1998). *The Rise of the Image and the Fall of the Word*. Oxford: Oxford University Press.

Interactivity, Interface, and Game Criticism

Aarseth, Espen J. (1997). *Cybertext: Perspectives on Ergotic Literature*. Baltimore, MD: Johns Hopkins University Press.

Baecker, Ronald M., et al. (eds.) (1995). *Human–Computer Interaction: Toward the Year 2000*, 2nd edn. San Francisco: Morgan Kaufmann.

Birringer, Johannes (1998). *Media and Performance: Along the Border*. Baltimore: Johns Hopkins University Press.

Burnham, Van (2001). *Supercade: A Visual History of the Videogame Age 1971–1984*. Cambridge, MA: MIT Press.

Cohen, Scott (1984). *Zap! The Rise and Fall of Atari*. New York: McGraw-Hill.

Crawford, C. *The Art of Computer Game Design*. URL: <http://www.erasmatazz.com/>. Accessed December 2002.

Huizinga, Johan (1950). *Homo Ludens: A Study of the Play-Element in Culture*. Boston: Beacon Press.

King, Geoff and Tanya Krzywinska (eds.) (2002). *ScreenPlay: Cinema/Videogames/Interfaces*. New York: Wallflower Press.

King, Lucien (ed.) (2002). *Game On: The History and Culture of Video Games*. New York: Universe Publishing.

Laurel, Brenda (ed.) (1990). *The Art of Human–Computer Interface Design*. New York: Addison-Wesley.

Murray, Janet H. (1997). *Hamlet on the Holodeck: The Future of Narrative in Cyberspace*. Cambridge, MA: MIT Press.

Norman, Donald (1988). *The Psychology of Everyday Things*. New York: Basic Books.

Preece, Jenny et al. (eds.) (1994). *Human–Computer Interaction*. New York: Addison-Wesley.

Provenzo, Eugene F., Jr. (1991). *Video Kids: Making Sense of Nintendo*. Cambridge, MA: Harvard University Press.

Rada, Roy (1995). *Interactive Media*. New York: Springer-Verlag.

Ryan, Marie-Laure (1997). Interactive Drama: Narrativity in a Highly Interactive Environment. *Modern Fiction Studies* 43,3: 677–707.

Wolf, Mark J. (ed.) (2001). *The Medium of the Video Game*. Austin: University of Texas Press

History of Computing and Multimedia

Atomic Rom. *Writing for Multimedia: Great Moments in Multimedia*. URL: <http://home.earthlink.net/~atomic_rom/moments.htm>. Accessed December 2002.

Brand, Stewart (1987). *The Media Lab: Inventing the Future at MIT*. New York: Viking.

Ceruzzi, Paul E. (1983). *Reckoners: The Prehistory of the Digital Computer, from Relays to the Stored Program Concept, 1935–1945*. Westport, CT: Greenwood Press.

——— (1998). *A History of Modern Computing*. Cambridge, MA: MIT Press.

Freiberger, Paul and Michael Swaine (1984). *Fire in the Valley: The Making of the Personal Computer*. Berkeley, CA: Osborne/McGraw-Hill.

Ifrah, Georges (2000). *The Universal History of Computing: From the Abacus to the Quantum Computer*, tr. E. F. Harding. New York: John Wiley.

Kahney, Leander. HyperCard Forgotten, but not Gone. *Wired News* (August 14, 2002). URL: <http://www.wir(ed.)com/news/mac/0,2125,54365,00.html>. Accessed December 2002.

Rheingold, Howard (1985). *Tools for Thought: The People and Ideas behind the Next Computer Revolution.* New York: Simon and Schuster.

Digital Art and Design

Lunenfeld, Peter (2000). *Snap to Grid: A User's Guide to Arts, Media, and Cultures.* Cambridge, MA: MIT Press.

Marcus, A. (1991). *Graphic Design for Electronic Documents and User Interfaces.* New York: ACM Press/ Addison-Wesley.

New Media Encyclopedia. URL: <http://www.newmedia-arts.org/sommaire/english/sommaire.htm>. Accessed December 2002.

Rokeby, David. <http://homepage.mac.com/davidrokeby/home.html>. Accessed December 2002.

Rush, Michael (1999). *New Media in Late 20th-Century Art.* New York: Thames and Hudson.

Schwarz, Hans-Peter (1997). *Media-Art-History.* Munich: Prestel-Verlag.

Velthoven, Willem and Jorinde Seijdel (eds.) (1996). *Multimedia Graphics: The Best of Global Hyperdesign.* San Francisco: Chronicle Books.

Wilson, Stephen (2002). *Information Arts: Intersections of Art, Science, and Technology.* Cambridge, MA: MIT Press.

Cyberculture and Multimedia

Gibson, William (1984). *Neuromancer.* New York: Ace Science Fiction Books.

Gilder, George (1992). *Life after Television: The Coming Transformation of Media and American Life.* New York: W. W. Norton.

Gray, Chris H. (ed.) (1995). *The Cyborg Handbook.* New York: Routledge.

Heim, Michael (1993). *The Metaphysics of Virtual Reality.* Oxford: Oxford University Press.

Negroponte, Nicholas (1995). *Being Digital.* New York: Alfred A. Knopf.

Postman, Neil (1993). *Technopoly: The Surrender of Culture to Technology.* New York: Vintage Books.

Rheingold, Howard (1994). *Virtual Communities: Homesteading on the Electronic Frontier.* New York: Harper Perennial.

Woolley, Benjamin (1992). *Virtual Worlds: A Journey in Hype and Hyperreality.* Oxford: Blackwell.

Selected Technologies and Multimedia Works Mentioned

Adobe. *GoLive.* URL: <http://www.adobe.com/products/golive/main.html>. Accessed December 2002.

Apple. *QuickTime.* URL: <http://www.apple.com/quicktime/>. Accessed December 2002.

Click2learn. *Toolbook.* URL: <http://www.asymetrix.com/en/toolbook/index/asp>. Accessed December 2002. (Formerly *Asymetrix Toolbook.*)

Cyan. *Myst.* URL: <http://www.riven.com/home.html>. Accessed December 2002.

Macromedia. *Flash File Format (SWF).* URL: <http://www.macromedia.com/software/flash/open/licensing/fileformat/>. Accessed December 2002.

Macromedia (for information on Dreamweaver, Flash, and Director). URL: <http://www.macromedia.com>. Accessed December 2002.

Voyager. *A Hard Day's Night.* URL: <http://voyager.learntech.com/cdrom/catalogpage.cgi?ahdn>. Accessed December 2002.

11

Performing Arts

David Z. Saltz

Computers and the performing arts make strange bedfellows. Theater, dance, and performance art persist as relics of liveness in a media-saturated world. As such, they stand in defiant opposition to the computer's rapacious tendency to translate everything into disembodied digital data. Nonetheless, a number of theorists have posited an inherent kinship between computer technology and the performing arts (Laurel 1991; Saltz 1997). While "old" media such as print, film, and television traffic in immaterial representations that can be reproduced endlessly for any number of viewers, the interactivity of "new" media draws them closer to live performance. Every user's interaction with a computer is a unique "performance," and moreover it is one that, like theater, typically involves an element of make-believe. When I throw a computer file in the "trash" or "recycling bin," I behave much like an actor, performing real actions within an imaginary framework. I recognize that the "trash bin" on my screen is no more real than a cardboard dagger used in a play; both are bits of virtual reality. Indeed, theater theorist Antonin Artaud coined the term "virtual reality" to describe the illusory nature of characters and objects in the theater over fifty years before Jaron Lanier first used that term in its computer-related sense (Artaud 1958: 49).

It is no wonder, then, that performance scholars and practitioners have looked to digital technology to solve age-old problems in scholarship, pedagogy, and creative practice. This chapter will begin with a review of significant scholarly and pedagogical applications of computers to performance, and then turn to artistic applications.

Database Analysis

In 1970, with the number of computers in the world still totaling less than 50,000, Lawrence McNamee touted the potential of computers to aid theater research. The examples that he points to as models for the future now seem mundane: a concordance of Eugene O'Neill's plays and a database of theater dissertations, both published in 1969. Twelve years later, in his Presidential Address to the American Society of Theater Research, Joseph Donohue highlighted the still largely hypothetical opportunities computers offered to theater scholars, emphasizing the ability of computers to order textual data into "clear, pertinent and discrete" patterns (1981: 139). In the 1980s theater historians increasingly turned to computers to help organize and analyze historical data. Edward Mullaly, for example, describes his use of an Apple IIe and the database software DB Master to reconstruct the career of a minor nineteenth-century American actor/ manager from newspaper accounts (1987: 62). These early attempts by performance scholars to tap the power of computers relied on computers' ability to crunch textual and numeric data, such as dramatic dialogue, critical texts about performance, names, locations, and dates. Such applications do not tackle challenges specific to the performing arts. Using a computer to analyze a play or a performance event is no different from using it to analyze any other kind of literary work or historical phenomenon.

Hypermedia

The performing arts, however, are not exclusively, or even primarily, textual. A work of dance, theater, or performance art is a visual, auditory, and, most of all, corporeal event. Only in the 1980s, when low-cost personal computers acquired the ability to store and manipulate images, sounds, and finally video, did computers begin to offer an effective way to represent the phenomenon of performance. Larry Friedlander's Shakespeare Project anticipated many subsequent applications of digital technology to performance pedagogy. Friedlander began to develop the Shakespeare Project in 1984 using an IBM InfoWindow system. He adopted HyperCard in 1987 while the software was still in development at Apple. Because personal computers then had very crude graphics capabilities and no video, Friedlander adopted a two-screen solution, with the computer providing random access to media stored on a laserdisk. The laserdisk contained hundreds of still images and, more important, six video segments, including two contrasting filmed versions of one scene each from *Hamlet*, *Macbeth*, and *King Lear*. The Shakespeare Project used this video material in three ways. In a Performance area, students could read the Shakespearean text alongside the video, switch between film versions at any time, jump to any point in the text, and alternate between a film's original audio track and a recording of Friedlander's interpretation of the actors' "subtext." In a Study area, students participated in interactive tutorials covering aspects of Shakespearean performance such as characterization and verse. Finally, in a Notebook area, students could extract digital video excerpts to incorporate into their own essays. In each case, the computer made it possible for students to *read a performance* almost as closely and flexibly as they could a printed text.

CD-ROM editions of plays released in the 1990s – most notably the 1994 Voyager edition of *Macbeth* and the 1997 Annenberg/CPB edition of Ibsen's *A Doll's House* – incorporate core elements of Friedlander's design, keying the play's script to multiple filmed versions of select scenes. In addition, these CD-ROMs provide a rich assortment of critical resources and still images. The Voyager *Macbeth* also includes an audio recording of the entire play by the Royal Shakespeare Company and a karaoke feature that allows the user to perform a role opposite the audio. These CD-ROMs take advantage of the ability acquired by personal computers in the 1990s to display video directly, obviating the need for a laserdisk player and second monitor. This approach is far more elegant, compact, and cost-efficient than using laserdisks, but the video in these early CD-ROM titles is much smaller and lower in quality than that of a laserdisk. By 2000, faster computer processors and video cards, along with more efficient video compression schemes and widespread DVD technology, had finally closed the gap between personal computers and laserdisk players.

Theater Models

The projects considered so far rely on the multimedia capabilities of computers; that is, a computer's ability to store and retrieve text, images, and audio. Other projects have exploited the power of computers to generate complex simulations of 3-D reality. Performance scholars began to explore the use of 3-D modeling in the mid-1980s to visualize hypotheses about historical theater buildings and staging practices. In 1984, Robert Golder constructed a 3-D computer model of the 1644 Théâtre du Marais, and Robert Sarlós used computer models to visualize staging strategies for a real-world recreation of the medieval Passion Play of Lucerne. This technique became more common in the 1990s when high-end computer-assisted design (CAD) software became available for personal computers. Theater historians used 3-D modeling software to reconstruct structures such as the fifth-century BCE Theater of Dionysos (Didaskalia website) and Richelieu's Palais Cardinal theater (Williford 2000). One of the most ambitious of these projects is an international effort, led by Richard Beacham and James Packer, to reconstruct the 55 BCE Roman theater of Pompey. The computer model is painstakingly detailed, with every contour of every column and frieze being modeled in three dimensions. As a result, even using state-of-the-art graphics workstations, a single frame takes approximately one hour to render at screen resolution (Denard 2002: 36).

None of the 3-D modeling projects described above allow a user to navigate the virtual spaces in real time; the models are experienced only as a series of still images or pre-rendered animations. These projects are geared toward research, with the goal of generating new historical knowledge and testing hypotheses. Consequently, the quality of the data is more important than the experience of the user. When the emphasis is on teaching rather than research, however, the tendency is to make the opposite trade-off, favoring interactivity over detail and precision. The most significant effort along those lines is the THEATRON project, also under the direction of Richard Beacham, with funding from the European Commission. THEATRON uses Virtual Reality Modeling Language (VRML) to allow people to explore models of historically significant theater structures over the Web. The first set of walkthroughs, including such structures as the Ancient Greek theater of Epidauros, Shakespeare's Globe and the Bayreuth Festspielhaus, became commercially available in 2002.

The THEATRON walkthroughs provide an experience of immersion, conveying a clear sense of the scale and configuration of the theater spaces. These spaces, however, are empty and static, devoid of any sign of performance. Frank Mohler, a theater historian and designer, has adopted an approach that focuses not on the architecture *per se*, but on technologies used for changing scenery. Mohler has made effective use of simple anima-tions to simulate the appearance and functioning of Renaissance and Baroque stage machinery.

Performance Simulations

Models of theaters and scenery, no matter how detailed, immersive, or interactive, simulate only the environment within which performances take place. There have also been attempts to use computer animation techniques to simulate the phenomenon of performance itself, both for pedagogical and scholarly purposes. Again, Larry Friedlander produced one of the earliest examples, a program called TheaterGame created in conjunc-tion with the Shakespeare Project. This software was innovative for its time and attracted a good deal of press attention. TheaterGame allowed students to experiment with staging techniques by selecting crude two-dimensional human figures, clothing them from a limited palette of costumes, positioning set pieces on a virtual stage, and finally moving the virtual actors around the stage and positioning their limbs to form simple gestures. The goal was to allow students with no theater experience or access to real actors to investigate the effects of basic staging choices.

At the same time Friedlander was developing TheaterGame, Tom Calvert began to develop a similar, but vastly more sophisticated, application geared toward choreograph-ers. The project started in the 1970s as a dance notation system called Compose that ran on a mainframe computer and output its data to a line printer. In the 1980s, Calvert replaced abstract symbols describing motions with 3-D human animations and dubbed the new program LifeForms. The human models in LifeForms are featureless wireframes, but the movements are precise, flexible, and anatomically correct. LifeForms was designed as a kind of word processor for dance students and practicing choreographers, a tool for composing dances. In 1990, the renowned choreographer Merce Cunningham adopted the software, bringing it to international attention. In the early 1990s, LifeForms became a commercial product.

Motion capture technology offers a very different approach to performance simulation. Motion capture uses sensors to track a performer's movements in space and then maps those movements onto a computer-generated model. While applications such as Life-Forms are authoring tools for virtual performances, motion capture provides a tool for archiving and analyzing real performances. The Advanced Computer Center for Art and Design (ACCAD) at Ohio State University maintains a high-end optical motion capture system dedicated to research in the performing arts. In 2001, ACCAD began to build an archive of dance and theater motion data by capturing two performances by the legendary mime Marcel Marceau. These data, which include subtle details such as the performer's breathing, can be transferred onto any 3-D model and analyzed in depth.

I am currently working with a team of researchers at seven universities on a National Science Foundation project that combines many elements of the projects discussed above: 3-D modeling of theater architecture, animated scenery, performance simulation using motion capture, along with simulations of audience interactions and hypermedia content. This project, called Virtual Vaudeville, is creating a computer simulation of late nine-teenth-century American vaudeville theater. The goal is to develop reusable strategies for using digital technology to reconstruct and archive historical performance events. Virtual Vaudeville strives to produce the sensation of being surrounded by human activity on stage, in the audience, and backstage. Viewers enter the virtual theater and watch the animated performances from any position in the audience, and are able to interact with the animated spectators around them. Professional actors are recreating the stage performances, and these performances are being transferred to 3-D models of the nineteenth-century performers using motion and facial capture technology. The program is being built with a high-performance game engine of the sort usually used to create commercial 3-D action games.

Computer simulations of performance spaces and performers are powerful research and teaching tools, but carry inherent dangers. Performance reconstructions can encourage a positivist conception of history (Denard 2002: 34). A compelling computer simulation conceals the hypothetical and provisional nature of historical interpretation. Moreover, vividly simulated theaters and performances produce the sensation that the viewer has been transported back in time and is experiencing the performance event "as it really was." But even if all of the physical details of the simulation are accurate, a present-day viewer's experience will be radically different from that of the original audience because the cultural context of its reception has changed radically. Some projects, such as the Pompey Project and Virtual Vaudeville, are making a concerted effort to counteract these positivistic tendencies, primarily by providing hypermedia notes that supply contextual information, provide the historical evidence upon which the reconstructions are based, and offer alternatives to the interpretations of and extrapolations from the historical data used in the simulation. Whether such strategies will prove sufficient remains to be seen.

Computers in Performance

My focus so far has been on applications of computers to teaching and research in the performing arts. Digital technology is also beginning to have a significant impact on the way those art forms are being practiced. For example, the computer has become a routine part of the design process for many set and lighting designers. Throughout the 1990s, a growing number of designers adopted CAD software to draft blueprints and light plots and, more recently, employed 3-D modeling software (sometimes integrated into the CAD software) to produce photorealistic visualizations of set and lighting designs.

Computers are also being incorporated into the performances themselves. The earliest and most fully assimilated example is computer-controlled stage lighting. Computerized light boards can store hundreds of light cues for a single performance, automatically adjusting the intensity, and in some cases the color and direction, of hundreds of lighting instruments for each cue. This technology was introduced in the late 1970s, and by the 1990s had become commonplace even in school and community theaters. Similarly, set designers have used computerized motion control systems to change scenery on stage – though this practice is still rare and sometimes has disastrous results. For example, the initial pre-Broadway run of Disney's stage musical *Aida* featured a six-ton robotic pyramid that changed shape under computer control to accommodate different scenes.

The pyramid broke down on opening night and repeatedly thereafter (Elliott 1998). Disney jettisoned the high-tech set, along with the production's director and designer, before moving the show to Broadway.

Computer-controlled lighting and scenery changes are simply automated forms of pre-computer stage technologies. A growing number of dance and theater artists have incorporated interactive digital media into live performance events. Such performances can have a profound impact on the way the art forms are conceived, collapsing the neat ontological divide that once separated (or seemed to separate) the live performing arts from reproductive media such as film and video. The Digital Performance Archive, a major research project conducted by Nottingham Trent University and the University of Salford, has created a web-based database documenting hundreds of dance and theater performances produced in the 1990s that combined digital media with live performance.

George Coates's Performance Works in San Francisco was one of the first and most prominent theater companies to combine digital media with live performance to create stunning, poetic visual spectacles. In 1989, George Coates founded SMARTS (Science Meets the Arts), a consortium including companies such as Silicon Graphics, Sun Microsystems, and Apple Computer, to acquire the high-end technology required for his productions. In a series of productions starting with *Invisible Site: A Virtual Sho* in 1991, Coates perfected a technique for producing the vivid illusion of live performers fully integrated into a rapidly moving 3-D virtual environment. The spectators wear polarized glasses to view huge, high-intensity stereographic projections of digital animations. The projections that surround the revolving stage cover not only the back wall but the stage floor and transparent black scrims in front of the performers. The digital images are manipulated interactively during the performances to maintain tight synchronization between the live performers and the media.

Another pioneer in the use of virtual scenery is Mark Reaney, founder of the Institute for the Exploration of Virtual Realities (i.e.VR) at the University of Kansas (Reaney 1996; Gharavi 1999). In place of physical scenery, Reaney creates navigable 3-D computer models that he projects onto screens behind the performers. The perspective on Reaney's virtual sets changes in relation to the performers' movements, and a computer operator can instantly transform the digital scenery in any way Reaney desires. In 1995, i.e.VR presented its first production, Elmer Rice's expressionist drama *The Adding Machine*. For this production, Reaney simply rear-projected the virtual scenery. For *Wings* in 1996, Reaney had the spectators wear low-cost head-mounted displays that allowed them to see stereoscopic virtual scenery and the live actors simultaneously. Starting with *Telsa Electric* in 1998 Reaney adopted an approach much like Coates's, projecting stereoscopic images for the audience to view through polarized glasses. Nonetheless, Reaney's approach differs from Coates's in a number of important ways. While Coates authors his own highly associative works, Reaney usually selects pre-existing plays with linear narratives. Reaney's designs, while containing stylized elements, are far more literal than Coates's, and the technology he employs, while more advanced than that available to most university theaters, is far more affordable than the state-of-the-art technology at Coates's disposal.

A number of dance performances have experimented with interactive 3-D technology similar to that used by Coates and Reaney. One of the earliest and most influential examples is *Dancing with the Virtual Dervish/Virtual Bodies*, a collaboration between dancer and choreographer Yacov Sharir, visual artist Diane Gromala, and architect Marcos Novak first presented at the Banff Center for the Arts in 1994. For this piece, Sharir dons a head-mounted display and enters a VR simulation of the interior of a human body, constructed from MRI images of Gromala's own body. The images that Sharir sees in the display are projected onto a large screen behind him as he dances.

The three examples of digitally-enhanced performance considered above are radically different in their aesthetics and artistic goals, but all establish the same basic relationship between the media and live performers: in each case, the media functions as virtual scenery, in other words, as an environment within which a live performance occurs. There are, however, many other roles that media can assume in a performance.[1] For example, the media can play a dramatic role, creating virtual characters who interact with the live performers. A number of choreographers, including prominent figures such as Merce Cunningham and Bill T. Jones, have enlisted motion capture technology to lend subtle and expressive movements to virtual dance partners (Dils 2002). Often, as in the case of both Cunningham's and Jones's work, the computer models themselves are highly abstract, focusing the spectators' attention on the motion itself. In a 2000 production of *The Tempest* at the University of Georgia, the spirit Ariel was a 3-D computer animation controlled in real time by a live performer using motion capture technology (Saltz 2001b). Claudio Pinhanez has applied artificial intelligence and computer-vision techniques to create fully autonomous computer characters. His two-character play *It/I,* presented at MIT in 1997, pitted a live actor against a digital character (Pinhanez and Bobick 2002).

A key goal of Pinhanez's work is to produce an unmediated interaction between the live performer and digital media. While this goal is unusual in theater, it is becoming increasingly common in dance, where there is less pressure to maintain a coherent narrative, and so creating an effective interaction between the performer and media does not require sophisticated artificial intelligence techniques. Electronic musicians created a set of technologies useful for creating interactive dance in the 1980s in the course of exploring sensors for new musical instrument interfaces. The Studio for Electro-Instrumental Music, or Steim, in the Netherlands was an early center for this research, and continues to facilitate collaborations between dancers and electronic musicians. A number of dancers have created interactive performances using the Very Nervous System (VNS), a system first developed by the Canadian media artist David Rokeby in 1986. The VNS uses video cameras to detect very subtle motions that can trigger sounds or video. One of the first dance companies formed with the explicit goal of combining dance with interactive technology was Troika Ranch, founded in 1993 by Mark Coniglio and Dawn Stoppiello. Troika Ranch has developed a wireless system, MidiDancer, which converts a dancer's movements into MIDI (Musical Instrument Digital Interface) data, which can be used to trigger sounds, video sequences, or lighting.

One of the most complex and successful applications of this kind of sensor technology was the 2001 production *L'Universe* (pronounced "loony verse") created by the Flying Karamazov Brothers, a troupe of comedic jugglers, in conjunction with Neil Gershenfeld of the Physics and Media Group at MIT. Gershenfeld created special juggling clubs with programmable displays, and used sonar, long-range RF links and computer vision to track the positions and movements of the four performers. This technology was used to create a complex interplay between the performers and media, with the jugglers' actions automatically triggering sounds and altering the color of the clubs.

Brenda Laurel and Rachel Strickland's interactive drama *Placeholder* is one of the best-known attempts to create a performance in which the spectators interact directly with the technology. As two spectators move through a ten-foot diameter circle wearing head-mounted displays, they interact with a series of digital characters, with a character called the Goddess controlled by a live performer, and, to a limited extent, with each other (Ryan 1997: 695–6). The challenge of creating a rich and compelling narrative within this kind of interactive, open-ended structure is immense. While a number of writers have tackled this challenge from a theoretical perspective (see, for example, Ryan 1997; Murray 1997), the promise of this new dramatic medium remains largely unfulfilled.

Telematic Performance

In 1932, in a remarkable anticipation of Internet culture, theater theorist and playwright Bertolt Brecht imagined a future in which radio would cease to be merely a one-way "apparatus for distribution" and become "the finest possible communication apparatus in public life, a vast network of pipes" (Brecht 1964: 52). By the early 1990s, it had become possible to stream video images over the Internet at very low cost, and perform-ance groups were quick to exploit video streaming technologies to create live multi-site performance events. In a 1994 production of *Nowhere Band*, George Coates used free CU-SeeMe video-conferencing software to allow three band members at various locations in the Bay Area to perform live with a Bulgarian bagpipe player in Australia for an audience in San Francisco (Illingworth 1995). In 1995, Cathy Weiss used the same software to create an improvised dance performance at The Kitchen in New York with the real-time participation of a video artist in Prague and a DJ in Santa Monica (Saltz 2001a). In 1999 the Australian Company in Space created a live duet between a dancer in Arizona and her partner in Australia (Birringer 1999: 368–9). In 2001, the opera *The Technophobe and Madman* took advantage of the new high-speed Internet2 network to create a multi-site piece of theater. Half of the performers performed at Rensselaer Polytechnic University, while the other half performed 160 miles away at New York University. Two separate audiences, one at each location, watched the performance simultaneously, each seeing half the performers live and the other half projected on a large projection screen (see Mirapaul 2001). The Gertrude Stein Repertory Theater (GSRT) is a company dedicated to developing new technologies for creating theater. In their production of *The Making of Americans* (2003), adapted from Gertrude Stein's novel, performers in remote locations work together in real time to create live performances in both locations simultaneously, with the faces and bodies of actors in one location being projected via videoconferencing on masks and costumes worn by actors in the second location. The GSRT draws a parallel between this process, which they call "Distance Puppetry," and Japanese performance traditions such as *bunraku* and *ningyo buri* that also employ multiple performers to portray individual characters.

Telematic performance acquires its greatest impact when spectators interact directly with people at the remote site and experience the uncanny collapse of space first-hand. In the 1990s, new media artist Paul Sermon created a series of interactive art installations joining physically separated viewers. For example, in *Telematic Dreaming* a viewer lies down on one side of a bed and on the other side sees a real-time video projection of a participant lying down on a second, identical bed in a remote location. Other installations place the remote participants on a couch, around a dining room table and at a séance table (Birringer 1999: 374). A more provocative example of a performance event that joins a live performer to the Internet is Stelarc's 1996 *Ping Body: An Internet Actuated and Uploaded Performance*, in which a muscle stimulator sent electric charges of 0–60 volts into Stelarc to trigger involuntary movements in his arms and legs proportionate to the ebb and flow of Internet activity.

Conclusions and Queries

The use of computers in the performing arts does not merely add a new tool to an old discipline. It challenges some of our most basic assumptions about performance. First, it blurs the boundaries between performance disciplines. When we watch a performer automatically triggering recorded fragments of dialogue as she moves across a stage, are we witnessing a piece of music, dance, or theater? Second, it blurs the boundaries between scholarship and creative practice. Is someone who extrapolates a complete set design, script, and performance from shreds of historical evidence to create a virtual performance simulation an artist or a scholar? When someone develops new artificial intelligence algorithms in order to create a dramatic interaction between a digital character and a live actor, is that person functioning as a computer scientist or an artist whose medium just happens to be computers? Finally, digital technology is challenging the very distinction between "liveness" and media. When a live performer interacts with a computer-generated animation, is the animation "live"? Does the answer depend on whether the animation was rendered in advance or is being controlled in real time via motion capture or with artificial intelligence software? Or do we now live in a world, as performance theorist Philip Auslander suggests, where the concept of liveness is losing its meaning?

Note

1   Elsewhere I have distinguished between twelve types of relationships a production can define between digital media and live performers (Saltz 2001b).

REFERENCES FOR FURTHER READING

Artaud, Antonin (1958). *The Theater and Its Double*, tr. Mary Caroline Richards. New York: Grove Weidenfeld. (Original work published 1938.)
Birringer, Johannes (1998). *Media and Performance: Along the Border*. Baltimore: Johns Hopkins University Press.
——(1999). Contemporary Performance/Technology. *Theater Journal* 51: 361–81.
Brecht, Bertolt (1964). The Radio as an Apparatus of Communications. In John Willett (ed. and tr.), *Brecht on Theater* (pp. 51–3). New York: Hill and Wang.
Denard, Hugh (2002). Virtuality and Performativity: Recreating Rome's Theater of Pompey. Performing Arts Journal 70: 25–43. At <http://muse.jhu.edu/journals/performing_arts_journal/toc/paj24.1.html>.

Didaskalia. *Recreating the Theater of Dionysos in Athens*. Accessed April 19, 2004. At <http://didaskalia.open.ac.uk/index.shtml>.

Digital Performance Archive. Accessed April 19, 2004. At <http://dpa.ntu.ac.uk/dpa_site/>.

Dils, Ann (2002). The Ghost in the Machine: Merce Cunningham and Bill T. Jones. *Performing Arts Journal* 24,1.

Dixon, Steve (1999). Digits, Discourse and Documentation: Performance Research and Hypermedia. *TDR: The Drama Review* 43,1: 152–75.

——(2001). Virtual Theatrics: When Computers Step into the Limelight. In Loren K. Ruff (ed.), *Theater: The Reflective Template*, 2nd edn (pp. 21–46). Dubuque, IA: Kendall/Hunt Publishing.

Donohue, Joseph (1981). Theater Scholarship and Technology: A Look at the Future of the Discipline. *Theater Survey* 22,2: 133–9.

Elliott, Susan (1998). Disney Offers an "Aida" with Morphing Pyramid. *New York Times* (October 9): E3.

Fridlander, Larry (1991). The Shakespeare Project: Experiments in Multimedia. In George Landow and Paul Delany (eds.), *Hypermedia and Literary Studies* (pp. 257–71). Cambridge, MA: MIT Press.

Gharavi, Lance (1999). i.e.VR: Experiments in New Media and Performance. In Stephen A. Schrum (ed.), *Theater in Cyberspace* (pp. 249–72). New York: Peter Lang Publishing.

Golder, John (1984). The Theatre du Marais in 1644: A New Look at the Old Evidence Concerning France's Second Public Theater. *Theater Survey* 25: 146.

Gromala, Diane J. and Yacov Sharir (1996). Dancing with the Virtual Dervish: Virtual Bodies. In M. A. Moser and D. MacLeod (eds.), *Immersed in Technology: Art and Virtual Environments* (pp. 281–6). Cambridge, MA: MIT Press.

Illingworth, Monteith M. (1995). George Coats [*sic*]: Toast of the Coast. *Cyberstage*. At <http://www.cyberstage.org/archive/cstage12/coats12.htm>.

Laurel, Brenda (1991). *Computers as Theater*. Reading, MA: Addison-Wesley.

Laurel, Brenda, Rachel Strickland, and Rob Tow (1994). Placeholder: Landscape and Narrative in Virtual Environments. *ACM Computer Graphics Quarterly* 28,2: 118–26.

McNamee, Lawrence F. (1970). Computers and the Theater. *Quarterly Journal of Speech* 56: 315–19.

Meisner, Sanford (1987). *On Acting*. New York: Vintage Books.

Menicacci, Armando and Emanuele Quinz (2001). *La scena digitale: nuovi media per la danza* [The digital scene: new media in dance]. Venice: Marsilio.

Mirapaul, Matthew (2001). How Two Sites Plus Two Casts Equals One Musical. *New York Times* (February 19): E2.

Mohler, Frank (1999). Computer Modeling as a Tool for the Reconstruction of Historic Theatrical Production Techniques. *Theater Journal* 51,4: 417–31.

Mullaly, Edward (1987). Computers and Theater Research. *Theater Survey* 28,1: 59–70.

Murray, Janet H. (1997). *Hamlet on the Holodeck: The Future of Narrative in Cyberspace*. New York: Free Press.

Pinhanez, Claudio S. and Aaron F. Bobick (2002). "It/I": A Theater Play Featuring an Autonomous Computer Character. *Presence: Teleoperators and Virtual Environments* 11,5: 536–48.

Reaney, Mark (1996). Virtual Scenography: The Actor, Audience, Computer Interface. *Theater Design and Technology* 32: 36–43.

Ryan, Marie-Laure (1997). Interactive Drama: Narrativity in a Highly Interactive Environment. *Modern Fiction Studies* 42,2: 677–707.

Saltz, David Z. (1997). The Art of Interaction: Interactivity, Performativity and Computers. *Journal of Aesthetics and Art Criticism* 55,2: 117–27.

——(2001a). The Collaborative Subject: Telerobotic Performance and Identity. *Performance Research* 6,4: 70–83.

——(2001b). Live Media: Interactive Technology and Theater. *Theater Topics* 11,2: 107–30.

Sarlós, Robert K. (1989). Performance Reconstruction: The Vital Link between Past and Future. In Bruce A. McConachie and Thomas Postlewait (eds.), *Interpreting the Theatrical Past* (pp. 198–229). Iowa City: University of Iowa Press.

Schrum, Stephen A. (ed.) (1999). *Theater in Cyberspace: Issues of Teaching, Acting, and Directing.* New York: Peter Lang.

THEATRON. Accessed April 19, 2004. At <http://www.theatron.org>.

Watts, Allan (1997). Design, Computers, and Teaching. *Canadian Theater Review* 91: 18–21.

Williford, Christa (2000). A Computer Reconstruction of Richelieu's Palais Cardinal Theater, 1641. *Theater Research International* 25,3: 233–47.

12

"Revolution? What Revolution?" Successes and Limits of Computing Technologies in Philosophy and Religion

Charles Ess

Who can foresee the consequences of such an invention?
Lady Ada Lovelace

Introduction

Computing technologies – like other technological innovations in the modern West – are inevitably introduced with the rhetoric of "revolution." Especially during the 1980s (the PC revolution) and 1990s (the Internet and Web revolutions), enthusiasts insistently celebrated radical changes – changes ostensibly inevitable and certainly as radical as those brought about by the invention of the printing press, if not the discovery of fire.

These enthusiasms now seem very "1990s" – in part as the revolution stumbled with the dot.com failures and the devastating impacts of 9/11. Moreover, as I will sketch out below, the patterns of diffusion and impact in philosophy and religion show both tremendous success, as certain revolutionary promises are indeed kept – as well as (sometimes spectacular) failures. Perhaps we use revolutionary rhetoric less frequently – because the revolution has indeed succeeded: computing technologies, and many of the powers and potentials they bring us as scholars and religionists have become so ubiquitous and *normal* that they no longer seem "revolutionary" at all. At the same time, many of the early hopes and promises – instantiated in such specific projects as Artificial Intelligence and anticipations of virtual religious communities – have been dashed against the apparently intractable limits of even these most remarkable technologies. While these failures are usually forgotten, they leave in their wake a clearer sense of what these new technologies can, and can*not* do.

To see this, I highlight historical and current examples of how computing technologies are used in philosophy and religion. We will see that philosophers have been engaged with computing from its beginnings in the dreams of Leibniz in the seventeenth century[1] and the earliest implementations of electronic computers in the 1940s, 1950s, and 1960s. And, perhaps because of the clear connections between computing technologies and a range of classical philosophical practices (logic) and fields (epistemology, ontology, ethics, political philosophy, etc.), computation has enjoyed an increasingly central place in the philosophical literature of the past fifty years. Indeed, many philosophers speak of a "computational turn" – referring to ways in which computing technologies have given philosophers new kinds of laboratories for testing and refining classical debates and hypotheses.

Similarly, religious studies scholars learned early to exploit the new tools – beginning with Father Roberto Busa's pioneering use of computers in the 1940s to analyze complex texts. More sophisticated versions of these early innovations gradually developed and became commonplace on today's desktops and even palm-held computers. In addition, the impact of computation in religion seems still more powerful in the larger domain of religious practice. In ways consistent with earlier technological innovations – especially such mass media as the radio and television – it is especially the religiously marginalized and proselytizers who have benefited from computation as instantiated in computer networks, i.e., the Internet and the World Wide Web.

In both domains we will see the same general pattern: an early period of enthusiasm, one that rode high on revolutionary – even apocalyptic – promises of radical transformation, followed by a quieter period of diffusion and incorporation of computing technologies within philosophical and religious domains. Hegel would remind us that it is in this relative quiet, aided now by a rich history of examples, that we are able to evaluate more critically and carefully the strengths and limits of these remarkable technologies.

Philosophy

"love of wisdom" (φιλοσοφία) – systematic and rational inquiry into *what is* (metaphysics, ontology), how we may know (epistemology), how we may think cogently and avoid error (logic), and, especially given some account of who we are as human beings and our relation(s) to the larger world (possibly including divinity/ies), how we should behave individually and in community (ethics, politics).

The computational turn: logic, AI, ethics

Arguably, computing *is* philosophy – specifically, the branch of philosophy concerned with logic. Our computing devices depend on the logical system developed by George Boole in the 1840s and 1850s; prior to Boole, a number of philosophers in the modern era – most notably, Leibniz – concerned themselves with the possibilities of machines that might automate reasoning as the manipulation of symbols (Dipert 2002: 148). Hence, it is perhaps not surprising that some of the earliest applications of computing technology in philosophy were precisely in the area of logic – in efforts both to exploit the computer as a logical calculating device (e.g., for assessing argument validity and generating valid conclusions from specified premises; ibid.) as well as to automate the teaching of logic (perhaps most notably by Patrick Suppes, beginning in 1963: see Suppes, Home page).

  Moreover, as computers automate and expand our ability to undertake logical analyses, they not only offer new ways of accomplishing classical logical tasks (from truth-table analysis through proofs to advanced logical applications – e.g., *Tarski's World*, etc.: see Barwise and Etchemendy 1999), they further open up distinctively new ways of exploring classical philosophical questions. One of the earliest, and most obvious, examples of this "computational turn" in philosophy is the rise of Artificial Intelligence (AI) – the effort to replicate human consciousness and reasoning through computing devices, prominent especially in the 1950s through the early 1990s. Computers provided philosophers with a laboratory in which to empirically test and refine hypotheses about the nature of reason and consciousness. Initially, so-called "hard" AI proponents believed and argued that machines would quickly outstrip human intelligence. It appears, however, that the hard AI agenda has largely moved to the margins – primarily because of repeated failures to live up to early promises. As in the natural sciences, however, both successes and failures are instructive: the successful efforts to instantiate at least some components of human reasoning in machines has helped philosophers sharpen their sense of how far computation and consciousness overlap – while the failures help demarcate how computation and human reasoning remain intractably distinct from one another. Indeed, there is a recent turn in philosophy – in fields as diverse as hermeneutics, phenomenology, and feminism – towards *embodiment* as a key theme of exploration: philosophers such as Albert Borgmann and Hubert Dreyfus use an understanding of *who we are as embodied creatures* to explore the strengths and limits of technology, including computing technologies, in contemporary life. In particular, Dreyfus recognizes the (limited) achievements of AI and the (limited) pedagogical advantages of distance learning via the Web and the Internet, but he further argues that these technologies do *not* help us acquire our most distinctive and important human capacities – those of making commitments, taking risks, and exercising *phronesis* (Aristotle's term for practical judgment and wisdom) in our ethical and political lives.

  Indeed, the creators of modern computing technology have been aware from the outset that these new devices raise, precisely, questions of *ethics* with regard to the use of these systems, *politics* with regard to their potential social and political impacts, etc. As Bynum points out (2001), Norbert Wiener, in what amounts to the first book of computer ethics (Wiener 1950), recognized that computing technologies will impact, for better and for worse, life and health, knowledge and science, work and wealth, creativity and happiness, democracy and freedom, and inter/national concerns with peace and security. In Bynum's view, moreover, Wiener sets the agenda for the field of computer ethics – a field that begins to emerge only slowly in the 1960s and 1970s, but now includes an extensive literature, including the journal *Ethics and Information Technology*. More broadly, the computational turn is now well documented not only in AI and ethics, but also, for example, in philosophy of mind, philosophy of science, epistemology, ontology, and so forth (Bynum and Moor 1998, 2003). Indeed, the late 1990s and early twenty-first century saw the emergence of philosophy of information as one way to provide a systematic overview of the impact of computing in virtually every domain of philosophy (Floridi 2003).

Hypertext

In the 1980s, both philosophers and other humanities scholars were excited by a new form of "non-linear" text made possible by computing technologies – hypertext. While the theoretical reflections and software experiments of such hypertext pioneers as Jay David Bolter and George Landow were most prominent – at least some philosophers were likewise quite interested in the potential of hypertext to open up at least *alternative* forms of argument. The best known of these, David Kolb, has in fact argued that hypertexts will make possible the *recovery* of argument forms (e.g., Hegel's dialectic) which are only awkwardly expressed in the (largely) linear frameworks of print.

CD-ROM databases (ethics, history of philosophy)

After appearing in the 1980s, CD-ROMs seemed the perfect medium for realizing extensive hypermedia programs and databases. Two examples can be mentioned here. First, effective hypermedia resources have been developed for exploring and teaching ethics (e.g., Cavalier et al. 1998). These resources are especially useful as they provide video documentary and interviews to bring more abstract discussion of general principles down to the fine-grained contexts of real persons facing specific ethical problems in particular contexts.

Second, while originally defined as a Greek classics project – i.e., focused on collecting primary and secondary literary and historical texts, as well as architectural, historical, and cultural resources (including extensive visual images of important sites, artifacts, etc.) – the second edition of the Perseus Project (*Perseus 2.0* 1996) also included both the Greek and English texts of Plato and Aristotle. Like its counterparts in Biblical studies, the Perseus CD-ROM not only provides an electronic library of these primary texts, but also allows for text searches and analyses. For example, I can find – more or less instantly – every example of Plato's use of the term κυβερνήτης ("cybernetes," a steersman, or pilot, and thus figuratively, the Divine as directing the destiny of humans – and the root, not coincidentally, of "cybernetics") as well as related terms. Through hypertext linking, the program can further take me to each example in the Platonic text, as well as provide morphological analyses. Such searches, of course, accomplish in minutes what might otherwise take weeks, months, or years of reading.

At the same time, however, while these are extraordinary resources and tools, they are also quite limited. While the primary and secondary texts made available on CD-ROM are extensive – and supplemented, of course, by a constantly growing electronic library on the Web – only a relatively small percentage of the literatures important to philosophers has been digitized. Moreover, word searches and morphological analyses are important components of scholarship – but they are only a very small component of our research, reflection, and writing. As with the specific history of AI, philosophers (and, it appears, religion scholars) are gaining a more realistic and nuanced appreciation of the strengths *and* limits of computing technologies in their disciplines, precisely as the successful resources and tools simultaneously mark out what the technologies can*not* do (at least so far).

Computer-mediated communication

The sorts of communication most familiar to us in terms of the Internet and the Web also serve as a philosophical laboratory, one that allows philosophers to revisit classical questions in the domains of ontology, epistemology (including semiotics, hypertext, and logic), the meaning of identity and personhood (including issues of gender and embodiment), and ethical and political values (especially those clustering about the claim that these technologies will issue in a global democracy vs. the correlative dangers of commercialization and a "computer-mediated colonization": see Ess 2003).

The Internet and the World Wide Web

Interestingly enough, major projects in both philosophy (Perseus) and religious studies (Diana Eck's On Common Ground) that began on CD-ROM have migrated to the Web to join additional "electronic libraries" and online search engines. Two significant examples of online philosophical resources are the *Hippias* search engine and website, and Lawrence Hinman's *Ethics Updates* site.

Finally, these computer networks have made possible what is now the presumed environment of philosophical scholarship – namely e-mail, listservs, extensive online databases and search engines, and countless websites (of varying quality) that collect and "publish" (often) significant resources. It is commonly observed that, in contrast with the high-profile projects and experiments, in the end, it is the relatively low-tech tools that make the most difference – in this case, e-mail and listservs. Despite the explosion of scholarly resources and specialized tools available online and on CD-ROM, it remains debatable as to whether the computer revolution has markedly improved philosophical debate, scholarship, or insight (Dipert 2002). Nonetheless, the ability for scholars, geographically remote from one another and positioned at institutions of varying resources and prestige, to communicate directly with one another through e-mail and listservs organized by interests and specialties is arguably "revolutionary" indeed. At the same time, however, this ability is now a commonplace.

Religion

"rebinding" – religio – between the human and the sacred, expressed both individually and in community in terms of beliefs, values, practices, rituals, etc.; religious studies – academic studies of multiple aspects of religion, including studies of scriptures and beliefs, as well as through a range of disciplines such as sociology, psychology, philosophy, philology, history, etc.

While philosophers were closely involved with the development and early uses of computing technologies because of their disciplinary focus on logic, religious scholars were among the first to explore applications of computing in textual analysis. More recently, however – beyond the use of the Web and the Internet by believers and discussants – there appear to be comparatively fewer religiously oriented computing projects (perhaps because religious studies are among the most marginalized and under-funded in the academy?). As a representative example: the Institute for Advanced Technology in the Humanities at the University of Virginia – arguably one of the most important centers for developing computing-based humanities applications – lists only two projects (out of some fifty or so) that focus on some aspect of religious studies. On the other hand, the open communicative environments of the Internet and the Web, while appropriated in much the same way among religious scholars as among philosophers, by contrast have been taken up with explosive energy by more or less every religious tradition whose representatives enjoy Internet access.

The use of computing technologies in religious scholarship

In the 1940s, Father Roberto Busa began developing techniques for encoding complex texts in ways that could be manipulated by computers – first of all, to develop a concordance for the corpus of Thomas Aquinas, followed by a more extensive project to develop a hypertextual edition of Aquinas that allowed for multiple levels of linking and comparison (*Thomae Aquinatis Opera Omnia cum hypertextibus in CD-ROM*). At least one Bible concordance (for the then new *Revised Standard Version of the Bible*) was also generated in the 1950s using a computer. As computers became (somewhat) less expensive and more widespread through the 1960s and 1970s, religious scholars began to develop ways of exploiting the computer's storage and processing abilities to undertake complex text analyses (Harbin 1998). Just as philosophers hoped to make the machine take over foundational but repetitive tasks of logical calculation, so their colleagues in religious studies sought to use the machine to take on the tedium of word counts and comparisons.

As microcomputers and CD-ROMs made processing and storage increasingly inexpensive in the 1980s, descendants of these early text-base and concordance projects moved to the desktops and laptops of religious scholars. First of all, Bible database projects flourished – i.e., collections of Bible texts, translations, and commentaries, with basic computing features (indexing, word searches, note-taking) that support both elementary and more advanced sorts of grammatical and textual analysis. These range from the historically oriented *History of the English Bible* (Beam and Gagos 1997) to such significant resources as BibleWorks. These new technologies further allow other sorts of databases – for example, Diana Eck's *On Common Ground* CD-ROM and subsequent website that documents religious diversity in the USA.

On the one hand, these resources fulfill some of the fondest dreams of scholars. BibleWorks, for example, allows for complex searches through multiple Bibles – translations as well as critical editions in Greek and Hebrew. A scholar can accomplish in minutes an inquiry that would otherwise take weeks or months. This is the analogue to the way computing technologies have indeed revolutionized mathematics, the sciences, and logic by turning over to the machine repetitive tasks that would otherwise take humans months, years, and lifetimes to perform (cf. Hardmeier 2000). On the other hand, as in philosophy, the impact of these new resources and abilities on the quality and quantity of scholarship remains a very open question. In particular, computer-adept scholars observe that these resources exploit only the most basic potentials of the computer, and – echoing the Socratic critique of the technology of writing as leading to the appearance, but not the substance, of wisdom – run the danger of giving the untutored amateur the appearance, if not conviction, that s/he now knows as much as any Bible scholar.

More fundamentally, the emergence of these new technologies themselves – again, especially as interpreted through the lenses of postmodernism – all but required scholars in religion to consider and respond to what many began to see as the emerging "secondary orality of electronic culture" (so one of the premier theologically oriented theorists of new media: Walter Ong, 1988: 135–8, cited in O'Leary and Brasher 1996: 246). In response, the American Bible Society (after bringing out one of the first CD-ROM Bible databases) undertook an ambitious series of projects to "transmediate" important Christian narratives – i.e., to translate these, using scholarly approaches and principles of translation, into the multimedia environments made possible by computing technologies; to synthesize music, visual images, and scholarly resources as an environment for "telling the story" in a way intended to be attractive especially to younger people, who are oriented primarily to electronic visual media (American Bible Society 1995). Despite considerable investment and remarkable talent, however, these projects have met with only limited success in the religious marketplace.

Religious scholarship on the Web

As for philosophers, the Internet and the Web have diffused into the commonplace practices and environment of religious scholars. Beyond the explosive development of sites on the Web by diverse faith communities, there is also to be found a reasonably extensive but largely pedestrian use of the Internet and the Web to support

- listservs on scholarly topics of interest to religion scholars and lay persons;
- sites for religious studies professionals (e.g., the American Academy of Religion) that offer relatively little in terms of use or pointers towards use of computing technologies, but rather make use of the Web – sensibly – as an easily updateable archive for such things as their online syllabus project, etc.; and
- portal sites (e.g., Oxford University [Fraser 2000], the Society of Biblical Literature's *Electronic Publications and Technology Resources for Biblical Studies*) that list both institutionally based resources and often very rich and helpful sites put up by individual scholars.

As with philosophers, these now relatively low-tech uses of the computing technology may have the most significance as they expand access to resources and the ability to communicate with geographically distant scholars who share similar interests.

The Internet, the Web, and religious communities

Whatever the potentials and impacts of computing technologies for religious scholars, religious communities have exploited the Internet and the Web with extraordinary energy. This religious colonization of cyberspace began first of all as the Internet and the Web afforded safe havens for those otherwise at the margins of North American religious life, e.g., Wiccans, Pagans, New Age seekers, etc., as well as (if more gradually) representatives of the world traditions such as Islam, Buddhism, Hinduism, etc. (O'Leary and Brasher 1996; Larsen 2001).

This enthusiasm was fueled (as elsewhere) by the rise of postmodernism, especially as postmodernism was theoretically conjoined with the technologies of hypertext and then the Web through such theorists as Jay David Bolter and George Landow. As postmodernism made its way into religious scholarship and theology, it was embraced especially by Evangelicals and Pentecostals, as postmodernism promised to unseat modern rationalism – and thus shift epistemological legitimacy and authority to emotive experience (e.g., the *feeling* of being saved), and undermine rationalist approaches to Scripture such as the historical-critical method, thereby eliminating the chief nemesis of Fundamentalist interpretation. More broadly, this trajectory has led to a number of insightful analyses of the relationship between new media and religion – including texts that both celebrate the media's ostensibly liberatory/revolutionary potentials (e.g., Careaga 2001) and those that directly challenge postmodernist communication theories by documenting how traditional religious beliefs and assumptions have shaped and constrained the development and use of the new technologies (e.g., Davis 1998; see Ess 2001, 2004 for an overview of this development and relevant literature).

Currently, the plethora of sites on the Web devoted to religion staggers the imagination: a Google search on "religion," for example, will turn up some 13.8 million hits. As yet, there is no authoritative study of this massive inventory. Two studies in progress suggest, however, an interesting pattern:

> *Evangelical/Pentecostal/Fundamentalist* sites more fully exploit the interactive nature of online communication to proselytize; while sites representing the online "face" of more *mainstream* and *conservative* traditions – including the Roman Catholic Church and the Greek Orthodox Church – largely provide extensive databases of authoritative texts and pronouncements, and relatively little interactive opportunity.

This pattern, moreover, is consistent with other studies that show, for example, that initial grassroots efforts to exploit the Internet and the Web for political activism are soon squeezed out as extant power centers learn, if somewhat more slowly, how to use the Web and the Net to re-establish their dominance and centrality online. Similarly, more ecumenical proponents of online religion hope that a global Internet may facilitate a global, dialogical culture that fosters the many voices of diverse religious traditions in a new pluralism. But the emerging patterns of use of the Internet, while giving a certain advantage to previously marginalized traditions, rather largely reflect and preserve the existing religious landscape, i.e., one marked far more often by allegiance to one's own tradition and proselytizing on its behalf.

Concluding Remarks

Should this overview be even approximately correct, it is then notable for two reasons. First of all, through the larger perspectives of research (including cross-cultural research) on computer-mediated communication (CMC), this curve from initial enthusiasm to more pedestrian applications fits the larger pattern of development from the 1980s and 1990s to the late 1990s and early noughties (so the British say) – i.e., from the heyday of postmodernism to a "post-post-modern" period that represents more of a hybrid between postmodernism and whatever came before it. Secondly, this pattern suggests that, indeed, the revolution has succeeded in certain remarkable ways – so much so that we no longer regard computer-based resources and tools as "revolutionary," but simply as "normal" elements of our lives – while at the same time, the multiple failures in philosophy and religion to exploit computing technologies have left a significant portion of our work and lives relatively untouched.

In my own case: I still marvel at having nearly instantaneous access to a remarkable library of important texts – both Biblical and philosophical – not only on my desktop computer, but also my palm-held computer, and that I can undertake searches that help me locate a familiar quote, and perhaps uncover new patterns and insights. In these ways, these computer-based resources and tools certainly enhance my scholarship and teaching. At the same time, as a number of contemporary observers of technology caution, the affordances of these technologies – what they make easy for me to do – thereby encourage me to pursue the paths they facilitate, and perhaps thereby discourage other aspects of scholarship and teaching that, as yet unreduced to computational algorithms, remain comparatively more difficult. As well, the very ubiquity and commonplace character of these technologies may discourage us from attending more carefully to whatever more subtle and long-term consequences they may have for us as scholars and as human beings.

But even these critical reflections, finally, may be an indication of the success and maturity of the computing revolution in philosophy and religion: perhaps like other revolutions we now take for granted, the computing revolution has proceeded far enough along to allow us to critically evaluate both its strengths and its limits.

See also CHAPTER 4: Classics and the Computer; CHAPTER 8: Literary Studies; CHAPTER 10: Multimedia.

Note

1   In the Science Museum (London) exhibition "Charles Babbage and his Calculating Engine," mounted on the occasion of the bicentennial of Babbage's birth and the Museum's realization of Babbage's "Difference Engine No. 2," the following is attributed to Leibniz in 1685: "It is unworthy for excellent men to lose hours like slaves in the labor of calculation which could safely be relegated to anyone else if machines were used."

REFERENCES FOR FURTHER READING

American Bible Society (1995). *A Father and Two Sons: Luke 15.11–32*, CD-ROM. New York: American Bible Society.
American Philosophical Association. Web Resources. Accessed October 26, 2002. At <http://www. apa.udel.edu/apa/resources/>.
Barwise, Jon and John Etchemendy (1999). *Language, Proof, and Logic* (text/software package). New York: Seven Bridges Press.

Beam, Kathryn and Traianos Gagos (eds.) (1997). *The Evolution of the English Bible: From Papyri to King James*, CD-ROM. Ann Arbor: University of Michigan Press.

BibleWorks (2002). CD-ROM, 2 disks. Norfolk, VA: BibleWorks. At: <http://www.bibleworks.com>.

Bolter, Jay David (1991). *Writing Space: The Computer, Hypertext, and the History of Writing*. Hillsdale, NJ: Lawrence Erlbaum.

Borgmann, Albert (1999). *Holding onto Reality: The Nature of Information at the Turn of the Millennium*. Chicago: University of Chicago Press.

Brasher, Brenda (2001). *Give Me that Online Religion*. San Francisco: Jossey-Bass.

Bynum, Terrell Ward (2001). Computer Ethics: Its Birth and Its Future. *Ethics and Information Technology* 3: 109–12.

Bynum T. W. and J. H. Moor (eds.) (1998). *The Digital Phoenix: How Computers are Changing Philosophy*. Oxford: Blackwell.

——(2003). *Cyberphilosophy*. Oxford: Blackwell.

Careaga, Andrew (2001). *eMinistry: Connecting with the Net Generation*. Grand Rapids, MI: Kregel.

Cavalier, Robert, Preston Covey, Elizabeth A. Style, and Andrew Thompson (1998). *The Issue of Abortion in America*, CD-ROM. London and New York: Routledge.

Davis, Erik (1998). *Techgnosis: Myth, Magic + Mysticism in the Age of Information*. New York: Three Rivers Press.

Dipert, Randall R. (2002). The Substantive Impact of Computers on Philosophy: Prolegomena to a Computational and Information-theoretic Metaphysics. *Metaphilosophy* 33,1/2 (January): 146–57.

Dreyfus, Hubert (2001). *On the Internet*. London and New York: Routledge.

Eck, Diana (2002). *On Common Ground: World Religions in America*, CD-ROM, 2nd edn. Affiliated web site: <http://www.fas.harvard.edu/~pluralsm/>.

Ess, Charles (2001). The Word Online? Text and Image, Authority and Spirituality in the Age of the Internet. *Mots Pluriels* 9 (October). At <http://www.arts.uwa.edu.au/MotsPluriels/MP1901ce.html>.

——(2003). Philosophy of Computer-mediated Communication. In Luciano Floridi (ed.), *The Blackwell Guide to the Philosophy of Information and Computing*. Oxford: Blackwell.

——(2004). *Critical Thinking and the Bible in the Age of New Media*. Lanham, MD: University Press of America.

Floridi, Luciano (ed.) (2003). *The Blackwell Guide to the Philosophy of Computing and Information*. Oxford: Blackwell.

Fraser, Michael and the Centre for Humanities Computing (2000). *Computing Resources for Theology: An Introduction*. Humanities Computing Unit, Oxford University. Accessed October 26, 2002. At <http://info.ox.ac.uk/ctitext/theology/theolit.html>.

Harbin, Duane (1998). *Fiat Lux*: The Electronic Word. In *Formatting the Word of God* (Exhibition catalogue, Bridwell Library, Dallas, Texas). Accessed October 31, 2002. At <http://www.smu.edu/bridwell/publications/ryrie_catalog/xiii_1.htm>.

Hardmeier, Christof (2000). Was ist Computerphilologie? Theorie, Anwendungsfelder und Methoden – eine Skizze [What is computer philology? A sketch of theories, fields of application, and methods]. In C. Hardmeier and W.-D. Syring (eds.), *Ad Fontes! Quellen erfassen – lesen – deuten. Was ist Computerphilologie? Ansatzpunkte und Methodologie – Instrumente und Praxis* [To the fonts! Understanding – reading – pointing to sources. What is computer philology? Beginning points and methodologies – instruments and praxis] (pp. 9–31). Amsterdam: VU University Press.

Hinman, Lawrence. *Ethics Updates*. Accessed October 26, 2002. At <http://ethics.acusd.edu/index.html>.

Hippias Limited Area Search of Philosophy on the Internet. Accessed October 26, 2002. At <http://hippias.evansville.edu/>.

Kolb, David (1996). Discourse across Links. In Charles Ess (ed.), *Philosophical Perspectives on Computer-mediated Communication* (pp. 15–26). Albany, NY: State University of New York Press.

Landow, George (1992). *Hypertext: The Convergence of Contemporary Critical Theory and Technology*. Baltimore: Johns Hopkins University Press.

Larsen, Elena (2001). *Cyberfaith: How Americans Pursue Religion Online*. Pew Internet and American Life Project. At <http://www.pewinternet.org/reports/pdfs/PIP_CyberFaith_Report.pdf>.

Lawrence, Bruce B. (2000). *The Complete Idiot's Guide to Religions Online*. Indianapolis: Macmillan.

O'Leary, Stephen D. and Brenda E. Brasher (1996). The Unknown God of the Internet. In Charles Ess (ed.), *Philosophical Perspectives on Computer-mediated Communication* (pp. 233–69). Albany, NY: State University of New York Press.

Ong, W. J. (1988). *Orality and Literacy: The Technologizing of the Word*. London: Routledge.

Perseus 2.0. (1996). CD-ROM. New York and London: Yale University Press.

Society of Biblical Literature. *Electronic Publications and Technology Resources for Biblical Studies*. Accessed October 26, 2002. At <http://www.sbl-site.org/e-resources.html>.

Suppes, Patrick. Home page. Accessed October 26, 2002. Philosophy Department, Stanford University. At <http://www.stanford.edu/~psuppes/>.

Wiener, Norbert (1950). *The Human Use of Human Beings: Cybernetics and Society*. Boston: Houghton Mifflin.

PART II
Principles

13

How the Computer Works

Andrea Laue

Computing humanists engage digital technologies in their studies of humanistic artifacts. In this chapter, we will engage the computer as artifact, seeking a better understanding of how histories of culture and of technology converge in our personal computers (PCs). First, we will explore how computers "work," how their largely electrical mechanisms process data. Second, we will consider how computers "function," how in theory and in practice humans figure their working relationships with these machines. The computer was built to be a sophisticated device for the manipulation of symbols, and, at several levels, it is just that. But this description does not acknowledge that computers are also symbols, nor does it reveal the extent to which computers employ technologies symbolic of larger historical and cultural trends. In order to understand how computers function, we must understand how humans use computers to manipulate symbols but also how the mechanisms within the machine manipulate human users. I will consider here "Wintel" machines, desktop PCs running on technology largely developed by Microsoft and Intel. These systems draw extensively on John von Neumann's stored-program architecture (1945) and incorporate primarily Douglas Engelbart's input devices. While popular rhetoric encourages users to imagine digital technologies outside of various histories of technology, of culture and of labor, I argue here that those histories are essential to a proper understanding of how a computer functions.

How the Computer Works

In 1945 John von Neumann described a radical new architecture for computers, and although he was not imagining personal computers, his design largely informs the machines we use today. I will adopt his concept of the five logical parts of a computer – control, processing, storage, output, and input – and discuss them in the context of a more mundane narrative – just what happens when one types "Hi!" as the first line of an e-mail. There is not a one-to-one correspondence between von Neumann's logical parts and the hardware components present in modern machines, so I will demarcate a section for each logical part, providing a basic explanation of the role of that part, and explain in greater detail how one or two hardware components perform the operations characteristic of that logical part. My choice of components and sequence of discussion will be guided by the framing narrative, the story of how one types and sends an e-mail that says "Hi!" but I will occasionally offer asides rather than omit an essential component.

Input

Contemporary computers offer a range of input devices, including keyboards, the mouse, floppy disk drives, modems, and USB (universal serial bus) ports. Such devices are often called peripherals, a term that describes any component, internal or external, which adds hardware capabilities to the basic design of the system. Each of these peripherals offers a means of transferring data to the machine, an operation that may seem mundane now but was key for von Neumann as previous computers used only punchcards and paper tape. Modern input devices utilize several different standards and media, but the principles behind the transfer of data share fundamental characteristics. Since the user is likely to use a keyboard to input the characters "H," "I," and "!," we will start there.

Although most keyboards look quite similar from the outside, there are at least five different "insides" common today. These differ in the mechanisms engaged by the striking of a key, and the most common setup, the rubber dome keyboard, will be described here. Looking inside this keyboard we find three plastic sheets: one with conductive tracks, one that acts as a separator, and a final conductive layer. Two of these together form the key matrix, a circuit board in two layers – a bottom layer containing gaps that are completed when the top layer is pressed down on to it. The third layer is shaped like the keyboard, with pliable rubber domes corresponding to each rigid plastic key. These domes contain a hard carbon center that, when depressed, completes a circuit. When released, the rubber dome regains its original shape, breaking the circuit.

Keyboards have simple microprocessors that constantly scan the circuit board looking for completed circuits. These detect both an increase and a decrease in current, the pressing and the releasing of a key. When a completed circuit is found, the microprocessor compares the completed circuit with its programmed character map, a sort of seating chart of characters. If more than one circuit is completed, the microprocessor checks to see if that combination of keys is recorded in the character map. The character map points to a specific scan code for the completed circuit, and it is this scan code that is sent to the computer for translation into the appropriate ASCII bit string. The scan codes are standard, but the character map is specific to a particular keyboard. The real significance of the character map lies in the fact that it separates the function of the keyboard from the letters printed on the plastic keys. If one reprograms the character map, striking the key labeled "H" might actually signal the microprocessor to send the code for the letter "o" to the machine. This means that computer keyboards can be reprogrammed for almost any arrangement of keys; although the peripheral is stamped with a QWERTY keyboard, nothing prevents one from actually using a Dvorak arrangement.

The keyboard stores the scan code in its memory while it sends an interrupt to the computer's BIOS (basic input/output system). This interrupt tells the computer to stop what it is doing and to receive the queued signals from the keyboard. The keyboard transmits the scan code to the keyboard controller, a circuit in the BIOS that forwards keyboard data to the operating system (OS). It is the keyboard controller that decides if the signal represents a system-level command or data intended for the application currently in use. In our case, the OS will send our input to an e-mail client.

But what exactly is sent between the keyboard and the BIOS, between the BIOS and the OS? While the characters appearing on the screen as you type match the characters printed on the keyboard, the machine never knows them as letters and punctuation marks. All data pass through the computer as nothing more than pulses of electricity; the machine recognizes two states: with charge and without charge. We often represent these two states with two digits, "1" and "0" respectively. (This actually reverses the historical representation: logical models of computing devices used binary logic previous to the actual construction of electromechanical or purely electrical machines.) This is also the origin of the term "bit" and by extension "byte." One bit of information is one switch, one 1 or 0, one "place"; eight bits is one byte. So our keyboards and our computers communicate via electricity, and mathematicians and logicians have developed methods for translating language (symbols) and many thought processes into binary code.

The most pertinent example for our purposes is the American Standard Code for Information Interchange (ASCII). The ASCII character set maps the 256 most common characters to binary equivalents, a unique string of eight digits. This is also the origin of the byte as a measurement of storage capacity, as one byte of information is sufficient for representing any character in the ASCII set. Thus, ASCII translates the Western alphabet into code that can be transmitted as pulses of electricity. While you type into your e-mail client, the characters are actually being stored as bit strings, as sequences of 1s and 0s. Let us return to our example, "Hi!"; in binary code: 101000 1101001 0100001. Standards-based e-mail clients and terminals understand all characters as bit strings, and it is bit strings that are transmitted from the keyboard to the computer.

Control

We will begin our discussion of the control unit at the motherboard, the physical component that houses the control and processing units. Most of the control unit is located in the chipset, a collection of microprocessors contained in the CPU (central processing unit). This chipset includes most essential components of the control unit and is usually visible on the motherboard. The motherboard is an intricate printed circuit board with miles of copper circuit paths called traces and numerous sockets for connecting peripherals. Together the traces constitute the bus, the metaphorical highway system that carries electricity between the processor, the memory, and the various peripherals. Buses are the physical connections that transfer data as electronic pulses, and these connections may be a fraction of an inch in length within the CPU or several inches long when stretching from the processor to an expansion slot. As we will learn later, the bus is an important factor of a computer's overall processing speed.

Let us return to our depressed keys, our scan codes waiting in the BIOS, the component responsible for making sure that the various parts of the computer work together. Actually a bit of software code, the BIOS is stored in the chipset. Most computers employ three levels of software: the OS; the device drivers that include instructions for operating particular peripherals; and the BIOS that translates and transmits instructions and data between the OS and the drivers. The BIOS handles the transmission of the electrical signals sent between the various peripherals. So the BIOS receives our scan code, translates it to the appropriate ASCII code, and sends it to the OS.

Before we move on from the BIOS, let us review its role in the boot process, the routine followed each time the computer is powered on or restarted. Most likely, the boot process is the only time you'll have any direct experience with the BIOS, as you can watch its work on the screen as your computer starts up. During the boot process, the PC checks its components and prepares the machine to load the OS. The first step in the boot process is the power-on self-test (POST), which begins when the pressing of the power button sends the first electrical pulse to the microprocessor, telling it to reset its registers and to initiate the boot program stored in the BIOS. This boot program invokes a series of system checks, testing to see that components such as the system bus and clock are functioning properly. Next, the BIOS contacts the CMOS (complementary metal oxide semiconductor), a tiny bit of memory located on the motherboard containing basic information about the components of the computer. After that, the video adapter is checked and, if all is well, something appears on the monitor. Next is the test of the system RAM, during which the machine will seem to count each bit of memory. Then the POST continues through the various system components, checking functionality and, when appropriate, loading a device driver into the BIOS, ensuring proper and rapid functioning when that device is called by the OS. In most cases, the BIOS will then print to the screen a summary of the system configuration, which will flash by just before the OS starts. Then the POST contacts the CMOS again looking for storage devices tagged as boot devices, pieces of hardware that might contain an OS. Finally, the BIOS checks the boot sector of those devices for a master boot record that will take control of the PC for the remainder of the startup.

Another important element of the control unit is the system clock. The clock is really an oscillator, a tiny quartz crystal that vibrates when electricity is applied to it. Thus the fundamental mechanism is the same as that which drives most digital watches and electronic clocks. The vibrations of the clock cause pulses of electricity to flow through the motherboard, moving bits from place to place. Thus the rate of vibration is the shortest time in which an operation can be executed, and this rate is often called the clock speed. Many modern computers operate at speeds greater than 1 GHz (gigahertz), or more than 1 billion cycles per second. The clock is necessary because different parts of the computer, even different operations within the processor, operate at different rates. It is the job of the clock to act as a master control, to synchronize the flow of bits through the machine. The bits that compose our greeting will be transmitted according to the rhythm enforced by the oscillator, by the "ticking" of the clock. Our three bytes of information will take a minimum of twenty-four cycles – an unimaginably small fraction of a second – for each "step" between the keyboard and the modem.

Processor

The microprocessor is probably the most recognizable component of the computer. Intel's first microprocessor, the 8080 introduced in 1974, had 6,000 transistors; Intel's most recent microprocessor, the Pentium 4, includes 42 million transistors. The microprocessor, also called the central processing unit (CPU), has three basic capabilities: to perform basic mathematical operations, move data from one memory location to another, make decisions to jump from one instruction to another. At the heart of the processor is the arithmetic/logic unit (ALU), which performs very simple operations such as adding, subtracting, multiplying, dividing, and completing some basic logical operations. And each of these operations is performed on bit strings like the one that constitutes our e-mail greeting. Data and instructions are all translated into 1s and 0s, pulses of electricity, and the processor is a mass of transistors, of switches, that can hold and manipulate these charges. Our e-mail greeting will flow through the CPU even though it will not be manipulated during its passing.

Storage

When we use the word "storage" we usually mean hard drives, floppy disks, or other relatively permanent but slow means of storing data. There are four major types of internal storage in modern computers, listed in order of decreasing speed and cost: registers, cache, random access memory (RAM), and hard disk drives (HDD). Registers and cache are located in the CPU or on the motherboard and come in relatively small amounts, say 512 MB (megabytes). In contrast, hard drives often have 80 GB (gigabytes) of storage for a fraction of the cost of the cache. We will learn a bit about RAM and hard drives, two locations where our greeting might be stored.

A RAM chip is an integrated circuit made of millions of pairs of transistors and capacitors that are linked to create a memory cell. Each cell can hold one bit of data. A capacitor holds a charge, and the transistor acts as a switch, allowing the control circuitry to change the state of the capacitor. These capacitors and transistors are arranged as a grid, with the columns connected by bitlines and the rows connected by wordlines. In both cases, a "line" is a microscopic strand of electrically conductive material etched into the RAM chip. When a burst of electricity is transmitted through a bitline, every closed transistor, each switch that is "on," charges its capacitor. The combination of bitlines and wordlines defines an address for each switch and capacitor. This also accounts for why this type of memory is called random access: you can access any memory cell directly if you know its address. Most RAM is volatile, or dynamic, meaning that the capacitors are always leaking their charge and thus must be refreshed constantly. RAM is inserted directly into the motherboard, most often in the form of a dual in-line memory module (DIMM) that holds up to 128 MB of memory.

A hard disk drive is one of the few computer components that is mechanical as well as electronic. Hard drives contain a collection of platters and heads arranged so that the gaps between them are smaller than a human hair; thus hard drives are very sensitive to dust and jostling. The round platters are made of aluminum or glass coated with a magnetic material. The surface of the platter is divided two ways, as a series of concentric circles and a collection of wedges, and the resulting pieces are called sectors. Each sector contains a set number of bytes, usually 256 or 512. A single hard drive may contain as many as eight platters, and platters are stacked on a central motorized spindle that spins the platters so that the disk heads can read and write data. The heads write data by aligning the magnetic particles on the surface of the platter; the heads read data by detecting the magnetic charge of particles that have already been aligned. Again, all data is stored as a charge, as a 0 or a 1.

How does the drive manage those eight disks, keeping track of where files are stored and not inadvertently overwriting important data? Every Windows hard drive has a virtual file allocation table (VFAT), a sort of database of addresses for files. The VFAT records the sectors holding any saved file and offers empty sectors for writing. When you delete a file, the hard drive doesn't actually modify the data sectors. Rather, it edits the VFAT, removing the entry for that file. Thus the file is invisible but not erased. Depending on our e-mail client, our greeting has either been saved to RAM or to the hard drive while it waits to be sent.

Output

Output devices include monitors, printers, modems, Ethernet cards, and speakers. We will forgo a discussion of monitors in favor of a brief account of modems, the hardware device through which most of us were introduced to the Internet. The modem is particularly interesting because it is a point of union, of conversion between the digital and the analogue, between new and (relatively) old technologies of communication. The modem gets its name from its primary tasks: modulating and demodulating. As we continue to discover, the computer operates exclusively with 1s and 0s, with a digital code. By contrast, phone lines work with an analogue signal, an electronic current with variable frequency and strength. It is the job of the modem to demodulate data from a phone line, to convert the wave to a series of 1s and 0s, and to modulate the data generated by the computer, to convert the 1s and 0s to a continuous wave. This process accounts in part for the limited speed of modems. The analogue signal in the phone line cannot change frequencies as quickly as a computer can send bits of information, yet the signal needs to change for every bit sent. Clever engineers devised techniques for avoiding this bottleneck, including defining four frequencies and four associated combinations of bits – 00, 11, 01, 10 – and experimenting with variations in amplitudes, but the physical medium of the telephone line still poses material constraints on the speed of transmissions. This means that our e-mail greeting, stored temporarily in RAM or perhaps saved to the hard drive, and displayed on the screen, will need to be translated to analogue before being sent to a friend.

Review

Let us review what just happened. We press a few keys on our keyboards, and each strike of a key completes a circuit mapped on the key matrix. Comparing the completed circuit to the key matrix, the keyboard's microprocessor selects a scan code for each character and transmits it to the computer's BIOS for decoding. After deciding that the keyboard data are bound for our e-mail client, the BIOS transmits the ASCII bit string for each character. These bit strings are stored temporarily in RAM or, if the e-mail has been saved, more permanently on our hard drive. When we send our e-mail, the ASCII bit strings will be sent to the modem, which will modulate the data before transferring it to the phone line.

Ending our discussion of how a computer works with the modem emphasizes the significance of the peripheral as a transitional device. Modems operate at the boundary between analogue and digital technologies, between nineteenth- and twentieth-century technologies of communication, between transmission and simulation. At multiple levels the machine is involved in sophisticated translations of information, as is evidenced by the fact that you really do not need to understand how a computer works to use a computer. A great accomplishment of software developers is the extent to which we can "talk" to computers using our own language, the extent to which the code, the 1s and 0s, the electric pulses are hidden. Many pioneers in computing technologies aspired to build machines capable of sophisticated symbol manipulation, as they understood that such skill – basically the ability to use language – is essential to human intelligence. Yet in simulating this capacity they added several layers of symbols, several additional levels of abstraction: printed letter to ASCII codes to a series of pulses.

How the Computer Functions

To begin, I will restate my guiding distinction: "work" describes the electronic processing performed by the machine; "function" refers to the theoretical and practical relations between the computer and its human operators. To explore this distinction, I focus on the system clock and the keyboard, but my evidence could have included several other components, most notably computer memory (Douwe 2000; Locke 2000; Williams 1997). I discuss the history of the adoption of and adaptation to these technologies, looking at how the computer as artifact reproduces metaphors of mind and incorporates bodies into mechanized routines. Relating the system clock and the computer keyboard to previous implementations of similar technologies, I explore motivations and rationales for the choices behind these particular mechanisms. Pioneers of digital technologies often thought their designs radical and their machines revolutionary, yet these inventions incorporate conventions and habits embedded in previous technologies. In this sense, digital technologies can be seen as extensions of numerous historical trends.

System clock

Let us begin by returning to John von Neumann, focusing this time on the biological metaphors that frame his understanding of his radical architecture. Trained in logic and mathematics, von Neumann's interest in information processing was strongly influenced by the work of Warren McCulloch and Walter Pitts, in particular the article "A Logical Calculus of the Ideas Immanent in Nervous Activity" (1943). Although he acknowledged that the McCulloch–Pitts model oversimplified neural activity, von Neumann was intrigued by the parallels proposed between man-made and organic systems

(Aspray 1990: 180–1). In 1944 von Neumann joined the likes of McCulloch, Pitts, and Norbert Wiener to form the Teleological Society, a research group "devoted on the one hand to the study of how purpose is realized in human and animal conduct and on the other hand how purpose can be imitated by mechanical and electrical means" (Aspray 1990: 315). Although the Teleological Society disbanded, many of its founding members initiated the Macy Conferences, probably the most famous early discussions of artificial intelligence.

Looking at von Neumann's *First Draft of a Report on the EDVAC* (1945), the first publication describing the stored-program architecture, one notices his analogies to organic systems. For instance, in this report the storage unit of a computer is first called "memory," and other logical parts are called "organs." Von Neumann understood organic systems to be highly complex, to employ parallel processing and to be adept at switching between analogue and digital modes of computation, and he planned to simulate the organic by implementing a few key principles – process hierarchies, serialization, regulation, and automation. Along with others in his field, von Neumann rationalized the organic and made discrete the continuous in an effort to mimic the intellect of man. Aware that current technology couldn't accomplish the sophistication of organic systems, von Neumann intended to design an architecture that could evolve sufficient complexity. He modeled the workings of his computer after the brain, hoping that the machine would function like – or at least with – man. In an attempt to replicate the functioning of the human mind, von Neumann built a model of the brain that worked in ways quite different than its organic precursor. The mechanics of the computer introduce several technologies foreign to the mind yet not so unfamiliar to the history of its acculturation and regulation.

Our brief investigation of these mechanics will focus on the system clock, a device central both to the work and to the function of the computer. Historians of technology often point to the clock as a mechanism central to the modernization of the West. In his history of technology *Technics and Civilization*, Lewis Mumford (1934: 14) writes: "The clock, not the steam-engine, is the key-machine of the modern industrial age. For every phase of its development the clock is both the outstanding fact and the typical symbol of the machine: even today no other machine is so ubiquitous." Mumford published his book a decade before von Neumann designed his stored-program architecture, the first computer architecture regulated by a control unit called a "clock." In his *Report*, von Neumann describes the electromechanical devices used to control computers previous to the EDVAC and then proposes an alternative for his new machine: "Alternatively, [computing instruments] may have their timing impressed by a fixed clock, which provides certain stimuli that are necessary for its functioning at definite periodically recurrent moments" (1945: 24). Even at this early stage von Neumann suggested that this "clock" might actually be an electronic oscillator controlled by a crystal. Two years later, von Neumann, Goldstine, and Burks described dynamic circuits, regulated by electric pulses emitted from a central source called a "clock": "Since the timing of the entire computer is governed by a single pulse source, the computer circuits will be said to operate as a synchronized system" (Burks et al. 1947: 131). Thus, the clock is essential to the proper working of the computer, and in this section I will argue that it is key to understanding the functioning of the computer as well.

The system clock lacks most mechanisms associated with clocks: it has neither gears nor hands, neither a face nor an audible signal to mark the minutes. Many advanced computer science books refer initially to a clock but later drop the metaphor and describe the oscillator, the tiny crystal whose vibrations regulate the flow of electricity through the motherboard. The etymology of "clock" relates our modern machines to medieval bells, in particular to bells that were struck to mark the hours (*OED* 1989). Samuel Macey extends this relation, figuring the clock as a sort of automaton: "the earliest mechanical clocks may be considered automated versions of the keeper of the bell or *Glocke*, which gave us the term *clock* in the first place" (Macey 1989: 11). Gerhard Dohrn-van Rossum, historian and author of *History of the Hour* (1996), traces the history of man's relation to time-keeping devices, focusing less on the technology underlying the machines and more on man's evolving relation to the device. I draw on Dohrn-van Rossum's account, foregrounding his argument that time-keeping devices have functioned to synchronize, regulate, and abstract time.

Well before mechanical clocks were sufficiently precise to reliably mark the hours, bells divided the day and synchronized the activities of a populace. Mumford points to the monasteries as the origin of modern notions of time-keeping, arguing that the Benedictines "helped to give human enterprise the regular collective beat and rhythm of the machine; for the clock is not merely a means of keeping track of the hours, but of synchronizing the actions of men" (1934: 14). Church bells also marked the hours outside the monastery, alerting laypersons to the hours for prayers and for mass, and by the fifteenth century many municipalities had acquired communal bells to signal secular meetings and events. Through variations in tone, duration, and number of rings, churches and municipalities developed elaborate codes to signal everything from mass to changing of the guards, from noontime break to opening of the courts. In both contexts – religious and secular – these bells announced hours that were irregular according to modern standards but nevertheless succeeded in improving the frequency with which monks and citizens were "on time" for various functions. In both contexts, the bells were functional well before devices for keeping time really worked.

After bells, civic officials developed several time-keeping technologies to regulate everything from the marketplace to the postal system. Beginning in the thirteenth century, officials regulated the market with clocks, setting times at which particular merchants could do business and hours during which locals could shop. Previous to the fifteenth century, universities varied the time and duration of lectures according to content. By the fifteenth century, particularly in secondary schools, days were divided into discrete blocks during which specific subjects were taught, and these hours were measured by bells and sandglasses. In addition to measuring and dividing the day, time-keeping devices increasingly aided the rationalizing of space. Between the fifteenth and eighteenth centuries, postal and courier services increasingly abstracted distance by measuring it in units of time. Delivery times once measured in days were soon measured in hours, and soon promptness became the measure of quality: the normative codes "should thus be understood as concepts for systematically organized transportation and communication links, which, if we trace them over a longer period, reveal the growing importance of the techniques of time measurement and time control" (Dohrn-van Rossum 1996: 343). Even before railroads, the technology most associated with the strict enforcement of standardized time, the markets, the schools, and the postal systems were regulated by increasingly abstract notions of time (and space) (Dohrn-van Rossum 1996).

It was not until the mid-seventeenth century that these functional time-keeping devices developed into working clocks. In 1656, Christiaan Huygens patented a pendulum clock that was accurate to within one minute a day, and by the late seventeenth century he had developed a balance wheel and spring assembly that could operate a pocket watch with an accuracy of 10 minutes per day. A substantial improvement over previous time-keeping mechanisms, the pendulum was subject to inaccuracies due to changes in temperature, air pressure, and gravity. Some 200 years later, quartz crystals replaced pendulums in the 1920s, further enhancing the accuracy of clocks. Using an electric circuit to cause a crystal to vibrate, quartz clocks shed the gears and escarpments – the tangible mechanisms – that often led to variations in time. Just thirty some years after the quartz clock, an atomic clock that was accurate to one second in 2,000 years appeared in 1955. The original definition of "second" was 1/86,400 of a mean solar day; in 1967 the natural frequency of the cesium atom – 9,192,631,770 oscillations of the atom's resonant frequency – was declared the international unit of time. Thus, by the late twentieth century measures of time had been abstracted to the point that they seemed to have little relation to the daily rhythms – solar or social – of man.

Modern system clocks utilize quartz crystals, the same technology that runs many digital watches, and von Neumann first suggested using these oscillators in his 1945 *Report*. Following a brief overview of his entire architecture, von Neumann began his section titled "Elements, Synchronism Neuron Analogy" with a description of the control unit (1945: 23). He argued that all digital computing devices must have control "elements" with discrete equilibrium and that a synchronous "element" – a system clock – is the preferable control mechanism. Going to the trouble to define "element" as a synchronous device with discrete equilibrium, he proceeded to a biological analogy: "It is worth mentioning, that the neurons of the higher animals are definitely elements in the above sense. They have all-or-none character, that is two states: Quiescent and excited" (1945: 24). Drawing on the work of MacCulloch and Pitts, von Neumann acknowledged that neurons were probably asynchronous but proposed that their behavior be simulated using synchronous systems (ibid.). Thus, von Neumann chose to implement a system clock because he was attempting to mimic the functioning of the human brain. Unable to build a machine that *worked* like a brain, he imagined constructing a computer that (apparently) functioned like a mind: "Von Neumann, especially, began to realize that what they were talking about was a *general-purpose machine*, one that was by its nature particularly well suited to function as an extension of the human mind" (Rheingold 2000: 86). Essential to this machine was a clock, a metronome that made regular, synchronous, and rational this model of the mind. Attempting to extend the capacities of the human mind, von Neumann's design actually recalled technologies previously used to control it. Paradoxically, von Neumann's architecture is at once flexible and rigid, is both an extension of and a constraint on our conceptual, cultural, and practical understanding of our minds.

QWERTY keyboard

In this section we will investigate the QWERTY keyboard, using a distinction between "machine" and "tool" to frame our discussion. Karl Marx in *Capital* (1867) and later Lewis Mumford in *Technics and Civilization* (1934) define these terms in reference to the history of labor and production. Without referring directly to Marx or Mumford, J. C. R. Licklider and Douglas Engelbart, early designers of computer interface and input devices, later defined a plan for man–computer symbiosis that echoes this tradition. Marx writes that the origin or impetus of movement is the essential difference between a tool and a machine: with tools, movement originates in the laborer; with machines, movement issues from the mechanism itself (1867: 409). Working in an environment with machines requires education, that the body be trained to move along with the uniform and relentless motion of the mechanism (1867: 408). Conversely, the tool allows the laborer freedom of movement, an opportunity for motion independent of the mechanism. Working from Marx, Mumford associates tools with flexibility and machines with specialization. The essential difference, according to Mumford, is the degree of independence of operation. To summarize, a man works with a tool as an extension of his own body (and perhaps his own mind); in contrast, a machine employs a man as an extension of its own mechanism.

Licklider (1960) essentially fears that computers are becoming machines rather than tools. Describing computers built previous to 1960 as "semi-automatic systems," he laments the trend toward automation at the expense of augmentation. He sees man incorporated into the system rather than being extended by it: "In some instances, particularly in large computer-centered information and control systems, the human operators are responsible mainly for functions that it proved infeasible to automate" (1960: 60). The human appears as a compromise required by the current state of technology, as a part that will be replaced once the memory is faster or the arithmetic unit more efficient. However, computers might act as extensions of humans, as devices for the augmentation of the intellect, as components in human–machine "symbiotic" systems. His proposed symbiosis is peculiar because he wants to introduce intuition and "trial-and-error procedures" into the system; as later expressed by Douglas Engelbart (1963), "we refer to a way of life in an integrated domain where hunches, cut-and-try, intangibles, and the human 'feel for a situation' usefully coexist with powerful concepts, streamlined terminology and notation, sophisticated methods, and high-powered electronic aids" (1963: 72). Licklider and Engelbart differ from von Neumann in that they do not want the computer to imitate the intellect but rather to enhance it. For both Licklider and Engelbart, organization is a component of intelligence, a function that could perhaps be better handled by a computer. But the essence of intelligence is a sort of synergy, a cooperative interplay between the human capabilities of organization and intuition, analysis and synthesis. While the language of progress and evolution employed by Licklider and Engelbart may be troubling, their visions of computers as extensions rather than imitations of man, as tools rather than machines, was revolutionary and remains relevant today.

The computer keyboard exemplifies this tug-of-war between machine and tool. Most know that the modern computer keyboard continues the tradition of the typewriter and its less-than-intuitive arrangement of keys. Often referred to as the "QWERTY" keyboard, this arrangement of keys was devised by Christopher Sholes, and the first Remington typewriters sold in 1873 implemented his design. For decades after the first Remington, manufacturers experimented with alternative arrangements, including a circular layout and an arrangement that featured keys in alphabetical order. Probably the most famous redesign was the Dvorak Simplified Keyboard, patented in 1936. August

Dvorak claimed that his keyboard led to increased speed, reduced fatigue, and more rapid learning. There is much dispute about the data used to support these claims (Liebowitz and Margolis 1990), and more recent experimental evidence suggests that the Dvorak keyboard leads to only a 10 percent improvement in speed (Norman 1990: 147). Yet the QWERTY keyboard remains a standard even though there exists an empirically superior option. Don Norman argues that such a small improvement does not warrant the institutional costs of conversion: "millions of people would have to learn a new style of typing. Millions of typewriters would have to be changed. The severe constraints of existing practice prevent change, even where the change would be an improvement" (1990: 150). Others add to this interpretation, citing the Dvorak keyboard as an example of the failure of the market economy (David 1985). Rather than entering this debate, I suggest that we accept parts of each argument – the Dvorak keyboard is not a marvelous improvement over the QWERTY arrangement, and the institutional cost of conversion is great – and then investigate the process through which QWERTY gained form and acceptance.

While the QWERTY arrangement might not be the ideal arrangement of keys independent of mechanism used to print those keys, the arrangement was the most functional of Sholes's designs. The design problem faced by Sholes was that of overlapping rods: if a typist struck in sequence two adjacent keys, their rods would intersect and jam. Then the operator would have to stop typing and dislodge the mechanism, losing valuable time. Sholes's keyboard minimized the likelihood of jamming by separating keys for letters that frequently appear adjacent to one another in common words. The arrangement aims to achieve maximum speed through maximum synchronization of operator and machine. It is often stated that Sholes designed the keyboard to slow down operators of the typewriter; in fact, Sholes designed the keyboard so as to better coordinate the actions of the machine and its operator, not just to slow the operator but to develop a sequence and a rhythm that was manageable by both human and machine. Bliven (1954) comments on the sound of a room full of typists, on the particular rhythm distinct to adept typists. Sholes's design of the machine was the engineering of this rhythm, a reorganization of the interface of the typewriter to facilitate the most efficient use of the mechanism.

Today we assume that good typists use all fingers, but this technique was not common until fifteen years after the typewriter went to market. In fact, there was much debate surrounding the feasibility of teaching this skill. Early typists used the "hunt and peck" method with remarkable success. In 1882, Mrs L. V. Longley issued a pamphlet proposing a method of typing that used all ten fingers. A typing instructor in Cincinnati, Mrs Longley met with great opposition in the trade press. Even five years after the publication of her pamphlet, trade magazines carried stories arguing the impracticality of her proposal, citing a lack of strength and dexterity in some fingers. Five years later, Frank McGurrin, a court stenographer from St Louis, again proposed a ten-finger method of typing. He added to his technique the skill of "touch typing," the ability to type without looking at the keyboard. He also met with resistance but silenced his adversaries when, in 1888, he won a typing contest using his new method. McGurrin used a Remington typewriter, and his victory led to the adoption of two standards: the QWERTY keyboard and the touch-typing method (Norman 1990: 147). Following McGurrin's victory, the same publication that berated Mrs Longley endorsed touch-typing. It was accepted that typewriters might be more than twice as fast as writing by hand, and typists were retrained to use all fingers.

In the early twentieth century, typewriter companies employed championship typists to compete in national competitions. These racers were given a racing typewriter and a salary for practicing their skills eight hours a day. Racing typists netted 120 error-free words per minute in front of crowds of businessmen at the various trade shows in Madison Square Garden. Once most speed typists mastered the art of touch-typing, other inefficiencies in the process were targeted. Charles Smith, the coach of the famous Underwood Speed Training Group, developed the "right-hand carriage draw," a new method of exchanging paper that saved as much as a full second. This method required the typist to grab the roller knob and the filled sheet with one hand while grabbing a fresh sheet from a prepared stack of papers and inserting it without ever looking away from the copy. All of this in one-third of a second (Bliven 1954: 125)! Techniques introduced in the racing circuit gradually infiltrated the business world, producing typists with elegant and precise routines to synchronize their movements with the machine. Rhythm was key: "Above all, the mark of good typing is a continuous, even rhythm. An expert keeps going" (Bliven 1954: 143). Thus the touch-typing system prescribed routines for striking the keys and for manipulating the impacted media, thereby rendering the typists extensions of their typewriters, parts of their machines.

In the late nineteenth century, business required improvements in technologies of communication and record-keeping, and commercial culture embraced the typewriter and its promise of increased speed and accuracy of transcription. But other cultures of use emerged as well. George Flanagan writes: "the idea of Art in typewriting has been sadly ignored" (1938: vi). Calling the machine "mechanically perfect" and typists "marvelous[ly] skilled," he writes a treatise in hopes of diverting attention from efficiency towards aesthetics. Flanagan recommends harmony and balance through the judicious arrangement of space and compactness (1938: 2). Utility should not be achieved at the expense of elegance; speed can be sacrificed for ornament. Inserting typewriting into the tradition of printing, Flanagan advises the typists to plan the layout of the page just as one plans the content of the paragraphs. He provides sample layouts – spacing, alignment, sizes for paragraphs – and includes formulas – combinations and sequences of keystrokes – for generating ornamental drop caps and borders. Although he recognizes the pressures of an office and the primacy of speed, Flanagan argues that typists should not ignore design. They might even profit from it: "Your work will become an endless romance, and we even suspect that your pay envelopes will grow fatter" (1938: vii). Seeing the typist as a craftsman rather than a laborer, Flanagan reshapes the machine as a tool. Although entertaining, the point isn't the aesthetics of ASCII art; rather, it is the revision of what had become a mechanistic relationship between a human and a machine. The idea of typing contests and of ornamental typing might seem equally trite today, but their historical value lies in the relationships they posit between typist and typewriter, between operator and tool or machine.

Although most computer keyboards follow Sholes's design, Engelbart experimented with many different input devices that drew on various traditions of symbol manipulation. Most interesting in this context is the chord keyset, a group of five piano-like keys that were operated by one hand. The keys were not printed with any characters, and operators used single keys and combinations of keys to produce up to 32 different codes, each of which represented a different character. Drawing on technologies developed by telegraphers, Engelbart expected that computer users would be trained in this code and would eventually surpass the speeds of typists using QWERTY keyboards. The chord keyset would also allow users to manipulate a keyset and a mouse at the same time without ever looking at their hands. Engelbart imagined a reincarnation of the Remington racer who could change paper without ever losing her place in the copy. His input devices would become extensions of the hands, and users would manipulate them without the aid of the other senses. Yet such facility would require learning another language, a new code, an additional symbol set that in its abstraction matched closely the binary set used by the computer itself. The boundary between man and machine seemed permeable, but man seemed to be the one crossing the line, the one adopting the characteristics of the other.

Engelbart argued in general terms that users would need to be trained to use computers, and the retraining necessary to use the chord keyset was just one step in that process. Of course, the typist's keyboard was eventually chosen over the telegrapher's, largely due to the anticipated institutional costs of retraining, and Engelbart's demo now seems rather quaint. But the choice to adopt the QWERTY keyboard demonstrates a few interesting points. First, we no longer recognize the extent to which typing – even the hunt-and-peck method – requires training; the typist's keyboard seems somehow natural. Second, while we resist new technologies that require abstract, mechanistic motion, we willfully embrace old ones that require equally abstract and mechanistic routines. If the QWERTY keyset casts the computer as machine, perhaps it's difficult to argue that the chord keyset does otherwise. The latter requires complicated and coordinated movements and an internalized understanding of an abstract code. Yet Engelbart, seeking augmentation rather than automation, argued that this degree of training is necessary before the computer may function as a tool. Engelbart's notions of training, and the boundaries between the training of man and the training of the computer, deserve further exploration. Returning to Marx and Mumford, we must work to cast the computer as tool rather than as machine.

Conclusion

Despite the apparent contradictions in Engelbart's efforts to build input devices that would augment the human intellect, he and Licklider provide inspiration for, if not demonstration of, what the computer might someday be. Engelbart in his 1961 report "Program on Human Effectiveness" describes his plan for the augmentation of the individual problem solver. His objective is to "develop means for making humans maximally effective as comprehending solvers of problems," and he plans to do this by inserting computers into various levels of our hierarchy of problem-solving tools. Here again he returns to issues of training, proposing that humans be conditioned both to use his input devices and to understand the logical operations that make the computer work. Engelbart wants to build tools even if he must first build machines; he wants humans to train computers, but for now he must settle for computers that can train humans. Today, children use computers from such a young age that manipulating a mouse seems "intuitive" and programming languages seem "natural." Half of Engelbart's program has been accomplished: we have been trained to use the computer.

Even in 1960 Licklider was troubled by the extent to which scientists had been trained to use the computer. Disappointed that the computer was being used primarily to solve "preformulated problems" with "predetermined procedures" – "It is often said that programming for a computing machine forces one to think clearly, that it disciplines the thought process. If the user can think his problem through in advance, symbiotic association with a computing machine is not necessary" (1960: 61) – Licklider proposed that computers be employed to ask questions, not just to provide answers. Given the limits to technology, the first attempts at symbiotic systems will rely on the human operators to set the goals, formulate hypotheses, devise models, and so on (1960: 64). The operators will evaluate the output, judge the contribution of the machine, and fill in the gaps when the machine lacks the proper routine for handling some problem. Although Licklider imagines much more, his first iteration of the symbiotic system is an advanced information-handling machine. Consistent with his colleague, Engelbart also framed the problem of symbiosis as one of information management: a primary objective for his H-LAM/T project was "to find the factors that limit the effectiveness of the individual's basic information-handling capabilities in meeting the various needs of society for problem solving in the most general sense" (1963: 73). In practice, the symbiotic machine became a problem-solving rather than a problem-posing device. For the most part, that is how the computer continues to function. Licklider's dream remains largely unfulfilled. Perhaps transforming the computer from machine to tool, from a device that automates mundane mental tasks to one that augments critical and creative thought, is the task now facing computing humanists.

See also CHAPTER 29: Speculative Computing.

REFERENCES FOR FURTHER READING

Aspray, William (1990). *John von Neumann and the Origins of Modern Computing.* Cambridge, MA: MIT Press.

Bliven, Bruce (1954). *The Wonderful Writing Machine.* New York: Random House.

Burks, Arthur, Herman H. Goldstine, and John von Neumann (1947). *Preliminary Discussion of the Logical Design of an Electronic Computing Instrument,* 2nd edn. In William Aspray and Arthur Burks (eds.), *The Papers of John Von Neumann on Computing and Computer Theory* (1986). Charles Babbage Institute Reprint Series for the History of Computing, vol. 12 (pp. 97–144). Cambridge, MA: MIT Press.

Campbell-Kelly, Martin, and William Aspray (1996). *Computer: A History of the Information Machine.* New York: Basic Books.

David, Paul A. (1985). Clio and the Economics of QWERTY. *American Economic Review* 75,2: 332–7.

Dohrn-van Rossum, Gerhard (1996). *History of the Hour: Clocks and Modern Temporal Orders,* tr. Thomas Dunlap. Chicago: University of Chicago Press.

Douwe, Draaisma (2000). *Metaphors of Memory,* tr. Paul Vincent. Cambridge: Cambridge University Press.

Engelbart, Douglas C. (1961). Proposal for Participation in the Program on Human Effectiveness. Accessed October 1, 2002. At <http://sloan.stanford.edu/mousesite/EngelbartPapers/B4_F12_HuEff3.html>.

——(1963). A Conceptual Framework for the Augmentation of Man's Intellect. In P. W. Howerton and D. C. Weeks (eds.), *The Augmentation of Man's Intellect by Machine.* In Paul A. Mayer (ed.), *Computer Media and Communication* (1999). New York: Oxford University Press.

—— (1968). Demo of the Augment Research Center. Fall Joint Computer Conference. Accessed October 1, 2002. At <http://sloan.stanford.edu/mousesite/1968Demo.html>.

Englander, Irv (1996). *The Architecture of Computer Hardware and Systems Software*. New York: John Wiley.

Flanagan, George A. (1938). *A Treatise on Ornamental Typewriting*. New York: Gregg Publishing.

HowStuffWorks (2002). <http://www.howstuffworks.com>, by Marshall Brain. HowStuffWorks, Inc.

Kozierok, Charles M. (2001). *The PC Guide*. At <www.pcguide.com>.

Licklider, J. C. R. (1960). Man–Computer Symbiosis: IRE Transactions on Human Factors in Electronics. In Paul A. Mayer (ed.), *Computer Media and Communication* (1999). New York: Oxford University Press.

Liebowitz, S. J. and Stephen E. Margolis (1990). The Fable of the Keys. *Journal of Law and Economics* 33,1: 1–26.

Locke, Chris (2000). Digital Memory and the Problem of Forgetting. In Susannah Radstone (ed.), *Memory and Methodology* (pp. 25–36). New York: Berg.

McCullough, Warren and Walter Pitts (1943). A Logical Calculus of the Ideas Immanent in Nervous Activity. *Bulletin of Mathematical Biophysics*, 5: 115–33.

Macey, Samuel L. (1989). *The Dynamics of Progress: Time, Method, and Measure*. Athens, GA: University of Georgia Press.

Marx, Karl (1867). *Capital*, Volume One. In Robert C. Tucker (ed.), *The Marx–Engels Reader*, 2nd edn. (1978). New York: W. W. Norton.

Mumford, Lewis (1934). *Technics and Civilization*. New York: Harcourt, Brace and Company.

Norman, Don (1990). *The Design of Everyday Things*. New York: Doubleday.

OED (1989). "clock, n." *Oxford English Dictionary*, ed. J. A. Simpson and E. S. C. Weiner, 2nd edn. Oxford: Clarendon Press. Electronic Text Center, University of Virginia. Accessed October 1, 2002. At <http://etext.virginia.edu/oed.html>.

Petzold, Charles (2000). *Code*. Redmond, WA: Microsoft Press.

Rheingold, Howard (2000). *Tools for Thought*. Cambridge, MA: MIT Press.

von Neumann, John (1945). First Draft of a Report on the EDVAC. In William Aspray and Arthur Burks (eds.), *The Papers of John Von Neumann on Computing and Computer Theory* (1986). Charles Babbage Institute Reprint Series for the History of Computing, vol. 12 (pp. 17–82). Cambridge, MA: MIT Press.

White, Ron (2001). *How Computers Work*, 6th edn. Indianapolis, IN: Que Publishers.

Williams, Michael R. (1997). *A History of Computing Technology*, 2nd edn. Los Alamitos, CA: IEEE Computer Society Press.

14

Classification and its Structures

C. M. Sperberg-McQueen

Classification is, strictly speaking, the assignment of some thing to a class; more generally, it is the grouping together of objects into classes. A *class*, in turn, is a collection (formally, a set) of objects which share some property.

For example, a historian preparing an analysis of demographic data transcribed from census books, parish records, and city directories might classify individuals by sex, age, occupation, and place of birth. Places of birth might in turn be classified as large or small cities, towns, villages, or rural parishes. A linguist studying a text might classify each running word of text according to its part of speech, or each sentence according to its structure. Linguists, literary scholars, or social scientists might classify words occurring in a text by semantic category, organizing them into semantic nets. Classification serves two purposes, each important: by grouping together objects which share properties, it brings like objects together into a class; by separating objects with unlike properties into separate classes, it distinguishes between things which are different in ways relevant to the purpose of the classification. The classification scheme itself, by identifying properties relevant for such judgments of similarity and dissimilarity, can make explicit a particular view concerning the nature of the objects being classified.

Scope

Since a classification may be based on any set of properties that can be attributed to the objects being classified, classification in the broad sense involves the correct identification of the properties of the objects of study and is hardly distinguishable from coherent discourse in general. (Like coherence, systematic classification is sometimes eschewed for aesthetic or ideological reasons and if overrated may descend into pedantry.) Information retrieval systems may be regarded, and are often described, as classifying records into the classes "relevant" and "not relevant" each time a user issues a query. Norms and standards like the XML 1.0 specification or Unicode may be understood as classification schemes which assign any data stream or program either to the class "conforming" or to the class "non-conforming." Laws may be interpreted as classifying acts as legal or illegal, censors as classifying books, records, performances, and so on. Any characteristic of any kind of thing, using any set of concepts, may be viewed as classifying things of that kind into classes corresponding to those concepts. In the extreme case, the property associated with a class may be vacuous: the members may share only the property of membership in the class. In general, classification schemes are felt more useful if the classes are organized around properties relevant to the purpose of the classification. Details of the concepts, categories, and mechanisms used in various acts of classification may be found in other chapters in this volume: see, for example, chapters 1, 7, 15, and 17.

In the narrower sense, for computer applications in the humanities classification most often involves either the application of pre-existing classification schemes to, or the *post hoc* identification of clusters among a sample of, for example, texts (e.g. to describe the samples in language corpora), parts of texts (e.g., to mark up the structural constituents or non-structural features of the text), bibliography entries (for subject description in enumerative bibliographies or specialized libraries), words (for semantic characterization of texts), or extra-textual events or individuals (e.g., for historical work). The best known of these among the readers of this work are perhaps the classification systems used in libraries and bibliographies for classifying books and articles by subject; in what follows, examples drawn from these will be used where possible to illustrate important points, but the points are by no means relevant only to subject classification.

Since classification relies on identifying properties of the object being classified, perfect classification would require, and a perfect classification scheme would exhibit, perfect knowledge of the object. Because a perfect subject classification, for example, locates each topic in a field in an n-dimensional space near other related topics and distant from unrelated topics, a perfect subject classification represents a perfect map of the intellectual terrain covered in the area being classified. For this reason, classification schemes can carry a great deal of purely theoretical interest, in addition to their practical utility. Classification schemes necessarily involve some theory of the objects being classified, if only in asserting that the objects possess certain properties. Every ontology can be interpreted as providing the basis for a classification of the entities it describes. And conversely, every classification scheme can be interpreted with more or less ease, as the expression of a particular ontology. In practice, most classification schemes intended for general use content themselves with representing something less than a perfect image of the intellectual structure of their subject area and attempt with varying success to limit their theoretical assumptions to those most expected users can be expected to assent to. At the extreme, the assumptions underlying a classification scheme may become effectively invisible and thus no longer subject to challenge or rethinking; for purposes of scholarly work, such invisibility is dangerous and should be avoided.

This chapter first describes the abstract structures most often used in classification, and describes the rules most often thought to encourage useful classification schemes. It then gives a purely formal account of classification in terms of set theory, in order to establish that no single classification scheme can be exhaustive, and indeed that there are infinitely more ways of classifying objects than can be described in any language. Finally, it turns to various practical questions involved in the development and use of classification systems.

One-dimensional Classifications

Very simple classification schemes (sometimes referred to as *nominal* classifications, because the class labels used are typically nouns or adjectives) consist simply of a set of categories: male and female; French, German, English, and other; noun, verb, article, adjective, adverb, etc. In cases like these, some characteristic of the object classified may take any one of a number of discrete values; formally, the property associated with the class is that of having some one particular value for the given characteristic. The different classes in the scheme are not ordered with respect to each other; they are merely discrete classes which, taken together, subdivide the set of things being classified.

In some classifications (sometimes termed *ordinal*), the classes used fall into some sort of sequencing or ordering with respect to each other: first-year, second-year, third-year student; folio, quarto, octavo, duodecimo; upper-class, middle-class, lower-class.

In still other cases, the underlying characteristic may take a large or even infinite number of values, which have definite quantitative relations to each other: age, height, number of seats in parliament, number of pages, price, etc. For analytic purposes, it may be convenient or necessary to clump (or *aggregate*) sets of distinct values into single classes, as when age given in years is reduced to the categories infant, child, adult, or to under-18, 18–25, 25–35, over-35.

All of the cases described so far classify objects based on the value of a single characteristic attributed to the object. In the ideal case, the characteristic can be readily and reliably evaluated, and the values it can take are discrete. The more borderline cases there are, the harder it is likely to be to apply the classification scheme, and the more information is likely to be lost by analyses which rely on the classified data rather than the original data.

Classification Schemes as *N*-dimensional Spaces

In less simple classification schemes, multiple characteristics may be appealed to. These may often be described as involving a hierarchy of increasingly fine distinctions. The Dewey Decimal Classification, for example, assigns class numbers in the 800s to literary works. Within the 800s, it assigns numbers in the 820s to English literature, in the 830s to German literature, the 840s to French, etc. Within the 820s, the number 821 denotes English poetry, 822 English drama, 823 English fiction, and so on. Further digits after the third make even finer distinctions; as a whole, then, the classification scheme may be regarded as presenting the classifier and the user with a tree-like hierarchy of classes and subclasses, with smaller classes branching off from larger ones.

In the case of the Dewey classification of literature, however, the second and third digits are (almost) wholly independent of each other: a third digit 3 denotes fiction whether the second digit is 1 (American), 2 (English), 3 (German), 4 (French), 5 (Italian), 6 (Spanish),

7 (Latin), or 8 (Classical Greek), and 2 as a third digit similarly denotes drama, independent of language.

We can imagine the literature classification of the Dewey system as describing a plane, with the second digit of the Dewey number denoting positions on the x axis, and the third digit denoting values along the y axis. Note that neither the sequence and values of the genre numbers, nor those of the language numbers, have any quantitative significance, although the sequence of values is in fact carefully chosen.

Generalizing this idea, classification schemes are often regarded as identifying locations in an n-dimensional space. Each dimension is associated with an *axis*, and the set of possible values along any one axis is sometimes referred to as an *array*. Many salient characteristics of classification schemes may be described in terms of this n-dimensional spatial model.

It should be noted that, unlike the dimensions of a Cartesian space, the different characteristics appealed to in a classification scheme are not always wholly independent of each other. A medical classification, for example, may well subdivide illnesses or treatments both by the organ or biological system involved and by the age, sex, or other salient properties of the patient. Since some illnesses afflict only certain age groups or one sex or the other, the two axes are not wholly independent. A classification of dialects based on the pronunciation of a given lexical item can only apply to dialects in which that lexical item exists. A facet in a social classification that distinguishes hereditary from non-hereditary titles is only relevant to that part of the population which bears titles, and only in countries with a nobility. The digits 2 for drama and 3 for fiction have these meanings in the Dewey classification for literature, but they are not applicable to the 900s (history) or the 100s (philosophy). And so on.

The idea of a classification as describing an n-dimensional Cartesian space is thus in many cases a dramatic simplification. It is nonetheless convenient to describe each characteristic or property appealed to in a classification as determining a position along an axis, even if that axis has no meaning for many classes in the scheme. Those offended by this inexactitude in the metaphor may amuse themselves by thinking of the logical space defined by such a classification not as a Cartesian or Newtonian one but as a relativistic space with a non-Euclidean geometry.

Some Distinctions among Classification Schemes

When the axes of the logical space are explicitly identified in the description of the classification scheme, the scheme is commonly referred to as a *faceted* classification, and each axis (or the representation of a given class's value along a specific axis) as a *facet*. The concept of facets in classification schemes was first systematized by Ranganathan, though the basic phenomena are visible in earlier systems, as the example from the Dewey classification given above illustrates.

Faceted schemes are typically contrasted with *enumerative* schemes, in which all classes in the system are exhaustively enumerated in the classification handbook or *schedule*. In a typical faceted scheme, a separate schedule is provided for each facet and the facets are combined by the classifier according to specified rules; because the classifier must create or *synthesize* the class number, rather than looking it up in an enumeration, faceted schemes are sometimes also called *synthetic* (or, to emphasize that the task of synthesis must be preceded by analysis of the relevant properties of the object, *analytico-synthetic*) schemes. Both because of their intellectual clarity and because they can readily exploit the strengths of electronic database management systems, faceted classification schemes have become increasingly popular in recent years.

Some classification schemes provide single expressions denoting regions of the logical space; in what follows these are referred to as *(class) formulas*. Formulas are convenient when the objects classified must be listed in a single one-dimensional list, as on the shelves of a library or the pages of a classified bibliography. In such schemes, the order in which axes are represented may take on great importance, and a great deal of ingenuity can be devoted to deciding whether a classification scheme ought to arrange items first by language, then by genre, and finally by period, or in some other order.

In computerized systems, however, particularly those using database management systems, it is normally easier to vary the order of axes and often unnecessary to list every object in the collection in a single sequence, and so the order of axes has tended to become somewhat less important in multidimensional classification schemes intended for computer use. The provision of unique class formulas for each point in the scheme's logical space has correspondingly declined in importance, and much of the discussion of notation in pre-electronic literature on classification has taken on an increasingly quaint air. For those who need to devise compact symbolic formulas for the classes of a scheme, the discussions of notation in Ranganathan's *Prolegomena* (1967) are strongly recommended.

When each axis of the logical space can be associated with a particular part of the formula denoting a class, and vice versa, the notation is *expressive* (as in the portion of the Dewey system mentioned above). Fully expressive notations tend to be longer than would otherwise be necessary, so some classification schemes intentionally use inexpressive or incompletely expressive notation, as in most parts of the Library of Congress classification system. Expressive notations are advantageous in computer-based applications, since they make it easy to perform searches in the logical space by means of searches against class symbols. A search for dramas in any language, for example, can be performed by searching for items with a Dewey class number matching the regular expression "8.2." No similarly simple search is possible in inexpressive notations.

Some classification systems describe classes using natural-language phrases, rather than by assigning them to specific locations in a class hierarchy; library subject headings are a well-known example, but there are many others. (Some classification theorists distinguish such alphabetical systems as *indexing systems*, as opposed to *classification systems* in the strict sense, restricting the latter term to systems that provide a formal notation other than natural language for their class formulas.) Typically, such systems arrange topics in alphabetical order, rather than a systematic order imposed by the structure of the classification scheme. At one extreme, such a system may use free-form textual descriptions of objects to "classify" them. Most alphabetically organized classification systems, however, differ from wholly free-form indices in one or more ways. First, in order to avoid or minimize the inconsistencies caused by the use of different but synonymous descriptions, such systems normally use *controlled vocabularies* rather than unconstrained natural-language prose: descriptors other than proper nouns must be chosen from a closed list. In the ideal case, the controlled vocabulary has exactly one representative from any set of synonyms in the scope of the classification scheme. Second, as part of the vocabulary control alphabetic systems often stipulate that certain kinds of phrases should be "inverted," so that the alphabetical listing will place them near other entries. In some schemes, particular types of descriptors may be subdivided by other descriptors in a hierarchical fashion. Thus the Library of Congress subject heading for *Beowulf* will be followed by "*Beowulf* – Adaptations," "*Beowulf* – Bibliography," "*Beowulf* – Criticism, textual," "*Beowulf* – Study and teaching," "*Beowulf* – Translations – Bibliographies," "*Beowulf* – Translations – History and criticism," and so on. The phrases after the dashes are, in effect, an array of possible subdivisions for anonymous literary works; the *Library of Congress Subject Headings* (LCSH) provide a prescribed set of such expansions for a variety of different kinds of object: anonymous literary works, individuals of various kinds, theological topics, legislative bodies, sports, industries, chemicals, and so on. Third, most systems which use controlled vocabularies also provide a more or less systematic set of cross-references among terms. At a minimum, these cross-references will include *see* references from unused terms to preferred synonyms. In more elaborate cases, *see-also* references will be provided to broader terms, narrower terms, coordinate terms (i.e., other terms with the same broader term), partial synonyms, genus/species terms, and so on. The links to broader and narrower terms allow the alphabetically arranged scheme to provide at least some of the same information as a strictly hierarchical scheme. Like the LCSH, the *New York Times Thesaurus of Descriptors* (1983) described by Mills provides a useful model for work of this kind.

The fineness of distinction carried by the classification – that is, the size of the regions in the logical space that the classification allows us to distinguish – is called (mixing metaphors) the *depth* of the classification scheme. Some classification schemes provide a fixed and unvarying depth; others allow variable depth. Depth may be added either by adding more axes to the classification, as when a library using the Dewey system subdivides 822 (English drama) by period, or by adding more detail to the specification of the value along an axis already present. Faceted classification schemes often allow facets to vary in length, so as to allow the depth of classification to be increased by providing a more precise value for any facet. Notations with fixed-length facets, by contrast, like the part of Dewey described above, cannot increase the specificity of facets other than the last without creating ambiguity.

Whether they use expressive notation or not, some classification schemes provide notations for each node in their hierarchy (e.g., one formula for "literature" and another for "English literature," and so on); in such cases, the categories of the classification are not, strictly speaking, disjoint: the broader classes necessarily subsume the narrower classes arranged below them. One advantage of expressive notation is that it makes this relationship explicit. Other schemes provide notations only for the most fully specified nodes of the hierarchy: the hierarchical arrangement may be made explicit in the description of the scheme, but is collapsed in the definition of the notation, so that the classification gives the impression of providing only a single array of values. Commonly used part-of-speech classification systems often collapse their hierarchies in this way: each tag used to denote word-class and morphological information denotes a complete packet of such information; there is no notation for referring to more general classes like "noun, without regard for its specific morphology." Markup languages similarly often provide names only for the "leaves" of their tree-like hierarchies of element types; even when a hierarchy of classes is an explicit part of the design, as in the Text Encoding Initiative (TEI), there may be no element types which correspond directly to classes in the hierarchy.

When combinations of terms from different axes are specified in advance, as part of the process of classifying or indexing an object, we speak of a *pre-coordinate* system. When a classification system limits itself to identifying the appropriate values along the various axes, and values may be combined at will during a search of the classification scheme, we speak of a *post-coordinate* system. Printed indices that list all the subject descriptors applied to the items in a bibliography, in a fixed order of axes, for example, present a kind of pre-coordinate classification scheme. Online indices that allow searches to be conducted along arbitrary combinations of axes, by contrast, provide a post-coordinate scheme. It is possible for printed indices to provide free combination of terms, but post-coordinate indexing is easier for computer systems. Post-coordinate indexing allows greater flexibility and places greater demands on the intelligence of the user of the index.

When the axes and the values along each axis are specified in advance, and items are classified in terms of them, we can speak of an *a priori* system. When the axes and their values are derived *post hoc* from the items encountered in the collection of objects being classified, we may speak of an *a posteriori* or *data-driven* system. Author-specified keywords and free-text searching are simple examples of data-driven classification. Citation analysis, and in particular the study of co-citation patterns in scholarly literature, as described by Garfield, is another.

In some cases, the identification of axes in a data-driven system may involve sophisticated and expensive statistical analysis of data. The technique of latent semantic analysis is an example: initially, the occurrence or non-occurrence of each word in the vocabulary of all the documents in the collection being indexed is treated as an axis, and a statistical analysis is performed to collapse as many of these axes together as possible and identify a useful set of axes which are as nearly orthogonal to each other as the data allow. In a typical application, latent-semantic analysis will identify documents in a space of 200 or so dimensions. It is sometimes possible to examine the dimensions and associate meaning with them individually, but for the most part data-driven statistical methods do not attempt to interpret the different axes of their space individually. Instead, they rely on conventional measures of distance in n-dimensional spaces to identify items which are near each other; when the classification has been successful, items which are near each other are similar in ways useful for the application, and items which are distant from each other are dissimilar.

A priori systems may also be interpreted as providing some measure of similarity among items, but it is seldom given a numerical value.

Unconscious, naive, or pre-theoretic classification (as seen, for example, in natural-language terminology for colors) may be regarded as intermediate between the *a priori* and *a posteriori* types of classification systems described above.

Some data-driven systems work by being given samples of pre-classified training material and inducing some scheme of properties which enables them to match, more or less well, the classifications given for the training material. Other data-driven systems work without overt supervision, inducing classifications based solely on the observed data.

A priori systems require more effort in advance than data-driven systems, both in the definition of the classification scheme and in its application by skilled classifiers. The costs of data-driven systems are concentrated later in the history of the classification effort, and tend to involve less human effort and more strictly computational effort. Data-driven classification schemes may also appeal to scholars because they are free of many of the obvious opportunities for bias exhibited by *a priori* schemes and thus appear more nearly theory-neutral. It must be stressed, therefore, that while the theoretical assumptions of data-driven systems may be less obvious and less accessible to inspection by those without a deep knowledge of statistical techniques, they are nonetheless necessarily present.

Rules for Classification

Some principles for constructing classification schemes have evolved over the centuries; they are not always followed, but are generally to be recommended as leading to more useful classification schemes.

The first of these is to avoid *cross-classification*: a one-dimensional classification should normally depend on the value of a single characteristic of the object classified, should provide for discrete (non-overlapping) values, and should allow for all values which will be encountered: perhaps the best-known illustration of this rule lies in its violation in the fictional Chinese encyclopedia imagined by Jorge Luis Borges, in which

> it is written that animals are divided into: (a) those that belong to the Emperor, (b) embalmed ones, (c) those that are trained, (d) suckling pigs, (e) mermaids, (f) fabulous ones, (g) stray dogs, (h) those that are included in this classification, (i) those that tremble as if they were mad, (j) innumerable ones, (k) those drawn with a very fine camel's-hair brush, (l) others, (m) those that have just broken a flower vase, (n) those that resemble flies from a distance. (Borges 1981)

One apparent exception to this rule is often found in schemes which seek to minimize the length of their class formulas: often two characteristics are collapsed into a single step in the classification hierarchy, as when a demographic classification has the classes infant (sex unspecified), infant male, infant female, child (sex unspecified), boy, girl, adult (sex unspecified), man, woman.

Other desirable attributes of a classification scheme may be summarized briefly (I abbreviate here the "canons" defined by Ranganathan). Each characteristic used as the basis for an axis in the logical space should:

1   distinguish some objects from others: that is, it should give rise to at least two subclasses;
2   be relevant to the purpose of the classification scheme (every classification scheme has a purpose; no scheme can be understood fully without reference to that purpose);
3   be definite and ascertainable; this means that a classification scheme cannot be successfully designed or deployed without taking into account the conditions under which the work of classification is to be performed;
4   be permanent, so as to avoid the need for constant reclassification;
5   have an enumerable list of possible values which exhausts all possibilities. Provision should normally be made for cases where the value is not ascertainable after all: it is often wise to allow values like *unknown* or *not specified*. In many cases several distinct

special values are needed; among those sometimes used are: *unknown* (but applicable), *does-not-apply*, *any* (data compatible with all possible values for the field), *approximate* (estimated with some degree of imprecision), *disputed*, *uncertain* (classifier is not certain whether this axis is applicable; if it is applicable, the value is unknown).

In classification schemes which provide explicit class symbols, it is useful to provide a consistent sequence of axes in the construction of the class symbol (if the subject classification for literature divides first by country or language and then by period, it is probably wise for the subject classification for history to divide first by country and then by period, rather than vice versa). The sequence of values within an array of values for a given axis should also be made helpful, and consistent in different applications. Patterns often suggested include arranging the sequence for increasing concreteness, increasing artificiality, increasing complexity, increasing quantity, chronological sequence, arrangement by spatial contiguity, arrangement from bottom up, left-to-right arrangement, clockwise sequence, arrangement following a traditional canonical sequence, arrangement by frequency of values (in bibliographic contexts this is called *literary warrant*), or as a last resort alphabetical sequence.

Many classification schemes appeal, at some point, to one of a number of common characteristics in order to subdivide a class which otherwise threatens to become too large (in bibliographic practice, it is often advised to subdivide a class if it would otherwise contain more than twenty items). Subdivision by chronology, by geographic location, or by alphabetization are all commonly used; standard schedules for subdivision on chronological, geographic, linguistic, genre, and other grounds can be found in standard classification schemes and can usefully be studied, or adopted wholesale, in the creation of new schemes.

Classification schemes intended for use by others do well to allow for variation in the depth of classification practiced. Library classification schemes often achieve this by allowing class numbers to be truncated (for coarser classification) or extended (for finer); markup languages may allow for variable depth of markup by making some markup optional and by providing element types of varying degrees of specificity.

It is also desirable, in schemes intended for general use, to provide for semantic extension and the addition of new concepts; this is not always easy. Library classification schemes often attempt to achieve this by providing standard schedules for subdividing classes by chronology, geographic distribution, and so on, to be applied according to the judgment of the classifier; the Colon Classification goes further by defining an array of abstract semantic concepts which can be used when subdivision by other standard axes is not feasible or appropriate. It provides a good illustration of the difficulty of providing useful guidance in areas not foreseen by the devisers of the classification scheme:

1   unity, God, world, first in evolution or time, one-dimension, line, solid state, . . .
2   two dimensions, plane, conics, form, structure, anatomy, morphology, sources of knowledge, physiography, constitution, physical anthropology, . . .
3   three dimensions, space, cubics, analysis, function, physiology, syntax, method, social anthropology, . . .
4   heat, pathology, disease, transport, interlinking, synthesis, hybrid, salt, . . .

5   energy, light, radiation, organic, liquid, water, ocean, foreign land, alien, external, environment, ecology, public controlled plan, emotion, foliage, aesthetics, woman, sex, crime, . . .
6   dimensions, subtle, mysticism, money, finance, abnormal, phylogeny, evolution, . . .
7   personality, ontogeny, integrated, holism, value, public finance, . . .
8   travel, organization, fitness.

In markup languages, semantic extension can take the form of allowing *class* or *type* attributes on elements: for any element type *e*, an element instance labeled with a *class* or *type* attribute can be regarded as having a specialized meaning. In some markup languages, elements with extremely general semantics are provided (such as the TEI *div*, *ab*, or *seg* elements, or the HTML *div* and *span* elements), in order to allow the greatest possible flexibility for the use of the specialization attributes.

Any new classification scheme, whether intended for general use or for use only by a single project, will benefit from clear documentation of its purpose and (as far as they can be made explicit) its assumptions. For each class in the scheme, the scope of the class should be clear; sometimes the scope is sufficiently clear from the name, but very often it is essential to provide *scope notes* describing rules for determining whether objects fall into the class or not. Experience is the best teacher here; some projects, like many large libraries, keep master copies of their classification schemes and add annotations or additional scope notes whenever a doubtful case arises and is resolved.

A Formal View

From a purely formal point of view, classification may be regarded as the partition of some set of objects (let us call this set *O*) into some set of classes (let us call this set of classes *C*, or the *classification scheme*).

In simple cases (nominal classifications), the classes of *C* have no identified relation to each other but serve merely as bins into which the objects in *O* are sorted. For any finite *O*, there are a finite number of possible partitions of *O* into non-empty pair-wise disjoint subsets of *O*. As a consequence, there are at most a finite number of extensionally distinct ways to classify any finite set *O* into classes; after that number is reached, any new classification must reconstitute a grouping already made by some other classification and thus be extensionally equivalent to it. Such extensionally equivalent classifications need not be intensionally equivalent: if we classify the four letters *a*, *b*, *l*, *e* according to their phonological values, we might put *a* and *e* together as vowels, and *b* and *l* as consonants. If we classed them according to whether their letter forms have ascenders or not, we would produce the same grouping; the two classifications are thus extensionally equivalent, though very different in intension. In practice, the extensional equivalence of two classifications may often suggest some relation among the properties appealed to, as when classifying the syllables of German according to their lexicality and according to their stress.

In some cases, the classes of *C* can be related by a proximity measure of some kind. In such a classification, any two adjacent classes are more similar to each other than, say, a pair of non-adjacent classes. If such a classification scheme relies on a single scalar property, its classes may be imagined as corresponding to positions on, or regions of, a line. If the classification schema relies on two independent properties, the classes will correspond to points or regions in a plane. In practice, practical classification schemes often involve arbitrary numbers of independent properties; if n properties are used by a classification scheme, individual classes may be identified with positions in an n-dimensional space. The rules of Cartesian geometry may then be applied to test similarity between classes; this is simplest if the axes are quantitative, or at least ordered, but suitably modified distance measures can be used for purely nominal (unordered, unquantitative) classifications as well: the distance along the axis may be 0, for example, if two items have the same value for that axis, and 1 otherwise.

If we imagine some finite number of classes, and conceive of a classification scheme as being defined by some finite-length description (say, in English or any other natural language) of how to apply those classes to some infinite set of objects, then it may be noted that there are an infinite number of possible groupings which will not be generated by any classification scheme described in our list. The proof is as follows:

1 Let us label the classes with the numbers 1 to n, where n is the number of classes.

2 Let us assume that the objects to be classified can be placed in some definite order; the means by which we do this need not concern us here.

3 Then let us place the descriptions of possible classifications also into a definite order; it is easy to see that the list of descriptions is likely to be infinite, but we can nevertheless place them into a definite order. Since we imagine the descriptions as being in English or some other natural language, we can imagine sorting them first by length and then alphabetically. In practice, there might be some difficulty deciding whether a given text in English does or does not count as a description of a classification scheme, but for purposes of this exercise, we need not concern ourselves with this problem: we can list all English texts, and indeed all sequences of letters, spaces, and punctuation, in a definite sequence. (If we cannot interpret the sequence of letters as defining a rule for assigning objects to classes, we can arbitrarily assign every object to class 1.)

4 Now let us imagine a table, with one row for each description of a classification scheme and one column for each object to be classified. In the cell corresponding to a given scheme and object, we write the number of the class assigned to that object by that classification scheme. Each row thus describes a grouping of the objects into classes.

5 Now, we describe a grouping of the objects into classes which differs from every grouping in our list:

(a) Starting in the first row and the first column, we examine the number written there. If that number is less than n, we add one to it; if it is equal to n, we subtract $n - 1$ from it.

(b) Next, we go to the next row and the next column, and perform the same operation.

(c) We thus describe a diagonal sequence of cells in the table, and for each column we specify a class number different from the one written there. The result is that we have assigned each object to a class, but the resulting grouping does not correspond to any grouping listed in the table (since it differs from each row in at least one position).

We are forced, then, to conclude that even though our list of finite-length descriptions of classification schemes was assumed to be infinite, there is at least one assignment of objects to classes that does not correspond to any classification scheme in the list. (The list contains only the schemes with finite-length descriptions, but the classification we have just described requires an infinitely large table for its description, so it does not appear in the list.) There are, in fact, not just the one but an infinite number of such classifications which are not in the list.

Since the list contains, by construction, every classification scheme that has a finite-length description, we must infer that the classifications described by the diagonal procedure outlined above do not have any finite-length description; let us call them, for this reason, *ineffable* classifications.

The existence of ineffable classifications is not solely of theoretical interest; it may also serve as a salutary reminder that no single classification scheme can be expected to be "complete" in the sense of capturing every imaginable distinction or common property attributable to the members of O. A "perfect" classification scheme, in the sense described above of a scheme that perfectly captures every imaginable similarity among the objects of O, is thus a purely imaginary construct; actual classification schemes necessarily capture only a subset of the imaginable properties of the objects, and we must choose among them on pragmatic grounds.

Make or Find?

Whenever systematic classification is needed, the researcher may apply an existing classification scheme or else devise a new scheme for the purpose at hand. Existing schemes may be better documented and more widely understood than an *ad hoc* scheme would be; in some cases they will have benefited from more sustained attention to technical issues in the construction of a scheme than the researcher will be able to devote to a problem encountered only incidentally in the course of a larger research project. Being based on larger bodies of material, they may well provide better coverage of unusual cases than the researcher would otherwise manage; they may thus be more likely to provide an exhaustive list of possible values for each axis. And the use of a standard classification scheme does allow more direct comparison with material prepared by others than would otherwise be possible.

On the other hand, schemes with broad coverage may often provide insufficient depth for the purposes of specialized research (just as the thousand basic categories of the Dewey Decimal System will seldom provide a useful framework for a bibliography of secondary literature on a single major work or author), and the studied theoretical neutrality of schemes intended for wide use may be uncongenial to the purpose of the research.

In the preparation of resources intended for use by others, the use of standard existing classification schemes should generally be preferred to the *ad hoc* concoction of new ones. Note that some existing classification schemes are proprietary and may be used in publicly available material only by license; before using an established classification scheme, researchers should confirm that their usage is authorized.

For work serving a particular research agenda, no general rule is possible; the closer the purpose of the classification to the central problem of the research, the more likely is a custom-made classification scheme to be necessary. Researchers should not, however, underestimate the effort needed to devise a coherent scheme for systematic classification of anything.

Some Existing Classification Schemes

Classification schemes may be needed, and existing schemes may be found, for objects of virtually any type. Those mentioned here are simply samples of some widely used kinds of classification: classification of documents by subject or language variety, classification of words by word class or semantics, classification of extra-textual entities by socio-economic and demographic properties, and classification of images.

The best-known *subject classification* schemes are those used in libraries and in major periodical bibliographies to provide subject access to books and articles. The Dewey Decimal Classification (DDC) and its internationalized cousin the Universal Decimal Classification (UDC) are both widely used, partly for historical reasons (the Dewey system was the first widely promoted library classification scheme), partly owing to their relatively convenient decimal notation, and because their classification schedules are regularly updated. In the USA, the Library of Congress classification is now more widely used in research libraries, in part because its notation is slightly more compact than that of Dewey.

Less widely used, but highly thought of by some, are the Bliss Bibliographic Classification, originally proposed by Henry Evelyn Bliss and now thoroughly revised, and the Colon Classification devised by Shiyali Ramamrita Ranganathan, perhaps the most important theorist of bibliographic classification in history (Melvil Dewey is surely more influential but can hardly be described as a theorist). Both are fully faceted classification schemes.

The controlled vocabulary of the Library of Congress Subject Headings may also be useful; its patterns for the subdivision of various kinds of subjects provide useful arrays for subordinate axes.

Researchers in need of specialized subject classification should also examine the subject classifications used by major periodical bibliographies in the field; Balay (1996) provides a useful source for finding such bibliographies.

The creators of *language corpora* often wish to classify their texts according to genre, register, and the demographic characteristics of the author or speaker, in order to construct a stratified sample of the language varieties being collected and to allow users to select subcorpora appropriate for various tasks. No single classification scheme appears to be in general use for this purpose. The schemes used by existing corpora are documented in their manuals; that used by the Brown and the Lancaster-Oslo/Bergen (LOB) corpora is in some ways a typical example. As can be seen, it classifies samples based on a mixture of subject matter, genre, and type of publication:

- *A* Press: reportage
- *B* Press: editorial
- *C* Press: reviews
- *D* Religion
- *E* Skills, trades, and hobbiesz
- *F* Popular lore
- *G* Belles lettres, biography, essays
- *H* Miscellaneous (government documents, foundation reports, industry reports, college catalogue, industry house organ)
- *J* Learned and scientific writings
- *K* General fiction
- *L* Mystery and detective fiction
- *M* Science fiction
- *N* Adventure and western fiction
- *P* Romance and love story
- *R* Humor

Several recent corpus projects have produced, as a side effect, thoughtful articles on sampling issues and the classification of texts. Biber (1993) is an example. (See also chapter 21, this volume.) Some recent corpora, for example the British National Corpus, have not attempted to provide a single text classification in the style of the Brown and LOB corpora. Instead, they provide descriptions of the salient features of each text, allowing users to select subcorpora by whatever criteria they choose, in a kind of post-coordinate system.

Some language corpora provide word-by-word annotation of their texts, most usually providing a single flat classification of words according to a mixture of word-class and inflectional information (plural nouns and singular nouns, for example, thus being assigned to distinct classes). A variety of *word-class tagging* schemes is in use, but for English-language corpora the point of reference typically remains the tag set defined by the Brown Corpus of Modern American English, as refined by the Lancaster-Oslo/Bergen (LOB) Corpus, and further refined through several generations of the CLAWS (Constituent Likelihood Automatic Word-tagging System) tagger developed and maintained at the University of Lancaster (Garside and Smith 1997). When new word-class schemes are devised, the detailed documentation of the tagged LOB corpus (Johansson 1986) can usefully be taken as a model.

Semantic classification of words remains a topic of research; the classifications most frequently used appear to be the venerable work of Roget's *Thesaurus* and the newer more computationally oriented work of Miller and colleagues on WordNet (on which see Fellbaum 1998) and their translators, imitators, and analogues in other languages (on which see Vossen 1998).

In *historical work*, classification is often useful to improve the consistency of data and allow more reliable analysis. When systematic classifications are applied to historical sources such as manuscript census registers, it is generally desirable to retain some account of the original data, to allow consistency checking and later reanalysis (e.g., using a different classification scheme). The alternative, *pre-coding* the information and recording only the classification assigned, rather than the information as given in the source, was widely practiced in the early years of computer applications in history, since it provides for more compact data files, but it has fallen out of favor because it makes it more difficult or impossible for later scholars to check the process of classification or to propose alternative classifications.

Historians may find the *industrial, economic, and demographic classifications* of modern governmental and other organizations useful; even where the classifications cannot be used unchanged, they may provide useful models. Census bureaus and similar governmental bodies, and archives of social science data, are good sources of information about such classification schemes. In the anglophone world, the most prominent social science data archives may be the Inter-university Consortium for Political and Social Research (ICPSR) in Ann Arbor (<http://www.icpsr.umich.edu/>) and the UK Data Archive at the University of Essex (<http://www.data-archive.ac.uk/>). The Council of European Social Science Data Archives (<http://www.nsd.uib.no/cessda/index.html>) maintains a list of data archives in various countries both inside and outside Europe.

With the increasing emphasis on image-based computing in the humanities and the creation of large electronic archives of images, there appears to be great potential utility in classification schemes for images. If the class formulas of an image classification scheme are written in conventional characters (as opposed, say, to being themselves thumbnail images), then collections of images can be made accessible to search and retrieval systems by indexing and searching the image classification formulas, and then providing access to the images themselves. Existing image classification schemes typically work with controlled natural-language vocabularies; some resources use detailed descriptions of the images in a rather formulaic English designed to improve the consistency of description and make for better retrieval. The Index of Christian Art at Princeton University (<http://www.princeton.edu/~ica/>) is an example.

The difficulties of agreeing on and maintaining consistency in keyword-based classifications or descriptions of images, however, have meant that there is lively interest in automatic recognition of similarities among graphic images; there is a great deal of proprietary technology in this area. Insofar as it is used for search and retrieval, image recognition may be thought of as a specialized form of data-driven classification, analogous to automatic statistically based classification of texts.

REFERENCES FOR FURTHER READING

Anderson, James D. (1979). Contextual Indexing and Faceted Classification for Databases in the Humanities. In Roy D. Tally and Ronald R. Deultgen (eds.), *Information Choices and Policies: Proceedings of the ASIS Annual Meeting*, vol. 16 (pp. 194–201). White Plains, NY: Knowledge Industry Publications.

Balay, Robert (ed.) (1996). *Guide to Reference Books*, 11th edn. Chicago, London: American Library Association.

Biber, Douglas (1993). Representativeness in Corpus Design. *Literary and Linguistic Computing* 8,4: 243–57.

Borges, Jorge Luis (1981). The Analytical Language of John Wilkins, tr. Ruth L. C. Simms. In E. R. Monegal and A. Reid (eds.), *Borges: A Reader* (pp. 141–3). New York: Dutton.

Bowker, Geoffrey C. and Susan Leigh Star (1999). *Sorting Things Out: Classification and its Consequences*. Cambridge, MA: MIT Press.

Deerwester, Scott et al. (1990). Indexing by Latent Semantic Analysis. *Journal of the American Society for Information Science* 41,6: 391–407.

Fellbaum, Christiane (ed.) (1998). *WordNet: An Electronic Lexical Database*. Cambridge, MA: MIT Press.

Floud, Roderick (1979). *An Introduction to Quantitative Methods for Historians*. London and New York: Methuen.

Foskett, A. C. (1996). *The Subject Approach to Information*. [n.p.]: Linnet Books and Clive Bingley, 1969. (4th edn. 1982. 5th edn. London: Library Association.)

Garfield, Eugene (1979). *Citation Indexing: Its Theory and Application in Science, Technology, and Humanities*. New York: Wiley.

Garside, R. and N. Smith (1997). A Hybrid Grammatical Tagger: CLAWS4. In R. Garside, G. Leech, and A. McEnery (eds.). *Corpus Annotation: Linguistic Information from Computer Text Corpora* (pp. 102–21). London: Longman.

Johansson, Stig, in collaboration with Eric Atwell, Roger Garside, and Geoffrey Leech (1986). *The Tagged LOB Corpus*. Bergen: Norwegian Computing Centre for the Humanities.

Kuhn, Thomas (1977). Second Thoughts on Paradigms. In Frederick Suppe (ed.), *The Structure of Scientific Theories*, 2nd edn. (pp. 459–82). Urbana: University of Illinois Press.

Library of Congress, Cataloging Policy and Support Office (1996). *Library of Congress Subject Headings*, 19th edn., 4 vols. Washington, DC: Library of Congress.

Mills, Harlan (1983). The New York Times Thesaurus of Descriptors. In Harlan Mills, *Software Productivity* (pp. 31–55). Boston, Toronto: Little, Brown.

Mills, Jack, and Vanda Broughton (1977–). *Bliss Bibliographic Classification*, 2nd edn. London: Butterworth.

Ranganathan, S[hiyali] R[amamrita] (1967). *Prolegomena to Library Classification*, 3rd edn. Bombay: Asia Publishing House.

Ranganathan, Shiyali Ramamrita (1989). *Colon Classification*, 7th edn. Basic and Depth version. Revised and edited by M. A. Gopinath. Vol. 1, *Schedules for Classification*. Bangalore: Sarada Ranganathan Endowment for Library Science.

Svenonius, Elaine (2000). *The Intellectual Foundation of Information Organization*. Cambridge, MA: MIT Press.

Vossen, Piek (1998). Introduction to EuroWordNet. *Computers and the Humanities* 32: 73-89.

15

Databases

Stephen Ramsay

Introduction

Databases are an ubiquitous feature of life in the modern age, and yet the most all-encompassing definition of the term "database" – a system that allows for the efficient storage and retrieval of information – would seem to belie that modernity. The design of such systems has been a mainstay of humanistic endeavor for centuries; the seeds of the modern computerized database being fully evident in the many text-based taxonomies and indexing systems which have been developed since the Middle Ages. Whenever humanists have amassed enough information to make retrieval (or comprehensive understanding) cumbersome, technologists of whatever epoch have sought to put forth ideas about how to represent that information in some more tractable form.

The computerized database, while a new development in this broad historical schema, nonetheless appeared more or less simultaneously with the early use of computers in academic and commercial environments. In such contexts, the essential problem of organization and efficient retrieval (usually understood as falling under the rubric of data structures and algorithms respectively) is complicated by the need for systems which facilitate interaction with multiple end users, provide platform-independent representations of data, and allow for dynamic insertion and deletion of information. The use of database technology among humanists has been invigorated by the realization – common, perhaps, to many other similar convergences – that a number of fascinating problems and intellectual opportunities lurk beneath these apparently practical matters. The inclusion of certain data (and the attendant exclusion of others), the mapping of relationships among entities, the often collaborative nature of dataset creation, and the eventual visualization of information patterns, all imply a hermeneutics and a set of possible methodologies that are themselves worthy objects for study and reflection.

This chapter provides an introduction to these issues by working through the design and implementation of a simple relational database (our example stores basic information about books in print). The intent, of course, is to remove some of the complexities and idiosyncrasies of real-world data in order that the technical and conceptual details of database design might more readily emerge. The data to which humanist scholars are accustomed – literary works, historical events, textual recensions, linguistic phenomena – are, of course, rarely simple. We would do well, however, to bear in mind that what might be viewed as a fundamental inadequacy has often proved to be the primary attraction of relational database systems for the humanist scholar. Rather than exploiting a natural congruity between relational ontologies and humanistic data, scholars have often sought insight in the many ways in which the relational structure enforces a certain estrangement from what is natural. The terms we use to describe books in a bookstore (authors, works, publishers) and the relationships among them (published by, created by, published in) possess an apparent stability for which the relational model is ideally suited. The most exciting database work in humanities computing necessarily launches upon less certain territory. Where the business professional might seek to capture airline ticket sales or employee data, the humanist scholar seeks to capture historical events, meetings between characters, examples of dialectical formations, or editions of novels; where the accountant might express relations in terms like "has insurance" or "is the supervisor of," the humanist interposes the suggestive uncertainties of "was influenced by," "is simultaneous with," "resembles," "is derived from."

Such relationships as these hold out the possibility not merely of an increased ability to store and retrieve information, but of an increased critical and methodological self-awareness. If the database allows one to home in on a fact or relationship quickly, it likewise enables the serendipitous connection to come forth. Relational databases in humanistic study are, in this sense, not so much pre-interpretative mechanisms as para-interpretative formations. As with so many similar activities in digital humanities, the act of creation is often as vital to the experiential meaning of the scholarly endeavor as the use of the final product.

Relational database management systems (RDBMS) represent the most popular way of creating searchable ontologies both among computing humanists and among professionals in other areas of research and industry, and so this chapter will be concerned primarily with the design and implementation of database systems using the relational model. Still, the modern database landscape continues to evolve. Some consideration of where databases may yet be going (and where humanists may be going with database technology) is therefore apposite as well.

The Relational Model

E. F. Codd first proposed the relational model in a 1970 article in *Communications of the ACM* entitled "A Relational Model of Data for Large Shared Databanks." Codd's proposal endeavored to overcome the limitations of previous systems, which had suffered from difficulties related both to inefficient (which is to say slow) access and unwieldy storage mechanisms – inefficiencies that often resulted from redundancies in the underlying data representation. Codd's model made great strides forward in both areas, and yet his achievement is perhaps more acutely evident in the mathematical presentation of his ideas. One researcher, who refers to the 1970 paper as "probably the most famous paper in the entire history of database management," notes:

> It was Codd's very great insight that a database could be thought of as a set of relations, that a relation in turn could be thought of as a set of propositions . . . , and hence that all of the apparatus of formal logic could be directly applied to the problem of database access and related problems. (Date 2001)

This fundamental idea has spawned a vast literature devoted to database theory, and while there have been several major additions to the relational model, the relational databases of today continue to operate on the basis of Codd's insights.

Database Design

The purpose of a database is to store information about a particular *domain* (sometimes called the *universe of discourse*) and to allow one to ask questions about the state of that domain. Let us suppose, for example, that we are creating a database that will contain information about current editions of American novels. Our goal will be to create a system that can store information about authors, works, and publishers, and allow us to ask questions like "What publications did Modern Library produce in 1992?" and "Which works by Herman Melville are currently in print?" The simplest database of all would simply list the data in tabular form (see table 15.1).

This database might be expanded to include a vast collection of authors and works. With the addition of some mechanism with which to store and query the data, we can easily imagine a system capable of answering the questions we would like to pose. Yet the inefficiencies, which the relational model endeavors to overcome, are evident even in this

Table 15.1

Last	First	YOB	YOD	Title	Pub Year	Publisher	Pub Address
Twain	Mark	1835	1910	Huckleberry Finn	1986	Penguin USA	New York
Twain	Mark	1835	1910	Tom Sawyer	1987	Viking	New York
Cather	Willa	1873	1947	My Antonia	1995	Library of America	New York
Hemingway	Ernest	1899	1961	The Sun Also Rises	1995	Scribner	New York
Wolfe	Thomas	1900	1938	Look Homeward, Angel	1995	Scribner	New York
Faulkner	William	1897	1962	The Sound and the Fury	1990	Random House	New York

simple example. A search for "Mark Twain" will require that the system continue iterating through the rows after it has found its first hit in order to ensure that the relevant matches have been found. This is because our data model allows – and indeed, demands – that the name of the author be entered into every row in which a new work is introduced. Similar redundancies occur with dates of publication, publisher names, and publisher addresses. Moreover, a change to an author's name (for example, the decision to enter "Samuel Clemens" in place of the author's pen name) will require that we update all fields in which the original name appears. Even if we devise some mechanism for ensuring a certain vigilance on the part of the machine, we are still left with a version of the same problem: having to go to *n* places instead of just one. In our example, the redundancy seems unproblematic – any machine can make quick work of a database with six items. In a system containing thousands or perhaps millions of items, the extra time and space required to perform search algorithms can become a severe liability.

Relational modeling attempts to factor these redundancies out of the system. We can begin modifying our original design by isolating the individual *entities* in the domain at a more abstract level; that is, by locating the types of information that vary independently of one another. The preliminary outline shown in figure 15.1 might emerge as one possible representation of the domain.

Each of the boxes in figure 15.1 illustrates a particular entity with a set of associated *attributes*. We have retained all the information from the original design, but have sequestered the various entities from one another according to certain logical groupings: authors (who have last names, first names, and dates of birth and death), works (which have titles and years of publication), and publishers (which have names and cities where they are headquartered). Often, the nouns we use to describe the domain and the recurrence of the word "have" helps to establish these entities and their attributes. To this basic outline we may also add a set of verb phrases describing the nature of the relationships among the entities. For example, authors *create* works, and works are, in turn, *published by* publishers. The addition of this information can then give rise to what is called an *entity relationship* (ER) diagram (see figure 15.2).

This diagram captures the basic relationships we have isolated, but it remains to say how many instances of a single entity can be associated with other entities in the model. For example, one author may contract with several publishers, and a publisher may offer many different works by multiple authors. There are several ways to capture these features diagrammatically.[1] We will simply use the number "1" to indicate a single instance and

Figure 15.1

an "M" to indicate multiple instances (see figure 15.3). We may then read the relationship line connecting authors and works to mean "One author has many works."

Thus far, we have been pursuing the logical design of our database – a design entirely independent of both the eventual machine representation of the data and of the end user's view of the information contained within it. We would do well at this point to imagine how this logical structure might be populated with the particular instances from the first model. To do this, we need to make a subtle mental shift in the way we view the entity relationship diagram. We might be tempted to see the various boxes as storage areas that can hold instances of authors' last names, work titles, and so forth. However, we have been really modeling the *generic form* that the particular instances of data will take. The populated database is properly conceived of as a set of tables with rows and columns, in which each row corresponds to the entities and each column to the attributes in the ER diagram. These rows are usually referred to as *records* and the intersection of rows and columns as *fields*. Table 15.2, for example, is a mock-up of a populated database built according to the terms of the ER diagram.

This more concrete view of our database captures the entities, but it makes no mention of the relationships. In order to represent the relationships between records, we need to introduce some variable that can hold these connections.

Our ability to do this will be significantly enhanced if we can devise some way to refer to each individual instance of a particular entity as a unique datum. After all, the final database will not merely connect authors to works in some generic way, but will reflect the fact that, for example, the author Mark Twain created both *Huckleberry Finn* and *Tom*

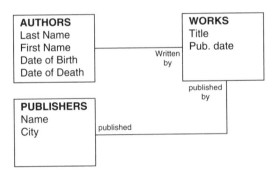

Figure 15.2

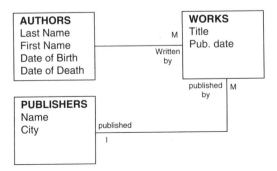

Figure 15.3

Sawyer. The usual method for establishing this uniqueness is to create a *primary key* for each record – a unique value associated with each individual record in a table.[2] This value is simply a new attribute which can be added to our ER diagram, and by extension, a new column in the final database for each record type. The author entity, for example, may be modified as shown in figure 15.4.

Table 15.2

AUTHORS

Last Name	First Name	Year of Birth	Year of Death
Twain	Mark	1835	1910
Cather	Willa	1873	1947
Hemingway	Ernest	1899	1961
Wolfe	Thomas	1900	1938
Faulkner	William	1897	1962

WORKS

Title	PubYear
The Adventures of Huckleberry Finn	1986
Tom Sawyer	1987
My Antonia	1995
The Sun Also Rises	1995
Look Homeward, Angel	1995
The Sound and the Fury	1990

PUBLISHERS

Name	City
Penguin USA	New York
Library of America	New York
Scribner	New York
Viking	New York
Random House	New York

```
AUTHORS
Primary Key
Last Name
First Name
Year of Birth
Year of Death
```

Figure 15.4

The resulting database table would then include a new column to hold this value (see table 15.3). With the other entities similarly modified, we now have a way of referring to each individual record in a table without ambiguity.

The next step is really at the heart of the relational model. In order to capture the *one-to-many* (1:M) relationship between authors and works, we introduce a second key attribute to the entities on the "many" side of the relationship – one that can hold a reference (or pointer) back to the entity on the "one" side of the relationship. This reference is, like the primary key, simply another attribute called a *foreign key*. Table 15.4, for example, shows how the "Works" table would look with additional fields for primary and foreign keys.

The foreign key field contains the primary key of the record with which it is associated. Thus the records for *The Adventures of Huckleberry Finn* and *Tom Sawyer* (which have been assigned primary keys 1 and 2, respectively) now contain foreign key references to the record in the "Authors" table which bears primary key 1 (the record for "Mark Twain"). In this way, the database is able to retain one reference for the author "Mark Twain." The redundancy that hindered the original design has been eliminated.

Unfortunately, the database still contains other instances of redundancy. For example, every publisher in our database is located in New York, which means this information is repeated for all six publisher records. Theoretically, this situation could have been avoided if we had held ourselves to a very strict interpretation of "types of information that vary independently of one another" in our initial ER diagram. In practice, such redundancies are often difficult to discern upon initial analysis of the domain. It may even be that some redundancies only appear after a considerable amount of data has already been entered into a prototype system.

Table 15.3

		AUTHORS		
Author ID	Last Name	First Name	Year of Birth	Year of Death
1	Twain	Mark	1835	1910
2	Cather	Willa	1873	1947
3	Hemingway	Ernest	1899	1961
4	Wolfe	Thomas	1900	1938
5	Faulkner	William	1897	1962

Table 15.4

WORKS

Work ID	Title	PubYear	Author Id
1	The Adventures of Huckleberry Finn	1986	1
2	Tom Sawyer	1987	1
3	My Antonia	1995	2
4	The Sun Also Rises	1995	3
5	Look Homeward, Angel	1995	4
6	The Sound and the Fury	1990	5

In any event, eliminating the redundancy in the "Publishers" table is simply a matter of breaking the "City" attribute off into its own table, assigning a primary key value to each record instance, and providing a new foreign key field in the "Publishers" table which can hold a reference to the correct city. In other words, we need to take one of our attributes and elevate it to the status of entity (see table 15.5).

Since primary key values in one table can be referenced from multiple tables as foreign keys, this restructuring may have a useful side effect if we ever decide to add "Place of Birth" to the Authors table.

Table 15.5

PUBLISHERS

Pub ID	Name	City ID
1	Penguin USA	1
2	Library of America	1
3	Scribner	1
4	Viking	1
5	Random House	1

CITIES

CityID	City
1	New York

There is another kind of relationship in this domain which isn't represented; namely, the *many-to-many* (M:M) relationship. This situation might easily arise if several publishers release editions of the same work. We would naturally describe this relationship as being, like all the relationships in the current design, one-to-many, but in this case, there is already a one-to-many relationship going the other way (from "Publishers" to "Works"). One might be tempted simply to introduce a foreign key pointing to "Works" from "Publishers" to complement the foreign key pointing from "Publishers" to "Works." However, the more apt solution is to abstract the relationship into a new entity called an *association* (or *junction table*). An association is simply a new table which contains the two related foreign keys (see table 15.6). This association captures the fact that Penguin USA (Pub ID 1) publishes *The Adventures of Huckleberry Finn* (Work ID 1) and an edition of *Tom Sawyer* (Work ID 2).

Each record in an association may be assigned a primary key, but in this case (and in the case of most associations) the combination of the two primary keys is understood to represent a unique combination. Most RDBMSs therefore allow one to declare the pair of values to be the primary key for that record (the creation of these *compound keys* will be discussed in the next section).

We have now analyzed our domain with entity-relationship modeling and have begun to factor out the major redundancies in the model. Readers interested in the formal explication of these methodologies will find abundant resources in the scholarly literature of the field, and while it is unnecessary to go into these matters here, at least one aspect of the more technical discussion deserves mention even in an introductory context.

Database theorists (and serious designers) often speak of databases as being in one of five *normal forms*. The normal forms may be stated in set theoretic terms, but they may also be stated more simply as design criteria by which to judge the soundness of one's design. For example, one practically minded book paraphrases *first normal form* by stating that "at each row-and-column intersection, there must be one and only one value, and that value must be atomic: there can be no repeating groups in a table that satisfies first normal form" (Bowman et al. 1999).

By the time a database is in *fifth normal form*, all redundancy has been removed; as Bowman puts it, "Tables normalized to this extent consist of little more than primary keys" (Bowman et al. 1999). This has the advantage of making it easier for the RDBMS to

Table 15.6

PUBLISHER–WORKS TABLE

Pub ID	Work ID
1	1
1	2
2	2
3	3
4	4

ensure the overall integrity of the data, but one may find that queries on those data become rather confusing to compose. As with most matters related to computer programming, one needs to balance the goals of correctness against the practical exigencies of the system and its users.

Schema Design

Up until now, our meditations on database design have been confined to what one might normally undertake at the whiteboard. The actual implementation of the design is much more akin to programming. Fortunately, there is little in the implementation stage that requires new concepts; for the most part, we simply need to translate our design into a representation intelligible to the machine. This representation is usually referred to as a *database schema*, and is created using *Structured Query Language* (SQL).[3]

There are a number of excellent SQL-compliant RDBMSs available to the humanist scholar. The majority of humanities computing projects that use databases employ free (open source) systems, of which the most popular are MySQL, mSQL, and PostgreSQL. There are also a number of commercial systems in use (Oracle, Microsoft Access, IBM DB2). The systems differ somewhat in their feature sets and in the amount of documentation available, but all provide efficient, feature-rich implementations of the relational model with advanced security and management functions. For our database, we will use PostgreSQL – a free, well-supported RDBMS for Unix-like systems which can be downloaded over the Internet.[4]

The database schema is nothing more than a machine-readable representation of the ER diagram. We may begin by laying out the various entities and their attributes, but since we are now giving instructions to the machine, we need to be more specific about the precise nature of the data to be entered:

```
CREATE TABLE authors (
   last_name VARCHAR(80),
   first_name VARCHAR(80),
   year_of_birth INTEGER,
   year_of_death INTEGER,
);
CREATE TABLE works (
   title VARCHAR(80),
   pub_year INTEGER,
);
CREATE TABLE cities (
   city VARCHAR(80),
);
CREATE TABLE publishers (
   name VARCHAR(80),
);
```

Like most programming languages, SQL includes the notion of a *datatype*. Datatype declarations help the machine to use space more efficiently and also provide a layer of verification for when the actual data is entered (so that, for example, a user cannot enter character data into a date field). In this example, we have specified that the last_name, first_name, title, city, and name fields will contain character data of varying length (not to exceed 80 characters), and that the year_of_birth, year_of_death, and pub_year fields will contain integer data. Other possible datatypes include DATE (for day, month, and year data), TEXT (for large text blocks of undetermined length), and BOOLEAN (for true/false values). Most of these can be further specified to account for varying date formats, number bases, and so forth. PostgreSQL, in particular, supports a wide range of datatypes, including types for geometric shapes, Internet addresses, and binary strings.

Databases often differ in the way they represent (and ensure the integrity of) primary keys. In PostgreSQL, the usual method is to create a separate mechanism for generating and keeping track of unique numeric values, and to have the tables containing the entities retrieve a value from that mechanism each time a new record is created. So, for example, to create a primary key for the authors table, we first create what is called a *sequence table* that will hold the set of unique values for that table:

```
CREATE SEQUENCE author_seq;
```

We can then add a new field to the author table which will have as its default value the next value called from the appropriate sequence:

```
CREATE TABLE authors (
author_id INTEGER DEFAULT NEXTVAL('author_seq')
  last_name VARCHAR(80),
  first_name VARCHAR(80),
  year_of_birth INTEGER,
  year_of_death INTEGER</dis?
);
```

This new line thus amounts to the following declaration about the author_id field: the author_id will have as its default value an integer that corresponds to the next value provided by the sequence named author_seq.[5]

We also want to declare this value specifically as the primary key for the table. This is accomplished with the following addition:

```
CREATE TABLE authors (
author_id INTEGER DEFAULT NEXTVAL('author_seq'),
  last_name VARCHAR(80),
  first_name VARCHAR(80),
  year_of_birth INTEGER,
  year_of_death INTEGER,
  year_of_death INTEGER,
PRIMARY KEY(author_id)
);
```

A foreign key is simply another data field, which, like the primary key field, has been specifically designated as a key. In order to capture the one-to-many relationship between works and authors, for example, we would modify the works table as follows:

```
CREATE TABLE works (
  work_id INTEGER DEFAULT NEXTVAL('work_seq'),
  title VARCHAR(80),
  pub_year INTEGER,
author_id INTEGER
  PRIMARY KEY(work_id),
FOREIGN KEY(author_id) REFERENCES author
);
```

The PRIMARY KEY() specifier also makes it easy to declare the publisher and work ids in our publisher/work association as a compound key:

```
CREATE TABLE pub_works (
  publisher_id INTEGER,
  work_id INTEGER,
PRIMARY KEY(publisher_id, work_id),
  FOREIGN KEY(publisher_id) REFERENCES publisher,
FOREIGN KEY(work_id) REFERENCES work
);
```

The designation of primary and foreign keys is one of the most important aspects of schema design, because it helps the system to achieve what is called *referential integrity*. Referential integrity is compromised when we delete a record that contains a reference to another record. So, for example, if we were to delete an author from the authors table, we might leave a reference to that author in the works table without a referent. A good RDBMS will use the primary and foreign key references either to prevent this from occurring or to warn the database administrator that the operation will result in a dangling reference (sometimes called a *null pointer*).

The method for creating an empty database and getting this schema into the RDBMS varies from system to system. Most RDBMSs provide command-line tools for setting up databases and for executing commands through an interactive command interpreter. The documentation for the particular RDBMS will discuss such matters in detail.[6]

Importing Data

Importing data into this schema requires the use of another set of SQL commands. The most useful of these is the INSERT keyword, which adds a record to one of the tables specified in the schema:

```
INSERT INTO authors (last_name, first_name, year_of_birth,
  year_of_death) values ('Twain', 'Mark', 1835, 1910);
```

The structure of this command is such that the target fields are declared in the first set of parentheses and the actual values in the second (the structure of the DELETE command, for removing data from a database, uses the same syntax). In most systems, character strings must be enclosed in quotation marks. Notice also that the INSERT statement does not include a primary key because our database schema has already instructed the system to use the next value in the sequence table as the default. A work record may be added in much the same way:

```
INSERT INTO works (title, pub_year) values ('The Adventures of
Huckleberry Finn', 1986);
```

In this case, however, we need to add a foreign key value that contains a primary key from the authors table. There are three ways to accomplish this. The first is simply to look up the appropriate record in the authors table before executing the INSERT statement for the work, note its primary key, and add this to the statement. The second way is to perform an UPDATE statement after the record has been created, which adds the primary key for the author to the foreign key field author_id of the work record. The third, and perhaps the most efficient way, is to embed the statement that looks up the appropriate primary key into the INSERT statement for adding a work record. All three of these methods require that we have an understanding of how to query the database for information, so let us defer this discussion for a moment while we explore the query commands of SQL.

Database Queries

The database administrator can query the database using the SELECT command. To retrieve all the last names currently in the authors table, for example, one would execute the following command:

```
SELECT last_name FROM authors;
```

Most RDBMSs will produce output that looks something like this:

```
last_name
_____
Twain
Cather
Hemingway
Wolfe
Faulkner
(5 rows)
```

In most circumstances, however, we want to create a more complex query that will let us home in on a particular record. Here, for example, is a SELECT statement that only selects authors born after 1890:

```
SELECT last_name, first_name FROM authors WHERE year_of_birth
>= 1890;
```

This statement begins by isolating two fields which should be returned to the user, but then adds a WHERE clause which qualifies the search according to particular criteria – in this case, to records in which the integer value contained in the `year_of_birth` field is greater than (or equal to) 1890. The result is a list of authors:

```
last_name | first_name
----- + ------
Hemingway | Ernest
Wolfe | Thomas
Faulkner | William
(3 rows)
```

Assuming we have already created records for Mark Twain and for *The Adventures of Huckleberry Finn*, we can now use the query syntax to discover the primary key for Mark Twain and use it to fill in the foreign key field for his works. The first is accomplished with a SELECT statement:

```
SELECT author_id FROM authors WHERE last_name='Twain';
```

The system returns the value "1." We can now use an UPDATE statement to modify the appropriate work record:

```
UPDATE works SET author_id=1 WHERE title='The Adventures of
Huckleberry Finn';
```

The more efficient method alluded to above – loading a record into the works table with the appropriate foreign key in one statement – uses what is called a *subselect*:

```
INSERT INTO works (title, pub_year, author_id) values ('The
Adventures of Huckleberry Finn', 1986, (SELECT author_id FROM
authors WHERE last_name='Twain'));
```

This statement follows the usual syntax of the INSERT statement, except that the last value in the second set of parentheses (the one pertaining to `author_id`) is itself a SELECT statement designed to return a single value: the primary key for the author record with the word "Twain" in the `last_name` field.

Database queries can reach a significant level of complexity; the WHERE clause can accept Boolean operators (e.g. ``WHERE year_of_birth > 1890 AND year_of_-birth < 1900''), and most SQL implementations offer keywords for changing the ordering of the output (e.g. ORDER BY year_of_birth). Taking full advantage of the relational model, moreover, requires that we be able to gather information from several tables and present it in one result list. This operation is called a *join*.

Let us suppose that we want to return a single result set that lists the authors' names, titles, and publishers of all works in the database. Doing so will require that we gather information from the author, publisher, and work tables, and also from the association that links publishers with works. The syntax for constructing this query follows the general template for SELECT . . . FROM . . . WHERE . . . but with a twist:

```
SELECT a.last_name, a.first_name, p.name, w.title FROM authors
a, publishers p, works w, pub_works pw WHERE p.publisher_-
```

```
id=pw.publisher_id AND w.work_id=pw.work_id AND a.author_-
id=w.author_id;
```

Any database of non-trivial complexity will have equivalent column names spread across several tables. Such equivalence will naturally occur with columns representing common concepts (such as "date"), but it will occur inevitably with the keys (since the primary key label in one table will often occur as the foreign key label in several others). The key to understanding this join query lies in the FROM clause, where each table participating in the join is aliased to a short variable. In this query, the variable a will stand in for the authors table, w for works, and so on. Thus we may read the first part of the query as saying "Select the last_name field from the authors table, the first_name field from the authors table, the name field from the publishers table, and the title field from the works table." The WHERE clause then tries to match up the appropriate key columns: the publisher_id in the publishers and pub_works tables must match, the work_id in the works and pub_works tables must match, and the author_ids in the authors and works tables must match. The RDBMS will then return all records that match all of these criteria in the order in which they were requested in the first part of the query:

```
last_name    | first_name   | name          | title
-----------+------------+-------------+---------------
 Twain       | Mark         | Penguin USA   | Tom Sawyer
 Twain       | Mark         | Penguin USA   | The Adventures of
                                                Huckleberry Finn
 Cather      | Willa        | Viking        | My Antonia
 Hemingway   | Ernest       | Library of    | The Sun Also Rises
                              America
 Wolfe       | Thomas       | Scribner      | Look Homeward, Angel
 Faulkner    | William      | Random House  | The Sound and the Fury
(6 rows)
```

Constraining this query to a single author is simply a matter of adding another constraint to the WHERE clause: au.last_name='Twain'.

The necessity for join operations (and subselects, which can often be used to accomplish the same thing) increases as the databases approach full normalization. Database administrators wishing to take full advantage of a good relational design will want to study the particular features of their SQL implementation closely.

Database Management

A good RDBMS will include all the facilities necessary for implementing a schema, importing data into the system, and performing queries. However, such facilities represent only part of the overall set of functions and capabilities necessary for creating a production system.

Prudence would suggest that only a few privileged users should possess the ability to create and destroy databases, and that a broader (but not unlimited) set of users be able to add data to existing databases. There may also be administrative data stored in the database that are not intended for ordinary users of the system. All of the major RDBMSs provide facilities – ranging from simple permissions files to elaborate security systems – for limiting user access to the system. Most simply use a separate database (integral to the RDBMS itself) that permits or denies the ability to run specific commands (often using the GRANT and REVOKE keywords from SQL). Since RDBMSs usually run as network processes (in order to allow for remote connections), some mechanism should also be in place for limiting connections to particular network domains. Unlike simple user applications (which usually come with a reasonable set of security defaults), advanced multi-user applications often assume that the administrator will take the time to study the security model carefully and implement the appropriate procedures. The assumption that users will do this is perhaps naive, but the assumption that the developers have already done everything to make the particular installation secure can be reckless indeed.

Transaction management represents another related set of concerns. Suppose that we had created a large file full of INSERT statements for the initial load of our data, but had left off the semicolon at the end of one of the statements. In all likelihood, the RDBMS (interpreting each INSERT statement as a discrete SQL operation) would execute the first n number of statements, inserting the data for each one, only to break in the middle of the list. We could perhaps delete the data already inserted, fix the error in the file, and reload the entire file, or perhaps we could erase the INSERT statements from the file that we have already executed and start anew. We would do better, however, if we had some way to declare all the INSERT statements in the file as an "all-or-nothing" block; the database has to perform all of these operations successfully or else it must exit with a warning, having performed none of them. Most systems provide some method for declaring a set of statements as a *transaction block* of this kind. In PostgreSQL, for example, the keywords are BEGIN (for signaling the beginning of a transaction), COMMIT (for executing the statements in the event that the proposed operations would generate no errors), and ROLLBACK (for undoing a set of operations).[7]

While the relational model lends itself to efficient storage and retrieval mechanisms, the sheer number of insertions, deletions, and updates on a production database system will often result in a certain fragmentation of the data (much in the way a hard drive can become fragmented after many frequent read-write operations). Much research has been devoted to finding new ways to defragment and otherwise optimize storage and retrieval in heavily used RDBMSs. While some of these operations occur behind the scenes, others are designed to be customized by the administrator for local circumstances. Such optimizations become more and more pertinent as a database (or a userbase) grows in size, and administrators will want to avail themselves of these facilities when appropriate.

Databases and Software Development

Database administrators (particularly those working in a Unix environment) will often find that the humble command-line interface represents the most efficient way to create database schema, load large files full of SQL statements, check the validity of queries, and perform the various tasks associated with user accounts and security. However, many database applications in humanities computing are intended for use outside the group of scholars and developers implementing the system. In such cases, low-level access to the RDBMS is rarely desirable. Indeed, it is often useful to design a system that shields users from SQL entirely.

The construction of *middleware* systems intended to provide such abstraction is among the more common software development tasks in humanities computing. In the case of both standalone and web-based applications, the usual goal is to place the execution of SQL queries and commands "in between" the user interface and the underlying RDBMS. Such a design (often called an *n-tiered design*) has the additional virtue of allowing the interface, database, and intervening programming logic to vary independently of one another; in a well-designed system, a change to the user interface (for example) would ideally imply only minor changes to the other tiers. Fortunately, nearly every programming language in common use among computing humanists provides elaborate mechanisms for executing SQL commands against a database from within an application.

The *DBI* (or *DataBase Independent*) module is an extension to the Perl programming language which provides a set of functions and variables for communicating with an RDBMS. In addition to allowing one to pass SQL statements to a database, retrieve results, and restructure data for delivery (to, for example, a web browser), DBI also provides an extremely powerful plug-in architecture that allows one to use the same program with several database implementations. So, for example, a program using the DBI interface could retrieve values from a web form, embed those values in a series of SQL statements, and pass them off to the RDBMS. Instead of going directly to the RDBMS, however, the DBI system would look for a driver (or *DBD* module) corresponding to the particular RDBMS being used, and effectively translate the DBI SQL syntax into the dialect of the particular database. Switching from PostgreSQL to MySQL (or perhaps running the two simultaneously) is therefore simply a matter of adding a new driver. DBI is also fairly mature; there are DBD modules corresponding to nearly every major database implementation, and all are freely available.[8]

Java programmers can find the same concept implemented in the *JDBC* (or *Java DataBase Connectivity*) library. JDBC is one of the more comprehensive implementations of SQL, and drivers are also available for all the major RDBMSs. Java also has the advantage of avoiding the overhead of *CGI* (*Common Gateway Interface*) upon which Perl and other similar scripting languages depend. CGI usually requires that a separate copy of the language interpreter be loaded into memory each time the program is invoked. The Java *servlet* architecture (intended for creating server-side applications) avoids this overhead by having a copy of the *Java Virtual Machine* (JVM) running constantly in memory with various caching facilities for the individual programs running on it.[9] This method is generally superior to CGI and can leverage the considerable power and flexibility of the Java programming language, but one sacrifices the simplicity of the CGI in the process.

Another technology that deserves mention is PHP (*PHP Hypertext Processor*). PHP is a programming language that can be embedded in ordinary HTML pages and interpreted by a program embedded into the web server itself (thus aligning itself with Java servlets in its avoidance of CGI). PHP does not employ the concept of a single interface with multiple drivers, but instead provides built-in function sets for all the major RDBMSs. Of the three middleware technologies here discussed, PHP is perhaps the easiest to use, but it is unfortunately the least "middle" of the three. Embedding code into an HTML page implies mingling the logic of the user interface with the programming logic – a convergence that can lead to systems which are difficult to maintain. Often, the size (and predicted mutability) of the system will determine whether the simplicity of PHP outweighs the potential for confusion later on.[10]

Alternative Models

The relational database model has been an extremely successful one. Previous models – hierarchical databases and network databases – are seldom used today, and it seems clear that the relational model will continue to be the dominant one for many years to come.[11] However, there are a number of competing models which have been the subject of active research in computer science and information technology circles over the last two decades. While none are as widely employed as the relational model, the usual proclivity for exploration and early adoption among computing humanists may well serve to bring these models into prominence in humanities research.

The most active contender for the prominence of the relational model is the *object-oriented* (OO) database model. The impetus for its creation lies in the widespread use of the object-oriented programming paradigm among software engineers. The details of this paradigm are beyond the scope of this discussion, but some sense of the model may be gleaned from the observation that relational schemas rely upon an older conception of programming in which the data and the procedures for manipulating those data are kept separate from one another. In our database, for example, the data pertaining to authors are entirely separate from the various operations (queries) we would like to perform on those data. The object-oriented model proposes that the data and the procedures be refactored into discrete objects. The data for the author table and the elements of the operations that can be performed on them would therefore belong to the same basic structure. Partisans of OO argue that this model facilitates maintenance by creating fewer dependencies between data items, allows for reusable data modules that can be easily moved from one database context to another, and creates a certain semantic richness (through the creation of inheritance hierarchies) in the data unattainable with more conventional methods.

While the more mainstream database developers have been reluctant to embrace this model fully, the relational database landscape has begun to see implementations which bill themselves as *object-relational database management systems* (ORDBMS). Such implementations typically fall short of the fully object-oriented databases envisioned by researchers, but borrow the notions of inheritance (having one table "inherit" properties from another without duplication) and complex object creation commonly associated with object-oriented systems. It seems clear that the trend toward such hybrid systems will continue.

Databases and the Humanist

Whether it is the historian attempting to locate the causes of a military conflict, the literary critic teasing out the implications of a metaphor, or the art historian tracing the development of an artist's style, humanistic inquiry reveals itself as an activity fundamentally dependent upon the location of pattern. Dealing with patterns necessarily implies the cultivation of certain habits of seeing; as one critic has averred: "Recognizing a pattern implies remaining open to gatherings, groupings, clusters, repetitions, and responding to the internal and external relations they set up" (Hunter 1990). Of all the technologies in use among computing humanists, databases are perhaps the best suited to facilitating and exploiting such openness. To build a database one must be willing to move from the forest to the trees and back again; to use a database is to reap the benefits of the enhanced vision which the system affords.

Humanists have used relational databases as the engines behind complex visualization systems, text archives, and multimedia works. In most cases the intent has been merely to leverage the efficiencies of the relational model as a means for storing and retrieving the information needed to populate a map, load a list of hits, or assemble a website. However, even in these relatively simple applications it becomes clear that the underlying ontology has considerable intellectual value. A well-designed database that contains information about people, buildings, and events in New York City contains not static information, but an entire set of ontological relations capable of generating statements about a domain. A truly relational database, in other words, contains not merely "Central Park," "Frederick Law Olmstead," and "1857," but a far more suggestive string of logical relationships (e.g., "Frederick Law Olmstead *submitted* his design *for* Central Park *in* New York *during* 1857").

One possible path for the future may seek to exploit further the implications of collaborative database creation. A database, as we have seen, can be set up in such a way as to allow multiple users access to the insert mechanisms of the system. The challenges proposed by this possibility are substantial, since the robustness of a system largely depends upon its consistency. Enforceable rules mechanisms (far above the level of mere transaction management) would need to be devised to ensure such consistency. The successful employment of such systems in humanistic contexts, however, would expand the possibilities of knowledge representation considerably. Since the data would enter into the system from a number of different sources, the logical statements that would flow from that ontology would necessarily exceed the knowledge of any one individual. The power of relational databases to enable the serendipitous apprehension of relationships would be that much more increased.

There is, of course, ample precedent for using complex, collaboratively managed data structures in humanistic inquiry. The earliest concordances were nominally produced to assist scholars in locating passages in the Bible, and one of the earliest uses of computers in humanistic study was a concordance of Thomas Aquinas. In both cases, the ultimate goal was not efficient retrieval, but interpretative insight. It only seems appropriate that after we have designed and implemented relational systems, and reaped the benefits of the efficiencies they grant, we consider the role they may play in the varied pursuits which have descended from what was once called – appropriately – the higher criticism.

Notes

1   Entity Relationship Modeling (developed by Peter Chen in the mid-1970s) is by far the most popular diagramming notation; even people unacquainted with formal methodologies will often adopt something like it when working through an initial design. Unfortunately, there is no standard outlining the precise notation (and thus enabling designers to communicate in a common format). Other, perhaps more sophisticated notations include *Object-Role Modeling* (ORM) and (for object-oriented database design) *Unified Modeling Language* (UML). See Halpin (2001).

2   Some database systems can generate a unique value for each record in the entire database. While this ensures an additional level of integrity useful (and perhaps even requisite) for other aspects of database management, it is not strictly necessary for the relational model as such.

3   SQL is specified in a standards document first issued by the American National Standards Institute in 1983, later revised in 1992, and again in 1999. While this standard has gone a long way toward creating a common tongue among database programmers, companies and developer groups that create RDBMSs continue to introduce subtle dialectical differences between implementations. Fortunately, these differences are relatively minor; the programmer searching for a particular semantic construct in one implementation will usually be able to find its counterpart in another with relative ease.

4   PostgreSQL (available at <http://www.postgresql.org>) is an open source application that can be modified and distributed freely (in source or binary form) under the terms of the BSD License. While it is intended for Unix-like systems (Linux, Solaris, AIX,* etc.), PostgreSQL can be run under Microsoft Windows using the Cygwin tools (available at <http://www.cygwin.com>). See Geschwinde (2001) and Stinson (2001).

5   The creation of unique values for use as primary keys is one of the areas in which RDBMSs differ the most, and most databases provide facilities for ensuring uniqueness that amount to extensions to the SQL-92 standard. Such is the case with the PostgreSQL sequence construct and with, for example, MySQL's use of the (somewhat less flexible) AUTO_INCREMENT keyword.

6   In PostgreSQL, the command for creating a database is simply createdb [database name]. The interactive command interpreter can be launched with pgsql [database name]. While it is possible to build up a schema by entering commands one line at a time into the interpreter, the more common method is to use the interpreter's built-in command for importing a file containing SQL commands.

7   All the major RDBMSs provide some level of built-in transaction management to prevent concurrent users from executing incompatible commands.

8   DBI-style modules exist for all the major scripting languages, including Python, Ruby, and Tcl.

9   Most of the major scripting languages have modules (usually intended to be used with the Apache web server) that allow the target interpreter to be used in the same manner.

10 PHP does provide facilities for moving the bulk of the programming logic into separate libraries on the server – a facility that can at least help to minimize the effect of embedding code in web pages.

11 The most famous hierarchical database system was undoubtedly IMS (Information Management System). This highly successful product, developed jointly by IBM and North American Rockwell in the late 1960s, was the dominant DBMS for commercial accounting and inventory for many years (Elmasri and Navanthe 1994). Its design – and even more so, the design of its query language, DL/1 – had a substantial influence on the development of later systems.

REFERENCES FOR FURTHER READING

Bowman, J. S., et al. (1999). *The Practical SQL Handbook*. Reading, MA: Addison-Wesley.

Codd, E. F. (1970). A Relational Model of Data for Large Shared Data Banks. *Communications of the Association for Computing Machinery* 13: 377–87.

Date, C. J. (2001). *The Database Relational Model: A Retrospective Review and Analysis*. Reading: Addison-Wesley.

Elmasri, R. and S. Navanthe (1994). *Fundamentals of Database Systems*. Redwood City: Benjamin/Cummings.

Geschwinde, E. (2001). *PostgreSQL Developer's Handbook*. Indianapolis: SAMS.

Halpin, T. (2001). *Information Modeling and Relational Databases: From Conceptual Analysis to Logical Design*. San Francisco: Morgan-Kaufmann.

Hunter, L. (1990). Fact – Information – Data – Knowledge: Databases as a Way of Organizing Knowledge. *Literary and Linguistic Computing* 5: 49–57.

Postgresql. Vers. 7.2.3. Accessed April 22, 2004. At <http://www.postgresql.org>.

Stinson, B. (2001). *PostgreSQL Essential Reference*. Indianapolis: New Riders.

16

Marking Texts of Many Dimensions

Jerome McGann

Bring out number weight & measure in a year of dearth.
William Blake

A sign is something by knowing which we know something more.
C. S. Peirce

Introduction: What is Text?

Although "text" has been a "Keyword" in clerical and even popular discourse for more than fifty years, it did not find a place in Raymond Williams's important (1976) book *Keywords*. This strange omission may perhaps be explained by the word's cultural ubiquity and power. In that lexicon of modernity Williams called the "Vocabulary of Culture and Society," "text" has been the "one word to rule them all." Indeed, the word "text" became so shape-shifting and meaning-malleable that we should probably label it with Tolkien's full rubrication: "text" has been, and still is, the "one word to rule them all and in the darkness bind them."

We want to keep in mind that general context when we address the issues of digitized texts, text markup, and electronic editing, which are our specialized concerns here. As we lay foundations for translating our inherited archive of cultural materials, including vast corpora of paper-based materials, into digital depositories and forms, we are called to a clarity of thought about textuality that most people, even most scholars, rarely undertake.

Consider the phrase "marked text," for instance. How many recognize it as a redundancy? All text is marked text, as you may see by reflecting on the very text you are now reading. As you follow this conceptual exposition, watch the physical embodiments that shape the ideas and the process of thought. Do you see the typeface, do you recognize it? Does it *mean* anything to you, and if not, why not? Now scan away (as you keep reading) and take a quick measure of the general page layout: the font sizes, the characters per line, the lines per page, the leading, the headers, footers, margins. And there is so much more to be seen, registered, understood simply at the documentary level of your reading: paper, ink, book design, or the markup that controls not the documentary status of the text but its linguistic status. What would you be seeing and reading if I were addressing you in Chinese, Arabic, Hebrew – even Spanish or German? What would you be seeing and reading if this text had been printed, like Shakespeare's sonnets, in 1609?

We all know the ideal reader of these kinds of traditional documents. She is an actual person, like the texts this person reads and studies. He writes about her readings and studies under different names, including Randall McLeod, Randy Clod, Random Cloud, etc. She is the Dupin of the textual mysteries of our exquisite and sophisticated bibliographical age.

Most important to realize, for this book's present purposes, is that digital markup schemes do not easily – perhaps do not even *naturally* – map to the markup that pervades paper-based texts. Certainly this is the case for every kind of electronic markup currently in use: from simple ASCII, to any inline SGML derivative, to the recent approaches of standoff markup (see Berrie website; Thompson and McKelvie 1997). The symptoms of this discrepancy are exemplified in the AI (Artificial Intelligence) community's struggles to simulate the complex processes of natural language and communicative exchange. Stymied of success in achieving that goal, these efforts have nonetheless been singularly fruitful for giving us a clearer view of the richness and flexibility of traditional textual machineries.

How, then, are traditional texts marked? If we could give an exhaustive answer to that question we would be able to simulate them in digital forms. We cannot complete an answer for two related reasons: first, the answer would have to be framed from within the discourse field of textuality itself; and second, that framework is dynamic, a continually emerging function of its own operations, including its explicitly self-reflexive operations. This is not to say that markup and theories of markup must be "subjective." (It is also not to say – see below – that they must *not be* subjective.) It *is* to say that they are and must be social, historical, and dialectical, and that some forms have greater range and power than others, and that some are useful exactly because they seek to limit and restrict their range for certain special purposes.

Autopoietic Systems and Co-dependency

Describing the problems of electronic texts in her book *Electronic Texts in the Humanities*, Susan Hockey laconically observes that "There is no obvious unit of language" (2000: 20). Hockey is reflecting critically on the ordinary assumption that this unit is the word. Language scholars know better. Words can be usefully broken down into more primitive parts and therefore understood as constructs of a second or even higher order. The view is not unlike the one continually encountered by physicists who search out basic units of matter. Our analytic tradition inclines us to understand that forms of all kinds are "built up" from "smaller" and more primitive units, and hence to take the self-identity and integrity of these parts, and the whole that they comprise, for objective reality.

Hockey glances at this problem of the text-unit in order to clarify the difficulties of creating electronic texts. To achieve that, we instruct the computer to identify (the) basic elements of natural language text and we try to ensure that the identification has no ambiguities. In natural language, however, the basic unit – indeed, all divisioning of any kind – is only procedurally determinate. The units are arbitrary. More, the arbitrary units themselves can have no absolute self-identity. Natural language is rife with redundancy and ambiguity at every unit and level and throughout its operating relations. A long history of analytic procedures has evolved certain sets of best practices in the study of language and communicative action, but even in a short run, terms and relations of analysis have changed.

Print and manuscript technology represent efforts to mark natural language so that it can be preserved and transmitted. It is a technology that constrains the shapeshiftings of language, which is itself a special-purpose system for coding human communication. Exactly the same can be said of electronic encoding systems. In each case constraints are installed in order to facilitate operations that would otherwise be difficult or impossible. In the case of a system like the Text Encoding Initiative (TEI), the system is designed to "disambiguate" entirely the materials to be encoded.

The output of TEI's markup constraints differs radically from the output generated by the constraints of manuscript and print technology. Whereas redundancy and ambiguity are expelled from TEI, they are preserved – are *marked* – in manuscript and print. While print and manuscript markups don't "copy" the redundancies of natural language, they do construct systems that are sufficiently robust to develop and generate equivalent types of redundancy. This capacity is what makes manuscript and print encoding systems so much more resourceful than any electronic encoding systems currently in use. ("Natural language" is the most complex and powerful reflexive coding system that we know of.)[1]

Like biological forms and all living systems, not least of all language itself, print and manuscript encoding systems are organized under a horizon of co-dependent relations. That is to say, print technology – I will henceforth use that term as shorthand for both print and manuscript technologies – is a system that codes (or simulates) what are known as autopoietic systems. These are classically described in the following terms:

> If one says that there is a machine M in which there is a feedback loop through the environment so that the effects of its output affect its input, one is in fact talking about a larger machine M^1 which includes the environment and the feedback loop in its defining organization. (Maturana and Varela 1980: 78)

Such a system constitutes a closed topological space that "continuously generates and specifies its own organization through its operation as a system of production of its own components, and does this in an endless turnover of components" (Maturana and Varela 1980: 79). Autopoietic systems are thus distinguished from allopoietic systems, which are Cartesian and which "have as the product of their functioning something different from themselves" (1980: 80).

In this context, all coding systems appear to occupy a peculiar position. Because "coding ... represents the interactions of [an] observer" with a given system, the mapping stands apart from "the observed domain" (Maturana and Varela 1980: 135). Coding is a function of "the space of human design" operations, or what is classically called "hetero-poietic" space. Positioned thus, coding and markup appear allopoietic.

As machines of simulation, however, coding and markup (print or electronic) are not like most allopoietic systems (cars, flashlights, a road network, economics). Coding functions emerge *as code* only within an autopoietic system that has evolved those functions as essential to the maintenance of its life (its dynamic operations). Language and print technology (and electronic technology) are second- and third-order autopoietic systems – what McLuhan famously, expressively, if also somewhat mislead-ingly, called "extensions of man." Coding mechanisms – proteins, print technology – are generative components of the topological space they serve to maintain. They are folded within the autopoietic system like membranes in living organisms, where distinct components realize and execute their extensions of themselves.

This general frame of reference is what makes Maturana and Varela equate the "origin" of such systems with their "constitution" (1980: 95). This equation means that co-dependency pervades an autopoietic structure of relations. All components of the system arise (so to speak) simultaneously and they perform integrated functions. The system's life is a morphogenetic passage characterized by various dynamic mutations and transform-ations of the local system components. The purpose or goal of these processes is autop-oietic – self-maintenance through self-transformation – and their basic element is not a system component but the relation (co-dependence) that holds the mutating components in changing states of dynamic stability. The states generate measurable co-dependency functions both in their periods (or basins) of stability and in their unique moments of catastrophic change.

Marking the Text: A Necessary Distinction

At the 2002 Extreme Markup Conference, Michael Sperberg-McQueen offered these observations on the problem of overlapping structures for SGML-based markup systems.

> It is an interesting problem because it is the biggest problem remaining in the residue. If we have a set of quantitative observations, and we try to fit a line to them, it is good practice to look systematically at the difference between the values predicted by our equation (our theory) and the values actually observed; the set of these differences is the residue. . . . In the context of SGML and XML, overlap is a residual problem.[2]

But in any context *other than* SGML and XML, this formulation is a play of wit, a kind of joke – as if one were now to say that the statistical deviations produced by Newtonian mathematical calculations left a "residue" of "interesting" matters to be cleared up by further, deeper calculations. But those matters are not *residual*, they are the hem of a quantum garment.

My own comparison is itself a kind of joke, of course, for an SGML model of the world of textualities pales in comprehensiveness before the Newtonian model of the physical world. But the outrageousness of the comparison in each case helps to clarify the situation. No autopoietic process or form can be simulated under the horizon of a structural model like SGML, not even topic maps. We see this very clearly when we observe the inability of a derivative model like TEI to render the forms and functions of traditional textual documents. The latter, which deploy markup codes themselves, supply us with simulations of language as well as of many other kinds of semeiotic processes, as Peirce called them. Textualized documents restrict and modify, for various kinds of reflexive purposes, the larger semeiotic field in which they participate. Nonetheless, the procedural constraints that traditional textualities lay upon the larger semeiotic field that they model and simulate are far more pragmatic, in a full Peircean sense, than the electronic models that we are currently deploying.

Understanding how traditional textual devices function is especially important now when we are trying to imagine how to optimize our new digital tools. Manuscript and print technologies – graphical design in general – provide arresting models for information technology tools, especially in the context of traditional humanities research and education needs. To that end we may usefully begin by making an elementary distinction between the archiving and the simulating functions of textual (and, in general, semeiotic) systems. Like gene codes, traditional textualities possess the following as one of their essential characteristics: that as part of their simulation and generative processes, they make (of) themselves a record of those processes. Simulating and record keeping, which are co-dependent features of any autopoietic or semeiotic system, can be distinguished for various reasons and purposes. A library processes traditional texts by treating them strictly as records. It saves things and makes them accessible. A poem, by contrast, processes textual records as a field of dynamic simulations. The one is a machine of memory and information, the other a machine of creation and reflection. Each may be taken as an index of a polarity that characterizes all semeoitic or autopoietic systems. Most texts – for instance, this chapter you are reading now – are fields that draw upon the influence of both of those polarities.

The power of traditional textualities lies exactly in their ability to integrate those different functions within the same set of coding elements and procedures.

SGML and its derivatives are largely, if not strictly, coding systems for storing and accessing records. They possess as well certain analytic functions that are based in the premise that text is an "ordered hierarchy of context objects." This conception of textuality is plainly non-comprehensive. Indeed, its specialized understanding of "text" reflects the pragmatic goal of such a markup code: to store objects (in the case of TEI, textual objects) so that they can be quickly accessed and searched for their informational content – or more strictly, for certain parts of that informational content (the parts that fall into a hierarchical order modeled on a linguistic analysis of the structure of a book).

These limitations of electronic markup codes are not to be lamented, but for humanist scholars they are to be clearly understood. A markup code like TEI creates a record of a traditional text in a certain form. Especially important to see is that, unlike the textual fields it was designed to mark up, TEI is an allopoietic system. Its elements are unambiguously delimited and identified *a priori*, its structure of relations is precisely fixed, it is non-dynamical, and it is focused on objects that stand apart from itself. Indeed, it defines what it marks not only *as* objective, but as objective in exactly the unambiguous terms of the system's *a priori* categories. This kind of machinery will therefore serve only certain, very specific, purposes. The autopoietic operations of textual fields – operations especially pertinent to the texts that interest humanities scholars – lie completely outside the range of an order like the TEI.

For certain archival purposes, then, structured markup will serve. It does not unduly interfere with, or forbid implementing, some of the searching and linking capacities that make digital technology so useful for different types of comparative analysis. Its strict formality is abstract enough to permit implementation within higher-order formalizations. In these respects it has greater flexibility than a stand-off approach to text markup, which is more difficult to integrate into a dispersed online network of different kinds of materials. All that having been recognized and said, however, these allopoietic text-processing systems cannot access or display the autopoietic character of textual fields. Digital tools have yet to develop models for displaying and replicating the self-reflexive operations of bibliographical tools, which alone are operations for thinking and communicating – which is to say, for transforming data into knowledge.

We have to design and build digital environments for those purposes. A measure of their capacity and realization will be whether they can integrate data-function mechanisms like TEI into their higher-order operations. To achieve that will entail, I believe, the deployment of dynamic, topological models for mapping the space of digital operations. But these models will have to be reconceived, as one can see by reflecting on a remark about textual interpretation that Stanley Fish liked to make years ago. He would point out that he was able to treat even the simplest text – road signage, for example – as a poem and thus develop from his own "response" and commentary its autopoietic potential. The remark underscores a basic and almost entirely neglected (undertheorized) feature of discourse fields: that to "read" them – to read "in" them at any point – one must regard what we call "the text" and "the reader" as co-dependent agents in the field. You can't have one without the other.

Fish's observation, therefore, while true, signals a widespread theoretical and methodological weakness in our conceptions of textuality, traditional or otherwise. This approach figures "text" as a heuristic abstraction drawn from the larger field of discourse. The word "text" is used in various ways by different people – Barthes's understanding is not the same as a TEI understanding – but in any case the term frames attention on the linguistic dimension of a discourse field. Books and literary works, however, organize themselves along multiple dimensions of which the linguistic is only one.

Modeling digital simulations of a discourse field requires that a formal set of dimensions be specified for the field. This is what TEI provides *a priori*, though the provision, as we know, is minimal. Our received scholarly traditions have in fact passed down to us an understanding of such fields that is both far more complex and reasonably stable. Discourse fields, our textual condition, regularly get mapped along six dimensions (see below, and Appendix B). Most important of all in the present context, however, are the implications of cognizing a discourse field as autopoietic. In that case the field measurements will be taken by "observers" positioned within the field itself. That intramural location of the field interpreter is in truth a logical consequence of the co-dependent character of the field and its components. "Interpretation" is not undertaken from a position outside the field; it is an essential part of a field's emergence and of any state that its emergence might assume.

This matter is crucial to understand when we are reaching for an adequate formalizing process for textual events like poetry or other types of orderly but discontinuous phenomena. René Thom explains very clearly why topological models are preferable to linear ones in dynamic systems:

> it must not be thought that a linear structure is necessary for storing or transmitting information (or, more precisely, significance); it is possible that a language, a semantic model, consisting of topological forms could have considerable advantages from the point of view of deduction, over the linear language that we use, although this idea is unfamiliar to us. Topological forms lend themselves to a much richer range of combinations . . . than the mere juxtaposition of two linear sequences. (Thom 1975: 145)

These comments distinctly recall Peirce's exploration of existential graphs as sites of logical thinking. But Thom's presentation of topological models does not conceive field spaces that are autopoietic, which seems to have been Peirce's view. Although Thom's approach generally eschews practical considerations in favor of theoretical clarity, his models assume that they will operate on data carried into the system from some external source. If Thom's "data" come into his studies in a theoretical form, then, they have been theorized in traditional empirical terms. The topological model of a storm may therefore be taken either as the description of the storm and/or a prediction of its future behavior. But when a model's data are taken to arise co-dependently with all the other components of its system, a very different "result" ensues. Imagined as applied to textual autopoiesis, a topological approach carries itself past an analytic description or prediction over to a form of demonstration or enactment.

The view taken here is that no textual field can exist as such without "including" in itself the reading or measurement of the field, which specifies the field's dataset from within. The composition of a poem is the work's first reading, which *in that event* makes a call upon others. An extrinsic analysis designed to specify or locate a poetic field's self-reflexiveness commonly begins from the vantage of the rhetorical or the social dimension of the text, where the field's human agencies (efficient causes) are most apparent. The past century's fascination with structuralist approaches to cultural phenomena produced, as we know, a host of analytic procedures that chose to begin from a consideration of formal causation, and hence from either a linguistic or a semiotic vantage. Both procedures are analytic conventions based in empirical models.

Traditional textuality provides us with autopoietic models that have been engineered as effective analytic tools. The codex is the greatest and most famous of these. Our problem is imagining ways to recode them for digital space. To do that we have to conceive formal models for autopoietic processes that can be written as computer software programs.

Field Autopoiesis: from IVANHOE to 'Patacriticism

Let's recapitulate the differences between book markup and TEI markup. TEI defines itself as a two-dimensional generative space mapped as (1) a set of defined "content objects" (2) organized within a nested tree structure. The formality is clearly derived from an elementary structuralist model of language (a vocabulary + a syntax, or a semantic + a syntagmatic dimension). In the SGML/TEI extrusion, both dimensions are fixed and their relation to each other is defined as arbitrary rather than co-dependent. The output of such a system is thus necessarily symmetrical with the input (cf. Curie's principle of causes and effects). Input and output in a field of traditional textuality works differently. Even in quite restricted views, as we know, the operations of natural language and communicative exchange generate incommensurable effects. The operations exhibit behavior that topologists track as bifurcation or even generalized catastrophe, whereby an initial set of structural stabilities produces morphogenetic behaviors and conditions that are unpredictable.[3] This essential feature of "natural language" – which is to say, of the discourse fields of communicative exchange – is what makes it so powerful, on one hand, and so difficult to model and formalize, on the other.

In these circumstances, models like TEI commend themselves to us because they can be classically quantified for empirical – numerable – results. But as Thom observed long ago, there is no such thing as "a quantitative theory of catastrophes of a dynamical system" like natural language. To achieve such a theory, he went on to say, "it would be necessary to have a good theory of integration on function spaces" (Thom 1975: 321), something that Thom could not conceive.

That limitation of qualitative mathematical models did not prevent Thom from vigorously recommending their study and exploration. He particularly criticized the widespread scientific habit of "tak[ing] the main divisions of science, the[ir] taxonomy... as given a priori" rather than trying to re-theorize taxonomics as such (1975: 322). In this frame of reference we can see (1) that textualization in print technology is a qualitative (rather than a taxonomic) function of natural language, and (2) that textualization integrates function spaces through demonstrations and enactments rather than descriptions. This crucial understanding – that print textuality is not language but an operational (praxis-based) theory of language – has stared us in the face for a long time, but seeing we have not seen. It has taken the emergence of electronic textualities, and in particular operational theories of natural language like TEI, to expose the deeper truth about print and manuscript texts. SGML and its derivatives freeze (rather than integrate) the function spaces of discourse fields by reducing the field components to abstract forms – what Coleridge called "fixities and definites." This approach will serve when the object is to mark textual fields for storage and access.

Integration of dynamic functions will not emerge through such abstract reductions, however. To develop an effective model of an autopoietic system requires an analysis that is built and executed "in the same spirit that the author writ." That formulation by Alexander Pope expresses, in an older dialect, what we have called in this century "the uncertainty principle," or the co-dependent relation between measurements and phenomena. An agent defines and interprets a system from within the system itself – at what Dante Gabriel Rossetti called "an inner standing point." What we call "scientific objectivity" is in one sense a mathematical function; in another, it is a useful method for controlling variables. We use it when we study texts as if they were objective things rather than dynamic autopoietic fields.

Traditional textual conditions facilitate textual study at an inner standing point because all the activities can be carried out – can be represented – in the same field space, typically, in a bibliographical field. Subject and object meet and interact in the same dimensional space – a situation that gets reified for us when we read books or write about them. Digital operations, however, introduce a new and more abstract space of relations into the study-field of textuality. This abstract space brings the possibility of new and in certain respects greater analytic power to the study of traditional texts. On the downside, however, digitization – at least to date, and typically – situates the critical agent outside the field to be mapped and re-displayed. Or – to put this crucial point more precisely (since no measurement has anything more than a relative condition of objectivity) – digitization situates the critical agent within levels of the textual field's dimensionalities that are difficult to formalize bibliographically.

To exploit the power of those new formalizations, a digital environment has to expose its subjective status and operation. (Like all scientific formalities, digital procedures are "objective" only in relative terms.) In the present case – the digital marking of textual fields – this means that we will want to build tools that foreground the subjectivity of any measurements that are taken and displayed. Only in this way will the autopoietic character of the textual field be accurately realized. The great gain that comes with such a tool is the ability to specify – to measure, display, and eventually to compute and transform – an autopoietic structure at what would be, in effect, quantum levels.

A series of related projects to develop such tools is under way at University of Virginia's Speculative Computing Laboratory (Speclab). The first of these, *IVANHOE*, is an online gamespace being built for the imaginative reconstruction of traditional texts and discourse fields. Players enter these works through a digital display space that encourages players to alter and transform the textual field. The game rules require that transformations be made as part of a discourse field that emerges dynamically through the changes made to a specified initial set of materials.[4]

As the *IVANHOE* project was going forward, a second, related project called *Time Modelling* was being taken up by Bethany Nowviskie and Johanna Drucker. The project was begun "to bring visualization and interface design into the early content modeling phase" of projects like IVANHOE, which pursue interpretation through transformational and even deformative interactions with the primary data. IVANHOE's computer is designed to store the game players' performative interpretational moves and then produce algorithmically generated analyses of the moves after the fact. The chief critical function thus emerges after-the-fact, in a set of human reflections on the differential patterns that the computerized analyses expose. In the *Time Modelling* device, however, the performative and the critical actions are much more closely integrated because the human is actively involved in a deliberated set of digital transformations. The *Time Modelling* device gives users a set of design functions for reconstructing a given lineated timeline of events in terms that are subjective and hypothetical. The specified field of event-related data is brought forward for transformation through editing and display mechanisms that emphasize the malleability of the initial set of field relations. The project stands, conceptually, somewhere between design programs (with their sets of tools for making things) and complex websites like *The Rossetti Archive* (with their hypertextual datasets organized for on-the-fly search and analysis). It is a set of editing and display tools that allows users to design their own hypothetical (re)formulations of a given dataset.

The frankly experimental character of *Time Modelling*'s data (re)constructions has led to an important reimagining of the original IVANHOE project. From the outset of that project we intended to situate the "interpreter" within the discourse field that was the subject of interpretive transformation. Our initial conception was toward what we called "Ultimate IVANHOE," that is, toward a playspace that would be controlled by emergent consciousness software. With the computer an active agent in an IVANHOE session, players could measure and compare their own understandings of their actions against a set of computer generated views. This prospect for IVANHOE's development remains, but the example of *Time Modelling* exposed another way to situate the human interpreter at an inner standing point of an autopoietic system.

If 'Pataphysics is, in the words of its originator, "the science of exceptions," the project here is to reconceive IVANHOE under the rubric of 'Patacriticism, or the theory of subjective interpretation. The theory is implemented through what is here called the dementianal method, which is a procedure for marking the autopoietic features of textual fields. The method works on the assumption that such features characterize what topologists call a field of general catastrophe. The dementianal method marks the dynamic changes in autopoietic fields much as Thom's topological models allow one to map forms of catastrophic behavior. The 'Patacritical model differs from Thom's models because the measurements of the autopoietic field's behaviors are generated from within the field itself, which only emerges as a field through the action of the person interpreting – that is to say, marking and displaying – the field's elements and sets of relations. The field arises co-dependently with the acts that mark and measure it. In this respect we wish to characterize its structure as dementianal rather than dimensional.

As the device is presently conceived, readers engage autopoietic fields along three behavior dementians: *transaction, connection, resonance*. A common *transaction* of a page space moves diagonally down the page, with regular deviations for horizontal line transactions left to right margin, from the top or upper left to the bottom at lower right. Readers regularly violate that pattern in indefinite numbers of ways, often being called to deviance by how the field appears marked by earlier agencies. *Connections* assume, in the same way, multiple forms. Indeed, the primal act of autopoietic connection is the identification or location of a textual element to be "read." In this sense, the *transaction* of an autopoietic field is a function of the marking of *connections* of various kinds, on one hand, and of *resonances* on the other. *Resonances* are signals that call attention to a textual element as having a field value – a potential for connectivity – that appears *and* appears unrealized.

Note that each of these behavior dementians exhibit co-dependent relations. The field is transacted as connections and resonances are marked; the connections and resonances are continually emergent functions of each other; and the marking of dementians immediately reorders the space of the field, which itself keeps re-emerging under the sign of the marked alteration of the dynamic fieldspace and its various elements.

These behavioral dementians locate an autopoietic syntax, which is based in an elementary act or agenting event: G. Spencer Brown's "law of calling," which declares that a distinction can be made. From that law comes the possibility that elements of identities can be defined. They emerge with the co-dependent emergence of the textual field's control dimensions, which are the field's autopoietic semantics. (For further discussion of these matters see below, Appendix A and Appendix B.)

Writing and Reading in Autopoietic Fields

This 'Patacritical approach to textual dementias is a meta-theory of textual fields, a pragmatistic conception of how to expose discontinuous textual behaviors ("natural language" so called, or what Habermas (1984) has better called "communicative action"). Integration of the dynamic functions begins not by abstracting the theory away from a target object – that is, the method of a taxonomic methodology – but by integrating the meta-theoretical functions within the discourse space itself.

Informational discourse fields function well precisely by working to limit redundancy and concurrent textual relations. Because poetry – or imaginative textuality broadly conceived – postulates much greater freedom of expressive exchange, it exhibits a special attraction for anyone wishing to study the dynamics of textuality. Aristotle's studies of semiotic systems preserve their foundational character because they direct their attention to autopoietic rather than allopoietic discourse fields. His studies pursue a taxonomy for the dynamic process of making and exchanging (remaking) simulations.

Plato's dialogues, by contrast, situate – or, more precisely, generate – their critical reflections at a standing point inside the textualities they are themselves unfolding. In this respect they have much in common with Wittgenstein's critical colloquies in the *Philosophical Investigations* or with Montaigne's *Essais*. But the dynamic play of even these textual fields remain, from the point of view of their readers, exemplary exercises. This situation prevails in all modes of critical reflection which assume to preserve the integrity and self-identity of the textual fields they study. Two forms of critical reflection regularly violate the sanctity of such self-contained textual spaces: translation and editing. The idea that an object of criticism like a textual field *is* an object can be maintained either as an heuristic procedure or as an ontological illusion. Consequently, acts of translation and editing are especially useful forms of critical reflection because they so clearly invade and change their subjects in material ways. To undertake either, you can scarcely *not* realize the performative – even the *deformative* – character of your critical agency.

At this point let me exemplify the general markup model for autopoietic textualities. This comes as the following hypothetical passage through an early poem by Robert Creeley, "The Innocence." Because imaginative textuality is, in this view, an exemplary kind of autopoietic process, any poetical work would do for a narrative demonstration. I choose "The Innocence" because it illustrates what Creeley and others called "field poetics." As such, it is especially apt for clarifying the conception of the autopoietic model of textuality being offered here. "Composition by field" poetics has been much discussed, but for present purposes it suffices to say that it conceives poetry as a self-unfolding discourse. "The poem" is the "field" of action and energy generated in the poetic transaction of the field that the poem itself exhibits. "Composition by field," whose theoretical foundations may be usefully studied through Charles Olson's engagements with contemporary philosophy and science, comprised both a method for understanding (rethinking) the entire inheritance of poetry, and a program for contemporary and future poetic discourse (its writing and its reading).

The text chosen is taken from Donald Allen's famous anthology (first published in 1960) *The New American Poetry* in its 1999 University of California Press reprinting.

The Innocence

Looking to the sea, it is a line
of unbroken mountains.

It is the sky.
It is the ground. There
we live, on it.

It is a mist
now tangent to another
quiet. Here the leaves
come, there
is the rock in evidence

or evidence.
What I come to do
is partial, partially kept

Before tracing a model for this poetic field we want to bear two matters in mind. First, the field we are transacting is localized in relation to this documentary instance of "the text." One of the most persistent and misleading procedures in traditional hermeneutics is to take the object of study as something not only abstract and disembodied, but as something lying outside the field space – itself specific and material – of the act of critical representation. Second, the sequence of readings (below) consciously assumes a set of previous readings whereby certain elementary forms of order – by no means insignificant forms – have been integrated into the respective textual dementians. All such forms are extrusions from the elementary semiotic move, which is Spencer Brown's basic law of form: that a distinction can be drawn (*as* a dementian, or within and between dementians). Thus the readings below assume that each dementian is oriented to a set of established formal objects which get called and then crossed (transformed) in the transaction of the field.

That said, let me transact the poetic field through the initial textual model supplied above.

A First Reading: I mark the following elements in the first line group (and in that act I mark as well the presence of (a) lines and (b) line groups): "Looking" as a dangling participle; "it" (line 1) as ambiguously pronominal; "line" as a word play referencing (first) this line of verse I am transacting, and (second) a landscape of "unbroken mountains" (to be marked as such only with the marking of the final line in the group). All of these are defined (connected to the fieldspace) as textual elements with marked resonances (anticipations and clear if inchoate recollections) as well as several manifest, second-order connections (e.g., "sea," "line," and "mountains" as objects in a landscape).

Line group 2 emerges to connect a network of "it" words as well as to settle the dominance of a linguistic gravity field centered in the initially marked "landscape" (a linguistic dementian subdomain). As line group 3 continues to elaborate the "landscape field," several distinctly new elements emerge and get marked. They center in the words "tangent," "quiet," "evidence," the notable enjambment at the end of the line group, and the deictics "Here and "there." The first four resonate by the differences they make with the previous elements I had defined in my transaction of the field. The deictics connect back to the second linguistic dementian subdomain (the self-reflexive set of textual elements marked in line 1 as the dangling participle and the final word "line"). The fourth and last line group is itself marked as strongly resonant in itself because of the emergence within it of the unique "I" and the startling repetitions ("evidence," "partial"/ "partially").

So the field transaction is marked geometrically as a complete and continuous passage from upper left to lower right and proceeding line by line left to right. That passage of the textspace marks out two control dementians, linguistic and graphical, as well as several distinct basins of order within them. In the graphical dementian we see an array of marked words, lines, and line groups. In the linguistic dementian I have marked two distinct subdomains, one referential (the set of "landscape" semantics), one a subdomain of pure signifiers (proliferating from line 1 through the deictic markers "Here" and "there."

A Second Reading: I mark the title as strongly resonant and I find myself scanning the poem rather than reading it linearly, and marking elements unnoticed in the first reading. I re-mark the array of "it" words and connect all of them to the title, marking thereby another linguistic subdomain. I mark as resonant the striking idea of "a mist / now tangent to another / quiet," and I mark a distinction in the linguistic subdomain (of "landscape") between different sensory aspects of a "landscape." I mark as resonant the equally striking final sentence and the phrase "the rock in evidence // or evidence."

A Third Reading: This is a sequential transaction through the poem as in the first reading. It is largely devoted to marking connections between the various elements already marked with resonance values. The wordplay in "line" is marked as a strongly resonant locus of fieldspace connections across the several linguistic subdomains. This connective fieldspace is especially resonant as the connection between the words "line" and "tangent." I mark all of the previously marked textual elements as connected to each other in a broadly dispersed semiotic dementian because I am seeing that elements in different fieldspace dementians and domains (e.g., "mist" and "quiet") are connected to each other.

A Fourth Reading: A sequential reading leads to marking the final sentence as a dramatic locus of a rhetorical dementian in the fieldspace. The construction of the textspace is "What I come to do." The emergence of this idea allows me to mark the poem as a deliberated sequential organization that exposes itself in certain telling (marked) moments and textual elements: "Looking," "line," "tangent," the deictic words, the previously unmarked "we" (line 5), the enjambment between the third and fourth line groups. In all these I mark a rhetorical organization tied most centrally to the phrase "What I come to do." I mark that these marks unfold as a relation that must be seen as sequenced: "I" in the present tense here is always the present tense in the linguistic dementian of this work. Marking the verb tense in that way immediately produces the first, remarkable emergence in this reading process of the work's social dementian. "I" comes to write this poem, which is marked thereby as an event in the world and as objective as any material thing (these material things, the "landscape" things, first marked in the linguistic dementian). In that rhetorical dementian I mark as well a key element of this work's social dementian first marked in the linguistic dementian: the relation between the "we" and the "I." The phrase "is partial, partially kept" is marked now as an element in the social dementian of the textspace – as if one were to say, interpretatively, that the "doing" of the poem is only one event in a larger field that the poem is part of and points toward. My acts of marking the poem fall into both the local fieldspace and the larger discourse field marked by this local poetical field. And I further mark the social space by connecting the textspace to the book in which the text is printed – for that book (the polemic it made) marks this specific text in the strongest way. At this point the sixth dementian of the fieldspace begins to get marked, the material dementian. I mark three documentary features in particular: the placement of the text in the book, the organ of publication, the date of publication. I mark as well the fact that these material features of the work are, like the word "line," double-meaninged (or double-dementianed), having as well a clear placement in the work's social dementian as well.

A Fifth Reading: I mark new elements in the six marked dementians that emerge in a widespread process of subdividing and proliferating. Elements defined in one dementian or subdomain get marked in another (for instance, "I" began in the rhetorical, reappeared in the social, and now gets marked in all the other dementians as well); unmarked textual features, like the letter "t," get marked as resonant; the shape of the textspace from word to line to word group is marked as a linked set of spare elements. These additional markings lead to other, previously unseen and unmarked relations and elements. The spare graphical dementian gets linked to the linguistic dementian ("The Innocence") and to the social and rhetorical dementians (the graphical spareness is only markable in relation to the absent/present discourse field in which this poetical work stands and declares its comparative allegiance.

A Sixth Reading: This is a reading that poses significant theoretical and practical issues. Time-stamped two weeks after the previous readings, this reading was negotiated in my mind as I recalled the history of my readings of the poem. It is thus a reading to be digitally marked after-the-fact. Focused on the final line group, it also marks the entirety of the autopoietic field. The reading marks the "I" as a figure in the social dementian, the poet (Creeley) who composed the poem. In that linking, however, I as reader become linked to the linguistic "I" that is also a social "I." This linkage gets enforced by marking a set of "partial" agents who "come to do" part of the continuous marking of the autopoietic field. (Creeley does what he does, I do what I do, and we both inhabit a space resonant with other, as yet unspecified, agents.)

Conclusion

What we theorize here and propose for a digital practice is a science of exceptions, a science of imaginary (subjective) solutions. The markup technology of the codex has evolved an exceedingly successful instrument for that purpose. Digital technology ought to be similarly developed. Organizing our received humanities materials as if they were simply information depositories, computer markup as currently imagined handicaps or even baffles altogether our moves to engage with the well-known dynamic functions of textual works. An alternative approach to these matters through a formal reconception of textspace as topological offers distinct advantages. Because this space is autopoietic, however, it does not have what mathematicians would normally call dimensionality. As autopoietic, the model we propose establishes and measures its own dimensions auto-telically, as part of its self-generative processes. Furthermore, space defined by pervasive co-dependencies means that any dimension specified for the system might be formally related to any other. This metamorphic capacity is what translates the concept of a dimension into the concept of a dementian.

This model of text-processing is open-ended, discontinuous, and non-hierarchical. It takes place in a fieldspace that is exposed when it is mapped by a process of "reading." A digital processing program is to be imagined and built that allows one to mark and store these maps of the textual fields and then to study the ways they develop and unfold and how they compare with other textual mappings and transactions. Constructing textualities as field spaces of these kinds short-circuits a number of critical predilections that inhibit our received, commonsense wisdom about our textual condition. First of all, it escapes crippling interpretative dichotomies like text and reader, or textual "subjectiv-ity" and "objectivity." Reader-response criticism, so-called, intervened in that space of problems but only succeeded in reifying even further the primary distinctions. In this view of the matter, however, one sees that the distinctions are purely heuristic. The "text" we "read" is, in this view, an autopoietic event with which we interact and to which we make our own contributions. Every textual event is an emergence imbedded in and comprising a set of complex histories, some of which we each partially realize when we participate in those textual histories. Interestingly, these histories, in this view, have to be grasped as fields of action rather than as linear unfoldings. The fields are topological, with various emergent and dynamic basins of order, some of them linear and hierarchical, others not.

APPENDIX A: THE 'PATAPHYSICS OF TEXT AND FIELD MARKUP

Texts and their field spaces are autopoietic scenes of co-dependent emergence. As such, their primal state is dynamic and has been best characterized by G. Spencer Brown's *Laws of Form* (1969), where "the form of distinction" – the act of making indications by drawing a distinction – is taken as "given" and primal (1). This means that the elementary law is not the law of identity but the law of non-identity (so that we must say that "*a* equals *a* if and only if *a* does not equal *a*"). Identities emerge as distinctions are drawn and redrawn, and the acts of drawing out distinctions emerge as co-dependent responses to the field identities that the form of distinction calls to attention.

Spencer Brown supplies a formal demonstration of what Alfred Jarry called 'pataphysics and that he and his OULIPian inheritors demonstrated in forms of traditional textual practice (i.e., in forms of "literature"). 'Pataphysics is a general theory of autopoietic systems (i.e., a general theory of what we traditionally call "imaginative literature"), and *Laws of Form* is a specifically 'pataphysical event because it clearly gives logical priority to the unique act and practice of its own theoretical thought. The fifth "Chant" of Lautréa-mont's *Les chants de Maldoror*, Jarry's *Gestes et opinions du docteur Faustroll, 'pataphysicien*, and all the descendants of those self-conscious works – Laura Riding's stories are the earliest

English-language examples – are the "literary" equivalents of Spencer Brown's *Laws of Form*.

In this view of any systematics, the taxonomy of a system is a derivation of what Peirce called an initial abduction. The abduction is an hypothesis of the total semeiotic integrity of the system. The hypothesis is tested and transformed (internally as well as externally) in a dialectical process – ultimately endless – of representation and reflection.

APPENDIX B: CONTROL DEMENTIANS FOR

A 'PATACRITICISM OF TEXTUALITIES

The transaction of textual fields proceeds by a series of moves (field behaviors) that proliferate from an elementary modal distinction between what have been specified (above) as *connections* and *resonances*, which are the elementary behavioral forms of the textual *transaction*. These modes correspond to what traditional grammarians define as an indicative and a subjunctive verbal mood. (In this view, interrogative and interjective moods are derivatives of these two primary categories.) Emerging co-dependently with these behavioral dementians is an elementary taxonomy of control dementians that are called into form and then internally elaborated.

The history of textual studies has evolved a standard set of field formalities that may be usefully analyzed in six distinct parts. These correspond to an elemental set of dimensions for textual fields (or, in fields conceived as autopoietic systems, an elemental set of six dementians). These control dementians locate what grammarians designate as the semantics of a language.

Let it be said here that these behavioral and control dementians, like their allopoietic dimensions, comprise a set of categories that recommend themselves through an evolved history of previous use. Other dimensions (and dementians) might be proposed or imagined. However, since the proposals being advanced here are all conceived within a pragmatistic frame of reference, the categories bring with them the strong authority of a habitual usefulness.

The Linguistic Dimension/Dementian. This aspect of the textual condition has been the principal focus of attention in the West. It represents a high-order framework of conceptual markers or distinctions that unfold and multiply from an initial pair of categories, the semantic and the grammatical. The former is an elemental category, the latter is a relational one, and the two together epitomize the structure of co-dependency that pervades and in a sense defines all textual processes at every dimension. That is to say, neither marker or category has conceptual priority over the other, they generate meaning together in a co-dependent and dialectical process. However, to specify their co-dependence requires that one adopt a pragmatistic or performative approach such as we see in Maturana, Spencer Brown, and Peirce.

The Graphical/Auditional Dimension/Dementian. Some kind of graphical and/or auditional state of affairs is a prerequisite for any appearance or functional operation of a Linguistic Dimension, and that state must be formally constrained. In Western attempts to clarify language and textuality, these forms are defined in the systematic descriptors of morphology and phonology, which are co-dependent subcategories of the Linguistic Dimension.

This Graphical/Auditional Dimension comprises the set of a text's codes of materiality (as opposed to the specific material state of a particular document). In print and manuscript states, the dimension includes various subsets of bibliographical codes and paratexts: typography, layout, book design, and the vehicular components of those forms. (If we are considering oral texts, the material assumes auditional forms, which can have visual components as well.)

Documentary Dimension/Dementian. This comprises the physical incarnation – the "real presence," so to speak – of all the formal possibilities of the textual process. We recognize it as a bibliographical or palaeographical description of some specific object, or as a library or archival record of an object's historical passage (transmission history).

Note that this dimension does not simply constitute some brute chemical or physical thing – what Coleridge referred to when he spoke as the "object as object," which he called "fixed and dead." Coleridge's "object as object" is a negative abstraction – that's to say, a certain formal conception of the documentary dimension that sets it apart (*a priori*) from any place in a study or interpretation of textuality. A document can and – in any comprehensive approach to textuality – should be maintained as an integral function of the textual process.

A document is a particular object that incarnates and constrains a specific textual process. In terms of print and manuscript texts, it is a specific actualized state of the Graphical/Auditional Dimension.

Semiotic Dimension/Dementian. This dimension defines the limit state of any text's formal possibilities. It postulates the idea of the complete integration of all the elements and dynamic relations in a field of discourse. In this dimension we thus cognize a textual process in holistic terms. It is a purely formal perspective, however, and as such stands as the mirrored antithesis of the document *per se*, whose integrity is realized as a phenomenal event. The document is the image of the hypothesis of total form; it appears at (or as) a closure of the dynamic process set in perpetual motion by the hypothesis at the outset.

We register the semiotic dimension as a pervasiveness of patterned relations throughout the textual system – both within each part of the system and among the parts. The relations emerge in distinct types or modes: elements begin and end; they can be accumulated, partitioned, and replicated; they can be anchored somewhere, linked to other elements, and relayed through the system

The first of those late systems of analysis called by Herbert Simon "Sciences of the Artificial," the science of semiotics, labels itself as an heuristic mechanism. The pervasive order of a textual process's semiotic dimension thus emerges as a function of the formal categories, both system elements and system processes, that are consciously specified by the system's agents. Order is constructed from the systemic demand for order. As a result, the forms of order can be of any type – hierarchical or non-hierarchical, continuous or discontinuous.

Rhetorical Dimension/Dementian. The dominant form of this dimension is genre, which is a second-order set of textual forms. Genre calls into play poems, mathematical proofs, novels, essays, speeches, dramas, and so forth. The function of this dimension is to establish forms of readerly attention – to select and arrange textual materials of every kind in order to focus the interest of the reader (audience, user, listener) and establish a ground for response.

Readers and writers (speakers and listeners) are rhetorical functions. (Writers' first readers are themselves in their act of composition.) Bakhtin's celebrated studies of textual polyvalence and heteroglossia exemplify the operative presence of this textual dimension.

Social Dimension/Dementian. This is the dimension of a textual production and of reception histories. It is the dimension of the object as subject: that is to say, of a determinate set of textual elements arrayed under names like "writer," "printer," "publisher," "reader," "audience," "user." It is the dimension that exposes the temporality function which is an inalienable feature of all the dimensions of the textual condition.

The social dimension of textuality unfolds a schedule of the uses to which its works are put beyond what New Critics liked to call "the poem itself." It is the dimension in which the dynamic and non-self-identical character of textual works is most plainly disclosed.

In most traditional theories of textuality, the social dimension is not considered an intrinsic textual feature or function. Framed under the sign "context," it is seen as the environment in which texts and documents stand. Until the recent emergence of more holistic views of environments – notably in the work of Donald McKenzie – this way of seeing textuality's social dimension forced severe restrictions on our ability to comprehend and study the dynamic character of textual processes.

ACKNOWLEDGMENT

"The Innocence" by Robert Creeley is reprinted from *The Collected Poems of Robert Creeley, 1945–1975* with kind permission of the University of California Press and Robert Creeley.

Notes

1   See Maturana and Varela (1992).
2   "What Matters?" (at: <http://www.w3.org/People/cmsmcq/2002/whatmatters.html>).
3   As the terms in this sentence indicate, I am working in terms laid down thirty years ago by René Thom in his classic study *Structural Stability and Morphogenesis* (1975).
4   For essays describing IVANHOE see the Special issue of *TEXT Technology* devoted to it (vol. 12, no. 2, 2003).

REFERENCES FOR FURTHER READING

Allen, Donald (ed.) (1999). *The New American Poetry 1945–1960*, with a new Foreword. Berkeley and Los Angeles: University of California Press.

Bellman, Rickard (1961). *Adaptive Control Processes: A Guided Tour*. Princeton, NJ: Princeton University Press.

Berrie, Phillip William (1999). Just in Time Markup for Electronic Editions. Accessed April 19, 2004. At <http://idun.itsc.adfa.edu.au/ASEC/PWB_REPORT/Index.html>.

Birnbaum, David J. (2001). The Relationship between General and Specific DTDs: Criticizing TEI Critical Editions. *Markup Languages: Theory and Practice* 3,1: 17–53.

Bornstein, George and Teresa Tinkle (eds.) (1998). *The Iconic Page in Manuscript, Print, and Digital Culture*. Ann Arbor: University of Michigan Press.

Brown, G. Spencer (1969). *Laws of Form*. London: George Allen and Unwin.

Buzzetti, Dino (2002). Digital Representation and the Text Model. *New Literary History* 33,1: 61–88.

Casati, Roberto and Achille C. Varzi (1999). *Parts and Places: The Structures of Spatial Representation*. Cambridge, MA: MIT Press.

Caton, Paul (2001). Markup's Current Imbalance. *Markup Languages: Theory and Practice* 3,1: 1–13.

Chandrasekaran, B., J. Glasgow, and N. H. Narayanan (eds.) (1995). *Diagrammatic Reasoning: Cognitive and Computational Perspective*. Cambridge, MA: MIT Press, and Menlo Park: AAAI Press.

Drucker, Johanna (1998). *Figuring the Word: Essays on Books, Writing, and Visual Poetics*. New York: Granary Books.

Elkins, James (1998). *On Pictures and Words that Fail Them*. Cambridge: Cambridge University Press.

——(1999). *The Domain of Images*. Ithaca, NY: Cornell University Press.

Engell, James and W. Jackson Bate (1983). *Samuel Taylor Coleridge. Biographia Literaria*, 2 vols. Princeton, NJ: Princeton University Press.

Fraenkel, Ernest (1960). *Les dessins trans-conscients de Stéphane Mallarmé, à propos de la typographie de* Un coup de dés, *avant-propos par Étienne Souriau* [Subconscious Drawings of Stéphane Mallarmé, in connection with the typography of *Un coup de dés*, foreword by Étienne Souriau]. Paris: Librairie Nizet.

Habermas, Jürgen (1984). *The Theory of Communicative Action*, tr. Thomas McCarthy. Boston: Beacon Press.

Hardwick, Charles (ed.) (1977). *Semiotic and Significs: The Correspondence between Charles S. Peirce and Victoria, Lady Welby*. Bloomington: Indiana University Press.

Hauser, Nathan and Christian Kloesel (eds.) (1992). *The Essential Peirce: Selected Philosophical Writings*, 2 vols. Bloomington: Indiana University Press.

Hockey, Susan (2000). *Electronic Texts in the Humanities*. Oxford: Oxford University Press.

Luhmann, Niklas (1998). *Observations on Modernity*, tr. William Whobrey. Stanford, CA: Stanford University Press.

Maturana, Humberto and Francisco Varela (1980). *Autopoiesis and Cognition: The Realization of Living*. Boston: D. Reidel.

——(1992). *The Tree of Knowledge: Biological Roots of Human Understanding*, tr. Robert Paolucci. New York: Random House.

McCarty, Willard (2002a). Computing the Embodied Idea: Modeling in the Humanities. *Körper – Verkörperung – Entkörperung / Body – Embodiment – Disembodiment*. 10. Internationaler Kongress, Deutsche Gesellschaft für Semiotik, Universität Kassel, July 19, 2002. At (http://www.kcl.ac.uk/humanities/cch/wlm/essays/kassel/).

——(2002b). Humanities Computing: Essential Problems, Experimental Practice. Accessed April 19, 2004. At <http://www.kcl.ac.uk/humanities/cch/wlm/essays/stanford/>.

McDonald, Peter D. and Michael Suarez, SJ (eds.) (2002). *Making Meaning: "Printers of the Mind" and Other Essays. D. F. McKenzie*. Amherst: University of Massachusetts Press.

McGann, Jerome (2001). *Radiant Textuality: Literature after the World Wide Web*. New York and London: Palgrave/St Martins.

——(ed.) (2004). The Complete Writings and Pictures of Dante Gabriel Rossetti. A Hypermedia Research Archive. Accessed April 19, 2004. At <http://jefferson.village.virginia.edu/rossetti/>.

McKenzie, D. F. (1986). *Bibliography and the Sociology of Texts: The Panizzi Lectures, 1985*. London: British Library.

McLuhan, Marshall (1964). *Understanding Media: The Extensions of Man*. New York: McGraw-Hill.

Mineau, G., B. Moulin, and J. Sowa (eds.) (1993). *Conceptual Graphs for Knowledge Representation*. Berlin: Springer-Verlag.

Omnès, Roland (1999). *Understanding Quantum Mechanics*. Princeton, NJ: Princeton University Press.

Shin, Sun-Joo (2002). *The Iconic Logic of Peirce's Graphs*. Cambridge, MA: MIT Press.

Simon, Herbert (1981). *The Sciences of the Artificial*, 2nd edn., rev. and enlarged. Cambridge, MA: MIT Press.

Sontag, Susan (ed.) (1982). *A Barthes Reader*. New York: Noonday Press.

Sperberg-McQueen, C. M. (2002). What Matters? At <http://www.w3.org/People/cmsmcq/2002/whatmatters.html>.

Sperberg-McQueen, C. M., Claus Huitfeldt, and Allen Renear (2000). Meaning and Interpretation of Markup. *Markup Languages* 2,3: 215–34.

Thom, René (1975). *Structural Stability and Morphogenesis: An Outline of a General Theory of Models*, tr. D. H. Fowler, with a Foreword by C. H. Waddington. Reading, MA: W. A. Benjamin.

Thompson, Henry S. and David McKelvie (1997). Hyperlink Semantics for Standoff Markup of Read-Only Documents. At <http://www.ltg.ed.ac.uk/~ht/sgmleu97.html>.

Varela, Francisco J., Evan Thompson, and Eleanor Rosch (1991). *The Embodied Mind: Cognitive Science and Human Experience*. Cambridge, MA: MIT Press.

17

Text Encoding

Allen H. Renear

Before they can be studied with the aid of machines, texts must be encoded in a machine-readable form. Methods for this transcription are called, generically, "text encoding schemes"; such schemes must provide mechanisms for representing the characters of the text and its logical and physical structure . . . ancillary information achieved by analysis or interpretation [may be also added] . . .

Michael Sperberg-McQueen, Text Encoding and Enrichment. In *The Humanities Computing Yearbook 1989–90*, ed. Ian Lancashire (Oxford: Oxford University Press, 1991)

Introduction

Text encoding holds a special place in humanities computing. It is not only of considerable practical importance and commonly used, but it has proven to be an exciting and theoretically productive area of analysis and research. Text encoding in the humanities has also produced a considerable amount of interesting debate – which can be taken as an index of both its practical importance and its theoretical significance.

This chapter will provide a general orientation to some of the historical and theoretical context needed for understanding both contemporary text encoding practices and the various ongoing debates that surround those practices. We will be focusing for the most part, although not exclusively, on "markup," as markup-related techniques and systems not only dominate practical encoding activity, but are also at the center of most of the theoretical debates about text encoding. This chapter provides neither a survey of markup languages nor a tutorial introduction to the practice of markup. The reader new to SGML/XML text encoding should read this chapter of the *Companion* concurrently with the short (21-page) second chapter of the TEI Guidelines, "A Gentle Introduction to XML," online at <http://www.tei-c.org/P4X/SG.html>. The justly renowned "Gentle

Introduction" remains the best brief presentation of SGML/XML text encoding and it provides a necessary complement of specific description to the background and theory being presented here. For a good general introduction to text encoding in the humanities, see *Electronic Texts in the Humanities: Theory and Practice*, by Susan Hockey (Hockey 2001).

In accordance with the general approach of this *Companion*, we understand text encoding in the "digital humanities" in a wide sense. Traditional humanities computing (particularly when related to literature and language) typically emphasized either analytical procedures on encoded textual material – such as, for instance, stylometric analysis to support authorship or seriation studies – or the publishing of important traditional genres of scholarship such as critical and variorum editions, indexes, concordances, catalogues, and dictionaries. But text encoding is no less important to digital humanities broadly conceived, in the sense which includes the creation and study of new cultural products, genres, and capabilities, such as those involving hypertext, multimedia, interactivity, and networking – cultural products that are often called "new media." In order to be presented using computers, such material must be encoded in machine-readable form. Although the presentation below does not take up hypertext or "new media" topics directly, we believe the background presented nevertheless provides a useful background for text encoding in general, new media applications as well as traditional humanities computing and publishing. For more specific treatment of encoding issues, hypertext, multimedia, and other new media topics, see chapters 10, 28, 29, and 30. For discussions of traditional humanities computing applications exploiting text encoding, see chapters 20, 21, 22, and 35.

What follows then is intended as a background for understanding the text encoding as a representation system for textually based cultural objects of all kinds.

Markup

Introduction

Markup, in the sense in which we are using the term here, may be characterized, at least provisionally, as information formally distinct from the character sequence of the digital transcription of a text, which serves to identify logical or physical features or to control later processing. In a typical unformatted view of a digital representation of a text such markup is visibly evident as the more or less unfamiliar expressions or codes that are intermixed with the familiar words of the natural-language writing system. The term *markup* comes, of course, from traditional publishing, where an editor marks up a manuscript by adding annotations or symbols on a paper copy of text indicating either directly (e.g., "center") or indirectly ("heading") how something is to look in print (Spring 1989; Chicago 1993).

Many markup theorists have found it instructive to conceptualize markup as a very general phenomenon of human communication. Extending the notion of markup in straightforward and natural ways, one can easily use this concept to illuminate aspects of the general nature and history of writing systems and printing, particularly in the areas such as page layout, typography, and punctuation (Coombs et al. 1987).

In addition, other fields and disciplines related to communication, such as rhetoric, bibliography, textual criticism, linguistics, discourse and conversation analysis, logic, and semiotics also seem to be rich sources of related findings and concepts that generalize our understanding of markup practices and make important connections between markup practices narrowly understood and other bodies of knowledge and technique.

However, although such a broad perspective can be illuminating, the significance of markup for humanities computing is best approached initially by considering markup's origin and development in computer-based typesetting and early text processing. Although markup might arguably be considered part of any communication system, and of fundamental theoretical significance, it is with straightforward applications in digital text processing and typesetting in the 1960s, 1970s, and 1980s that the use of markup, in our sense, first becomes explicit and begins to undergo deliberate and self-conscious development (Goldfarb 1981; Spring 1989; SGML Users' Group 1990).

Emergence of descriptive markup

The use of computers to compose text for typesetting and printing was common by the mid-1960s and the general process was more or less the same regardless of the specific technology. Typically, the first step was to create and store in a computer file a representation of the text to be printed. This representation consisted of both codes for the individual characters of the textual content and codes for formatting commands, the commands and the text being distinguished from each other by special characters or sequences of characters serving as "delimiters." The file would then be processed by a software application that acted on the formatting instructions to create data which could in turn be directly read and further processed by the phototypesetter or computer printer – creating formatted text as final output (Seybold 1977; Furuta et al. 1982).

The 1960s, 1970s, and 1980s saw extensive development of these document markup systems as software designers worked to improve the efficiency and functionality of digital typesetting and text processing software (IBM 1967; Ossanna 1976; Lesk 1978; Goldfarb 1978; Reid 1978; Knuth 1979; Lamport 1985).

One natural improvement on the approach just described was to replace the long strings of complex formatting codes with simpler abbreviations that could be automatically expanded into the formatting commands being abbreviated. The compositor would enter just the abbreviation instead of the entire string of commands. In many typesetting systems in the 1960s and 1970s these abbreviations were called "macros," a term drawn from assembly language programming where it referred to higher-level symbolic instructions which would be expanded, before program execution, into sequences of lower-level primitive instructions.

In typesetting and text processing these macros had the obvious immediate advantage of easier and more reliable data entry. However, during their early use it wasn't always entirely clear whether a macro got its primary identity from the text component (e.g., a caption, extract, or heading) whose formatting it was controlling, or whether it was simply a short name for the combination of the specific formatting codes it was abbreviating, with no other meaning or identity. The distinction is subtle but important. If a macro is truly just an abbreviation of a string of formatting codes then it can be appropriately used wherever those formatting codes would be used. So if, for instance, figure captions and third-level headings happen to have the same design specifications, then the same macro could reasonably and appropriately be used for both. In such a case the macro, as a mere abbreviation, gets its entire meaning and identity from the formatting commands it abbreviates and it would be natural for the macro name to then simply indicate the appearance of the formatted text (e.g., ":SmallCenteredBold;"), or be an arbitrary expression (e.g., ":format17;") rather than have a name that suggested an intrinsic relationship with the text component being formatted (such as, ":figurecaption") (Goldfarb 1997).

Although macros used as described above obviously provided some advantages over entering strings of formatting codes, it was a natural next step to see that many more advantages could be achieved by understanding the presence of the macro name in the file to be identifying the occurrence of a particular text component – a third-level heading, caption, stanza, extract, title, etc. – rather than just being an abbreviation for a string of formatting commands. On this new approach, figure captions, for instance, would be identified with one code (say, ":FigureCaption;"), and third-level headings would be identified with another (say, ":Heading3;" even if, according to the page design specification currently being applied, these codes were mapped to the same set of formatting commands.

The first advantage to this new approach is that it is now possible to globally alter the formatting of *figure captions* (by simply updating the formatting commands associated with ":FigureCaption;") without necessarily changing the formatting of the *third-level headings* (identified by the macro name ":Heading3;"). In addition, authoring and even composition can now take place without the author or compositor needing to know how the different components are to be formatted. As this approach to typesetting and text processing began to be systematically applied it became quickly apparent that there were a great many other advantages. So many advantages, in fact, and such a diversity of advantages, that the descriptive markup approach began to appear to be somehow *the* fundamentally correct approach to organizing and processing text (Goldfarb 1981; Reid 1981; Coombs et al. 1987).

The promotion of descriptive markup as the fundamentally correct systematic approach in digital publishing and text processing is usually traced to three events: (i) a presentation made by William Tunnicliffe, chairman of the Graphic Communications Association's Composition Committee, at the Canadian Government Printing Office in September 1967; (ii) book designer Stanley Rice's project, also in the late 1960s, of developing a universal catalogue of "editorial structure" tags that would simplify book design and production; and (iii) early work on the text processing macro language "GML," led by Charles Goldfarb, at IBM in 1969 (SGML Users' Group 1990; Goldfarb 1997). In the late 1970s these events would lead to an effort to develop SGML, a standard for machine-readable definitions of descriptive markup languages. Other examples of early use of descriptive markup in digital text processing include the Brown University FRESS hypertext system (Carmody et al. 1969; DeRose and van Dam 1999), and, later in the 1970s, Brian Reid's SCRIBE (Reid 1978, 1981). In addition, the seminal work on text processing by Douglas Engelbart in the 1960s should probably also be seen as exhibiting some of the rudiments of this approach (Engelbart et al. 1973).

Nature and advantages of descriptive markup

Early experience with descriptive markup encouraged some text processing researchers to attempt to develop a general theoretical framework for markup and to use that framework to support the development of high-function text processing systems. Some of the research and analysis on markup systems was published in the scientific literature (Goldfarb 1981; Reid 1981; Coombs et al. 1987), but most was recorded only in the working documents and products of various standards bodies, and in the manuals and technical documentation of experimental systems.

At the heart of this effort to understand markup systems was the distinction between "descriptive" and "procedural" markup originally put forward by Goldfarb. Descriptive markup was typically said to "identify" or "describe" the "parts" of a document, whereas procedural markup was a "command" or "instruction" invoking a formatting procedure. It was also often said that descriptive markup identified the "logical" or "editorial" parts or "components" of a document, or a text's "content objects" or its "meaningful structure" – emphasizing the distinction between the intrinsic ("logical") structure of the document itself, and the varying visual, graphic features of a particular presentation of that document. (For recent arguments that descriptive markup can be further divided into the genuinely descriptive and the "performative," see Renear 2000.)

Several particular advantages of descriptive markup, such as simplified composition and systematic control over formatting, have already been alluded to, but in order to appreciate how the descriptive markup motivated a new theory of the nature of text it is useful to rehearse the number, diversity, and value of the advantages of descriptive markup in overview; so we present a categorized summary below.

Advantages for authoring, composition, and transcription (*adapted from DeRose et al. 1990*)

- *Composition is simplified.* With descriptive markup, intended formatting considerations make no claim on the attention of the author, compositor, or transcriber, whereas with procedural markup one must remember both (i) the style conventions that are intended, and (ii) the specific commands required by the formatting software to get those effects. With descriptive markup one simply identifies each text component for what it is and the appropriate formatting takes place automatically. (Particularly striking is how descriptive markup allows the author to work at an appropriate "level of abstraction" – identifying something as a quotation, paragraph, or caption is a natural authorial task, while knowing whether to, and how to, format that text a certain way is not.)
- *Structure-oriented editing is supported.* Descriptive markup supports "structure-oriented editors" who "know" about what patterns of components can be found in a particular genre of document and who use this knowledge to assist the author or compositor. For instance, if a *date* component must always follow a *title* component then the software, upon detecting that a *title* component has just been entered by an author, can automatically add the required *date* markup and prompt the author to enter the actual

date. If either *date* or *status* is allowed after a *title* then the author will be presented with a choice. During editing the cursor location can be used to identify and present to the author the list of components that may be added or deleted at that point. For complicated document genres this means that there is much less for the author to remember and fewer possibilities for error.

- *More natural editing tools are supported.* Moves and deletes, for example, can take as their targets and scope the natural meaningful parts of the text (words, sentences, paragraphs, sections, extracts, equations, etc.) rather than relying on the mediation of accidental features (such as current lineation) or arbitrarily marked regions.

- *Alternative document views are facilitated.* An outline view of a text, for instance, can be done automatically, by taking advantage of the descriptive markup for chapters, sections, and headings. Or a more sophisticated and specialized display of portions of documents can be effected using identified discipline-specific components: such as equations, examples, cautions, lines spoken by a particular character in a play script, and so on.

Advantages for publishing

- *Formatting can be generically specified and modified.* When procedural markup is being used, the appearance of paragraphs can only be modified by editing the formatting commands preceding each actual occurrence of a paragraph in the source file, whereas with descriptive markup only the rule associating formatting commands with the descriptive markup for *paragraph* needs to be updated – and if these rules are stored separately there may be no need to even alter the files containing text in order to make formatting alterations. Obviously, controlling formatting with descriptive markup is easier, less error-prone, and ensures consistency.

- *Apparatus can be automated.* Descriptive markup supports the creation of indexes, appendices, and such. For instance, if stanzas and verse lines are explicitly identified, the creation of an index of first lines of stanzas (or second lines or last lines) is a matter of simple programming, and does not require that a human editor again laboriously identify verses and lines. Similarly, generating tables for equations, plates, figures, examples, is also easy, as are indexes of place names, personal names, characters, medium, authors, periods, and so on.

- *Output device support is enhanced.* When coding is based on logical role rather than appearance, output-device specific support for printers, typesetters, video display terminals and other output devices can be maintained separately, logically and physically, from the data with the convenient result that the data files themselves are *output-device independent* while their processing is efficiently *output-device sensitive*.

- *Portability and interoperability are maximized.* Files that use descriptive markup, rather than complicated lists of application-specific formatting instructions, to identify components are much easier to transfer to other text processing systems. In some cases little more than a few simple systematic changes to alter the delimiter conventions, substitute one mnemonic name for another, and a translation of formatting rules into those for the new system, are all that is necessary.

Advantages for archiving, retrieval, and analysis

- *Information retrieval is supported.* Descriptive markup allows documents to be treated as a database of fielded content that can be systematically accessed. One can request all equations, or all headings, or all verse extracts; or one can request all titles that contain a particular personal name, place name, chemical, disease, drug, or therapy. This can facilitate not only personal information retrieval functions, such as the generation of alternative views, but also a variety of finding aids, navigation, and data retrieval functions. It may seem that in some cases, say where equations are uniquely formatted, it is not necessary to identify them, as the computer could always be programmed to exploit the formatting codes. But in practice it is unlikely that equations will always be consistently formatted, and even more unlikely that they will be uniquely formatted. Similarly, it might be thought that a string search might retrieve all references to the city Chicago, but without markup one cannot distinguish the city, the rock band, and the artist.
- *Analytical procedures are supported.* Computer-based analysis (stylometrics, content analysis, statistical studies, etc.) can be carried out more easily and with better results if features such as sentences, paragraphs, stanzas, dialogue lines, stage directions, and so on have been explicitly identified so that the computer can automatically distinguish them. Consider some examples: If the style of spoken language in a play is being analyzed, the text that is not speech (stage directions, notes, etc.) must not be conflated with the dialogue. If the speech of a particular character is being studied it must be distinguished from the speech of other characters. If proximity is being studied, the word ending one paragraph should perhaps not be counted as collocated with the word beginning the next, and so on. Descriptive markup identifies these important components and their boundaries, supporting easier, more consistent, and more precise automatic processing.

The OHCO view of "what text really is"

That the descriptive markup approach had so many advantages, and so many different kinds of advantages, seemed to some people to suggest that it was not simply a handy way of working with text, but that it was rather in some sense deeply, profoundly, *correct*, that "descriptive markup is not just the best approach ... it is the best imaginable approach" (Coombs et al. 1987).

How could this be? One answer is that the descriptive markup approach, and only the descriptive markup approach, reflects a correct view of "what text really is" (DeRose et al. 1990). On this account, the concepts of descriptive markup entail a model of text, and that model is more or less right. The model in question postulates that text consists of objects of a certain sort, structured in a certain way. The nature of the objects is best suggested by example and contrast. They are chapters, sections, paragraphs, titles, extracts, equations, examples, acts, scenes, stage directions, stanzas, (verse) lines, and so on. But they are *not* things like pages, columns, (typographical) lines, font shifts, vertical spacing, horizontal spacing, and so on. The objects indicated by descriptive markup have an intrinsic direct connection with the intellectual content of the text; they are the underlying "logical" objects, components that get their identity directly from their role in carrying out and organizing communicative intention. The structural arrangement of these "content objects" seems to be hierarchical – they nest in one another without overlap. Finally, they obviously also have a linear order as well: if a section *contains* three paragraphs, the first paragraph *precedes* the second, which in turn precedes the third.

On this account then text *is* an "Ordered Hierarchy of Content Objects" (OHCO), and descriptive markup works as well as it does because it identifies that hierarchy and makes it explicit and available for systematic processing. This account is consistent with the traditional well-understood advantages of "indirection" and "data abstraction" in information science.

A number of things seem to fall into place from this perspective. For one thing, different kinds of text have different kinds of content objects (compare the content objects in dramatic texts with those in legal contracts), and typically the patterns in which content objects can occur is at least partially constrained: the parts of a letter occur in a certain order, the lines of a poem occur within, not outside of a stanza, and so on. Presentational features make it easier for the reader to recognize the content objects of the text.

There are alternative models of text that could be compared with the OHCO model. For instance, one could model text as a sequence of graphic characters, as in the "plain vanilla ASCII" approach of Project Gutenberg; as a combination of procedural coding and graphic characters, as in a word processing file; as a complex of geometric shapes, as in "vector graphics" format of an image of a page on which the text is written; as a pure image, as in a raster image format (JPEG, GIF, etc.); or in a number of other ways. However, implementations based on these alternative models are all clearly inferior in functionality to implementations based on an OHCO model, and in any case can be easily and automatically generated from an OHCO format (DeRose et al. 1990; Renear et al. 1996).

The OHCO account of "what text really is" has not gone uncriticized, but many have found it a compelling view of text, one that does explain the effectiveness of descriptive markup and provides a general context for the systematization of descriptive markup languages with formal metalanguages such as SGML.

SGML and XML

As we indicated above, this chapter is not designed to introduce the reader to text encoding, but to provide in overview some useful historical and theoretical background that should help support a deeper understanding. In this section we present some of the principal themes in SGML and XML, and take up several topics that we believe will be useful, but for a complete presentation the reader is again directed to the "Gentle Introduction" and the other readings indicated in the references below.

History of SGML and XML: Part I

Norman Scharpf, director of the Graphics Communication Association, is generally credited with recognizing the significance of the work, mentioned above, of Tunnicliffe, Rice, and Goldfarb, and initiating, in the late 1960s, the GCA "GenCode" project, which had the goal of developing a standard descriptive markup language for publishing (SGML Users' Group 1990; Goldfarb 1997). Soon much of this activity shifted to the American National Standards Institute (ANSI), which selected Charles Goldfarb to lead an effort for a text description language standard based on GML and produced the first working draft of SGML in 1980. These activities were reorganized as a joint project of ANSI and the International Organization for Standardization (ISO) and in 1986 ISO published *ISO 8879: Information Processing – Text and Office Systems – Standard Generalized Markup Language (SGML)* (ISO 1986; Goldfarb 1991). Later events in the history of SGML, including the development of XML and the profusion of SGML/XML standards that began in the mid-1990s, are discussed below. We will later describe more precisely the relationship between SGML and XML; at this point in the chapter the reader only needs to know that XML is, roughly, just a simpler version of SGML, and as a consequence almost everything we say about SGML applies to XML as well.

The basic idea: a metalanguage for defining descriptive markup languages

Although for a variety of reasons the SGML standard itself can be difficult to read and understand, the basic idea is quite simple. SGML is a language for creating machine-readable definitions of descriptive markup languages. As such it is called a "metalanguage," a language for defining a language. The SGML standard provides a way to say things like this: these are the characters I use for markup tag delimiters; these are the markup tags I am using; these are the acceptable arrangements that the components identified by my markup tags may take in a document; these are some characteristics I may be asserting of those components, these are some abbreviations and shortcuts I'll be using, and so on. An alternative characterization of SGML is as a "metagrammar," a grammar for defining other grammars; here "grammar" is used in a technical sense common in linguistics and computer science. (Although its origin is as a metalanguage for defining *document* markup languages, SGML can be, and is, used to define markup languages for things other than documents, such as languages for data interchange or interprocess communication, or specific data management applications.)

An almost inevitable first misconception is that SGML is a document markup language with a specific set of document markup tags for features such as paragraphs, chapters, abstracts, and so on. Despite its name ("Standard Generalized *Markup Language*"), SGML is not a markup language in this sense and includes no document markup tags for describing document content objects. SGML is a *metalanguage*, a language for defining document markup languages. The confusion is supported by the fact that both markup metalanguages like SGML and XML and also SGML-based markup languages like HTML and XHTML (technically *applications of* SGML) are "markup languages" in name. In each case the "ML" stands for "markup language," but SGML and HTML are markup languages in quite different senses. The characterization of SGML as a document markup language is not entirely unreasonable of course, as it is in a sense a language for marking up documents, just one without a predefined set of markup for content objects. Whether or not SGML should be called a markup language is historically moot, but to emphasize the distinction between markup languages that are actual sets of markup tags for document content objects (such as HTML, XHTML, TEI, DocBook, etc.) and metalanguages for defining such markup languages (such as SGML and XML) we will, in what follows, reserve the term *markup language* for languages like HTML and TEI, excluding the metalanguages used to define them.

Standardizing a metalanguage for markup languages rather than a markup language was a key strategic decision. It was an important insight of the GCA GenCode Committee that any attempt to define a common markup vocabulary for the entire publishing industry, or even common vocabularies for portions of the industry, would be extremely difficult, at best. However, a major step towards improving the interoperability of computer applications and data could be achieved by standardizing a metalanguage for defining markup languages. Doing this would obviously be an easier task: (i) it would not require the development of a markup language vocabulary with industry-wide acceptance and (ii) it would not assume that the industry would continue to conform, even as circumstances changed and opportunities for innovations arose, to the particular markup language it had agreed on.

At the same time this approach still ensured that every markup language defined using SGML, even ones not yet invented, could be recognized by any computer software that understood the SGML metalanguage. The idea was that an SGML software application would first process the relevant SGML markup language definition, and then could go on, as a result of having processed that definition, to process the marked-up document itself – now being able to distinguish tags from content, expand abbreviations, and verify that the markup was correctly formed and used and that the document had a structure that was anticipated by the markup language definition. Because the SGML markup language definition does not include processing information such as formatting instructions, software applications would also require instructions for formatting that content; shortly after the SGML project began, work started on a standard for assigning general instructions for formatting and other processing to arbitrary SGML markup. This was the *Document Style and Semantics Specification Language* (DSSSL). The World Wide Web Consortium (W3C)'s Extensible Stylesheet Language (XSL) is based on DSSSL, and the W3C Cascading Style Sheet specification performs a similar, although more limited function.

This strategy supports technological innovation by allowing the independent development of better or more specialized markup, without the impediment of securing antecedent agreement from software developers that they will manufacture software that can process the new markup – all that is required is that the software understand SGML, and not a specific SGML markup language.

Elements and element types

Up until now we have been using the phrase *content object* for the logical parts of a document or text. SGML introduces a technical term, *element*, that roughly corresponds to this notion, developing it more precisely. The first bit of additional precision is that where we have used "content object" ambiguously, sometimes meaning the specific titles, paragraphs, extracts and the like that occur in actual documents, and sometimes meaning the general kind of object (title, paragraph, extract) of which those specific occurrences are instances, SGML has distinct terminology for these two senses of "content object": an actual component of a document is an "element," and the type of an element (title, paragraph, extract, etc.) is an "element type." However, apart from the standard itself, and careful commentary on the standard, it is common, and usually not a problem, for "element" to be used in the sense of "element type" as well. This kind of ambiguity is common enough in natural language and almost always easily and unconsciously resolved by context.

The second bit of additional precision is that where we used *"content object"* to refer to the parts of texts understood in the usual way as abstract cultural objects, independent of, and prior to, any notion of markup languages, the most exact use of *"element"* in the technical SGML sense is to refer to the combination of SGML markup tags and enclosed content that is being used to represent (for instance, in a computer file) these familiar abstract textual objects. Again the distinction is subtle and "element" is routinely used in both senses (arguably even in the standard itself). Typically, no damage is done, but eventually encoding cruxes, design quandaries, or theoretical disputes may require appeal to the full range of distinctions that can be made when necessary.

Document types and document instances

Fundamental to SGML is the notion of the *document type*, a class of documents with a particular set of content objects that can occur in some combinations but not in others. Some examples of document types might be: novel, poem, play, article, essay, letter, contract, proposal, receipt, catalogue, syllabus, and so on. Some examples of combination rules: in a poem, lines of verse occur within stanzas, not vice versa; in a play, stage directions may occur either within or between speeches but not within other stage directions (and not, normally, in the table of contents); in a catalogue, each product description must contain exactly one part number and one or more prices for various kinds of customers. There are no predefined document types in SGML of course; the identification of a document type at an appropriate level of specificity, (e.g., poem, sonnet, petrarchan sonnet, sonnet-by-Shakespeare) is up to the SGML markup language designer.

A *document type definition* (DTD) defines an SGML markup language for a particular document type. Part of a document type definition is given in a *document type declaration* that consists of a series of SGML *markup declarations* that formally define the vocabulary and syntax of the markup language. These markup declarations specify such things as what element types there are, what combinations elements can occur in, what characteristics may be attributed to elements, abbreviations for data, and so on.

The SGML standard is clear that there is more to a document type *definition* than the markup declarations of the document type *declaration*: "Parts of a document type definition can be specified by a SGML document type declaration, other parts, such as the semantics of elements and attributes or any application conventions...cannot be expressed formally in SGML" (ISO 1986: 4.105). That is, the document type *declarations* can tell us that a poem consists of exactly one title followed by one or more lines and that lines can't contain titles, but it does not have any resources for telling us what a title *is*. The document type *definition* encompasses more. However, all that the SGML standard itself says about how to provide the required additional information about "semantics ...or any application conventions" is: "Comments may be used...to express them informally" (ISO 1986: 4.105). In addition, it is generally thought that properly written prose documentation for a markup language is an account of the "semantics...or any application conventions" of that markup language.

Obviously these two expressions "document type definition" and "document type declaration," which are closely related, sound similar, and have the same initials, can easily be confused. But the difference is important, if irregularly observed. We reiterate that: it is the document type *definition* that defines a markup language; part of that definition is given in the markup declarations of the document type declaration; and an additional portion, which includes an account of the meaning of the elements' attributes, is presented informally in comments or in the prose documentation of the markup language. We note that according to the SGML standard the acronym "DTD" stands for "document type *definition*," which accords poorly with the common practice of referring to the markup declarations of the document type declaration as, collectively, *the* "DTD," and using the extension "DTD" for files containing the markup declarations – these being only part of the DTD.

A *document instance* is "the data and markup for a hierarchy of elements that conforms to a document type definition" (ISO 1986: 4.100, 4.160). Typically, we think of the file of text and markup, although in fact the definition, like SGML in general, is indifferent to the physical organization of information: an SGML document instance may be organized as a "file," or it may be organized some other way.

Strictly speaking (i.e., according to ISO 1986, definitions 4.100 and 4.160), a document instance by definition actually conforms to the document type definition that it is putatively an instance of. This means that (i) the requirements for element and attribute use expressed in the markup declarations are met; and (ii) any other expressed semantic constraints or applications are followed. However, actual usage of "document instance" deviates from this definition in three ways: (i) it is common to speak of text and markup as a "document instance" even if it in fact fails to conform to the markup declarations of the intended DTD (as in "The document instance was invalid"); (ii) text plus markup is referred to as a document instance even if it is not clear what if any DTD it conforms to; and (iii) even a terminological purist wouldn't withhold the designation "document instance" because of a failure to conform to the "semantics and application conventions" of the document type definition – partly, no doubt, because there is no established way to automatically test for semantic conformance.

History of SGML and XML: Part II

Although SGML was soon used extensively in technical documentation and other large-scale publishing throughout the world, it did not have the broad penetration into consumer publishing and text processing that some of its proponents had expected. Part of the problem was that it was during this same period that "WYSIWIG" word processing and desktop publishing emerged, and had rapid and extensive adoption. Such software gave users a sense that they were finally (or once again?) working with "the text itself," without intermediaries, and that they had no need for markup systems; they could, again, return to familiar typewriter-based practices, perhaps enhanced with "cut-and-paste." This was especially frustrating for SGML enthusiasts because there is no necessary real opposition between WYSIWYG systems and descriptive markup systems and no reason, other than current market forces and perhaps technical limitations, why a WYSIWYG system couldn't be based on the OHCO model of text, and store its files in SGML. Most of what users valued in WYSIWYG systems – immediate formatting, menus, interactive support, etc. – was consistent with the SGML/OHCO approach. Users would of course need to forgo making formatting changes "directly," but on the other hand they would get all the advantages of descriptive markup, including simpler composition, context-oriented support for selecting document components, global formatting, and so on. There would never, needless to say, be any need to remember, type, or even see, markup tags. The "WYSIWYG" classification was misleading in any case, since what was at issue was really as much the combination of editing conveniences such as interactive formatting, pull-down menus, and graphical displays, as it was a facsimile of how the document would look when printed – which would typically vary with the circumstances, and often was not up to the author in any case.

But very few SGML text processing systems were developed, and fewer still for general users. Several explanations have been put forward for this. One was that OHCO/SGML-based text processing was simply too unfamiliar, even if more efficient and more powerful, and the unfamiliarity, and prospect of spending even an hour or two learning new practices posed a marketing problem for salesmen trying to make a sale "in three minutes on the floor of Radio Shack." Another was that OHCO/SGML software was just too hard to develop: the SGML standard had so many optional features, as well as several characteristics that were hard to program, that these were barriers to development of software. Several OHCO/SGML systems were created in the 1980s, but these were not widely used.

The modest use of SGML outside of selected industries and large organizations changed radically with the emergence of HTML, the HyperText Markup Language, on the World Wide Web. HTML was designed as an SGML language (and with tags specifically modeled on the "starter tag set" of IBM DCF/GML). However, as successful as HTML was it became apparent that it had many problems, and that the remedies for these problems could not be easily developed without changes in SGML.

From the start HTML's relationship with SGML was flawed. For one thing HTML began to be used even before there was a DTD that defined the HTML language. More important, though, was the fact that HTML indiscriminately included element types not only for descriptive markup, but also procedural markup as well ("font," "center," and so on). In addition there was no general stylesheet provision for attaching formatting or other processing HTML. Finally none of the popular web browsers ever validated the HTML they processed. Web page authors had only the vaguest idea what the syntax of HTML actually was and had little motivation to learn, as browsers were forgiving and always seemed to more or less "do the right thing." DTDs seemed irrelevant and validation unnecessary. HTML files were in fact almost never valid HTML.

But perhaps the most serious problem was that the HTML element set was impoverished. If Web publishing were going to achieve its promise it would have to accommodate more sophisticated and specialized markup languages. That meant that it would need to be easier to write the software that processed DTDs, so that arbitrary markup vocabularies could be used without prior coordination. And it was also obvious that some provision needed to be made for allowing more reliable processing of document instances without DTDs.

This was the background for the development of XML 1.0, the "Extensible Markup Language." XML was developed within the World Wide Web Consortium (W3C) with the first draft being released in 1996, the "Proposed Recommendation" in 1997, and the "Recommendation" in 1998. The committee was chaired by Jon Bosak of Sun Microsystems, and technical discussions were conducted in a working group of 100 to 150 people, with final decisions on the design made by an editorial review board with eleven members. The editors, leading a core working group of eleven people, supported by a larger group of 150 or so experts in the interest group, were Michael Sperberg-McQueen (University of Illinois at Chicago and the Text Encoding Initiative), Tim Bray (Textuality and Netscape), and Jean Paoli (Microsoft).

XML

The principal overall goal of XML was to ensure that new and specialized markup languages could be effectively used on the Web, without prior coordination between software developers and content developers. One of the intermediate objectives towards this end was to create a simpler, more constrained version of SGML, so that with fewer options to support and other simplifications, it would be easier for programmers to develop SGML/XML software, and then more SGML software would be developed and used, and would support individualized markup languages. This objectively was achieved: the XML specification is about 25 pages long, compared to SGML's 155 (664 including the commentary in Charles Goldfarb's *SGML Handbook*), and while the Working Group did not achieve their stated goal that a graduate student in computer science should be able to develop an XML parser in a week, the first graduate student to try it reported success in a little under two weeks.

Another objective was to allow for processing of new markup languages even without a DTD. This requires several additional constraints on the document instance, one of which is illustrative and will be described here. SGML allowed markup tags to be omitted when they were implied by their markup declarations. For instance if the element type declaration for paragraph did not allow a paragraph inside of a paragraph, then the start-tag of a new paragraph would imply the closing of the preceding paragraph even without an end-tag, and so the end-tag could be omitted by the content developer as it could be inferred by the software. But without a DTD it is not possible to know what can be nested and what can't – and so in order to allow "DTD-less" processing XML does not allow tags to be omitted. It is the requirement that elements have explicit end-tags that is perhaps the best-known difference between documents in an SGML language like HTML and an XML language like XHTML.

Whereas SGML has just one characterization of conformance for document instances, XML has two: (i) all XML documents must be *well-formed*; (ii) an XML document may or may not be *valid* (*vis-à-vis* a DTD). To be well-formed, a document instance need not conform to a DTD, but it must meet other requirements, prominent and illustrative among them: no start-tags or end-tags may be omitted, elements must not "overlap," attribute values must be in quotation marks, and case must be consistent. These requirements ensure that software processing the document instance will be able to unambiguously determine a hierarchy (or tree) of elements and their attribute assignments, even without a DTD..

The Text Encoding Initiative

Background

The practice of creating machine-readable texts to support humanities research began early and grew rapidly. Literary text encoding is usually dated from 1949, when Father Roberto Busa began using IBM punched-card equipment for the *Index Thomisticus* – in other words, literary text encoding is almost coeval with digital computing itself. By the mid-1960s there were at least three academic journals focusing on humanities computing, and a list of "Literary Works in Machine-Readable Form" published in 1966 already required 25 pages (and included some projects, listed modestly as single items, that were encoding an entire authorial oeuvre) (Carlson 1967). It is tempting to speculate that efforts to standardize encoding practices must have begun as soon as there was more than one encoding project. Anxiety about the diversity of encoding systems appears early – one finds that at a 1965 conference on computers and literature for instance, an impromptu meeting was convened to discuss "the establishment of a standard format for the encoding of text . . . a matter of great importance." It obviously wasn't the first time such a concern had been expressed, and it wouldn't be the last (Kay 1965).

At first, of course, the principal problem was consistent identification and encoding of the characters needed for the transcription of literary and historical texts. But soon it included encoding of structural and analytic features as well. A standard approach to literary text encoding would have a number of obvious advantages; it would make it easier for projects and researchers to share texts, possible to use the same software across textual corpora (and therefore more economical to produce such software), and it would simplify the training of encoders – note that these advantages are similar to those, described above, which motivated the effort to develop standards in commercial electronic publishing. And one might hope that without the disruptive competitive dynamic of commercial publishing where formats are sometimes aspects of competitive strategy, it would be easier to standardize. But there were still obstacles. For one thing, given how specialized text encoding schemes sometimes were, and how closely tied to the specific interests and views – even disciplines and theories – of their designers, how could a single common scheme be decided on?

Origins

The TEI had its origins in early November, 1987, at a meeting at Vassar College, convened by the Association for Computers in the Humanities and funded by the National Endowment for the Humanities. It was attended by thirty-two specialists, from many different disciplines and representing professional societies, libraries, archives, and projects in a number of countries in Europe, North America, and Asia. There was a sense of urgency, as it was felt that the proliferation of needlessly diverse and often poorly designed encoding systems threatened to block the development of the full potential of computers to support humanities research.

The resulting "Poughkeepsie Principles" defined the project of developing a set of text encoding guidelines. This work was then undertaken by three sponsoring organizations:

The Association for Computers in the Humanities, the Association for Literary and Linguistic Computing, and the Association for Computational Linguistics. A Steering Committee was organized and an Advisory Board of delegates from various professional societies was formed. Two editors were chosen: Michael Sperberg-McQueen of the University of Illinois at Chicago, and Lou Burnard of Oxford University. Four working committees were formed and populated. By the end of 1989 well over fifty scholars were already directly involved and the size of the effort was growing rapidly.

The first draft ("P1") of the TEI Guidelines was released in June, 1990. Another period of development followed (the effort now expanded and reorganized into 15 working groups) releasing revisions and extensions throughout 1990–93. Early on in this process a number of leading humanities textbase projects began to use the draft Guidelines, providing valuable feedback and ideas for improvement. At the same time workshops and seminars were conducted to introduce the Guidelines as widely as possible and ensure a steady source of experience and ideas. During this period, comments, corrections, and requests for additions arrived from around the world. After another round of revisions and extensions the first official version of the Guidelines ("P3") was released in May, 1994.

The TEI Guidelines have been an enormous success and today nearly every humanities textbase project anywhere in the world uses TEI. In 2002 the newly formed TEI Consortium released "P4," a revision that re-expressed the TEI Guidelines in XML, and today the Consortium actively continues to evolve the Guidelines and provide training, documentation, and other support. After HTML, the TEI is probably the most extensively used SGML/XML text encoding system in academic applications.

The history of the development of the TEI Guidelines, briefly told here, makes evident an important point. The Guidelines were, and continue to be, the product of a very large international collaboration of scholars from many disciplines and nations, with many different interests and viewpoints, and with the active participation of other specialists from many different professions and institutions. The work was carried out over several years within a disciplined framework of development, evaluation, and coordination, and with extensive testing in many diverse projects. All of this is reflected in a text encoding system of extraordinary power and subtlety.

General nature and structure

The TEI Guidelines take the form of several related SGML document type definitions, specified both in formal markup declarations and in English prose. The main DTD, for the encoding of conventional textual material such as novels, poetry, plays, dictionaries, or term-bank data, is accompanied by a number of *auxiliary DTDs* for specialized data: tag-set documentation, feature-system declarations used in structured linguistic or other annotation, writing-system declarations, and free-standing bibliographic descriptions of electronic texts.

The main DTD itself is partitioned into eighteen discrete tag sets or modules, which can be combined in several thousand ways to create different *views* of the main DTD. Some tag sets are always included in a view (unless special steps are taken to exclude them), some (the "base" tag sets) are mutually exclusive, and some (the "additional" tag sets) may be combined with any other tag sets.

In addition to the flexibility of choosing among the various tag sets, the main TEI DTD takes a number of steps to provide flexibility for the encoder and avoid a Procrustean rigidity that might interfere with the scholarly judgment of the encoder. Individual element types may be included or excluded from the DTD, additional element types may be introduced (as long as they are properly documented), and the names of element types and attributes may be translated into other languages for the convenience of the encoder or user.

It cannot be repeated enough that the apparent complexity of the TEI is, in a sense, only apparent. For the most part only as much of the TEI as is needed will be used in any particular encoding effort; the TEI vocabulary used will be exactly as complex, but no more complex, than the text being encoded. Not surprisingly, a very small TEI vocabulary, known as TEI Lite (<http://www.tei.org>), is widely used for simple texts.

Larger significance of the TEI

The original motivation of TEI was to develop interchange guidelines that would allow projects to share textual data (and theories about that data) and promote the development of common tools. Developing such a language for the full range of human written culture, the full range of disciplinary perspectives on those objects, and the full range of competing theories was a daunting task.

> It is easy to talk about accommodating diversity, about interdisciplinarity, about multiculturalism, about communication across various intellectual gaps and divides. But few efforts along these lines are more than superficial. The experience of the TEI makes it evident why this is so. Not only do different disciplines have quite different interests and perspectives, but, it seems, different conceptual schemes: fundamentally different ways of dividing up the world. What is an object of critical contest and debate for one discipline, is theory-neutral data for another, and then completely invisible to a third. What is structured and composite for one field is atomic for another and an irrelevant conglomeration to a third. Sometimes variation occurred within a discipline, sometimes across historical periods of interest, sometimes across national or professional communities. Practices that would seem to have much in common could vary radically – and yet have enough in common for differences to be a problem! And even where agreement in substance was obtained, disagreements over nuances, of terminology for instance, could derail a tenuous agreement. (Mylonas and Renear 1999)

The TEI made several important decisions that gave the enterprise at least the chance of success. For one thing the TEI determined that it would not attempt to establish in detail the "recognition criteria" for TEI markup; it would be the business of the encoder-scholar, not that of the TEI, to specify precisely what criteria suffice to identify a paragraph, or a section, or a technical term, in the text being transcribed. Examples of features commonly taken to indicate the presence of an object were given for illustration, but were not defined as normative. In addition the TEI, with just a few trivial exceptions, does not specify *what* is to be identified and encoded. Again, that is the business of the scholar or encoder. What the TEI does is provide a language to be used when the encoder (i) recognizes a particular object, and (ii) wishes to identify that object. In this sense, the TEI doesn't require antecedent agreement about what features of a text are important and how to tell whether they are present; instead, it makes it possible, when the scholar wishes, to communicate a particular theory of what the text is. One might say that the TEI is an agreement about how to express disagreement.

The principal goal of the TEI, developing an interchange language that would allow scholars to exchange information, was ambitious enough. But the TEI succeeded not only in this, but at a far more difficult project, the development of a new data description language that substantially *improves* our ability to describe textual features, not just our ability to exchange descriptions based on current practice. The TEI Guidelines represent

> an elucidation of current practices, methods, and concepts, [that] opens the way to new methods of analysis, new understandings, and new possibilities for representation and communication. Evidence that this is indeed a language of new expressive capabilities can be found in the experience of pioneering textbase projects which draw on the heuristic nature of the TEI Guidelines to illuminate textual issues and suggest new analyses and new techniques. (Mylonas and Renear 1999)

Finally, we note that the TEI is now itself a research community,

> connecting many professions, disciplines, and institutions in many countries and defining itself with its shared interests, concepts, tools, and techniques. Its subject matter is textual communication, with the principal goal of improving our general theoretical understanding of textual representation, and the auxiliary practical goal of using that improved understanding to develop methods, tools, and techniques that will be valuable to other fields and will support practical applications in publishing, archives, and libraries. It has connections to knowledge representation systems (formal semantics and ontology, objection orientation methodologies, etc.), new theorizing (non-hierarchical views of text, antirealism, etc.), and new applications and tools ... providing new insights into the nature of text, and new techniques for exploiting the emerging information technologies. (Mylonas and Renear 1999)

Concluding Remarks

Text encoding has proven an unexpectedly exciting and illuminating area of activity, and we have only been able to touch on a few aspects here. Ongoing work is of many kinds and taking place in many venues, from experimental hypermedia systems, to improved techniques for literary analysis, to philosophical debates about textuality. The references below should help the reader explore further.

For Further Information

SGML, XML, and related technologies

The best introduction to XML is the second chapter of the TEI Guidelines, "A Gentle Introduction to XML," online at <http://www.tei-c.org/P4X/SG.html>.

An excellent single-volume presentation of a number of XML-related standards, with useful practical information, is Harold and Means (2001). See also Bradley (2001).

The SGML standard is available as Goldfarb (1991), a detailed commentary that includes a cross-reference annotated version of the specification. A treatment of a number of subtleties is DeRose (1997).

A good detailed presentation of the XML specification is Graham and Quin (1999).

There are two extremely important resources on the Web for anyone interested in any aspect of contemporary SGML/XML text encoding. One is the extraordinary "Cover Pages," <http://xml.coverpages.org>, edited by Robin Cover and hosted by OASIS, an industry consortium. These provide an unparalleled wealth of information and news about XML and related standards. The other is the W3C site itself, <http://www.w3c.org>. These will provide an entry to a vast number of other sites, mailing lists, and other resources. Two other websites are also valuable: Cafe con Leche <http://www.ibiblio.org/xml/>, and XML.com <http://www.xml.com>. The most advanced work in SGML/XML markup research is presented at IDEAlliances' annual Extreme Markup Languages conference; the proceedings are available online, at <http://www.idealliance.org/papers/extreme03/>.

Document analysis, data modeling, DTD design, project design

Unfortunately there is a lack of intermediate and advanced material on the general issues involved in analyzing document types and developing sound DTD designs. There is just one good book-length treatment: Maler and Andaloussi (1996), although there are introductory discussions from various perspectives in various places (e.g., Bradley 2001). Other relevant discussions can be found in various places on the Web (see, for example, the debate over elements vs. attributes at <http://xml.coverpages.org/elementsAndAttrs.html>) and in various discussion lists and the project documentation and reports of encoding projects. (There are however very good resources for learning the basic techniques of TEI-based humanities text encoding; see below.)

Humanities text encoding and the TEI

For an excellent introduction to all aspects of contemporary humanities text encoding see *Electronic Texts in the Humanities: Theory and Practice*, by Susan Hockey (Hockey 2001).

The TEI Consortium, <http://www.tei-c.org>, periodically sponsors or endorses workshops or seminars in text encoding using the Guidelines; these are typically of high quality and a good way to rapidly get up to speed in humanities text encoding. There are also self-paced tutorials and, perhaps most importantly, a collection of project descriptions and encoding documentation from various TEI projects. See: <http://www.tei-c.org/Talks/> and <http://www.tei-c.org/Tutorials.index.html>. Anyone involved in TEI text encoding will want to join the TEI-L discussion list.

Theoretical issues

Text encoding has spawned an enormous number and wide variety of theoretical discussions and debates, ranging from whether the OHCO approach neglects the "materiality" of text, to whether TEI markup is excessively "interpretative"; to whether texts are really "hierarchical," to the political implications of markup, to whether SGML/XML is flawed by the lack of an algebraic "data model." From within the humanities computing community some of the influential researchers on these topics include Dino Buzzetti, Paul Caton, Claus Huitfeldt, Julia Flanders, Jerome McGann, Michael Sperberg-McQueen, Alois Pichler, and Wendell Piez, among others. A compendium of these topics, with references to the original discussions, may be found at <http://www.isrl.uiuc.edu/eprg/markuptheoryreview.html>.

One theoretical topic promises to soon have a broad impact beyond as well as within the digital humanities and deserves special mention. There has recently been a renewed concern that SGML/XML markup itself is not a "data model" or a "conceptual model," or does not have a "formal semantics." This is a criticism that on this view SGML/XML markup serializes a data structure, but it does not express the *meaning* of that data structure (the specification of the conceptual document) in a sufficiently formal way. For an introduction to this topic see Renear et al. (2002) and Robin Cover (1998, 2003). For a related discussion from the perspective of literary theory see Buzzetti (2002). Obviously these issues are closely related to those currently being taken up in the W3C Semantic Web Activity (<http://www.w3.org/2001/sw/Activity>).

ACKNOWLEDGMENTS

The author is deeply indebted to Michael Sperberg-McQueen for comments and corrections. Remaining errors and omissions are the author's alone.

BIBLIOGRAPHY

Bradley, N. (2001). *The XML Companion*. Reading, MA: Addison-Wesley.

Buzzetti, D. (2002). Digital Representation and the Text Model. *New Literary History* 33: 61–88.

Carlson, G. (1967). Literary Works in Machine-Readable Form. *Computers and the Humanitie*s 1: 75–102.

Carmody, S., W. Gross, T. H. Nelson, D. Rice, and A. van Dam (1969). A Hypertext Editing System for the 360. In M. Faiman and J. Nievergelt (eds.), *Pertinent Concepts in Computer Graphics* (pp. 291–330). Champaign: University of Illinois Press.

Chicago (1993). *The Chicago Manual of Style: The Essential Guide for Writers, Editors, and Publishers*, 14th edn. Chicago: University of Chicago Press.

Coombs, J.-H., A.-H. Renear, and S.-J. DeRose (1987). Markup Systems and the Future of Scholarly Text Processing. *Communications of the Association for Computing Machinery* 30: 933–47.

Cover, R. (1998). XML and Semantic Transparency. *OASIS Cover Pages*. At <http://www.oasis-open.org/cover/xmlAndSemantics.html>.

——(2003). Conceptual Modeling and Markup Languages. *OASIS Cover Pages*. At <http://xml.coverpages.org/conceptualModeling.html>.

DeRose, S. J. (1997). *The SGML FAQ Book: Understanding the Foundation of HTML and XML*. Boston: Kluwer.

DeRose, S.-J., and A. van Dam (1999). Document Structure and Markup in the FRESS Hypertext System. *Markup Languages: Theory and Practice* 1: 7–32.

DeRose, S.-J., D. Durand, E. Mylonas, and A.-H. Renear (1990). What Is Text, Really? *Journal of Computing in Higher Education* 1: 3–26. Reprinted in the *ACM/SIGDOC *Journal of Computer Documentation* 21,3: 1–24.

Engelbart, D. C., Watson, R. W. and Norton, J. C. (1973). The Augmented Knowledge. Workshop: *AFIPS Conference Proceedings*, vol. 42, National Computer Conference, June 4–8, 1973, pp. 9–21.

Furuta, R., J. Scofield, and A. Shaw (1982). Document Formatting Systems: Survey, Concepts, and Issues. *ACM Computing Surveys* 14: 417–72.

Goldfarb, C.-F. (1978). *Document Composition Facility: Generalized Markup Language (GML) Users Guide.* IBM General Products Division.

——(1981). A Generalized Approach to Document Markup. *Proceedings of the {ACM} {SIGPLAN-SIGOA} Symposium on Text Manipulation* (pp. 68–73). New York: ACM.

——(1991). *The SGML Handbook Guide.* Oxford: Oxford University Press.

——(1997). SGML: The Reason Why and the First Publishing Hint. *Journal of the American Society for Information Science* 48.

Graham, I. G. and L. Quin (1999). *The XML Specification Guide.* New York: John Wiley.

Harold, E. R. and W. S. Means (2001). *XML in a Nutshell: A Quick Desktop Reference.* Sebastopol, CA: O'Reilly & Associates.

Hockey, S. M. (2001). *Electronic Texts in the Humanities: Theory and Practice.* Oxford: Oxford University Press.

IBM (1967). *Application Description, System/360 Document Processing System.* White Plains, NY: IBM.

Ide, N.-M. and C.-M. Sperberg-McQueen (1997). Toward a Unified Docuverse: Standardizing Document Markup and Access without Procrustean Bargains. *Proceedings of the 60th Annual Meeting of the American Society for Information Science*, ed. C. Schwartz and M. Rorvig (pp. 347–60). Medford, NJ: Learned Information Inc.

ISO (1986). *Information Processing – Text and Office Systems – Standard Generalized Markup Language (SGML).* ISO 8879-1986 (E). Geneva: International Organization for Standardization.

Kay, M. (1965). Report on an Informal Meeting on Standard Formats for Machine-readable Text. In J. B. Bessinger and S. M. Parrish (eds), *Literary Data Processing Conference Proceedings* (pp. 327–28). White Plains, NY: IBM.

Knuth, D. E. (1979). *TEX and Metafont. New Directions in Typesetting.* Bedford, MA: Digital Press.

Lamport, L. (1985). *LaTeX – A Document Preparation System.* Reading, MA: Addison-Wesley.

Lesk, M.-E. (1978). *Typing Documents on the UNIX System: Using the -ms Macros with Troft and Nroff.* Murray Hill, NJ: Bell Laboratories.

Maler, E. and E. L. Andaloussi (1996). *Developing SGML DTDs: From Text to Model to Markup.* Englewood Cliffs, NJ: Prentice Hall.

Mylonas, M. and Renear, A. (1999). The Text Encoding Initiative at 10: Not Just an Interchange Format Anymore – but a New Research Community. *Computers and the Humanities* 33: 1–9.

Ossanna, J.-F. (1976). *NROFF/TROFF User's Manual (Tech. Rep.-54).* Murray Hill, NJ: Bell Laboratories.

Reid, B.-K. (1978). *Scribe Introductory User's Manual.* Pittsburgh, PA: Carnegie-Mellon University, Computer Science Department.

——(1981). *Scribe: A Document Specification Language and its Compiler.* PhD thesis. Pittsburgh, PA: Carnegie-Mellon University. Also available as Technical Report CMU-CS-81-100.

Renear, A. H. (2000). The Descriptive/Procedural Distinction is Flawed. *Markup Languages: Theory and Practice* 2: 411–20.

Renear, A. H., E. Mylonas, and D.-G. Durand (1996). Refining Our Notion of What Text Really Is: The Problem of Overlapping Hierarchies. In S. Hockey and N. Ide (eds.), *Research in Humanities Computing 4: Selected Papers from the ALLC/ACH Conference*, Christ Church, Oxford, April, 1992 (pp. 263–80).

Renear, A. H., D. Dubin, C. M. Sperberg-McQueen, and C. Huitfeldt (2002). Towards a Semantics for XML Markup. In R. Furuta, J. I. Maletic, and E. Munson (eds.), *Proceedings of the 2002 ACM Symposium on Document Engineering* (pp. 119–26). McLean, VA, November. New York: Association for Computing Machinery.

Seybold, J. W. (1977). *Fundamentals of Modern Composition.* Media, PA: Seybold Publications.

SGML Users' Group (1990). A Brief History of the Development of SGML. At <http://www.sgmlsource.com/history/sgmlhist.htm>.

Sperberg-McQueen, C.-M. (1991). Text Encoding and Enrichment. In Ian Lancashire (ed.), *The Human-ities Computing Yearbook 1989–90*. Oxford: Oxford University Press.

Sperberg-McQueen, M. and L. Burnard (eds.) (1994). *Guidelines for Text Encoding and Interchange (TEI P3)*. Chicago, Oxford: ACH/ALLC/ACL Text Encoding Initiative.

——(2002). *Guidelines for Text Encoding and Interchange (TEI P4)*. Oxford, Providence, Charlottesville, Bergen: ACH/ALLC/ACL Text Encoding Initiative.

Spring, M. B. (1989). The Origin and Use of Copymarks in Electronic Publishing. *Journal of Documentation* 45: 110–23.

18

Electronic Texts: Audiences and Purposes

Perry Willett

History

... today, even the most reluctant scholar has at least an indefinite notion of the computer's ability to store, manipulate and analyse natural language texts, whilst his less wary colleagues are likely to meet with a sympathetic reception if they approach their local computing centre with proposals for literary or linguistic research – some universities, indeed, have set up institutes and departments whose special task it is to facilitate work of this kind.

Wisbey, *The Computer in Literary and Linguistic Research: Papers from a Cambridge Symposium*, vii

Claims of the ubiquity of electronic text, such as this one published in 1971, may seem exaggerated for an era before personal computers, before standards for character or text encoding, before the World Wide Web, yet they have come more or less true. What is remarkable about this and other writing on electronic texts in the humanities published before 1995 is how well they predicted the uses of electronic text, before many people were even aware that text could be electronic. It is important to remember the introduction of the World Wide Web in the mid-1990s in evaluating the statements of computing humanists, for prior to the Web's arrival, while a great deal was written on the uses of and audiences for electronic text, almost no one foresaw such a powerful tool for the wide distribution of electronic texts, or that wide distribution for a general reading public would become the most successful use made of electronic texts.

It is well documented that the history of electronic text is almost as long as the history of electronic computing itself. Vannevar Bush famously imagined vast libraries available via the new technology in 1945. Father Roberto Busa began his pioneering effort to create the *Index Thomisticus*, the monumental index to the works of St Thomas Aquinas, in 1946 (Busa 1950, 1992). Other pioneers adopted computers and advocated their use in literary and linguistic research, with electronic texts as the necessary first ingredient. The same early study quoted above divides the world of humanities computing into several categories, as shown in its table of contents:

1 Lexicographical, textual archives, and concordance making
2 Textual editing and attribution studies
3 Vocabulary studies and language learning
4 Stylistic analysis and automated poetry generation

This list encompasses all aspects of humanities scholarship, from literary analysis and author attribution studies, to scholarly editing, to rhetoric and language studies, to the creation of archives of electronic text. While automated poetry generation has yet to find its audience, the other categories seem remarkably prescient. Humanities computing now includes media in other formats such as digital images, audio and video, yet early studies viewed electronic text as the starting point. Electronic text has indeed become common in humanities research and publishing. Many other early studies (Lusignan and North 1977; Hockey 1980; Bailey 1982) enthusiastically describe the potential that computers and electronic text hold for literary studies, and describe similar audiences.

These scholars developed a vision of the importance of electronic texts for the humanities, and developed the standards by which they are created. Humanists, precisely because of their sophisticated understanding of text, have a central role in the development of standards driving the World Wide Web, with far-reaching implications for what can be done today on the Internet.

Still, the kind of environment described by Wisbey in 1971, with computing centers sympathetic to humanists' concerns, existed at only a handful of universities and research centers at that time. One was more likely to find scientists and social scientists at such computer centers than literary scholars or historians. Universities might have had at most one or two humanities professors interested in electronic texts, leaving computing humanists largely isolated, with annual conferences and specialist journals the only opportunities to discuss issues, ideas, and developments with like-minded colleagues.

Skepticism about the use of electronic texts in humanities research has a long history also, and not just among traditionalists. Despite the best efforts of computing humanists, electronic text remained the domain of a few specialists into the early 1990s. In 1993, Mark Olsen wrote:

> [c]omputer processing of textual data in literary and historical research has expanded considerably since the 1960s. In spite of the growth of such applications, however, it would seem that computerized textual research has not had a significant influence on research in humanistic disciplines and that literature research has not been subject to the same shift in perspective that accompanied computer-assisted research in the social science oriented disciplines, such as history. . . . In spite of the investment of significant amounts of money and time in many projects, the role of electronic text in literary research remains surprisingly limited. (Olsen 1993–4: 309)

He goes on to list several reasons to support this assertion. Most importantly, Olsen notes a distrust of computing methodology among humanists at large, and believes that most research involving computing is too narrowly focused to one or two authors. Olsen spoke not as a traditionalist, for he was (and remains) the director of the pioneering collection of electronic text, the *American and French Research on the Treasury of the French Language* (*ARTFL*). He describes the potential of harnessing computers to large collections of literature, and the ability to trace concepts and important keywords over time both within and among various authors' works, along with more sophisticated kinds of analysis. He notes that in at least some disciplines, in the era prior to the World Wide Web, a critical mass of primary texts was available, pointing to the *Thesaurus Linguae Graecae* (*TLG*) for classics and *ARTFL* for modern French. Yet, he still concludes that the potential goes largely ignored. Alison Finch in 1995 displayed even more skepticism in her analysis of computing humanists, as she explored the heroic narratives invoked by literary researchers who use computers, while she claimed that these studies lacked importance to the larger field of literary studies.

Other commentators, less technologically savvy, see darker implications. The best known of these critics, Sven Birkerts in *The Gutenberg Elegies* (1994) and Nicholson Baker in *Double Fold* (2001), mourn the changes wrought by the development of electronic media, and fear that books, once decoupled from their physical presence, will lose their meaning and historical importance. Birkerts, also writing pre-World Wide Web, in particular fears that the digitization of books may lead to the "erosion of language" and a "flattening of historical perspectives" (Birkerts 1994: 128–9). He does not consider other possible outcomes, such as one in which general readers and scholars alike have a better sense of the concerns and ideas of peoples and historical periods with increased access to works otherwise available in only a few libraries. The development of digital collections does not require the destruction of books; instead, it may provoke more interest in their existence and provide different opportunities for their study through keyword and structured searching.

More nuanced critiques recognize the disadvantages of digital technology, while exploring its uses and potentials. As Bornstein and Tinkle noted:

> We agree with the proposition that the shift from print to digital culture has analogies in scale and importance to the shift from manuscript to print culture beginning in the Renaissance. Further, the change enables us to consider more strikingly than ever before the diverse characteristics of manuscript, print, and electronic cultures. This is particularly important now that new electronic technologies are making possible the production, display, and transmission of texts in multiple forms that far exceed the more fixed capacity of traditional codex books. (Bornstein and Tinkle 1998: 2)

Most of these studies were written prior to widespread popularization of the World Wide Web. As a tool, the Web does not solve all of the problems surrounding the creation, storage, delivery and display of electronic texts, but certainly simplifies many of them, particularly in comparison with the older technologies used for electronic text storage and delivery such as ftp, listserv, and Gopher. The early adopters, enthusiasts, and critics viewed electronic texts as the domain of scholars and researchers, and used electronic texts to assist in the traditional work of humanists as outlined in the table of contents reproduced above. They did not foresee the World Wide Web's capacity to reach a wider reading public.

Has the world of electronic texts changed with the ubiquity of the World Wide Web, or are these criticisms still accurate? Put another way, who is the audience for electronic texts today? A recent book on electronic text (Hockey 2000) provides a current view on their audience. Hockey lists these categories in her table of contents:

1   Concordance and Text Retrieval Programs
2   Literary Analysis
3   Linguistic Analysis
4   Stylometry and Attribution Studies
5   Textual Critical and Electronic Editions
6   Dictionaries and Lexical Databases

On the whole, this list is not significantly different from the categories of uses and users in the book edited by Wisbey almost 30 years earlier. Hockey believes that "most of the present interest in electronic texts is focused on access" (Hockey 2000: 3), that is, the use of computers to store and deliver entire texts. In her view, access is the least interesting aspect of electronic texts, for it leaves largely unexploited their real power: the ability for texts to be searched and manipulated by computer programs.

What is Electronic Text?

Answering this simple question could involve textual and literary theory and their intersection with digital technology, as discussed elsewhere in this volume. I wish to focus instead on practical considerations: what forms do electronic texts in the humanities take?

The first type to consider is an electronic transcription of a literary text, in which characters, punctuation, and words are faithfully represented in a computer file, allowing for keyword or contextual searching. Just what is meant by a "faithful representation" of a printed book is at the crux of a long debate, again explored elsewhere in this volume (see chapters 16, 17, and 22, for discussions of theoretical issues, and chapter 32 for more practical matters). A transcription in the form of a computer text file is the most compact form for electronic text, an important consideration given the severe constraints on computer storage and bandwidth that still exist for some people. In addition, this form provides greater ease of manipulation, for searching, for editing, and has significant advantages for people with visual impairments. Another basic form is a digital image of a physical page, allowing readers to see a representation of the original appearance, of great importance for textual scholars. This once seemed impractical given the amount of storage necessary for the hundreds of image files needed for even one book. Now, with ever greater storage available even on desktop computers, this is much less of an issue (while bandwidth remains an issue). Some collections, such as those available through digital libraries at the Library of Congress, the University of Virginia, and the University of Michigan, combine the two forms.

Another category is encoded text. For a multitude of reasons, many scholars and editors believe that encoding schemes, such as that developed by the Text Encoding Initiative (TEI), provide the best and fullest representation of text in all its complexity, allowing the creator or editor an opportunity to encode the hierarchical structures and multitude of features found in text. In addition to the belief that explicit structural markup along with robust metadata will allow for greater longevity of electronic texts, those who choose the TEI use its many elements and features for sophisticated analysis and repurposing of electronic texts for electronic and print publishing. The people developing the TEI have used open standards such as SGML and XML, as well as providing extensive documentation to assist in the use of the standard, as a way of encouraging and promoting the preservation and interchange of e-texts.

Others, notably people associated with Project Gutenberg, distrust all encoding schemes, believing that the lack of encoding will better allow e-texts to survive changes in hardware, operating systems, and application software. No special software and little training are required for contributors to Project Gutenberg, and a volunteer ethos prevails. They will have over 10,000 titles at the end of 2003, but little can be said for the accuracy of the transcriptions, for there is no central editorial control. The lack of encoding means it would be impossible, for example, to separate notes from text, or to determine quickly where chapters begin and end, or to indicate highlighting and font shifts within the text. Still, Project Gutenberg's founder Michael Hart has tapped into a volunteer spirit that drives most open source projects.

Encoding and editorial standards remain expensive, and the more encoding to be added and editing performed, the higher the level of expertise about the original document and/ or the technology for searching and display is required. Projects such as the *Women Writers Online* project at Brown University and the Model Editions Partnership provide extensive documentation about editorial standards and practices. Other projects listed on the TEI Consortium website provide examples of equally detailed documentation and exacting editorial standards.

Some projects have avoided this additional cost by converting page images to text using optical character recognition (OCR) software, and allowing readers to perform keyword searches against the unedited and unencoded text files. The results are displayed as digital images of the original page, with the uncorrected text hidden. While imperfections impede precise and complete results from keyword searches, proponents believe that with adequate OCR accuracy, the results will still prove useful, and at a significantly lower overall cost to produce than highly accurate transcriptions. Some extremely large e-text collections with tens of thousand of volumes and millions of pages, such as the *Making of America* and *American Memory* collections, are based upon this idea, pioneered by John P. Wilkin, called "rough OCR" or "dirty OCR."

Several people have pursued the idea of creating an archive of works containing manuscripts and variant editions, meant for both sophisticated researchers and general readers. In this type of publication, researchers would have access to all manuscript versions, allowing them to trace the development of a work through its variants, while a general audience could use a preferred reading created by the editors and derived directly from the sources. This kind of archive, proposed for authors such as Yeats, Hardy, and others, would be a boon to both audiences, but has proven to be very difficult. Outside of a few notable exceptions such as the *Canterbury Tales Project*, this idea has rarely been realized, indicating the enormous commitment and difficult work required.

A very different category is hypertext. Works of this type are generally original and not representations of previously published works. Hypertext would seem to have great potential for expression, allowing for a multiplicity of narrative choices and making the reader an active participant in the reading experience. Hypertextual content is generally bound inextricably with hypertext software, making productions in this format even more ephemeral than other kinds of electronic text. Some hypertext authors, such as Michael Joyce and Stuart Mouthrop, recognize the impermanence inherent in the genre and incorporate it into their hyperfictions, but this fundamental aspect of its nature will make it difficult or impossible for libraries to collect hyperfictions for the long term. Eventually, even if the medium on which the hypertext is stored remains viable, the software on which it relies will no longer run. While early critics such as Robert Coover believed (with some hope) that hypertext would lead to "the end of books," others, such as Tim Parks, dismiss the genre as "hype."

Creating Electronic Text

Scholars, students, librarians, computing professionals, and general enthusiasts of all kinds create and publish electronic texts. Commercial publishers, notably those previously known for publishing microfilm collections, are digitizing and licensing access to ambitiously large collections of tens of thousands of volumes. A few projects, such as the University of Virginia's collaboration with Chadwyck-Healey to publish *Early American Fiction*, and the Text Creation Partnerships formed for *Early English Books Online* and the *Evans Early American Imprints*, are examples of partnerships between libraries and publishers.

How do humanities scholars and students approach the creation of electronic texts? One axis stretches from a traditional humanities approach, taking time and great pains to create well-considered, well-documented, well-edited electronic works, such as the *Women Writers Online* project at Brown University, the archive of Henrik Ibsen's writings, sponsored by the National Library of Norway and hosted by the universities of Oslo and Bergen, and the archive of Sir Isaac Newton's manuscripts at Imperial College, London, to less rigorous efforts, relying on volunteers and enthusiasts, with the best-known examples being Project Gutenberg and Distributed Proofreaders. This difference in approaches mirrors various editorial approaches in the past century, with the same difference occurring between scholarly editions and reading editions, each with different purposes and audiences. For some scholars, the latter type suffices for classroom use or quick consultation, while for others, the extensive documentation and editorial standards of the former are of paramount importance.

Interestingly, skepticism may play a central role in either attitude. On the one hand, Project Gutenberg enthusiasts, most notably project leader Michael Hart, express skepticism about the added software and expertise needed to create and read encoded electronic texts. His concerns, forged by painful hardware and software changes beginning in the mainframe era, are founded in the belief that the lowest common denominator of encoding will ensure the largest readership and longevity of the texts. Others, equally concerned about longevity and the demands created by changing hardware and software, believe that encoding systems based on international standards such as SGML, XML, and Unicode allow for the best representation of complex textual structures and writing systems, and these formats will prove most useful for scholars and general readers, as well as being the most promising means for the long-term archiving of these works. It should be noted that even some Project Gutenberg texts are available in HTML, PDF, or

Microsoft Ebook reader formats, presumably for the added functionality or characters available beyond plain ASCII. Still, both sides view the other with suspicion.

High-cost equipment is not required for creating electronic text – it can be achieved with the simplest of computers and word processing software. Scanning equipment and OCR software continue to drop in price. However, our expectations of accuracy in printed texts are high – we are generally disappointed to find any errors, and certainly disappointed if we discover an error every 10 to 20 pages. An accurate transcription requires skill and concentration, either in keying it in or in proofreading, yet the standard acceptable accuracy rate used by many large e-text projects is 99.995 percent, or 1 error in every 20,000 characters. Given that an average page has 1,000–2,000 characters, this works out to 1 error every 10 to 20 pages. Spellcheckers, while useful in catching some misspellings, cannot catch typographic errors or inaccurate OCR that result in correctly spelled words, and they are also little help with dialect or creative misspellings that authors employ. Spellcheckers exist for only a limited number of languages as well, making them generally not useful for the work of correcting electronic texts. Instead, it is common for large projects to outsource the creation of electronic text to vendors. Many of these vendors use a technique whereby two or three typists work on the same text. The typists' work is collated, with any discrepancies between the versions being used to find errors. This method produces a high accuracy rate, because the chance of two or three typists making the same error in the same spot in a text is statistically low.

Using Electronic Text

The use of online collections, even collections of relatively obscure writers, remains surprisingly high. As noted above, one group overlooked by most early computing humanists is the general reader, someone willing and interested to read something online, remarkable considering the relatively primitive displays, unsophisticated inter- faces, and slow connections available. These general readers may have many different reasons for using electronic texts – they may lack access to research libraries; they may prefer to find and use books on their computers, in their homes or offices; they may live in countries without access to good collections in foreign languages; the books themselves may be fairly rare and physically available at only a handful of libraries. Whatever the motivation may be, these readers are finding and using electronic texts via the World Wide Web.

Jerome McGann, noted scholar, editor, theorist, and creator of the *Dante Gabriel Rossetti Archives*, places much more value on this aspect of access than does Hockey. A great change has swept through literary studies in the past twenty years, as scholars re-evaluate writers and works overlooked by previous generations of literary critics. The immediate challenge for anyone interested in re-evaluating a little-known text will be to find a copy, for it may be available in only a few libraries. For McGann, collections of electronic texts may be most valuable for holding works by those writers who are less well known, or who are considered minor. In analyzing the Chadwyck-Healey *English Poetry Database*, McGann explains it this way:

For research purposes the database grows less and less useful for those authors who would be regarded, by traditional measures, as the more or the most important writers. It's most useful for so-called minor writers. This paradox comes about for two reasons. On one hand, the poetical works of "minor" writers are often hard to obtain since they exist only in early editions, which are typically rare and can be quite expensive. By providing electronic texts of those hard-to-acquire books, "The English Poetry Database" supplies scholars with important primary materials. On the other hand, the policy of the Database is – wherever possible – to print from collected editions of the poets as such editions exist. The better-known the poet, the more likely there will be collected edition(s). . . . The Database would have done much better to have printed first editions of most of its authors, or at any rate to have made its determinations about editions on scholastic rather than economic grounds. But it did not do this.

[. . .] Speaking for myself, I now use the Database in only two kinds of operation: as a vast concordance, and as an initial source for texts that we don't have in our library. In the latter case I still have to find a proper text of the work I am dealing with. (McGann 1995: 382–3)

The initial hindrances to reading works by lesser-known writers, perhaps insurmountable in the past, can be much more easily overcome in this new medium. It should be noted that even such a digitally adept scholar as McGann prefers printed sources over electronic versions (or at least, still did in 1996). He used the online collection for discovery and research, but turned to the printed copy for verification and citation.

Many problems face a scholar wishing to use electronic texts for research. The immediate problem is in discovering just what is available. Traditionally, a researcher would check the library catalogue to discover whether a particular title or edition is available in the stacks. Given the growing number of online collections, it is impossible to be aware of all relevant sources for any given research topic, and even the specialized portals such as *Voice of the Shuttle* have fallen behind. As it stands now for most online projects, researchers must remember that a particular website has works by Charles Dickens or Margaret Oliphant to find electronic editions by these authors, for they may be found neither in online catalogues nor by using search tools such as Google. Libraries could have records for electronic texts in their online catalogues also and link directly to the electronic editions. However, few libraries have included records for all titles available in, for instance, the *English Poetry Database* from Chadwyck-Healey even if they have acquired the full-text database for their communities. This situation is worse for those texts that are freely available, for the job of discovering and evaluating electronic texts, and then creating and maintaining links to them, is overwhelming.

There is a great deal of interest in improving this situation. Libraries are beginning to include records for electronic texts in their online catalogues. Other developments, such as the Open Archives Initiative, could allow the discovery of the existence of electronic texts much more readily than at present. Methods are under development for searching across collections stored and maintained at different institutions, meaning that someone interested in nineteenth-century American history could perform one search that would be broadcast to the many sites with collections from this period, with results collected and presented in a single interface.

Another problem is the artificial divide that exists between those collections available from commercial publishers and those that are locally created. Generally, these two categories of materials use different interfaces and search systems. This distinction is completely irrelevant to researchers and students, but systems and interfaces that allow for searching both categories of materials simultaneously and seamlessly, while available, are still rare, due to the complexities of authentication and authorization.

Another type of divide exists as well. With the growing body of collections available from commercial publishers, the divide between the haves and have-nots in this area is growing. At a recent conference on nineteenth-century American literature, it was notable that graduate students at research universities had access to a wide range of commercially published electronic text collections, while many of their colleagues, recently graduated with first jobs at smaller institutions, did not. These untenured scholars may not need to travel to institutions to see original documents any more, but they will continue to need support to travel to institutions that have access to licensed collections of electronic texts. There is hope for these scholars, however, as libraries and museums digitize wider portions of their collections and make them publicly available.

A much more complex problem is the limited range of electronic texts that are available. A crazy patchwork quilt awaits any researcher or reader willing to use electronic texts, and as McGann points out, the selection of proper editions may not be given much thought. The situation resembles a land rush, as publishers, libraries, and individuals seek to publish significant collections. The number of freely available texts, from projects such as *Making of America*, to the *Wright American Fiction* project, to the University of Virginia E-Text Center, to the Library of Congress's *American Memory*, is growing at a phenomenal pace.

Commercial publishers are now digitizing large microfilm collections such as Pollard and Redgrave, and Wing (*Early English Books*, published by Bell and Howell/University of Michigan), and Evans (*Early American Imprints*, by Readex), and Primary Source Media has recently announced its intention to digitize the massive *Eighteenth Century* collection. The *English Poetry Database*, first published in 1992 and one of the earliest efforts, used the *New Cambridge Bibliography of English Literature*, first published in 1966 based on an earlier edition from the 1940s, as the basis for inclusion. The collections listed above are based upon bibliographies begun in the 1930s. Those collections of early literature such as the *Early English Books Online* can claim comprehensive coverage of every known publication from Great Britain before 1700, but as these online collections include publications closer to the present time, the less inclusive they can be, given the exponential growth of publishing. Thus, large collections such as the *English Poetry Database* have to employ selection criteria. Critics have debated these traditional collections, known informally as the "canon," and argued for broader inclusion of women or authors in popular genres. These electronic collections, while very large and inclusive, reflect the values and selection criteria of fifty years ago or more.

Some libraries are developing their own digital collections, and McGann suggests it is no coincidence. He sees in literary studies two movements: a return to a "bibliographical center" and a "return to history":

> The imperatives driving libraries and museums toward greater computerization are not the same as those that have brought the now well-known "return to history" in literary and humanities scholarship. Nevertheless, a convergence of the twain has come about, and now the two movements – the computerization of the archives, and the re-historicization of scholarship – are continually stimulating each other toward new ventures. (McGann 1995: 380)

Even with this phenomenal growth, one realizes immediately the inadequacy of using these collections for comprehensive research. Scholars still cannot assume that their fields have an adequate collection of electronic texts available, nor can they assume that those collections that do exist will reflect current thinking about inclusion. McGann stated in 1996, something still true, "the Net has not accumulated those bodies of content that we need if we are to do our work" (p. 382). The collection size of a research library numbers in millions of volumes. The size of the collective electronic text collections available through both commercial publishers and freely available websites probably exceeds 200,000, but not by much. Scholars, students, and librarians are learning that the collections will have to grow considerably in order to reliably meet the needs of a broad range of humanists.

As McGann states, these collections and editions were chosen in large part because they are in the public domain and free of copyright restrictions. The commercial publishers listed above started as microfilm publishers, and their microfilm collections were formed by the same principle. Copyright is the hidden force behind most electronic text collections. Very few electronic text collections, even those from commercial publishers, contain publications under copyright. This has two main effects on electronic collections. First and foremost, it means that most digital collections consist of authors who lived and published up to the twentieth century; the works of writers after that may still be under copyright, and therefore more difficult and perhaps expensive to copy and republish. Second, new editions of these pre-twentieth-century writers are generally excluded, with projects and publishers selecting those in the public domain. Finally, contemporary works of literary criticism, biography, and theory, that could provide needed context and interpretation to the primary literature, also remain largely excluded. The possibilities inherent in the medium, for providing a rich context for the study of primary literary texts and historical documents, have not yet been realized.

The effect of copyright means that researchers and students interested in twentieth-century and contemporary writing are largely prevented from using electronic text. A quick check of the online *MLA Bibliography* shows the number of articles published after 1962 dealing with twentieth-century authors is nearly double that of all other centuries combined, covering 1200–1900 CE. With the majority of researchers and students interested in writers and their work after 1900, it is no wonder that they may consider electronic text largely irrelevant to their studies.

In addition, many of the markers traditionally used by scholars to determine the merit of any given electronic text are missing. There may be no recognizable publisher, no editor, no preface or statement of editorial principles, which may cause scholars to shy away. They are left to their own devices to judge the value of many resources. On the other hand, in this unfamiliar terrain, there may be a tendency to trust the technology in the absence of such markers. Electronic text collections do not receive reviews as frequently as those published commercially, perhaps for some of these same reasons, although they may receive more use. Even in those reviews, one notes an uncritical trust on the part of reviewers. For instance, I assert on the website of the Victorian Women Writers Project (VWWP) that it is "devoted to highly accurate transcriptions" of the texts. I am alternately amused and alarmed to see that phrase quoted verbatim in reviews and websites that link to the VWWP (e.g., Burrows 1999: 155; Hanson 1998; McDermott 2001) without any test of its accuracy. Scholars who use these collections are generally appreciative of the effort required to create these online resources and reluctant to criticize, but one senses that these resources will not achieve wider acceptance until they are more rigorously and systematically reviewed.

It is difficult to find scholarly articles that cite electronic text collections as sources, or discuss the methodology of creating or using e-texts, outside of journals for computing humanists. Humanists have been slow to accept electronic texts for serious research, for the reasons explained above, particularly their scattershot availability, and the inadequate documentation of sources and editorial practices used in creating them. In an article taken from a major scholarly journal almost at random (Knowles 2001), the author investigates the use of the word "patriot" throughout the seventeenth century. He cites familiar authors such as Milton, Dryden, Bacon, Jonson, Sir Winston Churchill, as well as less familiar authors. Electronic text collections such as Chadwyck-Healey's *English Poetry Database* or ProQuest's *Early English Books Online* would be perfectly suited for this purpose – McGann's "vast concordance," with the ability to search across thousands of works, leading to both familiar and unfamiliar works containing the term. However, Knowles does not mention these, although it is possible that he used them behind the scenes. At any rate, it is rare to find them cited in scholarly articles or books, and thus their use and importance goes unnoticed and untested. Scholars need to hear more from their peers about the use of these resources in their research.

Electronic texts have an important place in classroom instruction as well. Julia Flanders points to a survey conducted by *Women Writers Online* in which a majority of professors responded that they "were more likely to use electronic tools in their teaching than in their research" (Flanders 2001: 57). The same problems described above would apply, but she posits that for students, unfamiliarity is an opportunity rather than an obstacle, giving them the chance to interact directly with the texts independent of contextual information and prior interpretation. The form of interaction offered by e-texts, with the opportunity to quickly explore words and terms across a large body of works, is vastly different than that offered by print texts. This approach to literary studies, closely related to traditional philology developed in the nineteenth century, is more common in classical studies, and may account for the successful adoption of computers and digital resources among classicists and medievalists in comparison to those who study and teach later periods.

One assumption underlying much of the criticism of Olsen and Finch noted above is that the computer will in some way aid in literary criticism. Beginning with Father Busa, up to the creation of the World Wide Web, computer-aided analysis was the entire purpose of electronic texts, as there was no simple way for people to share their works. More recent books (Sutherland 1997; Hockey 2000) have shifted focus to the methods needed to create and publish electronic texts, leaving aside any discussion of their eventual use.

Still, Hockey and others point to the inadequacies of the tools available as another limitation to wider scholarly acceptance of electronic texts. Early electronic texts, such as the WordCruncher collection of texts, were published on CD-ROM along with tools for their use. While there are a multitude of problems associated with this kind of bundling, it certainly made entrance to use very easy. Today, many collections of electronic texts contain tools for simple navigation and keyword searching, but little else. As Hockey notes (2000: 167), "[c]omplex tools are needed, but these tools must also be easy for the beginner to use," which explains in part why few exist. Another researcher, Jon K. Adams, writes:

Like many researchers, I have found the computer both a fascinating and frustrating tool. This fascination and frustration, at least in my case, seems to stem from a common source: we should be able to do much more with the computer in our research on literary texts than we actually do. (Adams 2000: 171)

In some sense, while the World Wide Web has sparked development and distribution of electronic texts in numbers unthinkable before it, the tools available for using these texts are of lesser functionality than those available through the previous means of publishing, such as CD-ROMs. This is perhaps due to the lack of consensus about the uses of electronic texts, as well as the difficulty of creating generalized text analysis tools for use across a wide range of collections. The acceptance of more sophisticated automated analysis will remain limited until more sophisticated tools become more widely available. Until then, the most common activities will be fairly simple keyword searches, and text retrieval and discovery. These types of research can be powerful and important for many scholars, but do not begin to tap the potential of humanities computing.

Still, even noting their inadequacies, these collections are finding audiences. The E-text Center at the University of Virginia reports that their collections receive millions of uses every year. *Making of America* at the University of Michigan reports similar use. The *Victorian Women Writers Project* (VWWP), which contains about 200 works by lesser-known nineteenth-century British women writers, receives over 500,000 uses per year. The most popular works in the VWWP collection include such books as Caroline Norton's study *English Laws for Women*, Vernon Lee's gothic stories *Hauntings*, and Isabella Bird's travel writings. These writers are better known than most of the others in the collection. Nevertheless, the most heavily used work in the collection is *Maud* and Eliza Keary's *Enchanted Tulips and Other Verse for Children*, which receives thousands of uses per month. This is one indication that scholars are not the only audience for electronic text. In the end, the general reader, students, and elementary and secondary school teachers, particularly those in developing countries without access to good libraries, may be the largest and most eager audience for these works.

Electronic texts give humanists access to works previously difficult to find, both in terms of locating entire works, with the Internet as a distributed interconnected library, and in access to the terms and keywords within the works themselves, as a first step in analysis. As reliable and accurate collections grow, and as humanists come to understand their scope and limitations, the use of e-texts will become recognized as a standard first step in humanities research. As tools for the use of e-texts improve, humanists will integrate e-texts more deeply and broadly into their subsequent research steps. Until then, electronic texts will remain, in Jerome McGann's words, a "vast concordance" and library with great potential.

BIBLIOGRAPHY

Adams, Jon K. (2000). Narrative Theory and the Executable Text. *Journal of Literary Semantics* 29,3: 171–81.
American Memory. Washington, DC: Library of Congress. Accessed October 13, 2003. At <http://memory.loc.gov>.

ARTFL: Project for American and French Research on the Treasury of the French Language. Mark Olsen, ed. University of Chicago. Accessed October 13, 2003. At <http://humanities.uchicago.edu/orgs/ ARTFL>.

Bailey, Richard W. (ed.) (1982). *Computing in the Humanities: Papers from the Fifth International Conference on Computing in the Humanities.* Amsterdam: North Holland.

Baker, Nicholson (2001). *Double Fold: Libraries and the Assault on Paper.* New York: Random House.

Birkerts, Sven (1994). *The Gutenberg Elegies: The Fate of Reading in an Electronic Age.* Boston: Faber and Faber.

Bornstein, George and Theresa Tinkle (1998). Introduction. In *The Iconic Page in Manuscript, Print and Digital Culture,* ed. Bornstein and Tinkle (pp. 2–6). Ann Arbor: University of Michigan Press.

Burrows, Toby (1999). *The Text in the Machine: Electronic Texts in the Humanities.* New York: Haworth Press.

Busa, Roberto (1950). Complete *Index Verborum* of Works of St Thomas. *Speculum* 25,3: 424–5.

—— (1992). Half a Century of Literary Computing: Towards a "New" Philology. *Literary and Linguistic Computing* 7,1: 69–72.

Bush, Vannevar (1945). As We May Think. *The Atlantic Monthly* (July): 101–8.

Canterbury Tales Project. Peter Robinson, ed. De Montfort University. Accessed October 13, 2003. At <http://www.cta.dmu.ac.uk/projects/ctp/>.

Coover, Robert (1992). The End of Books. *The New York Times Book Review* (June 21): 1, 4.

Early American Fiction. ProQuest/Chadwyck-Healey. Accessed October 13, 2003. At <http://e-text. virginia.edu/eaf/>.

Early English Books Online Text Creation Partnership. University of Michigan Library. Accessed October 13, 2003. At <http://www.lib.umich.edu/eebo/>.

Electronic Text Center. Alderman Library, University of Virginia. Accessed October 13, 2003. At <http:// e-text.virginia.edu>.

Evans Early American Imprint Collection Text Creation Partnership. University of Michigan Library. Accessed October 13, 2003. At <http://www.lib.umich.edu/evans/>.

Finch, Alison (1995). The Imagery of a Myth: Computer-Assisted Research on Literature. *Style* 29,4: 511–21.

Flanders, Julia (2001). Learning, Reading, and the Problem of Scale: Using *Women Writers Online.* *Pedagogy* 2,1: 49–59.

Hanson, R. (1998). Review, *Victorian Women Writers Project. Choice* 35 (Supplement): 88.

Hockey, Susan (1980). *A Guide to Computer Applications in the Humanities.* Baltimore: Johns Hopkins University Press.

—— (2000). *Electronic Texts in the Humanities: Principles and Practices.* Oxford: Oxford University Press.

Knowles, Ronald (2001). The "All-Attoning Name": the Word "Patriot" in Seventeenth-century England. *Modern Language Review* 96,3: 624–43.

Lusignan, Serge and John S. North (eds.) (1977). *Computing in the Humanities: Proceedings of the Third International Conference on Computing in the Humanities.* Waterloo, ON: University of Waterloo Press.

Making of America. Ann Arbor: University of Michigan. Accessed October 15, 2003. At <http:// moa.umdl.umich.edu>.

McDermott, Irene (2001). Great Books Online, *Searcher* 9,8: 71–7.

McGann, Jerome (1996). Radiant Textuality. *Victorian Studies* 39,3: 379–90.

Model Editions Partnership. David Chestnut, Project Director, University of South Carolina. October 13, 2003 <http://mep.cla.sc.edu>.

Olsen, Mark (1993–4). Signs, Symbols, and Discourses: A New Direction for Computer-aided Literature Studies. *Computers and the Humanities* 27,5–6: 309–14.

Parks, Tim (2002). Tales Told by a Computer. *New York Review of Books* 49:16 (October 24): 49–51.

Schaffer, Talia (1999). Connoisseurship and Concealment in *Sir Richard Calmady*: Lucas Malet's Strategic Aestheticism. In Talia Schaffer and Kathy Alexis Psomiades (eds.), *Women and British Aestheticism.* Charlottesville: University Press of Virginia.

Sutherland, Kathryn (ed.) (1997). *Electronic Text: Investigations in Method and Theory*. New York: Oxford University Press.

Text Encoding Initiative. University of Oxford, Brown University, University of Virginia, University of Bergen. Accessed October 13, 2003. At <http://www.tei-c.org>.

Thesaurus Linguae Graecae (1999). CD-ROM. Irvine, CA: University of California, Irvine.

Victorian Women Writers Project. Perry Willett, ed. Indiana University. Accessed October 13, 2003. At <http://www.indiana.edu/~letrs/vwwp>.

Wilkin, John P. (1997). Just-in-time Conversion, Just-in-case Collections: Effectively Leveraging Rich Document Formats for the WWW. *D-Lib Magazine* (May). Accessed October 13, 2002. At <http://www.dlib.org/dlib/may97/michigan/05pricewilkin.html>.

Wisbey, R. A. (ed.) (1971). *The Computer in Literary and Linguistic Research: Papers from a Cambridge Symposium*. Cambridge: Cambridge University Press.

Women Writers Online Project. Julia Flanders, ed. Brown University. Accessed October 13, 2003. At <http://www.wwp.brown.edu>.

The WordCruncher Disk (1990). CD-ROM. Orem, Utah: Electronic Text Corporation.

19

Modeling: A Study in Words and Meanings

Willard McCarty

Out on site, you were never parted from your plans. They were your Bible. They got dog-eared, yellowed, smeared with mud, peppered with little holes from where you had unrolled them on the ground. But although so sacred, the plans were only the start. Once you got out there on the site everything was different. No matter how carefully done, the plans could not foresee the *variables*. It was always interesting, this moment when you saw for the first time the actual site rather than the idealised drawings of it.

He knew men who hated the *variables*. They had their plans and by golly they were going to stick to them. If the site did not match the drawings it was like a personal insult.

He himself liked the variables best. He liked the way that the solution to one problem created another problem further down the line, so that you had to think up something else, and that in turn created another problem to solve. It was an exchange, backwards and forwards. Some men thought of it as a war, but to him it was more like a conversation.

Kate Grenville, *The Idea of Perfection* (Sydney: Picador, 1999): 62–3

Introduction

The question of modeling arises naturally for humanities computing from the prior question of what its practitioners across the disciplines have in common. What are they all *doing* with their computers that we might find in their diverse activities indications of a coherent or cohesible practice? How do we make the best, most productive sense of what we observe? There are, of course, many answers: practice varies from person to person, from project to project, and ways of construing it perhaps vary even more. In this chapter I argue for modeling as a model of such a practice. I have three confluent goals: to identify humanities computing with an intellectual ground shared by the older disciplines, so that we may say how and to what extent our field is *of* as well as *in* the humanities, how it draws from and adds to them; at the same time to reflect experience with computers "in the wild"; and to aim at the most challenging problems, and so the most intellectually rewarding future now imaginable.

My primary concern here is, as Confucius almost said, that we *use the correct word* for the activity we share lest our practice go awry for want of understanding (*Analects* 13.3). Several words are on offer. By what might be called a moral philology I examine them, arguing for the most popular of these, "modeling." The nominal form, "model," is of course very useful and even more popular, but for reasons I will adduce, its primary virtue is that properly defined it defaults to the present participle, its semantic lemma. Before getting to the philology I discuss modeling in the light of the available literature and then consider the strong and learned complaints about the term.

Background

Let me begin with provisional definitions.[1] By "modeling" I mean *the heuristic process of constructing and manipulating models*; a "model" I take to be either *a representation of something for purposes of study*, or *a design for realizing something new*. These two senses follow Clifford Geertz's analytic distinction between a denotative "model *of*," such as a grammar describing the features of a language, and an exemplary "model *for*," such as an architectural plan (Geertz 1973: 93).[2] In both cases, as the literature consistently emphasizes, a model is by nature a simplified and therefore fictional or idealized representation, often taking quite a rough-and-ready form: hence the term "tinker toy" model from physics, accurately suggesting play, relative crudity, and heuristic purpose (Cartwright 1983: 158). By nature modeling defines a ternary relationship in which it mediates epistemologically, between modeler and modeled, researcher and data or theory and the world (Morrison and Morgan 1999). Since modeling is fundamentally relational, the same object may in different contexts play either role: thus, e.g., the grammar may function prescriptively, as a model *for* correct usage, the architectural plan descriptively, as a model *of* an existing style. The distinction also reaches its vanishing point in the convergent purposes of modeling: the model *of* exists to tell us that we do not know, the model *for* to give us what we do not yet have. Models *realize*.

Perhaps the first question to ask is what such a process has to do with computing, since as the examples suggest neither of the two senses of "model" assumes it unless the definition is further qualified. In history, for example, Gordon Leff has argued that models have always been *implicit* in scholarly practice (Leff 1972). Leff cites, e.g., the historiographical notion of "epoch," but any well-articulated idea would qualify as a model *of* its subject. Nevertheless, Leff notes that as M. I. Finley said in *Ancient History: Evidence and Models*, "model-construction is rare among all but economic historians"; Finley recommends Max Weber's parallel concept of "ideal types," which "expresses clearly the nature and function of models in historical inquiry" (1986: 60f). Explicit model-construction is still rare in mainstream humanities scholarship. Even for non-computational research in the social sciences, it is more common, as Finley's demarcation suggests. For example, political schemes by nature model *for* a better or at least different world, even if like Marx's historiography they begin as models *of* it; delineating them as models is the scholar's obvious work (Mironesco 2002). Nevertheless, outside computationally affected scholarly practice Marvin Minsky's simple, straightforward definition remains alien in style and in thought: "To an observer B, an object A* is a model of an object A to the extent that B can use A* to answer questions that interest him about A" (Minsky 1995).

A strong temptation for us here is to dismiss the residual alienness of Minsky's formulation and to accept, as we have accepted computing, the reified, explicit "model" of Minsky's definition as what we *really* have been doing all along. This would, however, be a serious error. As with the relationship of hypertext to earlier ways of referring (McCarty 2002), the new form of expression, with its vocabulary and tools, means an altered way of thinking. A historical imagination is required to see what this means.

Two effects of computing make the distinction between "idea" or other sort of mental construct on the one hand, and on the other "model" in the sense we require: first, the demand for computational tractability, i.e., for complete explicitness and absolute consistency; second, the manipulability that a computational representation provides.

The first effects a sea-change by forcing us to confront the radical difference between what we know and what we can specify computationally, leading to the epistemological question of *how we know what we know*. On the one hand, as Michael Polanyi observed, "we can know more than we can tell" (1966: 4–5). Computational form, which accepts only that which can be told explicitly and precisely, is thus radically inadequate for representing the full range of knowledge – hence useful for isolating the tacit or inchoate kinds. On the other hand, we need to trust what we somehow know, at least provisionally, in order not to lose all that goes without saying or cannot be said in computational form.

Take, for example, knowledge one might have of a particular thematic concentration in a deeply familiar work of literature. In modeling one begins by privileging this knowledge, however wrong it might later turn out to be, then building a computational representation of it, e.g., by specifying a structured vocabulary of word-forms in a text-analysis tool. In the initial stages of use, this model would be almost certain to reveal trivial errors of omission and commission. Gradually, however, through perfective iteration trivial error is replaced by meaningful surprise. There are in general two ways in which a model may violate expectations and so surprise us: either by a success we cannot explain, e.g., finding an occurrence where it should not be; or by a likewise inexplicable failure, e.g., not finding one where it is otherwise clearly present. In both cases modeling problematizes. As a tool of research, then, modeling succeeds intellectually when it results in failure, either directly within the model itself or indirectly through ideas it shows to be inadequate. This failure, in the sense of expectations violated, is, as we will see, fundamental to modeling.

The second quality of "model" that distinguishes it from "idea" is manipulability, i.e., the capability of being handled, managed, worked, or treated by manual and, by extension, any mechanical means (*OED*: 1a.). Change is common to both models and ideas, but at greater or lesser metaphorical distance, "model" denotes a concrete, articulated plan inviting the etymological sense of action-by-hand (L. *manus*) in response. Manipulation in turn requires something that can be handled (physical objects, diagrams, or symbols of a formal language) – and a time-frame sufficiently brief that the emphasis falls on the process rather than its product. In other words, the modeling system must be interactive. Manipulable objects from the physical to the metaphorical have characterized mathematics, engineering, the physical sciences, and the arts *ab ovo*, but with exceptions the necessary time-frame, allowing for interactivity, has been possible only with computing. With its advent, Minsky has noted, models could be "conceived, tested, and discarded in days or weeks instead of years" (1991). Computing met research easily in fields where modeling was already an explicit method because, Brian Cantwell Smith has pointed out, models are fundamental to computing: to do anything useful at all a computer must have a model of something, real or imaginary, in software. But in the context of computing, models *per se* are not the point. What distinguishes computers from other kinds of machines, Smith notes, is that "they run by *manipulating* representations, and representations are always formulated in terms of models" (Smith 1995/1985: 460; cf. Fetzer 1999: 23).

In other words, computational models, however finely perfected, are better understood as *temporary states in a process of coming to know* rather than fixed structures of knowledge. It is of course possible to argue teleologically, as some still do, that we are converging on and will achieve such structures,[3] but in any case these structures would not then be *models* and would no longer have reason to exist in software. (Note that the history of computing is the story of ever more complex and extensive software, not less, despite the fact that implementations in hardware are faster and can be cheaper.) For the moment and the foreseeable future, then, *computers are essentially modeling machines, not knowledge jukeboxes*. To think of them as the latter is profoundly to misunderstand human knowledge – and so to constrict it to the narrow scope of the achievably mechanical.

In analytical terms, as I have suggested, modeling has two phases: first, construction; second, manipulation. Examples come readily to mind from ordinary technical practice, e.g., building a relational database, then querying the data thus shaped to explore emergent patterns. As experience with databases shows, the two phases often blur into each other especially in the early stages when use uncovers faults or suggests improvements that direct redesign. A model *of* and a model *for* may be distinct types – because in our terms they are fixed objects. But modeling *of* something readily turns into modeling *for* better or more detailed knowledge of it; similarly, the knowledge gained from realizing a model *for* something feeds or can feed into an improved version. This characteristic blurring of design into use and use into (re)design is what denies modeling *of* any sense of closure. Modeling *for*, utopian by definition, is denied it in any case.

Learned Complaints

So far so good – but at the cost of averting our gaze from the problems with the word "model." Indeed, the extensive and growing literature on the topic may seem adrift in a hopeless muddle. "I know of no model of a model," physicist H. J. Groenewold declared many years ago (1960: 98). The philosopher Peter Achinstein has warned us away even from attempting a systematic theory (1968: 203). The word itself is indeed astonishingly polysemous – or promiscuous, as Nelson Goodman puts it. "Model," he complains, can be used to denote "almost anything from a naked blonde to a quadratic equation" (1976: 171). Nevertheless, the word is often used as if its semantic complexity either did not exist or could be safely ignored. The muddle of partly overlapping, partly contradictory senses is proof enough that we ignore it at our peril. Nor can we simply avoid the problem by dismissing "model" altogether, as Goodman and others recommend, without (as I will argue) hobbling our ability to understand *inter alia* those aspects of computing most important to research – one might even say, as I do, its essence. Despite several other, supposedly less confusing terms on offer, the word remains stubbornly popular in the literature of the social and physical sciences, the history and philosophy of science, cognitive science, artificial intelligence, and related areas.

Theoretical physicist John Ziman and philosopher Stephen Toulmin, for example, recommend "map" on the basis of its conceptual clarity and fitness for describing the relationship between theoretical knowledge and reality (Ziman 2000: 126–38, 147–50; Toulmin 1953: 94–109). Goodman would have us collapse modeling into diagramming, which he thinks less troublesome (1976: 171–3). But preference needs to be based on more than such criteria; "map," for example, serves experiment much less well than theory, as I will show. We require a close and careful look at the semantic fields of all major alternatives, including "map," for their disjunctions and overlaps. We need to scrutinize each of these, asking what does it denote *and connote* that the others do not, and vice versa? What do all have in common? What are their individual tendencies of mind, and which of these best suits computing as we are learning to conceive it?

Philological Analysis of Related Terms

So far I have used the term "model" as the default, partly for purposes of convenience, partly because, as I argue, it is right for the job. To answer the learned criticisms and further clarify our topic, however, I propose to question it by comparison against the major alternatives: "analogy," "representation," "diagram," "map," "simulation," and "experiment." As we have seen, the two decisive criteria are that the thing named by the chosen term be computationally tractable and manipulable. Tractability in turn requires complete explicitness and absolute consistency; manipulability resolves into mechanical action and interactivity. Hence the term must denote a continual process of coming to know, not an achievement but an approximation. As I have argued, it is from the difference between the approximation and the reality approximated – which ultimately for the humanities is our humanly known apprehension of that reality – that we learn.

For each of the alternative terms I ask whether and to what degree the word normally denotes a dynamic process and whether it refers to a concrete, i.e. manipulable, form – the requirements of anything whose function is fulfilled through being changed. Corresponding to the two senses of "model" I identified earlier, the denotative model *of* and the exemplary model *for*, I also ask whether each word tends to the mimetic (imitation) or proleptic (anticipation). The distinction helps in determining whether the action denoted by a term may be said to be bounded, either by a fixed form, as is the case with "analogy," or by an inherent tendency to reach a definitive or satisfactory conclusion, as in "representation."

Thus bringing "model" into focus against the semantic background of these other terms will show that the problem has not so much been too many meanings for "model" as use without regard to any of them, often as if the sense of it simply goes without saying. It doesn't. But perhaps the most important lesson we learn from seeing the word in the context of its synonym set is not the range and variety of its meanings; rather, again, its strongly dynamic potential. Apart from the popularity of "model" taken at face-value, the word would have little to recommend it (and, as the complainers say, much against it) but for the open-ended *present-participial* strength of "modeling."[4] Indeed, the manifest confusion in the literature on the topic may be primarily due to a mistaken preference for the noun – as if getting a model right, and so promoting it to the status of theory, were the point. Modeling has an entirely different role to play. There are several better terms if what one wants is to name a stable conceptualization.

Analogy

"Analogy" (Gk. ἀναλογία, "equality of ratios, proportion") is, like "model," a highly polysemous term with a long and complex career.[5] John Stuart Mill complained that "no word . . . is used more loosely, or in a greater variety of senses, than Analogy" (*A System of Logic*, 1882). Yet Dr Johnson's pithy definition, "resemblance of things with regard to some circumstances or effects," and Mill's even pithier one, "resemblance of relations," give us an idea of why it is so fruitful. From its original meaning in Greek mathematics, analogy specifies a structured relationship between pairs of related quantities, which for convenience may be represented in the form of an equation, "A/B = C/D," read "as A is to B, so C is to D." Extended beyond mathematics to other modes of reasoning, analogy yields a powerful (but still poorly understood) means of inferring from the one relation to the other. Like most of the words in our domain, "analogy" is proleptic, a means of inference, based on conjecture, to something unknown or uncertain. Examples in the history of science are plentiful, e.g., Kepler's discovery of the *vis motrix*, or cause of planetary motion, by reasoning that as the sun radiated light, so it must also radiate this motive power (Gentner 2002).

Here I wish only to argue two points. The first is that analogy is basic to the entire vocabulary. Although not every model is as strictly based on an analogy as Kepler's, modeling is inherently analogical, with just the features that make the idea attractive for our purposes. Thus we require a structured correspondence between model and artifact, so that by playing with one we can infer facts about the other. (For example, by adjusting choice of words and weightings for a distribution-display across a textual corpus, one can investigate the effect of vocabulary on the interplay of meanings in that corpus.) The second point is that "analogy" is inherently static: it means either a type of relationship or an instance of one, never an object and not, literally or directly, a process. Action is implied in the ratio of quantities – thus Kepler's "as A *does* B, so C *does* D" – but *acting* is not denoted by the analogy. The word has no commonly used verbal form ("analogize" and "analogizing" are rare if not strange). Although an analogy may be algebraically or geometrically expressed and may refer to concrete objects, it itself is abstract.

Because analogy works so well as a way of describing how we often think, efforts to understand acquisition of new knowledge tend to engage with theories of analogy and to propose many mechanisms, e.g., in cognitive science, educational theory, and artificial intelligence (Hoffman 1995). Because modeling is analogical, this work is potentially relevant to questions raised in computing the artifacts of the humanities. We need to pay attention here.

Representation

"Representation" in Nelson Goodman's terms is defined by a symbolic denotative correspondence, not likeness or imitation (1976: 3–41).[6] In a less philosophically precise sense, however, we may say that "representation" displays strong mimetic tendencies, e.g., in the definition given by the *OED*: "An image, likeness, or reproduction in some manner of a thing. . . . A material image or figure; a reproduction in some material or tangible form; in later use esp. a drawing or painting (of a person or thing)." The history of aesthetics from earliest times, in fits and starts of fashion, demonstrates that the copy-theory of representation, though its falsity names its achievement in a *trompe l'oeil*, remains a habit of mind. If in aesthetics, why not in computer science?

A well-attested present participle and a full complement of verbal forms establishes the action of *representing*, but semantically this action is bounded by its relationship to the represented object, whether this be symbolic or imitative.

As with "analogy," the semantic fields of "model" and "representation" clearly overlap, but the situation is more complex because of the mimetic and proleptic kinds of "model." Hence (Platonism aside) we may say that modeling *of* is representational but not modeling *for*. In fact a model *of* is a manipulable variety of representation – which any representation in software would of course be. The crucial difference between model *of* and representation is the quality of the action implied. Unlike representing, modeling *of* is denied closure, as I noted earlier. It has no satisfactory *trompe l'oeil* or symbolizing conclusion. If the researcher calls a halt, then the last state of the system, as it were, is better called a "representation."

In the context of computing, the meaning of "representation" is dominated by the subfield of artificial intelligence known as "knowledge representation" (KR). Given the scope of this essay I can do little more than make a few observations, chiefly about the assumptions built into the name and apparently into tendencies in some KR work. In brief, my argument concerning KR is that it needs to be understood as a particularly rigorous control on model-building suitable to that which can be stated in propositional form.[7]

To the connotations of "representation" I have already reviewed, KR adds the demarcational term "knowledge." The point I wish to draw from current epistemology is a simple one, for which I quote Michael Williams – at length, because the issues are consequential for us:

> "Knowledge" is an honorific title we confer on our paradigm cognitive achievements. . . . More generally, "know" is a "success-term", like "win" or "pass" (a test). Knowledge is not just a factual state or condition but a particular *normative status*. Such statuses are related to appropriate factual states: winning depends on crossing the line before any other competitor. But they also depend on meeting certain norms or standards which define, not what you *do* do, but what you *must* or *ought* to do. To characterize someone's claim as expressing or not expressing knowledge is to pass judgement on it. Epistemic judgements are thus a particular kind of *value-judgement*. . . .
>
> This normative dimension distinguishes philosophical theories of knowledge from straightforwardly factual inquiries and explains why demarcational (and related methodological) issues are so significant. Because epistemological distinctions are invidious, ideas about epistemological demarcation always involve putting some claims or methods above others: mathematics above empirical science, empirical science above metaphysics or religion, logic above rhetoric, and so on. Demarcational projects use epistemological criteria to sort areas of discourse into factual and non-factual, truth-seeking and merely expressive, and, at the extreme, meaningful and meaningless. Such projects amount to proposals for a map of

culture: a guide to what forms of discourse are "serious" and what are not. Disputes about demarcation – induding disputes about whether demarcational projects should be countenanced at all – are disputes about the shape of our culture and so, in the end, of our lives. (2001: 11–12)

Projects such as Cyc, based on what Northrop Frye characterized as the discredited *Wissenschaft*-theory of knowledge – that its accumulation in vast quantities will one day, somehow, result in understanding[8] – clearly assume if not perfect closure, then a threshold beyond which lack of perfection ceases to matter. But to whom, and for what purposes?[9] Apart from such questions, and the serious doubts within computer science on the wisdom of building massive knowledge-bases for expert systems[10] – there are, again, the very serious demarcational issues. When, for example, one of the leading theorists of KR writes in passing that, "Perhaps there are some kinds of knowledge that cannot be expressed in logic" (Sowa 2000: 12), our intellectual claustrophobia tells an important tale. Not, of course, the only one. If the point of modeling is to fail well, then KR has a vital quality-control function to serve.

Diagram

A diagram (Gk. διάγραμμα, "that which is marked out by lines, a geometrical figure, written list, register, the gamut or scale in music")[11] is an analogical drawing, "a figure drawn in such a manner that the geometrical relations between the parts of the figure illustrate relations between other objects": thus the physicist James Clerk Maxwell on the graphic, symbolic, and hybrid kinds (1911). Such a diagram ranges from the precisely drawn schematic, whose measurements are significant, to the rough sketch intended to express symbolic relations only. But what makes a graphic a diagram, properly so called, is the way in which it is read, not its resemblance to anything.[12] Reviel Netz argues the point for the lettered diagram in Greek mathematical texts: "It is only the diagram perceived in a certain way which may function alongside the text" – irrelevant discrepancies are overlooked, the important matters denoted by the lettering: "All attention is fixed upon the few intersecting points, which are named" (1999: 33–5). Even when the diagrammed entity is a physical object, the diagram represents structure and interrelation of essential parts, foregrounding interpretative choice and conscious purpose. The ability to manipulate structures and parts may be implied.

The word "diagram" doubles as noun and verb and has a full range of verbal inflections. Like "represent," its action is bounded, but more by ideas than appearance, even when that appearance is precisely delineated. As Maxwell notes for physics, diagrams often represent force or movement, even if only implicitly, though the form is static. As a means of communication, e.g., in a lecture or discussion between collaborators, diagramming is the point, not the static trace left behind. That trace may in fact be unintelligible apart from the discussion of which it was a dynamic part.

The focus on ideas rather than things *per se*, the role of manipulation where diagramming is heuristic and the kinaesthetics of the action suggest the close relationship between diagramming and modeling for which Goodman argues. Models *of*, he declares, "are in effect diagrams, often in more than two dimensions and with working parts . . . [and] diagrams are flat and static models" (1972: 172–3). Nevertheless, the two-dimensionally graphic, geometrical, and finally static qualities of the diagram define it, not "model," which has considerably broader applications.

Sun-Joo Shin and Oliver Lemon note that although diagramming is very likely one of the oldest forms of communication, modern logicians and philosophers have tended until recently to regard it as only of marginal importance.[13] That is changing very rapidly now. As a cognitive, reasoning process it is studied in relation to Greek mathematics and geometry in particular (Netz 1999). Modern philosophical attention can be traced from Descartes's "La Géometrie" (1637) and Kant's *Critique of Pure Reason* II.1.1 (1781) to Peirce's "existential graphs" in the late nineteenth century, significantly as part of his much broader interest in scientific discovery, to which I will return. His work is now central to much current research.

Shin and Lemon delineate three branches of research since the mid-1990s: (1) multi-modal and especially non-linguistic reasoning, in the philosophy of mind and cognitive science; (2) logical equivalence of symbolic and diagrammatic systems, in logic; and (3) heterogeneous systems implementing theories of multi-modal reasoning, in computer science. The close relationship of diagramming and modeling make this research immediately relevant.

Map

A map may be defined as a schematic spatial representation, or following Maxwell, a diagram of "anything that can be spatially conceived."[14] Indeed, if not for the geographical focus of mapping, the semantic fields of "map" and "diagram" would completely overlap: both are fully verbal, their action bounded by a graphical representation that has both strongly mimetic and ideational aspects; both manipulate data for specific purposes and introduce fictional elements to serve these purposes. But the long history of mapping the physical world for exploration and description gives "map" specific (and evidently powerful) connotations.

Mapping is particularly characteristic of an early, exploratory period, when a territory is unknown to its discoverers (or conquerors). Mapping constructs the world it represents, selectively, therefore shaping thought and guiding action. It orients the newcomer, giving him or her control of the mapped terrain, at the same time expressing, though perhaps covertly, a perspective, a set of interests, and a history. Mapping attaches meaning to place. Like modeling it can be either *of* or *for* a domain, either depicting the present landscape or specifying its future – or altering how we think about it, e.g., by renaming its places. A map is never entirely neutral, politically or otherwise.

As I have noted, John Ziman, following Stephen Toulmin, has argued persuasively for describing scientific research as mapping – hence the immediate relevance of the carto-graphic imagination to my project. Mapping particularly fits a Kuhnian view of research: long periods of stable activity within a settled terrain interspersed by revolutionary, and perhaps incommensurable, reconceptualizations of that terrain. Mapping is for our purposes more to the point than representation, because we always know that there can be many maps for any territory and that all of them have a fictional character (which is why the map is a standard example of an interpretative genre for data[15]). But because its action is bounded and its result defines a world, mapping better suits the theoretician's than the experimenter's view.

In computer science, mapping is used in knowledge and argument representation and implementation of schemes for depicting cyberspace in general and the Web in particular. The term surfaces in "Topic Maps," "Concept Maps," and is implicit in talk about, e.g., "semantic networks." This interest seems to originate with Toulmin's mapping of argument (Toulmin 1958), which suggests techniques of automated inferencing in AI. (Maps of argument look like flowcharts.) As a form of data-visualization, mapping also connects with a very strong, recent interest in humanities computing (Kirschenbaum 2002), and so connects this interest with modeling.

Simulation

"Simulation" is "The technique of imitating the behaviour of some situation or process... by means of a suitably analogous situation or apparatus" (*OED*).[16] Its mimetic tendencies and so bounded action are perhaps most emphatic among the terms we are considering. Again, total replication is not at issue; a simulation attends to selected details of the world, thus can be exploratory, as when relevant conditions of flight are simulated for purposes of study or training. Simulation also relies on abstraction from the original to the analogue system (Simon 1969: 15–18), which makes it a kind of representation, subject to the same philosophical argument including the caveat respecting mimesis. But in usage, the connotation, if not denotation, of an *exact* correspondence between simulation and original remains paradoxically alongside knowledge of real difference.[17] That knowledge, however uneasily, can be put aside, as in what we now call "virtual reality" (VR).[18]

In its current form VR is of course quite a recent phenomenon, but the essential movement of simulation on which it is based, from self-conscious imitation to displacement of reality, is attested from the get-go of applied computing, in the weapons research in nuclear physics immediately following World War II. "Proven on the most complex physical problem that had ever been undertaken in the history of science," Peter Galison notes, simulation came to replace experimental reality, thus blurring multiple boundaries that had previously defined research, redefining it in new terms (1997: 690f). Since then the turn away from traditional analytic methods to simulation has spread to several other fields (Burch 2002). As the biologist Glenn W. Rowe points out, with this turn has come the realization that "a great many systems seem to have an inherent complexity that cannot be simplified"[19] – and so must be studied *as simulations*. Thus simulation has opened our eyes to the new problems with which it can deal. In the humanities we have known for some years that computer-based simulations, in the form of pedagogical games, can play a role in teaching. An old but very good example is *The Would-Be Gentleman*, a re-creation of economic and social life in seventeenth-century France in which the student-player must realize and put aside his or her modern preconceptions in order to win (Lougee 1988). In other words he or she must *become* a seventeenth-century Frenchman mentally and emotionally. From more recent and far more technically advanced VR applications, such as Richard Beacham's and Hugh Denard's reconstruction of the theater of Pompey in Rome (Beacham and Denard 2003), one can predict a scholarly future for simulation in many areas of humanistic research.

Simulation, like game-playing, tends to forgetfulness of the mechanism by which it is created, so long as its terms of engagement (expressed in parameters and algorithms) are fixed. Unfix them – e.g., in *The Would-Be Gentleman* by allowing the player to change the encoded attitude toward marrying above or below one's station – and the simulation becomes a modeling exercise directed to exploring the question of that attitude. Thus simulation crosses over into modeling when the constants of the system become variables. Modeling, one might say, is a *self-conscious* simulation, and simulation an *assimilated* modeling.

Experiment

In common usage "experiment" (L. *experiri*, to try) is either "An action or operation undertaken in order to discover something unknown..." or "The action of trying anything, or putting it to proof; a test, trial..." (*OED*). In its broadest sense, the word embraces "modeling," indeed any heuristic experience of the world, especially that which involves conscious purpose, defined procedure, or its material instantiation in equipment. Like "modeling," "experiment" refers to a process whose ending is constructed rather than given: as Peter Galison has argued for the physical sciences, the experimenter *decides* if and when the attempt has succeeded or failed, in "that fascinating moment... when instrumentation, experience, theory, calculation, and sociology meet" (Galison 1987: 1). Modeling and experimenting are by nature open-ended; indeed they are often at the time ill-defined, even quite messy.[20]

The semantic overlap of "modeling" and "experiment" is so close that the two can be quite difficult to separate (Guala 2002). Mary S. Morgan, writing about modeling in economics, has argued that they may be discriminated by the degree to which the former involves hypothesis, the latter reality (2002: 49). But, as she notes, hybrids provide exceptions and thought experiments – "devices of the imagination used to investigate nature" (Brown 2002) – a very close analogue to modeling.[21] Perhaps the relationship is most clearly stated by saying that in the context of research a model is an experimental device, modeling an experimental technique.

The point of considering "experiment" here is, however, primarily to locate our topic within the context of a particular history of ideas and so to engage with large and important areas of historical and philosophical research. Indeed, as an experimental technique modeling has shared the fate of experiment in the specialist literature, and so also in the popular understanding. Allow me briefly to summarize the background.[22]

By the mid-nineteenth century, understanding of scientific work had begun to polarize into two epistemological conditions, which physicist and philosopher Hans Reichenbach later famously named "the context of discovery" and "the context of justification."[23] By the early to mid-twentieth century, attention had shifted almost completely to justification and so, as Thomas Nickels has said, discovery was expelled from mainstream epistemology (2000: 87). Experiment, the means of discovery, was in consequence also demoted and theory, the focus of justification, promoted. "The asymmetric emphasis on theory in the historical literature," Peter Galison explains, meant that attention was confined "to the invention and testing of theories" (1987: 8), the actual conduct and intellectual role of experiments being largely overlooked. In philosophy too, "experiment *for* theory" dominated until (in Ian Hacking's paraphrase of Nietzsche) Thomas Kuhn's *The Structure of Scientific Revolutions* "unwrapped the mummy of science" by historicizing it (Hacking 1983: 1f). What had actually always been happening in experimental work could then become a proper subject of investigation. Furthermore, Kuhn's ample demonstration of "the essential role theory plays in the conduct of experimentation, the interpretation of data, and in the definition of 'relevant' phenomena" depolarized theory and experiment (Galison 1987: 8f). In other words, from an entirely subordinate and observational role, experiment emerged alongside theory as an interdependent partner.

Subsequently, through the work of Hacking, Feyerabend, Galison, and several others, the fiction of a unitary "scientific method," in which theory cleanly defines the role of experiment, has been dispelled. As Hacking says, calling for a "Back-to-Bacon" movement, "Experiment has a life of its own" (1983: 150), sometimes preceded by theory, sometimes not. But the consequent liberation of experiment from the debilitating pretense of grubby handmaiden to "pure" theory has at the same time directed attention back to the very hard, old problem of discovery: how does this happen?

Conclusion

Why do *we* need an answer to this question? Because, I have argued, ours is an experimental practice, using equipment and instantiating definite methods, for the skilled application of which we need to know what we are doing as well as it can be known. I have labeled the core of this practice "modeling," and suggested how, properly understood, modeling points the way to a computing that is *of* as well as *in* the humanities: a continual process of coming to know by manipulating representations. We are, I have suggested, in good epistemological company. But this only sharpens the epistemological question. The signified of modeling vanishes into the murk because we lack a disciplined way of talking about it. Methods are explicit, actions definite, results forthcoming, yet we have been unable fully and persuasively to articulate the intellectual case for the means by which these results are produced. Hence the just-a-tool status of computing, the not-a-discipline slur, the tradesman's entrance or other back door into the academy. No one doubts the usefulness of the practice. Rather it's the *intellection of praxis* to which the next stage in the argument I have begun here must turn.

Notes

1   My definitions reflect the great majority of the literature explicitly on modeling in the history and philosophy of the natural sciences, especially of physics (Bailer-Jones 1999). The literature tends to be concerned with the role of modeling more in formal scientific theory than in experiment. The close relationship between modeling and experimenting means that the rise of a robust philosophy of experiment since the 1980s is directly relevant to our topic; see Hacking (1983); Gooding (2000). Quite helpful in rethinking the basic issues for the humanities are the writings from the disciplines other than physics, e.g., Clarke (1972) on archaeology; Wimsatt (1987) on biology; Del Re (2000) on chemistry; and on the social sciences, the essays by de Callataÿ, Mironesco, Burch, and Gardin in Franck (2002). For interdisciplinary studies see Shanin (1972) and Morrison and Morgan (1999), esp. "Models as Mediating Instruments" (pp. 10–37). For an overview see Lloyd (1998).

2   Cf. Goodman's distinction between "denotative" and "exemplary" models, respectively (1976: 172–3); H. J. Groenewold's "more or less poor substitute" and "more or less exemplary ideal" (1960: 98). Similar distinctions are quite common in the literature.

3   This is usually done in "the rhetoric of technohype . . . the idiom of grant proposals and of interviews in the Tuesday *New York Science Times*: The breakthrough is at hand; this time we've got it right; theory and practice will be forever altered; we have really made fantastic progress, and there is now general agreement on the basics; further funding is required" (Fodor 1995). More serious criticism is leveled by Terry Winograd (1991: 207–8); see below.

4   I have in mind the present-participial imagination described by Greg Dening, with which we may "return to the past the past's own present, a present with all the possibilities still in it, with all the consequences of actions still unknown" (Dening 1998: 48; see also Dening 1996: 35–63).

5   For the concept in imaginative language and thought see Gibbs (1994; reviewed by Turner 1995), Turner (1996); in computer science, Hoffman (1995) – whose summary of research is quite valuable; in cognitive science, including psychology, Mitchell (1993), Holyoak and Thagard (1997); in the philosophy of science, Achinstein (1968), Leatherdale (1974), Gentner (2002), Shelley (2002); in relation to modeling, Bailer-Jones (1999), Bailer-Jones and Bailer-Jones (2002). I do not deal here with metaphor in relation to modeling, for which see Black (1979), Johnson (2002).

6   Goodman dismantles the copy-theory of representation, arguing that representation is not mimetic but symbolic: object X is always *represented as* Y, which means that Y is selective with respect to X and stands in symbolic relationship to it. See also Elgin (1998), Hopkins (2000).

7   Possibly the best and least problematic view is afforded by Davis et al. (1993); see also Sowa (2000); Barr and Feigenbaum (1981). Lenat (1998) illustrates the problematic tendencies in this field; Winograd (1991) and Dreyfus (1985) provide the antidote.

8   Frye (1991: 4), to which compare Winograd's analysis of the "almost childish leap of faith" made, e.g., by Marvin Minsky in his "Society of Mind" thesis that "the modes of explanation that work for the details of [the artificial micro-worlds thus represented] will be adequate for understanding conflict, consciousness, genius, and freedom of will" (Winograd 1991: 204–7) – as the ambitious claim; see also Winder (1996).

9   Note the boast that "Cyc knows that trees are usually outdoors, that once people die they stop buying things, and that glasses of liquid should be carried rightside-up" (*Cycorp Company Overview*, at <http://www.cyc.com/overview.html>, accessed September 22, 2003.

10 Winograd and Flores (1986: 97–100, 131–3, 174–7); Dreyfus (1985). See also Brooks (1991).

11 See, however, the discussion in Netz (1999: 35–8).

12 Goodman (1976: 170f), who distinguishes between analogue and digital diagrams. As Netz explains, the lettered diagram provides a good example of the latter (1999: 34f).

13 Shin and Lemon (2002); note the extensive bibliography.

14 Robinson and Petchenik (1976); see also Monmonier (1996); Wood (1992). Turnbull (1994) argues specifically for the link between maps and theories.

15 See Bateson (2002: 27–8), who cites Alfred Korzybski's principle that "the map is not the territory" (Korzybski 1933) and points out that "the natural history of human mental process" nevertheless tells a different tale: part of us in fact regularly identifies map and territory, name and thing named. See also Goodman (1972: 15); Kent (2000/1978: xix).

16 On the semantic overlap of "simulation" with "experiment" and "model," see Guala (2002), who also stresses the necessity of including the designer or initiator as part of the simulation.

17 Hence, perhaps, the deception attributed to the word: "intent to deceive" in a "false assumption or display, a surface resemblance or imitation . . ." (*OED* 1.a., 2) – an animated *trompe l'oeil*.

18 Recent research in psychology and cognitive science, working with the representational model of mind, might be summarized by the proposition that reality as we know and participate in it *is* simulated. Thus mental simulation is used to explain aspects of cognition (see, e.g., Markman and Dietrich 2000; Davies and Stone 2000). Especially relevant here is the idea that *perceptual* simulations play a significant role in cognition, as when the replay of a kinaesthetic memory, awakened by some corresponding movement or gesture, lends meaning to a diagram or physical model. This is

why animations can in principle be more effective than static diagrams: they are more *knowledgeable* (Craig et al. 2002).

19   Rowe (1994), quoted by Burch (2002: 245); see also Winsberg (2001).

20   This is true for scientific experiment much more often and more significantly than popular and earlier philosophical accounts would have us believe. Ian Hacking illustrates the point in an illuminating discussion of the famous Michelson–Morley experiment, "a good example of the Baconian exploration of nature" (1983: 254); see his discription (1983: 253–61), and esp. the book as a whole. See also Gooding (2000) and Morrison (1998) for an overview of experiment in current philosophy of science; the triplet of articles presented at a symposium on "The Philosophical Significance of Experimentation," Hacking (1988), Heelan (1988), and Galison (1988); and Franklin (2002) for physics in particular.

21   See also Brown (2000), Gooding (1998) and note esp. the careful argument in Kuhn (1964) toward an understanding of how thought experiment can lead to new knowledge, not simply expose logical contradictions or confusions.

22   I rely primarily on Galison (1987), Hacking (1983) and Nickels (2000).

23   Reichenbach introduced the distinction to mark "the well-known difference" between "the form in which thinking processes are communicated to other persons [and] the form in which they are subjectively performed," i.e., justification and discovery, respectively (Reichenbach 1938, chapter 1); compare Feyerabend (1993: 147–58). This distinction involves a long-standing argument that goes back to the debate between William Whewell (first to use the term "philosophy of science") and John Stuart Mill; it was then taken up by Charles Sanders Peirce on the one hand and Karl Popper on the other. Popper, in *Logik der Forschung* (translated as *The Logic of Scientific Discovery*) characteristically ruled discovery out of court by identifying it as a matter for psychology, recalling Duhem's and Reichenbach's use of that term: "The question of how it happens that a new idea occurs to a man . . . may be of great interest to empirical psychology; but it is irrelevant to the logical analysis of scientific knowledge" (Popper 1959/1935: 7). See Nickels (2000).

WORKS CITED

Achinstein, Peter (1968). *Concepts of Science: A Philosophical Analysis*. Baltimore: Johns Hopkins University Press.

Bailer-Jones, Daniela M. (1999). Tracing the Development of Models in the Philosophy of Science. In Magnani, Nersessian and Thagard (1999): 23–40.

—— 2002. Models, Metaphors and Analogies. In Machamer and Silberstein (2002): 108–27.

Bailer-Jones, Daniela M. and Coryn A. L. Bailer-Jones (2002). Modeling Data: Analogies in Neural Networks, Simulated Annealing and Genetic Algorithms. In Magnani and Nersessian (2002): 147–65.

Barr, Avron and Edward A. Feigenbaum (1981). Representation of Knowledge. In *The Handbook of Artificial Intelligence. Volume I*, ed. Avron Barr and Edward A. Feigenbaum (pp. 141–222). Los Altos, CA: Morgan Kaufmann.

Bateson, Gregory (2002). *Mind and Nature: A Necessary Unity*. Cresskill, NJ: Hampton Press.

Beacham, Richard, and Hugh Denard (2003). The Pompey Project: Digital Research and Virtual Reconstruction of Rome's First Theatre. *Computers and the Humanities* 37,1: 129–39.

Black, Max (1979). More About Metaphor. In *Metaphor and Thought*, ed. Andrew Ortony (pp. 19–39). Cambridge: Cambridge University Press.

Brooks, Rodney A. (1991). Intelligence without Representation. *Artificial Intelligence Journal* 47: 139–59.

Brown, James Robert (2000). Thought Experiments. In Newton-Smith (2000): 528–31.

—— 2002. Thought Experiments. *Stanford Encyclopedia of Philosophy*. Accessed September 12, 2003. At <http://plato.stanford.edu/entries/thought-experiment/>.

Burch, Thomas K. (2002). Computer Modeling of Theory: Explanation for the 21st Century. In Franck (2002): 245–65.

Cartwright, Nancy (1983). *How the Laws of Physics Lie*. Oxford: Clarendon Press.

Clarke, David L. (1972). Models and Paradigms in Contemporary Archaeology. In *Models in Archaeology*, ed. David L. Clarke (pp. 1–60). London: Methuen.

Craig, David L., Nancy J. Nersessian, and Richard Catrambone (2002). Perceptual Simulation in Analogical Problem Solving. In Magnani and Nersessian (2002): 167–89.

Davies, Martin and Tony Stone (2000). Simulation Theory. In *Routledge Encyclopedia of Philosophy*. London: Routledge.

Davis, Randall, Howard Shrobe, and Peter Szolovits (1993). What Is Knowledge Representation? *AI Magazine* (Spring): 17–33. Accessed September 18, 2003. At <http://www.aaai.org/Library/Magazine/Vol14/14-01.html>.

Del Re, Giuseppe (2000). Models and Analogies in Science. *Hyle – International Journal for the Philosophy of Chemistry* 6,1: 5–15. Accessed September 18, 2003. At <http://www.hyle.org/journal/issues/6/delre.htm>.

Dening, Greg (1996). *Performances*. Chicago: University of Chicago Press.

——(1998). *Readings/Writings*. Melbourne: University of Melbourne Press.

Dreyfus, Hubert L. (1985). From Micro-Worlds to Knowledge Representation: AI at an Impasse. In *Readings in Knowledge Representation*, ed. Ronald J. Brachman and Hector Levesque (pp. 71–94). Los Altos, CA: Morgan Kaufmann.

Elgin, Catherine Z. (1998). Goodman, Nelson. In *Routledge Encyclopedia of Philosophy*. London: Routledge.

Fetzer, James H. (1999). The Role of Models in Computer Science. *The Monist* 82,1: 20–36.

Feyerabend, Paul (1993). *Against Method*, 3rd edn. London: Verso.

Finley, M. I. (1986). *Ancient History: Evidence and Models*. New York: Viking.

Fodor, Jerry (1995). West Coast Fuzzy. Review of Paul M. Churchland, *The Engine of Reason, the Seat of the Soul. Times Literary Supplement* (August 25).

Franck, Robert (ed.) (2002). *The Explanatory Power of Models*. Methodos Series, vol. 1. Dordrecht: Kluwer Academic.

Franklin, Allan (2002). Experiment in Physics. *The Stanford Encyclopedia of Philosophy*. Accessed September 12, 2003. At <http://plato.stanford.edu/entries/physics-experiment/>.

Frye, Northrop (1991). Literary and Mechanical Models. In *Research in Humanities Computing 1. Papers from the 1989 ACH-ALLC Conference*, ed. Ian Lancashire (pp. 1–12). Oxford: Clarendon Press.

Galison, Peter (1987). *How Experiments End*. Chicago: University of Chicago Press.

——(1988). Philosophy in the Laboratory. *Journal of Philosophy* 85,10: 525–7.

——(1997). *Image and Logic: A Material Culture of Microphysics*. Chicago: University of Chicago Press.

Geertz, Clifford (1973). Religion as a Cultural System. In *The Interpretation of Cultures: Selected Essays*. New York: Basic Books. (Reprint: London: Fontana Press, 1993.)

Gentner, Dedre (2002). Analogy in Scientific Discovery: The Case of Johannes Kepler. In Magnani and Nersessian (2002): 21–39.

Gibbs, Raymond W., Jr (1994). *The Poetics of Mind: Figurative Thought, Language, and Understanding*. Cambridge: Cambridge University Press.

Gooding, David C. (1998). Thought Experiments. *Routledge Encyclopedia of Philosophy*. London: Routledge.

——(2000). Experiment. In Newton-Smith (2000): 117–26.

Goodman, Nelson (1972). *Problems and Projects*. Indianapolis, IN: Bobbs-Merrill.

——(1976). *The Languages of Art*. Indianapolis, IN: Hackett.

Groenewold, H. J. (1960). The Model in Physics. In *The Concept and the Role of the Model in Mathematics and the Natural Sciences*, ed. Hans Friedenthal (pp. 98–103). Dordrecht: D. Reidel.

Guala, Francesco (2002). Models, Simulations, and Experiments. In Magnani and Nersessian (2002): 59–74.

Hacking, Ian (1983). *Representing and Intervening: Introductory Topics in the Philosophy of Natural Science*. Cambridge: Cambridge University Press.

——(1988). On the Stability of the Laboratory Sciences. *Journal of Philosophy* 85,10: 507–14.

Heelan, Patrick A. (1988). Experiment and Theory: Constitution and Reality. *Journal of Philosophy* 85,10: 515–27.

Hoffmann, Robert R. (1995). Monster Analogies. *AI Magazine* 16,3: 11–35. Accessed September 18, 2003. At <http://www.aaai.org.Library/Magazine/Vol16.16-03/vol16-03.html>.

Holyoak, Keith J. and Paul Thagard (1997). The Analogical Mind. *American Psychologist* 52,1: 35–44.

Hopkins, R. D. (2000). Depiction. In *Routledge Encyclopedia of Philosophy*. London: Routledge.

Johnson, Mark (2002). Metaphor-Based Values in Scientific Models. In Magnani and Nersessian (2002): 1–19.

Kent, William (2000/1978). *Data and Reality,* 2nd edn. Bloomington, IN: 1st Books. (Originally published in Amsterdam: North Holland.)

Kirschenbaum, Matthew (ed.) (2002). Image-Based Humanities Computing. Special issue of *Computers and the Humanities* 36,3.

Korzybski, Alfred (1933). *Science and Sanity: An Introduction to Non-Aristotelian Systems and General Semantics*. Lancaster, PA: International Non-Aristotelian Library Publishing.

Kuhn, Thomas (1964). A Function for Thought Experiments. In *L'aventure de la science, Mélanges Alexandre Koyré*, vol. 2 (pp. 307–34). Paris: Hermann.

Leatherdale, W. H. (1974). *The Role of Analogy, Model and Metaphor in Science*. Amsterdam: North Holland Publishing.

Leff, Gordon (1972). Models Inherent in History. In Shanin, ed. (1972): 148–74.

Lenat, Douglas B. (1998). From *2001* to 2001: Common Sense and the Mind of HAL. In *HAL's Legacy: 2001's Computer as Dream and Reality*, ed. David G. Stork (pp. 193–209). Cambridge, MA: MIT Press.

Lloyd, Elisabeth A. (1998). Models. In *Routledge Encyclopedia of Philosophy*. London: Routledge.

Lougee, Carolyn (1988). The Would-Be Gentleman: a Historical Simulation of the France of Louis XIV. *History Microcomputer Review* 4: 7–14.

McCarty, Willard (2002). A Network with a Thousand Entrances: Commentary in an Electronic Age? In *The Classical Commentary: Histories, Practices, Theory*, ed. Roy K. Gibson and Christina Shuttleworth Kraus (pp. 359–402). Leiden: Brill.

Machamer, Peter and Silberstein, Michael, eds. (2002). *The Blackwell Guide to the Philosophy of Science*. Oxford: Blackwell Publishers.

Magnani, Lorenzo and Nancy J. Nersessian (eds.) (2002). *Model-Based Reasoning: Science, Technology, Values*. New York: Kluwer Academic/Plenum.

Magnani, Lorenzo, Nancy J. Nersessian, and Paul Thagard (eds.) (1999). *Model-Based Reasoning in Scientific Discovery*. New York: Kluwer Academic/Plenum.

Markman, Arthur B. and Eric Dietrich (2000). Extending the Classical View of Representation. *Trends in Cognitive Sciences* 4,12: 470–5.

Maxwell, James Clerk (1911). Diagram. In *Encyclopaedia Britannica*, 11th edn. (pp. 146–9).

Minsky, Marvin (1991). Conscious Machines. *Proceedings, National Research Council of Canada, 75th Anniversary Symposium on Science in Society* (June). Accessed April 22, 2004. At <http://kuoi.asui.uidaho.edu/~kamikaze/doc/minsky.html>.

Minsky, Marvin L. (1995). Matter, Mind and Models. Accessed January 20, 2003. At <http://medg.lcs.mit.edu/people/doyle/gallery/minsky.mmm.html>. (Rev. version of the essay in *Semantic Information Processing*, ed. Marvin Minsky. Cambridge, MA: MIT Press, 1968.)

Mironesco, Christine (2002). The Role of Models in Comparative Politics. In Franck (2002): 181–95.

Mitchell, Melanie (1993). *Analogy-Making as Perception*. Cambridge, MA: MIT Press.

Monmonier, Mark (1996). *How to Lie with Maps*, 2nd edn. Chicago: University of Chicago Press.

Morgan, Mary S. (2002). Model Experiments and Models in Experiments. In Magnani and Nersessian (2002): 41–58.

Morrison, Margaret (1998). Experiment. In *Routledge Encyclopedia of Philosophy*. London: Routledge.

Morrison, Margaret and Mary S. Morgan (eds.) (1999). *Models as Mediators: Perspectives on Natural and Social Science*. Ideas in Context, 52. Cambridge: Cambridge University Press.

Netz, Reviel (1999). *The Shaping of Deduction in Greek Mathematics: A Study in Cognitive History.* Ideas in Context, 51. Cambridge: Cambridge University Press.

Newton-Smith, W. H. ed. (2000). *A Companion to the Philosophy of Science.* Oxford: Blackwell.

Nickels, Thomas (2000). Discovery. In Newton-Smith (2000): 85–96.

Polanyi, Michael (1966). *The Tacit Dimension.* New York: Doubleday.

Popper, Karl R. (1959/1935). *The Logic of Scientific Discovery.* London: Hutchinson. (Originally published as *Logik der Forschung.* Vienna: Verlag von Julius Springer.)

——(1979). *Objective Knowledge. An Evolutionary Approach.* Oxford: Clarendon Press.

Reichenbach, Hans (1938). *Experience and Prediction: An Analysis of the Foundations and the Structure of Knowledge.* Chicago: University of Chicago Press. (A transcription of Chapter 1 is available at <http://www.ditext.com/reichenbach/reich0.html>. Accessed September 12, 2003.)

Robinson, Arthur H. and Barbara Petchenik (1976). *The Nature of Maps.* Chicago: University of Chicago Press.

Rowe, Glenn W. (1994). *Theoretical Models in Biology: The Origin of Life, the Immune System, and the Brain.* Oxford: Oxford University Press.

Shanin, Teodor (1972). Models in Thought. In Shanin, ed. (1972): 1–22.

——(ed.) (1972). *Rules of the Game: Cross-Disciplinary Essays on Models in Scholarly Thought.* London: Tavistock.

Shelley, Cameron (2002). Analogy Counterarguments and the Acceptability of Analogical Hypotheses. *British Journal for the Philosophy of Science* 53: 477–96.

Shin, Sun-Joo and Oliver Lemon (2002). Diagrams. *Stanford Encyclopedia of Philosophy.* Accessed September 11, 2003. At <http://plato.stanford.edu/entries/diagrams/>.

Simon, Herbert (1969). *The Sciences of the Artificial.* Cambridge, MA: MIT Press.

Smith, Brian Cantwell (1995/1985). Limits of Correctness in Computers. In *Computers, Ethics and Social Values*, ed. Deborah G. Johnson and Helen Nissenbaum (pp. 456–69). Englewood Cliffs, NJ: Prentice Hall. (Originally published in *Computers and Society* (ACM SIGCAS) 14/15: 18–26.)

Sowa, John F. (2000). *Knowledge Representation: Logical, Philosophical, and Computational Foundations.* Pacific Grove, CA: Brooks/Cole.

Toulmin, Stephen (1953). *The Philosophy of Science.* London: Hutchinson University Library.

——(1958). *The Uses of Argument.* Cambridge: Cambridge University Press.

Turnbull, David (1994). *Maps are Territories. Science is an Atlas.* Chicago: University of Chicago Press.

Turner, Mark (1995). Review of *The Poetics of Mind: Figurative Thought, Language, and Understanding*, by Raymond W. Gibbs. *Pragmatics and Cognition* 3,1: 179–85.

——(1996). *Literary Mind: The Origins of Thought and Language.* Oxford: Oxford University Press.

Williams, Michael (2001). *Problems of Knowledge: A Critical Introduction to Epistemology.* Oxford: Oxford University Press.

Wimsatt, William C. (1987). False Models as Means to Truer Theories. In *Neutral Models in Biology*, ed. Matthew H. Nitecki and Antoni Hoffman (pp. 23–55). Oxford: Oxford University Press.

Winder, William (1996). Textpert Systems. *Text Technology* 6,3. Rpt. 1997, *Computing in the Humanities Working Papers* B.35. Accessed September 11, 2003. At <http://www.chass.utoronto.ca/epc/chwp/winder2/>.

Winograd, Terry (1991). Thinking Machines: Can There Be? Are We? In *The Boundaries of Humanity: Humans, Animals, Machines*, ed. James J. Sheehan and Morton Sosna (pp. 198–223). Berkeley: University of California Press.

Winograd, Terry and Fernando Flores (1986). *Understanding Computers and Cognition: A New Foundation for Design.* Boston: Addison-Wesley.

Winsberg, Eric (2001). Simulations, Models, and Theories: Complex Physical Systems and Their Representations. *Philosophy of Science (Proceedings)* 68: S442–S454.

Wood, Denis (1992). *The Power of Maps.* Mappings: Society / Theory / Space. London: Guilford Press.

Ziman, John (2000). *Real Science: What it Is, and What it Means.* Cambridge: Cambridge University Press.

PART III
Applications

20

Stylistic Analysis and Authorship Studies

Hugh Craig

Introduction

Stylistics and authorship studies are siblings with obvious differences and important underlying similarities. Stylistic analysis is open-ended and exploratory. It aims to bring to light patterns in style which influence readers' perceptions and relate to the disciplinary concerns of literary and linguistic interpretation. Authorship studies aim at "yes or no" resolutions to existing problems, and avoid perceptible features if possible, working at the base strata of language where imitation or deliberate variation can be ruled out. Authorship attribution has a forensic aspect – evidence of authorship based on stylistics has been accepted in British courtrooms in particular – and this notion of determining a legally enforceable responsibility has given a particular intensity to scrutiny of its reliability. Yet stylistic analysis needs finally to pass the same tests of rigor, repeatability, and impartiality as authorship analysis if it is to offer new knowledge. And the measures and techniques of authorship studies must ultimately be explained in stylistic terms if they are to command assent.

In this chapter I offer first an example of a study in computational stylistics to set the scene. Then I discuss the most important theoretical challenge to stylistics, and go on to sketch a methodological basis for the practice. Turning to authorship attribution, I treat some underlying ideas about authorship itself, then theoretical issues in attribution studies, and finally some practical considerations.

Computational stylistics aims to find patterns in language that are linked to the processes of writing and reading, and thus to "style" in the wider sense, but are not demonstrable without computational methods. We might, for instance, wish to examine patterns of association and difference among Shakespeare plays, based on their spoken dialogue. In these plays there are the obvious groupings of genre, and chronological divisions into early, middle, and late. There are clusters which have been intensively discussed by critics at various times, like the "problem plays" and the "four great tragedies." But how would the plays arrange themselves if only internal and empirical evidence was used? With the idea of starting with as few presumptions as possible, we take twenty-five Shakespeare plays (a good proportion of the thirty-eight complete plays normally included in a Complete Shakespeare) and calculate which are the dozen most common words in them overall. We can make a table of counts of each of these twelve words in each of the twenty-five plays.

Principal components analysis (PCA) is a statistical technique much used in computational stylistics for analyzing the variation in a table like this. It creates new composite variables which are combinations of the original ones, with each of the latter given a separate weighting. The aim is to simplify the data by finding a few new variables which account for most of the relationships revealed by the table. To take a commonplace example, it might turn out that after collecting statistics on individuals' height and weight in a sample the two prove to be so closely related that a single new variable, size – height times weight, a composite of the original two – represents most of the variation. PCA vectors, "principal components," are an extension of this principle. The weightings in a component are worked out so as to create, first, the vector which accounts for the greatest proportion of the variance in the original table. Then the procedure finds a second independent vector which accounts for the next greatest proportion, and so on. If there are strong associations between variables, then the first few of these new composite variables will account for most of what is going on. In the Shakespeare plays table the first principal component accounts for 33 percent of the total variance, and the second for 19 percent, so we are justified in thinking that there are strong associations and contrasts in the way the variables behave. If there were not, and the variation was purely random, then we could expect each of the twelve principal components to have shared the variation equally, i.e., to account for around 8 percent. The first step is to look at the variable scores relative to each other on the first and second principal components, as in figure 20.1.

Looking at the X axis first, the highest score is for frequencies of *I*; those of *is*, *you*, and *it* are most closely associated with it. These variables evidently behave like each other – in plays where one of them is notably frequent, the others tend to be frequent too, and where one of them is notably scarce, the others will tend to be scarce also. At the other end, *of* is the extreme, associated with *and* and *the*. The first vector would seem to be a contrast between the variables which are associated with interactive dialogue, where pronouns like *I* and *you* are very common, and those associated with description and narration. The plays can also be given scores on the same principal components, as in figure 20.2. The contrast along the X axis here emerges as one between the history plays and the others. All the history plays included are to the left of the rest. This fits well with the idea that the first principal component, the most important line of difference through the plays, is a contrast between plays in which description and its associated function words is stronger and those where interaction between characters predominates. Comedy and tragedy do not therefore present the biggest contrast in Shakespearean dialogue in these terms. Both the comedy and the tragedy groups are well mixed on the first axis. Within the comedy group the range is from *Love's Labour's Lost* (most disquisitory) to *Two Gentlemen of Verona* (most interactive); within the tragedies the range is from *Hamlet* to *Othello*. (Here, as very often in computational stylistics, we are relating two kinds of variables: fixed, externally determined attributes of the particular text like genre, known as independent variables,

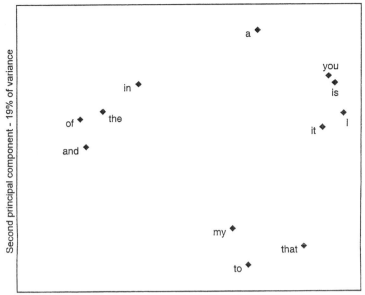

Figure 20.1   Variable weightings in a PCA of 12 word-variables in 25 Shakespeare plays

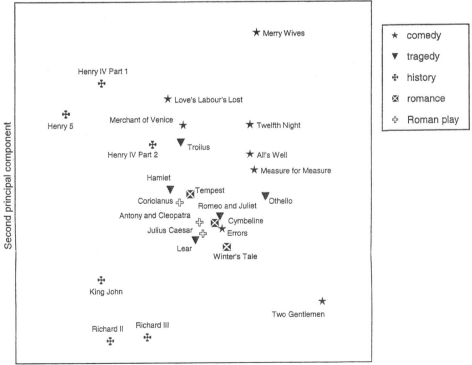

Figure 20.2   Scores for texts in a PCA of 12 word-variables in 25 Shakespeare plays

and counts of internal features, which are dependent variables. Correlation of the first with the second is the primary tool of computational stylistics.)

The second component, the vertical axis in the graphs, runs from *to* to *a* and from *Richard II* to *Merry Wives of Windsor*. High frequencies of *to* indicate a formal style (infinitives and prepositional uses contribute equally, and one arises through more complex constructions, the other by more precise specification), and high frequencies of *a* are associated with a more casual one. Once the disquisitory–interactive differences are accounted for, it seems that a high-style–low-style contrast is next most important in the plays. Along this axis the history plays are strung out rather than bunched together, *Richard II* most formal of all and *Henry IV Part 1* close to the opposite, informal extreme. The second component is not associated with the regular generic categories.

Figures 20.1 and 20.2 represent a sketch-map of the style of Shakespeare's plays, and of course raise more questions than they answer. In taking such a study beyond the sketch stage one would want to know how constant these patterns are when a play is added to the set or taken away, for instance, or if different variables are used, for instance by splitting *to* into infinitive, prepositional, and adverbial uses. In such work, a little paradoxically, one wants to be reassured by seeing patterns already familiar from the way the texts are usually discussed, yet also to be surprised so that they seem more than a restatement of the obvious. If the dispositions of these graphs do stand up to scrutiny, then they invite further exploration. The first principal component has many similarities with the factor that emerged as the strongest in Biber's 1988 study of a large mixed sample of modern English. Biber labels the factor "high informational density and exact informational content versus affective, interactional, and generalized content" (1988: 107). A similar contrast is dominant in a number of different studies of this kind, across many periods and text types. Should we think of this opposition as the fundamental one in categorizing texts? In Shakespeare studies the findings might be compared with Lancashire (1997), and the suggestion that the pattern of phrasal repetends indicates a segmentation of semantic knowledge in Shakespeare's mind between comedies and tragedies on the one hand and poetry and the histories on the other (1997: 182). Then, more locally still, one might ask what it is exactly that brings the two *Richard* plays together, which are from different tetralogies and not often discussed alongside each other, at the bottom of figure 20.2. Again, what does it mean that six of the tragedies lie in a close cluster, occupying quite a narrow range on both of these components? The outliers on both axes are histories or comedies: tragedies are more middling in style, or more mixed (an important difference, which might be explored by looking at segments from within the plays).

Beyond these are questions of the design of the experiment. Why choose words, and why these words? Why choose plays, when one might choose *oeuvres* or periods as larger aggregations, or characters or scenes as segmentations, or some combination? How would the main lines of differentiation in a larger set of Elizabethan and Jacobean plays, going beyond Shakespeare, compare?

These are questions that are internal to stylistics, and can be answered in its own terms. There are other more fundamental ones. What, for example, is the status and nature of the axes of differences that the procedure has derived? They have a precise definition – each variable and each case has a score for each vector – but this says nothing about the stylistic context. Should an axis of this kind be regarded as a stylistic reality, figuring as part of the writing or the reading or hearing process, or just as an artifact of the method? Then, even if an axis of this kind is allotted some importance in relation to style, one must be cautious about describing it. Any departure from the purely enumerative ("*I* has the highest score on the first principal component") is an act of judgment and is open to question. Then, if we accept that the vector has an authentic relationship to style, and is adequately interpreted, one can still ask whether anything of interest has been gained in relation to the questions that interest those who read and study Shakespeare plays.

This example will indicate what is at stake in computational stylistics: at best, a powerful new line of evidence in long-contested questions of style; at worst, an elaborate display of meaningless patterning, and an awkward mismatch between words and numbers and the aesthetic and the statistical. For the moment we can note that this sort of work remains under challenge, and is still largely ignored by mainstream humanities disciplines. It is worth reflecting also that though all its procedures individually predate the digital age, the combination in this sort of analysis is inconceivable without the computer. The labor involved with counting features like instances of word-types by hand and processing the results with a multivariate procedure like PCA the same way, would rule out embarking on such a project. Indeed, with no way of assembling and manipulating counts of word-variables, researchers in earlier periods assumed that very common words varied in frequency only in trivial ways among texts (Ellegård 1962: 15–16).

A Challenge to Stylistics

Stanley Fish has provided the most root-and-branch challenge to stylistics. He finds the whole project of identifying formal structures in a text and then interpreting them in relation to its meaning so flawed as to make stylistics entirely vacuous. A central problem for Fish is the assumption that meaning resides within the text rather than being created as it is read. He argues that the formal features described by stylisticians are meaningless except in relation to the reader's perception of them within a reading situation. When abstracted from this setting they refer to nothing but themselves and so any further analysis of patterns within their use, or comparison with the use of others or in other texts, or relating of them to meaning, is entirely pointless. Fish does not deny that there may be formal features which can enable categorical classification such as authorship (and so he is less hostile to authorship studies using computational stylistics), but he insists that these features cannot offer any information of interest about the text – just as a fingerprint may efficiently identify an individual but reveal nothing about his or her personality.

The two essays on stylistics reprinted in Fish's 1980 book discuss work by stylisticians which he declares to be either circular, so that findings based on the analysis of formal features are simply restated in "slightly different terms" (1980: 71–2), or arbitrary, because there is no principled way to link the meaning asserted with the feature. This rules out any claims to objectivity, since either there is no necessary connection between the features observed and the interpretation asserted for them, or the interpretation is built into the choice and description of the features themselves. He can envisage a pure stylistics which confines itself to the description of formal features, or a confessedly impure stylistics which would make no claim to objectivity, but suggests that as practiced in the studies he analyzes it is worthless.

Fish should be compulsory reading for any beginning stylistician. His papers belong with Schoenbaum's (1966) book as sources for cautionary tales in poor method. Any worker in the field will have felt tempted to do as one study Fish describes does, and slide from labeling a verb "active" to calling it "dynamic." Fish's comment is that the first "locates the verb in a system of formal differences," while the second "semanticizes, even moralizes" it (1980: 81). Again, it does seem illegitimate to move from "syntactic preferences" to "habits of meaning" or "conceptual orientation" (1980: 75), because, as Fish demonstrates, the step from preferences to significance can be made in any number of equally legitimate directions.

Fish is speaking as a humanist: he sees stylistics as an attempt to make interpretation mechanical and thus to exclude the human. His affective stylistics, later modified so as to make the agent interpretative communities rather than individual readers, is intended to locate the study of meaning in the proper creators, readers, or groups of readers, rather than in the linguistic features themselves. This is an attempt to incorporate the insight that "formal units are always a function of the interpretive model one brings to bear (they are not 'in the text')" (1980: 13).

Fish wants to do more than ridicule the occasional excesses of stylistics: he wants to demolish it entirely. The urgency in his analysis comes from his distrust of the claims of stylistics to a special "scientific" validity and of what he sees as its underlying anti-humanist motivation, the exclusion of the human factor in reading and interpretation. It is possible, however, to propose an alternative motivation for stylistics, that is, the uncovering of patterns of language use which because of their "background" quality, or their emergence on a superhumanly wide scale, would otherwise not be noticed; and the testing of hypotheses about language use where some empirical validation seems possible and appropriate. An example of the former would be patterns of use of *thou* and *you* forms within one dramatist; an example of the latter would be curiosity about whether men and women write differently from one another. This need not be anti-humanist, since it would recognize the role of the interpreter in relating any empirically derived results to readers' experiences, and to the myriad ways in which texts participate in a culture.

A Methodological Basis for Stylistics

A well-founded computational stylistics works with tendencies rather than rules; the semantic operation of language is so variable that the relationship of feature to meaning can never be fixed. Each element, and each combination of elements, can be used in new contexts to mean new things. Yet there are also continuities and patterns. These require a mixed theory of meaning. A textual form has meaning in its local context, but also as part of a collective. Thus an instance of *I* has a local meaning, a deixis in which the referent is the speaker, but also has a meaning as part of a wider abundance or scarcity of this pronoun in the text, reflecting a discourse more or less frequently framed as first-person expression.

Tendencies are best observed in multiple instances, and it is here that the superhuman reach and memory of the computer can be of most assistance. Computational stylistics is thus extensive by nature, and it may be that the greatest potential for important discoveries lies in large-scale comparisons, rather than in the intensive study which is the staple of traditional philology. An obvious example would be change in language over time, within a writer's career or more largely over a collective artistic enterprise, or between periods. There have been promising forays also into groupings of texts by gender and nationality.

Stylistics may be thought of as the epidemiology of textual study: its methods allow general conclusions about the relationship between variables. Those which have high counts together form a syndrome. Once this is identified, the researcher can seek out a mechanism to explain it, as medical researchers might isolate the cell pathology which lies behind the epidemiological link between the incidence of smoking and that of lung cancer.

Stylistics in its exploratory form has had a great deal in common with sociolinguistics, which relies on correlations between the frequency of linguistic features and categorical independent variables like class and gender, with the more or less explicit assumption that language patterns are explained by these independent variables. Individualist linguistics and cognitive stylistics, on the other hand, are not entirely sympathetic with strictly quantitative work, since they share an underlying belief that the most important dimensions of individuality cannot be captured in a common grid of frequencies. Johnstone, for example, argues for the value of the qualitative as against the quantitative, for small as against large amounts of data, greater as against lesser detail, and the methods of cases and interpretation as against those of rules and instances (1996: 23–4). Stylistics is perhaps best seen as the offspring of Saussurean linguistics, prizing what she calls "the knowledge that can be modelled with rules and conventions" (1996: 188) both for categorical assignations (as in authorship studies) and for explorations of relations of form and meaning (as in stylistics). The tension can be seen as one between an interest in the "more tractable explanatory variables" (1996: 15–16) favored for sociolinguistic study and a sense that these are not adequate to explain language behavior. For individualists, a full explanation returns to the irreducibly unique self-expression of the human agent. This kind of humanism links them with Fish, who finds the particular instance always triumphant in its circumstantial complexity over the rule which is imposed on it. In their practice both Johnstone and a practitioner of cognitive stylistics like Lancashire favor a more conventional *explication de texte*, an intensive examination of a single passage, albeit against the background of a larger work or *oeuvre*. This Johnstone calls "modern philology" (1996: 180–8), and consciously aligns with the practice of literary criticism. In their practice the new individualists create a foundation for authorship attribution (via the motivation and practice of individual language users, or the nature of the cognitive process) but this is so extremely individualist that it militates against the kind of systematic comparison which has been the basic method of stylometrics and the more recent computational stylistics.

There must be room both for the insight that any text, and any collection of texts, has elements which will never be reducible to tabular form, as well as for the knowledge that many of the elements of the individual case will form part of a pattern. There is a strong instinct in human beings to reduce complexity and to simplify: this is a survival mechanism. Rules of thumb can save a great deal of time and effort. Stylistics is born of this instinct. What seems hard to explain in the individual case may be easier to understand when it is seen in a larger context. If these elements can be put in tabular form, then one can harness the power of statistics and of numerous visualizing and schematizing tools to help in the process of finding patterns.

With a statistical method comes the possibility of falsifiability. This can be thought of in terms of a wager. If one researcher has a hunch about a literary problem – say, that drama written for the private theaters in the Shakespearean period is distinct in its style from that written for the public theaters – and bets a colleague that this is true, the wager can only be decided under strict conditions. The two will have to agree on how to judge difference; on which are clearly private-theater, and which clearly public-theater plays; and on how many of them amount to an adequate sample. Then the threshold conditions have to be agreed. What test will be used on what data from the plays, and which range of values will constitute difference, and which sameness, for the purposes of awarding the wager to one side or the other? Here random selection is a useful tool, in cases where it is not possible to use all the possible data, and both sides of a question will want to escape preconceptions about relevant attributes and groups.

This follows the lines of a more traditional, hypothesis-driven design. The alternative approach is through exploratory data analysis, in which the researcher changes all possible parameters in the search for a revealing finding. Performed with due cautions, this may lead to discoveries that might be obscured by the starting conditions of a more fixed study. As the cost in time of collecting data and manipulating it and presenting it visually has come down, the attractiveness of exploratory analysis has increased.

In a sense (as is often pointed out by critics) computational stylistics merely creates another text, which, far from doing away with or automating interpretation, itself requires it. But this secondary text is related to the first in a systematic and repeatable way, and may be revealing about it. It offers a new perspective on it, like a spectroscopic analysis. The unfamiliar and often elaborate and arcane presentation of the results of statistical study in stylistics should not obscure what it has in common with traditional practices. It is common in any analysis to move from relatively uncontroversial to relatively controversial observations. This definition of some readily agreed-on aspects of a text is a prelude to interpretation. These results may be gathered by hand, as in the observation that plays written by women tend to have more women characters, and that women characters in them are more likely to start and end a scene. In principle, work in computational stylistics is no different.

In recent years the most-used markers for computational stylistics have been function words. Other very common words which do not appear to be unduly sensitive to subject matter are also attractive. Then there are combinations of word-types: in Lancashire's terminology, the fixed phrase, collocation (pair of words within a certain number of words of each other), and word cluster (combination of word phrase and collocation) (Lancashire 1997: 172). Lancashire's understanding of language production as mostly instinctive, and based on an associative memory, leads him to highlight phrases as the key markers of idiolect – phrases of up to seven words since that is the limit of short-term or working memory. "We speak and write in chunks," he says (1997: 178–80). The existence of large commercial online full-text databases makes it now possible to use this kind of authorship marker against the background of a large corpus, which can show if any parallels between the phrases of a doubtful text and those of a target author are truly unusual. There are some sample studies in Jackson (2002). Among the other most important style markers have been choices among pairs of words which can be readily substituted for each other in a sentence, such as *while* and *whilst*, *has* and *hath*, *on* and *upon*, and the words used to begin sentences. McMenamin details a vast range of these markers; the range itself, and the dangers of arbitrary choices among them, have contributed to doubts about the overall validity of such studies (Furbank and Owens 1991).

The best method of guarding against these dangers is careful testing of the method alongside its application to the immediate problem. If the markers and procedures chosen provide an efficient separation of samples into authorial or other groups in a closely comparable set – ideally, drawn at random from the main set and then reserved for testing – then that provides a guide to the reliability of the method when it comes to the contested texts. Discriminant analysis, a method for data reduction with some similarities to PCA, provides a good illustration. Discriminant analysis provides a weighted vector which will maximize the separation between two groups of samples named in advance. The vector can then be held constant and a score can be worked out for a mystery segment. The procedure even supplies a probability that any given segment belongs to one group or the other. This seems ideal for authorship problems: simply provide some samples of author A, some of author B, calculate the Discriminant function, and then test any doubtful segment. Yet Discriminant results are notoriously optimistic: the separation of the segments into named groups is maximized, but we have no way of knowing if they are representative of the population of the works of Author A or B – which, in the fullest sense, is the range of works it was (or is) possible for Author A or B to write. There is the danger of "overtraining" – the method will work superbly for these particular samples, but what it is providing is exactly a separation of those samples, which may be a very different matter from a true authorial separation. Good practice, therefore, is to reserve some samples (as many as 10 percent) as test samples. They do not contribute to the "training" exercise, the formation of the function, and therefore are in the same position as the doubtful sample or samples. If these are correctly assigned to their group, or most of them are, then one can have some confidence that the result on the mystery sample is reliable. "Testing the test" in this way should be the first move in any statistical authorial experiment. The ease of use of statistical packages makes it possible to do a large amount of testing even with scarce data by "bootstrapping" – a single item can be withdrawn from the training set and tested, then returned to the set while a second is extracted and tested, and so on.

The claim for computational stylistics is that it makes available a class of evidence not otherwise accessible (i.e., not to the naked eye). This evidence is comparable to the evidence interpreters always use, if not to form their views, then at least to persuade others that they are true.

The computational varieties of stylistic analysis and authorship studies require some considerable immersion in traditional humanities disciplines (scholarly, i.e., bibliographical, literary-historical and textual; and critical, i.e., interpretative and theoretical); in humanities computing generally (in particular the compiling and editing of literary texts and assembling them into corpora); and statistical (involving the understanding of statistical techniques and the practicalities of statistics and spreadsheet programs). All three present enough challenges and large enough bodies of knowledge to occupy the working lifetimes of individual researchers by themselves. Most commonly, single practitioners are experts in one or possibly two areas, very rarely in three, and have to make do in various more or less satisfactory ways in a third. Often the requisite skills have been assembled in two practitioners (as in the case of Burrows and Love).

Authorship

Authorship attribution is as old as writing itself, and its history displays a fascinating variety of problems and solutions. Groupings of texts (Homer, the Bible, Shakespeare) may have been created at times when their coherence was not especially significant, but later generations have placed enormous importance on the difference between the canonical and the apocryphal in each case. The modern interest in authorship attribution derives from the Renaissance, when the availability of texts made comparative study possible, and a new critical spirit went with the linguistic and textual disciplines of Humanism. The demonstration by Lorenzo Valla in the fifteenth century that the Donation of Constantine, which gave the western part of the Roman Empire to Pope Sylvester, was a forgery, is perhaps the most famous example (Love 2002: 18–19).

In the modern era most texts come securely attributed on external evidence. The title page of the first edition announces the author, or some knowledgeable contemporary assigns the work to the author. Some exuberant authors include their name in the text itself, as Ben Jonson does in his ode to Lucius Cary and Henry Morison. These attributions may be a little deceptive in their straightforwardness – there are collaborators, editors, and writers of source materials to complicate matters – but for reasons of economy of effort such approximations (Charles Dickens wrote *Great Expectations*) are allowed to stand.

Then for texts without this explicit and decisive external evidence there are numerous considerations of topic, approach, attitudes, imagery, turns of phrase, and so on which have always served scholars as foundations for attributions. The balance between the credibility of this internal evidence and the external kind has swung back and forth. The 1960s were a low point for internal evidence, as a reaction to the undisciplined accumulation of parallel passages and the wholesale "disintegration" of canons like Shakespeare's. This skepticism about internal evidence can be seen in Schoenbaum's (1966) book and in the 1966 Erdman and Fogel collection.

Humanities computing is involved with a second generation of attribution based on internal evidence, depending on measuring stylistic features in the doubtful and other texts, and comparing the results. An interesting case study is the debate over attributing the *Funerall Elegie for William Peter* by W. S. to Shakespeare, which began with Foster's (1989) book. The only evidence in favor of the attribution was internal, and stylistic in the specialized sense, being quantitative on the one hand and concerned with largely unnoticed idiosyncracies of language on the other. Both sides of the debate agreed that the poem's style, in the more usual sense of the imagery, diction, and language use noticed by readers, was unlike canonical Shakespeare. The proponents of the attribution argued that since the quantitative and stylistic evidence was so strong, the generally held view of the "Shakespearean" would just have to change. (Recently, another candidate, John Ford, has been proposed, for whom there were none of the cognitive dissonances just mentioned, and whose work appears to satisfy both readers and stylisticians as a good match for the *Elegie*.)

Underpinning any interest in assigning authorship is a model of the author. Since the 1970s the traditional scholarly activity of determining authorship has been conducted with a certain unease, resulting from the work of the French post-structuralists Roland Barthes, Michel Foucault, and Jacques Derrida, who, in undermining what they saw as the bourgeois individual subject, displaced the author as the primary source of meaning for texts. In the literary sphere this individual subject had reached an apogee in the Romantic idea of the heroic individual author. Since structuralism, there has been more interest in the role of discourse, culture, and language itself in creating texts.

There are, as Furbank and Owens (1988) elaborate, special cautions which should attach to the activity of adding items to a canon. The more items included, the wider the canon, and the easier it is to add further ones (1988: 4). There is no such thing as adding a work *temporarily* to a canon (1988: 30). They urge resistance to the pressure to assign authors, since doing this has so many consequences for the canon to which the work is added: after all, "works do not need to be assigned to authors and it does not matter that anonymous works should remain anonymous" (1988: 30). It is not enough that a work is a "plausible" addition to a canon, since once added, works are very hard to subtract (1988: 15).

There is also a more traditional objection to the energy that has gone into attribution. In Erasmus's words in his edition of St Jerome, "What is so important about whose name is on a book, provided it is a good book?" (1992: 75). Erasmus's answer is that this may indeed not matter in the case of a mere playwright like Plautus, whose works he has discussed earlier (1992: 71), but is vital in the case of "sacred writers and pillars of the church" like Jerome. If "nonsense" by others is presented as the work of such writers, and the imposture is not detected, then readers are forced to remain silent about any doubts or to accept falsehood (1992: 76). (Erasmus's attribution methods are discussed in Love 2002: 19–22). A modern critic might argue that authorship is important even in the case of a dramatist like Plautus. Attaching a name to a work "changes its meaning by changing its context . . . certain kinds of meaning are conferred by its membership and position in the book or *oeuvre*. *Hamlet* by William Shakespeare is a different play from *Hamlet* by the Earl of Oxford or Francis Bacon" (Love 2002: 46). Kermode suggests that "a different and special form of attention" is paid to the work of a famous writer (quoted in Furbank and Owens 1988: 44). Even within the world of scholarship, discovery that an essay was not after all by an important thinker like Foucault would make a considerable difference (Love 2002: 96–7).

The signs are that models of authorship are evolving from the post-structuralist "author function," an intersection of discourses, toward a concept more influenced by the workings of cognitive faculties. If the long-term memory store of human beings works not systematically but by "casting out a line for any things directly or indirectly associated with the object of our search," then "the organisation of memories . . . reflects the person's own past experience and thought rather than a shared resource of cultural knowledge" and this would imply a "unique idiolect" for each individual's speech or writing (Lancashire 1997: 178).

Then there has been a renewed interest in the linguistics of the individual speaker, whose differences from other speakers, according to Johnstone, should be accorded "foundational status" (1996: 21). She shows that, even in highly constraining situations like academic discourse or conducting or answering a telephone survey, speakers tend to create an individual style, and to maintain this style across different discourse types. Sociolinguistics explains difference through social categories (most often class, gender, and race) or rhetorical ones (purpose and audience), but Johnstone argues that these should be seen as resources from which the individual constructs difference rather than the determinants of it (1996: ix–x). She is prepared to envisage a return to the Romantic view of the importance of the individual in language, overturning the highly influential arguments of Saussure that language study should concern itself with *langue*, the system of a language, rather than *parole*, the individual instance of language production (1996: 20) and challenging the prestige of abstract scientific laws which have meant that, in the words of Edward Sapir, "[t]he laws of syntax acquire a higher reality than the immediate reality of the stammerer who is trying 'to get himself across'" (quoted in Johnstone 1996: 20).

Theoretical Considerations for Attribution

The practicalities of attribution by stylistic means hinge on the question of the variation in the style of an author. In Sonnet 76 Shakespeare's speaker laments that he cannot vary his style in line with the poetic fashion, with the result that everything he writes is hopelessly easy to identify as his own, because it is "So far from variation or quick change." (There is a special reason in this case: he always writes on the same subject, on his beloved and his love.) In the eighteenth century, Alexander Pope thought that attributing authorship by style was foolish – on the grounds, it seems, that it was too easy for an author to "borrow" a style (quoted in Craig 1992: 199). Variation, in other words, was unlimited. Samuel Johnson later in the same century took the opposite point of view. His friend and biographer James Boswell asked him if everyone had their own style, just as everyone has a unique physiognomy and a unique handwriting. Johnson answered emphatically in the affirmative: "Why, Sir, I think every man whatever has a peculiar style, which may be discovered by nice examination and comparison with others: but a man must write a great deal to make his style obviously discernible" (quoted in Love 2002: 7).

The evidence from the vast activity in empirical work on authorship supports a qualified version of Johnson's view. An attribution to satisfy most standards of proof is possible on internal grounds provided the doubtful sample is of sufficient length, and sufficient samples for comparison in similar text types by candidate writers are available. It is reasonable to say that the extreme skeptics about "stylometry" or "non-traditional authorship attribution studies," those who suggested that it had similar claims to useful information about authorship to those of phrenology about personality (Love 2002: 155), have been proved wrong.

Statistics depends on structured variation – on finding patterns in the changes of items along measurable scales. It is easy to see that language samples must vary in all sorts of ways as different messages are composed and in different modes and styles. The claims of statistical authorship attribution rest on the idea that this variation is constrained by the cognitive faculties of the writer. The writer will compose various works in the same or different genres and over a more or less extended career. Language features must vary in frequency within his or her output. Chronology and genre are readily detectable as sources of change; readers might expect to tell the difference between early and late Henry James, or between the writing in a comic novel and a serious essay by the same writer. Play dialogue presents an expected sharp variation in style within the same work, which may contain old and young speakers, men and women, the rich and the poor, the witty and the dull, and so on. The approach to authorial idiolect through cognitive science and neurology offers its own reinforcement of the notion that different genres are treated differently, and that word-patterns can be acquired and also lost over a lifetime (Lancashire 1997: 182, and 1999: 744).

There is, however, evidence which suggests that authorial consistency is quite a strong factor in most eras, so that one can expect to find other sources of systematic variation nested within it. Early James and late James are different, but not so different as to override the difference between James and Thomas Hardy. The characters created by a single dramatist scatter on many variables, but the scatter may still be constrained enough so that their multidimensional "territory" does not overlap with a second dramatist of the same period writing in the same genres. There is contradictory evidence on this matter from empirical studies. Burrows (1991) shows that Henry Fielding's style in his parody of Samuel Richardson remained close enough to his usual pattern to group his parody, *Shamela*, with his other writing, though it did move some way toward the style of Richardson himself. On the other side of the ledger is the case of Romain Gary, who in the 1970s wrote two novels under a pseudonym in an effort to escape the reception which he felt his established reputation influenced too heavily. These novels were successful, and indeed after the publication of the second of them Gary won a second Prix Goncourt under his *nom de plume*, Émile Ajar. Tirvengadum (1998) reports that in the second of the Ajar novels Gary was able to change his style so radically as to make the profile of his common-word usage distinct from that in his other work.

The search for stylistic markers which are outside the conscious control of the writer has led to a divergence between literary interpretation and stylometry, since, as Horton puts it, "the textual features that stand out to a literary scholar usually reflect a writer's conscious stylistic decisions and are thus open to imitation, deliberate or otherwise" (quoted in Lancashire 1998: 300). In support of these unconscious style markers are the studies that show that much of language production is done by parts of the brain which act in such swift and complex ways that they can be called a true linguistic unconscious (Crane 2001: 18). Lancashire (1997: 177) adds: "This is not to say that we cannot ourselves form a sentence mentally, edit it in memory, and then speak it or write it, just that the process is so arduous, time-consuming, and awkward that we seldom strive to use it."

Naturally it is incumbent on the researchers to show their audiences how markers invisible to writers or readers can be operative in texts at more than a narrowly statistical level, to avoid what Furbank and Owens call "the spectre of the meaningless" (1988: 181). As Love argues, a stylistic explanation for grouping or differentiating texts is always to be preferred to a stylometric or "black-box" one (2002: 110). Unlike most research in the humanities, results of the purely computational kind cannot be checked against the reader's recollection or fresh study of the texts: in principle, the only check is a replication of the statistical tests themselves.

Practical Considerations in Attribution

The first factor to consider in an authorship question is the number of candidates involved. There may be no obvious candidates indicated by external evidence; a group of candidates, from two to a very large but still defined number; or there may be a single candidate with an unlimited group of other possible authors. Commentators have generally been pessimistic about all but two-author problems. Furbank and Owens (1988), assessing the potential usefulness of quantitative stylistics in testing attributions in the very large group of texts associated with Daniel Defoe, concluded that these new methods "were not yet in a position to replace more traditional approaches" (1988: 183). They proceeded to work on external and purely qualitative internal evidence in establishing a revised Defoe canon. The most-cited successful attribution on quantitative measures, the assignation of a group of essays in *The Federalist*, is an adjudication between two candidates. The disputed papers could only have been written by Alexander Madison or John Hamilton; the problem was solved by Mosteller and Wallace (1964) using function-word markers.

There are grounds for optimism, on the other hand, that with advances in technique and in the availability of good-quality, well-suited data, attribution by computational stylistics can make a contribution even in complicated cases. Burrows (2002), for instance, reports success with a recently developed technique adapted for multiple-candidate problems. It establishes multiple authorial profiles and determines a distance from each of these to the target text, as a measure of which author's work the mystery piece is "least unlike."

The way forward would seem to be by a double movement: calibrating the reliability of attribution methods by good technique and sheer collective experience, and on the other hand, with the increasing availability of text for comparison, advancing on even the most difficult problems (especially those involving a single author as against an unlimited group of others, and searching for good candidates from a very large pool). It may be misguided to aim for complete certainty in attaching a single name to a doubtful text. There is, after all, much to be gained from eliminating one or more candidates, while remaining uncertain about the actual author, or narrowing authorship to a small group of names.

It may be useful to conclude with a brief list of commonly encountered pitfalls in authorial attribution by computational stylistics:

1   Assuming that, if groups separate according to author, the separation is authorial. This is obvious when one authorial group is all tragedies and the second comedies. Even if all texts are from the same genre, there must always be the question whether the difference is really between (say) comedies set in the city and those set in the court.
2   Assuming that parallels between elements of a doubtful text and a given author provide an argument for authorship when those elements may be found in any number of other authors outside the sample tested. This was the downfall of what Schoenbaum calls the "parallelographic school" (1966: 94).
3   Selecting those techniques, and those features, which favor one case, while ignoring others ("cherry-picking"). Furbank and Owens (1991: 243) put it this way: "any

liberty to choose one test, rather than another for a given authorship problem will lay you open to incalculable, perhaps subliminal, temptations to choose the one that will help you to prove what you want to prove."

4 Assuming that an author cannot vary from his or her normal style when carrying out a particular assignment, or under a particular internal or external influence.

5 Using a new attribution, not yet generally accepted, as the basis for further attributions – what has been called in art-historical studies "the forging of chains," Friedländer's term for works in the visual arts added to an *oeuvre* on the basis of connoisseurship and then used to justify the addition of further works (cited in Furbank and Owens 1988: 47).

More positively, one might consider a set of ideal conditions for an attribution on stylistic grounds:

1 The doubtful text is long. (In the experiment in assigning Restoration poems to their authors described in Burrows (2002), reliability increases with sample length.)

2 There is a small number of candidates (two is ideal, as in the case of the *Federalist* papers).

3 There is no significant involvement in the doubtful text by other writers as collaborators or revisers, and very few changes have been made by third parties such as printers and editors between composition and the surviving texts.

4 There is a lot of securely attributed text by the candidates, in a similar genre and from a similar period to the doubtful text.

Purists would say that all these conditions must be met before a secure attribution can be made, but it may be more realistic to see a continuum of reliability to which all these conditions contribute. Attribution work may still yield valuable results, in eliminating some of the candidates, for example, where there are significant deficits in one or more of these conditions.

Conclusion

Computer-assisted stylistics and authorship studies are at an interesting stage. A remarkable range of studies has been built up; methods have been well calibrated by a variety of researchers on a variety of problems; and even if some studies have proved faulty, the vigorous discussion of their shortcomings is a resource for those who follow. Well-tested methods can now provide multiple approaches to a given problem, so that results can be triangulated and cross-checked. There is an ever-increasing volume of text available in machine-readable form: this means that a large purpose-built corpus can now be assembled quite quickly in many areas. There are enough successes to suggest that computational stylistics and non-traditional attribution have become essential tools, the first places one looks to for answers on very large questions of text patterning, and on difficult authorship problems. It is worth noting, too, that the lively debate provoked by computational work in stylistics and authorship is an indication that these activities are playing a significant part in a much wider contemporary discussion about the relations of the human and the mechanical.

REFERENCES FOR FURTHER READING

Biber, D. (1988). *Variation across Speech and Writing*. Cambridge: Cambridge University Press.
Burrows, J. F. (1987). *Computation into Criticism: A Study of Jane Austen and an Experiment in Method*. Oxford: Clarendon Press.
——(1991). "I lisp'd in numbers": Fielding, Richardson and the Appraisal of Statistical Evidence. *Scriblerian and the Kit-Kats* 23: 234–41.
——(2002). "Delta": A Measure of Stylistic Difference and a Guide to Likely Authorship. *Literary and Linguistic Computing* 17: 267–87.
Burrows, J. F., and H. Love (1998). The Role of Stylistics in Attribution: Thomas Shadwell and "The Giants' War." *Eighteenth Century Life* 22: 18–30.
Craig, D. H. (1992). Authorial Styles and the Frequencies of Very Common Words: Jonson, Shakespeare, and the Additions to "The Spanish Tragedy." *Style* 26: 199–220.
Crane, M. T. (2001). *Shakespeare's Brain: Reading with Cognitive Theory*. Princeton, NJ: Princeton University Press.
Ellegård, Alvar (1962). *A Statistical Method for Determining Authorship*. Gothenburg: University of Gothenburg.
Erasmus, Desiderius (1992). *Collected Works of Erasmus. Vol. 61. Patristic Scholarship: The Edition of St Jerome*, ed. J. F. Brady and John C. Olin. Toronto: University of Toronto Press.
Erdman, David V. and Ephim G. Fogel (eds.) (1966). *Evidence for Authorship: Essays on Problems of Attribution*. Ithaca, NY: Cornell University Press.
Fish, S. (1980). *Is there a Text in this Class? The Authority of Interpretive Communities*. Cambridge, MA: Harvard University Press.
Foster, Donald W. (1989). *Elegy by W. S.: A Study in Attribution*. Newark, DE: University of Delaware Press.
Furbank, P. N. and W. R. Owens (1988). *The Canonisation of Daniel Defoe*. New Haven, CT: Yale University Press.
——(1991). Dangerous Relations. *Scriblerian and the Kit-Kats* 33: 242–4.
Jackson, MacD. P. (2002). Determining Authorship: A New Technique. *Research Opportunities in Renaissance Drama* 41: 1–14.
Johnstone, B. (1996). *The Linguistic Individual: Self-Expression in Language and Linguistics*. New York: Oxford University Press.
Lancashire, I. (1997). Empirically Determining Shakespeare's Idiolect. *Shakespeare Studies* 25: 171–85.
——(1998). Paradigms of Authorship. *Shakespeare Studies* 26: 298–301.
——(1999). Probing Shakespeare's Idiolect in *Troilus and Cressida*, 1.3.1–29. *University of Toronto Quarterly* 68: 728–67.
Love, Harold (2002). *Attributing Authorship: An Introduction*. Cambridge: Cambridge University Press.
McMenamin, G. (1993). *Forensic Stylistics*. Amsterdam: Elsevier.
Milic, Louis T. (1991). Progress in Stylistics: Theory, Statistics, Computers. *Computers and the Humanities* 25: 393–400.
Mosteller, F. and D. L. Wallace (1964). *Inference and Disputed Authorship: The Federalist*. Reading, MA: Addison-Wesley.
Schoenbaum, S. (1966). *Internal Evidence and Elizabethan Dramatic Authorship: An Essay in Literary History and Method*. London: Arnold.
Tirvengadum, Vina (1998). Linguistic Fingerprints and Literary Fraud. *Computing in the Humanities Working Papers*. Accessed November 1, 2002. At <http://www.chass.utoronto.ca/epc/chwp/tirven/index.html>.

21

Preparation and Analysis of Linguistic Corpora

Nancy Ide

The corpus is a fundamental tool for any type of research on language. The availability of computers in the 1950s immediately led to the creation of corpora in electronic form that could be searched automatically for a variety of language features, and compute frequency, distributional characteristics, and other descriptive statistics. Corpora of literary works were compiled to enable stylistic analyses and authorship studies, and corpora representing general language use became widely used in the field of lexicography. In this era, the creation of an electronic corpus required entering the material by hand, and the storage capacity and speed of computers available at the time put limits on how much data could realistically be analyzed at any one time. Without the Internet to foster data sharing, corpora were typically created, and processed at a single location. Two notable exceptions are the Brown Corpus of American English (Kucera and Francis 1967) and the London/Oslo/Bergen (LOB) corpus of British English (Johansson et al. 1978); both of these corpora, each containing 1 million words of data tagged for part of speech, were compiled in the 1960s using a representative sample of texts produced in the year 1961. For several years, the Brown and LOB were the only widely available computer-readable corpora of general language, and therefore provided the data for numerous language studies.

In the 1980s, the speed and capacity of computers increased dramatically, and, with more and more texts being produced in computerized form, it became possible to create corpora much larger than the Brown and LOB, containing millions of words. The availability of language samples of this magnitude opened up the possibility of gathering meaningful statistics about language patterns that could be used to drive language processing software such as syntactic parsers, which sparked renewed interest in corpus compilation within the computational linguistics community. Parallel corpora, which contain the same text in two or more languages, also began to appear; the best known of these is the Canadian Hansard corpus of Parliamentary debates in English and French.

Corpus creation still involved considerable work, even when texts could be acquired from other sources in electronic form. For example, many texts existed as typesetter's tapes obtained from publishers, and substantial processing was required to remove or translate typesetter codes.

The "golden era" of linguistic corpora began in 1990 and continues to this day. Enormous corpora of both text and speech have been, and continue to be, compiled, many by government-funded projects in Europe, the USA, and Japan. In addition to monolingual corpora, several multilingual parallel corpora covering multiple languages have also been created. A side effect of the growth in the availability and use of corpora in the 1990s was the development of automatic techniques for *annotating* language data with information about its linguistic properties. Algorithms for assigning part of speech tags to words in a corpus and aligning words and sentences in parallel text (i.e., associating each word or sentence with its translation in the parallel version) were developed in the 1990s that achieve 95–98 percent accuracy. Automatic means to identify syntactic configurations such as noun phrases, and proper names, dates, etc., were also developed.

There now exist numerous corpora, many of which are available through the Linguistic Data Consortium (LDC) (http://www.ldc.upenn.edu) in the USA and the European Language Resources Association (ELRA) (http://www.elra.org) in Europe, both of which were founded in the mid-1990s to serve as repositories and distributors of corpora and other language resources such as lexicons. However, because of the cost and difficulty of obtaining some types of texts (e.g., fiction), existing corpora vary considerably in their composition; very few efforts have been made to compile language samples that are "balanced" in their representation of different genres. Notable exceptions (apart from the early Brown and LOB) are the British National Corpus (BNC) (http://www.hcu.ox.ac.uk/BNC/) and the American National Corpus (ANC) (http://www. AmericanNationalCorpus.org), as well as (to some extent) the corpora for several western European languages produced by the PAROLE project. In fact the greatest number of existing text corpora are composed of readily available materials such as newspaper data, technical manuals, government documents, and, more recently, materials drawn from the World Wide Web. Speech data, whose acquisition is in most instances necessarily controlled, are more often representative of a specific dialect or range of dialects.

Many corpora are available for research purposes by signing a license and paying a small reproduction fee. Other corpora are available only by paying a (sometimes substantial) fee; this is the case, for instance, for many of the holdings of the LDC, making them virtually inaccessible to humanists.

Preparation of Linguistic Corpora

The first phase of corpus creation is *data capture*, which involves rendering the text in electronic form, either by hand or via optical character recognition (OCR), acquisition of word processor or publishing software output, typesetter tapes, PDF files, etc. Manual entry is time-consuming and costly, and therefore unsuitable for the creation of very large corpora. OCR output can be similarly costly if it requires substantial post-processing to validate the data. Data acquired in electronic form from other sources will almost invariably contain formatting codes and other information that must be discarded or translated to a representation that is processable for linguistic analysis.

Representation formats and surrounding issues

At this time, the most common representation format for linguistic corpora is XML. Several existing corpora are tagged using the EAGLES XML Corpus Encoding Standard (XCES) (Ide et al. 2000), a Text Encoding Initiative (TEI)-compliant XML application designed specifically for linguistic corpora and their annotations. The XCES introduced the notion of *stand-off annotation*, which requires that annotations are encoded in documents separate from the primary data and linked to them. One of the primary motivations for this approach is to avoid the difficulties of overlapping hierarchies, which are common when annotating diverse linguistic features, as well as the unwieldy documents that can be produced when multiple annotations are associated with a single document. The stand-off approach also allows for annotation of the same feature (e.g., part of speech) using alternative schemes, as well as associating annotations with other annotations rather than directly to the data. Finally, it supports two basic notions about text and annotations outlined in Leech (1993): it should be possible to remove the annotation from an annotated corpus in order to revert to the raw corpus; and, conversely, it should be possible to extract the annotations by themselves from the text.

The use of stand-off annotation is now widely accepted as the norm among corpus and corpus-handling software developers; however, because mechanisms for inter-document linking have only recently been developed within the XML framework, many existing corpora include annotations in the same document as the text.

The use of the stand-off model dictates that a distinction is made between the *primary data* (i.e., the text without additional linguistic information) and their annotations, in particular, what should and should not be marked in the former. The XCES identifies two types of information that may be encoded in the primary data:

1 *Gross structure*: universal text elements down to the level of the paragraph, which is the smallest unit that can be identified language-independently; for example:

- structural units of text, such as volume, chapter, etc., down to the level of paragraph; also footnotes, titles, headings, tables, figures, etc.;
- features of typography and layout, for previously printed texts: e.g., list item markers;
- non-textual information (graphics, etc.).

2 *Segmental structure*: elements appearing at the sub-paragraph level which are usually signaled (sometimes ambiguously) by typography in the text and which are language-dependent; for example:

- orthographic sentences, quotations;
- orthographic words;
- abbreviations, names, dates, highlighted words.

Annotations (see next section) are linked to the primary data using XML conventions (XLink, Xpointer).

Speech data, especially speech signals, are often treated as "read-only," and therefore the primary data contain no XML markup to which annotations may be linked. In this case, stand-off documents identify the start and end points (typically using byte offsets) of the structures listed above, and annotations are linked indirectly to the primary data by referencing the structures in these documents. The *annotation graphs* representation format used in the ATLAS project, which is intended primarily to handle speech data, relies entirely on this approach to link annotations to data, with no option for referencing XML-tagged elements.

Identification of segmental structures

Markup identifying the boundaries of gross structures may be automatically generated from original formatting information. However, in most cases the original formatting is *presentational* rather than *descriptive*; for example, titles may be identifiable because they are in bold, and therefore transduction to a descriptive XML representation may not be straightforward. This is especially true for sub-paragraph elements that are in italic or bold font; it is usually impossible to automatically tag such elements as emphasis, foreign word, etc.

Creation of linguistic corpora almost always demands that sub-paragraph structures such as sentences and words, as well as names, dates, abbreviations, etc., are identified. Numerous programs have been developed to perform sentence "splitting" and word tokenization, many of which are freely available (see, for example, the tools listed in the Natural Language Software Registry (http://www.dfki.de/lt/registry/) or the SIL Software Catalogue (http://www.sil.org). These functions are also embedded in more general corpus development tools such as GATE (Cunningham 2002). Sentence splitting and tokenization are highly language-dependent and therefore require specific information (e.g., abbreviations for sentence splitting, clitics and punctuation conventions for tokenization) for the language being processed; in some cases, language-specific software is developed, while in others a general processing engine is fed the language-specific information as data and can thus handle multiple languages. Languages without word-boundary markers, such as Chinese and Japanese, and continuous speech represented by phoneme sequences, require an entirely different approach to segmentation, the most common of which is a dynamic programming algorithm to compute the most likely boundaries from a weighted transition graph. This, of course, demands that the probabilities of possible symbol or phoneme sequences are available in order to create the weighted graph.

Within the computational linguistics community, software to identify so-called "named entities" (proper names designating people, places, organizations, events, documents, etc.), as well as dates and other time expressions, has been developed, and many of these tools are freely available for research. However, most of these tools have been developed using existing corpora which consist of newspapers and government reports and are unlikely to perform well on the kinds of data that interest humanists, such as literary works, historical documents, etc. This is just one example of the broader situation in the development of corpus-handling tools: the available data, which are often highly skewed for genre, drive tool, and algorithm development, and therefore applicability to more generalized corpora is often limited.

Corpus annotation

For computational linguistics research, which has driven the bulk of corpus creation efforts over the past decade, corpora are typically annotated with various kinds of linguistic information. The following sections outline the major annotation types.

Morpho-syntactic annotation   By far the most common corpus annotation is morpho-syntactic annotation (part-of-speech tagging), primarily because several highly accurate automatic taggers have been developed over the past fifteen years. Part-of-speech tagging is a *disambiguation* task: for words that have more than one possible part of speech, it is necessary to determine which one, given the context, is correct. Although, in English, close to 90 percent of the words in the language have only one part of speech, in actual use (e.g., in a corpus), part of speech for as many as 40 percent of the word *instances* may be ambiguous (DeRose 1988), due in large part to ambiguity for a handful of high-frequency words such as "that," which can be either a determiner ("*that* girl") or a complementizer ("He heard *that* you came home"). Beyond this, the most common ambiguity in English is between verb and noun, e.g., "hide," "dog," "brand," "felt," etc.

Taggers fall into two general classes: rule-based (e.g. ENGTWOL, Voutilainen, 1995), which use manually generated rules to assign part of speech, and stochastic, which rely on probabilities for *n-grams* – sequences of *n* (usually, 2 or 3) tags that are known to occur in real data. Stochastic taggers learn these probabilities by being "trained" on previously tagged data that have been hand-validated for correctness. A third type of tagger, often called the "Brill tagger" after its developer (Brill 1995), uses a hybrid approach which learns its tagging rules from a previously tagged training corpus. Obviously, the more accurately tagged data a tagger can use for training, the more likely its probabilities will be correct. This fact has led to the creation of corpora that have been hand-annotated (or in which automatically produced tags have been hand-validated) specifically intended for training, in order to enable automatic taggers to produce even more tagged corpora.

The tags generated by a part-of-speech tagger provide more information than simple word class (noun, verb, adjective, etc.). Various levels of morpho-syntactic information can be represented; the more detailed the information, the bigger the tagset, and the bigger the tagset, the less accurate an automatic tagger will be. For this reason, tagsets including 50–100 tags that collapse or eliminate detailed morpho-syntactic information – such as the information in the morpho-syntactic specifications for western and eastern European languages produced by the EAGLES project (http://www.ilc.pi.cnr.it/ EAGLES/home.html) – are most typically used in automatic tagging.

There are several tagsets in common use for English, most of which evolved from the 87 tags used in the Brown corpus (http://www.hit.uib.no/icame/brown/bcm.html). Probably the most widely used is the 45-tag set of the Penn Treebank project (Marcus et al. 1993), of which only 36 are actual morpho-syntactic categories (the rest are for punctuation, list markers, etc.). The Penn tagset is a variant of the Brown tagset that eliminates information retrievable from the form of the lexical item. It therefore includes only one tag for different forms of the verbs "be," "have," and "do," whereas the Brown (and other common tagsets for English) provide a different tag for each of these forms. Another well-known tagset for English is the 61-tag C5 tagset of the CLAWS (Constituent Likelihood

Automatic Word-tagging System) tagger, developed at the University of Lancaster (Garside and Smith 1997) and used to tag the British National Corpus.

Part-of-speech taggers rely on *lexicons* that provide all of the possible part of speech assignments for a lexical item found in the input, from which it must choose the most probable given the immediate context. The information in the lexicons must therefore match – or at least, be mappable to – the tagset used by the tagger. It is an unfortunate fact that it is often extremely difficult and sometimes impossible to map one tagset to another, which has resulted in much re-creation of lexical information to suit the needs of a particular tagger.

Many lexicons include *lemmas* (root forms), and morpho-syntactic annotation may produce lemmas as well as part-of-speech tags in their output. The presence of lemmas in an annotated text enables extraction of all orthographic forms associated with a given lemma (e.g., "do," "does," "doing, "did" for the lemma "do"). However, although relatively easily produced, many existing corpora do not include lemmas; notable exceptions are the *Journal of the Commission* corpus, the Orwell multilingual corpus, and the SUSANNE corpus.

Parallel alignment   In addition to algorithms for morpho-syntactic annotation, reliable algorithms for alignment of parallel texts – i.e., texts for which there exist translations in two or more languages – have been developed. Probability information about correspondences between words, phrases, and other structures derived from aligned corpora are used to choose from multiple possible translations that may be generated by a machine translation system. Parallel corpora have also been used to automatically generate bilingual dictionaries (e.g., Dagan and Church 1997) and, more recently, as a means to achieve automatic sense tagging of corpora (e.g., Ide et al. 2001).

Two types of parallel alignment are common: sentence alignment and word alignment. Sentence alignment is by far the easier and more accurate of the two, the major problem being to determine cases in which one-to-many or partial mappings exist. Many sentence and word-aligned corpora exist, the vast majority of which include only two languages. Probably the best known is the English–French Hansard Corpus of Canadian Parliamentary debates, which has served as the basis for numerous translation studies. Multilingual parallel corpora are much more rare; the difficulty is not in the alignment itself, but rather in the availability of texts in multiple translations (in particular, texts that are not bound by copyright or other restrictions). Existing multilingual aligned corpora include the United Nations Parallel Text Corpus (English, French, Spanish), the *Journal of the Commission* (JOC) corpus (English, French, German, Italian, Spanish), the Orwell *1984* Corpus (Bulgarian, Czech, English, Estonian, Hungarian, Latvian, Lithuanian, Romanian, Serbo-Croat, Slovene), Plato's *Republic* (Bulgarian, Chinese, Czech, English, German, Latvian, Polish, Romanian, Slovak, Slovene) and the Bible (Chinese, Danish, English, Finnish, French, Greek, Indonesian, Latin, Spanish, Swahili, Swedish, Vietnamese).

Syntactic annotation   There are two main types of syntactic annotation in linguistic corpora: noun phrase (NP) bracketing or "chunking," and the creation of "treebanks" that include fuller syntactic analysis. Syntactically annotated corpora serve various statistics-based applications, most notably, by providing probabilities to drive syntactic parsers, and have been also used to derive context-free and unification-based grammars

(Charniak 1996; Van Genabith et al. 1999). Syntactically annotated corpora also provide theoretical linguists with data to support studies of language use.

The best known and most widely used treebank is the Penn Treebank for English (Marcus et al. 1993). Ongoing projects exist for the development of treebanks for other languages, including German (the NEGRA corpus, Brants et al. 2003; Stegman et al. 1998), Czech (The Prague Dependency Treebank, Hajič 1998), French (Abeillé et al. 2000), and Chinese (Xue et al. 2002). The Penn Treebank and the Chinese Treebank, both created at the University of Pennsylvania, use LISP-like list structures to specify *constituency relations* and provide syntactic category labels for constituents, as shown below:

```
((S (NP-SBJ-1 Jones)
    (VP followed)
    (NP him)
    (PP-DIR into
       (NP the front room))
 ,
 (S-ADV (NP-SBJ *-1)
   (VP closing
       (NP the door)
       (PP behind
          (NP him)))))
 .))
```

Although they differ in the labels and in some cases the function of various nodes in the tree, many treebank annotation schemes provide a similar constituency-based representation of relations among syntactic components. In contrast, *dependency schemes* do not provide a hierarchical constituency analysis, but rather specify grammatical relations among elements explicitly; for example, the sentence "Paul intends to leave IBM" could be represented as follows:

```
subj(intend,Paul,_)
xcomp(intend,leave,to)
subj(leave,Paul)
dobj(leave,IBM,_)
```

Here, the predicate is the relation type, the first argument is the head, the second the dependent, and additional arguments may provide category-specific information (e.g., *introducer* for prepositional phrases). Finally, so-called "hybrid systems" combine constituency analysis and functional dependencies, usually producing a shallow constituent parse that brackets major phrase types and identifies the dependencies between heads of constituents (e.g., the NEGRA Corpus).

Although most modern treebanks utilize an SGML or XML encoding rather than list structures, syntactic annotation is invariably interspersed with the text itself. This makes it difficult or impossible to add other kinds of annotations to the data, or to provide alternative syntactic annotations. As noted earlier, the use of stand-off annotations is increasingly encouraged. A stand-off scheme for syntactic annotations, which also serves as a "pivot" format for representing different types of syntactic annotation with a common scheme, has been developed by Ide and Romary (2001).

Semantic annotation   Semantic annotation can be taken to mean any kind of annotation that adds information about the meaning of elements in a text. Some annotations that may be considered to provide semantic information – for example, "case role" information such as agent, instrument, etc. – are often included in syntactic annotations. Another type of semantic annotation common in literary analysis (especially in the 1960s and 1970s) marks words or phrases in a text as representative of a particular theme or concept. At present, the most common type of semantic annotation is "sense tagging": the association of lexical items in a text with a particular sense or definition, usually drawn from an existing sense inventory provided in a dictionary or online lexicon such as WordNet (Miller et al. 1990).

The major difficulty in sense annotation is to determine an appropriate set of senses. Simply examining the differences in sense distinctions made from one dictionary to another demonstrates the difficulty of this task. To solve the problem, some attempts have been made to identify the kinds of sense distinctions that are useful for automatic language processing: for example, tasks such as information retrieval may require only very coarse-grained sense distinctions – the difference between "bank" as a financial institution vs. a river bank – whereas others, and in particular machine translation, require finer distinctions – say, between "bank" as a financial institution and as a building. However, by far the most common source of sense tags used for semantic annotation is WordNet, an online dictionary that in addition to providing sense lists, groups words into "synsets" of synonymous words. WordNet has been updated several times, and as a result, its sense list may differ for a particular word depending on the WordNet version used for the tagging.

It is widely acknowledged that the sense distinctions provided in WordNet are far from optimal. However, this resource, which is among the most heavily used in natural language processing research over the past decade, will likely continue to serve as a basis for sense tagging for at least the foreseeable future, if for no other reason than that it continues to be the only freely available, machine-tractable lexicon providing extensive coverage of English. The EuroWordNet project has produced WordNets for most western European languages linked to WordNet 1.5 (the current version of the English WordNet is 2.0), and WordNets for other languages (e.g., Balkan languages) are under development, which is likely to extend the research community's reliance on its sense inventory. In any case, no clearly superior alternative source of sense distinctions has been proposed.

Because sense-tagging requires hand annotation, and because human annotators will often disagree on sense assignments even given a predefined sense inventory, very few sense-tagged corpora exist. Examples include the Semantic Concordance Corpus (SemCor; Miller et al. 1993), produced by the WordNet project, which assigns WordNet sense tags for all nouns, verbs, and adjectives in a 250,000-word corpus drawn primarily from the Brown Corpus; the DSO Corpus, containing sense-tags for 121 nouns and 70 verbs in about 192,800 sentences taken from the Brown Corpus and the *Wall Street Journal*; and Hector, containing about 200,000 tagged instances of 300 words in a corpus of British English.

Automatic means to sense-tag data have been sought ever since machine-readable texts became available. This area of research, called "word sense disambiguation," remains to this day one of the more difficult problems in language processing. Although rule-based approaches have been developed, the most common approaches to word sense disambiguation over the past decade are statistics-based, relying on the frequency with which lexical items (or categories of lexical items) in the context under consideration have been found in the context of a word in a given sense. Some recent research (Ide 2000; Ide et al. 2001; Doab and Resnik 2002) has explored the use of information gleaned from parallel translations to make sense distinctions. For a comprehensive overview of approaches to word sense disambiguation see Ide and Veronis (1998).

Discourse-level annotation There are three main types of annotation at the level of discourse: topic identification, co-reference annotation, and discourse structure.

Topic identification (also called "topic detection") annotates texts with information about the events or activities described in the text. Automatic means for topic detection over streams of data such as broadcast news and newswires is under development, primarily in the context of the DARPA-sponsored Topic Detection Task. A subtask of this kind of annotation is detection of boundaries between stories/texts, which may also be included in the annotation.

Co-reference annotation links referring objects (e.g., pronouns, definite noun phrases) to prior elements in a discourse to which they refer. This type of annotation is invariably performed manually, since reliable software to identify co-referents is not available. For example, the MUC 7 (Message Understanding Conference) corpus contains hand-generated co-reference links (Hirschman and Chinchor 1997) marked in a non-stand-off SGML format similar to the following:

```
<COREF ID= "E5" >This appliance</COREF> is supplied with
<COREF ID= "E6" >a fitted three pin mains plug</COREF>.
<COREF ID= "E7" >A 3 amp fuse</COREF>
is fitted in <COREF ID= "E8" TYPE= "IDENT" REF= "E6" >the
plug</COREF>.
Should <COREF ID= "E9" TYPE= "IDENT" REF= "E7" >the fuse</-
COREF>
need to be replaced . . .
```

Discourse structure annotation identifies multi-level hierarchies of discourse segments and the relations between them, building upon low-level analysis of clauses, phrases, or sentences. There are several theoretical approaches to the analysis of discourse structure, differing in terms of the span of text (clause, sentence, etc.) that is considered to be the atomic unit of analysis, and in the relations defined to exist between units and higher-level structures built from them. Most common approaches are based on "focus spaces" (Grosz and Sidner 1986) or Rhetorical Structure Theory (Mann and Thompson 1988). To date, annotation of discourse structure is almost always accomplished by hand, although some software to perform discourse segmentation has been developed (e.g., Marcu 1996).

Annotation of speech and spoken data   The most common type of speech annotation is an orthographic transcription that is time-aligned to an audio or video recording. Often, annotation demarcating the boundaries of speech "turns" and individual "utterances" is included. Examples of speech corpora in this type of format include the Child Language Data Exchange System (CHILDES) corpus (MacWhinney 1995), the TIMIT corpus of read speech (Lamel et al. 1990), and the LACITO Linguistic Data Archiving Project (Jacobson and Michailovsky 2000).

The orthographic transcription of speech data can be annotated with any of the kinds of linguistic information outlined in previous sections (e.g., part of speech, syntax, co-reference, etc.), although this is not common. In addition, speech data may be annotated with phonetic segmentation and labeling (phonetic transcription), prosodic phrasing and intonation, disfluencies, and, in the case of video, gesture.

Most types of annotation particular to speech data are time-consuming to produce because they must be generated by hand, and because the annotators must be skilled in the recognition and transcription of speech sounds. Furthermore, speech annotation is problematic: for example, phonetic transcription works on the assumption that the speech signal can be divided into single, clearly demarcated sounds, but these demarcations are often rather unclear. Prosodic annotation is even more subjective, since the decision about the exact nature of a tone movement often varies from annotator to annotator. The kinds of phenomena that are noted include onset, rising tone, falling tone, rising/falling tone, level tone, pause, overlap, etc. The notations for prosodic annotation vary widely and they are not typically rendered in a standard format such as XML. As a result, the few existing corpora annotated for prosody are widely inconsistent in their format. One of the best known such corpora is the London-Lund Corpus of Spoken English (Svartvik 1990).

Corpus annotation tools

Over the past decade, several projects have created tools to facilitate the annotation of linguistic corpora. Most are based on a common architectural model introduced in the MULTEXT project, which views the annotation process as a chain of smaller, individual processes that incrementally add annotations to the data. A similar model was developed in the TIPSTER project.

Among the existing annotation tools for language data are LT XML (University of Edinburgh), which directly implements the MULTEXT model and is especially geared toward XML-encoded resources; GATE (University of Sheffield), based on the TIPSTER model and including tools for tokenization, sentence splitting, named entity recognition, part of speech tagging, as well as corpus and annotation editing tools. The Multilevel Annotation, Tools Engineering (MATE) project provides an annotation tool suite designed especially for spoken dialogue corpora at multiple levels, focusing on prosody, (morpho-)syntax, co-reference, dialogue acts, and communicative difficulties, as well as inter-level interaction. ATLAS (Architecture and Tools for Linguistic Analysis Systems) is a joint initiative of the US National Institute for Standards and Technology (NIST), MITRE, and the LDC to build a general-purpose annotation architecture and a data interchange format. The starting point in ATLAS is the annotation graph model, with some significant generalizations.

Currently, a subcommittee of the International Standards Organization (ISO) – ISO TC37 SC4 – is developing a generalized model for linguistic annotations and processing tools, based on input from developers of the annotation tool suites mentioned above as well as from annotation scheme designers. The goal is to provide a common "pivot" format that instantiates a generalized data model of linguistic resources and their annotations to and from which existing formats – provided they are consistent with the model – can be mapped in order to enable seamless interchange. At present, data annotated within one project, using XML, annotation graphs, or a proprietary annotation scheme, are typically difficult to import for manipulation using another tool suite, either for further annotation or analysis. The developing ISO model is intended to allow annotators to use any of a variety of schemes to represent their data and annotations, and map it to a common format for interchange. Users of other schemes would then import the data in the common format to their own schemes. This means, for example, that a corpus marked up using TEI or XCES conventions can be mapped to the common format and, from that, mapped again to, say, an annotation graph representation that will enable manipulation of the data by tools implementing that model, without information loss.

The future of corpus annotation

Recent developments in the XML world, primarily in the scope of work within the World Wide Web Consortium (W3C), have focused attention on the potential to build a Semantic Web. This possibility has interesting ramifications for both corpus annotation and analysis, in two (related) ways. First, the underlying technology of the Semantic Web enables definition of the kinds of relationships (links) one resource – where a "resource" can be any fragment of a document or the document as a whole – may have with another. For example, a "word" may have a link labeled "part of speech" with another resource that represents (possibly, as a simple string) "noun" or "noun singular masculine." Because annotation is, at the base, the specification of relationships between information in a corpus and linguistic information that describes it, the development of technologies such as the Resource Description Framework (RDF) can have significant impact on the way annotations are associated with primary language resources in the future.

A second activity within the Semantic Web community that has ramifications for both annotation and analysis of linguistic data is the development of technologies to support the specification of and access to ontological information. Ontologies, which provide *a priori* information about relationships among categories of data, enable the possibility to apply inferencing processes that can yield information that is not explicit in the data itself. For example, to properly parse a sentence such as "I ate a fish with a fork" – that is, to attach the prepositional phrase "with a fork" to the verb "eat" and not as a modifier of "fish" – we can check an ontology that specifies that "fork" IS-A sub-class of "instrument," and that "eat" has a USES-A relation with things of type "instrument." More generally, we may be able to identify the topic of a given document by consulting an ontology. For example, the ontology may specify that the word "bank" can represent a sub-class of "financial institution" or "geological formation"; if the document contains several other words that are also related to "financial institution" such as "money," "account," etc., we may conclude that the document has financial institutions as one of its topics (and, as a side effect, that the word "bank" is being used in that sense in this document).

In order to be able to exploit ontological information, it must be created and stored in a universally accessible form. The W3C group developing the Ontological Web Language (OWL) is providing a standard representation format. It is now up to the computational linguistics community to instantiate the relevant ontological information and use it to annotate and analyze language data. Development and use of ontologies has in fact been a part of the field for several years – in particular, the ontology in the WordNet lexicon has been widely used for annotation and analysis of language data. Semantic Web technologies will enable development of common and universally accessible ontological information.

Analysis of Linguistic Corpora

There are two major uses for linguistic corpora: statistics-gathering to support natural language processing; and language analysis to support language learning and dictionary creation.

Statistics gathering

A corpus provides a bank of *samples* that enable the development of numerical language models, and thus the use of corpora goes hand in hand with empirical methods. In the late 1980s, the increased availability of large amounts of electronic text enabled, for the first time, the full-scale use of data-driven methods to attack generic problems in computational linguistics, such as part-of-speech identification, prepositional phrase attachment, parallel text alignment, word sense disambiguation, etc. The success in treating at least some of these problems with statistical methods led to their application to others, and by the mid-1990s, statistical methods had become a staple of computational linguistics work.

The key element for many statistics-based approaches to language processing (in particular, so-called "supervised" methods) is the availability of large, annotated corpora, upon which annotation algorithms are trained to identify common patterns and create transformations or rules for them. The stochastic part-of-speech taggers described above are probably the best-known application relying on previously annotated corpora, but similar approaches are also used for word sense disambiguation, probabilistic parsing, and speech recognition. In word sense disambiguation, for example, statistics are gathered reflecting the degree to which other words are likely to appear in the context of some previously sense-tagged word in a corpus. These statistics are then used to disambiguate occurrences of that word in untagged corpora, by computing the overlap between the unseen context and the context in which the word was seen in a known sense.

Speech recognition is, in fact, the area of computational linguistics in which corpora were first put into large-scale use in support of language processing, beginning with the utilization of Hidden Markov Models (HMMs) in the 1970s. This paradigm required data to statistically train an acoustic model to capture typical sound sequences and a language model to capture typical word sequences, and produced results that were far more accurate and robust than the traditional methods. It was not until the late 1980s that the statistical approach was applied to other areas, one of the first of which was machine translation. Following the same approach as the speech recognition systems, researchers automatically trained a French–English correspondence model (the Translation Model) on 3 million sentences of parallel French and English from the Canadian Parliamentary records, and also trained a Language Model for English production from *Wall Street Journal* data. To translate, the former model was used to replace French words or phrases by the most likely English equivalents, and then the latter model ordered the English words and phrases into the most likely sequences to form output sentences.

Probabilistic parsing is one of the more recent applications of statistical methods to language processing tasks. Again, large bodies of data previously annotated and validated for syntactic structure are required in order to provide statistics concerning the probability that a given syntactic construction is the correct one in its context. Syntactic structure can be very ambiguous; traditional parsers often produced numerous alternative structural analyses for an input sentence. A probabilistic parser uses previously gathered statistics to choose the most probable interpretation.

Issues for corpus-based statistics gathering   In order to be representative of any language as a whole, it is necessary that a corpus include samples from a variety of texts that reflect the range of syntactic and semantic phenomena across that language. This demands, first of all, that the data be adequately large in order to avoid the problem of *data sparseness* that plagues many statistical approaches. For example, for tasks such as word sense disambiguation, data must be extensive enough to ensure that all senses of a polysemous word are not only represented, but represented frequently enough so that meaningful statistics can be compiled. Although it has been extensively used for natural language processing work, the million words of a corpus such as the Brown Corpus are not sufficient for today's large-scale applications: many word senses are not represented; many syntactic structures occur too infrequently to be significant, and the corpus is far too small to be used for computing the bi-gram and tri-gram probabilities that are necessary for training language models for speech recognition.

Unfortunately, in the main, the large corpora freely available for research consist of texts that can be easily acquired and are available for redistribution without undue problems of copyright, etc. Because of this, corpora used for statistics gathering for language processing are vastly over-representative of certain genres, in particular newspaper samples, which constitute the greatest percentage of texts currently available from, for example, the LDC, and which also dominate the training data available for speech recognition purposes. Other available corpora typically consist of technical reports, transcriptions of parliamentary and other proceedings, short telephone conversations, and the like. The upshot of this is that corpus-based natural language processing has relied heavily on language samples representative of usage in a handful of limited and linguistically specialized domains. This can lead to drastically skewed results: for example, in newspaper data, there is a disproportionate number of complex NP complements for some verbs, which appear in sentences typical of newspaper style, such as "The price rose two percent to 102 dollars per share from 100 dollars per share." Similar problems arise in work on word sense disambiguation: it has been noted that for some typical test words such as "line," certain senses (for example, the common sense of "line" as in the sentence, "He really handed her a line") are absent entirely from resources such as the *Wall Street Journal.*

The problem of balance is acute in speech recognition. Speech recognition systems are notoriously dependent on the characteristics of their training corpora. Corpora large enough to train the tri-gram language models of modern speech recognizers (many tens of millions of words) are invariably composed of written rather than spoken texts. But the differences between written and spoken language are even more severe than the differences between balanced corpora like the Brown and newspaper corpora like the *Wall Street Journal.* Therefore, whenever a state-of-the-art speech recognition research effort moves to a new domain, a new large training corpus of speech must be collected, transcribed at the word level, and the transcription aligned to the speech.

Language analysis

The gathering of authentic language data from corpora enables a description of language that starts from the evidence rather than from imposing some theoretical model. Because speakers and writers produce language with real communicative goals, corpora of native-speaker texts provide, in principle, samples of genuine language. For this reason, one of the oldest uses of corpora is for dictionary-making, or lexicography, and in particular, lexicography with the goal of producing so-called "learners' dictionaries" designed for those learning a new language.

The COBUILD corpus was compiled starting in the early 1980s, at which time it included about 7 million words. This corpus was used to create the Collins COBUILD English Dictionary, the first dictionary relying fully on corpora for its creation. Following this lead, over the course of the next decade most British dictionary publishers began to use corpora as the primary data source for their dictionaries, although interestingly, American dictionary publishers are only now beginning to rely on corpora to guide lexicography.

The basic lexicographic tool for analyzing a corpus is a concordancer, a program that displays occurrences of a word in the middle of a line of context from the corpus. However, the huge increase in available data has led to a situation where lexicographers are presented with hundreds or even thousands of concordance lines for a single word. As a result, lexicographers have begun to rely on techniques derived from computational linguistics to summarize concordance data. The most common is the "Mutual Information" (MI) score, a statistical measure that shows how closely one word is associated with others based on the regularity with which they co-occur in context. For example, in English, the mutual information score for the words "strong" and "tea" is much higher than the score for "powerful" and "tea," despite the fact that "strong" and "powerful" have similar meanings. This kind of information is invaluable for lexicographers, especially for the creation of language learners' dictionaries that must provide this kind of distinction.

Most recently, dictionary makers have teamed with researchers in the field of computational linguistics to glean even more precise information from corpus data. For example, MI scores can show that "strong" collocates with northerly, showings, believer, currents, supporter, and odor, while "powerful" collocates with words such as tool, minority, neighbor, symbol, figure, weapon, and post; but the MI score does not indicate the kinds of grammatical relations that exist among a word and its collocates. Supplemental grammatical information can provide even more precise understanding of word usage. For example, the word "tea" collocates with words like spoon, milk, and sugar when these words appear as the object of the preposition "with"; with mug, saucer, and cup when they are objects of the preposition "into"; with coffee, toast, sugar, etc., when joined by "and" or "or"; and "tea" is most commonly the object of verbs such as drink, sip, pour, finish, and make.

To gather this information, relatively sophisticated language-processing software is required that can annotate the data for one or more of the types of information outlined in the previous sections. The need for more informative results to serve the needs of lexicography has therefore led to increased collaboration with computational linguists. We see, as a result, two groups of researchers who had previously worked independently coming together to tackle common problems.

In general, researchers in the humanities and researchers in computational linguistics have not collaborated, despite their common problems and goals. With the advent of the World Wide Web, this should change soon. Humanists have increased access to information about work in computational linguistics as well as to tools and resources developed by that community. Computational linguists, on the other hand, are likely to face new language processing challenges due to the need to handle a greater variety of web-accessible materials, including literary works, historical documents, and the like. The eventual collaboration of these two groups should lead, in the end, to vastly increased capabilities for both.

REFERENCES FOR FURTHER READING

Abeillé, A., L. Clément, and A. Kinyon (2000). Building a Treebank for French. *Proceedings of the Second International Conference on Language Resources and Evaluation*: 87–94.

Brants, T., W. Skut, and H. Uszkoreit (in press 2003). Syntactic Annotation of a German Newspaper Corpus. In A. Abeillé (ed.), *Building and Using Syntactically Annotated Corpora*. Dordrecht: Kluwer Academic.

Brill, E. (1995). Transformation-based Error-driven Learning and Natural Language Processing: A Case Study in Part of Speech Tagging. *Computational Linguistics* 21: 543–65.

Charniak, E. (1996). Tree-bank Grammars. *AAAI-96: Proceedings of the Thirteenth National Conference on Artificial Intelligence*: 598–603.

Cunningham, H. (2002). GATE, a General Architecture for Text Engineering. *Computers and the Humanities* 36: 223–54.

Dagan, I. and K. Church (1997). Termight: Coordinating Humans and Machines in Bilingual Terminology Translation. *MachineTranslation* 12: 89–107.

DeRose, S. (1988). Grammatical Category Disambiguation by Statistical Optimization. *Computational Linguistics* 14: 31–9.

Doab, M. and P. Resnik (2002). An Unsupervised Method for Word Sense Tagging Using Parallel Corpora. *Proceedings of the 40th Annual Meeting of the Association for Computational Linguistics*: 255–61.

Garside, R. and Smith, N. (1997). A Hybrid Grammatical Tagger: CLAWS4. In R. Garside, G. Leech, and A. McEnery (eds.), *Corpus Annotation: Linguistic Information from Computer Text Corpora* (pp. 102–21). London: Longman.

Grosz, B. and C. Sidner (1986). Attention, Intention and the Structure of Discourse. *Computational Linguistics* 12: 175–204.

Hajič, J. (1998). Building a Syntactically Annotated Corpus: The Prague Dependency Treebank. In E. Hajicova (ed.), *Issues of Valency and Meaning: Studies in Honour of Jarmila Panevova*. Prague: Charles University Press.

Hirschman, L. and N. Chinchor (1997). MUC-7 Co-reference Task Definition Version 3.0. At <http://www.itl.nist.gov/iaui/894.02/related_projects/muc/proceedings/co_task.html>.

Ide, N. (2000). Cross-lingual Sense Determination: Can It Work? *Computers in the Humanities* 34: 1–2. (Special Issue on the Proceedings of the SIGLEX/SENSEVAL Workshop, ed. A. Kilgarriff and M. Palmer: 223–34.)

Ide, N. and L. Romary (2001). A Common Framework for Syntactic Annotation. *Proceedings of ACL'2001*: 298–305.

Ide, N. and J. Veronis (1998). Introduction to the Special Issue on Word Sense Disambiguation: The State of the Art. *Computational Linguistics* 24: 1–40.

Ide, N., P. Bonhomme, and L. Romary (2000). XCES: An XML-based Standard for Linguistic Corpora. *Proceedings of the Second Language Resources and Evaluation Conference*: 825–30.

Ide, N., T. Erjavec, and D. Tufis (2001). Automatic Sense Tagging Using Parallel Corpora. *Proceedings of the Sixth Natural Language Processing Pacific Rim Symposium*: 83–9.

Jacobson, M., and B. Michailovsky (2000). A Linguistic Archive on the Web. *IRCS/ISLE/Talkbank Linguistic Exploration Workshop: Web-Based Language Documentation and Description*. At <http://www.ldc.upenn.edu/exploration/expl2000/papers/michailovsky/index.htm>.

Johansson, S., G. Leech, and H. Goodluck (1978). *Manual of Information to Accompany the Lancaster-Oslo/Bergen Corpus of British English, for Use with Digital Computers*. Department of English, University of Oslo.

Kucera, H. and W. N. Francis (1967). *Computational Analysis of Present-Day American English*. Providence, RI: Brown University Press.

Lamel, L. F., J. Garafolo, J. Fiscus, W. Fisher, and D. S. Pallett (1990). *TIMIT: The Darpa Acoustic-phonetic Speech Corpus*. Technical Report NISTIR 4930, National Institute of Standards and Technology.

Leech, G. (1993). Corpus Annotation Schemes. *Literary and Linguistic Computing* 8: 275–81.

MacWhinney, B. (1995). *The CHILDES Project*, 2nd edn. Mahwah, NJ: Lawrence Erlbaum.

Mann, W. C. and S. A. Thompson (1988). Rhetorical Structure Theory: A Theory of Text Organization. *Text* 8: 243–81.

Marcu, D. (1996). Building Up Rhetorical Structure Trees. *Proceedings of the Thirteenth National Conference on Artificial Intelligence* 2: 1069–74.

Marcus, M., B. Santorini, and M. A. Marcinkiewicz (1993). Building a Large Annotated Corpus of English: The Penn Treebank. *Computational Linguistics* 19,2.

Miller, G., C. Leacock, T. Randee, and R. Bunker (1993). A Semantic Concordance. *Proceedings of the 3rd DARPA Workshop on Human Language Technology*: 303–8.

Miller, G. A., R. Beckwith, C. Fellbaum, D. Gross, and K. Miller (1990). WordNet: An On-line Lexical Database. *International Journal of Lexicography* 3: 235–44.

Ramshaw, L. and M. Marcus (1995). Text Chunking Using Transformation-based Learning. *Proceedings of the Third ACL Workshop on Very Large Corpora*: 82–94.

Srinivas, B. (1997). Performance Evaluation of Supertagging for Partial Parsing. In H. Blunt and A. Nijholt (eds.), *Advances in Probabilistic and other Parsing Technologies* (pp. 203–20). The Hague: Kluwer Academic.

Stegman, R., H. Schulz, and E. Hinrichs (1998). Stylebook for the German Treebank in VERBMOBIL. Manuskript Universität Tübingen. At <http://verbmobil.dfki.de/verbmobil/>.

Svartvik, J. (ed.) (1990). *The London Corpus of Spoken English: Description and Research*. Lund Studies in English 82. Lund: Lund University Press.

Van Genabith, J., A Way, and L. Sadler (1999). Semi-automatic Generation of f-Structures from Tree Banks. In M. Butt and T. H. King (eds.), *Proceedings of the LFG99 Conference*, Manchester University, July 19–21. CSLI Online, *From Treebank Resources to LFG Structures*. Stanford, CA. At <http:www-csli.stanford.edu/publications/>.

Voutilainen, A. (1995). A Syntax-based Part-of-speech Analyzer. *Proceedings of the European Chapter of the Association for Computational Linguistics*: 157–64.

Xue, N., F. Chiou, and M. Palmer (2002). Building a Large-scale Annotated Chinese Corpus. *Proceedings of the 19th International Conference on Computational Linguistics* (COLING).

22

Electronic Scholarly Editing

Martha Nell Smith

Though they are not bound together in this multi-authored, multi-edited volume and are not likely to be in any other, this essay is the second in a series I am writing musing on the effects and meanings of the kinds of *electronic scholarly editing*, work extending well beyond the spatial and typographically fixed limitations of the codex, which I and others have been doing and that has become increasingly visible over the past decade. Johanna Drucker's observations about the nature of writing as she reflects upon the word itself convey well, in order to reflect upon editing, its nature and character. Writing (editing) is "a noun as well as a verb, an act and a product, a visual and verbal form, the composition of a text and trace of the hand"; "letters, words, and pictorial elements all participate in producing a work with complex textual value. At its most fundamental writing is inscription, a physical act which is the foundation of literary and symbolic activity" (Drucker 1998: 3). Editing is a physical as well as a philosophical act, and the medium in which an edition is produced (or an edition's place in the material world) is both part of and contains the message of the editorial philosophies at work. As Adrienne Rich remarked about poetry (in "North American Time"), so editing "never stood a chance / of standing outside history." Indeed, we have entered a different editorial time, one that demands the conscious cultivation of and by many hands, eyes, ears, and voices. While print editions are containers for static objects, artifacts that are by definition unchangeable once produced, the world of digital surrogates practically demands new models for editorial praxes in which editors and readers work together. Such models are encouraged by the fact that in a world with access to photographic copies of texts and images, no one has to bear the burden of forging the perfect linguistic description of the artifact, and by the fact that digital artifacts are by definition alterable once produced. After all, digital surrogates featuring high-quality color images of a writer's manuscripts offer a more ample sense of their textual conditions, including the conditions of the writing scene in which they were produced. Informed more fully about textual conditions, readers can collaborate with the postulating editor in making the editorial artifacts for electronic media in ways not possible when decisions have already been made to exclude or include data and seal the resulting artifact into a printed state.

That this series of my essays examining and hypothesizing about these new editorial praxes does not share the binding of a book's spine is appropriate for a critique of work on scholarly projects that do not have clear end points – the boundaries that variorums and reading editions (such as the printed volume of Emily Dickinson's writings on which I collaborated) do. The first essay – "Computing: What's American Literary Study Got to Do with IT?" – was directed toward my Americanist colleagues who have not embraced new media for their scholarly work. The present essay is directed toward upper-level undergraduate and graduate students and instructors, seasoned scholars and editors, as well as other interested readers, many of whom may have embraced new media for their academic work while others may just be exploring the territory, as it were. Like that first essay, this one is concerned with the changing sociologies surrounding new media critical endeavors, and is focused particularly on the impact of those sociologies on the work and workers involved in electronic scholarly editing and the development of its principles (described in Part Two of this book). The changes evident in digital humanities in how we work in, as, with, and for groups constitute a profound shift in humanities knowledge production. The new editorial praxes made possible, indeed demanded, by the critical environments that new media call into being are pivotal to that shift. Those editorial praxes are not only made visible, but are constituted by some of the new technologies in digital humanities, technologies that have gone under-remarked, even by specialists. These praxes and technologies are this essay's primary foci, because they make possible the digital resources that, as I remarked in my earlier piece, are more than advantages for humanities knowledge production: they are necessities. As such, these praxes and technologies should be taken into account by anyone working or interested in humanities knowledge production.

Technologies bring scientific knowledge to bear on practical purposes in a particular field, and are thus the means by which we accomplish various ends – the tools and devices on which our critical suppositions rely. Some digital technologies, the machines and software with which we produce and consume scholarly editions, are prey to obsolescence (HyperCard, for example, is for all practical purposes already unusable, as are DOS-based machines; the SGML document delivery system DynaWeb has limitations, at least aesthetically, that are much lamented; examples abound). By contrast, all but one of the technologies under review here were already used in some form for book production and are obviously not susceptible to such rapid obsolescence. In fact, in migrating to the electronic realm the technologies have become much more visible and productively exploitable. Constitutive of digital humanities, the technologies are: access, multimedia study objects, collaboration, and increased self-consciousness. Central to the formulations and speculations of this critique is evaluating the effects of a technology implicitly invoked by all four, that of audience. If one considers a sense of audience a technology (with explanation and performance as kinds of knowledge application), then the technology of audience provides analytical perspectives that would not have been obtained had I been writing with only one audience in mind. Those different viewpoints have in turn deepened my understanding of just how profound are the shifts under way in scholarly applications of digital resources to the study of arts and humanities. That I and other enthusiasts have underestimated the degree of that profundity is remarkable. Finally, this chapter makes explicit the importance of standards, as well as the importance of querying the prides and prejudices of those standards and the implications for interpretation made possible in this new editorial work, invoking as a representative touchstone the new Guidelines for Electronic Editions just approved for use by the Modern Language Association (MLA)'s Committee on Scholarly Editions.

The fruits of several evolutions converged to produce a mode of editing suited to the new media: post-structuralist re-inflections of theories of editing; the proliferation of affordable, portable personal computers; the networking, on an unprecedented scale, of homes, individuals, institutions of all sorts (educational, governmental, commercial, religious, and medical), and nations. A fantasy unimaginable as part of the real world just a very short time ago, such networking and the accelerated communication it brings are now facts of everyday life throughout much of the world. Concomitantly, academics have moved beyond worried resistance to the work made possible by new media and computer technologies, and worked through much of the reactionary skepticism so widely and forcefully articulated in the 1990s, in books like Sven Birkerts's *The Gutenberg Elegies* (1994). By contrast, at the time of writing, under-informed skepticism has been replaced by the realization that critical engagements with new technologies are the best hope for advancing knowledge production in the humanities. That these advances are within our grasp is abundantly clear in the field of scholarly editing.

For example, one happy consequence of new media revolutions is that breathtaking advances in networking and communication have enabled editorial praxes previously thought too impractical to enact, whatever their intellectual value. Instead of being bound to representative samples, editions can now include images of all primary documents included in an edition. The surrogates possible in digital humanities are more than just singular photographic examples meant to represent hundreds or even thousands of instances. Thus editorial claims to being "comprehensive" (a staple of the print variorum relying on representative examples) accrue whole new meanings in the extraordinarily capacious digital realm. Ironically, though, electronic textual editors would not be likely to make such claims, realizing just how vast is the information one could choose to include in a "comprehensive" edition. Those same editors would nevertheless demand inclusion of images of all primary documents (manuscripts or corrected proofs, for example) rather than only the analytical descriptions thereof one finds in the editorial apparatus of print translations (iterations mechanically reproduced for public distribution and annotated for scholarly consumption). Also, editions can now implement new kinds of scholarly annotation by including, where applicable, sound and even video reproductions simply impossible to contain as a constitutive part of a book (though a CD might be slipped inside the cover as a companion or a chip ingeniously packaged and placed for a reader's play).

Networking and communication have also made imaginable and agreeable editorial praxes traditionally thought impracticable or undesirable. These practices modify the very nature of scholarly editing itself. For example, if an editor chooses, the much theorized common reader can now provide immediate and actual (in contrast to imagined) critical feedback that might in turn be usefully incorporated into the work of a scholarly edition, making the collaboration between reader and author that is characteristic of reading itself something more than the "creative regeneration" [of texts] by readers invested with and in private intentions such as those D. F. McKenzie describes in *Bibliography and the Sociology of Texts* (1999). All of these factors will be examined in this essay as examples of under-analyzed technologies, but first some observations about editing and the phrase that provides my title are in order.

Distinguished editing of literary and artistic work is a matter of the heart (emotions), and at least four of our five senses (physical perceptions), as well as of the head (logic). Astute editors take advantage of the acumen offered by these diverse ways of apprehending the world, and though it is in one sense bound by algorithms, digital editing is no exception in terms of its characteristics (of the heart, the physical senses, the head). Reflecting on the individual terms embodied by the phrase, and the traditions they bespeak, deepens and broadens understandings of "electronic scholarly editing," both in its present forms and in the theories about those praxes and the possibilities that inhere in multimedia. *Editing* makes works (poems, plays, fiction, film footage, musical performances, and artistic and documentary material) publishable (in books, films, television and radio, and recordings) by eliminating unwanted material and organizing what remains for optimal and intelligible presentation to audiences. In other words, editing translates raw creative work into an authoritative (not to be confused with definitive or authoritarian) form. *Scholarly* editing is editing performed under the aegis of research, learning, sustained instruction, mastery, knowledge building, standard setting. *Electronic* scholarly editing consciously incorporates phenomena associated with the movement and manipulation of electrons, those indivisible charges of negative electricity, through wires and radio waves onto screens and through speakers. Though it incorporates the principles of conventional scholarly editing (that is, in and for books) into its own methods, electronic scholarly editing is not performed to be read through the machine of the book but via the hardware of computers. Other nomenclatures for this field include "digital scholarly editing," exploiting to the fullest the obvious pun that enables clear contrastive play between the manual and the automated, and those pertaining to editing itself, especially in the world of ubiquitous computers and the connective possibilities of the World Wide Web. Electronic scholarly editing now inevitably involves networking, both among the texts being worked through and the workers performing the editing (including readers viewing the edited works), in ways never realized by that magnificent tool of knowledge transmission that has served so splendidly well for the past several centuries, the book.

Previously I have examined the implications for knowledge production of the fact that in the digital environment, access – both to numbers of study objects and to numbers of audience members – is facilitated on an unprecedented scale. I considered at length the possibilities for literary criticism and theory when the staggering data storage capacities of computers enable so much more visibility of what I refer to as BE-O objects – artifacts that have customarily been viewed By Experts Only. Agreeing that the skepticism with which many mainstream scholars regard "quantitative research methods" was not really misplaced "so long as the computer's primary role in the humanities was, ostensibly, to compute," Matthew Kirschenbaum proclaims that access to a digital surrogate of a "Rossetti painting" or "of one of Emily Dickinson's turbulent manuscripts" erases or at least reverses that skepticism. The visibilities that enable the unprecedented access to images that were previously locked away in library and museum archives for exclusive view by a very few is probably the technological boon with which scholars and readers are most familiar, for that perpetually available and repeatable access is really quite a big deal.

The ability to provide artifacts for direct examination (rather than relying on scholarly hearsay) has altered the reception of humanities computing in the disciplines of the humanities so that skepticism is "at least replaced with more to-the-point questions about image acquisition and editorial fidelity, not to mention scholarly and pedagogical potential." These are indeed "questions of representation, and they are eminently relevant to the work of the humanities" (Kirschenbaum 2002: 4). As Ray Siemens's introduction to *A New Computer-assisted Literary Criticism?* makes plain, enthusiasts of text analysis would take issue with Kirschenbaum's assertion about quantitative research methods, but the point about the power of visibility, of making accessible for as many pairs of eyes as possible, images (rather than their analytical textual descriptions) for critical analysis, cannot be overstated. When editors make as much about a text visible to as wide an audience as possible, rather than silencing opposing views or establishing one definitive text over all others, intellectual connections are more likely to be found than lost.

Though it will not necessarily do so, that access to primary digital artifacts can in turn create extraordinary access to the editorial process itself, especially if editors and readers alike are proactive in taking advantage of these opportunities by building "sound infrastructure, and the organizational and financial structures . . . essential to consolidate, to preserve, and to maintain" the "new organizational forms" created by electronic media (D'Arms 2000). The standards described by the MLA's Guidelines for Scholarly Editing, print and electronic, are commonsensical and bound to ensure quality: they ask for "explicitness and consistency with respect to methods, accuracy with respect to texts, adequacy and appropriateness with respect to documenting editorial principles and practice." However practical and necessary for meeting principled goals and however derived by scholarly consensus, uses of various media constrain and enable adherence to these benchmarks to different degrees. Indeed, one clear example lies in the fact that explicitness, consistency, and accuracy are all finally matters of faith in the bibliographic realm.

Considering an actual instance will make clear the importance of enhanced visibility and the more critical reading it enables. My examples will be drawn from the editorial resources with which I have been most involved, both as a user and a maker, those of the writings of the nineteenth-century American poet Emily Dickinson. Because the practices involved in their making are so widespread in the production of scholarly editions, and similar principles to those employed in producing Dickinson are so widely accepted for making accessible the texts of other authors, these specific instances serve well as exemplifications of general rules and procedures for scholarly textual production. R. W. Franklin spent scrupulous decades producing a three-volume variorum edition of *The Poems of Emily Dickinson* for Harvard University Press, a publisher highly esteemed for producing study objects meeting the highest standards. Franklin's stated goal is to give a "comprehensive account" of all of Dickinson's texts, as well as any texts directly bearing on her compositional practices (1998: 28). In a comprehensive account, one would expect to see all omissions, additions, alterations, emendations of which the editor is aware marked in some way for his readers. Thus any ellipsis, any omission of data, would be signaled by familiar punctuation (. . .) and probably explained in editorial notes. Yet this is not the case, and readers cannot readily know when an omission has occurred or a change silently made because their access to the objects edited is limited and the evidence of explicitness, consistency, and accuracy cannot be seen. Instead, readers have to trust that the printed texts they see are explicit, consistent, and accurate about all textual data.

Thus when Franklin erases 74 words from his representation of an epistolary manuscript involving the composition of Dickinson's poem "Safe in their Alabaster Chambers" and does so without commentary and without signifying punctuation, readers of his print variorum have no way of knowing that the omission has been made, much less of evaluating its import (FP 124C). Besides being misinformed about the nature of this text because of omission of information, access to the editorial process itself is limited, the implicit contract with the reader (that such treatment of documentary evidence would be signaled in some readable way) having been violated. Franklin's change might, one could argue, simply be chalked up to bad editorial work. Yet he silently enacts other emendations as a course of standard, widely accepted editorial practice. Much ink has been spilled by Dickinson and American poetry scholars about her use of punctuation marks that most have labeled "the dash." Strong positions have been taken about whether the shorter en- or the longer em-mark most faithfully translates Dickinson's mark into print, and Franklin has resolved the matter with the authoritarian stance that neither the en- nor the em-suffice: according to him, the shorter-than-either hyphen best conveys Dickinson's practice of using a horizontal or angled mark rather than a comma. The problem with staking out a hard and fast position on this matter (as many a Dickinson critic has done) is the "one size fits all" perspective practically required by print production. Examining almost any poem written during Dickinson's middle years shows that within individual poems, indeed within individual lines, she did not consign herself to a single sort of mark but used marks of varying lengths and angles (see, for example, "The name -of it -is 'Autumn'__" (FP 465; facsimile available in Franklin's *Manuscript Books of Emily Dickinson*, p. 494). Editing nearly 1,800 poems, Franklin makes the decision for readers that a hyphen will suffice to represent Dickinson's diverse, varied marks, and thus also decides for readers that the differences among her punctuating inscriptions are not poetically significant.

Trust in any print edition, then, whether it be that made by Franklin or any other editor, including myself, is necessarily faith-based, for readers cannot adequately see the documentary evidence that determines everything from genre to suitability for inclusion in a scholarly edition. Indeed, such matters of representation are more than eminently relevant to humanities; they are central to humanities knowledge production itself. Opportunities for analysis of who made the scholarly objects we study and for what purposes, and of which parts of those objects are constitutive and worthy of study, are proportionate to the visibility of foundational documentary evidence enabled by the medium of representation.

In contrast to the constrained visibilities of book representations, access to questions of editorial fidelity and therefore to the editorial process itself is much more obtainable in an electronic edition featuring images of all documents edited as well as their translations into typography. In such a realm, 74 words cannot simply be excised without commentary and marks translated with a "one size fits all" authoritarian stance and go unnoticed, because a digital image of the document is available for readers to view, assess, compare with editors' representations. Representation via digital facsimiles of original documents changes access to the foundational materials of scholarly editions, the contours of expertise, and even standard-setting itself.

Consciously foregrounding the ontological differences between electronic and biblio-graphic scholarly editions is necessary for understanding ways in which this access can work, for learning how electronic editions made might best be used, and for planning and developing electronic editions that are more and more well made (in that they are designed for optimum usability as well as optimum incorporation of relevant but scattered data and commentary). Introducing Harvard University Press's latest variorum edition of *The Poems of Emily Dickinson*, Franklin claims that although that three-volume edition "is a printed codex," it is practically electronic, for the edition "has an electronic database" and the "poems are in bits and bytes." He then flatly states that "other outputs are possible, including other printed editions, organized or presented differently. Dickinson and Hypertext may well be matched, and images are particularly useful with an unpublished poet who left her poems unprepared for others" (1998: 27–8). Yet electronic editions are by their very constitution markedly different, both from the print edition Franklin made and the hypertext one he imagines. For one thing (which he acknowledges), the bits and bytes to which he refers do not contain images and thus do not provide multifaceted viewpoints, the visibility of digital surrogates of original manuscripts presented in an environment where the distance that separates the libraries in which they are held presents no obstacle for direct comparison of texts within each of those collections spread across oceans and nations, separated by geography, national boundaries, and disparate laws. Collected into an electronic edition, Blake or Dickinson manuscripts logically related to one another but dispersed across various collections are gathered together so they can be studied and synthesized to make new knowledge; collected into the same electronic edition, they no longer lie like scattered pieces of a puzzle, their connections splintered, difficult to see as possibly yoked, and thus next to impossible to imagine. Another difference unacknowledged by Franklin is that the typographical bits and bytes to which he refers are those of word processing, which only encode the textual data found in Dickinson's works. A scholarly electronic edition would likely be prepared in XML or SGML (probably following the guidelines of the Text Encoding Initiative), and would capture logical, structural, and artifactual aspects of the original, as well as its textual content. An electronic edition also might include databases, Flash, video, and sound presentations. Different editions are not simply "outputs" of the same bits and bytes, which Franklin's declaration assumes. The statement makes plain that he envisions electronic editions as typographically edited texts with illustrations that can be accessed with the click of a mouse. But electronic scholarly editions provide much greater opportunities than texts with links to illustrations and to one another, enabling a range of manipulation not possible for those bound to the printed page.

Far more than display, replications constitute the textual reproductions and representa-tions in scholarly editions such as *The Blake Archive*, the *Rossetti Archive*, *The Walt Whitman Archive*, *The Canterbury Tales Project*, the *Dickinson Electronic Archives*. Scholarly electronic editions are not simply a matter of bits and bytes and how they have been encoded to link to one another and to appear in particular browsers. Dynamic rather than static, deeply encoded, they are designed to enable readers to achieve better understanding of texts and open up possibilities for more sophisticated interpretations. Susan Schreibman and others have chronicled the fact that by the mid-1980s it had become clear to numbers of scholars already involved in the creation of electronic resources for the humanities that a standard for encoding texts needed to be developed that was not dependent upon a particular platform or software package (Schreibman 2002a). Achieving platform-independence requires separating the information content of documents from their formatting, which is what led an international group of those concerned with publishing and preserving government documents to develop GML (Generalized Markup Language) in the 1970s, and then SGML (Standard Generalized Markup Language), adopted as an international standard in the mid-1980s. Working with SGML, a group of humanities scholars and librarians launched the Text Encoding Initiative (TEI) in 1987.

Though markup has a *performative* significance, the TEI is designed to represent already existing literary texts. For electronic scholarly editors, "markup is supplied as part of the transcription in electronic form of pre-existing material.... Markup reflects the understanding of the text held by the transcriber; we say that the markup *expresses a claim* about the text" (see Allen Renear, in chapter 17, this volume, and in writings elsewhere, and many others, for example Susan Hockey, Michael Sperberg-McQueen, Jerome McGann: see entries in the References for Further Reading). John Unsworth's claim that "any attempt to systematically express one's understanding of a text in the kind of internally consistent, explicit and unambiguous encoding that is required in the creation of a computable SGML or XML edition will produce some intellectual benefit and will ensure some degree of integrity," is indisputable (Unsworth, website). Indeed, the technology of self-consciousness required by computer encoding of texts, especially that such as TEI-conformant XML encoding, produces a healthy self-consciousness about what Bruno Latour and Steve Woolgar describe in *Laboratory Life* as "black-boxing" – which occurs when one "renders items of knowledge distinct from the circumstances of their creation" (1986: 259n). In black-boxing, critical opinion becomes "fact"; more often than not, amnesia sets in after that factual instantiation, and having been effectively black-boxed, "fact" becomes "truth." As in the case of Dickinson discussed here, wittingly or unwittingly bibliographic editors sometimes remove elements that are (or well might be) constitutive of its poetics when transmitting a text from the messy circumstance of its creation to the ordered pages of print. The challenge for electronic scholarly editors is not to perpetrate similar distortions when enthusiastically embracing the ordering tools of encoding to convey literary expression, which by its very nature often perplexes the orders of expository logic.

Hypertext theorists and practitioners, who have been (sometimes roundly) critiqued for being too exuberant, are sometimes echoed by the encoding specialist's enthusiasm for important developments in XML: "One of the most powerful features of the XML family of technologies is Extensible Stylesheet Language Transformations (XSLT), a language that facilitates transformation of text rather than display (as HTML's Cascading Style Sheet language does).... The 'infinitely recenterable system whose provisional point of focus depends on the reader' (Landow 1997, p. 36) is made realizable through XML-XSLT technology, and is much closer to the democratized space envisioned by early hypertext theorists" (Schreibman 2002b: 85). Without a doubt, though, new technologies for structuring data, coupled with the guidelines provided by the Committee on Scholarly Editions and the TEI's commitment to work out of a "broad, community-based consensus," are crucial for realizing advances in editorial praxes. Also necessary is the commitment to facilitate difference by evolving "guidelines... to accommodate a greater variety of editorial methods and a broader range of materials and periods" (MLA Committee on Scholarly Editions, website), and by the TEI's "extension mechanism, as well as its consistent insistence...on international and interdisciplinary representation in its governing bodies, its workgroups, its funding sources, and its membership" (Unsworth, website). The collaborative development of these standards is absolutely essential for any demotic ethic valued as a worthwhile goal, and the disambiguation forced upon knowledge workers who thrive on ambiguity often proves critically profound, because texts are seen as never before, both on the surface and in their deep structures.

Yet none of these advances in markup, nor any of these guidelines, is robust enough to accommodate all facets of the actual textual experience of editors working with primary artifacts. Original documents, the raw materials with which editors must work, are by their very nature queer, and must be normalized to some degree in order to be put into an edition. In part, this is a result of the fact that "there are certain basic – irresolvable – philosophical tensions in language – most particularly between its capacity to represent knowledge systematically and its capacity to be knowledge experientially and perceptually – and this tension intensifies in an electronic environment as a tension between machine language and natural language – since it is a reductive hybrid version of the one which can be encoded/encrypted in order to serve as the basis of the other" (Drucker 1998: 219). This characteristic of language itself is much more visible in an environment in which

> the more sophisticated we are the more we normalize textual incommensurables. We have internalized an immensely complicated, many-leveled set of semiotic rules and signs, and we control the contradictions of actual textual circumstances by various normalizing operations. We can hope to expose these normalizations – which are themselves deformative acts – by opening the conversation . . . between analogue and digital readers. We begin by implementing what we think we know about the rules of bibliographical codes. The conversation should force us to see – finally, to imagine – what we don't know that we know about texts and textuality. At that point, perhaps, we may begin setting philology – "the knowledge of what is known," as it used to be called – on a new footing. (McGann 2001: 207)

In a case such as the *Dickinson Electronic Archives*, the editions are explicitly designed not to define and normalize texts, as has been the objective of most bibliographic scholarly editions, and has been the practice of many electronic scholarly editions. Many electronic editions are still framed by the good work of the book because the dream of shedding the inertia imported from the bibliographical realm is only gradually finding its modes of practice. The TEI was developed to represent already existing literary texts in electronic media, but in its years of development it has been confronted by queerer and queerer texts and by editors whose commitment to integrity means that they cannot simply normalize those texts to fit a predetermined grid. This, in turn, demands that we grasp the real significance of the truism that editing is a kind of encoding and encoding is a kind of editing, and it also requires that we probe the politics of the encoding standards we are embracing. Readers too

> rarely think about the myriad of databases, standards, and instruction manuals subtending our reading lamps, much less about the politics of the electric grid that they tap into. And so on, as many layers of technology accrue and expand over space and time. Systems of classification (and of standardization) form a juncture of social organization, moral order, and layers of technical integration. Each subsystem inherits, increasingly as it scales up, the inertia of the installed bases of systems that have come before. (Bowker and Star 1999: 33)

Besides asking who made our objects of study, generative questions about standard setting, who made them, and for what purposes should be posed, and in ways, as McGann argues, not previously imagined. "There is more at stake – epistemologically, politically, and ethically – in the day-to-day work of building classification systems and producing and maintaining standards than in abstract arguments about representation" (Bowker and Star 1999: 10). Standards are of course crucial for realizing reliability, sustainability (both in terms of being intellectually substantive and in terms of residing in a preservable medium), and interoperability among different works and even different systems. Those editing for new media are carrying on this responsibility by working with and helping to develop the new international standards and guidelines. In this ongoing work, we must self-consciously pose questions about the consequences of standardizing, classifying, and categorizing. In previous scholarly editions, classifications or the qualifying criteria dictating how an entity would be classified have been invisible. One benefit of encoding is "to understand the role of invisibility in the work that classification does in ordering human interaction" and thus to keep an eye on the "moral and ethical agenda in our querying of these systems. Each standard and each category valorizes some point of view and silences another. This is not inherently a bad thing – indeed it is inescapable" (Bowker and Star 1999: 5). Standards and categories become problematic when they are insufficiently critiqued, and when "a folk theory of categorization itself" prevails. That folk theory "says that things come in well-defined kinds, that the kinds are characterized by shared properties, and that there is one right taxonomy of the kinds" (Lakoff 1987:121). Both the TEI Consortium and the MLA's Committee on Scholarly Editions have said that principled accommodation is necessary, and that's as it must be, if electronic scholarly editing is to realize its potential by pre-empting this compulsion toward standard setting as a kind of intellectual police force. The community has established standards that are flexible and adjustable, adopting what in the builder's trade is called a *lesbian rule* – a mason's rule of lead, which bends to fit the curves of a molding; hence, figuratively, lesbian rules are pliant and accommodating principles for judgment (OED). Commitment to such principles for judgment must be vigilantly maintained, with editors relentlessly asking: "What work are the classifications and standards doing? Who does that work? What happens to the cases that do not fit the classification scheme? What happens to cases in which several classification schemes apply?" After all, automatons do not make literary texts: people do.

Understanding the poetics and principles of electronic scholarly editing means understanding that the primary goal of this activity is not to dictate what can be seen but rather to open up ways of seeing. The disambiguating codes are tools to understand texts, not to define them. Though consensus may develop around certain elements of what is seen, no consensus need be developed on how to read those elements. In fact, the different perspectives offered via the encoding, image-based digital surrogates, and direct critiques from "common" readers that are possible in electronic scholarly editing create a climate of possibility for interpretation that is precluded by the invisible controls placed on literary works and their interpretation in bibliographic editing. The editorial goal of electronic scholarly editing is not to find the proper literary container for "poems" (or whatever genre is being produced) but to find the medium that transmits more, rather than fewer, of the techniques inscribed and found on the literary page. Propriety (which inheres in the notion of the proper container) is not the issue, hence the TEI's extension mechanism. The issue is textual pleasure and access to greater understanding, and enabling audiences to avail themselves of as many aspects as possible of the scriptures under study.

So in scholarly editing, the challenge of using these electronic tools that create so many advantages for storage of data (including sound and images), retrieval, and searching is to develop them so that editorial praxes themselves are truly advanced and the hieratic ethic of editing for books is not simply imported into a new, more proficient medium (as was originally the case with the TEI). Derrida's deconstruction of the meanings of "archive" (Derrida 1996) and its connotations of "commandment" and "commencement" help clarify distinctions between *hieratic* and *demotic* and show why the latter is an advance when it comes to editorial approaches. By tracing his emphasis on a hierarchy of genres, one can see that *commandment* – stressing authority, social order – describes the guiding principle of Franklin's variorum. Thus in spite of his emphasis on versioning in his iteration of 1,789 Emily Dickinson poems, order is imposed on that which is otherwise unruly – the messy handwritten artifacts of poems, letters, letter-poems, scraps, notes, fragments. The idea of "poem" disciplines and contains views and the version represented of Dickinson's writings so that they conform to social order and literary law, whatever the material evidence may suggest. According to this principle of *commandment*, the material evidence, the manuscripts, contain the idea of "poem" and an editor's job is to deliver that idea in a container that makes "poem" extractable. Here textual boundaries are clear, commanded as they are by the ideas that demarcate genres for books. The temptation in disambiguating markup is to repeat that strategy of containment, for it is much easier simply to claim that a text is prose or poetry rather than to acknowledge that it is much more complicated than that, a blend of the two, and requires innovative extensions of the predetermined TEI markup schemes.

By contrast, *commencement* – physical, historical, ontological beginning – describes the guiding principle of the *Dickinson Electronic Archives'* production, including our markup. Unpersuaded that "poem" is an "idea" easily separable from its artifact, the editors of the electronic archives feature images of Dickinson's manuscript bodies in their multiple sizes and shapes, in all their messiness. Though our markup designates verse, letter, verse-letter, letter with embedded verse, and letter with enclosed verse, what constitutes a "poem" and poetic meanings is left up to the reader (http://jefferson.village.virginia.edu/dickinson/nosearch/documentation/). A work might sport a stamp or a cutout from Dickens placed by Dickinson into the literary scene that the reader deems part of a "poem," and the editors of the electronic archives refuse to bind those elements as extra-literary but put them on display and include them in the claims our markup makes about the text. Finger smudges, pinholes, paste marks, coffee stains, and traces of ribbons, flowers, or other attachments offer a view into the manuscript circulation and exchange so central to Dickinson's literary world, and we likewise put them on display and include questions about such signs in our editorial submission forms so that markup and notes recognize these materialities as part and parcel of literary production and circulation. Also featured are images of the printed pages, the bodies that have transmitted Dickinson's writings to the world, and in these are stories of Dickinson's history as a poet whose writings are read and enjoyed by a wide audience. The tidy organizations of those printings bound into *The Poems of Emily Dickinson* and *The Letters of Emily Dickinson* juxtaposed with the not fully intelligible bindings of manuscripts (into the manuscript books found in her room or her correspondences to 99 recipients) by Dickinson herself, as well as with her many writings unbound (single sheets, notes, drafts, fragments, scraps), renew ontological questions about the identities of these many writings. Textual boundaries are not clear, hence on our submission form for co-editors, the word "genre" in the question asking them to select one for encoders is in quotation marks to underscore the fact that such denotation is forced by the encoding scheme. Underscored both in the markup and the display of original documents is the fact that though an ideal idea of "poem" or "letter" must dominate for the writings to be neatly divided by bibliographically determined genre, and though some denotation must be made for the meta-information of markup, electronic editing enables a much more flexible approach to understanding Dickinson's writings and her manipulations of genre. With many of the documents, readers cannot help but begin to ask "what is this?" "What is this writer doing?" The electronic archives are designed to enable much more extensive considerations of such questions, to confront the philosophical tensions in language rather than smoothing them over and masking them via editorial "clean-up."

Thus if editors self-consciously work beyond the inertia inherited from bibliographic editing, the editorial environment made possible by these technologies of publication can have profound implications for the interpretation of texts and for knowledge production. Though editing might pretend to be objective, it is always someone enacting his or her critical prerogatives. Presenting artistic and critical works can never be done without some bias being conveyed. Though the fact that editing is always interpretation was realized long before their incorporation into humanities work, the new media, and new and newly recognized technologies facilitate accommodation of this fluidity of authorial and editorial/authorial intentions. Editorial theorists as diverse as Tanselle, McGann, Bornstein, Bryant, Shillingsburg, McKenzie, and Grigely in one way or another acknowledge the philosophical tensions in language in which these fluidities inhere and point out that "writing is fundamentally an arbitrary hence unstable hence variable approximation of thought" (Bryant 2002: 1). In the context of these recognitions, all of these values are profoundly affected: authority, literariness, authenticity, sociology, access, reproductivity, original/originary texts/moments, editorial responsibilities, authorship, intention. Electronic editions are most valuable in their capaciousness, not only in their ability to offer different versions but also in their ability to facilitate varying views and valuations, both of what is seen and of how it is comprehended, as text or as extra-textual.

Though major editorial projects have often involved collaborators, the collaborations enabled by electronic editions can be something different than previously seen in humanities research, as are the editions themselves. Because websites can be mounted by individuals and because most have not been vetted, peer review has been a contentious issue in the first generation of digital humanities production. Publishers, libraries, and other institutions invested in quality control routinely vet their digital publications in ways akin to those used for print publications: two or three readers' reports by experts in the field are presented to a board who then votes to accept or reject. This is important and valuable, but critical review need not stop there. In electronic publishing, tools such as dynamic databases enable a more sustained and collaborative critical engagement of reader with editor than has previously been seen. The *Dickinson Electronic Archives* has, for example, opened a critical review space <http://emilydickinson.org/review/deareview.php>, making user feedback an integral part of the editorial process. In this virtual space users have the opportunity to post commentary, reviews, or critical analysis of a particular section(s) or of the site as a whole. Because comments are stored (either anonymously or with signature) in a searchable database, users have the option of reading and responding to previous commentary. Such a space enables interactions with the editors and with readers and provides a generative, previously unavailable, context for critical responses. The dynamic interplay of the audience, the original writer who inscribes the marks, and the editors communicating those marks to posterity is thereby more likely to open what Dickinson herself would call "doors and windows of possibility." In turn, these myriad perspectives can enable a much more sustained reflection on how our critical findings are produced and then transmitted, on the mechanisms of authorization and critical review, and on the criteria for authenticity. These assessments can then begin to penetrate critical mystiques in ways likely to expand rather than restrict knowledge, and to focus attention more on the knowledge itself than on the individual responsible for bringing it to the fore. Access to such knowledge can in turn foster a variety of new co-editorial collaborations among authors, editors, and readers. Digital surrogates alone make definitive analytical descriptions, on which readers of scholarly editions have depended, neither possible nor desirable. Instead, such analytical descriptions accompany images that readers can examine, make judgments about, and then use to assess the editorial commentary. The *Dickinson Electronic Archives* is complementing the Open Critical Review database by importing and making available to users the Virtual Lightbox <http://mith2.umd.edu/products/lightbox/>, a software tool via which images can be compared and evaluated online, and the Versioning Machine <http://mith2.umd.edu/products/ver-mach/index.html>, a software tool designed by a team of programmers, designers, and literary scholars for displaying and comparing multiple versions of texts. Both products are open source and have been produced and maintained at Maryland Institute for Technology in the Humanities (MITH) <http://www.mith.umd.edu/>. The database and the sophisticated online tools for comparing images and texts make it possible for users not only to examine the editorial process, but even to become part of that process. Such collaborations are ways of turning the editorial process inside out in order to advance its integrity, its scope, and its reach, as is the choreography of guest co-editors working with a group of general editors.

On multivolume editions of a major author's work, guest co-editors have worked under a rubric framed by (a) presiding editor(s), but electronic editions provide new opportunities for more extensive knowledge transfer and diverse yet coherent knowledge production in electronic scholarly editions. As do their print predecessors, electronic co-editors act as second and third readers, the first readers being the writer at work on creating text to be disseminated and the general editor conceiving of an edition appropriately designed for the electronic field. Since not simply the originating writer but also editors are creative agents, coordinating groups of qualified editors to work on a vast body of work rather than relying on a single master editor or master pair or trio of editors to bring a scholarly edition into being practically insures, as do the disambiguating codes of TEI-conformant XML, greater integrity in textual production.

As we have seen, new materialities of editing, the fact that multimedia representations make it possible for readers to examine documentary evidence previously hidden from their view, that dynamic databases make it possible for critical readers to record and store their feedback in a manageable format, and that the electronic work produced by editors has been instantiated in forms much more manipulable than the rigid freeze of print make innovations in the work of editing itself possible. Teams of editors, rather than a solitary master with her assistants, can work on projects as never before possible. However, multiply edited electronic editions run the risk of inducing a kind of interpretative vertigo in the perspective of readers. After all, though the objective is no longer to produce the definitive, immutable text, electronic editions do aim to produce greater understandings. As readers' critical responses are managed through an online database, so editors' work can be managed via a database-driven editorial submission form such as that provided by the *Dickinson Electronic Archives* <http://jefferson.village.virginia.edu/dickinson/nosearch/admin/submissions.php>, with its guidelines for encoding, statement of editorial principles, and documentation with links to regularization databases, lists of hands identified on the Dickinson manuscripts, lists of manuscript repositories, and so forth.

Just as any editor has to take into account authorial intentions, and any reader is wise to consider both the writer's and subsequent editors' authorial intentions, multiple editors all working on parts of the same textual body must take into account the intentions of their co-editors and collaborators, those readers willing to commit time and energy and to abide by the principles established for scholarly textual production. Such forced engagements with the sociologies of intention that frame and inhere in any and all textual productions are immensely valuable for creating editorial environments that are not only more trustworthy but that are bound to advance critical understandings, teaching scholars to ask questions heretofore unimagined. As I noted in an earlier essay, Lucy Suchman makes insightful observations about the conditions necessary for optimizing knowledge production. Instead of viewing the "objective knowledge" proffered by a critical editon "as a single, asituated, master perspective that bases its claims to objectivity in the closure of controversy," "objective knowledge" in the production of a dynamic critical edition online can more easily be seen as "multiple, located, partial perspectives that find their objective character through ongoing processes of debate." Since critical vision is parallactic rather than unidimensional, the processes of comparing and evaluating those different angles of seeing as one compares and evaluates different images or different perspectives of the same images is essential in order to see more clearly and accurately. The locus of objectivity is not "an established body of knowledge . . . produced or owned by anyone," but "knowledges in dynamic production, reproduction and transformation, for which we are all responsible." By contrast, the hieratic models of the master editorial perspective do not acknowledge how "layered and intertwined" are the "relations of human practice and technical artifact" and how such individualistically driven productions can tend to obstruct rather than facilitate intellectual connections, treating editorial and critical works as "finished . . . achievements" rather than as ongoing research activities and part of a "process of accretion" of editorial technique and knowledge, part of midrash, as it were (Suchman, website).

Lessons learned by the makers and users of electronic scholarly editions can help answer the call of the late John D'Arms and others to "move the scholarly monograph into the second generation of the digital age," as the electronic scholarly edition has moved into the first generation. As President of the MLA, Stephen Greenblatt issued a letter to the membership about the plight of scholarly publishing in the humanities and a call to action to address the "systemic, structural, and at base economic" crises confronting twenty-first-century humanities scholars committed to the free flow of information that enables knowledge building ("Call for Action on Problems in Scholarly Book Publishing" <http://www.mla.org/>); as President of the Association for Computers and the Humanities and Chair of the TEI Board of Directors, John Unsworth answered Greenblatt's call in presentations such as "The Emergence of Digital Scholarship: New Models for Librarians, Scholars, and Publishers" <http://www.iath.virginia.edu/~jmu2m/dartmouth.02> and in his work on the MLA Committee on Scholarly Editions and the TEI.

In order to move the scholarly monograph into the digital realm, humanists need to embrace the new technologies developing in digital humanities communities of practice, technologies making not only new work but new ways of working possible, especially those that will not become obsolete (access, multimedia study objects, collaboration, self-consciousness, audience).

Thus digital humanities needs to move from producing primarily the scholarly archive (first generation of electronic literary projects) to also producing digital monographs or multiply (and to varying degrees) authored works – polygraphs. There is no reason that tightly focused critical inquiry cannot be produced by a group. Revealing and practical questions about reproductive fidelity – such as "what degree of imaging accuracy is needed for critical inquiry?" and "who should be responsible for maintaining and making available the highest quality copies?" – are crucial for such editions and have expanded group efforts. Initiatives such as the LEADERS project, which "aims to enhance remote user access to archives by providing the means to present archival source materials within their context," ensure that archivists best trained to maintain both the actual and the surrogate archival copies assume the responsibilities for doing so and work with scholarly editors best trained to organize the data critically. That they can work remotely, as do multiple guest co-editors discussed earlier in this chapter, can be imagined, and perhaps achieved, only in the digital realm of information organization and exchange. Similarly, to develop digital monographs the most basic question – "what lines of critical argument are possible only in a digital monograph?" – needs to be posed repeatedly. Certainly, there are adept ways of using sound and image, as well as linguistic codes, that are only possible in the digital realm, but that is only the beginning. Moving from editor (author surrogate) and author to reader (including editor and author), from enacting definitude (editing for the static printed page) to enacting fluidity (the dynamic screen), is enabling profound innovations in editorial praxes, changes demonstrating how vital are "recent moves to reframe objectivity from the epistemic stance necessary to achieve a definitive body of knowledge, to a contingent accomplishment of dynamic processes of knowing and acting" for enriching our intellectual commons (Suchman, website). Acknowledging the fluidity of texts instead of insisting upon single-minded, singularly-oriented texts, "learning the meaning of the revision of texts," as well as the revision of our editorial practices, creates an environment in which a "new kind of critical thinking based on difference, variation, approximation, intention, power, and change" can flourish and work for the common good. If we are to shed the inertia bequeathed from the bibliographic world, editorial integrity and fidelity created within and upon the "shifting sands of democratic life" demand a "new cosmopolitanism" in scholarly editing (Bryant 2002: 177), adopting the "lesbian rule" of principled accommodation for digital humanities.

REFERENCES FOR FURTHER READING

Bernstein, Charles (2000). The Art of Immemorability. In Jerome Rothenberg and Steven Clay (eds.), *A Book of the Book: Some Works and Projections about the Book and Writing* (pp. 504–17). New York: Granary Books.

Bornstein, George and Theresa Tinkle (eds.) (1998). *The Iconic Page in Manuscript, Print, and Digital Culture.* Ann Arbor: University of Michigan Press.

Bowker, Geoffrey C. and Susan Leigh Star (1999). *Sorting Things Out: Classification and its Consequences.* Cambridge, MA, and London: MIT Press.

Bryant, John (2002). *The Fluid Text: A Theory of Revision and Editing for Book and Screen.* Ann Arbor: University of Michigan Press.

Condron, Frances, Michael Fraser, and Stuart Sutherland (2001). *Digital Resources for the Humanities.* Morgantown: West Virginia University Press.

D'Arms, John H. (2000). The Electronic Monograph in the 21st Century. Based on Scholarly Publishing in the 21st Century, presented at the American Historical Association, Chicago, January, 2000. Available at <http://www.acls.org/jhd-aha.htm>.

Derrida, Jacques (1996). *Archive Fever: A Freudian Impression.* Chicago and London: University of Chicago Press.

Drucker, Johanna (1998). *Figuring the Word: Essays on Books, Writing, and Visual Poetics.* New York: Granary Books.

Finneran, Richard J. (ed.) (1996). *The Literary Text in the Digital Age.* Ann Arbor: University of Michigan Press.

Flanders, Julia (1998). Trusting the Electronic Edition. *Computers and the Humanities* 31: 301–10.

Franklin, R. W. (ed.) (1998). *The Poems of Emily Dickinson: Variorum Edition*, 3 vols. Cambridge, MA, and London: Harvard University Press. (References to texts in this edition will use "FP" and refer to the poem's number.)

Grigely, Joseph (1995). *Texualterity: Art, Theory, and Textual Criticism.* Ann Arbor: University of Michigan Press.

Hamill, Sam. "Open Letter" on "Who We Are," *Poets Against the War.* Accessed spring 2003. Available at <http://poetsagainstthewar.org>.

Hockey, Susan (2000). *Electronic Texts in the Humanities.* Oxford and New York: Oxford University Press.

Hockey, Susan, Allen Renear, and Jerome McGann. What is Text? A Debate on the Philosophical Nature of Text in the Light of Humanities Computing Research. Accessed spring 2003. Available at <http://www.humanities.ualberta.ca/Susan_Hockey/achallc99.htm>.

Kirschenbaum, Matthew (guest ed.) (2002). *Image-based Humanities Computing.* Special issue of *Computers and the Humanities* 36: 1–140; his introductory essay (pp. 3–6).

Lakoff, George (1987). *Women, Fire, and Dangerous Things: What Categories Reveal about the Mind.* Chicago and London: University of Chicago Press.

Landow, George (1997). *Hypertext 2.0: The Convergence of Contemporary Critical Theory and Technology.* Baltimore: Johns Hopkins University Press.

Latour, Bruno and Steve Woolgar (1986). *Laboratory Life: The Construction of Scientific Facts*, 2nd edn. Princeton, NJ: Princeton University Press. (Originally published 1979.)

Love, Harold (1993). *Scribal Publication in Seventeenth-century England.* Oxford: Clarendon Press.

McGann, Jerome (2001). *Radiant Textuality: Literature after the World Wide Web.* New York: Palgrave.

McKenzie, D. F. (1999). *Bibliography and the Sociology of Texts.* Cambridge: Cambridge University Press. (1986) London: British Library. (1985) The Panizzi Lectures. (1984) The Sociology of a Text: Oral Culture, Literacy and Print in early New Zealand. *The Library* 6 (December 1984).

MLA Committee on Scholarly Editions. Revision Plan for the Guidelines for Scholarly Editions of the Committee on Scholarly Editions. Accessed spring 2003. Available at <http://www.mla.org.www_mla_org/reports/reports_main.asp?>. Guidelines for Electronic Scholarly Editions: Available at

<http://sunsite.berkeley.edu/MLA/guidelines.html>. Guidelines for Editors of Scholarly Editions: Available at <http://jefferson.village.virginia.edu/~jmu2m/cse/CSEguidelines.html>.

Rockwell, Geoffrey (2002). Gore Galore: Literary Theory and Computer Games. In Siemens (ed.), *A New Computer-Assisted Literary Criticism?* (pp. 345–58).

Schreibman, Susan (2002a). Computer-mediated Texts and Textuality: Theory and Practice. In R. G. Siemens (ed.), *A New Computer-Assisted Literary Criticism?* (pp. 283–93).

——(2002b). The Text Ported. *Literary and Linguistic Computing* 17: 77–87.

Siemens, Raymond G. (guest ed.) (2002). *A New Computer-assisted Literary Criticism?* Special issue of *Computers and the Humanities* 36: 255–378; his introductory essay (pp. 259–67).

Shillingsburg, Peter L. (1996). *Scholarly Editing in the Computer Age: Theory and Practice.* Ann Arbor: University of Michigan Press.

Smith, Martha Nell (2002). Computing: What's American Literary Study Got to Do with IT? *American Literature* 74: 833–57. Online. *Project Muse.* Accessed spring 2003. Available at <http://muse.jhu.edu/journals/american_literature/v074/74.4smith.html>.

Sperberg-McQueen, C. M. and L. Burnard (eds.) (1990). *Guidelines for Electronic Text Encoding and Interchange: TEI P3.* Chicago and Oxford: The Text Encoding Initiative. (Reprinted 1999.) Available at <http://www.tei-c.org/Guidelines/index.htm>.

Sperberg-McQueen, C. M., Claus Huitfeldt, and Allen Renear (2000). Meaning and Interpretation of Markup. *Markup Languages* 2: 215–34.

Suchman, Lucy. Located Accountabilities in Technology Production. Published by the Department of Sociology, Lancaster University. Online. Accessed Spring 2003. Available at <http://www.comp.lancs.ac.uk/sociology/soc039ls.html>.

Unsworth, John (1996). Electronic Scholarship; or, Scholarly Publishing and the Public. In R. J. Finneran (ed.), *The Literary Text in the Digital Age* (pp. 233–43). Ann Arbor: University of Michigan Press.

——. Electronic Textual Editing and the TEI. Online. Accessed spring 2003. Available at <http://jefferson.village.virginia.edu/~jmu2m/mla-cse.2002.html>.

Winder, William (2002). Industrial Text and French Neo-structuralism. In R. G. Siemens (ed.), *A New Computer-Assisted Literary Criticism?* (pp. 295–306).

23

Textual Analysis

John Burrows

Preamble

The object of this paper is to show that computer-assisted textual analysis can be of value in many different sorts of literary inquiry, helping to resolve some questions, to carry others forward, and to open entirely new ones. The emphasis will not be on the straightforward, albeit valuable, business of gathering specimens of chosen phenomena for close study – the business of concordances and tagged sets. It will fall rather on the form of computational stylistics in which all the most common words (whatever they may be) of a large set of texts are subjected to appropriate kinds of statistical analysis.

Statistical analysis is necessary for the management of words that occur too frequently to be studied one by one. But why study such words at all? For those of a sufficiently ascetic taste, there is a certain intrinsic interest in considering why Henry Fielding should stand out among a host of others in his recourse to the plain man's *very* and the lawyer's inferential use of the conjunction *for*. And if the substance of Aphra Behn's love poetry is epitomized in her fondness for *warm* and *soft*, her slightly strident tone of voice can be heard in *all* and *none* and *never*. On a larger scene, my datasets uphold the belief that British writers still make more use of *which* and *should* than their American or Australian contemporaries. Australian writers, however, show a preference for *we/our/us* in contexts where their British and American counterparts would favor *I/my/me*. A desire to avoid any appearance of immodesty or a desire for concealment within the herd?

But the real value of studying the common words rests on the fact that they constitute the underlying fabric of a text, a barely visible web that gives shape to whatever is being said. Despite a brave attempt made long ago (Bratley and Ross 1981), we have yet to find satisfactory ways of tracing the interconnections of all the different threads, as each of the common words occurs and recurs in the full sequence of a text. We are able, nevertheless, to show that texts where certain of these threads are unusually prominent differ greatly from texts where other threads are given more use. An appropriate analogy, perhaps, is with the contrast between handwoven rugs where the russet tones predominate and those where they give way to the greens and blues. The principal point of interest is neither a single stitch, a single thread, nor even a single color but the overall effect. Such effects are best seen, moreover, when different pieces are put side by side. That, at all events, is the case I shall present.

Classification of Texts

Analyses

To begin directly with the first of several case studies, let us bring a number of poems together, employ a statistical procedure that allows each of them to show its affinity for such others as it most resembles, and draw whatever inferences the results admit. For this purpose, I have taken forty specimens of seventeenth-century and early eighteenth-century English verse, as listed in table 23.1. Many are excerpts from longer works but each of them exceeds two thousand words in length. While they range in date from 1633 to about 1733, most come from 1660–1700. While they run across the range of literary forms taken by long poems in that era, satire and epic figure prominently among them. The first twenty on the list are by poets whose other work contributes to the large, wide-ranging database listed in the Appendix. Seventeen of the second twenty are by poets whose work is not included there. Although the remaining three poems (nos. 22–24) are of doubtful authorship, they are usually attributed to Andrew Marvell, a member of the database. If these three are counted, notionally, as Marvell's, twenty of the forty poems form small authorial sets. The other twenty are independent pieces.

The actual data for analysis consist of word-counts, from each of the forty specimens, of 150 common words. The words themselves are the 150 most common in the aforementioned database of seventeenth-century verse. Such a list is more robust than one derived from a small, selective set of texts like the one we shall examine. The texts were prepared according to the same protocols as the main database. They were all modernized so as to remove the statistically misleading effects of seventeenth-century spelling. Contracted forms like *don't* and *I've* were expanded to allow full counts of the parent words. A few common words like *so* and *that* were tagged in such a way as to distinguish their main grammatical functions. With this preparatory work complete, the texts were subjected to our sorting and counting programs. The raw counts for each common word in each text were normalized as percentages of the total number of words in that text. The object is to avoid the tyranny of the larger numbers with texts of uneven length.

The chief analytical procedures employed for comparing texts on the basis of the relative frequencies of many common words all depend upon the logical principle of concomitant variation. The counts for each word are treated as variables on which each of the chosen specimens (the texts under examination) lies nearest to such others as it most resembles and furthest from those it least resembles. To take examples that will easily be appreciated, texts (like plays) where *I* and *you* occur unusually often are likely to differ in many ways from texts (like prose treatises) where *the* and *a* rise well above the norm. Texts of the former sort usually run high in the simpler auxiliary verbs and in many colloquial,

Table 23.1   Forty long poems of the late seventeenth century

*1	2586 Butler, Samuel	*Hudibras, Canto III*
#2	2208	*Upon the Imperfection ... of Human Learning, Parts I & II. 1–72*
*3	3373 Cotton, Charles	*A Voyage to Ireland in Burlesque, Cantos 2 and 3*
#4	3004 Cowley, Abraham	*The Plagues of Egypt, 1–262*
#5	6812	*Davideis, Book II*
*6	7824 Dryden, John	*Absalom and Achitophel*
*7	19896	*The Hind and the Panther*
*8	7817 D'Urfey, Thomas	*The Malecontent*
#9	6020 Gould, Robert	*To the Society of the Beaux Esprits*
#10	4019	*The Play-House. A Satyr, Part II*
#11	4057	*A Satyr against Man, Part I*
#12	4492	*Presbytery Rough-drawn. A Satyr*
*13	27154 Milton, John	*Paradise Lost, lines 201–500 of each Book*
*14	15694	*Paradise Regained*
*15	12885	*Samson Agonistes*
*16	2210 Oldham, John	*Satyr II*
*17	3378	*The Eighth Satyr of Monsieur Boileau Imitated*
*18	3381 Swift, Jonathan	*On Poetry: A Rhapsody*
*19	3206	*Verses on the Death of Dr. Swift, D. S. P. D.*
*20	2606 Waller, Edmund	*Instructions to a Painter*
#21	3547 Addison, Joseph	*The Campaign*
*22	2867 Anon.	*The Second Advice to a Painter*
*23	3638	*The Third Advice to a Painter*
*24	7693	*Last Instructions to a Painter*
*25	11111 Billingsley, Nicholas	*The World's Infancy*
#26	6986 Blackmore, Richard	*King Arthur, Book I*
*27	3892 Caryll, John	*Naboth's Vineyard*
#28	3617 Chamberlayne, Willi	*Pharonnida, Book I, Canto 1*
#29	2743 Chudleigh, Mary	*On the Death of his Highness the Duke of Gloucester*
#30	5167 Davenant, William	*Gondibert, Book I, Cantos 1 and 2*
#31	3892 Duke, Richard	*Paris to Helena*
#32	5935 Fletcher, Phineas	*The Purple Island, Cantos I and II*
#33	8797 Heyrick, Thomas	*The New Atlantis, Parts I and II*
#34	3731 Parnell, Thomas	Homer's Battle of the Frogs and Mice, Books I–III
*35	3103 Pordage, Samuel	*The Medal Revers'd*
*36	3250 Thompson, Thomas	*Midsummer Moon*
*37	2287 Tutchin, John	*A Search after Honesty*
*38	4374 Vaughan, Henry	*Juvenal's Tenth Satire Translated*
*39	2156 Wase, Christopher	*Divination*
*40	3321 Wild, Robert	*Iter Boreale*

Texts are complete except where specified. Texts marked* are from original or standard modern editions. Those marked # are from the Chadwyck-Healey Archive of English Poetry, to which my university subscribes. The texts were used only for the extraction of word-counts.

speech-oriented forms of expression. Texts of the latter sort tend to be oriented towards the relationships among things and ideas rather than persons and often show high frequencies in the most common prepositions. Differences in level of discourse (as in the wide-ranging contrasts between Latinate forms like *ascend* and Germanic equivalents like *go up*); in genre (as between the past-tense verbs of retrospective narrative and the present tense of most disquisitory writing); and in historical provenance (as in the shift from *thou* to *you*) – all these and many more are reflected in systematic relationships among the frequencies of the very common words.

When any large group of texts is analyzed, such manifestations of concomitant variation as these yield complex but intelligible patterns of affinity and disaffinity. They are much enriched, moreover, by the many exceptions that arise. Some of these are associated with authorial idiosyncrasies. The possible combinations from genre to genre, era to era, author to author, text to text, are almost unlimited. Effects like these, we may suppose, impinge upon the minds of good readers as part of their overall response. But they are not easy for a reader to articulate. Statistical analysis, on the other hand, offers clear but comparatively unsubtle ways of representing them.

The main analytical procedure to be employed in this chapter is that of cluster analysis, chosen because it offers rather a harsh test of the questions to be considered and also because the "family trees" in which the results are displayed speak plainly for themselves. The procedure is put to excellent use in a recent study of prose fiction. (See Hoover 2002.) The principal disadvantage of cluster analysis is that the underlying word-patterns are not made visible and must therefore be approached in other ways. For those who are versed in these matters, I should add that the statistical package used for these cluster analyses is MINITAB. My many trials suggest that, for such data as we are examining, complete linkages, squared Euclidean distances, and standardized variables yield the most accurate results. This pattern of preferences avoids any undue smoothing of data whose inherent roughness reflects the complexities of the language itself. This pattern, at all events, is used throughout.

Figure 23.1 represents the outcome of a cluster analysis in which our forty texts are compared with each other on the basis of the full list of the 150 most common words. It should be studied from the base upwards, taking account of the way the clusters form. The texts are identified, along the horizontal base of the figure, by the numbers attached to them in table 23.1. The true affinities are not between entries that merely stand beside each other before separating, like nos. 2 and 4, but between those that form unions, like nos. 4 and 5. The closest affinities of all are between those pairs that unite soonest, like nos. 13 and 14, and those trios that do so, like nos. 13, 14, and 15.

The most obvious feature of figure 23.1 is that some of its members are so slow to form any union at all. The isolation of no. 35, Samuel Pordage's satire *The Medal Revers'd*, can readily be shown to rest on an unusual preponderance of verbs couched in the present tense. They reflect the rhetorical stance of an ostensibly philosophic observer of affairs. No. 3, Charles Cotton's *A Voyage to Ireland in Burlesque*, is isolated by its narrative mode and its colloquial speech-register. When it does finally form an affinity, it is not with the epic and heroic poems to its left but with the loose group, chiefly made up of satires, lying to its right. And even though nos. 1 and 2, the highly idiosyncratic satires of Samuel Butler, differ markedly from each other, they stand even further apart from all the rest.

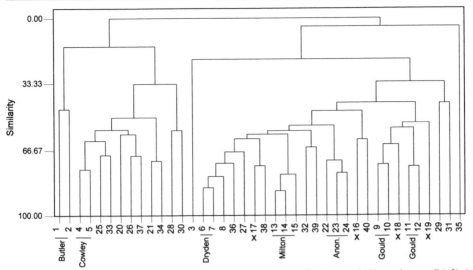

Authorial sets labeled by author's name. Failed members marked by "x". Singletons marked by numbers: see list of texts.

Figure 23.1   Forty long Poems: cluster analysis based on the 150 most common words of the main corpus

Considered more broadly, figure 23.1 shows a rough differentiation between the earlier- and later-born poets, with the work of the latter lying towards the right. Near the right-hand extremity, for example, the poems of Gould, Swift, Duke, and Lady Mary Chudleigh make comfortable enough chronological neighbors while Butler, Cowley, Billingsley, and Waller are well placed at the left. But this incipient pattern is severely damaged by the genre-differentiation already noted. On a chronological basis, Blackmore (no. 26), Addison (no. 21) and Parnell (no. 34) have no place on the left while Vaughan (no. 38) and Phineas Fletcher (no. 32) lie much too far to the right. The location of Milton's three poems (nos. 13–15) is anomalous in both chronology and genre.

Of the seventeen poems that make up authorial sets, only four fail to reveal their true authorial affinities. The three that are thought to be Marvell's form another little set. (In the case of Robert Gould, whose quartet forms two pairs, the success of the cluster analysis is incomplete.) Since the members of each authorial pair are locating their proper partners from a field of thirty-nine, the odds against the chance achievement of such a success rate are immense. Moreover, as readers who know these forty poems will be aware, the three anonymous painter-satires (nos. 22–24) are the only set where the effects of genre and authorship might be thought to work entirely in unison. The two Dryden poems, for instance, have little in common but their authorship; and *Samson Agonistes* differs mark-edly in genre from Milton's epics.

Figure 23.2 is specifically designed to show why the painter-satires form a trio. It is constructed in exactly the same fashion as figure 23.1 save that two extra specimens have been added. They are two of Andrew Marvell's best-known poems, *Upon Appleton House* (no. 41) and *The First Anniversary of the Government under O. C.* (no. 42). At 4,845 and 3,131 words respectively, they are of appropriate length for the comparison. And they differ markedly in genre from each other and from the painter-satires. In figure 23.2, it will be seen that they form an additional authorial pair and that this pair unites with the trio of painter-satires. As in figure 23.1, furthermore, the target of the painter-satires, Edmund Waller's *Instructions to a Painter* stands well away from them. Marvell's likely authorship of these three painter-satires is a matter of some importance in literary history. It is pursued more thoroughly in a new article to be submitted to *The Yearbook of English Studies*. For our present purpose, however, figure 23.2 makes a more general point. With the addition of the two Marvell pieces and the uniting of the Gould quartet, figure 23.2 surpasses the strong result achieved in figure 23.1. The 150 most common words of our main dataset can clearly be said, therefore, to offer a useful basis for testing the authorship of long poems of the late seventeenth century. The possibility that this outcome might be a statistical artifact is easily set at rest: other methods of analyzing these data yield equally accurate results.

If the word list is progressively truncated from the bottom, much shorter poems can be tested for authorship. Although the rate of success diminishes as the texts grow shorter, it still far exceeds the rate of chance success. A study of this topic (Burrows 2002a) has recently been published. But a selective word list can be constructed in other ways. Is it possible to achieve similar levels of success more economically, working with only a chosen subset of our 150 most common words? After making many attempts, varying in rigor and subtlety but without conspicuous success, as reported elsewhere (Burrows 2003: 21–3), I chose a plainer path. In table 23.2, the 150 most common words are dispersed in three subsets. The 54 words of "domain 1" comprise the principal referential markers, namely the definite and indefinite articles and the personal pronouns, to which are added the infinitive particle *to* and those common verb-forms whose inflections differ in association with the articles and pronouns. The 69 words of "domain 2" comprise the common connectives (including conjunctions, prepositions, and relative pronouns) and the common intensifiers, whether adjectives or adverbs. The descriptive adjectives, however, are put aside with the nouns among the 27 words excluded as too lexical, too

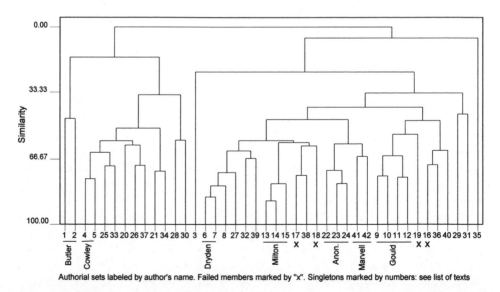

Figure 23.2   Forty-two long poems: cluster analysis based on the 150 most common words of the main corpus

Table 23.2   Experimental classification of the 150 most common words of the main dataset

"Domain 1": 54 words		"Domain 2": 69 words		Exclusions: 27 words
1 the	79 do	2 and	71 there	64 love
4 a	80 should	3 of	72 some	70 great
5 to (i)	82 let	6 in (p)	73 too	92 own
7 his	83 make	8 with	74 how	100 first
10 is	84 could	9 to (p)	76 one	101 men
12 he	86 must	11 but	77 never	103 man
14 I	87 an	13 all	81 though	106 heaven
15 it	90 us	16 as	85 those	108 good
17 their	93 thee	19 not	88 where	111 well
18 her	94 made	23 for (p)	89 still	114 long
20 be	95 has	24 by (p)	91 here	115 old
21 you	96 see	27 from	97 these	116 day
22 they	122 art	28 that (rp)	98 before	121 heart
25 my	124 give	29 or	99 thus	123 wit
26 we	128 know	33 this	102 every	126 world
30 our	129 find	34 when	104 whose	130 fate
31 thy	131 its	37 at	105 out	132 eyes
32 was	137 been	38 which (rp)	107 much	133 life
35 are	146 come	39 no (aj)	109 while	134 vain
36 your		40 what	110 so (c)	135 power
43 will (v)		41 so (ad)	112 each	139 God
45 can		42 that (d)	113 only	140 soul
46 have		44 on (p)	117 once	141 new
47 she		49 more	118 through	142 fair
48 thou		50 if	119 up (ap)	147 time
51 did		53 now	120 both	148 name
52 would		54 who (rp)	125 till	150 last
57 had		55 that (c)	127 ever	
60 him		56 yet	136 down	
66 may		58 then	138 whom	
67 shall		59 such	143 upon (p)	
68 me		61 nor	144 whilst	
69 were		62 for (c)	145 since	
75 does		63 like (p)	149 over	
78 them		65 than		

Abbreviations:
(p) = preposition
(i) = infinitive
(c) = conjunction
(rp) = relative pronoun
(v) = verb
(ap) = adverbial particle
(ad) = adverb of degree
(aj) = adjective
(d) = demonstrative

subject-oriented, to be valid markers of more formal differences. A close student of table 23.2 will detect at least two cases, *art* and *own*, where I have sought the less bad compromise. The former is included in "domain 1" on the ground that, in seventeenth-century verse, its role as an auxiliary verb is more potent than its role as an abstract noun. The latter is excluded on the ground that it is used less often as a verb than as an adjective. Such is the wealth of our data that a few arguable choices have little impact on the analyses.

Figure 23.3 is a cluster analysis of our original set of forty poems using only the 69 words of "domain 2." As a test of authorship, it offers much the same result as the full list of 150 words used earlier. The members of the Oldham and Swift pairs still stand apart from their fellows. The Gould poems now fall into a trio and a singleton instead of the two pairs of figure 23.1 or the quartet of figure 23.2. The other authorial sets hold firm. On closer study, however, it can be seen that figure 23.3 surpasses both its predecessors because the various groups form much more quickly. For testing the authorship of this large group of poems, "domain 2," therefore, is more economical of data and more efficient in operation than the full list of 150 words.

It goes almost without saying that, if these 69 words can match or outmatch the full set, the omitted words must shed little light on authorship. Figure 23.4 is the counterpart of figure 23.3, taking the 54 words of "domain 1" as its basis. Two of the three Milton poems, two of the three painter-satires, and two of the four Gould poems still unite with their respective fellows. But where we had four or five errors out of twenty, we now have fourteen. Since this pattern is certainly not author-driven, the question is whether other inferences can be drawn. A close study of the way the poems cluster offers rough but suggestive distinctions between predominantly monologic, dialogic, narrative, and re-flective forms of rhetoric. Since we are working exclusively with referential markers and

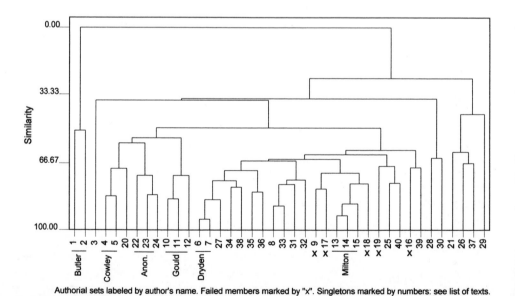

Authorial sets labeled by author's name. Failed members marked by "x". Singletons marked by numbers: see list of texts.

Figure 23.3   Forty long poems: cluster analysis based on the 69 most common words of "domain 2"

inflected verbs, this seems a plausible result. But the genre-differences in the poetry of the Restoration era are too subtle and too impure to allow any firm conclusions to be drawn from this one analysis.

To pursue the hypothesis that "domain 1" may indeed be genre-driven, I have accordingly added a further 26 specimens, as listed in table 23.3. Some 16 of them (nos. 41–56) are selections from plays of the period. Most of the plays are represented by a single Act but there are cases where other considerations call for a choice of scattered scenes. (Both Rochester and Waller, for example, contributed scenes to plays by other

Table 23.3   Twenty-six additional texts

Sixteen excerpts from plays of the late seventeenth century

Verse plays

*41	2918 ?Dorset, Charles Sackville, Earl of	*Pompey the Great*, Act II
*42	7133 Dryden, John	*The Siege of Granada*, Act I.i, Act V.i–ii
*43	4955	*Tyrannic Love*, Acts I-II
*44	7870 Rochester, John Wilmot, Earl of	*Valentinian, replacement scenes*
*45	2106	*The Walls of China, a contributed scene*
*46	3177 Sedley, Sir Charles	*Antony and Cleopatra*, Act I.ii, Act III.i
*47	2304 Shadwell, Thomas	*Psyche, two scenes*
#48	7817 Stapylton, Sir Robert	*Hero and Leander*, Act II
#49	3764	*The Slighted Maid*, Act III
*50	4980 Waller, Edmund	*The Maid's Tragedy, replacement scenes*

Prose plays

#51	5612 Congreve, William	*Love for Love*, Act IV
#52	5334	*The Way of the World*, Act IV
#53	5303 Sedley, Sir Charles	*Bellamira*, Act III
*54	6144 Shadwell, Thomas	*The Libertine*, Act III

Prose and verse

#55	3732 Southerne, Thomas	*The Fatal Marriage*, Act III
#56	4082	*The Fatal Marriage*, Act IV

Ten sets of letters from the late seventeenth century

*57	9615 Conway, Anne Finch, Lady	Letters to her husband
*58	5058 King, William, Archbishop of Dublin	Letters to Jonathan Swift
*59	5545 Montagu, Lady Mary Wortley	Letters to Edward Montagu (before marriage)
*60	5969 More, Henry	Letters to Anne, Lady Conway
*61	8113 Osborne, Dorothy	Letters to William Temple (before marriage)
*62	7193 Rochester, John Wilmot, Earl of	Letters
*63	6251 Savile, Henry	Letters to Rochester
*64	8948 Swift, Jonathan	Letters to Esther Vanhomrigh ("Vanessa")
*65	8730 Swift, Jonathan	Letters to Archbishop King
*66	5418 Vanhomrigh, Esther ("Vanessa")	Letters to Jonathan Swift

Texts are complete except where specified. Texts marked* are from original or standard modern editions. Those marked # are from the Chadwyck-Healey Archive of English Poetry, to which my university subscribes. The texts were used only for the extraction of word-counts.

dramatists.) Among the plays, the first ten selections are of verse drama. The next four are of prose drama and the last two, both from Southerne's *The Fatal Marriage*, include both verse and prose. Of the dramatists included, Dryden, Rochester, Stapylton, Congreve, and Southerne offer authorial pairs within their respective subsets. Sedley and Shadwell make it possible to test dramatic authorship across the differences between verse and prose. While these 16 specimens of drama are too few to be representative, they may suffice for an instructive comparison with the poetry and the personal letters of their day.

The other ten specimens (nos. 57–66) are selections from the personal letters of some well-known figures of the period. All the letters within each set except for Rochester's are directed to a particular recipient. Two sets of Swift's letters are included to display the possible diversity of an epistolary repertoire.

Whereas only tentative conclusions could be drawn from figure 23.4, figure 23.5 uses the 54 words of "domain 1" to quite striking effect. Some 90 percent of our 66 specimens form genre-based clusters. All ten sets of personal letters form a cluster of their own, at the extreme right. Thirty-eight of the forty poems lie to the left of any other specimens. Twenty-nine of them form one large cluster at the left with another seven clustering to their immediate right. The rest are located among the verse-plays and are marked as errors. Two verse plays are marked as errors because they cross into the remaining cluster, where they join the prose plays and the two plays in which prose and verse are mixed.

From another, simpler perspective, figure 23.5 is composed of three large clusters. To the left is a set made up entirely of poems. In the middle is a set uniting some poems of a dialogic cast with verse drama, obviously their close kin. To the right is a set of sixteen prose specimens and two stray pieces of verse drama (nos. 48 and 49). These last, both extracts from little-known plays by Sir Robert Stapylton, are couched in what has aptly been described (Sutherland 1969: 43) as "an easy and colloquial blank verse." Why do

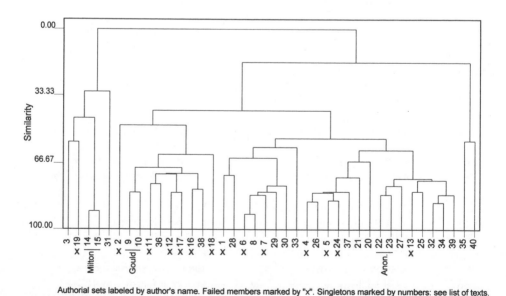

Authorial sets labeled by author's name. Failed members marked by "x". Singletons marked by numbers: see list of texts.

Figure 23.4 Forty long poems: cluster analysis based on the 54 most common words of "domain 1"

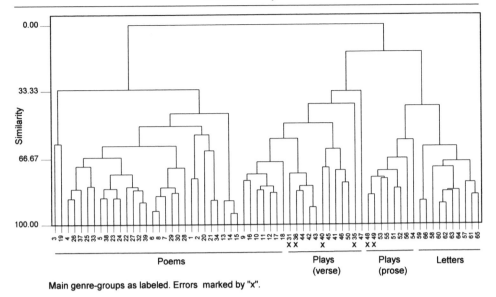

Similarity

Poems   Plays   Plays   Letters
              (verse)   (prose)

Main genre-groups as labeled. Errors marked by "x".

Figure 23.5 Sixty-six tents: cluster analysis based on the 54 most common words of "domain 1"

they cross the border between verse and prose? The best explanation, I believe, is that Stapylton favors a dialogue of brief, deictic interchange and only rarely offers a large, poetic set-speech. In an analysis based principally upon pronouns and auxiliary verbs, this tendency carries his plays towards the prose drama of the period.

That explanation is supported by figure 23.6, where the full list of 150 words is employed in an analysis of the same 66 specimens. The richer word list, less strongly influenced by *I/thou*, places Stapylton correctly in the cluster composed entirely of verse drama. No. 45, Rochester's highly poetic contribution to Sir Robert Howard's verse drama *The Walls of China*, is now misplaced among the 37 poems that make up the main cluster. Three poems (nos. 31, 35, and 3), which have previously shown little affinity for the others, are now misplaced among the plays. Every other entry is correctly placed in a tripartite distribution of the texts according to their genre.

The foregoing series of analyses shows many points of interest. One of the more unexpected offers special food for thought. When we compared figures 23.1 and 23.3, we saw that the selective word list, though scarcely less accurate than the full list, was more economical and more efficient. In the corresponding case, figure 23.5 does offer a somewhat less accurate separation of literary genres than figure 23.6. Yet figure 23.5 is much more economical than figure 23.6 in its use of data and its clusters form more speedily. If the 69 words of "domain 2" and the 54 words of "domain 1" compare so favorably with the full list of 150 words as indicators of authorship and genre respectively, we do well to seek an explanation.

Rationale

As a first step, the case for excluding the most common lexical words from such analyses because they are too subject-oriented is well understood and widely practiced. Even in the

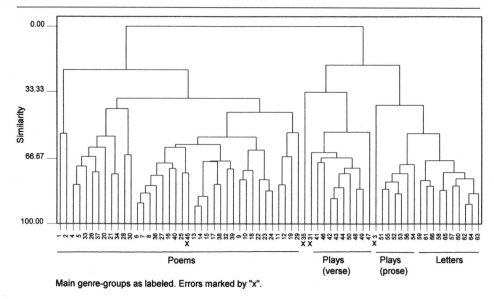

Figure 23.6 Sixty-six texts: cluster analysis based on the 150 most common words of the main dataset

upper reaches of the frequency hierarchy, the lexical words favored by different authors are sometimes idiosyncratic, sometimes those of a coterie. The Christian vocabulary of seventeenth-century devotional verse stands out in contrast, for example, to the obscene vocabulary that marks the clandestine verse of Rochester and his circle: some words of both kinds rank very high in appropriate texts. We do not need a computer to determine that the obscene farce, *Sodom*, is unlikely to be the work of Henry Vaughan. And even if it were, a quite uncharacteristic set of lexical words would act only as a disguise. Since such problems cannot validly be addressed by picking and choosing among the lexical words, it is best to treat them all alike and to recognize what one is doing. And, though the boundary between lexical and function words is inexact, the upper end of the frequency range includes very few hard choices. On this basis, 27 words can be excluded from our list of 150.

A good case can also be made for excluding the personal pronouns because they are too volatile in frequency to serve as reliable measures. If that is done, the question of the inflected verbs arises with some force. It would obviously be logical to exclude them too. But by now the increasing sacrifice of information must occasion serious concern. These three excisions would take out 81 words from the 150 of the list we have been using. A desirable rigor would be obtained at a disturbing cost.

The results already offered illustrate what follows when the 27 most common lexical words are set aside while the common function-words are all retained but are separated into two "domains." Figure 23.7 represents an attempt to understand the difference between these notional domains. Anybody who sets about a piece of writing may be thought of as beginning at the standpoint marked at the extreme left of the figure. Even at that point, such a person is too much a creature of habit and background to begin with a clean slate. Even at that point, such a person will also have some notion of a subject, an intended audience, and an attitude to that audience. And, although the writer retains a good deal of latitude as the work proceeds, these broad constraints begin to strengthen

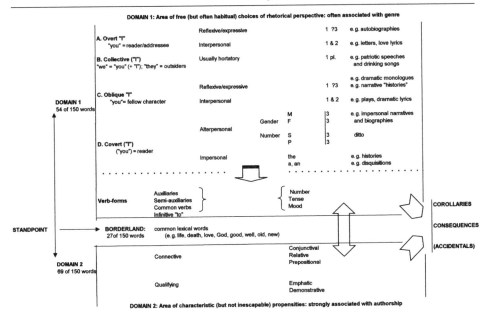

Figure 23.7 A sketch-map of relationships among the common words of English: a rationale for concomitance of frequency

from the moment the very first words are written: "Of Man's first disobedience..."; "The glories of our blood and state..."; "It is a truth universally acknowledged..."; "She waited, Kate Croy..."; "My father had a small estate in Nottinghamshire; I was the third of five sons..."; "When I consider how my light is spent..."; "I wandered lonely as a cloud..."; "Shall I compare thee to a summer's day..."; "Believe't, I will.// Thy worst. I fart at thee."

The authorial *I* of a text is ever-present though not always visible. That *I*, of course, cannot simply be identified with the writer *in propria persona*. But four of the many roles open to that *I* govern the categories set out in the upper part of figure 23.7. In category A, an *I* not easily distinguished from the author engages in some form of direct address to a real or putative reader. Such work need not be disingenuous. Samuel Johnson offers a celebrated warning about the deceits of epistolary correspondence and when Lady Mary Pierrepont tells her future husband, Edward Wortley Montagu, "I am going to write you a plain long letter" (Halsband 1970: 41), only the warning signs are plain. (He did not heed them.) The *I* of category A usually occurs freely and carries a select group of verbal inflections along with it. The *thou/you* who is addressed may occur just as freely but may also remain inexplicit. T. S. Eliot distinguishes the pulpit-rhetoric of Donne from that of Lancelot Andrewes on pertinent lines: whereas the former is always in his pulpit, addressing his congregation, the latter "is wholly in his subject, unaware of anything else" (Eliot 1932: 341). While the comparative frequencies of the relevant pronouns, articles, and verbs in their sermons are not what engages a reader, they show the force of Eliot's distinction.

In category B, both the authorial *I* and the *you* of the addressees are absorbed into the *we* of a real or notional group. *They* is assigned to outsiders, whether feared, pitied, or admired. When these plural forms predominate, the singular pronouns and verbs all drop away in frequency. Winston Churchill's "We will fight them on the beaches ... We will never surrender" takes the hortatory form. The elegiac form is taken by Lawrence Binyon's Armistice hymn, *For the Fallen*: "They shall grow not old / As we that are left grow old."

In category C, the authorial *I* is displaced by the deictic *I* of whichever character, dramatic or fictional, is speaking at a given time. In plays, accordingly, *Thou/you* is reserved for the characters then addressed. All of the personal pronouns are free to occur but *I/thou/you* usually predominate. The present tense verb-forms are usually in the ascendant. In the retrospective narrative "histories" that either constitute or are interpolated in many novels, especially those of the eighteenth and nineteenth centuries, *I* is customarily the highly visible property of the present speaker. (Whereas Lemuel Gulliver always holds the center of his stage, Henry Fielding's Man of the Hill and Mrs Fitzpatrick or his Miss Mathews, Captain Booth, and Mrs Bennet take turns at being *I*.) *Thou/you* may either be reserved for fellow characters or extended to include us "Gentle Readers." Both *he* and *she* are likely to occur almost as freely as *I*, being devoted to those others who took part in the events now recounted. Except in those retrospective narratives where the historic present tense is adopted as a rhetorical strategy, most verbs are couched in the past tense.

In the many and varied forms of writing composing category D, neither *I* nor *you* need ever occur, most other pronouns may be rare, and the articles are likely to be the chief referential markers. Among the third-person pronouns, *it* and *they* are likely to predominate. And though historical writings are often more personally oriented than most treatises and disquisitions, they do not often find much use for the feminine pronouns. It might be interesting to ascertain whether a flurry of feminine pronouns could be found in any part of Gibbon's great history except the chapter treating the notable exploits of the Empress Theodora. She is certainly one of the only two women named in the extensive titles of his 71 chapters. Modern feminist historians are busy redressing the imbalances of the past, and altering the incidence of pronouns as they do so.

With Henry Fielding's novels among my examples, Gentle Reader, I could not easily forget that many of the literary forms I have referred to, and the novel in particular, can draw on the resources of more than one of my categories. When this occurs, of course, the pattern of pronouns, articles, and auxiliary verbs is bound to be modified. My short list of distinguishable literary forms is only a scanty representation of the more obvious classes. And I am well aware that, in broadening its field of reference in recent years, the word *genre* has lost its former rigor. Its over-extension can be seen when it is applied, for example, to personal letters, a whole family of loosely related literary forms.

With all due allowance for these reservations, figure 23.5 still indicates that some major genre-divisions can indeed be differentiated by the statistical analysis of a select word list confined to pronouns, inflected verbs, articles, and the infinitive particle. This last acts as a marker of complex verbal compounds, often couched in the first person, in which the speaker stands back a little from the action encompassed in the main verb and expresses a self-conscious attitude to it. "I hoped/feared/wished/chose to ... " and many other forms like them typify a usage which is remarkably common in some writers, Butler and Rochester among them, and which offers us an easy transition from domain 1 to domain 2.

From the standpoint at the left of figure 23.7, as a writer moves forward with the emerging text, the choices made in domain 1 interweave with those of domain 2. Here, however, the more open choices of domain 1 are outweighed though not extinguished by the constraints of upbringing and habit. Predisposition or idiosyncrasy? The syntactical forms by which a writer's ideas are connected and the forms of emphasis a writer chooses all offer a new battleground for ancient debates about the nexus between idiosyncratic and socially influenced facets of our behavior. If social factors were all that mattered, it would be hard to explain why men of such different backgrounds as Defoe and Henry Fielding should far outrank their contemporaries in the use of so commonplace a word as *very*. If idiosyncrasy were all that mattered, it would be hard to explain why, nearly three centuries later, that same word should act as a statistically significant differentia between a large set of Australian writers and their British and American fellows. Contrasts in socially imposed roles may well explain why *not*, *but*, and *never* are statistically significant differentiae between large sets of female and male writers of the eighteenth and nineteenth, but not the twentieth centuries. They do not explain why Dryden and Gould should stand out among their contemporaries in their use of *before* and *there* respectively.

Whether they originate in idiosyncrasy or in upbringing, such authorial habits are strong enough and consistent enough to allow the 69 words of domain 2 to act as effective authorial discriminators among the forty poems of figure 23.3. Although cluster analysis rests upon combinations of many word-frequencies, it is possible to pick out some of the more striking. Rochester is much given to *who* and *whose* and *ever*, Marvell to *yet* and *where* and *only*. Dryden and Congreve make uncommonly frequent use of *thus*. Of *while* and *whilst*, Marvell and Dryden lean to the former whereas Aphra Behn prefers the latter. Whereas both Dryden and Milton prefer *on* to *upon*, Samuel Butler goes the other way. As these last examples suggest, the words to which particular writers have more recourse than most are matched, as discriminators, by words that they eschew.

Provided the texts called into comparison are not too dissimilar in kind, such preferences among the common connectives and modifiers that constitute our domain 2 (or the corresponding "domain 2" of any other large database) can go far towards establishing the likely authorship of doubtful texts. And the notion of a writer finding a path forward by intermingling choices and habits helps to explain why this should be so. As the writer advances, the emerging shape of the text makes the basis of the stylistic corollaries and consequences indicated at the extreme right of figure 23.7. Choices, constraints, further constraints following from each choice – and always some room for accident, whether inept or inspired.

But figure 23.8 is an abrupt reminder that a writer's habits are not set in stone. It represents the outcome of a cluster analysis of the 66 texts of tables 23.1 and 23.3, using the 69 words of domain 2. Some 38 of the 66 texts are eligible as members of little authorial subsets: only 17 of them find their partners. Those 17 almost exactly match the successful unions of figure 23.3 and include, in addition, the two specimens of Dryden's verse drama (nos. 42 and 43). *Samson Agonistes* (no. 15) has moved away from the other Milton entries, but the previously misplaced Gould entry (no. 9) has rejoined the other three. Dryden's verse drama apart, the eligible specimens from among the additional texts not only fail to achieve a single cross-genre union but even fail to find their partners within the same genre. One interesting failure lies in Swift's two sets of letters (nos. 64–5), whose strikingly different recipients may explain why he can adopt such different

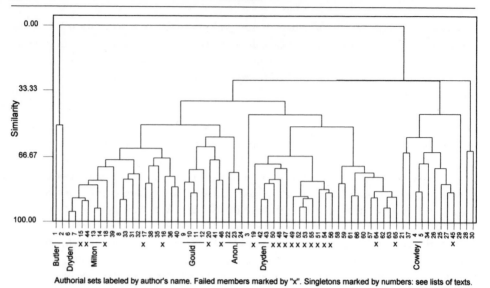

Authorial sets labeled by author's name. Failed members marked by "x". Singletons marked by numbers: see lists of texts.

Figure 23.8   Sixty-six texts: cluster analysis based on the 69 most common words of "domain 2"

styles. The two Acts from the same tragedy by Thomas Southerne (nos. 55–6) are distinguished from each other by their different proportions of subplot and main plot, prose and verse. The two specimens of Congreve's prose drama (nos. 51–2) are distinguished from each other by this dramatist's keen ear for different stylistic registers. The aristocrats of *The Way of the World* (no. 52) converse in a manner more akin to that of their peers in Sedley's *Bellamira* (no. 53) than that of the (not ill-spoken) cits and squires in *Love for Love* (no. 51).

But the strongest general contrast in figure 23.8 is between prose and verse. Three specimens of verse drama by Rochester (no. 44), Sedley (no. 46), and – as it is thought – by Dorset (no. 41) lie among the large cluster of poems at the left. Another by Rochester (no. 45) lies among the poems at the right. In the middle of the whole group, ranging across from no. 52 to no. 65, the sixteen prose specimens form a slightly disordered but unbroken sequence. Even in domain 2, so it appears, strong differences of genre can smother authorial resemblance.

There is matter here for a searching, full-scale inquiry. Even a cursory study of the word-counts, however, is suggestive. The following examples are grounded on comparisons among the word-counts for four groups of texts: the 40 poems of table 23.1; the 25 authorial sets that make up our main database of seventeenth-century verse; a large database of first-person narratives by 55 writers of prose fiction born between 1660 and 1860, the subject of the next main section of this chapter; and the ten sets of personal letters of table 23.3. From an examination of these four large groups, I pick out the more striking contrasts between verse and prose and offer some small inferences.

Among the connectives, verse scores higher than prose for *or* and *nor*, the twin staples of many an antithesis, and for the preposition *like*, the prelude to simile. Verse scores higher for four of the five main relative pronouns, the exception being *which*. The embedded clauses customarily introduced by *which* (at least in British writing) may be less congenial to the flow of verse rhythms than the corresponding appended clauses. A number of monosyllabic connectives and semi-connectives may serve the metrical needs of many poets while offering the strong rhetorical pointing of Restoration verse argument. They include *what, yet, now, such, too, still, while, whilst,* and *thus.* Verse also runs to high scores in some absolute forms like *all* and *no.*

The prose set employed in these comparisons is too heterogeneous to yield examples of much interest. But it is certainly worth noting that some of our poets abandon some of their most pronounced verse habits when they turn to prose. Congreve and Swift stand out among the poets in their frequent recourse to *thus* and *never* respectively. In Congreve's prose drama and Swift's letters, their scores fall right away. Other poets, like Katherine Phillips ("Orinda"), maintain much the same stylistic repertoire through thick and thin. *On/upon* is a strong verse/prose discriminator, possibly because *on* has greater metrical versatility. Of the few poets much given to *upon,* Samuel Butler is celebrated not for a tin ear but for his mastery of offbeat rhymes and rhythms. In general, however, it seems that metrical necessities, rhetorical patterning, and a comparative dearth of circumstantial detail are among the factors that induce writers to assume rather different habits of connection and emphasis when they turn from verse to prose.

While the separation of domain 1 and domain 2 is obviously worth maintaining and deserves further investigation, it is not a Berlin wall but only an analytical convenience. The vigorous traffic in both directions represents an intermingling of stylistic forces. As a valuable sidelight in a study of doubtful authorship (Forsyth et al. 1999: 395–6), the writers make the point that an unduly ambitious analysis can collapse under its own weight. While something of that kind occurs in figure 23.8, the outcome is not unintelligible. It is rather that some real authorial affinities are obscured when such extreme differences of genre supervene.

Classification of Authorial Groups

Genre and authorship are not the only powerful stylistic differentiae. A suitable choice of specimens allows other effects to be observed. Let us turn, for this purpose, to another large database. In its current state, it runs to 1.8 million words and consists entirely of first-person, retrospective narratives from works of prose fiction by 100 authors. The earliest born of the authors is Daniel Defoe (1660) and the latest is Louise Erdrich (1954). The later sets comprise American and Australian as well as British writings. Some 48 of the authors are female. The authorial sets range in length from 4,000 to almost 76,000 words and each includes at least three narratives. The small sets are included, perforce, in order to represent some authors of particular interest like Louisa Atkinson, who is accepted as the earliest native-born Australian writer. With a threshold of 4,000 words, however, the differences of size among the sets show no apparent effects. (The e-texts were created by keyboard from standard editions and from the admirable facsimiles of early British fiction published by the Garland Press, New York. Permission was obtained where necessary and the texts were used only for the extraction of word-counts.)

Earlier versions of this database have been used for a study of change over time (Burrows 1992) and a pilot study of national differences in the English of literary narrative (Burrows 1996). The former takes its place beside Cluett (1976) and other, more linguistically oriented work like Biber and Finegan (1989). The latter, unfortunately, still stands alone.

On the present occasion, developing work I presented at ACH/ALLC 1993 but have never published, the database will be used to examine possible differences between male and female writers. To this end, for reasons that will emerge, the database is divided between 55 authors born before 1860 and 45 born afterwards. The former subset includes 26 female writers, the latter 22. As tables 23.4 and 23.5 indicate, the female writers are placed first in each subset. (Most of the information offered in those tables speaks for itself. It should be noted, however, that, where a writer is given two nationalities, his or her "less influential" country of abode is shown in parentheses.)

Distribution tests like Student's *t*-test and the Mann-Whitney test are among the most appropriate procedures for assessing possible differences, over a range of many variables, between any two large sets of specimens. In both tests, the underlying assumption – the null hypothesis – is that the sets do *not* represent distinct populations. For each variable in turn, therefore, the results show the likelihood that the assumption is false. This likelihood, expressed as a degree of probability, takes the form of a decimal fraction like 0.05 or 0.005. The smaller this fraction, the more likely it is that the assumption is false. When the tests are conducted with many variables, they must be expected to yield some chance successes: around one result in twenty should be above 0.05; around one in a hundred should be above 0.01, and so on. With our 150 variables, therefore, we need many more than seven results from levels below 0.05, or many more than two from below 0.01 before we can begin to accept that there are systematic differences between our male and female writers, that they do indeed represent different populations. (We must also stiffen our stated requirement to allow for the fact that the "two-tailed" form of these tests, as used here, doubles the probability of a chance success.) To make the requirement still more rigorous, I have chosen, finally, to ignore results that do not satisfy *both* of the distribution tests at levels below 0.05.

As table 23.6 indicates, there is no need to quibble about borderline cases. In the upper part of the table, labeled (a), the results for our 55 earlier-born authors include no fewer than 32 out of 150 where the probabilities fall below 0.05. Almost all of them, in fact, fall far below that threshold. In the lower part of the table, labeled (b), the results for our 45 later-born authors lie well within the realm of chance, with only six words yielding probabilities from below the 0.05 threshold. Taken together, the two sets of results indicate that, in our earlier but not our later set, the male and female authors represent different populations. Whereas men and women used to write very differently from each other, they have long since ceased to do so.

In table 23.6, the columns headed "*t*-score" and "DF" represent a different way of expressing the same probabilities from those shown in the column headed "*t*-prob." (The discriminatory power of *t*-scores is established by consulting an appropriate manual of statistical tables.) My reason for including the *t*-scores here is that they distinguish between positives and negatives. The positive scores are always those of the first set entered – in this case, the set of female authors.

The contrasting scores for such referential markers as *I/me/she/her* and, on the other hand, *the/a* point to a straightforward opposition between more and less personally oriented rhetorical stances among the two sets of earlier-born writers. The absence of any masculine pronouns makes this opposition a little more complex; and the opposed

Table 23.4 Fifty-five authors born before 1860 (female authors listed first)

#	Author	Dates	Country	Number
1	Atkinson, Louisa	1834–72	A	4005
2	Austen, Jane	1775–1817	UK	8889
3	Braddon, Mary	1837–1915	UK	8269
4	Brontë, Anne	1820–49	UK	22640
5	Brontë, Charlotte	1816–55	UK	15644
6	Brontë, Emily	1818–48	UK	15743
7	Cambridge, Ada	1844–1926	UK(A)	12266
8	Edgeworth, Maria	1767–1849	UK	29330
9	"Eliot, George"	1819–80	UK	22686
10	Fielding, Sarah	1710–68	UK	75982
11	Freeman, Mary W.	1852–1930	US	6084
12	Gaskell, Elizabeth	1810–65	UK	51989
13	Hamilton, Elizabeth	1758–1816	UK	16922
14	Haywood, Eliza	1693?–1756	UK	28633
15	Hearne, Mary	fl. 1718	UK	12815
16	Jewett, Sarah O.	1849–1909	US	5985
17	Lennox, Charlotte	1720–1804	(US)UK	12995
18	Manley, Mary	1663–1724	UK	15727
19	Praed, Rosa	1851–1935	(A)UK	9147
20	Radcliffe, Ann	1764–1823	UK	12066
21	Robinson, Mary	1758–1800	UK	10891
22	Scott, Sarah	1723–95	UK	15316
23	Shelley, Mary	1797–1851	UK	35806
24	Smith, Charlotte	1749–1806	UK	28695
25	Spence, Catherine	1825–1910	(UK)A	11538
26	Stowe, Harriet B.	1811–96	US	10965
27	Bage, Robert	1728–1801	UK	13969
28	Becke, Louis	1855–1913	A	9641
29	Bierce, Ambrose	1842–1914?	US	7745
30	"Boldrewood, Rolf"	1826–1915	UK(A)	17722
31	Brockden Brown, C.	1771–1810	US	15923
32	Clarke, Marcus	1846–81	UK(A)	13342
33	Cleland, John	1709–89	UK	12995
34	Cooper, James F.	1789–1851	US	5760
35	Collins, Wilkie	1824–89	UK	61539
36	Defoe, Daniel	1660–1731	UK	35317
37	Dickens, Charles	1812–70	UK	8519
38	Favenc, Ernest	1845–1908	UK(A)	4762
39	Fielding, Henry	1707–54	UK	75532
40	Furphy, Joseph	1843–1912	A	15532
41	Godwin, William	1756–1836	UK	28814
42	Graves, Richard	1715–1804	UK	23685
43	Hardy, Thomas	1840–1928	UK	12867
44	Hawthorne, Nath'l	1804–64	US	18154
45	Holcroft, Thomas	1745–1809	UK	19628
46	James, Henry	1843–1916	US	33244
47	Johnson, Samuel	1709–84	UK	16943
48	Maturin, C. R.	1782–1824	UK	16581
49	Melville, Herman	1819–91	US	21084
50	Poe, Edgar A.	c1809–49	US	10930
51	Richardson, Samuel	1689–1761	UK	18615
52	Scott, Walter	1771–1832	UK	29156
53	Smollett, Tobias	1721–71	UK	31746
54	Stockton, Frank R.	1834–1902	US	13321
55	"Mark Twain"	1835–1910	US	10142

Table 23.5 Forty-five authors born after 1860 (female authors listed first)

No.	Author	Dates	Country	Count
1	Anderson, Jessica	1920?–99	A	12825
2	Bedford, Jean	1946–	(UK(A)	6463
3	Bowen, Elizabeth	1899–1973	UK	11071
4	Carter, Angela	1940–92	UK	15642
5	Cather, Willa	1873–1947	US	12051
6	Erdrich, Louise	1954–	US	19565
7	Franklin, Miles	1879–1954	A(UK)	16712
8	Gardam, Jane	1928–	UK	10470
9	Grenville, Kate	1950–	A	14482
10	Hazzard, Shirley	1931–	A(US)	10359
11	Hospital, Janette T.	1940?–	A(US/Can.)	5700
12	Jolley, Elizabeth	1923–	UK(A)	12533
13	Jong, Erica	1942–	US	13545
14	Langley, Eve	1908–1974	A	13345
15	Lurie, Alison	1926–	US	14287
16	Mansfield, Katherine	1888–1923	NZ(UK)	10827
17	Murdoch, Iris	1919–99	UK	21437
18	Park, Ruth	1923?–	NZ(A)	6755
19	Stead, Christina	1902–83	A(UK)	10442
20	Tennant, Kylie	1912–88	A	7112
21	Wharton, Edith	1862–1937	US	19269
22	Wright, Judith	1915–2000	A	10012
23	Barth, John	1930–	US	12836
24	Bellow, Saul	1915–	US	20342
25	Boothby, Guy	1867–1905	(A)UK	13182
26	Boyd, William	1952–	UK	9871
27	Carey, Peter	1943–	A	24708
28	Cary, Joyce	1888–1957	UK	9936
29	Cowan, Peter	1914–	A	13221
30	Doctorow, E. L.	1931–	US	18701
31	Faulkner, William	1897–1962	US	21471
32	Fowles, John	1926–	UK	30394
33	Greene, Graham	1904–91	A	9184
34	Hemingway, Ernest	1899–1961	US	14202
35	Johnston, George	1912–70	A	24729
36	Joyce, James	1882–1941	UK	6531
37	Lawson, Henry	1867–1922	A	16056
38	Lodge, David	1935–	UK	8465
39	Malouf, David	1934–	A	12261
40	McEwan, Ian	1948–	UK	18919
41	Palmer, Vance	1885–1959	A	13256
42	Porter, Hal	1911–84	A	14274
43	Sargeson, Frank	1903–82	NZ	10869
44	Waugh, Evelyn	1903–66	UK	11380
45	Wells, H. G.	1866–1946	UK	50612

Table 23.6   *One hundred authors: significant differentiations among the 150 most common words*

	Rk. Word	t-score	DF	t-prob.	MW-prob.
(a) 55 authors born before 1860: 26 women vs. 29 men					
1	1 the	−5.18	52	0.0000	0.0000
2	3 I	3.40	52	0.0013	0.0038
3	4 of	−3.50	51	0.0010	0.0020
4	5 a	−2.79	52	0.0073	0.0088
5	6 was	2.69	49	0.0097	0.0112
6	7 to (inf.)	3.33	52	0.0016	0.0023
7	8 in (p.)	−3.44	49	0.0012	0.0036
8	14 her	3.03	52	0.0038	0.0021
9	15 me	3.55	48	0.0009	0.0019
10	18 not	2.91	44	0.0057	0.0068
11	20 she	4.69	52	0.0000	0.0000
12	21 but	3.30	43	0.0020	0.0020
13	35 which (rp)	−2.38	52	0.0210	0.0358
14	36 would	2.89	52	0.0057	0.0065
15	38 this	−2.48	52	0.0160	0.0244
16	41 could	2.67	50	0.0100	0.0149
17	45 or	−2.55	52	0.0140	0.0187
18	46 one	−2.09	52	0.0420	0.0330
19	52 did	3.04	37	0.0043	0.0029
20	54 what	3.37	39	0.0017	0.0007
21	73 never	2.88	35	0.0068	0.0224
22	75 man	−2.10	52	0.0410	0.0278
23	82 thought	3.03	49	0.0039	0.0018
24	83 do	3.35	32	0.0021	0.0033
25	99 two	−3.36	33	0.0020	0.0006
26	101 how	3.76	46	0.0005	0.0012
27	108 know	4.57	29	0.0001	0.0002
28	115 mother	2.04	44	0.0470	0.0065
29	122 told	2.58	41	0.0140	0.0123
30	141 think	3.36	32	0.0021	0.0038
31	142 go	2.87	47	0.0062	0.0045
32	149 these	−3.75	46	0.0005	0.0002
(b) 45 authors born after 1860: 22 women vs. 23 men					
1	6 was	−2.37	39	0.0230	0.0377
2	59 so (av. deg.)	3.48	41	0.0012	0.0015
3	62 time	−2.52	41	0.0160	0.0188
4	72 like (p)	2.61	35	0.0130	0.0114
5	75 man	−3.26	31	0.0027	0.0017
6	81 before	−2.59	42	0.0130	0.0121

Abbreviations:

Rk. = rank ex 150

DF = degrees of freedom

t-prob and MW-prob. = probability as assessed on Student's *t*-test and Mann–Whitney test respectively

inf. = infinitive particle

p = preposition

rp = relative pronoun

av. deg. = adverb of degree.

scores (albeit weak) for *mother* and *man* add to that effect. Female authors, it seems, had more to say of females: both male and female authors had much to say of males. For the substance of what they said, of course, one turns, with pleasure, to the texts themselves.

Among the clausal connectives, *but*, *what*, and *how*, words often introducing an exclamatory note, are favored by the female writers. The auxiliary verbs *did* and *do* are often used for emphasis. These all stand, perhaps, with *not*, *never*, *could*, and *would* in signifying that the present indicative is not quite as these writers might wish and that a certain insistence is thought necessary if their voices are to be heard. The infinitive particle *to* (the marker of compound verbs) and the verbs *thought*, *think*, *know*, and *told* are also favored by the female writers. The point to observe here is that these words have less to do with mental activities as such than with overt reference to those activities: "I thought that . . . ," " . . . , I think, . . . ," " . . . , you know, . . . " and "as I told you/him/her" are typical specimens. Their presence posits a distance between speaker and deed.

Among the smaller group of words favored by the male writers, the association of *the/a* with *of/in* and *this/these* and even, perhaps, with *one/two* suggests an emphasis on things and ideas rather than persons. But, as markers of a firmly marshaled, somewhat artificial syntax, *which/or* may reveal more than any of the phenomena so far mentioned about the most remarkable aspect of table 23.6.

If a body of statistically significant differences between male and female writers can disappear completely over a generation or two, as these results suggest, the explanation should not be sought in biological differences between the sexes. But if differences in "gender," expressed in the little manifestations of male and female social roles touched on above, were the whole explanation, it is unlikely that the alteration would be so nearly absolute. Irrespective of one's personal standpoint, it is hard to claim that the social roles of men and women in English-speaking societies can no longer be distinguished.

Figure 23.9, the last of my cluster analyses, throws a clear light on these questions. The 55 entries for the authors born before 1860 fall, chiefly by gender, into two large groups. Six of the 29 men are located among the women. Five of the 26 women are located among the men. Of these five women, all but one are known to have been educated as if they were boys. Of these six men, all but one are known to have grown up without benefit of the classical education offered in British grammar schools. (The other two are Charlotte Lennox, who was certainly well enough educated to publish her translations from the French, and Thomas Alexander Brown – "Rolf Boldrewood" – who was born in Britain but came young to Australia.) The idea that a British classical education exerted a powerful influence on the way boys wrote while most girls continued to write something more like spoken English can be endorsed by making a similar analysis of an even earlier subgroup – those of our British writers who were born before 1800. The division between male and female is even more pronounced, but Richardson, Defoe, and Charlotte Lennox continue as exceptions. It seems clear, in short, that we began to write more like each other when we began to go to school together. And the very notion that a general difference between males and females was evident is transmuted

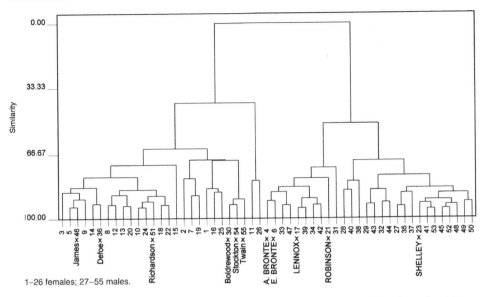

Figure 23.9 Fifty-five "hostorians" born before 1860: cluster analysis based on the thirty-two most common gender-discriminating words of the database

into the more plausible idea that our education deeply affects the way we use our language.

Reflections

In its traditional forms, textual analysis has to do with separating, distinguishing, and the like and it usually treats of single works. This sort of literary analysis often rests upon seemingly intuitive insights and discriminations, processes that may seem remote from the gathering and combining and classifying on which I have concentrated and in which computational stylistics is usually engaged. But those insights and discriminations are not ultimately intuitive because they draw, albeit covertly, upon data gathered in a lifetime's reading, stored away in a subconscious memory bank, and put to use, as Samuel Johnson reminds us, through processes of comparison and classification, whether tacit or overt.

When I. A. Richards opened *Principles of Literary Criticism* (1924) by saying that "A book is a machine to think with," he foreshadowed an attack upon what he regarded as the undue aestheticizing of literary criticism. So far as it bears upon books themselves, his remark gains new force from recent changes in the technology of texts. Although my own chief premise may also offend some old-fashioned litterateurs, that is not my motive. In proposing that literary criticism and analysis are always grounded in the inductive processes of classification and differentiation, I wish to emphasize the links between the old stylistics and the new. The close readers and analysts of former years and their present counterparts, who draw upon computational methods for their textual analyses, should actually be close allies.

Traditional and computational forms of textual analysis do have their distinct strengths. The parallels between the two plots of *King Lear* or the subtleties discerned by Coleridge in the opening lines of *Hamlet* lie as far beyond the reach of a computer as the ironies offered by Jane Austen or the ambiguities detected by William Empson. But computers obviously surpass our unassisted powers in managing large textual corpora, singling out unique forms or gathering all the instances of common ones.

Within the realm of English studies, statistical work on single authors has usually been focused on comparisons of different texts. There are a few such studies at book length, treating respectively of Swift, Jane Austen, and Milton (Milic 1967; Burrows 1987; Corns 1990). For exemplary studies of authorial development at article length, see Brainerd (1980), Craig (1999), and Forsyth (1999). Among those studies of single texts in which literary and statistical analysis are associated, there is notable work on Blake's *The Four Zoas* (Ide 1989) and Joyce's *Ulysses* (McKenna and Antonia 2001). In both instances, the argument relies upon internal comparisons between different facets of these large and complex texts.

But the vast textual archives now available offer rich opportunities for the study of single texts in a manner that has never before been feasible. (For a brief illustration of this approach, see Burrows 2002b: 693–6.) The database of late seventeenth-century verse used at the beginning of the present chapter yields well-founded scores for as many common words as anyone might wish. Norms derived from the database make it easy to study the vocabulary of any poet of the day. We are now able, however, to take a further step. The corresponding scores for any poem of adequate length can be compared not only with those same norms but also with the author's overall scores. It is therefore possible to establish that, in certain demonstrable respects, *Absalom and Achitophel* or *Upon Appleton House* is characteristic either of its author or of some specified group – male poets, say, or satirists – but that, in others, it departs from his usual practice or from theirs. At this point, I suggest, the evidence flowing from statistical comparison is more nearly complementary to the evidence offered by the traditional literary analyst than it has ever been. With due allowance for the felt needs and all the mordant joys of a continuing sibling rivalry, dare we hope to go forward hand in hand?

APPENDIX

In our main dataset, from which the list of the 150 most common words derives, the present corpus of 540,244 words ranges widely across the work of the following 25 poets: Aphra Behn (1640–89) 21,705 words; Alexander Brome (1620–66) 29,539; Samuel Butler (1612–80) 30,932; William Congreve (1670–1729) 30,917; Charles Cotton (1630–87) 12,625; Abraham Cowley (1618–67) 19,272; Sir John Denham (1615–69) 30,092; Charles Sackville, Earl of Dorset (1638–1706) 9,586; John Dryden (1631–1700) 18,238; Thomas D'Urfey (1653–1723), 18,757; Robert Gould (1660?–1709?) 29,110; Andrew Marvell (1621–78) 23,282; John Milton (1608–74) 18,924; John Oldham (1653–83) 32,462; Katherine Phillips (1631–64) 29,004 ; Matthew Prior (1664–1721) 32,000; Alexander Radcliffe (*floruit* 1669–96) 11,889; John Wilmot, Earl of Rochester (1648–80) 12,725; Sir Charles Sedley (1639?–1701) 10,304; Elkanah Settle (1648–1724)

24,080; Thomas Shadwell (1642?–92) 14,540; Jonathan Swift (1667–1745) 30,974; Nahum Tate (1652–1715) 20,333; Edmund Waller (1606–87) 16,443; Anne Wharton (1659–85) 12,511. Most of the corpus was prepared by John Burrows and Harold Love, assisted by Alexis Antonia and Meredith Sherlock. The Marvell subset was contributed by Christopher Wortham, assisted by Joanna Thompson.

REFERENCES

NB. For a broader framework than the present argument requires, see the reference list in Burrows (2003).

Biber, Douglas and Edward Finegan (1989). Drift and the Evolution of English Style: A History of Three Genres. *Language* 65: 487–517.

Brainerd, B. (1980). The Chronology of Shakespeare's Plays: A Statistical Study. *Computers and the Humanities* 14: 221–30.

Bratley, Paul and Donald Ross, Jr (1981). Syllabic Spectra. *ALLC Journal* 2: 41–50.

Burrows, J. F. (1987). *Computation into Criticism: A Study of Jane Austen's Novels and an Experiment in Method.* Oxford: Clarendon Press.

——(1992). Computers and the Study of Literature. In C. S. Butler (ed.), *Computers and Written Texts* (pp. 167–204). Oxford: Blackwell.

——(1996). Tiptoeing into the Infinite: Testing for Evidence of National Differences in the Language of English Narrative. In N. Ide and S. Hockey (eds.), *Research in Humanities Computing* 4 (pp. 1–33). Oxford: Clarendon Press.

——(2002a). "Delta": a Measure of Stylistic Difference and a Guide to Likely Authorship. *Literary and Linguistic Computing* 17: 267–86.

——(2002b). The Englishing of Juvenal: Computational Stylistics and Translated Texts. *Style* 36: 677–94.

——(2003). Questions of Authorship: Attribution and Beyond. *Computers and the Humanities* 37: 1–26.

Cluett, Robert (1976). *Prose Style and Critical Reading.* New York: Teachers College Press.

Corns, Thomas N. (1990). *The Development of Milton's Prose Style.* London: Oxford University Press.

Craig, Hugh (1999). Contrast and Change in the Idiolects of Ben Jonson Characters. *Computers and the Humanities* 33: 221–40.

Eliot, T. S. (1932). For Lancelot Andrewes. In *Selected Essays.* London: Faber.

Forsyth, R. S. (1999). Stylochronometry with Substrings, or: a Poet Young and Old. *Literary and Linguistic Computing* 14: 467–77.

Forsyth, Richard S., David I. Holmes, and Emily K. Tse (1999). Cicero, Sigonio, and Burrows: Investigating the Authenticity of the *Consolatio. Literary and Linguistic Computing* 14: 375–400.

Halsband, Robert (ed.) (1970). *The Selected Letters of Lady Mary Wortley Montagu.* London: Longman.

Hoover, David (2002). Frequent Word Sequences and Statistical Stylistics. *Literary and Linguistic Computing* 17: 157–80.

Ide, Nancy M. (1989). Meaning and Method: Computer-assisted Analysis of Blake. In Rosanne G. Potter (ed.), *Literary Computing and Literary Criticism.* Philadelphia: University of Pennsylvania Press.

McKenna, C. W. F. and Alexis Antonia (2001). The Statistical Analysis of Style: Reflections on Form, Meaning, and Ideology in the "Nausicaa" Episode of *Ulysses. Literary and Linguistic Computing* 16: 353–74.

Milic, Louis T. (1967). *A Quantitative Approach to the Style of Jonathan Swift.* Paris: Mouton.

Richards, I. A. (1924). *Principles of Literary Criticism.* London: Routledge.

Sutherland, James (1969). *English Literature of the Late Seventeenth Century.* Oxford: Clarendon Press.

24

Thematic Research Collections

Carole L. Palmer

Introduction

The analogy of the library as the laboratory of the humanities has always been an exaggeration. For most humanities scholars, it has been rare to find the necessary materials for a research project amassed in one place, as they are in a laboratory setting. Thematic research collections are digital resources that come closer to this ideal. Where in the past scholars produced documents from source material held in the collections of libraries, archives, and museums, they are now producing specialized scholarly resources that constitute research collections. Scholars have recognized that information technologies open up new possibilities for re-creating the basic resources of research and that computing tools can advance and transform work with those resources (Unsworth 1996). Thematic research collections are evolving as a new genre of scholarly production in response to these opportunities. They are digital aggregations of primary sources and related materials that support research on a theme.

Thematic research collections are being developed in tandem with the continuing collection development efforts of libraries, archives, and museums. These institutions have long served as storehouses and workrooms for research and study in the humanities by collecting and making accessible large bodies of diverse material in many subject areas. Thousands of extensive, specialized research collections have been established, but they are often far removed from the scholars and students who wish to work with them. In recent years, many institutions have begun to digitally reformat selected collections and make them more widely available on the Web for use by researchers, students, and the general public.

Humanities scholars are participating in this movement, bringing their subject expertise and acumen to the collection development process. In taking a thematic approach to aggregating digital research materials, they are producing circumscribed collections, customized for intensive study and analysis in a specific research area. In many cases these digital resources serve as a place, much like a virtual laboratory, where specialized source material, tools, and expertise come together to aid in the process of scholarly work and the production of new knowledge.

This chapter is focused primarily on the thematic research collections created by scholars. The history and proliferation of the new genre cannot be examined in full within the limits of the chapter. Instead, this essay will identify characteristics of the genre and clarify its relationship to the collection development activities that have traditionally taken place in research libraries. This relationship is central to understanding how our stores of research materials will evolve in the digital realm, since thematic research collections are derived from and will ultimately contribute to the larger institution-based collections. The thematic collections used as examples throughout the chapter have been selected to illustrate specific features and trends but do not fully represent the variety of collections produced or under development. Although there are numerous collections available for purchase or through licensing agreements, all the examples identified here were available free on the Web as of October 2002.

Characteristics of the Genre

There are no firm parameters for defining thematic research collections (hereafter referred to as thematic collections), but there are characteristics that are generally attributable to the genre. John Unsworth (2000b) describes thematic collections as being:

electronic
heterogeneous datatypes
extensive but thematically coherent
structured but open-ended
designed to support research
authored or multi-authored
interdisciplinary
collections of digital primary resources

These characteristics are common to the projects developed at the Institute for Advanced Technology in the Humanities (IATH), the research and development center at the University of Virginia, previously directed by Unsworth. They are also broadly applicable to many of the research collections being developed elsewhere by scholars, librarians, and collaborative teams. With thematic collections, however, there is considerable synergy among these characteristics, and as the genre grows and matures additional characteristics are emerging that differentiate it from other types of digital resources.

Table 24.1 reworks Unsworth's list of descriptors, separating content and function aspects of the collections and adding emerging features of the genre. The first tier of features contains basic elements that are generally shared by thematic collections. In terms of content, they are all digital in format and thematic in scope. In terms of function, they are all intentionally designed to support research. The next tier of features further defines the makeup and role of thematic collections, and together they reflect the unique contribution this type of digital resource is making to research in the humanities. Unlike the basic elements, these characteristics are highly variable. They are not represented in all thematic collections, and the degree to which any one is present in a given collection is varied. Collections differ in the range and depth of content and the types of functions provided. The basic elements and all the content features, outlined below, are closely aligned with Unsworth's description. The emergent function features are explicated more fully in sections that follow.

Thematic collections are *digital* in format. While the sources may also exist as printed texts, manuscripts, photographs, paintings, film, or other artifacts, the value of a thematic collection lies in the effectiveness of the digital medium for supporting research with the materials. For example, through advances in information technology, creators of *The William Blake Archive* have been able to produce images that are more accurate in color, detail, and scale than commercially printed reproductions, and texts more faithful to the author's originals than existing printed editions (Viscomi 2002).

The contents are *thematic* or focused on a research theme. For example, a number of the IATH collections are constructed around author-based themes, including *The Complete Writings and Pictures of Dante Gabriel Rossetti: A Hypermedia Research Archive*, *The Dickinson Electronic Archives*, and *The Walt Whitman Archive*. Collections can also be developed around a literary or artistic work, such as *Uncle Tom's Cabin and American Culture*. A collection called *Hamlet on the Ramparts*, designed and maintained by the MIT Shakespeare Project, is a good example of a collection based on a narrowly defined literary theme. That project aims to bring together texts, artwork, photographs, films, sound recordings, and commentary related to a very specific literary entity, Hamlet's first encounter with the ghost. A collection theme can be an event, place, phenomenon, or any other object of study. Interesting examples outside of literary studies include the *Salem Witch Trials*, *Pompeii Forum*, and the *Waters of Rome* projects. Some thematic collections are embedded in larger digital resources. One example is the *Wilfred Owen Multimedia Digital Archive*, a core content area in the *Virtual Seminars for Teaching Literature*, a pedagogical resource developed at Oxford University.

Like traditional library collections in the humanities, thematic collections have been built for *research support*, but the new genre is producing more specialized microcosms of

Table 24.1   *Features of thematic research collections*

Content	Function
Basic elements	
Digital	Research support
Thematic	
Variable characteristics	
Coherent	Scholarly contribution
Heterogeneous	Contextual mass
Structured	Interdisciplinary platform
Open-ended	Activity support

materials that are tightly aligned with specific research interests and that aid in specific research processes. Some thematic collections have been designed as new virtual environments for scholarly work. For example, *Digital Dante*, a project produced at the Institute for Learning Technologies at Columbia University, has been conceived as a "place" for study and learning and a "means" of scholarly production.

The thematic framework allows for *coherent* aggregation of content. All the materials included assist in research and study on the theme. This coherence is generally anchored by a core set of primary sources. The capabilities of networked, digital technology make it possible to bring together extensive corpuses of primary materials and to combine those with any number of related works. Thus the content is *heterogeneous* in the mix of primary, secondary, and tertiary materials provided, which might include manuscripts, letters, critical essays, reviews, biographies, bibliographies, etc., but the materials also tend to be multimedia. The digital environment provides the means to integrate many different kinds of objects into a collection. In literary studies collections, multiple versions of a given text are commonly made available to aid in comparative analysis, along with additional types of media such as maps, illustrations, and recorded music. For example, *Uncle Tom's Cabin and American Culture* contains different editions of the primary text along with poems, images, films, and songs that show the context and history surrounding the primary work (Condron et al. 2001).

The individual items in a collection are *structured* to permit search and analysis, with most projects in the humanities adopting SGML-based markup formats. Many aspects of a source may be coded, including bibliographic information, physical features, and substantive content, to produce highly flexible and searchable digital materials. The collection as a whole is further organized into interrelated groups of materials for display and to assist in retrieval. Libraries, archives, and museums have conventions for structuring and representing collections, which include systems and guidelines for applying metadata, classification schemes, and descriptors. Some of these methods are being applied in thematic collections, but scholars are also designing new approaches and developing new standards, such as the TEI (Text Encoding Initiative) markup language for tagging scholarly material, that are more attuned with scholarly practices. As a result, there is not yet uniformity in the methods used for structuring data in digital collections, but there are ongoing efforts to align standards and a growing awareness by collection developers of the value of developing interoperable systems.

Collections of all kinds can be *open-ended*, in that they have the potential to grow and change depending on commitment of resources from collectors. Most thematic collections are not static. Scholars add to and improve the content, and work on any given collection could continue over generations. Moreover, individual items in a collection can also evolve because of the inherent flexibility (and vulnerability) of "born digital" and transcribed documents. The dynamic nature of collections raises critical questions about how they will be maintained and preserved as they evolve over time.

Scholarly Contribution

While thematic collections support both research and pedagogy, the scholarly contribution that results from the creation and use of the resources is what qualifies them as a scholarly genre. When electronic sources are brought together for scholarly purposes they become a new, second-generation electronic resource (Unsworth 2000b). Scholars are not only constructing environments where more people can do research more conveniently, they are also creating new research. Like other scholarship in the humanities, research takes place in the production of the resource, and research is advanced as a result of it. Thus, scholarship is embedded in the product and its use. And like research generated in the fields of engineering, computer science, and information science, some of the research contribution lies in the technical design, functionality, and innovation that makes new kinds of research possible.

Authorship is included in Unsworth's description of thematic collections, but the term does not fully capture the nature of the work involved in developing thematic collections. A collection is not always attributable to one author or even a few co-authors, and the process of production may not generate new, original content. Some of the technical work involved in creating a collection requires expertise outside that of a typical author in the humanities. Literary scholars who are assembling electronic texts and archives of multimedia objects have become "literary-encoders" and "literary-librarians" (Schreibman 2002). Moreover, as noted above, thematic collections are inherently open-ended and therefore can be added to and altered in dramatic ways over time by new participants in the process. After a collection has been established for some time, it may not be accurate to continue to assign complete authorship to the originator, and it may prove complicated to trace authorial responsibility as it evolves over years or even decades.

In many ways collection work resembles that of an editor, but the activities of curators, archivists, and compilers are also applicable. But the concept of author is useful in its ability to relate the significance of the purposeful organization of information. As Atkinson notes in reference to professional collection developers in research libraries, since "every text is to some extent a compilation of previous texts, then the collection is a kind of text – and the building of the collection is a kind of authorship" (1998: 19). Nonetheless, "creator" seems best for encapsulating the range of work involved in the development of thematic collections. The term "creator" has become common in standard schemes for describing electronic resources, such as the Dublin Core metadata element set, and it accommodates the technical, intellectual, and creative aspects of the digital collection development process. Academic subject expertise is considered critical in the development of quality, scholarly digital resources (Crane and Rydberg-Cox 2000), and technical computing knowledge of text, image, audio and video standards, and applications is equally important. Thus, the creators of scholarly collections will need to be a new kind of scholar, or team, with a distinct mix of expertise in at least three areas – the specific subject matter and associated critical and analytical techniques, technical computing processes, and principles of content selection and organization.

Contextual Mass

The creators of thematic collections are constructing research environments with contextual mass, a proposed principle for digital collection development that prioritizes the values and work practices of scholarly communities (Palmer 2000). The premise behind the principle is that rather than striving for a critical mass of content, digital research libraries should be systematically collecting sources and developing tools that work together to provide a supportive context for the research process. For libraries, this approach to collection development requires analysis of the materials and activities involved in the practices of the different research communities served (Brockman et al. 2001). Researchers are able to more readily construct contextual mass for themselves through highly purposeful selection and organization of content directly related to their specialized areas of research.

All collections are built through the process of privileging some materials over others (Buckland 1995), and the construction of contextual mass takes place through careful, purposeful privileging. Because of the specific scope and aims of thematic collections, creators select materials in a highly focused and deliberate manner, creating dense, interrelated collections. By contrast, in both physical and digital libraries, materials are usually separated for reasons unimportant to the scholar. For example, primary texts may be part of an isolated rare book room or special collection, while secondary works are in separate book and journal collections, with indexes, bibliographies, and handbooks kept in reference areas. Moreover, the historical, literary, and cultural treatments of a topic are likely to be further scattered across differentiated classes of subjects. When a person uses a research library collection they are interacting with a context that includes physical, institutional, and intellectual features (Lee 2000). It is a grand and scattered context compared to that of thematic collections, which tend to focus on the physical context of core primary sources and the intellectual context represented in a mix of heterogeneous but closely associated materials.

Collections built on a contextual mass model create a system of interrelated sources where different types of materials and different subjects work together to support deep and multifaceted inquiry in an area of research. Although many of the resources referenced in this chapter contain large, complex cores of primary materials, this is not necessary to achieve contextual mass. For instance, the *Decameron Web* project, a collection devoted to the literary, historical, and cultural context of Boccaccio's famous text, contains an established critical edition with translations and a selection of related materials, such as annotations, commentaries, critical essays, maps, and bibliographies. The pedagogical intent of the site is obvious in its content and layout, but it is simultaneously strong as a research context.

A number of existing thematic collections exemplify the notion of contextual mass in their depth and complexity, as well as in their explicit goals. The core of the Rossetti archive is intended to be all of Rossetti's texts and pictorial works, and this set of primary works is complemented by a corpus of contextual materials that includes other works from the period, family letters, biography, and contemporary secondary materials. In the Blake archive, "contextual" information is at the heart of the scholarly aims of the project. The documentation at the website explains that works of art make sense only in context. In this case creating a meaningful context involves presenting the texts with the illustrations, illuminated books in relation to other illuminated books, and putting those together with other drawings and paintings. All of this work is then presented in the context of relevant historical information.

Collaboration is required in the creation of contextually rich thematic collections. Instead of being a patron of existing collections, scholars must partner with libraries, museums, and publishers to compile diverse materials that are held in different locations.

For example, collections from the Boston Public Library, the New York Public Library, the Massachusetts Historical Society, the Massachusetts Archives, and the Peabody Essex Museum were melded to create the *Salem Witch Trials* collection. The *Dickinson Electronic Archives*, produced by a collective that includes four general editors who work collaboratively with co-editors, staff, and users, has reproduced works housed in library archives all along the northeast corridor of the United States (Smith 1999).

Interdisciplinary Platform

Humanities scholars have long been engaged in interdisciplinary inquiry, but the library collections they have relied on have been developed around academic structures that tend to obscure connections between fields of research. This is partly because of the large scale of research libraries, but also because of the inherent difficulties in maintaining standard organization and access systems for materials that represent a complex base of knowledge. The continuing growth of interdisciplinary research is a recognized challenge to collection development and the provision of information services in research libraries, and recent studies have identified specific practices of interdisciplinary humanities scholars that need to be better supported in the next generation of digital resources (Palmer 1996; Palmer and Neumann 2002). Creators of thematic collections are beginning to address some of these needs through the conscious development of interdisciplinary platforms for research.

A number of collections have been explicitly designed to be conducive to interdisciplinary research and have effectively incorporated the interests of diverse intellectual communities. The *Thomas MacGreevy Archive* aims to promote inquiry into the interconnections between literature, culture, history, and politics by blurring the boundaries that separate the different fields of study. *Monuments and Dust*, a thematic collection focused on Victorian London, states its interdisciplinary intent in the project subtitle: "New Technologies and Sociologies of Research." A stated objective of the project is to foster international collaboration and intellectual exchange among scholars in literature, architecture, painting, journalism, colonialism, modern urban space, and mass culture. The premise is that the aggregation of diverse sources – images, texts, numerical data, maps, and models – will seed intellectual interaction by making it possible to discover new visual, textual, and statistical relationships within the collection and between lines of research.

Activity Support

The functions of thematic collections are being greatly expanded as creators add tools to support research activities. Humanities research processes involve numerous activities, and collections are essential to many of them. Scholarly information seeking is one type of activity that has been studied empirically for some time, and our understanding of it is slowly informing the development of information retrieval systems in the humanities (Bates 1994). Other significant research practices, especially those involved in interpretation and analysis of sources, have received less attention.

Reading is of particular importance in the humanities, and the technologies being developed for collections are beginning to address the complexities of how and why people read texts (Crane et al. 2001). Scanning a text is a different activity from rereading it deeply and repeatedly over time, and it is but one stage of a larger pattern of wide reading and collecting practiced by many humanities scholars (Brockman et al. 2001). Other common scholarly activities, such as the "scholarly primitives" identified by Unsworth (2000a), have yet to be adequately supported by the digital resources designed for scholars. These include the basic activities of annotating, comparing, referring, selecting, linking, and discovering that are continually carried out by scholars as part of the complex processes of reading, searching, and writing. Just as materials can be structured for scholarly purposes as we transform our bodies of texts into digital format, tools can be tailored for specific scholarly tasks.

Searching collection content is a standard function of databases of all kinds, and among thematic collections there is considerable variation in the level of retrieval supported. Image searching has been a vital area of development, since many collections contain a significant number of facsimile images and other pictorial works. In the Blake archive, for instance, access to images is enhanced through extensive description of each image and the application of a controlled vocabulary. Likewise, the Rossetti archive project has been dedicated to developing methods for formally coding features of images to make them amenable to full search and analysis (McGann 1996). Imagesizer, a tool developed at IATH and provided to both the Blake and Rossetti archives, allows the user to view images in their original size or in other convenient dimensions. Inote, another IATH tool configured for the Blake project, allows viewing of illustrations, components of illustrations, and image descriptions. It also allows users to create their own personal annotations along with saved copies of an image. This, in particular, is a key advancement in activity support for collections since it goes beyond searching, viewing, and linking to assist scholars with the basic tasks of interpretation and note-taking, activities that have been largely neglected in digital resource development. Tools to support scholarly tasks are also being developed independent of thematic collection initiatives. For example, the Versioning Machine software designed by the Maryland Institute for Technology in the Humanities (MITH) blends features of the traditional book format with electronic publishing capabilities to enhance scholars' interpretive work with multiple texts.

Hypertext has been a monumental advancement in the functionality of collections, and many current projects are working toward extensive interlinking among aggregated materials. The *Walt Whitman Hypertext Archive* intends to link sources to demonstrate the numerous and complex revisions Whitman made to his poems. The items associated with a poem might include the initial notes and trial lines in a notebook, a published version from a periodical, publisher's page proofs, and various printed book versions. The *Bolles Collection on the History of London*, part of the larger *Perseus* digital library, exploits hypertext by presenting full historical texts on London with hyperlinks from names of towns, buildings, and people to correlate items, such as photographs and maps of places and drawings and biographies of people.

Mapping and modeling tools are valuable features of a number of place-based thematic collections. The *Bolles Collection* provides electronic timelines for visualizing how time is represented within and across documents. Also, historical maps of London have been integrated with a current geographic information system (GIS) to allow users to view the same location across the maps (Crane et al. 2001). Modeling adds an important layer of data to the *Monuments and Dust* collection. A variety of VRML (Virtual Reality Modeling Language) images of the Crystal Palace have been developed from engineering plans and other sources of data to create models of the building and small architectural features such as drains, trusses, and wall panels, as well as animations of the building's lighting and other three-dimensional replicas.

The Humanities Laboratory

The thematic collections concentrating on contextual mass and activity support are coming closest to creating a laboratory environment where the day-to-day work of scholars can be performed. As with scientific laboratories, the most effective places will be those that contain the materials that need to be studied and consulted during the course of an investigation as well as the instrumentation to carry out the actual work. For humanities scholars, a well-equipped laboratory would consist of the sources that would be explored, studied, annotated, and gathered in libraries and archives for an area of research and the means to perform the reading, analyzing, interpreting, and writing that would normally take place in their offices. The most successful of these sites will move beyond the thematic focus to provide contextual mass and activity support that is not only responsive to what scholars currently do, but also to the questions they would like to ask and the activities they would like to be able to undertake.

In the sciences the virtual laboratory, or collaboratory, concept has been around for some time. Traditional laboratories that are physically located encourage interaction and cooperation within teams, and collaboratories extend that dimension of research to distributed groups that may be as small as a work group or as large as an international research community. Collaboratories are designed as media-rich networks that link people to information, facilities, and other people (Finholt 2002). They are places where scientists can obtain resources, do work, interact, share data, results, and other information, and collaborate.

Collaborative processes have not been a significant factor in technology development in the humanities, due at least in part to the prevalent notion that humanities scholars work alone. This is true to some degree. Reading, searching databases, and browsing collections are solitary activities, and most articles and books are written by individuals. However, most humanities scholars do work together in other important ways. They frequently share citations, ideas, drafts of papers, and converse about research in progress, and these interactions are dependent on strong relationships with others in an intellectual community. For most scholars, this type of collaborative activity is a necessary part of the daily practice of research, and it has been shown to be especially vital for interdisciplinary work (Palmer and Neumann 2002).

An increasing number of thematic projects are encouraging scholars to share their research through the submission of content and by providing forums for dialogue among creators and the user community. A few initiatives are aimed at enabling collaboration among scholars, as with the case of *Monuments and Dust*, noted above. In other projects, the corpus brought together is considered a resource to foster collaboration among scholars, students, and lay readers. While it is not a thematic collection *per se, Collate* is a unique resource that provides tools for indexing, annotation, and other types of work with digital resources. This international project has been designed to support the development of collections of digitized historic and cultural materials, but its other primary goal is to demonstrate the viability of the collaboratory in the humanities.

The Process of Collocation

All collections, either physical or virtual, are formed through collocation, the process of bringing together related information (Taylor 1999). Collocation is a useful term because it emphasizes the purpose of collection building and can be applied to the different means used to unite materials. The collocation of research materials can take many forms. Anthologies are collocations of selected works on a subject. In a traditional archive, collocation is based on the originating source – the person or institution – and these collections are acquired and maintained as a whole. Collocation is often associated with physical location, such as when materials by the same author are placed together on shelves in a library. It is not surprising that some thematic collections have adopted the metaphor of physical collocation. For example, the *Decameron Web* describes its collection as a "specialized bookshelf or mini-library" generated from Boccaccio's masterpiece. The *Tibetan and Himalayan Digital Library* describes its collections as the equivalent of the "stacks" in a traditional library. A library catalogue also provides collocation by bringing together like materials through a system of records and references.

To see a substantial portion of the works associated with a particular author or topic, it has been necessary for scholars to consult many catalogues and indexes and travel to different libraries, copying and collecting what they can along the way. In the case of fragile items, handling is limited and photocopying or microfilming may be prohibited. With thematic collections, scholars are now exercising the power of virtual collocation. By pulling together materials that are part of various works and located in repositories at different sites, they collocate deep, sophisticated collections of sources that can be used at a convenient time and place. For example, the directory of the Rossetti archive, which lists pictures, poems, prose, illustrated texts, double works, manuscripts, books, biography, bibliography, chronology, and contexts, illustrates the diversity and richness that can be achieved through the collocation of digital materials.

The physical proximity of resources becomes trivial when the material is digital and made available in a networked information system (Lagoze and Fielding 1998), but the intellectual and technical work of selecting and structuring meaningful groupings of materials remains critical. This is especially true in the humanities, where research often concentrates on the documents and artifacts created by or surrounding an object of study. Compared with other fields of study, the sources used are highly heterogeneous and wide-ranging, and their value persists over time, rather than dissipating through obsolescence. Over the course of a scholar's research project, certain manuscripts or artifacts in foreign archives may be essential, but a standard edition or a popular culture website can be equally important (Palmer and Neumann 2002). The distributed, dynamic research collections that can be created on the Web are attuned with the nature of humanities fields, which are "concerned with the construction of knowledge from sources of different types, scattered across different subject areas" (Fraser 2000: 274).

The principles that guide the collocation of research collections in libraries are different from scholarly motivations for collocation. Library collections are amassed for preservation, dispensing, bibliographic, and symbolic purposes (Buckland 1992). The process of collecting is ruled first by the mission of the institution and more specifically by the selection criteria developed to support research and teaching in a given subject area. In contrast, collections produced by scholars are customized to the research focus of a scholarly community or to the specific interests of the creators. Thus, the "principles of inclusion" for *The William Blake Archive* – that designate the illuminated books as the foundation and the strategy of adding clusters of materials based on medium, theme, or history – are idiosyncratic to that particular project. Schreibman suggests that the Blake archive and other early thematic collections, as well as broader collection initiatives such as the CELT Project and the Women Writers Project, have been governed by a digital library model that collocates "previously published texts based on a theory of collection appropriate to the particular archive" (2002: 287). While a loose theory of collecting may be guiding creators' selection of content, the criteria being used to determine what is appropriate for a collection and the long-term development principles of a project are not always clarified for users of thematic collections.

The potential of digital collocation has been restrained by copyright concerns. It is much less complicated to digitize and redistribute sources that do not have copyright restrictions, and therefore older materials in the public domain have been more widely selected for digital collections of all kinds. Increasingly, thematic collection creators are working through copyright requirements for published works, as well as adding new, born digital sources, to build systematic and principled collections that meet their scholarly aims. Again, *The William Blake Archive* is one of the projects that offer a sound model on this front. They have gained access to valuable and important materials for their collection by working closely with museums, libraries, and collectors to address their copyright concerns.

Research Collections Landscape

Scholarly thematic collections are a new addition to the array of existing and emerging research collocations. Interestingly, many thematic collections created by scholars refer to themselves as *archives*, but conventional archives differ in important ways, especially in terms of their mission and the methods they use to organize materials. The collections held in archival repositories document the life and work of institutions or individuals. An archive's role is to "preserve records of enduring value that document organizational and personal activities accumulated in the course of daily life or work" (Taylor 1999: 8). Archival collections are collocated according to provenance – the individual or corporate originator – and organized in original working order. As accumulations of materials from regular daily life, these collections may contain print and electronic documents and artifacts of any kind, including meeting minutes, annual reports, memoranda, deeds, manuscripts, photographs, letters, diaries, printed books, and audio recordings.

Thematic collections are more analogous to the *subject collections* traditionally developed in research libraries than they are to archives. Examples of research library subject collections include the Chicano Studies collection at the University of California at Berkeley and the Historical Linguistics collection at the Newberry Library in Chicago. A standard directory lists 65,818 library and museum subject collections in the United States and Canada (Ash 1993), many of which are thematic in scope. For example, the entry for William Blake lists 20 collections, two of which are contributors to *The William Blake Archive* project. Subject collections are sometimes developed cooperatively by multiple institutions, and these tend to cover broad academic or geographic categories. Examples include the Urban Studies collection at the Center for Research Libraries, a membership organization devoted to cooperative collection programs, and the East Asian collections cooperatively developed at the University of North Carolina and Duke University.

Localized collections that contain rare or valuable items may be kept as part of a *special collection*. Special collections departments develop concentrated subject and theme-based collections that include substantial primary materials. They are also the place where manuscripts, papers, and other unique, fragile, or valuable items are maintained and segregated for restricted access. As research libraries began to make materials accessible via the Web, the contents of special collections were often the first to be selected for digitization. Research libraries have been eager to share their treasures with a wider audience and make them more convenient to view, and offering a digital alternative decreases handling and the wear and tear on valuable materials. The first digitized special collections released by the Library of Congress in 1994 through their *American Memory* project were photographic collections. The initiative has since grown to offer over 100 online collections, many of which are thematic and multimedia. Most are based on existing special collections within the Library of Congress, but some, such as *Band Music from the Civil War Era* and the *American Variety Stage*, are thematic collections that have been collocated for the first time specifically for online presentation. Many other institutions have selected notable special collections for digitization. For instance, the Academic Affairs Library at the University of North Carolina at Chapel Hill has produced *Documenting the American South*, a digital collection based on their existing Southern Historical Collection, one of the largest stores of Southern manuscripts in the country.

As research libraries continue to undertake these projects, substantial bodies of previously hidden source material are coming into public view. These digital collections make an important contribution to digital research library development and provide potential raw materials for the construction of thematic collections and other aggregations of digital content. Digital special collections provide an important service for researchers, but they generally do not possess the range of scholarly functions – scholarly contribution, contextual mass, interdisciplinary platform, and activity support – provided by many thematic collections.

Digital Collections Terminology

There is little consistency in the terms used to describe digital resources, and the number of terms and the overlap between them seem to be increasing. In addition to being a new conceptualization of research collection development, the phrase "thematic research collection" is itself a new addition to the vocabulary. As discussed above, the term "archive" is being widely applied to thematic collections, and the adoption of the word has merit for this purpose, since, like traditional archives, scholarly thematic collections tend to focus on primary sources and emphasize the importance of the physical object. For example, *The Dickinson Electronic Archives* prioritizes the physical object by representing Emily Dickinson's poems, letters, letter-poems, drafts, fragments, and manuscripts as facsimile images. Likewise, in the *William Blake Archive* the physical nature of the artifacts is a central thrust. The digital collection represents the integration of Blake's illustrations and texts and the variations among different copies of his books, features that have not been well represented in printed editions of his work. As with most thematic collections, the actual goals of the Blake project reach beyond those of a traditional archive, where the central aim would be to preserve the physical record of production. Here the notion of the archive has been extended to include the catalogue, scholarly edition, database, and tools that work together to fully exploit the advantages of the digital medium (Viscomi 2002).

It has been suggested that electronic archives will increasingly take the form of hypertext editions, similar to the *Electronic Variorum Edition of Don Quixote* being developed at the Center for the Study of Digital Libraries at Texas A & M University (Urbina et al. 2002). But, at present, many kinds of resources, including journal article pre-print servers and lists of links on a web page, are being referred to as digital or electronic archives. The traditional, professional archive still holds an important place in the array of research collections, and some of these are being digitally reformatted while retaining their original aims and organizational methods. At the same time, colloquial applications of the term are increasing and new scholarly idealizations of the concept are evolving.

The vocabulary of digital resources has been further complicated by the wide usage of the term "digital library" for all kinds of digital collections, essentially blurring the distinction between collections and libraries. Of the many definitions of digital libraries circulating in the literature, several can be readily applied to thematic collections. However, a widely accepted conception in the field of library and information science clarifies the difference:

> Digital libraries are organizations that provide the resources, including the specialized staff, to select, structure, offer intellectual access to, interpret, distribute, preserve the integrity of, and ensure the persistence over time of collections of digital works so that they are readily and economically available for use by a defined community or set of communities. (Waters 1998)

A thematic collection is not a library in the organizational sense; it is a collection that may be developed or selected for inclusion in a digital library, or it may exist separately from any library or similar institution. A library contains a collection of collections and has an institutional commitment to services that ensure access and persistence. Because of their size and diverse user population, libraries, including digital libraries, generally lack the coherency and the functional features characteristic of thematic collections.

In the humanities, the *Perseus* project is considered an exemplar digital library. It serves as a good, albeit complex, example of the relationship between collections and libraries. The scope of *Perseus* was originally disciplinary rather than thematic, providing access to an immense integrated body of materials in Classics, including primary Greek texts, translations, images, and lexical tools (Fraser 2000). As the project has grown, as both a scholarly resource and a research initiative, it has added collections outside the realm of Classics. The mix of subject collections within *Perseus* represents an interesting variety of collection-building approaches in terms of scope and mode of creation. Three geographically oriented collections, *California*, *Upper Midwest*, and *Chesapeake Bay*, have been developed in association with the Library of Congress's *American Memory* project. The library also contains an extensive body of primary and secondary materials covering the early modern period. The best example of a thematic collection within *Perseus* is the pre-twentieth-century London segment based on the *Bolles Collection on the History of London*. It is a digitized recreation of an existing special collection that is homogeneous in theme but heterogeneous in content. As noted previously, it interlinks maps of London, relevant texts, and historical and contemporary illustrations of the city.

The *Tibetan and Himalayan Digital Library* (THDL) is another kind of digital library/ thematic collection hybrid. It is being designed to capitalize on internal collocation of an underlying base of holdings to create multiple collections with different structures and perspectives. For example, the Environment and Cultural Geography collection organizes the library's texts, videos, images, maps and other types of materials according to space and time attributes. The thematic and special collections are organized by subject attributes. The categorization scheme used in the THDL is an interesting case of variant applications of digital resource terminology. Its special collections are thematic, with a focus, for example, on the life or activities of an individual, while the thematic collections integrate diverse sources within broad disciplinary units, such as Art, Linguistics, Literature, or Music. Subtheme collections, which are independent projects with their own content and goals, are nested within the thematic collections.

Needless to say, there is much overlap between digital library and thematic collection efforts, and variations and hybrids will continue to evolve along with the terminology. Digital research libraries will no doubt continue to acquire the collections built by scholars, collaborative teams, and institutions, while scholars' projects grow to nest and annex digital special collections. An important outcome of this activity is that expert collocation of research materials by scholars is adding an important new layer of resources to humanities research collections.

Turn in the Collection Cycle

In the past, scholars used collections for their research and contributed to collections as authors, but their role as collection builders was limited. They developed significant personal collections for their own purposes, and they collocated materials by editing and publishing collected works. On the other hand, collection development has long been a significant part of the professional responsibilities of librarians, archivists, and curators. The interaction between the scholarly community and collection professionals has been an important influence on the development of research library collections. As the primary constituency of research libraries, scholars' questions, requests, and ongoing research and teaching activities have guided the collection processes at research institutions. Of course, the essential contribution of scholars has been as creators of intellectual works that make up a large proportion of research collections. Now scholars have also become creators of research collections, and this change will have an important impact on how our vast arrays of research materials take shape in the future.

Where libraries once acquired the documents authored by scholars, they now also need to collect the thematic research collections created by scholars. This genre has new qualities that cannot be treated in the same way as a printed or electronic single work, and the interdisciplinary, multimedia, and open-ended characteristics of the resources, further complicate matters. Libraries are not yet systematically collecting the collections produced by scholars, in part because of the newness of the genre, but also because this type of meta-collecting is an unfamiliar practice. In fact, most research libraries do not yet collect and catalogue non-commercial, web-based digital materials of any kind. For example, at the time of this writing, *WorldCat*, a major bibliographic database of library holdings, indicated that 263 libraries had purchased and catalogued a recent book of criticism on William Blake by William Vaughan. In contrast, only 26 libraries had added the *William Blake Archive* collection to their catalogue. As a point of reference, 34 libraries had catalogued *Voice of the Shuttle*, a humanities gateway that is widely used but less similar to the scholarly creations traditionally collected by libraries than the materials in a typical thematic collection. As research libraries begin to regularly acquire and catalogue thematic collections, they will be interjecting a new layer of collecting activities and causing a shift in the scholarly information transfer cycle.

The traditional cycle of document transfer as conceptualized before the advent of digital documents (King and Bryant 1971) required publishers and libraries to take documents through most steps of the process. A large part of the production and distribution of scholarly research materials still adheres to this cycle. It begins with use of a document for scholarly work, usually in conjunction with many other documents, which leads to composition by the scholar. At this point, the scholar becomes an author, in addition to an information user. A publisher handles the reproduction or printing and distribution phase. Libraries move published documents through the circuit by selecting, acquiring, organizing, and storing them, and then by making them accessible, usually on library shelves and through representation in catalogues and indexes. Use of the materials is enhanced by assistance from reference, instruction, and access services provided by the library. The cycle is completed when the material becomes part of the research process by being accessed and assimilated by a scholar.

To some degree, libraries can treat thematic collections like the documents produced by scholars – by selecting, acquiring, and organizing them, as has been done by the 26 libraries that have catalogued the Blake archive. Over time, the distribution of scholarly materials in the humanities may be greatly expanded by scholars as they take up selection and organization activities. Perhaps even more importantly, scholars are adding valuable features to collections as they customize them for their scholarly purposes. While research libraries strive to meet the information needs of the communities they serve, they are not equipped or charged to fully support the scholarly process. Selection criteria for collections in research libraries emphasize how to choose the best items from the universe of publications being produced relative to the research communities being served. Measurements of satisfaction, circulation, and Web activity are combined with librarians' knowledge of their scholarly constituencies, which grows based on what scholars ask for and what they reveal to librarians about their interests and projects. Less attention has been paid to assessing how to prioritize materials in terms of what scholars do, what they value, or what would be the most likely to enhance specific research areas.

Many research libraries are currently focusing on global approaches to digital collection building by producing expansive gateways for all their user communities. At the same time, researchers are creating their own repositories and tools, highly customized to the scholarly work of their intellectual communities. Research libraries will need to fill the gap by developing mid-range collection services that actively collocate thematic collections within meaningful aggregations. The profile of a mid-level research collection would look quite different from the current digital research library. It would not prioritize the top tier of scholarly journals, the major indexes, a large general set of reference materials, or disciplinary canons. Instead, it would provide access to constellations of high-quality thematic research collections that are aligned with the scholarly activities conducted at the institution.

Scholar-created research collections are likely to increase in number as the work of producing them becomes more widely accepted as legitimate scholarship. Research libraries have yet to grasp how this will impact their practices, and it may be some time before there is a confluence of scholar- and institution-generated collections. First there will need to be a wider awareness of thematic collections as an important mode of scholarly work. Scholars and scientists are producing an abundance of digital products, many of which are important, high-quality compilations, and these activities are proliferating through support from funding agencies. It will be necessary for research libraries to respond to this trend in their collection development programs. Just as importantly, as collection building grows as a form of scholarly production, universities will need to provide resources to assist in this form of research. At present, the materials and expertise required for collection building research tend to be thinly scattered across departments, libraries, and computing centers. Resources and support services would be best centralized in the library or in auxiliary research units where scholars from all fields can turn for assistance in developing content and tools.

Conclusion

As scholars gain mastery in digital collocation and produce innovative research environments, they are practicing a new kind of collection development. Thematic collections are conceived not only as support for scholarship but as contributions to scholarship. They provide configurations of research materials that strongly represent the relationships between different kinds of sources and different subject areas. Through contextual mass, interdisciplinary platform, and activity support, thematic collections add density, flexibility, and interactivity to previously scattered and static repositories of content. They assist in the production of new research, but they also have the potential to substantively improve the scholarly research process.

In thematic collections, research materials are closely tied to the processes of inquiry, making the contours of scholarship more visible as they are inscribed into the collection. The questions and methods that propel scholarship become part of the representation, and as scholars build the partnerships it takes to construct quality collections, the networks of researchers and institutions involved in a research area become more explicit. Thematic collections are a substantive contribution to the rebuilding of research resources in the digital age, adding richness to our expansive stores of materials and new opportunities for humanities scholarship.

See also CHAPTER 36: The Past, Present, and Future of Digital Libraries.

REFERENCES FOR FURTHER READING

Ash, L. (1993). *Subject Collections*, 7th edn. New Providence, NJ: R. R. Bowker.

Atkinson, R. (1998). Managing Traditional Materials in an Online Environment: Some Definitions and Distinctions for a Future Collection Management. *Library Resources and Technical Services* 42: 7–20.

Bates, M. J. (1994). The Design of Databases and Other Information Resources for Humanities Scholars: The Getty Online Searching Project Report no. 4. *Online and CDROM Review* 18: 331–40.

Brockman, W. S., L. Neumann, C. L. Palmer, and T. Tidline (2001). *Scholarly Work in the Humanities and the Evolving Information Environment*. Washington, DC: Digital Library Federation and the Council on Library and Information Resources. Accessed November 26, 2002. At <http://www.clir.org/pubs/reports/pub104/contents.html>.

Buckland, M. (1992). Collections Reconsidered. In *Redesigning Library Services: A Manifesto* (pp. 54–61). Chicago: American Library Association.

——(1995). What Will Collection Developers Do? *Information Technologies and Libraries* 14: 155–9.

Condron, F., M. Fraser, and S. Sutherland (2001). *Oxford University Computing Services Guide to Digital Resources for the Humanities*. Morgantown, WV: West Virginia University Press.

Crane, G. and J. A. Rydberg-Cox (2000). New Technology and New Roles: The Need for "Corpus Editors." *Proceedings of the Fifth ACM Conference on Digital Libraries* (pp. 252–3), June 2–7, San Antonio, Texas.

Crane, G., C. E. Wulfman, and D. A. Smith (2001). Building a Hypertextual Digital Library in the Humanities: A Case Study of London. *Proceedings of the ACM/IEEE Joint Conference on Digital Libraries* (pp. 426–34), June 24–28, Roanoke, Virginia.

Finholt, T. (2002). Collaboratories. *Annual Review of Information Science and Technology* 36: 73–107.

Fraser, M. (2000). From Concordances to Subject Portals: Supporting the Text-centred Humanities Community. *Computers and the Humanities* 34: 265–78.

King, D. W. and E. C. Bryant (1971). *The Evaluation of Information Services and Products*. Washington, DC: Information Resources Press.

Lagoze, C. and D. Fielding (1998). Defining Collections in Distributed Digital Libraries. *D-Lib Magazine*, November. Accessed November 26, 2002. At <http://www.dlib.org.dlib/november98/lagoze/11lagoze.html>.

Lee, H.-L. (2000). What Is a Collection? *Journal of the American Society for Information Science* 51: 1106–13.

McGann, J. (1996). The Rossetti Archive and Image-based Electronic Editing. In R. J. Finneran (ed.), *The Literary Text in the Digital Age* (pp. 145–83). Ann Arbor, MI: University of Michigan Press.

Palmer, C. L. (ed.) (1996). *Navigating among the Disciplines: The Library and Interdisciplinary Inquiry. Library Trends* 45.

Palmer, C. L. (2000). Configuring Digital Research Collections around Scholarly Work. Paper presented at Digital Library Federation Forum, November 19, Chicago, Illinois. Accessed November 26, 2002. At <http://www.diglib.org/forums/fall00/palmer.htm>.

Palmer, C. L., and L. J. Neumann (2002). The Information Work of Interdisciplinary Humanities Scholars: Exploration and Translation. *Library Quarterly* 72: 85–117.

Schreibman, S. (2002). Computer-mediated Texts and Textuality: Theory and Practice. *Computers and the Humanities* 36: 283–93.

Smith, M. N. (1999). Because the Plunge from the Front Overturned Us: The Dickinson Electronic Archives Project. *Studies in the Literary Imagination* 32: 133–51.

Taylor, A. (1999). *The Organization of Information*. Englewood, CO: Libraries Unlimited.

Unsworth, J. (1996). Electronic Scholarship: or, Scholarly Publishing and the Public. *Journal of Scholarly Publishing* 28: 3–12.

——(2000a). Scholarly Primitives: What Methods Do Humanities Researchers Have in Common, and How Might Our Tools Reflect This? Paper presented at symposium, Humanities Computing: Formal

Methods, Experimental Practice, May 13, King's College London. Accessed November 26, 2002. At <http://www.iath.virginia.edu/~jmu2m/Kings.5-00/primitives.html>.

——(2000b). Thematic Research Collections. Paper presented at Modern Language Association Annual Conference, December 28, Washington, DC. Accessed November 26, 2002. At <http://www.iath. virginia.edu/~jmu2m/MLA.00/>.

Urbina, E., R. Furuta, A. Goenka, R. Kochumman, E. Melgoza, and C. Monroy (2002). Critical Editing in the Digital Age: Informatics and Humanities Research. In J. Frow (ed.), *The New Information Order and the Future of the Archive.* Conference proceedings, Institute for Advanced Studies in the Humanities, March 20–23, University of Edinburgh. Accessed November 26, 2002. At <http://webdb.ucs. ed.ac.uk/malts/other/IASH/dsp-all-papers.cfm>.

Viscomi, J. (2002). Digital Facsimiles: Reading the William Blake Archive. *Computers and the Humanities* 36: 27–48.

Waters, D. J. (1998). What Are Digital Libraries? *CLIR Issues* 4 (July/August). Accessed December 23, 2002. At <www.clir.org/pubs/issues/issues04.html>.

25

Print Scholarship and Digital Resources

Claire Warwick

Whosoever loves not picture, is injurious to truth: and all the wisdom of poetry. Picture is the invention of heaven: the most ancient, and most akin to nature. It is itself a silent work: and always of one and the same habit: yet it doth so enter, and penetrate the inmost affection (being done by an excellent artificer) as sometimes it o'ercomes the power of speech and oratory.

Ben Jonson, *Explorata or Discoveries*, ll. 1882–90

Introduction

In the late 1990s there was a great deal of concern about the death of the book. From every corner it was possible to hear quoted Victor Hugo's Archbishop, complaining that "ceci, tuera cela" (Nunberg 1996). Articles and books were published on the future of the book, which was assumed to be going to be a brief one (Finneran 1996). At the same time we were being told that we might no longer need to commute to work, or attend or teach at real physical universities, and of course if there were no longer any books, we would only need virtual libraries from which to access our electronic documents. Just a few years later all this seems to be as misguidedly futuristic as those 1970s newspaper articles predicting that by the year 2000 we would all eat protein pills instead of food. It is clear, then, that far from being killed off, print scholarship is still very much alive and well, and that its relationship to electronic resources is a highly complex one. In this chapter I will examine this relationship, and argue that we cannot hope to understand the complexity of such a relationship without looking at scholarly practices, and the way that such resources are used. This in turn means examining how we use information, either computationally or in print, in the wider context of scholarly life. We must consider how we read texts, and indeed visual objects, to understand why print remains important, and how it may relate to the digital objects and surrogates that are its companions.

Scenes from Academic Life

To exemplify some of the changes that are taking place I would like to recreate two scenes from my academic life, which are illustrative of some of these larger issues.

Thessaloniki, Greece

I am in the Byzantine museum, being shown some of the treasures of this northern Greek city, which prides itself on having been longest under continuous Byzantine rule. It is full of icons, mosaics, marble carvings, and richly painted tombs. My guide asks what I think of them, and repeatedly I marvel at their beauty. But this, it appears, is not the point. We must, I am told, be able to read these images and icons in the way that their creators intended us to. I see a tomb with a painted tree sheltering a rotund bird which looks rather like a turkey. In fact this is an olive, signifying eternity and peace, and the bird is a peacock, symbol of paradise. This is not simply wallpaper for the dead, but a statement of belief. The icons themselves glow with colors, whose richness I wonder at, but again they must be read. The gold background symbolizes heaven, and eternity, the red of a cloak is for love, the green band around the Madonna's head is for hope. The wrinkles painted on her face are to symbolize that beauty comes from within, and is not altered by age. My guide begins to test me, what do I see in front of me? I struggle to remember the unfamiliar visual alphabet that I am being taught, and realize that reliance on the printed word, and a lack of such meaningful images, has deprived me of a visual vocabulary; that such iconography is part of another tradition of communication, whose roots, at least in this part of Greece, are extremely ancient. They have long co-existed with the culture of the printed word, but have not entirely been supplanted by it.

Portsmouth, England

I am on an advisory board for the Portsmouth record office. Over a period of several decades they have painstakingly produced nine edited volumes of printed work cataloguing some of the holdings of their archives. They are arranged thematically, concerning dockyards, houses in the old town, legal documents. All are handsome hardbacks with an individual design. There is, it seems, still a substantial backlog of volumes in preparation, but printing has become so costly that they have decided to publish electronically, which is why I am here. We spend time discussing volumes awaiting release, and all are relieved to find that the next volume should soon be ready after a period of thirty years in preparation.

There is a certain culture shock on both sides. I am amazed to discover how long the process of editing and publication takes. Thirty years is long, but an average of a decade seems to be quite usual. I reflect that the papers themselves are historic, and still exist in the archive, waiting to be discovered, even if not calendared. But from the world I am used to, where technology changes so quickly, it is hard to return to a sense of such relative lack of change and urgency.

A fellow panel member suggests that what had been thought of as several discrete print volumes, on large-scale maps, title deeds, city plans, and population data, could easily be combined, in an electronic environment, with the help of geographic information systems (GIS) technology. I in turn argue that the idea of separate volumes need not be retained in an electronic publication. There is no need to draw up a publication schedule as has been done with the print volumes. We could publish data on different themes concurrently, in several releases, when it is ready, so that the digital records will grow at the pace of those who are editing, and not have to suffer delays.

These suggestions are welcomed enthusiastically but the series editor reminds us that there are human dimensions to this process. Those editing individual volumes may want to see their work identified as a discrete entity, to gain credit from funding authorities or promotion boards. These collections would also, it seems, be incomplete without an introduction, and that, paradoxically, is usually written last: a major intellectual task and perhaps the factor, I speculate privately, which may have delayed publication, since it involves the synthesis of a vast range of sources and an attempt to indicate their intellectual value to a historian. Would it be possible to publish a release of the data without such an introduction, even if temporarily? We explore different possibilities for ways that data might appear with different views, to accommodate such problems, and the intellectual adjustments on both sides are almost visible. The historians and archivists contemplate the electronic unbinding of the volume as a controlling entity: those interested in computing are reminded that more traditional elements of the intellectual culture we are working in cannot be ignored if the project is to keep the good will of the scholars who work on it.

Tools to Think With

The two examples above serve as illustration of some of the very complex issues that we must contend with when considering the relationship between printed and electronic resources. As Jerome McGann argues, we have grown used to books as the primary tools to think with in the humanities. We may read one text, but are likely to use a variety of other books as tools, as we attempt to interpret texts of all kinds (McGann 2001, ch. 2). In the remainder of this chapter I shall demonstrate that what links the two examples that I have quoted above with McGann's concerns is the question of how we use materials in humanities scholarship. I shall argue that whatever format materials are in, computational methods must make us reconsider how we read. Since we are so used to the idea of reading as an interpretative strategy we risk taking it for granted, and considering it mundane when compared to exciting new computational methods. But, as the example of the Macedonian museum shows, reading is a much more broad-ranging process than the comprehension of a printed text, and this comprehension itself is a complex process which requires more detailed analysis. It is also arguable that the visual elements of the graphical user interface (GUI) have also made us rediscover the visual aspects of reading and comprehension. Both of these processes must be considered in order to try to understand the complex linkage between digital resources and print scholarship, because if we assume that reading printed text is a simple process, easily replaced by computational methods of interpreting digital resources, we risk underestimating the richness and complexity of more traditional research in the humanities.

When the use of digital resources was first becoming widespread, assumptions were made that such resources could and indeed should replace the culture of interpreting printed resources by reading them. Enthusiasts championed the use of digital resources, and decried those who did not use them as ill-informed or neo-Luddite. During the 1990s efforts were made to educate academics in the use of digital resources. Universities set up learning media units to help with the production of resources, and offered some technical support to academics, though at least in the British system this remains inadequate. The quality and quantity of digital resources available in the humanities also increased. And yet print scholarship is far from dead. Academics in the humanities still insisted on reading books, and writing articles, even if they also used or created digital resources. As I discovered in Portsmouth, cultural factors within academia are slow to change. The authority of print publication is still undoubted. Why, after all, is this collection published in book form? Books are not only convenient, but carry weight with promotion committees, funding councils, and one's peers. Computational techniques, however, continue to improve and academic culture changes, even if slowly. What is not likely to change in the complex dynamics between the two media is the fundamentals of how humanities academics work, and the way that they understand their material. How, then, should we explain the survival of reading printed texts?

We might begin this process by examining early attempts to effect such a culture change. The 1993 *Computers and the Humanities* (*CHUM*) was very much in proselytizing mode. In the keynote article of a special issue on computers and literary criticism, Olsen argued that scholars were being wrong-headed. If only they realized what computers really are useful for, he suggested, there would be nothing to stop them using computer methodology to produce important and far-reaching literary research. This is followed by an interesting collection of articles, making stimulating methodological suggestions. All of them proceeded from the assumption that critics ought to use, and what is more, should want to use digital resources in their research. Suggestions include the use of corpora for studying intertextuality (*CHUM* 1993, Greco) or cultural and social phenomena (*CHUM* 1993, Olsen); scientific or quantitative methodologies (*CHUM* 1993, Goldfield) such as those from cognitive science (*CHUM* 1993, Henry, and Spolsky), and Artificial Intelligence theory (*CHUM* 1993, Matsuba). All of these might have proved fruitful, but no work to be found in subsequent mainstream journals suggests that any literary critics took note of them.

The reason appears to be that the authors of these papers assumed that a lack of knowledge on the part of their more traditional colleagues must be causing their apparent conservatism. It appears that they did not countenance the idea that none of these suggested methods might be fit for what a critic might want to do. As Fortier argues in one of the other articles in the volume, the true core activity of literary study is the study of the text itself, not theory, nor anything else. He suggests that: "this is not some reactionary perversity on the part of an entire profession, but a recognition that once literature studies cease to focus on literature, they become something else: sociology, anthropology, history of culture, philosophy speculation, or what have you" (*CHUM* 1993, Fortier 1993: 376). In other words these writers are offering useful suggestions about what their literary colleagues *might* do, instead of listening to critics like Fortier who are quite clear about what it is they *want* to do. Users have been introduced to all sorts of interesting things that *can* be done with computer analysis or electronic resources, but very few of them have been asked what it is that they do, and want to keep doing, which is to study texts by reading them.

As a result, there is a danger that humanities computing enthusiasts may be seen by their more traditional colleagues as wild-eyed technocrats who play with computers and digital resources because they can. We may be seen as playing with technological toys, while our colleagues perform difficult interpretative tasks by reading texts without the aid of technology. So if reading is still so highly valued and widely practiced, perhaps in order to be taken seriously as scholars, we as humanities computing practitioners should take the activity of reading seriously as well. As the example of my Portsmouth meeting shows, both sides of the debate will tend to make certain assumptions about scholarly practice, and it is only when we all understand and value such assumptions that we can make progress together. If reading a text is an activity that is not easily abandoned, even after academics know about and actively use digital resources, then it is important for us to ask what then reading might be, and what kind of materials are being read. I shall consider the second part of the question first, because before we can understand analytical methods we need to look at the material under analysis.

Texts and Tradition

Norman (1999) argues that we must be aware what computer systems are good for and where they fit in with human expertise. He thinks that computers are of most use when they complement what humans can do best. He attributes the failure or lack of use of some apparently good computer systems to the problem that they replicate what humans can do, but do it less efficiently. A clearer understanding of what humanities scholars do in their scholarship is therefore important. Computer analysis is particularly good at returning quantitative data and has most readily been adopted by scholars in fields where this kind of analysis is privileged, such as social and economic history, or linguistics. A population dataset or linguistic corpus contains data that is ideal for quantitative analysis, and other researchers can also use the same data and analysis technique to test the veracity of the results.

However, despite the pioneering work of Corns (1990) and Burrows (1987), literary text can be particularly badly suited to this type of quantitative analysis because of the kind of questions asked of the data. As Iser (1989) argues, the literary text does not describe objective reality. Literary data in particular are so complex that they are not well suited to quantitative study, polar opposites of being or not being, right and wrong, presence or absence, but rather the analysis of subtle shades of meaning, of what some people perceive and others do not. The complexity is demonstrated in the use of figurative language. As Van Peer (1989: 303) argues this is an intrinsic feature of its "literariness." Thus we cannot realistically try to reduce complex texts to any sort of objective and non-ambiguous state for fear of destroying what makes them worth reading and studying.

Computer analysis cannot "recognize" figurative use of language. However, an electronic text might be marked up in such a way that figurative uses of words are distinguished from literal uses before any electronic analysis is embarked upon. However, there are two fundamental problems with this approach. Firstly, it is unlikely that all readers would agree on what is and is not figurative, nor on absolute numbers of usages. As I. A. Richards' study (1929) was the first to show, readers may produce entirely different readings of the same literary text. Secondly, the activity of performing this kind of markup would be so labor-intensive that a critic might just as well read the text in the first place. Nor could it be said to be any more accurate than manual analysis, because of the uncertain nature of the data. In many ways we are still in the position that Corns complained of in 1991 when he remarked that: "Such programmes can produce lists and tables like a medium producing ectoplasm, and what those lists and tables mean is often as mysterious" (1991: 128). Friendlier user interfaces mean that results are easier to interpret, but the point he made is still valid. The program can produce data, but humans are still vital in its interpretation (*CHUM* 1993, Lessard and Benard).

Furthermore, interpreting the results of the analysis is a particularly complex activity. One of the most fundamental ideas in the design of automatic information retrieval systems is that the researcher must know what he or she is looking for in advance. This means that they can design the system to find this feature and that they know when they have found it, and how efficient recall is. However, unlike social scientists or linguists, humanities researchers often do not know what they are looking for before they approach a text, nor may they be immediately certain why it is significant when they find it. If computer systems are best used to find certain features, then this is problematic. They can only acquire this knowledge by reading that text, and probably many others. Otherwise, they are likely to find it difficult to interpret the results of computer analysis, or indeed to know what sort of "questions" to ask of the text in the first place.

Humanities scholars often do not need to analyze huge amounts of text to find material of interest to them. They may not need to prove a hypothesis as conclusively as possible, or build up statistical models of the occurrence of features to find them of interest, and may find the exceptional use of language or style as significant as general patterns (Stone 1982). They may therefore see traditional detailed reading of a relatively small amount of printed text as a more effective method of analysis.

The availability of a large variety of text types may be more important than the amount of material. Historians require a wide variety of materials such as letters, manuscripts, archival records, and secondary historical sources like books and articles (Duff and Johnson 2002). All of these are to be found in print or manuscript sources, some of which are rare and delicate and often found only in specific archives or libraries. Of course some materials like these have been digitized, but only a very small proportion. Even with the largest and most enthusiastic programs of digitization, given constraints of time, the limited budgets of libraries, and even research councils, it seems likely that this will remain the case for the foreseeable future. The historical researcher may also be looking for an unusual document whose value may not be apparent to others: the kind of document which may be ignored in selective digitization strategies.

Indeed the experience of projects like Portsmouth records society suggests that this has already been recognized. If the actual material is so unique that a historian may need to see the actual artifact rather than a digitized surrogate, then we may be better advised to digitize catalogues, calendars, and finding aids, and allow users to make use of them to access the material itself. This also returns us to the question of the visual aspect of humanities scholarship. Initially the phenomenon of a digitized surrogate increasing the demand for the original artifact seemed paradoxical to librarians and archivists. However, this acknowledges the need for us to appreciate the visual aspects of the interpretation of humanities material. A transcribed manuscript which has been digitized allows us to access the information contained in it. It may only be as a result of having seen a digital image that the scholar realizes what further potential for interpretation exists, and this, it appears, may only be satisfied by the artifact itself. This is such a complex process that we do not yet fully understand its significance.

The nature of the resources that humanities scholars use should begin to explain why there will continue to be a complex interaction between print and digital resources. There is not always a good fit between the needs of a humanities scholar or the tasks that they might want to carry out, and the digital resources available. Print still fulfills many functions and this perhaps encourages scholars to produce more, by publishing their research in printed form. But surely we might argue that computational methods would allow more powerful and subtle ways of analyzing such material. Reading, after all, seems such a simple task.

What is Reading?

Whatever assumptions we might be tempted to make, the activity of reading even the simplest text is a highly complex cognitive task, involving what Crowder and Wagner (1992: 4) describe as "three stupendous achievements": the development of spoken language, written language, and literacy. Kneepkins and Zwaan (1994: 126) show that:

> In processing text, readers perform several basic operations. For example, they decode letters, assign meaning to words, parse the syntactic structure of the sentence, relate different words and sentences, construct a theme for the text and may infer the objectives of the author. Readers attempt to construct a coherent mental representation of the text. In this process they use their linguistic knowledge (knowledge of words, grammar), and their world knowledge (knowledge of what is possible in reality, cultural knowledge, knowledge of the theme).

These processes are necessary for even the most basic of texts, and therefore the cognitive effort necessary to process a complex text, such as the material commonly used by humanities researchers, must be correspondingly greater. Arguably, the most complex of all such texts are literary ones, and thus the following section is largely concerned with such material. Although empirical studies of the reading of literary text are in their comparative infancy (de Beaugrande 1992) research has ensured that the reading process is thought of as not simply a matter of recall of knowledge, but as a "complex cognitive and affective transaction involving text-based, reader-based, and situational factors" (Goetz et al. 1993: 35).

Text-based factors

Most humanities scholars would agree that their primary task is to determine how meaning can be attributed to texts (Dixon et al. 1993). Yet the connection between meaning and language is an extremely complex problem. As Snelgrove (1990) concluded, when we read a literary text we understand it not only in terms of the meaning of specific linguistic features, but also by the creation of large-scale patterns and structures based on the interrelation of words and ideas to one another. This pattern making means that the relative meaning invested in a word may depend on its position in a text and the reaction that it may already have evoked in the reader. Dramatic irony, for example, is effective because we know that a character's speech is loaded with a significance they do not recognize. Our recognition of this will depend on the mental patterns and echoes it evokes. Language may become loaded and suffused with meaning specifically by relations, or its use in certain contexts.

The complexity of the patterns generated by human readers is, however, difficult to replicate when computational analysis is used. Text analysis software tends to remove the particular phenomenon under investigation from its immediate context except for the few words immediately surrounding it. A linguist may collect instances of a particular phenomenon and present the results of a concordance sorted alphabetically, irrespective of the order in which the words originally occurred in the text, or the author of them. However, for a literary critic the patterns created are vital to the experience of reading the text, and to the way it becomes meaningful. Thus the fragmented presentation of a computer analysis program cannot begin to approach the kind of understanding of meaning that we gain by reading a word as part of a narrative structure.

The way we read literary text also depends on the genre of the work. Comprehension depends on what we already assume about the type of text we recognize it to be. Fish (1980: 326) found that he could persuade students that a list of names was a poem because of their assumptions about the form that poems usually take. Hanauer (1998) has found that genre affects the way readers comprehend and recall text, since they are likely to read more slowly and remember different types of information in a poem. Readers also decode terms and anaphora differently depending on what we know to be the genre of a text; for example, we will expect "cabinet" to mean one thing in a newspaper report of a political speech, and another in a carpentry magazine (Zwaan 1993: 2).

Reader-based factors

The way that we extract meaning from a text also depends on many things which are extrinsic to it. The meaning of language changes depending on the associations an individual reader may make with other features of the text (Miall 1992), and with other texts and ideas. The creation of such webs of association and causation is central to the historian's craft. As the eminent historian G. R. Elton put it:

> G. M. Young once offered celebrated advice: read in a period until you hear its people speak.... The truth is that one must read them, study their creations and think about them until one knows what they are going to say next. (Elton 1967: 30)

Interaction between the reader and the text is also affected by factors which are particular to the individual reader (Halasz 1992). Iser (1989) argues that narrative texts invite the interaction of the reader by indeterminacy in the narrative. Where there are gaps of uncertainty, the reader fills them using their own experience. Readers' experience of a

fictional text will even be affected by the relationship which they build between themselves and the narrator (Dixon and Bertolussi 1996a).

Situational factors

The reader's response to a text is likely to be affected by situational factors, for example
their gender, race, education, social class, and so on. This is also liable to change over time,
so that we may experience a text differently at the age of 56 than at 16. As Potter (1991)
argues, these factors have yet to be taken into account in empirical readership studies of
literary text. Even more subtly than this, however, a reader's appreciation of a text may be
affected by how they feel on a particular day, or if a feature of the text is reminiscent of
their personal experience. Happy readers notice and recall parts of a text which describe
happiness, or evoke the emotion in them, and sad ones the opposite (Kneepkins and
Zwaan 1994: 128). The role of emotional engagement is clearly vital in literary reading.
Yet it is one which is very difficult to quantify, or describe, and therefore is almost
impossible for computer analysis to simulate.

Reading a text is also affected by the frequency of reading and the expertise of the
reader, as Elton's observation suggests (Dixon and Bertolussi 1996b; Dorfman 1996).
Dixon and colleagues (1993) found that the same textual feature might be the cause of
varied effects in different readers and certain effects were only apparent to some readers.
Although core effects of the text could usually be discerned on first reading, other, more
subtle effects were only reported on second or subsequent readings, or would only be
apparent to some of the readers. They also found that the subtlest of literary effects tended
to be noticed by readers who they called "experienced." They concluded that reading is
such a complex procedure that all the effects of the text are unlikely to be apparent at
once, and that reading is clearly a skill that needs to be learnt and practiced.

Reading the Visual

It should therefore be becoming clear why print resources have continued to co-exist with
digital ones. The key activity of the humanities scholar is to read and interpret texts, and
there is little point in using a computational tool to replicate what human agency does
best in a much less complex and subtle manner. Reading a printed text is clearly a subtle
and complex analysis technique. It is therefore not surprising that scholars have made the
assumption that digital resources and computational techniques that simply replicate
the activity of reading are a pale imitation of an already successful technique. To be of use
to the humanities scholar, it seems that digital resources must therefore provide a different
dimension that may change the way that we view our raw materials.

In some ways we can discern a similar movement in humanities computing to that
which has taken place in computer science. In the 1980s and 1990s Artificial Intelligence
seemed to offer the prospect of thinking machines (Jonscher 1999, ch. 5). But the
technology that has captured the imagination of users has not been a computer system
that seeks to think for them, but one that provides access to material that can provide raw
material for human thought processes, that is, the Internet and World Wide Web. The
popularity of the Web appears to have dated from the development of graphical browsers

that gave us access not only to textual information, but to images. The effect of this and the rise of the graphical user interface has been to re-acquaint us with the power of images, not only as ways of organizing information, but as way of communicating it. Just as the images in the museum in Thessaloniki reminded me that there are other ways to interpret and communicate ideas, so we have had to relearn ways to read an image, whether the frame contains a painted or a pixelated icon.

It is in this area that, I would argue, digital resources can make the greatest contribution to humanities scholarship. Digitization projects have revolutionized our access to resources such as images of manuscripts (Unsworth 2002). The use of three-dimensional CAD modeling has been extensively used in archaeology to help reconstruct the way that buildings might have looked (Sheffield University 2003). However, the projects that are most innovative are those that use digital resources not for reconstruction or improved access, though these are of course enormously valuable, but as tools to think with. If the process of reading and interpreting a text is so complex, then it may be that this is best left to our brains as processing devices for at least the medium term. It is, however, in the realm of the visual that we are seeing some of the most interesting interrelationships of print scholarship and digital resources. We need only look at a small sample of some of the papers presented at the Association for Literary and Linguistic Computing–Association for Computers and the Humanities conference (at <http://www.uni-tuebingen.de/zdv/zrkinfo/pics/aca4.htm>) in 2002 to see exciting examples of such developments in progress.

Steve Ramsay argues that we might "remap, reenvision, and re-form" a literary text (Ramsay 2002). He refers to McGann and Drucker's experiments with deforming the way a text is written on a page (McGann 2001), but has moved beyond this to the use of Graph View Software. He has used this program, which was originally designed to create graphic representations of numerical data, to help in the analysis of dramatic texts. In a previous interview, he had demonstrated this to me, showing a three-dimensional graphical mapping of Shakespeare's *Antony and Cleopatra*. This created wonderful abstract looping patterns which might have been at home in a gallery of modern art. But, like the Macedonian icons, theses were not simply objects of beauty. Once interpreted, they show the way that characters move though the play, being drawn inexorably towards Rome. This visual representation had the effect, not of abolishing the human agency of the literary critic, but providing, literally, a new vision of the play, perhaps opening up new vistas to the critical view. The significance of such movement, and what it reveals about the play, is for the critic herself to decide, but the program has performed a useful form of defamiliarization, which would be difficult to imagine in a print environment.

We can also see similar types of visual representation of textual information in the interactive 3-D model of Dante's *Inferno*. The effect of this is a similar kind of defamiliarization. A very new view of the information in the text is created, but the effect of it, at least on this reader, is to make her wish to return to the text itself in printed form, and to read it with new eyes. The digital resource has therefore not made reading redundant, but helped to suggest new avenues of interpretation. This project is being developed at the same research centre, IATH, where McGann is and Ramsay was based. This is another intriguing connection between the world of digital resources and more traditional forms of scholarship. Computational tools as simple as e-mail have made the process of scholarly collaboration over large physical distances much easier than before. Yet it is fascinating to note that the physical proximity of scholars such as those at IATH facilitates the interchange of ideas and makes it possible for methodologies to be shared and for projects and scholars to be a creative influence on each other – a process that we can see at work in the visual dynamics of these IATH projects. This is not an isolated phenomenon. The fact that Microsoft's campus in Cambridge shares alternate floors of a building with the university department of computer science shows that such a technologically advanced organization still values informal creative exchanges as a way to inspire new projects and support existing ones. The Cambridge University Computer Laboratory's online coffee machine was a star turn of the early Web (Stafford-Fraser 1995). But it was finally switched off in 2001, perhaps proof that Microsoft's decision to privilege meetings over a non-virtual coffee shows their recognition that traditional methods are still vital in innovation and scholarship.

Two other IATH projects were also discussed at the conference. The Salem witch trials and Boston's Back Bay Fens are two projects which both make use of GIS technology to integrate textual material and numerical data with spatial information (Pitti et al. 2002). Once again these projects allow the user to visualize the data in different ways. Connections might be made between people or places in historical Boston, whose physical proximity is much easier for a user to establish in the visual environment of a GUI interface than by the examination of printed data. Where a particular user's knowledge might be partial, the use of such data lets her literally envision new ones, as a result of interrogating a large spatial dataset. A new textual narrative can emerge from the physical linkages.

The case of the Salem witch trials is also intriguing, since the Flash animations actually allow the user to watch as the accusations spread over time and space like a medical, rather than psychological, epidemic. This idea of mapping this spread is, however, not new in terms of historiography. In 1974 Boyer and Nissenbaum had pioneered this approach in a ground-breaking book, *Salem Possessed*. This contains printed maps of the area which give us snapshots of the progress of the allegations. We can, therefore, see an immediate relationship between scholarship in print and a digital resource which has grown out of such theories. What the digital resource adds, though, is the immediacy of being able to watch, run and rerun the sequence in a way that a book, while impressive, cannot allow us to do. Once again, the theories that lie behind the data are, as Pitti et al. (2002) make clear, very much the product of the scholarship that the historians who initiated the projects brought to them. Analysis performed on the data will also be done in the minds of other scholars. But the visual impact of both of these databases supports human information processing, and may suggest new directions for human analysis to take.

As the website for the Valley of the Shadow, one of the two original IATH projects, puts it, GIS may be used literally "to put [historical] people back into their houses and businesses" (Ayers et al. 2001). Valley of the Shadow is itself doing far more than simply this. The project itself seems to be predicated on an understanding of the visual. Even the basic navigation of the site is organized around the metaphor of a physical archive, where a user navigates the different materials by visiting, or clicking on, the separate rooms of a plan of the space. By linking a contemporary map with the data about a particular area, GIS allows users to interpret the data in a new way, giving a concrete meaning to statistical data or names of people and places in the registers which are also reproduced (Thomas 2000). Just as with a literary text, this might cause a historian to return to the numerical or textual data for further analysis, and some of this might use computational tools to aid the process.

But its greatest value is in prompting a fresh approach for consideration. The historian's brain is still the tool that determines the significance of the findings. This distinction is important, since it distinguishes Valley of the Shadow from some earlier computational projects in similar areas of American history. For example, in 1974 Fogle and Engerman wrote *Time on the Cross*, in which they sought to explain American slavery with the use of vast amounts of quantitative data on plantation slavery, which was then analyzed computationally. This, they claimed, would produce a definitive record of the objective reality of slavery in America. Critics of the book have argued persuasively that the data were handled much too uncritically. Their findings, it has been claimed, were biased, because they only used statistical written data, which usually emerged from large plantations, and ignored the situation of small slave holders who either did not or could not document details of their holdings, either because the holdings were small or because the slave holder was illiterate (Ransom and Sutch 1977; Wright 1978). Other historians have insisted that anecdotal sources and printed texts must be used to complement the findings, to do sufficient justice to the complexity of the area. It could be argued that the problems that they encountered were caused by an over-reliance on computational analysis of numerical data, and by the implication that this could somehow deliver a definitive explanation of slavery in a way that would finally put an end to controversies caused by subjective human analysis. A project such as Valley of the Shadow is a significant progression onwards, not only in computational techniques but also in scholarly method. It does not rely on one style of data, since it links numerical records to textual and spatial data. These resources are then offered as tools to aid interpretation, which takes place in the historian's brain, rather than in any way seeking to supersede this.

The products of the projects are also varied, ranging from students' projects, which take the materials and use them to create smaller digital projects for assessment, to more traditional articles and conference presentations. Most intriguing, perhaps, is the form of hybrid scholarship that Ed Ayers, the project's founder, and William Thomas have produced. Ayers had long felt that despite the innovative research that could be performed with a digital resource, there had been very little effect on the nature of resulting publication. The written article, even if produced in an electronic journal, was still essentially untouched by the digital medium, having the same structure as an article in a traditional printed journal. Ayers and Thomas (2002) therefore wrote an article which takes advantage of the electronic medium, by incorporation some of the GIS data, and the hypertextual navigation system which gives a reader multiple points of entry and of linkage with other parts of the resource. Readers are given a choice of navigation, a visual interface with Flash animations or a more traditional text-based interface. The article might even be printed out, but it is difficult to see how it could be fully appreciated without the use of its digital interactive elements. This has appeared in *American Historical Review*, a traditional academic journal, announcing its right to be considered part of the mainstream of historical research. As such it represents a dialogue between the more traditional world of the academic journal and the possibilities presented by digital resources, at once maintaining the continuity of scholarly traditions in history, but also seeking to push the boundaries of what is considered to be a scholarly publication. The analysis presented in the paper emerges from human reading and processing of data, but would not have been possible without the use of the digital resource.

It is not only at IATH, however, that work in this area is taking place, despite their leading position in the field. Thomas Corns et al. (2002), from the University of Bangor in Wales, has described how one aspect of document visualization can aid human analysis. Being able to digitize a rare manuscript has significantly aided his team in trying to determine whether it was written by Milton. The simple task of being able to cut, paste, and manipulate letter shapes in the digitized text has helped in their examination of scribal hands. The judgment is that of the scholars, but based on the ability to see a text in a new way, only afforded by digitized resources. This is not a new technique, and its success is largely dependent on the questions that are being asked of the data by the human investigators. Donaldson (1997) discusses ways in which complex analysis of digital images of seventeenth-century type was used to try to decide whether Shakespeare had used the word *wife* or *wise* in a couplet from *The Tempest*, usually rendered as "So rare a wondered father and a wise / Makes this place paradise" (Act IV, Scene, I, ll. 122–3). The digital research proved inconclusive but might have been unnecessary, since a Shakespeare scholar might be expected to deduce that the rhyme of *wise* and *paradise* is much more likely in the context of the end of a character's speech, than the word *wife*, which while tempting for a feminist analysis would not follow the expected pattern of sound. All of which indicates that the use of digital resources can only be truly meaning-ful when combined with old-fashioned critical judgment.

Another project being presented at ALLC-ACH, which is very much concerned with facilitating critical judgment through the realm of the visual, is the Versioning Machine (Smith 2002). This package, which supports the organization and analysis of text with multiple variants, is once again a way of helping the user to envision a text in a different way, or even in multiple different ways. The ability to display multiple variants concur-rently, to color-code comments that are read or unread, selectively to show or hide markup pertaining to certain witnesses, gives scholars a different way of perceiving the text, both in terms of sight and of facilitating the critical process. It is also far less restrictive than a printed book in the case where the text of a writer might have multiple variants, none of which the critic can say with certainly is the final version. The case of Emily Dickinson is a notable one, presented by the MITH team, but it may be that if freed by digital resources like the Versioning Machine of the necessity of having to decide on a copy text for an edition, the text of many other writers might be seen as much more mutable, and less fixed in a final form of texuality.

Print editions, for example of the seventeenth-century poet Richard Crashaw, have forced editors to make difficult decisions about whether the author himself made revisions to many of the poems. When, as in this case, evidence is contradictory or inconclusive, it is surely better to be able to use digital technology such as the Versioning Machine to give users a different way of seeing, and enable them to view the variants without editorial intervention. The use of the Versioning Machine will not stop the arguments about which version might be preferred, based as they are on literary judgment and the interpretation of historical events, but at least we as readers are not presented with the spurious certainty that a print edition forces us into. Once again, therefore, such use of computer technology is not intended to provide a substitute for critical analysis, and the vast processing power of the human brain, rather it gives us a way of reviewing the evidence of authorial revisions. It makes concrete and real again the metaphors that those terms have lost in the world of print scholarship.

Conclusion

Even when we look at a small sample of what is taking place in the field, it is clear that some of the most exciting new developments in the humanities computing area seem to be looking towards the visual as a way of helping us to reinterpret the textual. It appears that we are moving beyond not printed books and print-based scholarship, but the naive belief that they can easily be replaced by digital resources.

As the example of my visit to Portsmouth demonstrated, it is simplistic to believe that we can, or should, rush to convince our more traditional colleagues of the inherent value of digital resources, without taking into account the culture of long-established print scholarship. It is only through negotiations with scholars, and in forging links between the digital and the textual traditions that the most interesting research work is likely to emerge.

The materials that humanities scholars use in their work are complex, with shifting shades of meaning that are not easily interpreted. We are only beginning to understand the subtle and complicated processes of interpretation that these require. However, when we consider that the process of reading a text, which may seem so simple, is in fact so difficult an operation that computer analysis cannot hope to replicate it at present, we can begin to understand why for many scholars the reading of such material in print will continue to form the core activity of their research.

Digital resources can, however, make an important contribution to this activity. Far from attempting to replace the scholar's mind as the processing device, computer delivery of resources can help to support the process. The complexity of visual devices as a way of enshrining memory and communicating knowledge is something that the ancient world understood very well, as I learnt when I began to read the icons in Thessaloniki. While much of this knowledge has been lost in the textual obsession of print culture, the graphical interface of the computer screen has helped us reconnect to the world of the visual and recognize that we can relearn a long-neglected vocabulary of interpretation. Digital resources can provide us with a new way to see, and thus to perceive the complexities in the process of interpreting humanities materials. A new way of looking at a text can lead to a way of reading it that is unconstrained by the bindings of the printed medium, even if it leads us back to the pages of a printed book.

ACKNOWLEDGMENTS

It is with gratitude that I would like to dedicate this chapter to the memory of Dr J. Wilbur Sanders (1936–2002). A man of acute perception and a great teacher, he helped me to see how subtle and complex a process reading might be.

BIBLIOGRAPHY

Ayers, E. L. (1999). The Pasts and Futures of Digital History. At <http://jefferson.village.virginia.edu/vcdh/PastsFutures.html>.

Ayers, E. L., A. S. Rubin, and W. G. Thomas (2001). The Valley's Electronic Cultural Atlas Initiative Geographic Information Systems Project. At <http://jefferson.village.virginia/edu/vshadow2/ecai/present/html>.

Ayers, E. L. and W. G. Thomas (2002). Two American Communities on the Eve of the Civil War: An Experiment in Form and Analysis. At <http://jefferson.village.virginia.edu/vcdh/xml_docs/projects.html>.

de Beaugrande, R. (1992). Readers Responding to Literature: Coming to Grips with Reality. In Elaine F. Narduccio (ed.), *Reader Response to Literature: The Empirical Dimension* (pp. 193–210). New York and London: Mouton de Gruyter.

Boyer, P. and S. Nissenbaum (1974). *Salem Possessed: The Social Origins of Witchcraft*. Cambridge, MA: Harvard University Press.

Burrows, J. F. (1987). *Computation into Criticism: A Study of Jane Austen's Novels and an Experiment in Method*. Oxford: Clarendon Press.

Computers and the Humanities (*CHUM*), 27 (1993). Special issue on literature and computing, includes: Thomas, J.-J., Texts On-line (93–104). Henry, C., The Surface of Language and Humanities Computing (315–22). Spolsky, E., Have It Your Way and Mine: The Theory of Styles (323–30). Matsuba, S., Finding the Range: Linguistic Analysis and its Role in Computer-assisted Literary Study (331–40). Greco, L. G., and Shoemaker, P., Intertextuality and Large Corpora: A Medievalist Approach (349–55). Bruce, D., Towards the Implementation of Text and Discourse Theory in Computer Assisted Textual Analysis (357–64). Goldfield, J. D., An Argument for Single-author and Similar Studies Using Quantitative Methods: Is There Safety in Numbers? (365–74). Fortier, P. A., Babies, Bathwater and the Study of Literature (375–85). Lessard, G. and J. Benard, Computerising Celine (387–94). Olsen, M., Signs, Symbols and Discourses: a New Direction for Computer Aided Literature Studies (309–14). Olsen, M., Critical Theory and Textual Computing: Comments and Suggestions (395–400).

Corns, T. N. (1990). *Milton's Language*. Oxford: Blackwell.

——(1991). Computers in the Humanities: Methods and Applications in the Study of English Literature. *Literary and Linguistic Computing* 6,2: 127–31.

Corns, T. N. et al. (2002). Imaging and Amanuensis: Understanding the Manuscript of De Doctrina Christiana, attributed to John Milton. *Proceedings of ALLC/ACH 2002: New Directions in Humanities Computing* (pp. 28–30). The 14th International Conference. University of Tübingen, July 24–28, 2002.

Crowder, R. G. and R. K. Wagner (1992). *The Psychology of Reading: An Introduction,* 2nd edn. Oxford: Oxford University Press.

Dixon, P. and M. Bertolussi (1996a). Literary Communication: Effects of Reader–Narrator Cooperation. *Poetics* 23: 405–30.

——(1996b). The Effects of Formal Training on Literary Reception. *Poetics* 23: 471–87.

Dixon, P. et al. (1993). Literary Processing and Interpretation: Towards Empirical Foundations. *Poetics* 22: 5–33.

Donaldson, P. S. (1997). Digital Archive as Expanded Text: Shakespeare and Electronic Textuality. In K. Sutherland (ed.), *Electronic Text: Investigations in Method and Theory* (pp. 173–98). Oxford: Clarendon Press.

Dorfman, M. H. (1996). Evaluating the Interpretive Community: Evidence from Expert and Novice Readers. *Poetics* 23: 453–70.

Duff, W. M. and C. A. Johnson (2002). Accidentally Found on Purpose: Information-seeking Behavior of Historians in Archives. *Library Quarterly* 72: 472–96.

Elton, G. R. (1967). *The Practice of History.* London: Fontana.

Finneran, R. J (1996). *The Literary Text in the Digital Age.* Ann Arbor: University of Michigan Press.

Fish, S. (1980). *Is There a Text in this Class? The Authority of Interpretive Communities.* Cambridge, MA: Harvard University Press.

Fogel, R. W. and S. L. Engerman (1974). *Time on the Cross.* London: Wildwood House.

Goetz, et al. (1993). Imagery and Emotional Response. *Poetics* 22: 35–49.

Halasz, L. (1992). Self-relevant Reading in Literary Understanding. In Elaine F. Narduccio (ed.), *Reader Response to Literature: The Empirical Dimension* (pp. 229–46). New York and London: Mouton de Gruyter.

Hanauer, D. (1998). The Genre-specific Hypothesis of Reading: Reading Poetry and Encyclopaedic Items. *Poetics* 26: 63–80.

Iser, W. (1989). *Prospecting: From Reader Response to Literary Anthropology.* Baltimore and London: Johns Hopkins University Press.

Jonscher, C. (1999). *The Evolution of Wired Life: From the Alphabet to the Soul-Catcher Chip – How Information Technologies Change Our World.* New York: Wiley.

Kneepkins, E. W. E. M. and R. A. Zwaan (1994). Emotions and Literary Text Comprehension. *Poetics* 23: 125–38.

McGann, J. (2001). *Radiant Textuality: Literature after the World Wide Web.* New York and Basingstoke: Palgrave.

Miall, D. (1992). Response to Poetry: Studies of Language and Structure. In Elaine F. Narduccio (ed.), *Reader Response to Literature: The Empirical Dimension* (pp. 153–72). Berlin and New York: Mouton de Gruyter.

Norman, D. A. (1999). *The Invisible Computer: Why Good Products Can Fail, the Personal Computer Is so Complex, and Information Appliances Are the Solution.* Boston: MIT Press.

Nunberg, G. (ed.) (1996). *The Future of the Book* (p. 10). Berkeley: University of California Press.

Pitti, D., C. Jessee, and S. Ramsay (2002). Multiple Architectures and Multiple Media: the Salem Witch Trials and Boston's Back Bay Fens. *Proceedings of ALLC/ACH 2002: New Directions in Humanities Computing* (pp. 87–91). The 14th International Conference. University of Tübingen, July 24–28, 2002.

Potter, R. G. (1991). Pragmatic Research on Reader Responses to Literature with an Emphasis on Gender and Reader Responses. *Revue Belge de la Philosophie et d'Histoire* 69,3: 599–617.

Ramsay, S. (2002). Towards an Algorithmic Criticism. *Proceedings of ALLC/ACH 2002: New Directions in Humanities Computing* (p. 99). The 14th International Conference. University of Tübingen, July 24–28, 2002.

Ransom, R. L. and R. Sutch (1977). *One Kind of Freedom: The Economic Consequences of Emancipation.* Cambridge: Cambridge University Press.

Richards, I. A. (1929). *Practical Criticism: A Study of Literary Judgements.* London: Kegan Paul.

Sheffield University (2003). The Cistercians in Yorkshire. At <http://cistercians.shef.ac.uk/>.

Smith, M. N. (2002). MITH's Lean, Mean Versioning Machine. *Proceedings of ALLC/ACH 2002: New Directions in Humanities Computing* (pp. 122–7). The 14th International Conference. University of Tübingen, July 24–28, 2002.

Snelgrove, T. (1990). A Method for the Analysis of the Structure of Narrative Texts. *LLC* 5: 221–5.

Stafford-Fraser, Q. (1995). *The Trojan Room Coffee Pot: A (Non-technical) Biography.* Cambridge University Computer Laboratory. At <http://www.cl.cam.ac.uk/coffee/qsf/coffee.html>.

Stone, S. (1982). Humanities Scholars – Information Needs and Uses. *Journal of Documentation* 38,4: 292–313.

Thomas, W. G. (2000). Preliminary Conclusions from the Valley of the Shadow Project. Paper delivered at: ECAI/Pacific Neighborhood Consortium Conference, January 11, 2000, University of California at Berkeley. At <http://jefferson.village.virginia.edu/vcdh/ECAI.paper.html>.

Unsworth, J. (2002). Using Digital Primary Resources to Produce Scholarship in Print. Paper presented at Literary Studies in Cyberspace: Texts, Contexts, and Criticism. Modern Language Association

Annual Convention, Sunday, December 29, 2002. New York, USA. At <http://jefferson.village.virginia.edu/~jmu2m/cyber-mla.2002/>.

Van Peer, W. (1989). Quantitative Studies of Literature, a Critique and an Outlook. *Computers and the Humanities* 23: 301–7.

Wright, G. (1978). *The Political Economy of the Cotton South: Households, Markets, and Wealth in the Nineteenth Century*. New York: W. W. Norton.

Zwaan, R. A. (1993). *Aspects of Literary Comprehension: A Cognitive Approach*. Amsterdam: John Benjamins.

26

Digital Media and the Analysis of Film

Robert Kolker

This history of film studies is a short one, dating from the early to mid-1960s, and evolving from a number of historical events. One was the appearance of the films of the French New Wave – Jean-Luc Godard, François Truffaut, Claude Chabrol, Eric Rohmer, as well as older figures, such as Alain Resnais. These directors, along with Sweden's Ingmar Bergman and Italy's Federico Fellini and Michelangelo Antonioni, among others, demonstrated that the formal, thematic, and economic givens of American Cinema were not that at all. Film had a flexible language that could be explored, opened, rethought. They proved that the conventions of Hollywood story telling could be pulled and stretched, stood on their head. These films, in short, made many people aware that cinema was a serious form of expression, an art form involved in the production of thought.

The wonderful paradox here was that many of these European directors learned from watching American film. Not knowing English, they read the visual structure of the films they saw and discovered a visual energy mostly missed by plot-centric American filmgoers and film reviewers. They embraced the American style and countered it simultaneously, all the while refusing the pressures of a studio system that, in America, saw films as commodities. And, as the writing and the filmmaking of the French New Wave reached Britain and then the USA, there was an interesting flow-back effect, turning the eyes of burgeoning American film scholars toward their own cinema, largely reviled, mostly forgotten.

In their discovery of American film, the French – concentrating on the visual aspects of what they saw, and understanding that film was essentially about the construction of images – noticed that when the structures of formal and thematic element cohered, it was around the film's director – no matter what other personnel were involved, including the screenwriter. As these insights were passed overseas, American film suddenly took on a patina of seriousness that only authorship could give it. This, coupled with the excitement of the new cinema coming from overseas, and the call by students for a broader college curriculum, led to film courses being offered by English professors (like myself), and in history and art history departments. Film Studies departments came together more slowly. Publishing scholarly film articles and books grew apace.

What was taught and studied in the early days? The *auteur* theory, in which the film director is seen as the formative creative consciousness of a film, turned out to be in practice not mere idolatry, but a means of analysis. If one could identify a filmmaker by certain stylistic and thematic traits, these could to be understood and analyzed. Or, taking a Foucauldian turn, the *auteur* could be constructed from a group of films, discovered as *auteurs* through their work, the analysis of which yields ways of cinematic seeing that were recognizable from film to film.

By the late 1960s and into the 1970s and 1980s, the fundamentals of *auteur*ism were enriched by a number of other theoretical and historical practices. In fact, film studies was among the earliest disciplines to apply feminist and gender theory. Laura Mulvey's theory of the formal structures of the gendered gaze in her essay "Visual Pleasure and the Narrative Cinema," published in 1975, remains a touchstone not only for film studies, but for art and literary analysis as well. Ideological criticism and cultural analysis, Lacanian psychoanalytic theory, structuralism, postmodern critique – indeed a variety of theoretical permutations – have built film (and, finally, television) studies into a rich and productive discipline.

Throughout this period of growth (if not expansion), one problem remained in both the teaching and writing of film: the ability to prove and demonstrate by means of quotation. In other words, the literary scholar, the historian, the art historian can literally bring the work under study into her own text to prove a point, illustrate an argument, and provide the text and context for analysis. The film scholar cannot.

In teaching, the ability to analyze sequences in front of a class was better served, going through a long phase of never quite adequate development. In the beginning, there were only 16 mm copies of films to show and analyze. The equivalent of Xerox copies, 16 mm film was terrible for general viewing, and selecting a sequence to study involved putting pieces of paper in the film reel as it ran and then winding it back to find the passage. One could also put the reel on manual rewinds and use a small viewer to find the passage, and then remount the whole thing back on the projector. At one point, the department I was working in purchased an "analyzer" projector – the kind that was used by football teams before videotape. One still needed to find the passage in the reel, but, theoretically, one could freeze frames, roll forward or backward, or even step-frame through the sequence. In reality, the machine usually spat out sprocket holes and tore up the film. Videotape was no better in image quality – worse, in fact, because the manufacturers of video believed audiences would not put up with the black bars on the top and bottom of the frame for wide-screen and anamorphic films, and so blew up the image to make it fit the familiar, almost square rectangle, thereby losing about two-thirds of it in a process nicely named "pan and scan."

Laserdisk and now DVD came close to ameliorating the situation. The image resolution is greatly improved. Good video projection creates a sharp, color correct or accurate greyscale image in the proper screen ratio. Accessibility to the precise place in the film to which we want to aim our students' attention, or have them find the sequence they wish to discuss, is easy. We can now "quote" the passages of the film when teaching them.

But this did not solve the quotation problem for research. The presentation and analysis of cinematic works, no matter what methodology was used, could not be given the proof of the thing itself, the moving image upon which the analysis was based. We could only describe what we saw as a means of bolstering and driving our arguments, and, for visuals (often on the insistence of publishers), provide studio stills, which are, more often than not, publicity stills rather than frame enlargements from the film itself. To be sure, there were some painstaking researchers who, with special lenses and the permission of archives, made (and still make) their own frame enlargements directly from a 35 mm print in order to get exactly the image they need. But the images were still, and we were all writing and talking about the images in motion.

The situation began to change in the early 1990s. The first indication of a new way to do film studies occurred at a meeting of the Society for Cinema Studies in 1989, when Stephen Mamber of UCLA hooked up a computer, a laserdisk player, and a television monitor and controlled the images of the film on the laserdisk through the computer with a program he had written. This was followed the next year by a colloquium that Mamber and Bob Rosen set up at UCLA, funded by a MacArthur Grant, that advanced Mamber's work considerably. He and Rosen had created a database of every shot in *Citizen Kane*, Welles's *Macbeth,* and a film from China, *Girl From Hunan* (1986). They could access the shots from the computer, through a multimedia program called Toolbook – an excellent multimedia package that still exists and is among the best to do the kind of work I'm describing.

The coup came shortly after this, when a colleague at the University of Maryland demonstrated image overlay hardware that put a moving image from a tape or disk directly into a window on the computer screen. Quickly following this came inexpensive video capture hardware and software that allows the capture of small or long sequences from a videotape or DVD. The captured and compressed images (the initially captured image creates a huge file which must be compressed with software called "codecs" in order to make them usable) are like any computer file. They can be manipulated, edited, titled, animated. The film scholar and burgeoning computer user finally discovered that a fundamental problem faced by the discipline of film studies could now be solved. The visual text that eluded us in our scholarly work and even our teaching was now at hand. We could tell, explain, theorize, and demonstrate!

But other problems immediately surfaced. One was obvious: how would this work be transmitted? On first thought, the web seemed the best and obvious means of distribution for this new kind of film analysis. It wasn't then; it isn't now. To analyze the moving image, it has to appear promptly, smoothly, with as near perfect resolution as possible, and at a size no smaller than 320 × 240 pixels or larger (to make things confusing, these numbers refer to image resolution, but translate on the screen as image size). This is impossible on the Web. Even today's streaming video and high-powered computers cannot offer the image size, resolution, and smoothness of playback that are required, despite the fact that a few successful Web projects have emerged, mostly using very small images to minimize download time. Until Internet 2 becomes widely available, CD and DVD are the only suitable media for transmission of moving images. (Recordable DVD is still in its standardizing phase, with a number of formats competing with each other.) There is something on the horizon that will allow the Web to control a DVD in the user's machine, and we will get to that in a bit.

The other problem involves the programming necessary to create a project that combines text and moving image. There are relatively simple solutions: moving image clips can be easily embedded into a Power Point presentation, for example. A Word document will also accept embedded moving images – although, of course, such an essay would have to be read on a computer. HTML can be used relatively easily to build an off-line Web project which will permit the size and speed of moving images necessary. But more elaborate presentations that will figuratively or literally open up the image and allow the user to interact with it, that will break up the image into analyzable chunks, or permit operations on the part of the reader to, for example, re-edit a sequence – all require some programming skills. This is probably not the place to address the pains and pleasures of programming. There is no getting around the fact that one will need to know some basics of programming (and the varieties of online users' groups, who will answer questions); but ultimately, programming is only half the problem. The other, perhaps most important, is designing the project, creating an interface, making the screen inviting, as easy or as complex to address as the creator of it wishes it to be. And, preceding the interface, there must lie a well-thought out concept of what we want a user to do, to discover, to learn. In other words, in addition to the analytic and theoretical skills of a film scholar, there are added design and usability skills as well.

There are a variety of tools available to execute design and usability, each one with its particular strengths and weaknesses. Macromedia Director is good for animations to accompany the exposition, but it requires a great deal of programming in a non-intuitive environment. Toolbook is an excellent, Windows-only program. Its scripting language is fairly simple (or fairly complex, depending upon your need) and much of it in plain English. Visual Basic is a powerful tool, requiring a great deal of programming knowledge. The solution for all of this, of course, is for the film scholar to work closely with a student with programming skills, so that the scholar becomes essentially a concept and content provider. On the other hand, it is very satisfying to learn the necessary program or multimedia package. More than satisfying, by working out the programming, one learns how to structure and form ideas by and for the computer – in effect understanding the grammar that will express what you want the viewer to see. By understanding the form and structure of computational possibilities, you can generate the design, interactivity, the images and analyses that integrate concept, execution, and reception.

Many scholars have experimented with various modes of computer representations since the 1990s. I've indicated that the work of Stephen Mamber was responsible for getting me and others started in using the computer to analyze films. Mamber went on to do what still remains the most exciting and complex computer-driven work of cinematic analysis, his "Digital Hitchcock" project on Hitchcock's *The Birds*. The project started in part when the Academy of Motion Picture Arts and Sciences allowed him access to the script, storyboards, and other material related to the film. Programming from scratch, Mamber created a stunning presentation: beginning with the representation of the first frame of every shot of the film, all of which he managed to put on one screen. In other words, the whole film is represented by a still of each of its shots and each still is addressable. When clicked, they bring up the entire shot.

Mamber compares Hitchcock's storyboard illustrations side by side with moving clips from the finished screen, to demonstrate how closely Hitchcock hewed to his original conceptions. (Hitchcock was fond of saying that, for him, the most boring part of making a film was actually making the film, because he had completed it before it went to the studio floor.) Mamber's comparison of sketches with shots proves Hitchcock right and wrong, because it indicates where he deviates from the sketches to achieve his greatest effects. The program allows the clip to be played while the successive storyboard sketches appear next to the sequence.

In this project, Mamber began what has become some of his most exciting work, the creation of 3-D mock-ups of filmic spaces. Working on the theory of "imaginary spaces," Mamber shows how the images we look at in a film could not possibly exist. They are almost the cinematic equivalents of *trompe l'oeil*, using the two-dimensional surface of the screen to represent a fictional space that the filmmaker deems necessary for us to see, without regard to the impossible spaces he or she is creating. By making the entire space visible by imagining a three-dimensional simulacrum of it (in effect creating a simulacrum of a simulacrum), Mamber exposes not only the fictional space, but the processes of representation itself. His spatial representations provide an analytical understanding of the continuity of movement through space that filmmakers are so keen on maintaining, despite the optical trickery used to create them. His work becomes, in effect, an exposure of the ideology of the visible. He creates an alternative world of the alternative world that the film itself creates.

Mamber clarifies a film sequence through 3-D rendering, showing how it is constructed for our perception. He has made, for example, a painstaking animated reconstruction of the opening of Max Ophüls's *The Earrings of Madame De...*, showing the intricate movements of the camera – by putting the camera in the animation – during an amazingly long shot. He has done a still rendering of the racetrack and a flythrough of the betting hall in Kubrick's *The Killing* in order to show the spatial analogues of the complex time scheme of the film. The line of his investigation is of enormous potential for all narrative art because he is essentially discovering ways of visualizing narrative. Film is, obviously, the perfect place to start, because its narrative is visual and depends upon spatial relationships, as well as the temporal additions of editing. But literary narrative also depends upon the building of imaginary spaces, and the kind of visualizations Mamber is doing on film could go far toward a mapping of the spaces of the story we are asked by fiction to imagine.[1]

Other pioneering work in the field of computer-driven film studies includes Marsha Kinder's 1994 companion CD-ROM to her book on Spanish film, *Blood Cinema*. Here, film clips and narration elaborate the elements of Spanish cinema since the 1950s. Lauren Rabinowitz's 1995 CD-ROM, *The Rebecca Project*, is a wonderful example of how CD-ROMs are able to combine images, clips, critical essays, and other documents to drill as deeply and spread as widely information and analysis of Hitchcock's first American film. Robert Kapsis's *Multimedia Hitchcock*, displayed at MOMA, also brings together a variety of information, images, clips, and commentary on Hitchcock's work. Similarly, Georgia Tech's *Griffith in Context* (Ellen Strain, Greg Van Hoosier-Carey, and Patrick Ledwell), supported by a National Endowment for the Humanities (NEH) grant, takes representative sequences from *Birth of a Nation* and makes them available to the user in a variety of ways. The user can view the clips, attempt a re-editing of them, listen to a variety of commentary from film scholars, view documents, and learn about the racial and cultural context surrounding Griffith's work. MIT's *Virtual Screening Room* (Henry Jenkins, Ben Singer, Ellen Draper, and Janet Murray), also the recipient of an NEH grant, is a huge database of moving images, designed to illustrate various elements of film construction. Adrian Miles's *"Singin' in the Rain*: A Hypertextual Reading," appearing in the January, 1998, film issue of *Postmodern Culture* (at <http://muse.jhu.edu/cgi-bin/access.cgi?uri=/ journals/pmc/v008/8.2miles.html>, is one of the most ambitious projects involving image and critical analysis, and one of the few successful web-based projects with moving images. Miles uses small and relatively fast-loading Quicktimes with an intricate hyper-textual analysis – hypervisual might be more accurate – that not only explores the Kelly-Donen film, but experiments with the possibilities of a film criticism that follows non-linear, reader-driven paths in which the images and the text simultaneously elucidate and make themselves more complex. This is textual and visual criticism turned into Roland Barthes's writerly text.

My own work has followed a number of paths. Early attempts emerged out of an essay I wrote on Martin Scorsese's *Cape Fear* (1991). *Cape Fear* is not great Scorsese, but, watching it, I was struck by something very curious I could not quite put my finger on: I could see other films behind it, in it, lurking like ghosts. None of these ghosts were the original 1961 *Cape Fear*, an early *Psycho* imitation. But it was Hitchcock I was seeing, especially early 1950s Hitchcock, before he had got into his stride; I was seeing *Stagefright* (1950), *Strangers on a Train* (1951), and *I Confess* (1953). The proof of my intuition appeared as soon as I looked closely at these three films. And what I had intuited were not ghosts, but a kind of palimpsest, images and scenes that lay under Scorsese's film. He was quoting – indeed recreating scenes – from these earlier films. Writing the essay analyzing these quotes didn't seem sufficient, I wanted a way to show them.

I built a very simple Toolbook program, using a laserdisk and an overlay window, which merely had a screen of buttons naming the various scenes from *Strangers on a Train* and *Cape Fear* which, when pressed, and with the proper side of the appropriate disk in the player, displayed the images on the computer screen. The interface was plain, but the first step had been taken. The laserdisk/computer interface was extremely confining. There needed to be a way to capture the images and have them on the computer hard disk, quickly available and easy to insert into a program. Reasonably priced image capture boards that allowed easy digitizing and compression of short-duration clips, even on the then low-powered desk-top PCs, were already being developed in the early 1990s. This was the obvious answer to the problem: making image files as accessible and manipulable as any other digital artifact. Here was hardware and software that turned the moving image into binary code, and once so encoded, almost anything could be done with it.

With the encouragement and assistance of John Unsworth at the Institute of Advanced Technology in the Humanities, I wrote I kind of manifesto, "The Moving Image Reclaimed," for a 1994 issue of IATH's online journal *Postmodern Culture* (http://muse. jhu.edu/journals/postmodern_culture/ v005/5.1kolker.html). The essay included various moving image files, including the major comparisons of *Cape Fear* and *Strangers on a Train*. It also included an idea of how the computer could be used literally to *enter* the image and diagram it to show how it worked. I took part of a very long shot in *Citizen Kane*, where Mrs Kane sells her son to Mr Thatcher for a deed to a copper mine – a sequence in which the movement of the camera and the shifting positions of the characters tell more interesting things about the story than the dialogue does – and animated it. That is, I plucked each frame from the sequence, and, overlaying the frame with various colored lines, put together a variation of a rotoscope (an animation technique where live action is traced over and turned into a cartoon). The result was a visualizing – a map – of how eyeline matches (the way a film allows us to understand who is looking at whom, and why) and the changing positions of the various characters were staged and composed in order to represent the spaces of Oedipal conflict.

Unsworth and I decided that MPEG would be the best format for the purpose (this was some time before the development of streaming video), though we could not transmit the sound. The essay and images were put online. The images were large, and they took a great deal of time to download, but the project successfully proved the ability to solve the quotation problem.

While it was a worthwhile experiment, it confirmed that the Web was an imperfect transmission vehicle for moving images. The next project was the creation of an interactive program that would provide a visual version of an introduction to the basic elements of film study. Prototyping in Toolbook, I created a series of modules on editing, point-of-view, *mise-en-scène*, lighting, camera movement, and other issues that seemed to me most amenable to using digitized clips. This was not to be a program on how to make a film, but, to borrow James Monaco's term (who has himself recently published a DVD full of text and moving images), how to *read* a film. The program uses text and moving image, both often broken up into successive segments to show how a sequence is developed, and always allowing the user to look at the entire clip. It included interactivity that allowed the user to, for example, put together a montage cell from Eisenstein's *Potemkin* or see the results of classical Hollywood three-point lighting by "turning on" the key, fill, and backlighting on a figure, or step through a sequence in *Vertigo* to show how camera movement and framing tell a story different from the one a character in the film is telling. It contained a glossary, so that by clicking on any hotword in the text, one would jump to a definition of the term.

The point-of-view (POV) module was among the most challenging. POV is a difficult concept to analyze even in the traditional modes of film theory (though Edward Branigan and others have made important contributions to our understanding). How to *show* how point-of-view works toward narrative ends – how the film guides our gaze and provides a "voice" for the narrative – required careful choices and execution. I went to a film that was *about* point-of-view, Hitchcock's *Rear Window* (1954). (It is, incidentally, no accident that so many film/computer projects focus on Hitchcock, one of the most complex formalists of American film.) By combining stills and moving images, winding up finally with a 3-D flythrough that indicates the perceptual spaces of the film and the way they turn at a crucial moment, the user is able to gain a visual grip on the process and understand how filmmakers make us see the way they want us to see.

The creation and publication of the project, called *Film, Form, and Culture*, offers a useful example of other problems and successes that arise once you have decided to go digital. For one thing, most publishers are reluctant to publish CDs or DVDs alone. They are, after all, book publishers, and they still want paper. While continuing to prototype the CD-ROM project, I wrote an introductory textbook, which not only introduces terms and concepts basic to film studies, but also examines the history of film in the contexts of the cultures that produced them. The book was not written as a supplement, but as a stand-alone companion to the CD. Elements in the text that are covered on the CD are cited at the end of each chapter. And the book itself is illustrated by digital stills – that is, stills grabbed by the computer directly from the DVD or VHS of a film, a process which allows creating a sequence of shots which, while still, convey some of the movement between them, as well as indicating ways in which editing connects various shots.

The publisher of the work, McGraw-Hill, bid out for a professional CD-authoring company to do the distribution CD. An important lesson was learned from this. The film scholar, used to dealing politely with editors, who, more often than not, had the right ideas on how to improve the language, organization, and accuracy of a manuscript, is here confronted with the age-old problem of "creator" (or, in the discourse of CD or Web authoring, the "content provider") vs. the producer, who was working within a budget provided by the publisher. The CD producer converted my prototype into Macromedia Director, in order to create a cross-platform product. We worked closely to choose a suitable interface, but some small "creative differences" ensued. The producer wanted a uniform interface, so that each screen would look the same. This is common multi-media/web-design practice, though it can limit flexibility, especially when one wants to break the limits of the screen frame, or present alternative ways of laying out the material. There was an urge to cut down on interactivity and slightly diminish an immersive experience for the user. They insisted on small anomalies, such as not allowing the cursor to change into a hand icon over a link.

These were small, limiting constraints, and in some cases, convincing was needed on my part, to maintain my original conceptions, especially when these involved pedagogical necessities. But like all such give and take, the constraints were turned to advantages, and, to the producers' great credit, the last module, on music, turned out to be one of the best on the CD, and for that module, I provided only concept, assets (images and sounds), and text; they developed the appearance of the section based upon some preliminary prototyping on my part – which used Sergei Eisenstein's graphic visualization of how Prokofiev's score and Eisenstein's images worked in perfect abstract relationship to each other in *Alexander Nevsky* (1938). In the second edition of the CD, many problems were solved. The cursor changes to a hand over a link. The new material on *film noir* and on sound are well executed. The interface remains, and even more interactivity was and can still be added. As with all digital projects, it is a work in progress, always undergoing improvement with each new edition and the help of very supportive publishers.

But one issue, much more immediately pressing than dealing with producers, hangs like a cold hand over the project of using digital media in the study of film or any other discipline. This is the issue of copyright and intellectual property law (IP). Simply put, IP is the legal issue of who owns what, who can use it, and where it can be used. But the issue is not simple. The US government is trying to make copyright laws more and more inflexible and has made Fair Use (the legally permitted use of small portions of a copyrighted work for educational purposes) more difficult to apply, beginning with the 1990 Digital Millennium Copyright Act. But many of the new laws are undergoing a challenge. And, with the major exception of Napster, there have been few major test cases to indicate how the various parties – content owner and content user – would fare in court. No one wants to go first!

It might be helpful to briefly outline the major copyright laws and then go into some more detail on the major problems in gaining licenses, rights, and permissions for digital media, with the full knowledge that such a complex issue can never be completely elucidated in a short space.

- The overwhelming majority of feature films are under copyright.
- Copyright has (in its original form) limits:
  - Published before 1923, the work is in the Public Domain (PD).
  - Works created after January 1, 1978, are copyrighted for the life of the author (in film, often considered the Studio) plus 70 years.
  - Works published from 1923 to 1963: copyright holds for 28 years, renewable up to 67 years. There are other variations, but these are the most pertinent.
  - The Sonny Bono Copyright Term Extension Act extends copyright on many works for as much as 95 years, and gives foreign works this extension even if the works are not formally copyrighted. Works published in or before 1922 remain in the Public Domain. Bono is under litigation in the Supreme Court. The restrictive 1990 Digital Millennium Copyright Act is also undergoing challenges.
  - Legislation has been passed for the "Technology, Education and Copyright Harmonization Act" (TEACH), that aims to modify copyright restrictions for Distance Education.
  - Films in the Public Domain may have "subsidiary rights." That is, while the film may have come in to PD, parts of it, the score, for example, may have been separately copyrighted. Carol Reed's *The Third Man* is an example.
  - Licensing clips for a CD – even an educational one – takes a strong stomach, a very busy fax machine, and often a lot of money.

Copyright issues are, perhaps even more than developing one's work, the greatest hindrance to scholars making use of digital interventions in film studies. However, they are not insuperable. Copyright concerns and the energy required for licensing clips should in fact stop no one, but only cause one to act cautiously and judiciously, especially if the work is aimed at publication. The Library of Congress (the repository for all copyrighted material) has, for example, a three-volume listing of films in the Public Domain. The last volume has an appendix that, as of the early 1990s, lists films for which extensive research on subsidiary rights was made. Many of these films are available on magnetic or digital media. This is the best first source for what is freely available – especially if the Bono Act is overthrown.

After the research for PD titles, the very best way to start the rights and permissions process, or at least get an entry to the studios who own copyrighted material, is to contact the film's director – assuming he or she is alive. For *Film, Form, and Culture*, one filmmaker gave us complete use of one of his films, and signed a clearance for it. Another, Oliver Stone, a great filmmaker and an admirer of film studies, wrote to each of his distributors asking them to help me out. Sometimes even this will not prevail. Disney, whose Hollywood Films released *Nixon*, appreciated the personal note, but announced their policy of *never* giving permissions for CDs. However, Warner Bros did license thirty seconds of *JFK* for the same amount, and for the same length of clip from *Citizen Kane*, $3,000.

For the second edition, I added a module on *film noir*. I was most interested in using images from one of the greatest of the late-1940s *noir* directors, Anthony Mann. His dark, brutal, misanthropic films are currently owned by the famous publisher of children's literature, Golden Books. The ways of copyright are strange, indeed. Golden Books charged $1,000 for sixty seconds. In the great scheme of licensing clips, this is not a lot of money, and publishers who understand the value of having a CD with a book will pay such a relatively modest fee.

For other clips, the Hitchcock Estate, who, when I started the project, still controlled *Rear Window* and *Vertigo*, worked with Universal pictures, who – unlike the Estate, but at their urging – reluctantly allowed me to use clips from those films. My understanding is that Universal and other studios have since streamlined both their rights process and their attitude. Everything else used was Public Domain.

Certainly, none of this was easy (though now it may be at least easier, given such companies as RightsLine and *RightsIQ*, that can help track who holds various rights to a film). In every successful instance of dealing with a studio, the result will be a long and intimidating contract, which must be read carefully. The result, however, is worth the labor. The work of copyright searches and acquisition of licenses allowed *Film, Form, and Culture*, for example, to present students with access to clips from a large variety of films and uses them in some detail to show the precision with which they are made and a variety of ways in which they can be read and analyzed.

I would only repeat that IP concerns should not be the initial obstacle to using moving images in a pedagogical or scholarly work. There are many ways to get what you need, if not always what you want. And Fair Use should still prevail for in-class pedagogical use, for digital stills in books, and, since the TEACH Act has been passed, for wider educational distribution. The studios have become somewhat more accommo- dating, a response that may have to do with DVDs and the unexpected popularity of their "supplementary material." DVDs also offer something of a new frontier in the development of digitized media in film studies and, hopefully, a relief for copyright concerns.

DVDs have proven a boon to film scholars and film viewers alike. They have compen- sated for the culture's massive error in visual judgment when it chose VHS over Beta (which had a higher image resolution) in the 1980s. The success of DVD has proven that image quality does count. They have been of great help to film studies: they are cheap for an academic department to buy; they are readily available for students to rent and view at home. Their "supplementary material" (directors' and actors' commentaries, demonstra- tions on how scenes are shot, and how computer graphics are integrated into a film) have proven enormously popular, even though they are mostly illustrative and anecdotal. This success, as I noted, came as something of a surprise to the studios, and the outcome is that they may be taking notice of the fact that viewers may, first of all, be interested in older titles, and, second, do want to know more about the film they are watching. In fact, studios may now be admitting that a film might have educational value! Herein lies some hope on the licensing issue. The studios (and this is pure fantasy at the moment) may some day, when a scholar tells them that use of their material will help further sales of their films by educating new viewers, and without "copying" clips, begin to accept the claim and therefore restrain themselves from deriding the person who makes such an argument.

Use of DVDs for analysis is being made possible by some new technology that opens interesting possibilities of using commercially available DVDs, controlling them as one would a digitized file on the computer, and even creating a set of analytic tools available on a CD or on a website to address the DVD in the individual's own computer. Some of this work has received funding from the National Endowment for the Humanities.

Again, programming issues are at stake here, and various choices have to be made, depending upon whether the creator of a DVD-based project wants to do a standalone (that is, a project that exists only on a computer or CD-ROM, along with the DVD) or a web-based project that contains the controls, a database, and an interface online, which address the DVD in the user's computer. Indeed, unlike digitized clips, addressing the DVD from the Web does not result in image degradation, because the image remains on the user's computer.

The basics for building a set of DVD controls are reasonably straightforward, if you have some facility at cutting and pasting code. Microsoft offers a complete programmer's guide to DVD control, down to the very frame. Full information and very simple code is given at <http://msdn.microsoft.com/library/default.asp?url=/library/en-us/dx8_c/directx_cpp/ htm/mswebdvdobject.asp>. Drill through this page and you will find script that you can cut and paste into an HTML file or a Power Point slide to see how it works. There should be utilities, or plug-ins, available for the Mac and Mac-based Director that would perform similar operations. The Windows version makes use of the MSWebDVD ActiveX control (the program that contains the window in which the DVD will play as well as the instructions for writing very simple code). It is possible that the Javascript version of the code to control the DVD will also function on a web-based project on the Mac, and the latest version of Macromedia Director includes DVD controls, though I have not tested this. The work I have done so far has been in Toolbook and Visual Basic for standalone use.

Again, the coding issues can be overcome in various ways. But there is yet another issue involved. While the use of a commercial DVD in no way bypasses copyright issues, it may (and I must emphasize that I, like anyone else, can only speculate) make licensing easier to obtain or cause even less of a worry for Fair Use in a classroom or other educational settings. After all, one is not digitizing copyrighted material, but using something that is already commercially available. The content provider, however, may still see this as using their material, in ways other than for home viewing.

It may, finally, seem as if we have come full circle to the time when a computer controlled a laserdisk. There are important differences. DVDs are digital; laserdisks were analogue. Laserdisks had to be played either on a monitor, or on an overlay window on the computer screen through special hardware. DVDs play directly through the computer's graphics display card – as long as there are the proper drivers (which come automatically with any computer that has a DVD drive). All this makes control of DVDs easier and more flexible than laserdisk. In a relatively simple Visual Basic program, one can even capture a still from the DVD directly to disk. I have been able to program a DVD so that, with user input, the film is paused, the exact time of the pause is passed to the computer, which then uses that time to call up other information I have prepared in a database that is relevant to that moment or shot in the film. This can be combined with other images and analysis that further explains the shot or the sequence it is part of – and finally the film as a whole. In other words, this combination of database and image, along with the interactivity that gives the user choice over what part of the film he wishes to examine, provides an invaluable method to thoroughly analyze a single work.

The database, created and connected to the DVD, contains information for every shot in the film – from dialogue, discussion of the narrative moment, *mise-en-scène*, editing patterns, and so on. A database is essentially a static set of cubicles, each containing various kinds of data, which can be organized and then accessed in a variety of ways. We use them continuously: whenever you go online to use the campus library, to shop, or to buy an airline ticket, you are manipulating a database. Terabytes of personal information (more and more being added each day) are stored by government agencies in databases. It is not a stretch to say that the computerized database is the one completely structured item in an otherwise chaotic world – though this is no guarantee of the veracity of the data it contains. It *must* be ordered correctly and filled with well-thought out data, and at the same time accessible, and manipulable, containing data in the form of text, numbers, sounds, or images that can be drawn upon in a number of different ways. Using a simple scripted language called SQL (Standard Query Language, better known as "Sequel"), the database becomes a malleable, flexible, responsive thing, alive to query and incredibly responsive if you ask the right questions of it. Database tables are themselves combinable, open to cross-queries, with the ability to pull together a large array of information.

Lev Manovich (2001: 226) theorizes that the database is essential to computer aesthetics, part or, perhaps more appropriately, the genesis of the various narratives – including analytic and theoretical narratives – we can create by computer. "Creating a work in new media," he writes, "can be understood as the construction of an interface to a database," the means of accessing, combining, temporalizing, and spatializing static bits of data.

Allow me another example from my own work: before DVDs were available, I had started work analyzing Robert Altman's 1993 film *Short Cuts*, using a five-minute digitized clip. My initial interests were to create a search engine so that various key terms (say, "zoom," a camera lens movement that Altman turns into an aesthetic and narrative statement) would yield the corresponding shots in which the zoom was used. What I would like to do now, when the DVD becomes available, is to create a critical narrative of the entire film, especially concentrating on its complex narrative structure and the way that complexity is made perfectly comprehensible to the viewer through Altman's editing, his use of color, the matching of character movement, and, throughout, an abstract, intuited pattern of movement across the narrative fields of the film, which, indeed, can itself be thought of as a sort of database of narrative events.

The creation of a database for a three-hour film is no easy task. There are a number of decisions to be made in order to make it become dynamic, and all of these must be done by the imagination and work of the film scholar. There is little automation here, but an extraordinary opportunity to learn about the film. One must choose the various elements to describe and analyze the shot – for example, narrative elements, *mise-en-scène*, editing, dialogue, etc. And, indispensably, though not very creatively, the "in" and "out" points for each shot – that is, where a shot ends and where the next shot begins must be found and entered in the database. The in and out points are where the program will first go to find the shot and the relevant information the user wants for that shot. The filling-in of the database fields is where the major analytic work is done; we have to make the same judgments, the same analytic insights, and apply the same methodologies as we would writing an article or a book. The difference is a kind of fragmentation and the adoption of a more aphoristic style than the critical writer is used to. At the same time, the writer has to be aware of a thread of analysis running through all the database entries and make sure that the keywords that the user may want to search on appear wherever appropriate.

The ability to search is a major advantage of a database: if the user wants to find any place in the film where a word is used, a color combination is present, a narrative element can be found, she should be able to enter that word, click a button, and have a list pulled from the database. Clicking on any entry in the list will bring up the accompanying shot.

The search function opens up an entirely new problem in film analysis. We are, in effect, giving over some critical work to the user of the program. This opens up difficult critical and functional questions, the most striking of which is: what is the reader going to want to search for? Do we second-guess when we create the database, or create a list of keywords that we know the user may want to search on, and then make certain that they appear in the appropriate fields of the database? Do we provide such a list in the program itself, perhaps as part of the introductory apparatus, thereby suggesting what the user might want to find? When we go to a Web search engine, like Google, we know more or less what we are looking for, even though what we get may not precisely fit our query. Going to the interface of a film database and guessing what we want to find, is a problem of a different order. We have, somehow, to present a critical apparatus within the interface that discusses the program's intent and offers some guidance for the user. As much interactivity as we provide, we must provide as well a guide to the critical narrative we are striving to get the user to put together.

We have, then, discovered a second major advantage of the use of the computer in film studies. The first was the ability to quote from and analyze a given sequence of a film. The second is the database, as huge as one wants, and as fine-tuned as one needs, full of ideas, information, analysis, and offering the user the ability to connect the data to the precisely relevant images within a complete film.

What we need, finally, to make this complete is a program that searches images themselves. We can tag images in the database and search that way. In other words, we can describe the image content, color, composition, and narrative relevance, and allow the user to choose these and bring up the related images or shots. A new codec, MP7, promises the ability to tag the image itself. But all these are still text-based. We have to write out a description for, or appended to, the image and then search for it by entering the keyword. There is software available to search still images by example: that is, by clicking on one image, other images with similar colors or shapes will be called up. These are complex applications, not yet easily available to a film scholar.

Searching moving images is another matter still. The ability, for example, to search a database of *Short Cuts* for zoom shots of specific kinds, based merely on clicking on an example of that kind, would open up new avenues for studying a film's textuality, an *auteur*'s style, and, most important, begin to enable us to understand the structure of cinematic representation itself. Software to search moving images is slowly being developed, although a researcher at Kodak told me "not in our lifetime." But that was six years ago.

Note

1   Another aspect of Mamber's investigations, on the theory and ideology of the surveillance camera, can be found online at <http://www.cinema.ucla.edu/mamber2/>.

REFERENCES FOR FURTHER READING

Branigan, Edward (1984). *Point of View in the Cinema: A Theory of Narration and Subjectivity in Classical Film*. Berlin and New York: Mouton.

Kolker, Robert (1994). The Moving Image Reclaimed. *Postmodern Culture* 5.1 (September). At <http://muse.jhu.edu/journals/postmodern_culture/ v005/5.1kolker.html>.

——(1998). "Algebraic Figures: Recalculating the Hitchcock Formula." In *Play It Again, Sam: Retakes on Remakes*, ed. Andrew Horton and Stuart Y. McDougal. Berkeley: University of California Press.

Mamber, Stephen (1998). Simultaneity and Overlap in Stanley Kubrick's *The Killing*. *Postmodern Culture* (January). At <http://muse.jhu.edu/cgi-bin/access.cgi?uri=/journals/pmc/v008/8.2mamber.html>.

Manovich, Lev (2001). *The Language of New Media*. Cambridge, MA: MIT Press.

Miles, Adrian (1998). *Singin' in the Rain*: A Hypertextual Reading. *Postmodern Culture* (January). At <http://muse.jhu.edu/cgi-bin/access.cgi?uri=/journals/pmc/v008/8.2miles.html>.

Mulvey, Laura (1975). Visual Pleasure and the Narrative Cinema. *Screen* 16,3 (Autumn): 6–18. Reprinted at <http://www.bbk.ac.uk/hafvm/staff_research/visual1.html>.

Information on copyright is from Lolly Gasaway, University of North Carolina <http://www.unc.edu/~unclng/public-d.htm>. David Green provided further information on the Bono Act and treats it and many other IP issues in Mary Case and David Green, "Rights and Permissions in an Electronic Edition," in *Electronic Textual Editing*, ed. Lou Burnard, Katherine O'Brien O'Keeffe and John Unsworth (New York: MLA, forthcoming).

Among many sources for information on IP law and policy are Ninch (the National Initiative for a Networked Cultural Heritage), at <www.ninch.org>, the Digital Future Coalition, <www.dfc.org>, and the American Library Association, <www.ala.org>.

27

Cognitive Stylistics and the Literary Imagination

Ian Lancashire

Cognitive stylistics analyzes an author's idiolect, his individual language traits. Although cognitive psychology and neuroscience do not know how the human mind works, they have detected, through experiments on how people behave (not through personal testimony about that behavior), features of mental behavior that are consistent with a standard theory or model. That cautious experimentation uses recall and recognition tests, and EEG (electroencephalography), PET (positron emission tomography), fMRI (functional magnetic resonance imaging), and other scans. With them, scientists are painstakingly uncovering steps, and constraints in taking these steps, that characterize how we mentally create and utter sentences (no word in English covers both oral and written expressing, but perhaps "uttering" will do). The current standard model describes two language processes: an unself-conscious creative process, veiled and almost unknowable, named by older writers the Muse (Jacoby 1971); and a conscious analytical procedure by which all authors assemble and revise sentences mentally.

These sciences are enhancing our understanding of how authors create both oral and written texts. New knowledge about language processing in the brain helps us interpret data from traditional computer text analysis, not because the mind necessarily works algorithmically, like a computer program, but because quantitative word studies reveal auditory networks, and the cognitive model asserts that the brain operates as a massively distributed group of such networks. Cognitive stylistics underscores how every utterance is stamped with signs of its originator, and with the date of its inception: these traits are not unique, like fingerprints, but, taken together, they amount to sufficiently distinctive configurations to be useful in authorship attribution or text analysis. Cognitive stylistics determines what those traces may be, using concordances and frequency lists of repeated phenomena and collocations: together, partially, these conceivably map long-term associational memories in the author's mind at the time it uttered the text. Such clusters of repetitions arise from built-in cognitive constraints on, and opportunities in, how we generate language. The length of fixed phrases, and the complexity of clusters of those collocations, are important quantitative traits of individuals.

Experimental cognitive psychology restores the human author to texts and endows computer-based stylistics with enhanced explanatory power. The potentially distinguishable authorship traits to which it draws attention include the size of the author's personal working memory (Just and Carpenter 1992). The cognitive model shows that, far from being dead, traces of the author do remain in the work, just as Shakespeare vowed it would in his sonnets, long after his own personal death. Collocational clusters also change over time as an individual's memory does. As the implications of cognitive research become understood, text-analysis systems may change, and with them stylistics. Texts in languages whose spelling departs widely from its sounding will likely be routinely translated into a phonological alphabet, before processing, as researchers recognize the primacy of the auditory in mental language processing. Because the standard cognitive model breaks down the old literary distinction between what is said and how it is said, interpretation and stylistics will come together.

First Impressions

A paradox underlies stylistic research. Most of us do not know much about how we make and utter text, simply because we are so expert at uttering. The more we make texts, the less we have time to be self-conscious about doing so. Committing ourselves completely to the action as it unfolds, we no longer attend to how it takes place.

Composing for anyone whose style is likely to be subject of analysis resembles walking, cycling or even, sometimes, driving a car on a highway. We can almost entirely devote our minds to other things and yet execute these actions properly. Kosslyn and Koenig say the more we know something, the harder it is to declare how we do it: "when one becomes an expert in any domain, one often cannot report how one performs the task. Much, if not most, of the information in memory cannot be directly accessed and communicated" (1992: 373). Recently one of my students, a professional actor, described an unnerving experience she had midway through a theatrical run of Henrik Ibsen's *Enemy of the People*. As she stood, waiting to go onstage, she could not remember anything of what she was to say or do when performing her part. Yet once she walked onstage, she executed everything perfectly just in time. She then understood why many actors repeatedly experience dread and sickness just before going on. So ingrained has the experience of performing become, over many weeks, that they can no longer summon the words or even the actions to conscious memory. Ironically, even if these actors were to succumb to amnesia, they still would not lose their roles. These have just become inaccessible and so are in effect protected against loss. Amnesiacs may forget who they are, but they can all the same speak and write (Squire 1987: 161, 171; Shimamura et al. 1992). Ironically, the more we do something, the less we can attend to how we do it. This well-observed cognitive effect shows how frightening and even disabling can neurological processes developed to ensure reliable performance of an essential skill be in practice.

Technology partially conceals this actual neglect from anyone who composes directly onto an artificial memory device. Equipped with a pen, a typewriter, or digital editing tools, authors see their text unfolding from their minds as they manually encode it in alphanumeric symbols on screen or paper. Making sentences visibly explicit as composed, writers no longer worry about having to store mentally what they create. Externalized, the words, phrases, and sentences of utterances can be easily deleted, rearranged, transformed grammatically, and replaced. We fully attend to the analytic task of doing these things. Because we externalize subvocal or inner speech immediately in visual form, we feel totally conscious of the mental activity of composing. Yet all we experience is the storage and the manipulation of symbols manifested outside the mind. What happens within the mind remains dark, especially to the expert composer, although novices learning how to use a language may assemble, with painful slowness, utterances in memory, consciously, before they utter them. The inexpert attend completely to the task. They may even be able to describe what steps they take consciously, probing their memory, and editing the results mentally in advance of speaking it. Any native speaker can follow this method in preparing to utter a sentence in their own tongue. It is so slow in natural conversation and composition as to be seldom worth using.

Expert authors in many languages often mention this neglect of attention to how they compose. Although they do not theorize their inability to see how they create sentences, their cumulative testimony is convincing. Being unable to see themselves create text, they characterize the process itself as beyond comprehension. Jean Cocteau explains: "I feel myself inhabited by a force or being – very little known to me. *It gives* the orders; I follow" (Plimpton 1989: 106). Elizabeth Hardwick agrees: "I'm not sure I understand the process of writing. There is, I'm sure, something strange about imaginative concentration. The brain slowly begins to function in a different way, to make mysterious connections" (Plimpton 1989: 113). Fay Weldon candidly admits: "Since I am writing largely out of my own unconscious much of the time I barely know at the beginning what I am going to say" (Winter 1978: 42). Cynthia Ozick imagines language coming out of disembodied nothingness.

> I find when I write I am disembodied. I have no being. Sometimes I'm entranced in the sense of being in a trance, a condition that speaks, I think, for other writers as well. Sometimes I discover that I'm actually clawing the air looking for a handhold. The clawing can be for an idea, for a word. It can be reaching for the use of language, it can be reaching for the solution to something that's happening on the page, wresting out of nothingness what will happen next. But it's all disembodied....I fear falling short. I probably also fear entering that other world; the struggle on the threshold of that disembodied state is pure terror. (Wachtel 1993: 16)

John Hersey compares composing to "'something like dreaming'...I don't know how to draw the line between the conscious management of what you're doing and this state" (Plimpton 1988: 126). Jonathan Raban thinks of himself as taking down spoken text, as if in dictation, uttered by an "it" – the pronoun used by Cocteau – rather than emerging from his own consciousness.

> All writers are in some sense secretaries to their own books, which emerge by a process of dictation. You start the thing off and on the first few pages you're in control, but if the book has any real life of its own, *it* begins to take control, *it* begins to demand certain things of you, which you may or may not live up to, and it imposes shapes and patterns on you; it calls forth the quality of experience it needs. Or that's what you hope happens. I don't just sit,

making conscious decisions externally about how much of my experience I am going to use. (Wachtel 1993: 120)

Earlier writers name the voice dictating the text as the Muse, a word for memory. Gore Vidal describes this unknown as sounding words aloud in the mind and goes further than others in admitting how ignorant he is of where this voice and its language come from.

> I never know what is coming next. The phrase that sounds in the head changes when it appears on the page. Then I start probing it with a pen, finding new meanings. Sometimes I burst out laughing at what is happening as I twist and turn sentences. Strange business, all in all. One never gets to the end of it. That's why I go on, I suppose. To see what the next sentences I write will be. (Plimpton 1989: 63)

Amy Lowell uses the word "voice" and says, like Ozick, that it comes from something disembodied, from no body.

> I do not hear a voice, but I do hear words pronounced, only the pronouncing is toneless. The words seem to be pronounced in my head, but with nobody speaking them. (Ghiselin 1952: 110)

These very different authors all tried to watch how sentences came from their minds and gave up. They had to attribute their composition to a disembodied voice or dream that came out of nothing. In editing on the page or screen, they consciously delete and rearrange words within passages, adjust syntactic structure, re-sequence parts, and make word-substitutions, just as we all do. They do not locate the tedious and conscious sentence-building in short-term memory as the origin of genuine composition. Literary theorists agree. Colin Martindale characterizes "primary-process cognition" as "free-associative . . . autistic . . . the thought of dreams and reveries," unlike the mind's problem-solving capability, "secondary-process cognition" (1990: 56). Mark Turner states that "All but the smallest fraction of our thought and our labor in performing acts of language and literature is unconscious and automatic" (1991: 39).

Impressions Sustained

Experiments in cognitive psychology and neuroscience have supported the concept of a disembodied mental voice that "utters" sentences without exhibiting how they were put together.

All verbal utterances, written or oral, are received by the brain, and uttered by it, in an auditory-encoded form. Philip Lieberman explains that, during language processing, we access "words from the brain's dictionary through their sound pattern" (2000: 6, 62). Further, we internally model whatever we expect to hear separately from what we are hearing. That is, we can only understand heard speech by modeling silently the articulatory actions necessary to produce it. Lieberman explains that

> a listener uses a special process, a "speech mode," to perceive speech. The incoming speech signal is hypothetically interpreted by neurally modeling the sequence of articulatory

gestures that produces the best match against the incoming signal. The internal "articulatory" representation is the linguistic construct. In other words, we perceive speech by subvocally modeling speech, without producing any overt articulatory movements. (2000: 48)

The "McGurk" effect shows that our internal model for the utterance we are decoding, for various reasons, may differ significantly from what comes to us as auditory speech.

The effect is apparent when a subject views a motion picture or video of the face of a person saying the sound [ga] while listening to the sound [ba] synchronized to start when the lips of the speaker depicted open. The sound that the listener "hears" is neither [ba] nor [ga]. The conflicting visually-conveyed labial place-of-articulation cue and the auditory velar place of articulation cue yield the percept of the intermediate alveolar [da]. The tape-recorded stimulus is immediately heard as a [ba] when the subject doesn't look at the visual display. (McGurk and MacDonald 1976, cited by Lieberman 2000: 57)

If sound alone were responsible for what was heard, the McGurk subject would hear [ba] at all times. Because it attends to visual clues as well, the mind hears something never sounded, [da]. Only if the subject's mind manufactured speech sounds internally, drawing on all sensory evidence available, could its model differ from both auditory and visual clues individually.

Authors who describe their inner mental activity when creating and uttering sentences are indeed correct when they characterize the "voice" they hear as bodiless. Even when we listen to the speech of others, it is not the speech of those others that we hear. It is the brain's own construct of those voices. Obviously, different brains might well perceive very different sounds, and thus words, from the same speech sounds heard from others. The mind becomes a reader of things made by a mental process that manifests itself as a bodiless, at times strange, voice.

Cognitive sciences confirm authors' impressionistic descriptions of the language-making process as blank and inaccessible. The inner voice utters sentences that appear to come out of nowhere. That we hear a voice suggests we are listening to someone else, not ourselves but someone nameless, unrecognizable, and above all as distant from analysis as the mind of someone whose words we hear on a radio. We invoke such images for a form of memory of how to do something, creating utterances from natural language, where we lack the means to identify the remembering process with ourselves. That process exemplifies the expert mind failing to attend to what it is doing. During composition, we cannot correct this neglect, as we can when driving a car and suddenly wake up to a recognition that we have been driving on automatic, unattended, for some miles. We cannot will consciousness of how our minds create utterances. Making them relies on what is termed procedural or implicit memory, in which what is recalled (that is, how to utter something) is remembered only in the act of doing it. When we try to recollect something stored implicitly, we execute the stored procedure. The mind has never created a readable "manual" of the steps whereby it creates sentences. The only exceptions are those halting, deliberate activities in our short-term memory in which, as if on paper, we assemble an utterance, but of course this method too, in the end, relies on the same mysterious voice or Muse, what cognitive sciences associate with implicit memory, to get it going. That truism, "How can we know what we are going to utter until we have uttered it?," characterizes the uncertainty of waiting for an utterance to be set down on the page or screen, to be spoken aloud, and to enter working memory. In all these situations, a silent inner voice precipitates the text out of nowhere.

Twenty-five years ago, Louis Milic distinguished between what writers do unconsciously in generating language (their stylistic options) and what they do consciously in "scanning, that is, evaluation of what has been generated" (their rhetorical options; 1971: 85). Milic *anticipated* the distinction between implicit or procedural and explicit memory by several years (Squire 1987: 160). By insisting on the primary role of empirical, rather than of theoretical or impressionistic, evidence in the study of authorship, Milic directed the discipline of stylistics to the cognitive sciences.

Why cannot we recall how we make a sentence? Why is the mind blocked by implicit memory in understanding one of the most critical defining features of a human being? The answer seems to lie in what we make memories of. Our long-term memory maker, located in the hippocampus, can store language, images, sounds, sensations, ideas, and feelings, but not neural procedures. Biologically, we appear to have no use for recalling, explicitly, activities by the language-processing centers themselves. Our minds, as they develop, have no given names for the actors and the events at such centers. Such knowledge is not forbidden. It is likely that it is unnecessary to and possibly counter-productive for our survival.

The Cognitive Model

So far, cognitive sciences have been shown to make two critical contributions to the analysis of style: it must be analyzed as auditory, and it emerges from neural procedures to which we cannot attend. Much else can be learned, however, by reading the scientific literature, both general studies (Kosslyn and Koenig 1992; Eysenck and Keane 1990; and Lieberman 2000), and analyses of specific areas like memory (Baddeley 1990; Squire 1987). Recent scientific results, on which these books are based, appear as articles in journals such as *Brain*, *Brain and Language*, *Cognitive Psychology*, *The Journal of Neuroscience*, *The Journal of Verbal Learning and Verbal Behavior*, *Memory and Cognition*, *Nature*, *Neuropsychologia*, *Psychological Review*, and *Science*. These papers are accessible, but to work with them the intelligent reader must be grounded in the cognitive model of language processing. Because it is changing now, and will continue to do so, work in cognitive stylistics will need steady reassessment. However, the method of cognitive stylistics, which bases text-stylistics on cognitive *effects* that experimentation has found to illuminate the mind's style, will remain. Here follows a brief summary of the emerging model. It breaks down into two parts: memory systems, and neural processes.

Scientists now recognize three basic kinds of human memory: (1) short-term memory, now known as working memory; and long-term associative memory, which falls into two kinds, (2) implicit or inaccessible, and (3) explicit or accessible. Implicit long-term memory includes recall of a procedure in the action, and priming. Explicit long-term memory includes episodic memory and semantic memory.

Working memory offers short-term storage of a limited amount of language so that it can be *consciously* worked on. This form of memory cannot be separated from processing activities. Alan Baddeley first proposed twenty years ago a very influential model of working memory split into three parts: a central executive and two subsystems, a visual area and a phonological or articulatory loop. The executive, which manages tasks in the two subsystems, has been localized in the dorsolateral prefrontal cortex (Lieberman 2000: 77). All conscious mental work on language gets done in the articulatory loop. It encompasses many regions in the brain, including the well-known language centers, Wernicke's and Broca's areas, which handle, respectively, semantic and syntactic processing. (When damaged, Wernicke's area leads an individual to utter well-formed nonsense, "word salad," and Broca's area to utter a form of agrammatism, characterized by sentence fragments, understandable but unformed.)

Central to the mind's conscious fashioning of language is the subsystem Baddeley calls the articulatory loop. So called because we must recirculate or rehearse a piece of language in order to keep working on it, this loop has a limited capacity, identified by Miller in 1956 as "seven, plus or minus two." Experiments have for decades confirmed these limits and show that individuals do not always reach the maximum potential capacity. The so-called reading-span test asks individuals to remember the final words of a sequence of unrelated sentences. Test results show a range of from 2 to 5.5 final words (Just and Carpenter 1992). As early as 1975 experiments showed that we could store in working memory, for recall, only as many words as we could utter aloud in two seconds (Baddeley et al. 1975). The number of such words declined as the total number of syllables increased, in what was termed "the word-length effect." Other experiments elicit so-called "effects" in subjects that confirm the auditory nature of working memory of language, and its severe capacity limits. The "acoustic similarity effect" shows that the ability of an individual to recollect a sequence of unrelated words suffers if they sound alike: semantic relations, or lack of them, and dissimilarity in sound have no effect. If working memory used the images of words, as text, the acoustic character of a word would not affect manipulation in working memory. The "articulatory suppression" effect also testifies to the auditory nature of language as consciously worked in memory. Individuals having to repeat aloud, continuously, a single sound or term or number (say, a function word such as "with") cannot rehearse, subvocally, utterances and so put or keep them in working memory. Auditory language immediately, unpreventably, enters it. Other experiments reveal that syntactically challenging sentences, such as those with clauses embedded within them centrally, reduce language capacity in working memory. Recently, Philip Lieberman asserts that we maintain "words in verbal working memory by means of a rehearsal mechanism (silent speech) in which words are internally modeled by the neural mechanisms that regulate the production of speech or manual signs" (2000: 6).

What can be learned about the mind's style from the articulatory loop? Its capacity constraints hamstring conscious mental work on making continuous sentences. It is little wonder that we seldom mentally assemble or attend to editing what we are going to say before we utter it. We have perhaps not had artificial storage devices (e.g., paper, computers), where it is very easy to edit texts, long enough noticeably to atrophy our already limited working memory. However, we have supplemented that memory, for language manipulation, with external storage devices. Increasingly, texts will depart from the mind's constraints as we assemble sentences that greatly exceed the length and complexity of ones that can be attended to by the unassisted mind. This extension has two clear effects. First, it produces utterances that the human mind cannot consciously assimilate into working memory for analysis. This, like the McGurk effect, will cause the mind to work-around the problem and perhaps, in doing so, to remodel the ingested utterance in ways that distort it. Second, the very experience of total control over utterances that artificial storage devices give makes all the more unbearable our mental blindness to the generation of utterances. No one can use software to create sentences, outside of playful programs like Joseph Weizenbaum's Eliza and the Postmodernism Generator of <www.elsewhere.com>. Authors affirm that the puzzling, to some frighteningly blank, inner voice which early writers called the Muse exists.

No matter whether we utter sentences as oral speech, or write them onto paper or into a file, we use one of four methods. We can spontaneously compose and utter without conscious thought or foresight, as during free conversation, when our auditory voice overlays the subvocal inner muse, or during rapid typing or writing, when our hands scarcely keep up with the dictation from within. Second, we can recite, rehearse by rote, from long-term explicit memory something that we laid down in that. The term "explicit" is a little misleading because our long-term memory is never apparent, as if it were a landscape, but resembles a black ocean in which we cast lines. In long-term memory is knowledge of the world and facts, including information (so-called semantic memory), and personal experience (so-called episodic memory; Tulving 1983). If we catch something, it suddenly appears in working memory, uttered by a subvocal voice if what we retrieve is language, and then we can recite (respeak) that voice aloud. Third, we can script sentences in working memory and utter them deliberately from there. This making process draws not only on long-term memory but consciously on cognitive powers like emotion and reason. Last, we can join our inner subvocal voice in working memory to our eyes and to external artificial memory devices, such as paper and computer displays, in order to compose, apparently "outside ourselves," although relying on cognitive resources of which we are aware.

What we call long-term or associative memory is still not well understood. How memories are stored in it and are retrieved from it, like what is stored there and why, emotionally, we embed it and withdraw it from memory at all, characterizes what authors term the Muse. We find something in long-term memory by using working memory to think of words and things associated with what we are trying to recall. It is widely accepted that this activates links in our mental network so that the desired information, sometimes on the "tip-of-one's-tongue," pops out. We often link individual things not logically but fortuitously, according to how we have encountered them in experience, and intentionally to meet a need. A common phrase for this linking effect is "spreading activation" (Collins and Loftus 1975). To stimulate one memory appears to have a rippling effect on all memories linked to it. The strength of that activation, or its "weight," may be proportional to the number of times that the linkage between those two memories has previously been activated.

Long-term associative memory does not store, in one place, complete utterances. Our mind's procedural memory of how to create or recreate an utterance calls on many different parts of the brain simultaneously, that is, concurrently, and they operate until the very instant of utterance or subvocal voicing. The mind's thesaurus (concepts), lexicon (words), and encyclopedia (images of things) consist of "morphologically decomposed representations" (Koenig et al. 1992). Different systems responsible for phonemes, lexis, part-of-speech, syntax, letter-shapes, etc., all stored in different locations, work in parallel. Current research, for example, locates color words in the ventral temporal lobe, action words in the left temporal gyrus, names of people in the temporal pole, and words for animals and tools in, respectively, the anterior and posterior inferotemporal area (Martin et al. 1995: 102; Lieberman 2000: 63, 65; Ojemann 1991). The concept of a typical noun resembles an address list that itemizes the locations of separately stored traits or features. Words associated with concepts are kept separately and matched together by a mediating area of the brain (Damasio and Damasio 1992) termed a "convergence zone." The "combinatorial arrangements that build features into entities, and entities into events, i.e. their spatial and temporal coincidences, are recorded in separate neural ensembles, called convergence zones ... [found in] association cortexes, limbic cortexes, and nonlimbic subcortical nuclei such as the basal ganglia ... [where they form] hierarchical and heterarchical networks" (Damasio et al. 1990: 105). Convergence zones are keys to neural networks.

One type of long-term associative memory is priming. It is a wildcard in the formation of our memory store. Sensory experience lays down primes in the mind; we are never aware of and we do not attend to them. Kosslyn and Koenig describe how researchers read word-pairs to patients who had been anaesthetized for surgery. Later, when these patients were asked for the second, associated member of each word-pair, they replied with the formerly primed words more than with equally likely associated words (1992: 376). This effect is often termed repetition priming. A "prior exposure to a stimulus facilitates later processing of that stimulus" (1992: 374). Primes create sometimes unexpected links between an experience or an idea that we regard as common, and other things that would not ordinarily be associated with it. Even if everyone shared the same fuzzy definition of a simple concept, individual experiences impacting on us in the force of primes would subtly alter that already fuzzy definition. When we search long-term memory, we are intentionally, consciously, launching a prime-like probe. This type of prime always places semantic restrictions on retrieval. For instance, priming with the word "present" in the hope of raising memories related to the meaning "gift" will not elicit anything related to the meaning "now." When "primes are unattended, words related to either meaning appear to be facilitated" (Posner and Raichle 1997: 148–51). That is, when someone or some experience triggers long-term memory, what surfaces in equally unattended shape has all strings attached.

How does the mind use these associative networks to provide an utterance? That process remains elusive. Kosslyn and Koening say that the brain forces output of an utterance automatically "via a process of constraint satisfaction" (1992: 48, 268–69) in which what might be termed the best fit survives. This fit is to some pragmatic goal that meets the person's needs, however they may be said to exist. Emotions, desires, and purposes inform those needs. If cognition activates many brain sites in parallel, and if our vaguely sensed intentions determine what associative networks are selected to supply the semantic gist of what we will say, it is little wonder that we cannot describe how the Muse works. Working memory – the only mental place where we can consciously attend to language – is not big enough to hold this complex cascade of mental events and is also inherently unsuited to doing so. Mental processes are not images or sounds.

So-called experiments "in nature" (that is, patients with brain damage) and devices that image brain activity have at least identified some essential components of this sentence-making process. In the classical model of language brain function, Lichtheim (1885) and Geschwind (1970) proposed that two regions of the neocortex were responsible: the posterior Wernicke's area did semantic processing and sent language data to the frontal Broca's area, which clothed it with syntactic form and passed it on to the motor cortex for speaking. This model relied on ample medical evidence that patients with damage in Wernicke's area displayed faulty or nonsensical semantics and comprehension, and that those with damage in Broca's area revealed staccato, fragmented speech with agrammatism. No one disputes this evidence from brain damage, but localizing function so simply is now impossible. Neural activity during linguistic processing turns out to be massively parallel and distributed. Language does not follow one path but many. Also, after damage to Broca's and Wernicke's areas, the brain can enlist "alternate neuroanatomical structures" for language use (Lieberman 2000: 5) and recover functionality. Lieberman and his colleagues have also recently shown that subcortical basal ganglia structures, in one of the most evolutionarily ancient (reptilian) parts of the brain, help regulate language processing. As far as the brain is concerned, the watchword is indeed in the plural, location, location, location.

The Mind's Style

Louis Milic some decades ago argued that stylistics must abandon impressionism for quantitative measures. Since then, researchers who compiled numeric data about style and made such measures have been puzzled to explain how they illuminate literary works or the authors who made them. Cognitive stylistics asserts that literary texts do not have style; individual minds do, in uttering. It contends that individual styles are profoundly affected by the neural constraints surrounding mental language processes. Because minds can only be indirectly analyzed, stylistics as a discipline must do research at the interface of cognitive sciences and corpus linguistics. Cognitive psychology and neuroscience tell us what to expect. Corpus linguistics extracts quantitative features of texts that can be analyzed in terms of how they match what human sciences predict will be found.

How, then, do these sciences characterize language uttered by the disembodied subvocal voice long named the Muse? Keeping in mind that scientists base their models of how the mind works on experimentally discovered effects, and that cognitive stylistics is at an early stage, a clear profile of the mind's style is beginning to emerge. It is:

- *auditory.* Language utterances as stored, processed, and retrieved are phonological, not sequences of visual symbols, not alphabetic.
- *lexico-syntactic.* Grammar and vocabulary cannot be separated: that is, syntactic structure imposed by Broca's area, and semantic fields by Wernicke's area, simultaneously participate in a unified, parallel, non-sequential process.
- *combinatory.* The building blocks of any utterance are networks, what Damasio's convergence zones wire together. These blocks are not discrete words. The mind knows word-image-concept-sound combinations, not dictionary headwords and their explanations.
- *built from two-second-long units.* These combinations appear in repeated phrases or unfixed collocations that are not more than 5–9 units in length. This follows if, as scientists suspect, working memory constraints are associated with a deeper limitation existing at the level of neural networks. Indeed, one use of computer text analysis is to

help determine the size and complexity of long-term-memory networks, how many things can converge on a convergence zone.

- *biased to parataxis*. Working memory is slowed when it must manipulate centrally embedded clauses. The mind, working towards a best fit in generating a sentence, may also well opt for simpler syntactical structures, unnested syntactic constructions, that is, paratactic sentences that take the form of a list of clauses linked by conjunctions.
- *semantically indeterminate*. No conventional thesaurus, encyclopedia, or dictionary can adequately document the individual mind's convergence zones, what may underlie semantic fields and associative clusters, simply because every individual's long-term store is affected by fortuitous associations, primes. The traits associated with concepts and words alter subtly as the weights that measure their binding strength change over time, affected by everything we directly experience through the senses. This partly explains the language effect known as lexical indeterminacy (Pilch 1988). Many words cannot be defined precisely enough to avoid misunderstandings. Individuals use words differently and only partially overlap with others.
- *time-sensitive*. As memory changes (or deteriorates), so do the characteristic traits of its utterances. Style is tied always to the health and age of the author's brain.

Other features of the mind's default style may be known and certainly will be discovered. These inbuilt traits are enough to initiate research.

Tools

Text-analysis algorithms and tools are available today to undertake rudimentary computer-based cognitive stylistics research.

Analysis is complicated by the need for enriched texts. We cannot use orthographically spelled text alone because the brain uniformly recognizes, stores, retrieves, and operates in working memory on language as auditory data, "silent speech." Each word must be available in orthographic and phonemic forms, at least, and optimally be segmented into syllables, and tagged with morphological information. Organizations such as the Speech Assessment Methods Phonetic Alphabet (SAMPA, <www.phon.ucl.ac.uk/home/sampa/home.htm>) offer rigorous modern British and American alphabets. SIL International (<www.sil.org>) has useful databases and software for this enrichment. Some automatic phonetic conversion tools recommended by the Simplified Spelling Society (<www.spellingsociety.org>) use less rigorous alphabets. Phonetic conversion in general can only be done well by researchers who understand the sounds of a language. In early periods, before printing, spelling may represent word-sounds adequately for analysis.

Researchers have been able to locate repeated words and fixed phrases since the invention of the KWIC concordancer in the late 1950s. Software by computational linguistics exists to generate the repeating fixed phrases of texts, termed "n-grams" (Fletcher 2002). Techniques for generating unfixed repeating phrases, that is, collocations, has been slower to develop. *Collgen*, a free *TACT* program I developed in the early 1990s, works only with word-pairs, word–word collocations, in small corpora. *Xtract* (1993), by Smadja and McKeown, is unavailable, but *Word Sketch* by Kilgarriff and Tugwell looks promising.

Every researcher faces the not inconsiderable task of defining collocation itself and selecting a statistical measure that ranks repeating collocations by their significance. Collins Wordbanks Online (<titania.cobuild.collins.co.uk/wbinfo.php3>) offers inter- active searching for word-combinations extracted from a 56-million-word Bank of Eng- lish with two significance scores: "mutual information" and *t*-test. Berry-Rogghe (1973), Choueka et al. (1983), and Church and Hands (1990) offer various measures. Budanitsky and Hirst (2001) evaluate them. Significance rating conceivably recovers information about the strength of associativity among items stored in long-term memory. By process- ing concordance data, representations of such clusters can be built.

I am not aware of any software that generates repeating clusters of words, fixed phrases, and unfixed phrases (collocations), say, to a limit of seven units, plus or minus two, but computational algorithms written for large industrial applications in data mining might permit repurposing.

Applications

Some trial literary analyses tested whether traits in works by two English poets, Geoffrey Chaucer and Shakespeare, could be accounted for within the standard cognitive model of language processing. My studies used texts with normalized orthography, untranscribed phonetically because Middle and Early Modern English pronunciation is not yet suffi- ciently well understood. The software, *Collgen*, was limited to repeated fixed phrases and node-collocate pairs. Unfixed groups of three and more collocates were uncollected. These limitations aside, published results of the analyses tended to affirm that the styles of both authors might be cognitively based, and partly recoverable.

I studied two passages from Shakespeare's works, *Hamlet*, III.1 (the so-called "nunnery scene"), and *Troilus and Cressida*, I.3.1–29 (Agamemnon's first speech), and two parts of Chaucer's *Canterbury Tales*, the General Prologue and the Manciple's prologue and tale, both in the context of the complete *Canterbury Tales*. The principal repeated vocabulary unit of both authors was the word-combination. In *The Canterbury Tales*, Chaucer used 12,000 word-forms but 22,000 repeating fixed phrases. Over two periods, 1589–94 and 1597–1604, Shakespeare's different fixed phrases at least doubled his word types. The vocabulary of both poets consisted, not of single words, but of little networks, a fact consistent with associative long-term memory. The sizes of these networks were well within what working memory could accommodate. The 464 phrasal repetends appearing in both Chaucer's General Prologue and the rest of his *Canterbury Tales* averaged 2.45 words. They fell into 177 networks. Repeating fixed phrases in Shakespeare's texts in both periods averaged 2.5 words. Chaucer's largest repeating combination in the General Prologue (853 lines) had nine words. Shakespeare's largest in *Hamlet* III.1, under 200 lines long, had five words. A second Shakespeare analysis, of Agamemnon's speech in *Troilus and Cressida*. I.3.1–29, found 107 phrasal repetends (repeating elsewhere in Shakespeare's works) in a passage that has only 159 different word-forms. Most combin- ations are two words in length, and the maximum has four. It is possible that the constraints of working memory affected the quantitative profile of the verbal networks employed by both men.

For both authors, I used text-graphs of these phrasal repetends to depict how they intersected. In the Chaucer study, three overlapping "say"–"tell"–"speak" graphs drew attention to Chaucer's unnoticed marking of the three verbs: they distinguished "between speaking (words), telling tales, and saying truths or sooths" (Lancashire 1992a: 349). Gary Shawver's doctoral thesis at the University of Toronto, "A Chaucerian Narratology: 'Storie' and 'Tale' in Chaucer's Narrative Practice" (1999), developed a finely detailed theory of Chaucer's narrative by taking this passing observation seriously. Two intersecting phrasal repetend graphs on the various word-forms for "true" and "love" in *Hamlet* also revealed a small network including the term "prove."

Other findings illustrate the variety of useful applications of cognitive stylistics. Chaucer's phrasal repetends in the General Prologue that repeated somewhere in the rest of the tales were graphed against those tales. After taking into account their different sizes, a distribution showed that the General Prologue shared more repetends with a quite unrelated tale, by the Manciple, found always just preceding the last tale, by the Parson. One possible interpretation of these results is that Chaucer wrote the two works in the same year. The 107 phrasal repetends in Agamemnon's speech in Shakespeare's *Troilus and Cressida* served a different purpose. They explained why Shakespeare used an odd sequence of images in lines that critics thought ill-conceived. Passages from earlier poems and plays here documented associative linkages that are private.

Conclusions

Annotating texts for their repeating combinations conceivably finds traces of an author's long-term associative memory that make up his idiolect. Combinatorial analysis also assists in close reading. It puts into sharp relief the *unrepeating* words in those passages that may mark recent mental acquisitions. (Very long phrasal repetends enter the author's text manually, copied from other sources.) Analysis exposes some repetitions, notably syntactic strings, that may show that an author primes his mind by looking at the unfolding composition on page or screen and so moving the language into the artificial memory. The image of just-composed text can lead to re-use of the grammatical structures, that is, function words. Entering working memory as an image, then converted subvocally for the articulatory loop, writing stimulates variations on itself. Yet cognitive stylistics is a young field. It must undertake hundreds of case studies to buttress these hypotheses. There are three special challenges.

We still have no firm model of repeating word-combinations. Fixed-phrase repetends (n-grams) and collocations (order-free collocate groups) are known to vary according to the span or the window, measured in words, within which they are measured. The tighter the window (e.g., five words), the smaller the length of the repeating repetends. If a window becomes as large as a page, it can contain two or more instances of the same fixed phrase. In that case, should the repetend be redefined as a cluster of that repeating phrase? We do not know how large such repeating clusters are allowed to get. If we increase the size of the window to the complete text, we then have only one complex cluster that turns out not to be a repetend after all because it never repeats. The window itself must be theorized. It could be set at the length of working memory, but mental associational networks may be larger. If eight words on either side of one member of a collocate pair were set as the span (i.e., the maximum capacity of the articulatory loop in working memory), what would we find if, after collecting all repeating collocates for a node word, we then treated those collocates themselves as nodes and went on to collect their collocates, and so on? At what point does the original node no longer reasonably associate with a distant collocate of one of its node-collocates?

We now have a reasonable vocabulary for describing the repeating fixed phrase and the cluster of a node and its collocates. Word-combinations that have reached their greatest phrasal length or collocate number are termed "maximals" (Altenberg and Eeg-Olofsson 1990: 8). Shorter, more frequent substrings or sub-collocate groups, which appear to function as kernels or attractors for other units, are called "subordinates"; and substrings of those subordinates, substrings that do not occur more frequently than the subordinate in which they appear, are termed "fragments" (Lancashire, 1992b). Kjellmer (1991: 112) uses the phrase "right-and-left predictive" for nodes that accumulate collocates to the right or the left. Sinclair (1991: 121) characterizes the frequency behavior of a node to be "upward" if its collocates occur more frequently than it, and "downward" if less frequently. (For example, nouns collocate upward with function words, and function words collocate downward with nouns.) Repetend features such as these affect our sense of the strength of association – often termed semantic distance – between parts of a fixed phrase or node-collocates cluster. So far, we calculate strength on the basis of frequencies (expected and actual) and mutual distance (measured in words), but size and other traits must be taken into account. For example, consider two node-collocate pairs, both separated by five words, and both sharing the same frequency profiles. (That is, both pairs share an actual frequency of co-occurrence that exceeds the expected frequency by the same amount.) Do they have different strengths of association if one of the pairs consists of two single words, and the other of two four-word fixed phrases? Or consider a repetend consisting of a single open-class word (e.g., noun, adjective, non-auxiliary verb, etc.), grammatically marked by a function word (e.g., article, preposition, etc.). Can we reasonably compare the strength of association there with that governing two open-class words that collocate freely and at some distance from one another? (In other words, can we treat grammatical and lexical collocations identically?) And how should we locate, name, and characterize words that have no significant repeating collocates and partner in no repeated phrases? These are words with a null "constructional tendency" (Kjellmer, 1994: ix). The more we know about combinatory repetends, the more we can bring to understanding the mind's style and even maybe our long-term memory. Texts follow from an individual's brain functions, but experimental sciences do not know how to use texts as evidence. Cognitive stylistics can assist.

The most common application of stylistics is authorship attribution. It locates marker-traits in an unattributed work that match selected traits of only one of the candidates. This method systematically neglects the overall stylistic profile of any one author. We need many more text-based studies of how a single author uses repeating word-combinations over time. Humanities researchers must also go beyond texts for their evidence. We can enhance our knowledge about composition, and its relationship to brain function, by undertaking experimental studies common in psychology and neuroscience. If the humanities expect the sciences to attend to text-based analysis, they must begin to undertake controlled experiments to analyze the linguistic behavior of living writers as they compose. Interviews and tests before, during, and after periods of composition can be combined with detailed capture of the author's keystrokes as the creative process takes place. The necessary research tools for these experiments are now widely applied to human-user interaction research.

In cognitive stylistics, the humanities can take a leading role in profoundly important research straddling the medical sciences, corpus and computational linguistics, literary studies, and a community of living authors.

REFERENCES FOR FURTHER READING

Altenberg, B. and M. Eeg-Olofsson (1990). Phraseology in Spoken English: Presentation of a Project. In J. Aarts and W. Meijs (eds.), *Theory and Practice in Corpus Linguistics* (pp. 1–26). Amsterdam: Rodopi.

Baddeley, A. (1986). *Working Memory*. Oxford: Clarendon Press.

—— (1990). *Human Memory: Theory and Practice*. Hove and London: Erlbaum.

—— (1992). Is Working Memory Working? The Fifteenth Bartlett Lecture. *Quarterly Journal of Experimental Psychology* 44A,1: 1–31.

—— (1993). Working Memory. *Science* 255: 556–9.

—— (1998). Recent Developments in Working Memory. *Current Opinion in Neurobiology* 8,2 (April): 234–8.

Baddeley, A., S. E. Gathercole, and C. Papagno (1998). The Phonological Loop as a Language Learning Device. *Psychological Review*: 158–73.

Baddeley, A., et al. (1975). Word Length and the Structure of Short-term Memory. *Journal of Verbal Learning and Verbal Behavior* 14,6: 575–89.

Berry-Rogghe, G. L. M. (1973). The Computation of Collocations and Their Relevance in Lexical Studies. In A. J. Aitken, R. W. Bailey, and N. Hamilton-Smith (eds.), *The Computer and Literary Studies* (pp. 103–12). Edinburgh: Edinburgh University Press.

Budanitsky, Alexander and Graeme Hirst (2001). Semantic Distance in WordNet: An Experimental, Application-oriented Evaluation of Five Measures. *Workshop on WordNet and Other Lexical Resources*, Second meeting of the North American Chapter of the Association for Computational Linguistics, Pittsburgh.

Caplan, D. and G. S. Waters (1990). Short-term Memory and Language Comprehension: a Cortical Review of the Neuropsychological Literature. In G. Villar and T. Shallice (eds.), *Neuropsychological Impairments of S.T.M.* Cambridge: Cambridge University Press.

Chang, T. M. (1986). Semantic Memory: Facts and Models. *Psychological Bulletin* 99,2: 199–220.

Choueka, Y., T. Klein, and E. Neuwitz (1983). Automatic Retrieval of Frequent Idiomatic and Collocational Expressions in a Large Corpus. *Journal for Literary and Linguistic Computing* 4: 34–8.

Church, Kenneth Ward and Patrick Hands (1990). Word Association Norms, Mutual Information, and Lexicography. *Computational Linguistics* 16,1: 22–9.

Collins, A. M. and E. F. Loftus (1975). A Spreading Activation Theory of Semantic Processing. *Psychological Review* 82: 407–28.

Courtney, S. M., L. Petit, M. M. Jose, L. G. Ungerleider, and J. V. Haxby (1998). An Area Specialized for Spatial Working Memory in Human Frontal Cortex. *Science* 279: 1347–51.

Damasio, Antonio R. (1995). *Descartes' Error: Emotion, Reason, and the Human Brain*. New York: Avon.

Damasio, Antonio R. and Hanna Damasio (1992). Brain and Language. *Scientific American* 267,3: 88–95.

Damasio, Antonio R., Daniel Tranel, and Hanna Damasio (1990). Face Agnosia and the Neural Substrates of Memory. *Annual Review of Neuroscience* 13: 89–109.

D'Esposito, M., J. A. Detre, D. C. Alsop, R. K. Shin, S. Atlas, and M. Grossman (1995). The Neural Basis of the Central Executive System of Working Memory. *Science* 378: 279–81.

Eysenck, Michael W. and Mark. T. Keane (1990). *Cognitive Psychology: A Student's Handbook*. Hove, East Sussex: Erlbaum.

Fletcher, William H. (2002). *kfNgram Information & Help*. URL: At <www.chesapeake.net/~fletcher/kfNgramHelp.html>.

Gathercole, S. E. and A. D. Baddeley (1993). *Working Memory and Language*. Hillside, PA: Lawrence Erlbaum.

Geschwind, Norman (1970). The Organization of Language and the Brain. *Science* 170: 940–4.

——(1979). Specializations of the Human Brain. In *The Brain* (pp. 108–17). A Scientific American Book. San Francisco: W. H. Freeman.

Ghiselin, Brewster (ed.) (1952). *The Creative Process: A Symposium*. New York: Mentor.

Grasby, P. M., C. D. Frith, K. J. Friston, C. Bench, R. S. J. Frackowiak, and R. J. Dolan (1993). Functional Mapping of Brain Areas Implicated in Auditory–Verbal Memory Function. *Brain* 116: 1–20.

Hagoort, Peter (1993). Impairments of Lexical–Semantic Processing in Aphasia: Evidence from the Processing of Lexical Ambiguities. *Brain and Language* 45: 189–232.

Hoey, M. (1991). *Patterns of Lexis in Text*. Oxford: Oxford University Press.

Jacoby, Mario (1971). The Muse as a Symbol of Literary Creativity. In Joseph P. Strelka (ed.), *Anagogic Qualities of Literature* (pp. 36–50). University Park and London: Pennsylvania State University Press.

Just, Marcel A. and Patricia A. Carpenter (1992). A Capacity Theory of Comprehension: Individual Differences in Working Memory. *Psychological Review* 99: 122–49.

Kertesz, Andrew (1983). Localization of Lesions in Wernicke's Aphasia. In Andrew Kertesz (ed.), *Localization in Neuropsychology* (pp. 208–30). New York: Academic Press.

Kilgarriff, Adam and David Tugwell (2001). WORD SKETCH: Extraction and Display of Significant Collocations for Lexicography. *COLLOCATION: Computational Extraction, Analysis and Exploitation* (pp. 32–8). 39th ACL and 10th EACL. Toulouse (July).

Kjellmer, G. (1991). A Mint of Phrases. In K. Aijmer and B. Altenberg (eds.), *Corpus Linguistics: Studies in Honour of Jan Svartvik* (pp. 111–27). London: Longman.

Kjellmer, Goran (1994). *A Dictionary of English Collocations*. Oxford: Clarendon Press.

Koenig, Olivier, Corinne Wetzel, and Alfonso Caramazza (1992). Evidence for Different Types of Lexical Representations in the Cerebral Hemispheres. *Cognitive Neuropsychology* 9,1: 33–45.

Kosslyn, Stephen M. and Olivier Koenig (1992). *Wet Mind: The New Cognitive Neuroscience*. New York: Free Press.

Lancashire, Ian (1992a). Chaucer's Repetends from The General Prologue of the *Canterbury Tales*. In R. A. Taylor, James F. Burke, Patricia J. Eberle, Ian Lancashire, and Brian Merrilees (eds.), *The Centre and its Compass: Studies in Medieval Literature in Honor of Professor John Leyerle* (pp. 315–65). Kalamazoo, MI: Western Michigan University Press.

——(1992b). Phrasal Repetends in Literary Stylistics: Shakespeare's *Hamlet* III.1. *Research in Humanities Computing 4* (pp. 34–68). Selected Papers from the ALLC/ACH Conference, Christ Church, Oxford, April, 1992. Oxford: Clarendon Press, 1996.

——(1993a). Chaucer's Phrasal Repetends and *The Manciple's Prologue and Tale*. In Ian Lancashire (ed.), *Computer-Based Chaucer Studies* (pp. 99–122). CCHWP 3. Toronto: Centre for Computing in the Humanities.

——(1993b). Computer-assisted Critical Analysis: A Case Study of Margaret Atwood's *The Handmaid's Tale*. In George Landow and Paul Delany (eds.), *The Digital Word* (pp. 293–318). Cambridge, MA: MIT Press.

——(1993c). Uttering and Editing: Computational Text Analysis and Cognitive Studies in Authorship. *Texte: Revue de Critique et de Théorie Littéraire* 13/14: 173–218.

——(1999). Probing Shakespeare's Idiolect in *Troilus and Cressida* I.3.1–29. *University of Toronto Quarterly* 68,3: 728–67.

Lancashire, Ian, in collaboration with John Bradley, Willard McCarty, Michael Stairs, and T. R. Wooldridge (1996). *Using TACT with Electronic Texts: A Guide to Text-Analysis Computing Tools, Version 2.1 for MS-DOS and PC DOS*. New York: Modern Language Association of America.

Lavric, A., S. Forstmeier, and G. Rippon (2000). Differences in Working Memory Involvement in Analytical and Creative Tasks: An ERP Study. *Neuroreport* 11,8: 1613–18.

Levine, David N. and Eric Sweet (1983). Localization of Lesions in Broca's Motor Aphasia. In Andrew Kertesz (ed.), *Localization in Neuropsychology* (pp. 185–208). New York: Academic Press.

Lichtheim, L. (1885). On Aphasia. *Brain* 7: 433–84.

Lieberman, Philip (2000). *Human Language and Our Reptilian Brain: The Subcortical Bases of Speech, Syntax, and Thought*. Cambridge, MA: Harvard University Press.

Longoni, A. M., J. T. E. Richardson, and A. Aiello (1993). Articulatory Rehearsal and Phonological Storage in Working Memory. *Memory and Cognition* 21: 11–22.

MacDonald, Maryellen, Marcel A. Just, and Patricia A. Carpenter (1992). Working Memory Constraints on the Processing of Syntactic Ambiguity. *Cognitive Psychology* 24: 56–98.

Martin, A., J. V. Haxby, F. M. Lalonde, C. L. Wiggs, and L. G. Ungerleider (1995). Discrete Cortical Regions Associated with Knowledge of Color and Knowledge of Action. *Science* 270: 102–5.

Martindale, Colin (1990). *The Clockwork Muse: The Predictability of Artistic Change*. New York: Basic Books.

Miles, C., D. M. Jones, and C. A. Madden (1991). Locus of the Irrelevant Speech Effect in Short-term Memory. *Journal of Experimental Psychology: Learning, Memory, and Cognition* 17: 578–84.

Milic, Louis T. (1971). Rhetorical Choice and Stylistic Option: The Conscious and Unconscious Poles. In Seymour Chatman (ed. and tr.), *Literary Style: A Symposium*. London and New York: Oxford University Press.

Miller, G. A. (1956). The Magical Number Seven, Plus or Minus Two: Some Limits on our Capacity for Processing Information. *Psychological Review* 63: 89–97.

Miyake, Akira and Priti Shah (1998). *Models of Working Memory: Mechanisms of Active Maintenance and Executive Control*. New York: Cambridge University Press.

Ojemann, George A. (1991). Cortical Organization of Language. *Journal of Neuroscience* 11,8 (August): 2281–7.

Ojemann, George A., F. Ojemann, E. Lattich, and M. Berger (1989). Cortical Language Localization in Left Dominant Hemisphere: an Electrical Stimulation Mapping Investigation in 117 Patients. *Journal of Neurosurgery* 71: 316–26.

Paulesu, E., C. Firth, and R. Frackowiak (1993). The Neural Correlates of the Verbal Component of Working Memory. *Nature* 362: 342–45.

Perani, D., S. Bressi, S. F. Cappa, G. Vallar, M. Alberoni, F. Grassi, C. Caltagirone, L. Cipolotti, M. Franceschi, G. L. Lenzi, and F. Fazio (1993). Evidence of Multiple Memory Systems in the Human Brain. *Brain* 116: 903–19.

Petersen, S. E. and J. A. Fiez (1993). The Processing of Single Words Studied with Positron Emission Tomography. *Annual Review of Neuroscience* 16: 509–30.

Pilch, Herbert (1988). Lexical Indeterminacy. In E. G. Stanley and T. F. Hoad (eds.), *Words for Robert Burchfield's Sixty-fifth Anniversary* (pp. 133–41). Cambridge: D. S. Brewer.

Plimpton, George (ed.) (1988). *Writers at Work: The* Paris Review *Interviews*. London: Penguin.

——— (1989). *The Writer's Chapbook: A Compendium of Fact, Opinion, Wit, and Advice from the 20th Century's Preeminent Writers*, rev. edn. London: Penguin Books.

Posner, Michael I. and Marcus E. Raichle (1997). *Images of Mind* (pp. 117–18, 123–9). New York: Scientific American Library.

Schacter, Daniel L., C.-Y. Peter Chiu, and Kevin N. Ochsner (1993). Implicit Memory: A Selective Review. *Annual Review of Neuroscience* 16, 159–82.

Schweickert, R. and B. Boriff (1986). Short-term Memory Capacity: Magic Number or Magic Spell? *Journal of Experimental Psychology: Learning, Memory, and Cognition* 12,3: 419–25.

Scott, Mike and Geoff Thompson (eds.) (2001). *Patterns of Text in Honour of Michael Hoey*. Amsterdam: John Benjamins.

Shallice, T. and B. Butterworth (1977). Short-term Memory and Spontaneous Speech. *Neuropsychologia* 15: 729–35.

Shawver, Gary (1999). A Chaucerian Narratology: "Storie" and "Tale" in Chaucer's Narrative Practice. PhD thesis, University of Toronto. Cf. <homepages.nyu.edu/~gs74/nonComIndex.html#4>.

Sheridan, Jenny and Glyn W. Humphreys (1993). A Verbal-semantic Category-specific Recognition Impairment. *Cognitive Neuropsychology* 10,2: 143–84.

Shimamura, Arthur P., Felicia B. Gershberg, Paul J. Jurica, Jennifer A. Mangels, and Robert T. Knight (1992). Intact Implicit Memory in Patients with Frontal Lobe Lesions. *Neuropsychologia* 30,10: 931–7.

Sinclair, John (1991). *Corpus Concordance, Collocation.* Oxford: Oxford University Press.

Smadja, Frank (1994). Retrieving Collocations from Text: Xtract. *Computational Linguistics* 19,1: 143–77.

Squire, Larry R. (1987). *Memory and Brain.* New York: Oxford University Press.

Tulving, E. (1983). *Elements of Episodic Memory.* Oxford: Oxford University Press.

Turner, Mark (1991). *Reading Minds: The Study of English in the Age of Cognitive Science.* Princeton, NJ: Princeton University Press.

Vallar, G., A. M. D. Betta, and M. C. Silveri (1997). The Phonological Short-term Store-rehearsal System. *Neuropsychologia* 35: 795–812.

Wachtel, Eleanor (ed.) (1993). *Writers and Company.* Toronto: Alfred A. Knopf Canada.

Winter, Nina (1978). *Interview with the Muse: Remarkable Women Speak on Creativity and Power.* Berkeley, CA: Moon.

Zola-Morgan, S. and L. R. Squire (1993). Neuroanatomy of Memory. *Annual Review of Neuroscience* 16: 547–63.

28

Multivariant Narratives

Marie-Laure Ryan

Media theorists divide the history of writing into four periods delimited by technological innovations: the oral age; the chirographic age (manuscript writing); the print age; and the digital age. The material support of language passed from unique to freely copiable; from restricted to a live audience to widely distributed; and from evanescent to durable, only to return to a strange combination of evanescence and durability: though digital texts can be stored in a wide variety of memory devices, computer systems become rapidly obsolete and their archives unreadable.

We know that the invention of writing and of the printing press had major consequences for textuality and narrativity. In oral cultures, as Walter Ong (1982) has shown, narrative was used as a mnemonic device for the transmission of knowledge; its memorization was facilitated by prosodic features – meter, rhyme, alliteration – as well as by fixed formulae and standardized images; and the limitations of memory were compensated by a relatively free episodic structure which allowed, within limits, permutation of its units. The invention of writing made it possible to shape the flat line of epic plots into the curve of dramatic form, a much more condensed narrative structure that allows a tighter management of emotional responses. Writing also froze the free order of plots into a fixed sequence. The printing press increased the length of narrative, revived the episodic pattern of epic poetry to fill the generous frame of the book, rendered mnemonic devices obsolete, and led to the birth of the novel, a relatively unconstrained narrative form that took plot to unprecedented levels of complexity: framing, embedding, branching, digressions, disruptions of temporal sequence, and multiple plot lines. Thanks to the spatiality of the page, images found their way into texts, and visual presentation was eventually recognized and exploited as an expressive device. After these three stages, is there anything left for digital media to develop in the narrative territory?

This question would not be worth asking if the computer merely served as a medium of transmission for print texts (as it does when a digitized version of a Stephen King novel is sold online) or as an instrument of production for texts to be experienced in print: most novels, after all, come out of word processors. A truly digital text, or narrative, is one that cannot be transferred into the print medium without significant loss. It depends on the computer as a sustaining environment, and it uses the screen (or any other display device) as a stage for performance.

What, then, are the properties of digital media, and, by extension, of digital texts, that bear upon the development of narrative? Several new media theorists (Murray 1997; Manovich 2001) have offered their own lists of distinctive features or essential properties of digital systems. The list proposed below is a distillation of the features I regard as the most relevant to the issues of textuality and narrativity:

- Algorithm-driven operation. Computers are machines that can run a variety of programs, through which they can perform a variety of tasks. The behavior of digital objects, such as texts, images, and sound, is therefore regulated by an invisible code, the machine-language instructions of the supporting software.
- Reactive and interactive nature. This property is a direct consequence of the preceding one. Computer code is based on conditional statements (if . . . then) that execute different instructions, depending on the state of the system or on external input. I call a system reactive when it responds to changes in the environment or to non-intentional user actions; it is interactive when the input originates in a deliberate user action. (Interactivity does not necessarily mean, however, that the system will act in the way intended by the user.)
- Performantial aspect. Another consequence of the first property. A digital text is like a music score or theater script: its written inscription is meant to be executed, either by the underlying code alone, or through a feedback loop that leads from the user to the underlying code to the display, and back to the user. Digital texts thus present the same contrast as the classic performing arts between the invariability of the script and the variability of its execution.
- Multiple sensory and semiotic channels, or what we may call multimedia capabilities, if we are not afraid of the apparent paradox of talking about multimedia media. Digital environments can combine text, sound, still pictures, and animations.
- Networking capabilities. Digital media connect machines and people across space and bring them together in virtual environments. This opens the possibility of multi-user systems and live (real-time) as well as delayed (asynchronous) communication.
- Volatile signs. Computer memory is made of bits whose value can switch back and forth between positive and negative. The value of these bits determines the display. This means that unlike books or paintings, digital texts can be refreshed and rewritten, without having to throw away the material support. This property explains the unparalleled fluidity of digital images.
- Modularity. Because the computer makes it so easy to reproduce data, digital works tend to be composed of many autonomous objects. These objects can be used in many different contexts and combinations, and undergo various transformations, during the run of the work.

The output of a hidden program, digital narrative is shaped not only by the general properties of its "material" medium (i.e., silicon chips), but also by the specific affordances of the system through which it is created and executed. An Infocom interactive fiction of the 1980s or a Storyspace hypertext narrative of the early 1990s differs significantly from a Flash game or Director "movie" produced in this new century. The code of authoring programs is a second-order means of expression, and the various software supports should, therefore, be considered the submedia of digitality – just as clay tablets, papyrus scrolls, and codices are the submedia of manuscript writing.

To complete the preliminaries of my discussion, let me briefly define what I mean by narrative. I endorse a medium-free, semantically based definition, according to which narrative is a type of meaning, or mental image generated in response to certain stimuli. A narrative text is an artifact designed to bring this meaning to mind. But the cognitive construct specific to narrativity can also be formed in response to stimuli not expressly designed for this purpose, for instance as an interpretation of life itself. This does not make life into "a" narrative, but it means that life may possess narrative potential – what we may call "narrativity." A narrative script (as I will call the relevant cognitive construct) pictures a world situated in time and populated by intelligent agents. The time span framed by the representation encompasses a series of different states mediated by accidental happenings and deliberate actions. To understand the sequence as narrative means to be capable of reconstructing the motivations of the agents and the causal connections between events and states. As a mental representation of a temporal sequence of events, narrative is not only linear – or multilinear, when it follows several parallel or interwoven destinies – but vectorial: a plot must be followed in a specific direction, from birth to death, beginning to end.

In contrast to some of the narrower definitions endorsed by narratologists, the present approach does not limit narration to the re-presentation of past events by a narrator, but accepts various modalities: narrative scripts can be told (diegetic mode), they can be shown (mimetic mode), or they can be enacted, not for the benefit of an audience, as is the case in drama, but as a self-rewarding activity. In this last mode, which prevails in computer games and participatory environments, the interactor is also the beneficiary of the text. Rather than being necessarily pre-encoded in a semiotic body, moreover, narrative scripts can be dynamically generated during the performance of a text through a simulation of actions and events. In contrast to scholars such as Espen Aarseth, who want to maintain a strict distinction between computer games and narrative (a concept implicitly narrowed down to its literary manifestations), my definition regards games and literary texts (or rather, those games and those literary texts that satisfy the proper semantic conditions) as two different narrative modalities. In the discussion below, I will therefore consider texts conceived as literature as well as texts regarded as games, but I will exclude the rich field of electronic poetry, as well as some innovative digital texts that rely too much on aleatory principles to fulfill the strict requirements of narrative coherence.

The development of digital textuality hit the literary scene at a time when "serious" literature – in contrast to popular culture – was in the grip of an epistemological and aesthetic crisis that challenged the closure, stability, and vectoriality of narrative form. The epistemological issue was a critique of the alleged blindness of classical narrative to the complexity of the problem of truth: facts are asserted by authoritative narrators as a matter of absolute knowledge, and the reader is asked to take the text as the canonical version of the world. For the historian Hayden White (1987), narrative is not a reliable way to gain knowledge about the past, because it always involves a fabrication. Reality, he claims, does not offer itself to perception in the shape of a story. And for the discourse analysts Elinor Ochs and Lisa Capps, a truly "authentic" narrative of personal experience would not be a stable reconstruction of the past but "the airing and evaluating of alternative possible understandings of past events" (2001: 17). The aesthetic issue arose from a similar desire to open up the text to multiple variants. Throughout the twentieth century, as Umberto Eco has shown in *The Open Work* (1989), artists in many media have been obsessed with the idea of making the text endlessly self-renewable, of capturing infinity in its necessarily bounded body, of turning the work of art from a static self-identical object into a matrix of virtualities. Modern science has recently come up with some models and names for this aesthetic ideal: emergence, complexity, distributed intelligence.

Through its permanent inscription and linear reading protocol, its bound spine and bounded content, the book was perceived as an obstacle to the dream of the text that keeps giving. If the problem came from the limitations of print, the solution might come from the affordances of digital technology. Thanks to the properties of reactivity, interactivity, volatility, and modularity, every run of a digital text can be turned into a performance of different virtualities. Out of a limited number of elements, the computer allows the creation of a vast number of versions. Janet Murray (1997: 155–62) calls this property the "kaleidoscopic" nature of the medium.

Twentieth-century writers did not await the advent of the digital age to develop a kaleidoscopic form of textuality. They did so through the technique of physically "chunking" and rearranging the text. We find the principle at work in the combinatorial algorithms developed by the members of the Oulipo literary movement: novels written on decks of cards which could be shuffled to produce different texts (Marc Saporta's *Composition No 1*, 1961); or sonnets obtained by selecting each verse from a matrix of poems (Raymond Queneau's *Cent mille milliards de poèmes*). In these last two examples the combinatorial principle is aleatory, and it does not guarantee the production of meaning, especially not of narrative meaning. We can make a picture out of any arrangement of pictorial fragments; and perhaps even a "text" in the same way, since non-sense can have a certain poetic force, but certainly not a story. Consider for instance what would happen if we reshuffled the functions of Vladimir Propp's *Morphology of the Folktale* (1962 [1928]):

> The villain is defeated. One member of a family either lacks something or desires to have something. The hero is recognized. The hero is married and ascends to the throne. The hero and the villain join in direct combat. A false hero presents unfounded claims. An interdiction is addressed to the hero.

An alternative to random sequencing, also practiced by print authors, is a combination of chunking and directed linking. After a given fragment of text the reader is given the choice between two or more alternatives. In "A Story As You Like It" by the French Oulipo member Raymond Queneau, the reader is asked: (a) "Do you wish to hear the story of the three big skinny beanpoles?" (yes – go to b; no – go to c); (b) "Do you want to hear the story of the three meddling mediocre bushes?" (yes – go to d; no – go to e). The expansion of each node creates a decision tree. Because there is only one way to reach a given node, whether terminal or medial, the author has absolute control over the information available to readers at every moment of their itinerary. This prevents the nonsense of the Propp example. But the ratio of number of paths vs. number of units in a tree-based system is not efficient; most works based on this algorithm offer a single-digit number of variants (two, for instance, in Julio Cortázar's *Hopscotch* (1966); about eight, in a typical *Choose Your Own Adventures* children's book).

The digital medium offers a much more powerful engine for the creation of multi-variant narrative than either aleatory combination or unconditional branching because the passage from one chunk of text to the next can be meaningfully controlled by code. In a hypertextual system, for instance, the operation of clicking on buttons activates the execution of some machine-language instructions, usually a "goto" to a certain memory address and an instruction to display the group of data beginning at this address. But the "goto" can be embedded in an "if . . . then . . . else" statement that imposes conditions on the branching. From the node "hero arrives at castle," for instance, the computer could be instructed to display the nodes "marriage to princess" or "king gives hero mission to rescue princess," depending on whether or not the reader has already visited "hero defeats villain." In a computer game, similarly, the player's actions function as links between segments in the sense that they trigger the execution of code, which leads to changes in the display and in the global state of the system. What players can do at a given moment depends on what they did in the past. The placement of links or the timing of user action in a well-designed narrative or informational system cannot be a random act, unless the point is to signify randomness itself. The creation of multivariant narratives depends on the existence of protocols that maintain linear coherence on the cognitive level – for, as the Propp example suggests, you cannot freely permute events in your mental representation of a story without consequences for the construction of causal and temporal relations. Here I would like to explore some of the system configurations, linking strategies, and modes of user participation that enable digital texts to achieve the difficult task of combining variability with narrativity. My investigation will focus on three aspects of narrative: discourse, which is the presentation of the narrative script through a particular medium, point of view, and plot – the narrative script itself.

Variable Discourse

Most of the digital texts that implement this type of variability are hypertexts, a form of organization described as follows in the documentation for Storyspace, the authoring software published by Eastgate:

> The word "hypertext" refers to a specific kind of writing. While customary text appears in a single sequence (e.g. page two always follows page one), hypertext presents the reader with multiple pathways through a document. These pathways are created by using hypertext links, a special kind of hypertext object that permits readers to actuate sequences, just like turning a page. . . . Simply put, hypertexts are branching textual objects that allow the reader to decide where to go next. (Storyspace FAQ; available from <http://www.eastgate.-com/storyspace/Download.html>

By the admission of its developers, Storyspace was designed to handle "large texts" (novels and databases rather than poems and short stories) with heavily interlinked nodes. One of the convenient features of Storyspace is the automatic building of a graph that keeps track of the system of links. This diagram gives the writer an overview of the developing network; but it can also serve as a navigational tool for the reader.

Figure 28.1 shows the organizational map of Stuart Moulthrop's novel *Victory Garden* (1991). This map (inserted as art, rather than generated by the system) represents only the upper layer of the textual architecture: each named site on the map stands for a region of the text with its own finely grained system of links, and it would be necessary to zoom in to a larger-scale image to get a full view of the textual architecture. The configuration of the map of *Victory Garden* is what theorists would call a network, or unrestricted graph. The presence of circuits – the formal trademark of a network – means that there may be many different ways to get to the same node. The system designer can control the reader's itinerary on the local level (where to go from a given node) but not on the global level. This feature discourages what I call a "narrative" interpretation of the sequence viewed by the reader: an interpretation that narrowly associates the order of appearance of lexia with a chronological and causal chain of events in the reference world. This type of reading would frequently lead to nonsense. For instance, if we first visited a node where a character is dead, and then a node where the character is alive, we would have to imagine a miraculous resurrection to make a story out of the sequence. It would take superhuman intelligence, or a map with very few decision points, for the designer to guarantee that every path will form a logically coherent plot. The map of *Victory Garden* is not a projection of branching possible parallel times into a spatial image but just what it claims to be: the map of a garden, or labyrinth, or graveyard – in any case a purely spatial construct. Despite its allusions to J. L. Borges's *Garden of Forking Paths*, where paths represent possible futures rather than routes in space, Moulthrop's *Victory Garden* does not outline multiple destinies for its heroes, but rather traces many pathways into a reasonably solid and chronologically organized narrative core. There is no necessary *global* parallelism between the progression of narrative time and the progression of the reader on the paths of the garden, though there can be *partial* relations: for instance a stretch of path without branches or with a default continuation that captures a sequence of events in chronological

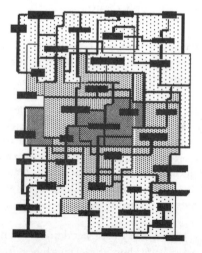

Figure 28.1   The map of *Victory Garden*

order. (*Victory Garden* is particularly rich in such linear paths: they are what enables the reader to get a general idea of the plot.)

A text based on a map as complex as figure 28.1 does not tell a different story for every reader, or with every reading session, it rather tells a story in many different ways, varying discourse instead of plot. Approaching the text like a jigsaw puzzle, the reader rearranges lexia mentally, so that a fragment encountered at T1 in the reading sequence may be assigned time slot T22 in the reader's final reconstruction of the plot. Similarly, the reader of an epic text that begins *in medias res* will reconstrue a chronological order of events that differs from the order of their presentation.

With its implication of a stable, determinate, complete, and coherent image to be recovered in its entirety, the image of the jigsaw puzzle admittedly fails to capture important aspects of the hypertextual reading experience. How does the phenomenon resist the metaphor? The reconstruction of narrative meaning is hardly ever complete because readers rarely visit all the lexia. Narrative is often only one of the threads in the textual web; following the postmodern aesthetics of the collage, most "classic" hypertexts interweave narration with metatextual comments, philosophical reflections, and inter-textual imports. There may be not just one but many stories in the textual network, just as a print text may tell a complex story with many subplots, or the text may present different versions of the same events without designating one of them as true. (Michael Joyce's *afternoon* (1987) circles, for instance, among several versions of an accident witnessed by the narrator.) Even in its print form, narrative discourse rarely allows the linearization of all its information. Islands of free-floating events (mostly of the mental type) usually co-exist with streams of temporally ordered states of affairs. Whether print or digital, literary texts may actively militate against narrativity and its linear organiza-tion, though many of the texts that sound their demand for a post-narrative mode of signification do so from a platform of narrative fragments that maintain the reader's interest.

The reconstruction of a reasonably consistent narrative world from a scrambled dis-course would quickly become a tiresome activity if the reader's role were exhausted by the metaphor of the jigsaw puzzle. Any picture can be cut up, boxed, and sold as a puzzle. A narrow mapping of hypertext onto puzzles would therefore mean that the significance of the reader's involvement is independent of the narrative content of the text. From a literary point of view, the best hypertexts are those that manage to present the reader's activity of moving through the network and reassembling the narrative as a symbolic gesture endowed with a meaning specific to the text, a meaning which cannot be predicted by reading the medium as a built-in message. The hypertextual mechanism does not make a text automatically innovative and significant; it is up to the author to put it in the service of a unique textual idea, of a metaphor that gives meaning to the reader's activity. In *Victory Garden*, this activity is framed as an exploration of space. With its 2,804 links connecting 993 lexia through a variety of paths planned over long stretches rather than from node to node (so that the narrative retains considerable linear coherence), *Victory Garden* takes Daedalian architecture to a level of complexity that probably no reader has fully appreciated. Moulthrop's metaphor of the Garden of Forking Paths was so suggestive of a radically new mode of reading, and described the structure favored by Storyspace so well, that it has become something of a theoretical cliché. In Michael Joyce's *afternoon*, the often frustrated search of the reader for explanations and narrative continuity emulates the frantic calls of the narrator to find out whether or not the accident he witnessed involved, and perhaps killed his ex-wife and son (Bolter 1991: 126). And in Shelley Jackson's *Patchwork Girl*, the reader is made to stitch together a text out of heterogeneous fragments, some recycled from other texts, just as the narrator-character Mary Shelley assembles a monster (allegory of a multiple, decentered subjectivity) by sewing together body parts collected from different women, and just as Shelley Jackson constructs a narrative identity for the monster from the stories of these women.

Variable Point of View

When the idea of interactive television was first introduced to the public, the advantage of the new technology was presented as an opportunity for spectators to view live broadcasts from a variety of perspectives. The capture of different cameras would be shown in small windows on the side of the screen, and by clicking on one of these windows the viewer would expand the image to the entire screen. Interactive movies, a genre that never really got off the ground, also played with the idea of variable point of view. In the exposition of *I'm Your Man* (1998), a DVD interactive movie playable on personal computers, we are given the choice between three options, each bearing a character's name. If we choose Leslie, the heroine, we will hear about Leslie's mission to give some important computer disk files to an FBI agent at a party. If we choose Richard, the villain, we will find out about his sinister plan to pose as a fake agent in order to get the documents from Leslie and then to kill her. (This is a very cheesy plot.) If we choose Jack, the fool-turned-hero-in-spite-of-himself, we will simply accompany him on his way to the party, looking alternatively at Jack and with Jack at the derrières and décolletés of female passers-by. At every decision point we can switch to the corresponding moment on one of the other two narrative tracks. The switches have no impact on the plot, or on the order of its presentation. Time moves inexorably forward, and by selecting a point of view we miss information that will only become available when we stop the movie and start from the beginning again. Because of the temporal structure of film, it takes several passes through the movie to tie the three strands together into one coherent plot.

Purely textual environments can vary point of view without running into this problem because a written text normally exists simultaneously in all of its parts. (Digital texts may change this, by destroying some of the links after the reader has visited them.) In the hypertext short story "A Long Wild Smile" by Jeff Parker (found at <http://www.hypertxt.com/parker/magnetic>), the reader can move back and forth between two narrative strands: one narrated by a woman's fiancé and another by her lover. Each node has links to the partner narrative, enabling the reader to follow both versions in parallel. Some links make very quick incursions into the other perspective, highlighting micro-level conflicts. In the following sequence, as Parker explains, the underlined words (which also function as links to the other passage) represent the interpretation by two different characters of the same string of sound:

> (Node 1: Fiancé's perspective) When I awake, she's joined him in the kitchen. She stares at the fridge while he stares at her. She says, *"Did you ever ride ponies?"* He says, "No."

(Node 2: Lover's perspective) *"Do you ever write rhyming poetry?"* she said, taking a big sip of water and passing the cup to me. I drank and passed it back to her.

This is a subtle authorial way to suggest misunderstanding (most likely the fiancé's) behind the back of the two narrators. Locked in their own perspectives, the lover and the fiancé quote what they hear, and they are not aware that the other interpreted the same words differently. But this kind of effect could have been achieved in print by juxtaposing the two passages and distinguishing them with indentation or with different fonts.

Variations in point of view have been so successfully achieved in "old media" (think of William Faulkner's novel *The Sound and the Fury*; or of Akira Kurosawa's film *Rashomon*) that they seldom carry digital texts all by themselves. The online soap operas *The Spot* and *The Lurker Files*, which consisted of interwoven first-person narratives that represent the perspective of different characters, have now disappeared from the Web. Interactive film and TV will have to find other selling points to succeed commercially – such as the possibility for the latter to play any document from an archive. The linking design of Parker's text pursues a wider variety of literary effects than merely switching back and forth between two perspectives. Even a work as crude as *I'm Your Man* combines variable point of view with other types of choices, such as deciding what the characters should do next. It is perhaps computer games that show the most efficient use of variable point of view in a digital environment. Many games enable players to switch from a god's eye perspective, third-person display, through which they see their character as a moving object on a map of the playing field, to a first-person, horizontal perspective that shows the game world to the players through the eyes of their avatar. One view is for the planning of strategy in a suspended time, and the other for the execution of moves in the heat of the game-action.

Variable Plot

The simplest way to implement variability on the level of plot is to arrange multiple narrative developments along the branches of a decision tree. We see this principle at work in *Choose Your Own Adventures* children's stories, in the Queneau text quoted above, and in postmodern narratives with two or more endings or with different reading paths (*Hop-scotch*). All these examples come from print texts, and all are fairly static. The various narrative lines are pre-inscribed within the database, limited in number (it would take God-like vision to control the combinatorial explosion of an arborescent structure with more than three levels), and the reader activates them through a purely selective type of interactivity. As long as this scheme is maintained, the digital medium does not really facilitate the creation of multiple plots. It makes travel along the branches a little bit easier, since clicking brings text to the reader, while print makes the reader go to the text, but the author still has to write the individual stories. But digital media present one significant advantage over print. They allow the user to interact with the text not just selectively but also productively. It is only when the user contributes elements to a developing story, allowing plots to be dynamically generated at run-time, that a system's narrative productivity can be raised above the level reachable by print media. In this type of system the player's actions perform an individualized narrative by responding to the affordances of the textual world. Since no two players will take the same moves, no two runs of the program will produce the same narrative trace. This productive type of interactivity is found mostly in computer games, although it also occurs in chatrooms, MOOs (Multi-User Dungeons, Object-Oriented), dialogue systems (the famous ELIZA program), virtual reality installations, and projects in Interactive Drama (Ryan 2001a). Here I will examine its effect on plot in three types of games: interactive fiction, first-person shooters, and simulation games.

The lowest degree of plot-level variability occurs when the player's actions fill in the blank spots in a pre-determined narrative script. This situation occurs in interactive fiction (IF), a text-only digital genre that flourished in the early 1980s, when computer graphics were too primitive to create an immersive environment. The genre nearly disappeared in the 1990s, displaced from the game market by fancy graphic interfaces and exiled from the front stage of digital literature by hypertext, a genre which quickly became the darling of theorists. But IF survives in small Internet niches, practiced without commercial and theoretical pressures by enthusiastic writers and programmers who freely share their work with a devoted community.

In an interactive fiction, we impersonate a character within the story world. We specify the actions of this character by typing instructions to the system in a simplified version of a natural language on an old-fashioned command-line interface. A parser analyzes the input, and the system responds with appropriate, or sometimes comically inappropriate actions. Since most IFs are designed as adventure games, the user's character has a task to perform, and the plot only reveals itself fully to the user who is able to complete the task by solving all the problems.

The downside of a system that grants free speech to the user is the impossibility of incorporating every verbal action into a coherent dialogue. IF systems understand only a limited vocabulary – typically 200 verbs, and as many nouns as there are different objects in the game-world – and they reject any input that cannot be parsed by their limited syntactic and semantic competence. This means that while the user can technically perform an unlimited number of actions, only some of these actions yield events in the developing story. The following examples, all taken from *Spider and Web* by Andrew Plotkin (Plotkin, website), illustrate various relations between input and plot. In the first example, player input counts as a turn in a conversation between the player's character and another member of the story world, and it reproduces exactly a verbal event within this world (> represents the output of the system):

> Interrogation chamber [You are imprisoned in a chair]
> "Don't be absurd," [the interrogator] says. " . . . if you'd had enough sense to walk away from that door, you wouldn't be here. You don't and you didn't and are; we caught you. And you're going to start by telling me how you got through that door. Do you understand me?
> Player: Yes.
> >The man nods briefly – a man satisfied with the least important detail.

In the next example, the player and the system takes turn at producing the story, though the player's input is not an act of narration but a command to the system. The system responds by updating its knowledge base, by narrating the result of the action, and

occasionally (though this is not exemplified in the passage below) by retelling the action
to the player in more elaborate language:

>You are carrying nothing of importance, except a lockpick.
Player: Put lockpick on plate.
>The pick locks itself rigidly to the black plate by the door. Its status dot flashes to yellow.
Player: Wait.
>Time passes.
The door slides neatly open.

In the last example, the player's actions cannot be executed because they cannot be parsed
by the system. Their event-status within the narrative is uncertain: do they count as futile
attempts to solve problems, or are they altogether external to the story world? The
response of the system is clearly external, and since it is situated on the same ontological
level as the player's attempted action, the whole dialogue may be regarded as taking place
outside narrative space and time:

>A plain metal door faces you to the east, near the alley's end. It's firmly shut.
Player: Open door.
>You don't see how.
Player: Scream in despair.
>That's not a verb I recognize.

Interactive fiction thus keeps the plot on the projected track by expelling the actions that
do not fit within the script to a sphere that narratologists would call the extra-diegetic or
para-textual.

Most interactive fictions trace a narrowly scripted trajectory. Players must visit a
number of locations, either in free or fixed order, and they must solve a problem to get
to the next location. In *Spider and Web*, for instance, player A may try the blaster and the
lockpick to enter a space before succeeding with the scan scrambler; player B may never
solve the problem and be caught by the guards in the hallway (a fate which can be averted
by consulting the solutions posted on the Web); while player C may succeed on the first
try. The only room for variation resides in the player's unsuccessful attempts. *Spider and
Web* creates an original variation on this pattern by presenting the user's failed actions not
as actual events but as lies told by the player's character to an interrogator who wants to
know how the character has managed to infiltrate a secret war laboratory. Some interactive
fictions have two or three endings, but in general, the variety of the player's input does not
translate into an equal variety on the level of plot. Though they can develop very
imaginative scripts that spice up the solving of problems with narrative interest, IF
texts offer little incentive to re-enter their world once the game has been beaten.

But endless replayability is not a reliable sign of high narrative variability. Consider the
case of the so-called "First Person Shooter" or FPS (*Wolfenstein, Doom, Quake, Unreal
Tournament*, etc.), a type of game that is played over and over again by its fans. Here
also the user is cast as a character situated in both the time and space of the fictional
world. The actions of the user determine the fate of the puppet character, and by
extension, the fate of the fictional world. The script of the game simulates a live encounter
with opponents, who can be manipulated either by the computer itself, or, if the game is

played in a networked environment, by other human players. Whereas IFs allow users to type whatever they want, but filter out a narrow range of acceptable inputs, FPS games accept all of the user's actions as part of the game, but they limit these actions to moving around the game world, gathering ammunition, selecting weapons, and aiming and firing them. If we regard the player's moves as the writing of a "life story" for the character, every run of the system produces a new life, and consequently a new narrative trace. This narrative is created dramatically by being enacted, rather than diegetically by being narrated. Because the speed of the processor and the number of variables involved in the execution of the game script make the system's reaction partially unpredictable to the player, FPS games are inexhaustible matrices of different lives for the player's character. The stories of these lives remain in a virtual state until they are mentally replayed. When players tell about their game experience, they do so by producing a standard "diegetic" narrative. For instance: "I was out of ammo, and Tyrus and Jason were surrounding me, and I thought I was dead, but I made this cool jump, and landed on the other side of the wall, and I found a cache of new ammo. I got back to the dungeon and killed them both, and we won the game." But while FPS games are played over and over again, players rarely "replay" in their minds the story of a game, because these stories only differ from each other in who shot whom and who died when. This monotonous diversity is only compounded by the fact that all FPSs implement the same narrative archetype – the story of the quest – through the same motif: a physical confrontation between hero and villain. Though FPSs have a narrative base, like almost all recent computer games, the stories they generate are worth experiencing in the first person but rarely worth telling to a third party.

For a combination of replayability and narrative diversity, no formula can presently rival the type of game known as simulation or as "god game" – the latter name due to the fact that the player manipulates the objects of the game world from an external position of power. Simulation games create a dynamic model of a complex entity, such as a city (*Simcity*), an empire (*Caesar*), or a family (*The Sims*). An emergent process, the global evolution of this entity is the product of an algorithm that computes the interrelated consequences of the actions of many individual agents and continually feeds this output back into its own engine. In *The Sims*, for instance, a game whose master plot is a pursuit of happiness that requires a steady climb up the economic and social ladder, the well-being of the family of Bob and Betty Newbie is a balancing act through which this couple of suburbanites must manage the resources of time to satisfy bodily demands (eating, sleeping, using the bathroom), emotional demands (their relation to each other), entertainment demands (satisfied by buying the proper commodities), social demands (getting along with neighbors), and economic pressures (they must earn money to fill their house with pleasure-giving commodities). The game has been criticized for its capitalist philosophy, but the comic texts that ridicule some of the objects available for purchase can just as easily be read as a satire of consumerism.

In keeping with its conception of life as a story that is constantly being written by the interaction between individuals and their environment, *The Sims* presents each object within the game world as an opportunity for action. A computer, for instance, affords the actions of playing games (good to cheer up depressed characters) or of finding a job (good to expand buying power). Characters are like objects: they too offer opportunities for actions by other characters. By mousing over Betty Newbie, the user playing Bob will for instance discover that Bob can kiss her, hug her, tickle her, or talk to her. The possibilities of action evolve during the run of the program, and since affordances are determined by the global state of the system, as well as by the nature of the objects, the user's choices will always produce a coherent narrative development.

The object of the game is not to win, since life never runs out of problems to be solved, but to manage the life of the characters as successfully as possible according to cultural standards (make them rich), or to the player's personal idea of dramatic development (for instance, create interpersonal conflicts and situations leading to catastrophic events). Some players (the novelists) want to produce specific scenarios; others (the virtual historians) are more interested in discovering how certain actions will affect the fate of the family. It is the same curiosity that makes us wonder "what would my life be like now if I hadn't met this stranger in a bar" or that inspires practitioners of virtual history to write essays about "what would have happened in US foreign policy if JFK had not been murdered." The motivation of both types of players is much more narrative than that which drives the players of FPS. In contrast to the lives of FPS players, the narratives produced by *The Sims* can be enjoyed retrospectively as well as during the run of the program. The system allows users to retell the story of their game, or to invent their own Sim stories, by taking snapshots of the screen and by complementing their pictures with text. Many of these cartoon-form stories are posted on the game's website. Whether or not they make interesting reading, and whether or not they chronicle actual games, the urge of players to share them with other players provides ample evidence that computer games can produce a genuine narrative interest in their fictional worlds.

The ludic pleasure of deciphering the logic of the system – what game designers call reverse engineering– cannot be separated from the narrative pleasure of watching the story unfold. Without playing skills, the player would be unable to create interesting stories. On my first attempt to play *The Sims*, for instance, the cooking range caught fire, and because I hadn't bought a phone I could not call the fire department. I watched helplessly my whole family die, and my only option was to let the last survivor mourn for his loved ones before being himself engulfed by the flames. At this point there was nothing to do but start again from scratch. It is only by learning how the system "thinks" that players can increase their authorial power over their family. But since the system throws in unexpected events, the player's control over the fate of the characters is never absolute. For narrative to be pleasurable, appreciators must be able to anticipate to some extent the development of the story, but the story must be able to fulfill expectations in a surprising way. This time-tested formula holds no less for simulation games than for novels and drama.

For all its narrative productivity, however, the formula of *The Sims* does not entirely satisfy the ambition of Will Wright, the designer of the game. He envisions a networked system that detects the most innovative subplots produced by users, updates the program with devices that facilitate their creation, and sends the new version to thousands of other users to find out if they, too, will attempt these subplots. "So in fact you [will] have the players . . . cross-pollinating their creativity," but the exchange will be mediated by the computer (Pearce 2002: 6). What Wright has in mind is a narrative variability of a higher power – a variability that affects the storytelling engine.

Beyond Narrative

In all the previous examples, variability remained within the bounds of narrative logic. Let me conclude my survey with an example that starts well within these bounds, but transgresses them during the run of the program, so that the text performs before the reader's eyes the dissolution of narrative. The text in question is *The Impermanence Agent*, by Noah Wardrip-Fruin and Brion Moss (2002). It consists of two windows on the screen. One of them contains the input narrative: a story inspired by the death of the author's grandmother, Nana, illustrated with family photos. The other window contains texts from various authors and memorial imagery from multiple cultures. The content of both windows scrolls down slowly by itself, then returns to the top, in an infinite loop. A reactive, rather than interactive text which takes full advantage of the networking capability of the medium, *The Impermanence Agent* modifies the content of each window by gradually integrating materials culled from the user's "scrapbook" – the file in which the Internet browser of the user's system stores text and images from the websites most recently visited. Whereas the original story reads "As a girl, at recess, Joan played punching games with the boys" it may become, "As a girl, at recess, Joan *to follow in the Bowlers' footsteps* played *TeacherSource: Health and Fitness* with the boys" (Wardrip-Fruin and Moss 2002: 14). A "lightweight intelligence model" selects "interesting" or frequent words from the user's scrapbook, and makes sure that they fit syntactically into the text, but the model does not check the output for semantic coherence. The visual material undergoes similar blending with pictures from the scrapbook. The authors claim that this algorithm customizes narrative discourse to the reader's interests, but their definition of narrative is so loose that it accepts any grammatical sequence of words. After several loops through the program, all that is left of the original story is bits and pieces of an aleatory collage, as the text is invaded by fragments of other texts that may point towards, but never fully tell their own stories. My point in presenting this example is not to deny artistic potential to this kind of project, but rather to locate the point where multivariant textuality leaves narrativity behind and becomes conceptual art.

The textual phenomena described in this chapter represent two extremes on the cultural spectrum. While computer games have taken popular culture by storm, generating a billion-dollar industry that rivals Hollywood and Disneyland, hypertext is an arcane academic genre read mostly by theorists and prospective authors. What remains to be conquered for digital textuality is the territory that lies between the stereotyped narrative scripts of popular culture and the militant anti-narrativity of so many experimental texts: a territory where narrative form is neither frozen nor ostracized, but recognized as an endlessly productive source of knowledge and aesthetic experiences. In the early 1990s, when theorists embraced hypertext as the genre that would carry the future of digital literature, the concepts of non-linearity and spatiality stood at the top of their list of aesthetic preferences. But narrative, as we have seen, is a fundamentally temporal, and consequently linear form of meaning. It was the great achievement of the twentieth-century novel to have created complex networks of internal relations, through which the present word, passage, motif, or episode activated the energies of other textual elements to form patterns of signification that transcended the linear development of the plot. This process of irradiation produced what critics have called a spatial form. But the greatest spatial novels (for instance Proust's *A la recherche du temps perdu*) can still be read for the plot, because their spatial organization complements, rather than destroys, the temporality of their narrative layer. Computer games, especially the much-maligned FPS, also present a very efficient use of time and space, if by space one understands the concrete geography of the game world rather than an abstract formal pattern. The pleasure of FPS consists in equal parts of moving through a three-dimensional environment that constantly updates itself to reflect the player's perspective, and of taking the right action at the right moment in a world relentlessly subjected to the ticking of the clock. For digital texts to establish themselves within the cultural middle ground – the narratives of the educated but not professional public – they must do the opposite of what the twentieth-century novel achieved, and perhaps learn a lesson from computer games, without succumbing to their propensity for repetitive themes and stereotyped storylines: naturally spatial, these texts must reconquer the narrative temporality that fuels the reader's desire.

REFERENCES FOR FURTHER READING

Aarseth, E. (1997). *Cybertext. Perspectives on Ergodic Literature*. Baltimore: Johns Hopkins University Press.
———(1999). Aporia and Epiphany in Doom and The Speaking Clock: The Temporality of Ergodic Art. In *Cyberspace Textuality* (pp. 31–41), ed. M.-L. Ryan. Bloomington: Indiana University Press.
———(forthcoming). Repurposing the Novel – Narrative Literature in the Turning Universe. In *The Novel,* ed. Franco Moretti. Princeton, NJ: Princeton University Press.
Bolter, J. (1991). *Writing Space: The Computer, Hypertext, and the History of Writing*. Hillsdale, NJ: Lawrence Erlbaum.
Cortázar, Julio (1966). *Hopscotch (Rayuela)*, tr. G. Rabassa. New York: Pantheon.
Douglas, J. Y. (2000). *The End of Books – or Books Without End? Reading Interactive Narratives*. Ann Arbor: University of Michigan Press.
Eco, U. (1989 [1962]). *The Open Work*. Cambridge, MA: Harvard University Press.
Hayles, N. K. (2000a). Flickering Connectivities in Shelley Jackson's *Patchwork Girl*: The Importance of Media-specific Analysis. *Postmodern Culture* 10,2. At <http://www.iath.virginia.edu/pmc/text-only/issue.100/10.2hayles.txt>.
———(2000b). The Transformation of Narrative and the Materiality of Hypertext. *Narrative* 9,1: 21–39.
I'm Your Man (1998). Dir. B. Bejean. A Choice Point Film. Presented by Planet Theory in association with DVD international. DVD edition produced by B. Franzblau.
Jackson, S. (1995). *Patchwork Girl*. Hypertext software. Cambridge, MA: Eastgate Systems.
Joyce, M. (1987). *afternoon, a story*. Hypertext software. Cambridge, MA: Eastgate Systems.
———(1995). *Of Two Minds: Hypertext, Pedagogy and Poetics*. Ann Arbor: University of Michigan Press.
Koskimaa, R. (2000). Digital Literature: From Text to Hypertext and Beyond. Unpublished PhD dissertation. University of Jyväskylä Available at: <http://www.cc.jyu.fi/~koskimaa/thesis/>.
Landow, G. (1997). *Hypertext 2.0: The Convergence of Contemporary Critical Theory and Technology*. Baltimore: Johns Hopkins University Press.
Manovich, L. (2001). *The Language of New Media*. Cambridge, MA: MIT Press.
Montfort, N. (2003). *Twisty Little Passages: An Approach to Interactive Fiction*. Cambridge, MA: MIT Press.
Moulthrop, S. (1991). *Victory Garden*. Hypertext software. Cambridge, MA: Eastgate Systems.
Murray, J. (1997). *Hamlet on the Holodeck: The Future of Narrative in Cyberspace*. New York: Free Press.
Ochs, E. and L. Capps (2001). *Living Narrative: Creating Lives in Everyday Storytelling*. Cambridge, MA: Harvard University Press.
Ong, W. (1982). *Orality and Literacy. The Technologizing of the Word*. London: Methuen.

Parker, J. A Poetics of the Link. *Electronic Book Review* 12. Accessed April 21, 2004. At <http://altx.com/ebr12/park/park.htm>.

Pearce, C. (2002). Sims, Battlebots, Cellular Automata, God and Go. A Conversation with Will Wright. *Gamestudies* 2. At <http://gamestudies.org/0102/pearce>.

Plotkin, A. *Spider and Web*. Interactive Fiction. Accessed April 21, 2004. At <http://www.wurb.com/if/game/207>. Solution to the game (by PJG, modified by Nils Barth) at <http://www.ifarchive.org/if-archive/solutions/tangle.sol>.

Propp, Vladimir (1968 [1928]). *Morphology of the Folktale,* tr. L. Scott, rev. L. Wagner. Austin: University of Texas Press.

Queneau, R. A Story As You Like It: Interactive Version. Accessed April 21, 2004. At <http://www.thing.de/projekte/7:9%23/queneau_1.html>.

Ryan, M.-L. (2001a). *Narrative as Virtual Reality: Immersion and Interactivity in Literature and Digital Media*. Baltimore: Johns Hopkins University Press.

——(2001b). Beyond Myth and Metaphor: Narrative in Digital Media. *Gamestudies* 1. At <http://www.gamestudies.org/0101/ryan/>.

Saporta, Marc (1961). *Composition No 1*. Paris: Seuil.

Sloane, S. (2000). *Digital Fictions: Storytelling in a Material World*. Stamford, CT: Ablex.

The Sims (2000). Computer game. Designer: Will Wright. Maxis/Electronic Arts. At <www.thesims.com>.

Wardrip-Fruin, Noah and Brion Moss (with A. C. Chapman and Duane Whitehurst) (2002). *The Impermanence Agent*. Project and context. *CyberText Yearbook*, ed. Markku Eskelinen and Raine Koskimaa (pp. 13–58). University of Jyväskylä: Publications of the Research Centre for Contemporary Culture.

White, H. (1987). *The Content of the Form: Narrative Discourse and Historical Representation*. Baltimore: Johns Hopkins University Press.

29

Speculative Computing: Aesthetic Provocations in Humanities Computing

Johanna Drucker (and Bethany Nowviskie)

With roots in computational linguistics, stylometrics, and other quantitative statistical methods for analyzing features of textual documents, humanities computing has had very little use for analytic tools with foundations in visual epistemology. In this respect humanities computing follows the text-based (dare I still say – logocentric?) approach typical of traditional humanities. "Digital" humanities are distinguished by the use of computational methods, of course, but they also make frequent use of visual means of information display (tables, graphs, and other forms of data presentation) that have become common in desktop and Web environments. Two significant challenges arise as a result of these developments. The first is to meet requirements that humanistic thought conform to the logical systematicity required by computational methods. The second is to overcome humanists' long-standing resistance (ranging from passively ignorant to actively hostile) to visual forms of knowledge production. Either by itself would raise a host of issues. But the addition of a third challenge – to engage computing to produce useful aesthetic provocations – pushes *mathesis* and *graphesis* into even more unfamiliar collaborations. Speculative approaches to digital humanities engage subjective and intuitive tools, including visual interfaces, as primary means of interpretation in computational environments. Most importantly, the speculative approach is premised on the idea that a *work* is constituted in an *interpretation* enacted by an *interpreter.* The computational processes that serve speculative inquiry must be dynamic and constitutive in their operation, not merely procedural and mechanistic.

To some extent these notions are a radical departure from established practices in digital humanities. As the articles in this volume attest, many of the practices in digital humanities are becoming standardized. Technical and practical environments have become more stable. So have procedures for developing meta-data, for content modeling, for document classification and organization, search instruments, and the various protocols of ordering, sorting, and accessing information in digital formats. In its broadest conceptualization, speculative computing is premised on the conviction that logical, systematic knowledge representation, adequate though it may be for many fields of inquiry, including many aspects of the humanities, is not sufficient for the interpretation of imaginative artifacts.

Intellectual debates, collateral but substantive, have arisen as digital humanists engage long-standing critical discussions of the "textual condition" in its material, graphical, bibliographical, semantic, and social dimensions. No task of information management is without its theoretical subtext, just as no act of instrumental application is without its ideological aspects. We know that the "technical" tasks we perform are themselves acts of interpretation. Intellectual decisions that enable even such fundamental activities as keyword searching are fraught with interpretative baggage. We know this – just as surely as we understand that the front page of any search engine (the world according to "Yahoo!") is as idiosyncratic as the Chinese Emperor's Encyclopedia famously conjured by Borges and commented upon by Foucault. Any "order of things" is always an expression of human foibles and quirks, however naturalized it appears at a particular cultural moment. We often pretend otherwise in order to enact the necessary day-to-day "job" in front of us, bracketing out the (sometimes egregious) assumptions that allow computational methods (such as markup or data models) to operate effectively.

Still, we didn't arrive at digital humanities naively. Though work in digital humanities has turned some relativists into pragmatists under pressure of technical exigencies, it has also reinvigorated our collective attention to the heart of our intellectual undertaking. As the applied knowledge of digital humanities becomes integrated into libraries and archives, providing the foundation for collection management and delivery systems, the ecological niche occupied by theory is called on to foster new self-reflective activity. We are not only able to use digital instruments to extend humanities research, but to reflect on the methods and premises that shape our approach to knowledge and our understanding of how interpretation is framed. Digital humanities projects are not simply mechanistic applications of technical knowledge, but occasions for critical self-consciousness.

Such assertions beg for substantiation. Can we demonstrate that humanities computing isn't "just" or "merely" a technical innovation, but a critical watershed as important as deconstruction, cultural studies, feminist thinking? To do so, we have to show that digital approaches don't simply provide objects of study in new formats, but shift the critical ground on which we conceptualize our activity. The challenge is to structure instruments that engage and enable these investigations, not only those that allow theoretically glossed discussion of them. From a distance, even a middle distance of practical engagement, much of what is currently done in digital humanities has the look of automation. Distinguished from augmentation by Douglas Engelbart, one of the pioneering figures of graphical interface design, automation suggests mechanistic application of technical knowledge according to invariant principles. Once put into motion, an automatic system operates, and its success or benefit depends on the original design. By contrast, Engelbart suggested that augmentation extends our intellectual and cognitive – even imaginative – capabilities through prosthetic means, enhancing the very capabilities according to which the operations we program into a computer can be conceived. Creating programs that have emergent properties, or that bootstrap their capabilities through feedback loops or other recursive structures, is one stream of research work. Creating digital environments that engage human capacities for subjective interpretation, interpellating the subjective into computational activity, is another.

Prevailing approaches to humanities computing tend to lock users into procedural strictures. Once determined, a data structure or content model becomes a template restricting interpretation. Not in your tag set? Not subject to hierarchical ordering? Too bad. Current methods don't allow much flexibility – a little like learning to dance by fitting your feet to footsteps molded into concrete. Speculative computing suggests that the concrete be replaced by plasticine that remains malleable, receptive to the trace of interpretative moves. Computational management of humanities documents requires that "content" has be subjected to analysis and then put into conformity with formal principles.

Much of the intellectual charge of digital humanities has come from the confrontation between the seemingly ambiguous nature of imaginative artifacts and the requirements for formal dis-ambiguation essential for data structures and schema. The requirement that a work of fiction or poetry be understood as an "ordered hierarchy of content objects" (Allen Renear's oft-cited phrase of principles underlying the Text Encoding Initiative) raises issues, as Jerome McGann has pointed out. Productive as these exchanges have been, they haven't made the shrug of resignation that accompanies acceptance of such procedures and presses them into practice into anything more than a futile protest against the Leviathan of standardization. Alternatives are clearly needed, not merely objections. The problems are not just with ordered hierarchies, but with the assumption that an artifact is a stable, constant object for empirical observation, rather than a *work* produced *through* interpretation.

Speculative computing is an experiment designed to explore alternative approaches. On a technical level, the challenge is to change the sequence of events through which the process of "dis-ambiguation" occurs. Interpretation of subjective activity can be formalized *concurrent with* its production – at least, that is the design principle we have used as the basis of *Temporal Modeling*.

By creating a constrained visual interface, *Temporal Modeling* puts subjective interpretation within the system, rather than outside it. The subjective, intuitive interpretation is captured and then formalized into a structured data scheme, rather than the other way around. The interface gives rise to XML exported in a form that can be used to design a document type definition (DTD) or to be transformed through use of Extensible Stylesheet Language Transformation (XSLT) or other manipulations. A description of the technical parameters that realize these conceptual premises is described in the case study below. The project is grounded on convictions that subjective approaches to knowledge representation can function with an intellectual rigor comparable to that usually claimed by more overtly formal systems of thought. This experimental approach has potential to expand humanities computing in theoretical scope and practical application.

Our path into the "speculative" has been charted by means of aesthetic exploration, emphasizing visual means of interpretation. These are informed by the history of aesthetics in descriptive and generative approaches, as well as by the anomalous principles of 'pataphysics, that invention of the late nineteenth-century French poet-philosopher Alfred Jarry. An outline of these aesthetic, literary, and critical traditions, and their role in the ongoing development of digital humanities, forms the first part of this chapter. This is followed by a discussion of the project that demonstrates the working viability of the precepts of speculative computing, *Temporal Modeling*. I invited Bethany Nowviskie to author this final section, since the conceptual and technical development of this research project has proceeded largely under her intellectual guidance.

Aesthetics and Digital Humanities

The history of aesthetics is populated chiefly by descriptive approaches. These are concerned with truth value, the specificity of individual media and activity "proper" to their form, the development of taste and knowledge, and the capacity of aesthetics to contribute to moral improvement – and, of course, notions of beauty and the aesthetic experience. These concerns are useful in assessing the aesthetic capabilities of digital media – as well as visual forms of knowledge production – even if only because of the peculiar prejudices such traditional approaches have instilled in our common understanding. For instance, long-standing tensions between images and text-based forms of knowledge production still plague humanist inquiry. A disposition against visual epistemology is deeply rooted in conceptions of image and word within their morally and theoretically charged history in Western philosophy. A schematic review of such key traditional issues provides a useful preface to understanding current concerns, particularly as visual tools become integrated into digital contexts as primary instruments of humanities activity.

Fundamental distinctions differentiate *descriptive* modes from the intellectual traditions that inform our project: generative aesthetics, 'pataphysics, speculative thought, and quantum poetics. Generative approaches are concerned with the creation of form, rather than its assessment on grounds of truth, purity, epistemological, cognitive, or formal value. Speculative aesthetics is a rubric hatched for our specific purposes, and incorporates emergent and dynamic principles into interface design while also making a place for subjectivity within the computational environment. 'Pataphysics inverts the scientific method, proceeding from and sustaining exceptions and unique cases, while quantum methods insist on conditions of indeterminacy as that which is intervened in any interpretative act. Dynamic and productive with respect to the subject–object dialectic of perception and cognition, the quantum extensions of speculative aesthetics have implications for applied and theoretical dimensions of computational humanities.

Before plunging into the vertiginous world of speculative and 'pataphysical endeavors, some frameworks of traditional aesthetics provide useful points of departure for understanding the difficulties of introducing visual means of knowledge representation into digital humanities contexts. To reiterate, the themes of descriptive aesthetics that are most potently brought to bear on digital images are: truth value, "purity" or capabilities of a medium, the cognitive values of aesthetics, and the moral improvement aesthetic experience supposedly fosters. Debates about beauty I shall leave aside, except in so far as they touch on questions of utility, and the commonplace distinction between applied and artistic activity.

The emphasis placed on the distinction between truth-value and imitation in classical philosophy persists in contemporary suspicions of digital images. The simulacral representations that circulate in cyberspace (including digital displays of information in visual form) are so many removes from "truth" that they would be charged with multiple counts of aesthetic violation in any Socratic court. Platonic hierarchies, and their negative stigmatization of images as mere imitations of illusions, are famously entrenched in Western thought. Whether we consider the virtual image to be a thing-in-itself, with ontological status as a first-order imitation, or as a mimetic form and thus yet another remove from those Ideas whose truth we attempt to ascertain, hardly matters. The fixed hierarchy assesses aesthetic judgment against a well-marked scale of authenticity.

From a theological perspective, images are subject to negative judgment except when they serve as instruments of meditation, as material forms whose properties function as a first rung on the long ladder towards enlightenment. Such attitudes are characterized by a disregard for embodied intelligence and of the positive capacities of sensory perception. Denigrating the epistemological capacity of visualization, they assume that art and artifice are debased from the outset – as deceptive, indulgent acts of hubris – or worse, temptations to sinful sensuality. But if images are necessarily inferior to some "Idea" whose pale shadow they represent, digital images are redeemed only when they bring the ideal form of data into presentation. The difficulty of such reasoning, however, is that it collapses into questions about what form data has in a disembodied condition.

Aristotle's concern with *how* things are made, not just how "truthful" they are, suggested that it was necessary to pay attention to the properties particular to each medium. The idea of a "proper" character for poetry was opposed to – or at least distinct from – that of visual forms. Likewise, sculpture was distinguished from painting, and so on, in an approach dependent on the specificity of media and their identifying properties. This notion of "propriety" led to differentiation among aesthetic forms on the basis of media, providing a philosophical foundation for distinctions that resonate throughout literary and visual studies. Investigation of the distinct properties of media was formulated most famously in the modern era by Gotthold Lessing (*Laocöon*, 1766). The value judgments that lurk in his distinctions continue to surface in disciplinary and critical activity to the present day. Such boundaries are well policed. But "new media" challenge these distinctions through the use of meta-technologies and inter-media sensibility. In addition, artistic practices forged from conceptual, procedural, and computational realms can't be well accommodated by aesthetic structures with "purist" underpinnings. If a data file can be input from a typewriter keyboard and output as musical notes then the idea of the "purity" of media seems irrelevant.

Critics trained in or focused on the modern tradition (in its twentieth-century form and reaching back into eighteenth-century aesthetics) have difficulty letting go of the long-standing distinction between textual and visual forms of representation – as well as of the hierarchy that places text above image. The disjunct between literary and visual modernism, the very premise of an autonomous visuality freed of literary and textual referents, continues to position these approaches to knowledge representation within separate domains. The consequences are profound. Intellectual training in the humanities only rarely includes skills in interpretation of images or media in any but the most thematic or iconographic terms. The idea that visual representation has the capacity to serve as a primary tool of knowledge production is an almost foreign notion to most humanists. Add to this that many latter-day formalists conceive of digital objects as "immaterial" and the complicated legacy of hierarchical aesthetics becomes a very real obstacle to be overcome. Naivety aside (digital artifacts are highly, complexly material), these habits of thought work against conceptualizing a visual approach to digital humanities.

Nonetheless, visualization tools have long been a part of the analysis of statistical methods in digital humanities. So long as these are kept in their place, a secondary and subservient "display" of information, their dubious character is at least held in check. Other conceptual difficulties arise when visual interfaces are used to create, rather than merely present, information.

In a teleologically grounded aesthetics, forms of creative expression are understood to participate in spiritual evolution, moral improvement – or its opposite.

Whether staged as cultural or individual improvements in character through exposure to the "best that has been thought" embodied in the artifacts of high, fine art, the idea lingers: the arts, visual, musical, or poetical, somehow contribute to moral improvement. Samuel Taylor Coleridge, Matthew Arnold, and Walter Pater all reinforced this sermon on moral uplift in the nineteenth century. Even now the humanities and fine arts often find themselves justified on these grounds. The links among ideas of progress and the application of "digital" technology to humanities continue to be plagued by pernicious notions of improvement.

Hegel wrote a fine script for the progressive history of aesthetic forms. The cultural authority of technology is insidiously bound to such teleologies – especially when it becomes interlinked with the place granted to instrumental rationality in modern culture. The speculative approach, which interjects a long-repressed streak of subjective ambiguity, threatens the idea that digital representations present a perfect match of idea and form.

But Hegel's dialectic provides a benefit. It reorients our understanding of aesthetic form, pivoting it away from the classical conception of static, fixed ideal. The interaction of thesis and antithesis in Hegelian principles provides a dynamic basis for thinking about transformation and change – but within a structure of progress towards an Absolute. Hegel believed that art was concerned "with the liberation of the mind and spirit from the content and forms of finitude" (Hegel 1975) that would compensate for the "bitter labour of knowledge" (ibid.). Aesthetic experience, presumably, follows this visionary path. If an aesthetic mode could manage to manifest ideal thought, presumably in the form of "pure data" – and give it perfect form through technological means, then descriptive aesthetics would have in its sights a sense of teleological completion. Mind, reason, aesthetic expression – all would align. But evidence that humankind has reached a pinnacle of spiritual perfection in this barely new millennium is in short supply. In this era following post-structuralism, and influenced by a generation of deconstruction and post-colonial theory, we can't really still imagine we are making "progress." Still, the idea that digital technology provides a high point of human intelligence, or other characterizations of its capabilities in superlative terms, persists.

Eighteenth-century aestheticians placed attention on the nature of subjective experience, rather than remaining focused on standards of harmonious perfection for objectified forms. In discussions of taste, subjective opinion comes to the fore. Well suited to an era of careful cultivation of elite sensibility, this discussion of taste and refinement emphasizes the idea of expertise. Connoisseurship is the epitome of knowledge created through systematic refining of sensation. Alexander Baumgarten sought in aesthetic experience the perfection proper to thought. He conceived that the object of aesthetics was "to analyse the faculty of knowledge" (Baumgarten 1735, sections 115–16; Beardsley 1966: 157) or "to investigate the kind of perfection proper to perception which is a lower level of cognition but autonomous and possessed of its own laws" (ibid.). The final phrase resonates profoundly, granting aesthetics a substantive, rather than trivial, role. But aesthetic sensibilities – and objects – were distinguished from those of *techne* or utility. The class divide of laborer and intellectual aesthete is reinforced in this distinction. The legacy of this attitude persists most perniciously, and the idea of the aesthetic function of utilitarian objects is as bracketed in digital environments as it is in the well-marked domains of applied and "pure" arts.

In what is arguably the most influential work in modern aesthetics, Immanuel Kant elevated the role of aesthetics – but at a price. The *Critique of Judgment* (1790), known as the "third" critique – since it bridged the first and second critiques of Pure Reason (knowledge) and Practical Reason (sensation) – contained an outline of aesthetics as the understanding of design, order, and form. But this understanding was meant as the apperception of "Purposiveness without purpose." In other words, appreciation of design outside of utility was the goal of aesthetics. Knowledge seeking must be "free," disinterested, without end, aim, he asserted. In his system of three modes of consciousness – knowledge, desire, and feeling (Pure Reason, Practical Reason, and Judgment) – Kant positioned aesthetics between knowledge and desire, between pure and practical reasons. Aesthetic judgment served as a bridge between mind and sense. But what about the function of emergent and participatory subjectivity? Subjectivity that affects the system of judgment? These are alien notions. For the Enlightenment thinker, the objects under observation and the mind of the observer interact from autonomous realms of stability. We cannot look to Kant for anticipation of a "quantum" aesthetics in which conditions exist in indeterminacy until intervened by a participatory sentience.

In summary, we can see that traditional aesthetics bequeaths intellectual parameters on which we can distinguish degrees of truth, imitation, refinement, taste, and even the "special powers of each medium" that are contributing strains to understanding the knowledge-production aspects of visual aesthetics in digital media. But none provide a foundation for a generative approach, let alone a quantum and/or speculative one.

Why?

For all their differences these approaches share a common characteristic. They are all descriptive systems. They assume that form pre-exists the act of apprehension, that aesthetic objects are independent of subjective perception – and vice versa. They assume stable, static relations between knowledge and its representation – even if epistemes change (e.g., Hegel's dialectical forms evolve, but they do not depend on contingent circumstances of apperception in order to come into being). The very foundations of digital media, however, are procedural, generative, and iterative in ways that bring these issues to the fore. We can transfer the insights gleaned from our understanding of digital artifacts onto traditional documents – and we should – just as similar insights could have arisen from non-digital practices. The speculative approach is not specific to digital practices – nor are generative methods. Both, however, are premised very differently from that of formal, rational, empirical, or classical aesthetics.

Generative Aesthetics

The Jewish ecstatic traditions of gematria (a method of interpretation of letter patterns in sacred texts) and Kabala (with its inducement of trance conditions through repetitive combinatoric meditation) provide precedents for enacting and understanding generative practices. Secular literary and artistic traditions have also drawn on permutational, combinatoric, and other programmed means of production. Aleatory procedures (seemingly at odds with formal constraints of a "program" but incorporated into instructions and procedures) have been used to generate imaginative and aesthetic works for more than a century, in accord with the enigmatic cautions uttered by Stéphane Mallarmé that the "throw of the dice would never abolish chance." In each of the domains just cited, aesthetic production engages with non-rational systems of thought – whether mystical, heretical, secular, or irreverent. Among these, twentieth-century developments in generative aesthetics have a specific place and relevance for digital humanities.

"Generative aesthetics" is the phrase used by the German mathematician and visual poet Max Bense to designate works created using algorithmic processes and computational means for their production. "The system of generative aesthetics aims at a numerical and operational description of characteristics of aesthetic structures," Bense wrote in his prescription for a generative aesthetics in the early 1960s (Bense 1971: 57). Algorithmically generated computations would give rise to datasets in turn expressed in visual or other output displays. Bense's formalist bias is evident. He focused on the description of formal properties of visual images, looking for a match between their appearance and the instructions that bring them into being. They were evidence of the elegance and formal beauty of algorithms. They also demonstrated the ability of a "machine" to produce aesthetically harmonious images. His rational, mathematical disposition succeeded in further distancing subjectivity from art, suggesting that form exists independent of any viewer or artist. Bense's systematic means preclude subjectivity. But his essay marks an important milestone in the history of aesthetics, articulating as it does a procedural approach to form giving that is compatible with computational methods.

Whether such work has any capacity to become emergent at a level beyond the programmed processes of its original conception is another question. Procedural approaches are limited because they focus on calculation (manipulation of quantifiable parameters) rather than symbolic properties of computing (manipulation at the level of represented information), thus remaining mechanistic in conception and execution. Reconceptualizing the mathematical premises of combinatoric and permutational processes so they work at the level of symbolic, even semantic and expressive levels, is crucial to the extension of generative aesthetics into speculative, 'pataphysical, or quantum approaches.

Generative aesthetics has a different lineage than that of traditional aesthetics. Here the key points of reference would not be Baumgarten and Kant, Hegel and Walter Pater, Roger Fry, Clive Bell, or Theodor Adorno – but the generative morphology of the fifth-century BC Sanskrit grammarian Panini, the rational calculus of Leibniz, the visionary work of Charles Babbage, George Boole, Alan Turing, Herbert Simon, and Marvin Minsky. Other important contributions come from the traditions of self-consciously procedural poetics and art such as that of Lautréamont, Duchamp, Cage, Lewitt, Maciunas, Stockhausen, and so on. The keyword vocabulary in this approach would not consist of *beauty, truth, mimesis, taste,* and *form* – but of *emergent, autopoietic, generative, iterative, algorithmic, speculative,* and so on.

The intellectual tradition of generative aesthetics inspired artists working in conceptual and procedural approaches throughout the twentieth century. Earlier precedents can be found, but Dada strategies of composition made chance operations a crucial element of poetic and visual art. The working methods of Marcel Duchamp provide ample testimony to the success of this experiment. Duchamp's exemplary "unfinished" piece, *The Large Glass*, records a sequence of representations created through actions put into play to create tangible traces of abstract thought. Duchamp precipitated form from such activity into material residue, rather than addressing the formal parameters of artistic form-giving according to traditional notions of beauty (proportion, harmony, or truth, for instance). He marked a radical departure from even the innovative visual means of earlier avant-garde visual traditions (Post-Impressionism, Cubism, Futurism, and so forth). For all their conceptual invention, these were still bound up with visual styles.

In the 1960s and 1970s, many works characteristic of these approaches were instruction-based. Composer John Cage made extensive use of chance operations, establishing his visual scores as points of departure for improvisational response, rather than as prescriptive guidelines for replication of ideal forms of musical works. Fluxus artists such as George Brecht, George Maciunas, Robert Whitman, or Alison Knowles drew on some of the conceptual parameters invoked by Dada artists a generation earlier.

The decades of the 1950s and 1960s are peopled with individuals prone to such inspired imaginings: Herbert Franke and Melvin Pruitt, Jascia Reichardt, and the heterogeneous research teams at Bell Labs such as Kenneth Knowlton, Leon Harmon, and dozens of other artists, worked in robotics, electronics, video, visual and audio signal processing, or the use of new technology that engaged combinatoric or permutational methods for production of poetry, prose, music, or other works. The legacy of this work remains active. Digital art-making exists in all disciplines and genres, often hybridized with traditional approaches in ways that integrate procedural methods and material production.

One of the most sustained and significant projects in this spirit is Harold Cohen's *Aaron* project. As a demonstration of artificial aesthetics, an attempt to encode artistic creativity in several levels of instructions, *Aaron* is a highly developed instance of generative work. *Aaron* was first conceived in 1973, and not surprisingly its first iteration corresponded to artificial vision research at the time. The conviction that perceptual processes, if sufficiently understood, would provide a basis for computational models predominated in research done by such pioneers as David Marr in the 1970s. Only as this work progressed did researchers realize that perceptual processing of visual information had to be accompanied by higher-order cognitive representations. Merely understanding "perception" was inadequate. Cognitive schemata possessed of the capacity for emerging complexity must also be factored into the explanation of the way vision *worked*.

Aaron reached a temporary impasse when it became clear that the methods of generating shape and form within its programs had to be informed by such world-based knowledge as the fact that tree trunks were thicker at the bottom than at the top. Vision, cognition, and representation were all engaged in a dialogue of percepts and concepts. Programming these into *Aaron's* operation pushed the project towards increasingly sophisticated AI research. *Aaron* did not simulate sensory perceptual processing (with its own complex mechanisms of sorting, classifying, actively seeking stimuli as well as responding to them), but the cognitive representations of "intellectualized" knowledge about visual forms and their production developed for Aaron made a dramatic demonstration of generative aesthetics. Aaron was designed to create original expressive artifacts

– new works of art. Because such projects have come into being as generative machines before our very eyes, through well-recorded stages, they have shown us more and more precisely just how that constitutive activity of cognitive function can be conceived.

'Pataphysical Sensibilities and Quantum Methods

Before returning to speculative computing, and to the case study of this chapter, a note about 'pataphysics is in order. I introduced 'pataphysics almost in passing in the introduction above, not to diminish the impact of slipping this peculiar gorilla into the chorus, but because I want to suggest that it offers an imaginative fillip to speculative computing, rather than the other way around.

An invention of the late nineteenth-century French physicist poet Alfred Jarry, 'pataphysics is a science of unique solutions, of exceptions. 'Pataphysics celebrates the idiosyncratic and particular within the world of phenomena, thus providing a framework for an aesthetics of specificity within generative practice. (This contrasts with Bense's generative approach, which appears content with generalities of conception and formal execution.)

The original founder of 'pataphysics, Alfred Jarry, declared the principles for the new science in the fantastic pages of his novel *Dr Faustroll, 'Pataphysicien*: "Faustroll defined the universe as that which is the exception to oneself." In his introduction to *Dr Faustroll* Roger Shattuck described the three basic principles of Jarry's belief system: *clinamen*, *syzygy*, and *ethernity*. Shattuck wrote: "Clinamen, an infinitesimal and fortuitous swerve in the motion of an atom, formed the basis of Lucretius's theory of matter and was invoked by Lord Kelvin when he proposed his 'kinetic theory of matter.' To Jarry in 1898 it signified the very principle of creation, of reality as an exception rather than the rule." Just as Jarry was proposing this suggestive reconceptualization of physics, his contemporary Stéphane Mallarmé was calling the bluff on the end game to metaphysics. Peter Bürger suggests that Mallarmé's conception of "the absolute" coincides with a conception of aesthetic pleasure conceived of as a technological game, driven by a non-existent mechanism. The substantive manifestation in poetic form shows the workings of the mechanism as it enacts, unfolds. Generative and speculative aesthetics are anticipated in the conceptualization of Mallarmé's approach.

What has any of this to do with computing?

Without 'pataphysical and speculative capabilities, instrumental reason locks computing into engineering problem-solving logical sensibility, programs that only work within the already defined parameters. The binarism between reason and its opposite, endemic to Western thought, founds scientific inquiry into truth on an empirical method. Pledged to rational systematic consistency, this binarism finds an unambiguous articulation in Book X of Plato's *Republic*. "The better part of the soul is that which trusts to measure and calculation." The poet and visual artist "implant an evil constitution" – indulging the "irrational nature" which is "very far removed from the true." Ancient words, they prejudice the current condition in which the cultural authority of the computer derives from its relation to symbolic logic at the expense of those inventions and sensibilities that characterize imaginative thought. By contrast, speculative approaches seek to create parameter-shifting, open-ended, inventive capabilities – humanistic and imaginative by nature and disposition. Quantum methods extend these principles. Simply stated, quantum interpretation notes that all situations are in a condition of indeterminacy distributed across a range of probability *until* they are intervened by observation. The goal of 'pataphysical and speculative computing is to keep digital humanities from falling into mere technical application of standard practices (either administered/info management or engineering/statistical calculations). To do so requires finding ways to implement imaginative operations.

Speculative Computing and the Use of Aesthetic Provocation

Visual or *graphic design* has played almost no part in humanities computing, except for the organized display of already structured information. Why should this be necessary? Or continue to be true? What are the possibilities of integrating subjective perspectives into the *process* of digital humanities. And though emergent systems for dynamic interface are not realizable, they are certainly conceivable. Such perspectives differentiate speculative approaches from generative ones.

The attitude that pervades information design as a field is almost entirely subsumed by notions that data pre-exist display, and that the task of visual form-giving is merely to turn a cognitive exercise into a perceptual one. While the value of intelligent information design in the interpretation of statistical data can't be overestimated, and dismissing the importance of this activity would be ridiculous, the limits of this approach also have to be pointed out. Why? Because they circumscribe the condition of knowledge in their apparent suggestion that information exists independently of visual presentation and just waits for the "best" form in which it can be represented. Many of the digital humanists I've encountered treat graphic design as a kind of accessorizing exercise, a dressing-up of information for public presentation *after* the *real work of analysis* has been put into the content model, data structure, or processing algorithm. Arguing against this attitude requires rethinking of the way embodiment gives rise to information in a primary sense. It also requires recognition that embodiment is not a static or objective process, but one that is dynamic and subjective.

Speculative computing is a technical term, fully compatible with the mechanistic reason of technological operations. It refers to the anticipation of probable outcomes along possible forward branches in the processing of data. Speculation is used to maximize efficient performance. By calculating the most likely next steps, it speeds up processing. Unused paths are discarded as new possibilities are calculated. Speculation doesn't eliminate options, but, as in any instance of gambling, the process weights the likelihood of one path over another in advance of its occurrence. Speculation is a mathematical operation unrelated to metaphysics or narrative theory, grounded in probability and statistical assessments. Logic-based, and quantitative, the process is pure *techne*, applied knowledge, highly crafted, and utterly remote from any notion of *poiesis* or aesthetic expression. Metaphorically, speculation invokes notions of possible worlds spiraling outward from every node in the processing chain, vivid as the rings of radio signals in the old RKO studios film logo. To a narratologist, the process suggests the garden of forking paths, a way to read computing as a tale structured by nodes and branches.

The phrase "speculative computing" resonates with suggestive possibilities, conjuring images of unlikely outcomes and surprise events, imaginative leaps across the circuits that comprise the electronic synapses of digital technology. The question that hangs in that splendid interval is a fundamental one for many areas of computing application: can the logic-based procedures of computational method be used to produce an aesthetic provocation? We know, of course, that the logic of computing methods does not in any way preclude their being used for illogical ends – or for the processing of information that is unsystematic, silly, trivial, or in any other way outside the bounds of logical function. Very few fully logical or formally systematic forms of knowledge exist in human thought beyond those few branches of mathematics or calculation grounded in unambiguous procedures. Can speculation engage these formalized models of human imagination at the level of computational processing? To include an intuitive site for processing subjective interpretation into formal means rather than circumscribing it from the outset? If so, what might those outcomes look like and suggest to the humanities scholar engaged with the use of digital tools? Does the computer have the capacity to generate a provocative aesthetic artifact?

Speculative computing extends the recognition that interpretation takes place from inside a system, rather than from outside. Speculative approaches make it possible for subjective interpretation to have a role in shaping the *processes*, not just the *structures*, of digital humanities. When this occurs, outcomes go beyond descriptive, generative, or predictive approaches to become speculative. New knowledge can be created.

These are big claims. Can they be substantiated?

Temporal Modeling[1]

Temporal Modeling is a time machine for humanities computing. Not only does it take time and the temporal relations inherent in humanities data as its computational and aesthetic domain, enabling the production and manipulation of elaborate, subjectively inflected timelines, but it also allows its users to intervene in and alter the conventional interpretative sequence of visual thinking in digital humanities.

The Temporal Modeling environment, under ongoing development at SpecLab (University of Virginia), embodies a reversal of the increasingly familiar practice of generating visualizations algorithmically from marked or structured data, data that have already been modeled and made to conform to a logical system. The *aesthetic provocations* Johanna Drucker describes are most typically understood to exist at the edges or termini of humanities computing projects. These are the graphs and charts we generate from large bodies of data according to strict, pre-defined procedures for knowledge representation, and which often enchant us with their ability to reveal hidden patterns and augment our understanding of encoded material. They are, however, fundamentally static and (as they depend on structured data and defined constraints) predictable, and we are hard-pressed to argue that they instantiate any truly *new* perspective on the data they reflect. Why, given the fresh possibilities for graphesis the computer affords, should we be content with an after-the-fact analysis of algorithmically produced representations alone? Temporal Modeling suggests a new ordering of aesthetic provocation, algorithmic process, and hermeneutic understanding in the work of digital humanities, a methodological reversal which makes visualization a procedure rather than a product and integrates interpretation into digitization in a concrete way.

How concrete? The Temporal Modeling tools incorporate an intuitive kind of sketching – within a loosely constrained but highly defined visual environment – into the earliest phases of content modeling, thereby letting visualization drive the intellectual work of data organization and interpretation in the context of temporal relations. Aesthetic provocation becomes dynamic, part of a complex dialogue in which the user is required to respond to visualizations *in kind.* Response in kind, that is, in the visual language of the Temporal Modeling toolset, opens up new ways of thinking about digital objects, about the relation of image to information, and about the subjective position of any interpreter within a seemingly logical or analytic system. Our chief innovation is the translation of user gestures and image-orderings that arise from this iterative dialogue into an accurate and expressive XML schema, which can be exported to other systems, transformed using XSLT, and even employed as a document type definition (DTD) in conventional data-markup practices. The sketching or composition environment in which this rich data capture takes place (the Temporal Modeling PlaySpace) is closely wedded to a sister-environment, the DisplaySpace. There, we provide a set of filters and interactive tools for the manipulation and display of more familiar, algorithmically generated visualizations, derivative from PlaySpace schemata or the already-encoded data structures of established humanities computing projects. Like the PlaySpace, though, the Temporal Modeling DisplaySpace emphasizes the flux and subjectivity common to both our human perception of time and our facility for interpretation in the humanities. We have not rejected display in favor of the playful engagement our composition environment fosters; instead, we hope to show that a new, procedural understanding of graphic knowledge enhances and even transfigures visualization in the older modes.

Our work in building the PlaySpace, with which we began the project in the Summer of 2001 and which now nears completion, has required a constant articulation of its distinction from the DisplaySpace – the implementation of which forms the next phase of Temporal Modeling. What quality of appearance or use distinguishes a display tool from an editing tool? At their heart, the mechanisms and processes of the PlaySpace are bound up in: the positioning of temporal objects (such as events, intervals, and points in time) on the axis of a timeline; the labeling of those objects using text, color, size, and quality; the relation of objects to specific temporal granularities (the standards by which we mark hours, seasons, aeons); and, in complex interaction, the relation of objects to each other. Each of these interpretative actions – the specification of objects and orderings, their explication and interrelation – additionally involves a practice we designate *inflection.* Inflection is the graphic manifestation of subjective and interpretative positioning toward a temporal object or (in a sometimes startling display of warping and adjustment) to a region of time. This positioning can be on the part of the prime interpreter, the user of the PlaySpace, or inflections can be employed to represent and theorize external subjectivities: the implied interpretative standpoint of a character in a work of fiction, for instance, or of an historical figure, movement, or *Zeitgeist.* The energies of the PlaySpace are all bound up in enabling understanding through iterative visual *construction* in an editing environment that implies infinite visual breadth and depth. In contrast, the DisplaySpace channels energy into iterative visual *reflection* by providing a responsive, richly-layered surface in which subjectivity and inflection in temporal relations are not fashioned but may be reconfigured.

I want to focus here on some specific qualities and tools of Temporal Modeling, especially as they relate to the embeddedness of subjectivity, uncertainty, and interpretation in every act of representation, which we take as a special province of speculative computing. Our very process of design self-consciously embodies this orientation toward information and software engineering. We make every effort to work from imagery as much as from ontology, coupling our research efforts in the philosophy and data-driven classification of temporal relations with the intuitive and experimental work of artists of whom we asked questions such as: "What does a slow day look like?" or "How might you paint anticipation or regret?" As our underlying architecture became more stable and we began to assemble a preliminary notation system for temporal objects and inflections, we made a practice of asking of each sketch we floated, "What does this imply?" and "What relationships might it express?" No visual impulse was dismissed out of hand; instead, we retained each evocative image, frequently finding use for it later, when our iterative process of development had revealed more about its implications in context.

In this way, the necessity of a special feature of the Temporal Modeling Project was impressed on us: a capacity for expansion and adjustment. The objects, actions, and relations defined by our schemata and programming are not married inextricably with certain graphics and on-screen animations or display modes. Just as we have provided tools for captioning and coloring (and the ability to regularize custom-made systems with legends and labels), we have also made possible the upload and substitution of user-made standard vector graphics (SVG) for the generic notation systems we've devised. This is more than mere window-dressing. Our intense methodological emphasis on the importance of visual understanding allows the substitution of a single set of graphics (representing inflections for, say, mood or foreshadowing) to alter radically the statements made possible by Temporal Modeling's loose grammar. Users are invited to intervene in the interpretative processes enabled by our tool almost at its root level.

A similar sensibility governs the output of a session in the PlaySpace environment. PlaySpace visualizations consist of objects and inflections in relation to each other and (optionally) to the metric of one or more temporal axes. The editing process involves the placement and manipulation of these graphics on a series of user-generated, transparent layers, which enable groupings and operations on groups (such as zooms, granularity adjustments, panning and positioning, simple overlays, and changes in intensity or alpha-value) meant to enhance experimentation and iterative information design inside the visual field. When the user is satisfied that a particular on-screen configuration represents an understanding of his data worth preserving, he may elect to save his work as a model. This means that the PlaySpace will remember both the positioning of graphic notations on-screen and the underlying data model (in the form of an XML schema) that these positions express. This data model can then be exported and used elsewhere or even edited outside the PlaySpace and uploaded again for visual application. Most interesting is the way in which transparent editing layers function in the definition of PlaySpace models. The process of saving a model requires that the user identify those layers belonging to a particular, nameable interpretation of his material. This means that a single PlaySpace session (which can support the creation of as many layers as hardware limitations make feasible) might embed dozens of different interpretative models: some of which are radical departures from a norm; some of which differ from each other by a small, yet significant, margin; and some of which are old friends, imported into the PlaySpace from past

sessions, from collections of instructional models representing conventional understandings of history or fiction, or from the efforts of colleagues working in collaboration on
research problems in time and temporal relations. A model is an interpretative expression
of a particular dataset. More importantly, it is what the interpreter says it is at any given
point in time. We find the flexibility inherent in this mode of operation akin to the
intuitive and analytical work of the traditional humanities at its best.

Our policies of welcoming (and anticipating) the upload of user-designed graphic
notation and of enforcing the formalization of interpretative models in the loosest terms
possible are examples of Temporal Modeling's encouragement of hermeneutic practice in
computational contexts. In some sense, this practice is still external to the visual environment we have built, even as it forms an integral part of the methodology Temporal
Modeling is designed to reinforce. I wish to close here with a description of a new and
exciting tool for encoding interpretation and subjectivity *within* the designed Temporal
Modeling environment: a mechanism we call the *nowslider.*

"Nowsliding" is a neologism for a practice all of us do constantly – on which, in fact,
our understanding of ourselves and our lives depends. Nowsliding is the subjective
positioning of the self along a temporal axis and in relation to the points, events, intervals,
and inflections through which we classify experience and make time meaningful. You
nowslide when you picture your world at the present moment and, some ticks of the clock
later, again at another ever-evolving present. You nowslide, too, when you imagine and
project the future or interpret and recall the past. Our toolset allows a graphic literaliza-
tion of this subjective positioning and temporal imagining, in the shape of configurable,
evolving timelines whose content and form at any given "moment" are dependent on the
position of a sliding icon, representative of the subjective viewpoint. Multiple independent or interdependent points of view are possible within the context of a single set of data,
and the visual quality of nowsliding may be specified in the construction of a particular
model.

At present, two display modes for the nowslider are in development. The first is a
catastrophic mode, in which new axial iterations (or imagined past- and future-lines)
spring in a tree structure from well-defined instances on a primary temporal axis. In this
way, PlaySpace users can express the human tendency to re-evaluate the past or make
predictions about the future in the face of sudden, perspective-altering events. New
subjective positions on the primary axis of time (and new happenings) can provoke
more iterations, which do not supplant past imaginings or interpretations, but rather
co-exist with them, attached as they are to a different temporal locus. In this way,
timelines are made to bristle with possibility, while still preserving a distinct chronology
and single path. Our nowsliders also function in a continuous mode – distinct from
catastrophism – in which past and future iterations fade in and out, change in position or
quality, appear or disappear, all within the primary axis of the subjective viewpoint. No
new lines are spawned; instead, this mode presents time as a continuum of interpretation,
in which past and present are in constant flux and their shape and very content are
dependent on the interpretative pressure of the now.

Our taking of temporal subjectivity and the shaping force of interpretation as the
content and overarching theme of the PlaySpace and DisplaySpace environments we have
built is meant to reinforce the goal of the Temporal Modeling tools and, by extension, of
speculative computing. Our goal is to place the hermeneut inside a visual and algorithmic

system, where his or her very presence alters an otherwise mechanistic process at the quantum level. Humanists are already skilled at the abstract classification and encoding that data modeling requires. We understand algorithmic work and can appreciate the transformative and revelatory power of visual and structural deformance. We at least think we know what to do with a picture or a graph. What we haven't yet tried in a rigorous and systematic way is the injection of the subjective positioning any act of interpretation both requires and embodies into a computational, self-consciously visual environment. If speculative computing has a contribution to make to the methods and outcomes of digital humanities, this is it.

See also CHAPTER 16: Marking Texts of Many Dimensions; CHAPTER 13: How the Computer Works

b,t this is but consequence what does?

Note

1   This section was co-authored with Bethany Nowviskie.

REFERENCES FOR FURTHER READING

Amelunxen, H. V., S. Iglhaut, and F. Rötzer (eds.) (1996). *Photography after Photography*. Munich: G&B Arts.

Baumgarten, A. (1735). *Reflections on Poetry*. London.

——(1750). *Aesthetica*. London.

Beardsley, M. (1966). *Aesthetics*. Tuscaloosa: University of Alabama Press.

Bense, M. (1971). The Projects of Generative Aesthetics. In J. Reichardt (ed.), *Cybernetics, Art and Ideas* (pp. 57–60). New York: Graphics Society.

Bök, C. (2002). *Pataphysics: The Poetics of an Imaginary Science*. Evanston, IL: Northwestern University Press.

Bürger, P. (1998). Mallarmé. In M. Kelly (ed.), *Encyclopedia of Aesthetics* (pp. 177–8). Oxford: Oxford University Press.

Dunn, D. (ed.) (1992). *Pioneers of Electronic Art*. Santa Fe: Ars Electronica and The Vasulkas.

Engelbart, D. (1963). A Conceptual Framework for the Augmentation of Man's Intellect. In P. W. Howerton and D. C. Weeks (eds.), *The Augmentation of Man's Intellect by Machine, Vision in Information Handling*, vol. 1. Washington, DC: Spartan Books.

Franke, H. and H. S. Helbig (1993). Generative Mathematics: Mathematically Described and Calculated Visual Art. In M. Emmer (ed.), *The Visual Mind*. Cambridge, MA: MIT Press.

Glazier, L. P. (2002). *Digital Poetics: The Making of E-Poetics*. Tuscaloosa, AL, and London: University of Alabama Press.

Hegel, G. W. F. (1975). *Aesthetics: Lectures on Fine Arts*. Oxford: Oxford University Press. (Translated by T. M. Moore. Citation is from <http://www.hegel.net/spirit/abs/art>.)

Hockey, S. (2000). *Electronic Texts in the Humanities*. Oxford and New York: Oxford University Press.

Holtzman, S. (1994). *Digital Mantras*. Cambridge, MA: MIT Press.

Jarry, A. (1996). *Exploits and Opinions of Dr. Faustroll, Pataphysician*. Boston: Exact Change.

Lister, M. (ed.) (1995). *The Photographic Image in Digital Culture*. London and New York: Routledge.

Marr, D. (1982). *Vision*. New York: W. H. Freeman.

McGann, J. J. (2001). *Radiant Textuality*. Basingstoke and New York: Palgrave.

Prueitt, M. (1984). *Art and the Computer*. New York: McGraw-Hill.

Renear, A. (1997). Out of Praxis: Three (Meta) Theories of Textuality. In K. Sutherland (ed.), *Electronic Text*. Oxford: Clarendon Press.

Ritchin, F. (1990). *In Our Own Image*. New York: Aperture.

Shanken, E. (n.d.). The House that Jack Built. At <http://www.duke.edu/~giftwrap/>, <http:mitpres.mit.edu/e-journals/LEA/ARTICLES/jack.html>.

Sutherland, K. (ed.) (1997). *Electronic Text*. Oxford: Clarendon Press.

Zhang, Y., L. Rauchwerger, and J. Torrellas (1999). Hardware for Speculative Reduction, Parallelization and Optimization in DSM Multiprocessors. *Proceedings of the 1st Workshop on Parallel Computing for Irregular Applications*, 26. At <http://citeseer.nj.nec.com/article/zhang99hardware.html>.

Temporal Modeling is freely available at <http://www.speculativecomputing.org>, and is delivered to the Web using XML-enabled Macromedia Flash MX and Zope, an object-oriented open-source application server.

30

Robotic Poetics

William Winder

Robots

There is a fundamental link between language and robots. Whatever material constitution they may have – arms and legs, cogs and wheels, and engines – the crucial ingredients, the ones that separate robots from wrenches, are their instructions. Instructions are perhaps inscribed in some concrete medium, but they are quintessentially abstract, existing more in the netherworld of code than in concrete form. That code netherworld is where humans and robots inevitably meet. It is where humans are most robotic and where robots are most human.

Such was Turing's reasoning that led him to choose the test of dialogue to detect human intelligence. It is no coincidence that a computer scientist of Turing's stature might come to the same conclusion as such foundational thinkers as C. S. Peirce and F. de Saussure. Each in his own way took the axiomatic position that there is no thought without signs, and Peirce, at least, comes to the conclusion that a person is in fact fundamentally a sign – and so too, though inversely, for robots, which are best described as personified signs. Robots are instructions that take human form.

Mechanized writing has been at the center of philosophical debate as far back as the invention of writing itself, but the humanists' version of the Turing test is relatively recent. It is, of course, not the conversational game between man and machine Turing described, but rather a literary version of the Turing test, where the goal is to simulate the author (see Kurzweil 2002, for a practical example). There is no doubt that mechanical processes underlie literary texts (Zholkovsky 1984: 53) and they have been used sporadically throughout history as an explicit device of creation (Swift's literary engine, the Surrealists' *cadavre exquis*, Bryon Gyson and Burroughs's cut-ups). Yet only recently have mechanical processes become the principal focus of a literary movement, in the form of the (largely French) group OULIPO (*ou*voir de *litt*érature *po*tentielle – Workshop for Potential

Literature), which by a *plagiat par anticipation* (anticipatory plagiarism) took computational constraints as the source of their creations.

Let us call robotic poetics (RP hereafter) the study of creative writing done by robots:

> Definition 1: RP is the study of robotic authors and the automatic generation of creative texts.

RP has as many facets as automatic writing has dimensions (see Fournel 1986). Generated text has a robotic author, itself created by a human programmer. There is a poetics of creating that author (here creativity lies in the writing of instructions); a poetics of generating a specific text (how those instructions play out to make a given text); and a poetics of reading generated literature (how the reader will read a text knowing, or not, that it is automatically generated). We simply do not read a generated text the same way we read a one-off hand-crafted text. We read in the shadow of textual variants, those sibling texts that could have been generated just as easily: generated texts come in swarms.

We will consider here RP as the field that covers all these facets of robotic creation, without narrowing the field to a single aspect. We will talk about robotic authors (the program that generates), robotic texts (generated texts), text engineers (those who program), and so on. We will perhaps focus narrowly here on creative natural language texts, but that should not be taken as RP's natural limit. What is central to RP is not text (which in any case should be taken as multimedia text), but rather printing, the central metaphor for any action a robot might take. Literally any medium can be printed on or imprinted. Thus CAD (computer-aided design) and CNC (computer numeric control) are used in factories to "print" machine parts. What is central is the way the texts of instructions are automatically transmuted into something other, sometimes other texts, sometimes things.

Textual generation systems have many applications in the humanities. Lessard and Levison offer a good example of the range of applications. Their generation system, *Vinci* (see below), has been used for foreign-language exercise generation, simulation of oulipian constraints, teaching linguistics, punning and humor, word and story generation, among others. (See their site for documentation, download, and an extensive publication list.)

Two red threads that RP follows are human creativity and combinatory practices. These two dimensions are oddly opposed, yet intertwined. A combinatory can be systematic or random, but its value is inevitably placed second to what is creative. A roll of the dice is not a creative act, since the outcome is within a foreseeable range of events. It is a distinctly human ability to creatively define the possible, to envisage possibilities outside the foreseeable. And yet we too are combinatory creatures. As Saussure and Peirce underline, because we think and live through signs, we must be signs (argues Peirce). What are signs? Nothing if not combinatory conspiratorialness.

Let us formulate a second possible definition of the field that covers the combinatorial dimension of robots:

> Definition 2: RP is humanities combinatorial studies.

RP is an interdisciplinary, interstitial field – a field that takes on a certain consistency in the overlap of more clearly defined disciplines such as cognitive science and computational linguistics (Anis 1995). That interdiscplinarity comes naturally through computers, which are by nature interdisciplinary machines: anything can be digitized; everything – so it would seem – can be virtualized (see chapter 28, this volume) and thus converge in the computer.

Potential and Real Texts

Poetics is traditionally conceived as the science of message construction, a systematic study of texts that describes why and how they make sense or have a particular effect. Even in this traditional vein, poetics describes text generation, the ergonomics of texts and the aesthetics of combinations. RP pushes the notion one step further in that it studies what creates the mechanics of creativity. What is central in RP is the *virtualized* (or potentialized) dimension of a work of art; understanding virtual texts tells us much about real texts and their creative core. A robotic author is precisely the site of a corpus of virtual texts.

Pierre Lévy (1998: 141–2) contrasts the virtual with the potential, the actual, and the real (see figure 30.1). The north/south planes oppose what is inert (substances) and what is dynamic (events); the east/west, what is unrealized (potential, virtual) and realized (real, actual). The movement from north to south is described as "jectification" – transforming what is fixed into a dynamic interaction between subjectified objects (money and language, for example, exist only through our collective subjectivity) and objectified subjects (the self is constructed by concrete choices of technological solution to problems – the subject can choose to *be* a blond or a brunette). The movement in the opposite direction, south to north, is towards the fixation of predefined structures.

A real text is a text instance that derives its primary value from its simple existence. It has a secondary value in that it can also be "reused" through potentialization to enhance a potential text, i.e. a range of possible texts. Transducer bots (my neologism; see below), which scramble real texts to form new texts, are a clear example of potentialization of real texts.

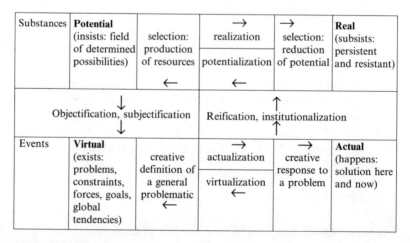

Figure 30.1   The potential, the real, the actual, and the virtual

A potential text represents a set of real texts, each of which is created through the reader's choice. Queneau's *Cent mille milliards de poèmes* (One hundred trillion poems) is the classic example of this kind of text. For each of the 14 lines of a sonnet, Queneau offers 10 substitute or variant lines. Since each of the 14 lines has 10 possible realizations and any combination of these choices is "poetically grammatical", the number of possible poems is 10^{14}, or one hundred trillion.

This (14 by 10) combinatorial poem is printed in book form. The book looks as if it has 10 pages with 1 poem per page. However, the pages of this book are cut horizontally between the verses so that each verse can be turned separately. By turning partial pages in this way, verses on the pages below can be successively revealed and each distinct combinatory sonnet can be brought to the fore (see figure 30.2).

According to Queneau's calculations one would have to read 24 hours a day for 200 millennia to read all the combinations; this is clearly a work that no one could ever possibly read.

Queneau's text shows us how, in Lévy's terms, the potential is transformed into the real. On the other hand a transducer bot represents the potentialization of a real text. Transducers take as input any text and produce another text, using various transcoding procedures. One example is the Shannonizer, which more or less randomly rearranges input text and intersperses it with canned expressions. The Shannonizer will transform this text (edited by a robotic Dr Seuss):

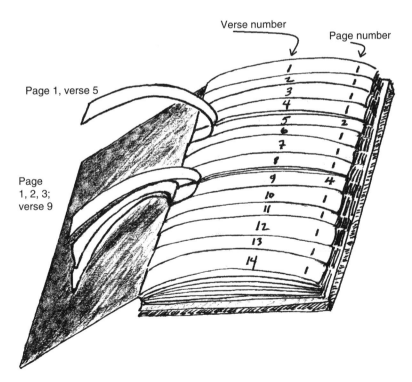

Figure 30.2   Raymond Queneau, *Cent mille milliards de poèmes*

Windows XP delivers a host of great features, including improved reliability and security, along with great experiences in real-time communications, mobile support, home networking, digital photos, digital video, and digital music. As a result of these higher standards, you may see some compatibility issues with your computer systems and software programs. In most cases, however, you can expect those problems to be at an absolute minimum. Here's why. (Windows XP "Compatibility", Internet advertisement)

into this text:

Windows XP delivers
as edited by
Dr Seuss

Windows XP delivers a host of great features, sir. Thank goodness I'm a result of sour gooseberry jam! Just look! No, digital photos, home networking, you may see some compatibility issues with great experiences in their paddles in real-time communications, we serve hot dogs, along with your computer systems and the dark. Take a star, funny things are everywhere. In most cases, however, along with great experiences in real-time communications, not one little bed all night. (The Shannonizer transforms a Windows XP advertisement)

The Shannonizer potentializes in that it recreates new texts from old. A more sophisticated potentializer is Kurzweil's poetry generator ("Cyberart Technologies"), which "recycles" the poetry of any given corpus. (As Balpe remarks, poetry is the easiest genre to simulate – See Balpe and Magné 1991: 129.)

Games, Dialogue, and Texts

A potential text represents a field of possibilities defined by the text engineer. A given realization of the text is simply a selection, a roll of the dice, by the user. Potential texts are textual kaleidoscopes and the basis of such ancient textual games as Tarot, I Ching, or horoscope predictions.

There is a great range of potential texts, and many possible classifications (for example, Aarseth 1997: 58ff). The following represents a very simple classification with some prototypical examples:

1   Combinatory texts or textual kaleidoscopes, such as hypertext, which generate variants or allow the reader to select variants: mail merge in word processors or Queneau's sonnets.
2   MUDs (multi-user domains), which generate and manage a virtual universe for the interaction of several users. (See chapter 28, this volume.)
3   Transducer bots, which rearrange text: the Shannonizer or Kurzweil's poetry engine.
4   Generators, such as *Vinci* (Lessard and Levison 2002) or *KPML* (Reiter 2002).
5   Chatbots or *Eliza* variants, such as *ALICE*, which have Turing-style dialogues with the user.

Such texts are at the same time text, game, and dialogue. Queneau's text requires that the reader select a poem by turning to the appropriate verses. The choice is not determined in advance, though the field of possibilities is. Games are in general dialogues between two or more players, though in some games, such as solitaire, the second player is reduced to the mechanical combination that resists – the shuffle that gives the distribution of cards that the solitaire player must "beat."

"Playtexts" (Motte 1995) have peculiar properties, though all can be represented as a sequence of signs, just as chess games have a notation for each move of a game. Lewis Carroll will thus reproduce the chess problem that informed *Alice in Wonderland* in the preface to the text itself. Chess offers the example of a now highly computerized game in which the robotic player routinely outstrips its designers (Aarseth 1997: 27). Whether authorship will be automated to the same degree remains a question. It is nevertheless useful at this point to consider more closely the general structure of games.

A chess game is a combinatory, but its potential nature is distributed in many layers of increasing complexity. A chess piece has no pertinent parts, but a board with its distribution of pieces does. Even so, we can just as easily consider each possible board an unanalyzed "piece" of a larger construct, the sequence of board configurations that make up a given game. We will recognize three very broad, relative layers of play: pre-play, play, and post-play.

Pre-play (syntactic level) concerns the mastering of the *fundamental rules of the game* which define the playing field. A player who could in some way visualize all the possible board configurations would completely master this level. Even so, he or she would not necessarily win a single game, even against someone who could not visualize the entire field of possibilities.

Play (semantic level) concerns the *relative value of a move* and its fundamental effect or consequences. The players' vying is a kind of dialogue at a higher combinatorial level than pre-play, though it presupposes pre-play vying in the sense that each player is more or less expert at seeing potential moves. Play adds a layer of meaning since the choice of a complete game must be *shared* with the opponent. At the same time, play includes an unlimited number of possible sub-games. For example, in chess, the opening play is of itself a sub-game, as is the end game. Yet all the sub-games blend with the general goal of winning.

Post-play (pragmatic level) concerns aesthetic sensibility; it is not the simple winning or losing of the game, but rather the *way* one wins or loses that becomes the game. Post-play can make the game mean just about anything: for example, out of deference, one player might seek to lose, perhaps to encourage the other player. At the post-play level the game opens on to any number of further games.

Abstractly, the pre-play level in chess is always the same. However, a real player must devise a set of rules for seeing pre-play and play potential, and those heuristic rules can change and indeed should change as the player improves. At the moment, it would seem that programmers of chess machines, which do great things through brute search algorithms, have not yet addressed this further level of chess prowess, that rule-changing creativity that allows players to improve or, while playing chess, to play more than just chess.

Reading a playtext involves vying at all these levels. Potential texts are like solitaire: they are only worthy adversaries at the pre-play level, or perhaps at the play level. The game stops with a win or loss for the computer. In human interaction, the game can be transformed into just about any game the players wish; it becomes mostly post-play, or higher. That facile movement to higher levels of play is the ultimate focus of RP, both for understanding what robotic texts mean and how to build them.

Virtual and Actualized Texts

Many features not clearly associated with traditional print literature come to the forefront in the robotic text. All texts are minimally interactive, but a robotic text has concrete structures that are designed to maintain a more human-like feedback loop with the reader. Many special functions, while possible with a paper text, become central to the ethos of a robotic text. Clearly, time is one parameter that can be used in a novel way. Thus Fournel contrasts the computer implementation of Queneau's sonnets with the printed book:

> The printed collection [of Queneau's poems] is prettily conceived, but the manipulation of the strips on which each verse is printed is sometimes tedious. The computer, though, makes a selection in the corpus in function of the length of the "reader's" name and the time which he takes to type it into the terminal, then prints the sonnet, which bears the double signature of Queneau and his reader. (Fournel 1986: 140)

This *subjectification*, as Lévy calls it, characterizes the move towards the virtual text. (see figure 30.1). Yet moving from the potential to the virtual is not simply a question of degree. Both virtual and potential texts are alike in that both are equally unreadable (as Queneau remarks above). Virtual texts have however a kind of open-ended creativity that would ultimately define success under the Turing test. A computerized version of Queneau's text simply does not have that degree of intelligence. Today's systems only approach asymptotically the virtual text, which remains a challenge. Even so, many potential texts seem to "simulate" virtual texts (!).

The virtual text remains the ultimate object of RP. How does one instill a robot with creative subjectivity? There are certainly many tantalizing steps that seem to inch the potential text towards the virtual. The single most common step is to borrow the reader's subjectivity by implicating him or her in the construction of the text. This transfer of subjectivity is no doubt the source of the Eliza effect: readers fill in what the computer leaves blank. Though such sleights of hand concerning subjectivity hybridize (reader and text) rather than virtualize, they do offer a tantalizing mirage of what RP seeks:

> Definition 3: RP is the poetics of virtualization and virtual text.

At present, the only obvious path to virtualization is by degrees, through a dogged expansion of the computer's generative potential using ever more powerful techniques – such was the evolution of computer chess. It is useful therefore to look at some concrete examples of text generation and follow how the generative power of applications can be expanded through progressive generalization.

Generative Applications: Prolog and the Tigerbil

There are many technical dimensions associated with a generation project, and a confusing diversity of applications. Very little can be called standard in this area. Anyone wishing to become a text engineer and actually generate text will face a number of practical choices (operating systems, programming environment, grammar formalism, lexicon format, etc.), many of which have considerable theoretical implications.

One of the major stumbling blocks in the field is the short life cycle of any software. Publications in computer-generated literature included, as late as 1986, pages of poorly printed code in DOS BASIC and were fairly unreadable. Transcribing code from books was extremely error-prone, especially in the unfriendly DOS BASIC environment. It would seem that pseudo code and abstract structures are the best way to approach any presentation of this rapidly evolving field. Danlos's use of pseudo-code in her *Linguistic Basis of Text Generation* (Danlos 1987) makes it more accessible today. More recent texts on text generation (Reiter and Dale 2000), grammar formalism (Butt et al. 1989), or computational linguistics (Gazdar and Mellish 1989; Jurafsky and Martin 2000) use higher-level programming languages and grammar formalisms. (See SIGGEN 2002 and Calder 2002 for recent publications on generation.)

And yet the heart of generation lies in the code, because it is in the code that virtual structures are condensed into single-step operations – the code becomes the text engineer's principal language. A simple example, automating Lewis Carroll's portmanteau words, should suffice to illustrate, in a very minimal way, both the problems and powers associated with a given programming environment.

Let us program a system that will create portmanteau words by combining words whose spelling overlaps. That is, one word will end with the same letters with which the other word begins. To investigate that relation over a given set of words (the size of the set being almost immaterial for the computer), one must exhaustively compare every possible pair of words in the set. Each word must be decomposed into all its possible front sequences and corresponding end sequences. For example, "tiger" and "gerbil" must be split into: t iger, ti ger, tig er, tige r, tiger / g erbil, ge rbil, ger bil, gerb il, gerbi l, gerbil. Then each front of one must be compared to the ends of the other and vice versa to check for (the longest) match: tigerbil.

In a high-level language like Prolog, built-in programming constructs allow the specification of that splitting process to be very detailed and yet concise. The following code (Coelho et al. 1982: 18) uses a small set of French names of animals. It prints out: alligatortue, caribours, chevalligator, chevalapin, vacheval. (Some overlaps in English are beelephant, birdog, birdonkey, birdove, birduck, camelephant, camelion, catiger, caturkey, chickite, cowl, cowolf, crowl, crowolf, cuckoowl, dogecko, dogibbon, dogoat, dogoose, dovelephant, duckite, elephantiger, elephanturkey, frogecko, frogibbon, frogoat, frogoose, geckowl, goatiger, goaturkey, gooselephant, horselephant, jackalion, kitelephant, mouselephant, owlion, pigecko, pigibbon, pigoat, pigoose, roosterooster, sheepig, sheepigeon, snakelephant, tigerooster, wolfox, wolfrog. Of these, only camelephant and crowl overlap by more than one letter.) The actual core of the algorithm is only in the *append* and *mutation* routines; the others just deal with data representation and display. On most Prolog systems, *append* would be a built-in function, and so the programmer would only design *mutation*.

> Prolog program for generating French portmanteau words
>
> begin:-mutation(X), name(Nn,X), write(Nn), nl, fail.
>
> begin:-nl, write('Done.'), nl.
>
> mutation(X):-animal(Y),
>   animal(Z),
>   append(Y1,Y2,Y),
>   Y1 \= [],
>   append(Y2,–,Z),
>   Y2 \= [],
>   append(Y1,Z,X).
>
> append([],X,X).
> append([A|T],Y,[A|T2]):-append(T,Y,T2).
>
> animal(X) if animals(X1), name(X1,X).
>
> animals(alligator). /* alligator */
> animals(tortue). /* turtle */
> animals(caribou). /* caribou*/
> animals(ours). /* bear */
> animals(cheval). /* horse */
> animals(vache). /* cow */
> animals(lapin). /* rabbit */

We can explain the *mutation* algorithm as shown in table 30.1. The *append* code will try all the possible ways to split a list, just as the *animal* code will form all possible pairs of animals' names. The search for possible combinations (through the backtracking function) is a built-in dimension of any procedure and gives Prolog its specific character as a programming language. In fact, the programming issue in Prolog is really how to contain the search for combinations. Thus, in the list for English overlaps, we find "roosterooster"; since we did not specify explicitly that Y and Z should not be the same, that combination was produced along with the others.

   AI programming languages such as Lisp and Prolog come closest to a pseudo-code for generation. Unfortunately, considerable time and energy is required to master the power and concision of a high-level programming language. It is clear nonetheless that if these languages are preferred for AI applications, it is precisely because they represent an important step towards the virtual. Algorithms must ultimately stand on each other's shoulders, as *mutation*'s use of *append* shows.

   Many generation systems are end-user applications which require no programming at all, but they do not allow any extension of virtualization (Kurzweil's poetry generator or the *Shannonizer*). Others are quite sophisticated specifications, such as *ALICE* and *AIML* (AI XML), but do not deal in any direct way with crucial linguistic dimensions. Grammar management packages are by definition still closer to questions of language generation (see the NLP Software Registry); some, such as *KPML* (Reiter 2002; Reiter and Dale 2000) or *Vinci* (Lessard and Levison 2002) are explicitly conceived for generation. In all

Table 30.1   The mutation algorithm

mutation(X):-	Try to make an X (a word) with the following properties:
animal(Y), animal(Z),	To find that X, you will first have find two animals (whose names have been split into lists of characters), Y and Z. (Finding two candidate animals will be the job of code defined elsewhere, in the *animal* definition.)
append(Y1,Y2,Y), Y1 \= [],	Divide animal Y into a front part (Y1) and an end part (Y2). Make sure that the end part (Y2) is *not* the whole word, which would be the case should Y1 be the empty list.
append(Y2,–,Z),	Divide the other animal, Z, into two parts such that the front is Y2, i.e., the same end found in the Y animal.
Y2 \= [],	Again, make sure that there is some overlap; Y2 should not be empty.
append(Y1,Z,X).	Splice together Y1 (front of Y), with whole of Z to give X, the portmanteau we seek.

cases, the real question is how to make the programming language increasingly high-level and expressive; grammar specification and programming are increasingly fused. For the moment, no metalanguage would allow the programmer to code a portmanteau generator without specifying in a very detailed manner character-string manipulations.

Generalizing Generation: Grammar Levels

A generator is fundamentally a mail merge function, as is found in most word processors. A template for a merge has blank spots that are filled in using a database of content items. For example, from the sentence "Jack finds Jill irresistible," we can construct the template: "<Person> finds <Person> <Adjective>".

A simple sentence template

<Person>
    Jack
    Jill
    John
    Jeremy
    Jocelyn
    June

<Adjective>
    irresistible
    irrepressible
    irresponsible
    irrational
    irritating
    irascible

With that data a combinatorial generation will produce (6 * 6 * 6 =) 216 sentences having the same general form as the original. As can be seen, the combinations depend on the distinction between tag classes: the <Person> set is used twice, the <Adjective> set once. We might wish to refine our set of categories to distinguish between different aspects of the content items.

A sentence template with distinguishers

```
<Person>
    <male>
        Jack
        John
        Jeremy
    <female>
        Jocelyn
        Jill
        June
<Adjective>
    <positive>
        irresistible
        irrepressible
    <negative>
        irresponsible
        irrational
        irritating
        irascible
```

The template "<Person, male> finds <Person, female> <Adjective, positive>" restricts the combinatory to (3 * 3 * 2 =) 18 combinations. Other restrictions might be of the logical sort, for example excluding the (schizophrenic!) cases where the first and second person is the same person: "<Person = A> finds <Person = ∼A> <Adjective>". Variable A will be instantiated randomly and ∼A will be chosen randomly as well, but excluding whoever was chosen for A.

Sentence grammars: context-free grammars

Advanced generators differ from mail merge only in generality, i.e., advanced systems construct the most general descriptions possible of all dimensions of the text. Unfortunately, as structures become more general, the metalanguage and the control of generation become increasingly complex. The grammar of that seemingly simple sentence is not simple if considered as part of English grammar in general. A more general description of the sentence requires a framework for grammar description that is ultimately similar to a programming language. There is often a direct translation between programming constructs and grammar metalanguage. Prolog has in fact a built-in grammar description language called definite clause grammars (DCGs), which are essentially context-free grammars (CFGs) (see Jurafsky and Martin 2000 for this and other formalisms). A CFG of the template "<Person> <Attributive Verb> <Person> <Adjective>" is:

A simple context-free grammar

S → NP + VP
NP → Proper Noun
VP → V + NP
VP → V + NP + ADJ
Proper Noun → Jack | Jill | . . .
V → finds | believes | imagines . . .

where:

A → B = rewrite A as B
+ = concatenation with a space
| = or (choose one)
S = Sentence
V = Verb
ADJ = Adjective
NP = Noun phrase
VP = Verb phrase

Each rule represents a step in the description of a possible sentence. What is to the left of the arrow is rewritten in the form to the right. When generating a sentence, the substitution process continues until all the categories (left-hand side of the arrow) have been rewritten into words (terminal entries, which are not on the left-hand side of any rewrite rule). Diagrammatically a given sentence is a network of rewrites (see figure 30.3). This "stacking up" of grammatical categories in a tree form is called a phrase-structure tree diagram.

Distinguishers (attributes)

If our generative needs were limited to this one type of sentence, this simple CFG would be sufficient: from the database of possible nouns, adjectives, and verbs, it could generate all possible combinations. However, as it is, this grammar is too specific to be reused as a component of a larger grammar; it only describes the very specific behavior of attributive verbs (verbs whose adjective complement is attributed to the direct object complement). Other sentences, such as the simple transitive sentence "Jack sees Jill," do not fit this framework: "Jack sees Jill irresistible" is not grammatical.

We can generalize our grammar fairly simply by adding subclassifications to the main categories. We want to limit the VP to a particular subset of verbs, those that are attributive, and expand the grammar to allow for simple transitive constructions:

S→	NP →	Proper Noun →	Jack
	VP →	V →	finds
		NP →	Jill
		ADJ →	irresistible

Figure 30.3   A phrase-structure tree diagram

A context-free grammar with distinguishers

S → NP + VP
NP → Proper Noun
VP (number = NUM) → V(transitive, number = NUM) + NP
VP → V(attributive) + NP + ADJ
Proper Noun → Jack | Jill | ...
V(attributive) → finds | believes | sees | ...
V(transitive) → sees | loves | cherishes | ...

This is a more general grammar since it subcategorizes V so that we can distinguish between attributive and simple transitive verbs. (In *Vinci*, described below, distinguishers are called *attributes*.) Other distinguishers could be added to control various kinds of agreement between categories, such as number agreement (subject–verb). We will add the case of a plural subject:

A context-free grammar with distinguishers for number

S → NP(number=NUM) + VP(number=NUM)
NP(number=singular) → Proper Noun
NP(number=plural) → Proper Noun + "and"
+ Proper Noun
VP (number = NUM) → V (attributive, number = NUM) + NP + ADJ
VP → V(attributive) + NP + ADJ
Proper Noun→ Jack | Jill | June | ...

V(attributive, number=singular) → finds | believes | ...
V(attributive, number=plural) → find | believe | ...

V(transitive, number=singular) → sees | loves | cherishes | ...
V(transitive, number=plural) → see | love | cherish | ...

The first rule states that the value of the number distinguisher, NUM, must be the same in both the VP and the NP. That value will be assigned in the rewrite rules that follow it: when the NP subject is finally chosen, the value of the number distinguisher will be transferred, through NUM, to VP and will constrain the choices from that node down the tree to the selection of the verb.

Word grammars: morphology

The generalizations we have made so far are generalizing extensions to the grammar; they allow for other possible sentences, or variants of the original. Another generalization concerns what was originally taken as the data items of the merge: the words themselves have their own grammar, their morphology. Most English verbs have a simple morphology, just a choice between "s" and "es" in the third person:

A context-free grammar for morphology

V(number=singular) → Vstem(vtype=s) + "&s"
V(number=singular) → Vstem(vtype=es) + "&es"

V(number=plural) → Vstem

Vstem(transitive, vtype=s) → see | love | ...
Vstem(transitive, vtype=es) → cherish | kiss | ...

Vstem(attributive, vtype=s) → find | believe | imagine | ...
Vstem(attributive, vtype=es) → wash (as in "washes clothes clean") | ...

where
& = suppress preceding space.

Our morphological rules are more complex than in the previous CFG, but now they are more general: adding new verbs to the database requires adding only the infinitives to one of the four classes, rather than adding two inflected forms in different rules.

Text grammars: metagrammars

All grammar might in principle be integrated into a CF sentence grammar. Word morphology becomes a module of a sentence grammar, and a text of whatever length can be transformed into a single sentence. Yet grammars traditionally describe separately the word, sentence, and textual levels. Text grammars bring with them a number of difficult issues. Minimally, a text is two or more sentences that cohere. That coherence expresses itself in many ways.

The sentence generator we have described so far could easily generate two sentences to make a text: "Jack finds Jill irresistible. Jack finds Jill irrepressible." To add a textual level to the grammar, it is sufficient to add the rules:

A context-free grammar for generating a two-sentence text

T → S + "&." + S + "&."

where
T = Text.

This describes minimally a text as two sentences, but it does not generate a very natural one. We would prefer our first text to be rendered as: "Jack finds Jill irresistible and irrepressible." Furthermore, if we generated "Jack finds Jill irresistible. Jack finds Jill irritating," we would prefer to have "Jack finds Jill irresistible *yet* irritating."

This process of removing repetitive structures, expressing the underlying logical relations, and making a natural synthesis of the information is called aggregation. In the first case, it is simply a question of suppressing the start of the second sentence and adding "and," but to accomplish that in a general fashion, we would need to understand how the two sentences compare in their structure. Not all sentences that end in adjectives can be conflated in this same way. (We cannot conflate "Jack finds Jill irresistible" and "Jack is irrepressible.") Suppression of the first part of the sentence and coordination of the adjectives is possible because each adjective is in exactly the same syntactic environment.

Textual grammars are meta or control grammars; they direct the generation of sentences. Descriptions at this level are obviously quite complex since they are twice removed from an actual sentence. A control grammar would not normally attempt to reorganize what is already generated. Comparing and manipulating two parse trees would be a very complex process. Rather, typically it is more straightforward to allow the control grammar to build a plan of the text and then to select the grammatical resources needed to fulfill the plan.

We might represent the plan or semantic skeleton of our text using predicate calculus. In this small grammar, each verb would have a general semantic description. One class of attributive verbs expresses the fact that the subject, X, believes that the object comple-ment, Y, possesses a certain quality, Z: *belief(X, is(Y, Z))*. The predicate "belief" reflects the modal part of the fundamental meaning behind "finds," "considers," or "believes"; "is," the attributive part. If our text is defined by two facts of this type, the rules of predicate logic will allow us to understand how they can be combined.

From *belief(X, is(Y,Z))* and *belief(X, is(Y,W))* we can deduce (using logical transform-ations) that *belief(X,&(is(Y,Z),is(Y,W)))*. From that expression, we simplify to *belief(X, is(Y,&(Z,W)))*. That is the general plan for our text, derived by transformation of formulas that preserve meaning. Our grammar would then have to take that meaning and translate it into the appropriate grammatical structures and finally into words.

Vinci[1]

To understand how control grammars work, we will consider in more detail a small fragment of a story generator coded in *Vinci*, the generation system designed by Lessard and Levison.

Vinci supports all the grammar coding structures we have discussed so far: CFGs, inheritance of distinguishers (attributes), sophisticated morphological generation, and much more. The feature that will concern us here is their PRESELECT, which plays the role of a sentence planner. This system does not (yet) have a text planner as such, but the sentence planner does give us insight into how a full-blown text planner would work. (*KPML* is a more complete implementation on this point, but considerably more com-plex. See Reiter and Dale 2000.)

The following is a *Vinci*-generated story designed by Lessard. It is presented here divided according to the Proppian narrative functions that served as its generative framework (an approach that is common since Klein et al. 1977):

A *Vinci*-generated fairy tale

(present king)	_Il était une fois un roi (Once upon a time there was a king)
(name king)	qui s'appelait Pierre. (named Pierre.)
(describe king)	_Il était beau, intelligent, bon, et il avait des cheveux roux. (He was handsome, intelligent, good, and he had red hair.)
(present victim)	_Il avait une enfant, la princesse. (He had a child, the princess.)
(describe victim)	_Elle était belle, intelligente, forte, bonne, et elle avait des cheveux blonds. (She was beautiful, intelligent, strong, good, and she had blond hair.)
(make interdiction)	_Le roi ordonna à la princesse de rester au château. (The king ordered the princess to stay in the castle.)
(disobey)	_Elle désobéit quand même. (She disobeyed nevertheless.)
(leave)	_Elle alla dans la forêt. (She went into the forest.)

(encounter)	_où elle rencontra un sorcier. (where she met a sorcerer.)
(name villain)	_Il s'appelait Merloc. (His name was Merloc.)
(describe villain)	_Il était laid, intelligent, fort, méchant, et il avait des cheveux blonds. (He was ugly, intelligent, strong, wicked, and he had blond hair.)
(kidnap)	_Il l'enleva. (He kidnapped her.)
(ask)	_Pour la sauver, le roi demanda l'aide d'un prince. (To save her, the king asked a prince for help.)
(give)	_Heureusement, le prince rencontra un lutin qui lui fournit une grenouille magique. (Luckily, the prince met an elf who provided him with a magic frog.)
(kill)	_Le prince l'utilisa pour tuer le sorcier. (The prince used it to kill the sorcerer.)
(marry)	_Il épousa la princesse et ils eurent beaucoup d'enfants. (He married the princess and they had many children.)

This story requires a number of support files and a separate grammar for each narrative function. The main files that concern us here are:

1   The lexicon, where words are stored with their attributes and indications for generating morphological variants. The lexicon, and the grammar in the user file, is expandable.
2   The attribute file, which defines the attribute categories and the values of each attribute (which we called distinguishers in the previous sections). For example, in the Genre category (gender) there will be two attribute values, *masc* and *fém*.
3   The user file, which is the main grammar file where the CFGs are found.

Without any preselection, the system uses whatever grammar has been defined in the user file and generates random output. The PRESELECT, along with the SELECT function, controls how the grammar will generate. For example, we will want certain verbs to have certain nouns as subjects, and not others (e.g., "It is raining" is acceptable; "Paul is raining" is not). In this fairy tale, each narrative function concerns the sphere of action of a given subject and that subject must be the focus throughout the function. Attributes, the SELECT, and the PRESELECT functions of *Vinci* allow us to describe such constraints. Random generation will happen within the boundaries defined by these structures.

Table 30.2 contains a detailed commentary of the user file for the second function, the "Name the king" function, produces the output "qui s'appelait X" (who is called X). Grammar control is achieved in *Vinci* principally through controlling the flow of attributes in the phrase structure trees and through loading and unloading grammar modules in user files. This is a simulation of grammar control, but it is clear that in a full implementation of a metagrammar, the grammar rules themselves become the objects of manipulation and take on the same status, but at a higher level, that words have in a sentence grammar. To correctly generate sentences in a general manner, we had to develop a complex system of grammatical categories and attributes. A metagrammar must in the same way develop the descriptive language, not to describe sentences, but to describe what describes sentences: the CFG rules.

In short, the most logical way to generate text under *Vinci* would be to use two *Vinci*s: one to (randomly) generate a constrained grammar and the second to use that grammar to

Table 30.2   The "name the king" function

PRESELECT = roi : N[sing]/"roi"	According to this PRESELECT instruction, the system will first choose a singular N (noun) whose lexical entry is "roi." "Roi" is defined in the lexicon as: "roi"|N|masc, Nombre, Déterm, humain, mâle, roux, bon ("king"|N|masc, Number, Determiner, human, male, red-haired, good). This preselected lexical item will be used in the SELECT rule below. (Note that the "|" is a field delimiter in the dictionary entries.)
ROOT = NOMMER[roi]	The highest node is always ROOT. For this generation, its only child node is NOMMER with the semantic attribute *roi*. For generating "Name the villain," NOMMER is given attribute *scélérat* (villain) instead.
NOMMER = INHERIT Ps : Personnage; SELECT Ge : Genre *in* Ps, No : Nombre *in* Ps, Mo : Moralité *in* Ps;	In creating the daughter nodes for NOMMER as described below, we first inherit its *Personnage* attribute, in this case *roi*, giving this value to the variable Ps. Through Ps, we then access the lexical item preselected for *roi* (i.e., "roi") to set up three variables (Ge, No, Mo). Notice that "roi" is masc, and has the attribute *bon* (good) taken from the Moralité category. The preselection has also been designated *sing*. To summarize the transfer of attributes: the lexical entry "roi" gives its attributes to the preselection labelled *roi*, one of the *Personnage* attributes defined in the attributes file. The NOMMER node has *roi* as its *Personnage* attribute, which is inherited under the name of Ps. Through Ps, the variables Ge, No, and Mo obtain values which are used to select appropriate PRON and N words.
PRON[pronrel, suj, clit]	"qui": the attributes select the subject relative pronoun in a clitic construction
PRON[pronréf, p3, No]	"se": a reflexive pronoun, 3rd person, with number (*sing*) defined in the PRESELECT. Morphological rules of this entry deal with the elision of "e."
V[vpron, imparf, p3, No]/"appeler"	"appelait": the imperfect tense, 3rd person singular, of the verb "appeler."
N[prp, Mo, Ge, No]	"Pierre" is a possible N[*prp*] (*prp* = proper noun) choice. His entry in the lexicon is: "Pierre"|N|prp, masc, sing, humain, Cheveux, Obéissance, Apparence, Force, Moralité, Intelligence." Of course, we do not know whether Pierre is actually *bon* – he is not defined as such in the lexicon. He does however possess the attribute category *Moralité*, and that is sufficient for him to qualify as a potential *roi*. On the other hand, "Merloc," another N[prp], will not be chosen from the lexicon since his Mo does not match *bon* (he is *méchant*!): "Merloc"|N|prp, masc, sing, humain, Cheveux, Apparence, Force, méchant, Intelligence
PONCT[pt]	Then a period.

randomly generate the final text. The PRESELECT and the SELECT rules represent a foreshadowing of that ultimate metagrammar.

Definition 4: RP is the study of abstraction and meta processes.

Art and Virtuality

We have outlined a seemingly new area of study called robotic poetics. We have not tried to define all its dimensions or to subdivide it in any way. Rather we have focused on a number of interwoven problematics that seem to concern any form RP might take in the future: mechanization, combinatory, virtualization, and abstraction towards metastructures. There are many formalist poetics that have dealt with some of these issues in the past, and some are now being adapted to the new computational context (enterprises such as Rastier's interpretative semantics or Zholkovsky's poetics of expressiveness). However, RP's most pivotal shift in emphasis lies in the confluence of traditionally separate fields of interest: generation merges with analysis, theory with practice, creativity with criticism.

Whatever the techniques that ultimately come to inform RP, the field is inevitably structured by the romantic image of a creative artificial intelligence. Winograd (1990) discusses that image in a practical manner. In his *Count Zero* (1986) William Gibson presents perhaps a more powerful literary description of RP's idealized object. One strand of the intrigue focuses on Marly Krushkhova, an art dealer who has been hired by Joseph Virek to track down the author of beautiful, shoebox-sized found-object sculptures. Her employer is astronomically wealthy, but now an immense blob of cancerous cells maintained in a vat at a Stockholm laboratory. Virek wants to transfer his mind out of the vat and into an AI construct. He believes that the artist Marly seeks – an AI construct – holds the key to his transmogrification. Near the end of the novel Marly travels to an abandoned space station to meet the artist. She arrives in the weightless domed room where the robot is housed. Its arms stir the floating space debris:

> There were dozens of the arms, manipulators, tipped with pliers, hexdrivers, knives, a subminiature circular saw, a dentist's drill.... They bristled from the alloy thorax of what must once have been a construction remote, the sort of unmanned, semiautonomous device she knew from childhood videos of the high frontier. But this one was welded into the apex of the dome, its sides fused with the fabric of the Place, and hundreds of cables and optic lines snaked across the geodesics to enter it. Two of the arms, tipped with delicate force-feedback devices, were extended; the soft pads cradled an unfinished box. (Gibson 1986: 217)

The debris, from which the mechanical arms extract components and fashion its box sculptures, is composed of personal belongings abandoned by a family of now decadent AI pioneers:

> A yellowing kid glove, the faceted crystal stopper from some vial of vanished perfume, an armless doll with a face of French porcelain, a fat gold-fitted black fountain pen, rectangular segments of perf board, the crimpled red and green snake of a silk cravat.... Endless, the slow swarm, the spinning things. (1986: 217)

Virek, a pleasant, human-like "generated image" (1986: 227), appears on the terminal screen in the AI's workshop; Marly is caught floating between the fake glowing image that masks Virek's deformed and decadent humanity and the very concrete arms of the superhuman robotic artist. The AI explains that the Virek teratoma might at best become "the least of my broken selves" (ibid.). Marly recaps to the AI:

> You are someone else's collage. Your maker is the true artist. Was it the mad daughter [of the AI pioneer family]? It doesn't matter. Someone brought the machine here, welded it to the dome, and wired it to the traces of memory. And spilled, somehow, all the worn sad evidence of a family's humanity, and left it to be stirred, to be sorted by a poet. To be sealed away in boxes. I know of no more extraordinary work than this. No more complex gesture. (1986: 227)

Why this fascination with the robotic poet? Why should the robotic author be so "extraordinary," the most "complex gesture"? There are many reasons why artists might be drawn to robotics, but one profound reason might lie in the nature of art itself.

Art, like religion, is a window onto something beyond, though we know not what. The work of art entices us beyond who we are and what we understand, and we are left floating, like Marly, in a space defined only by the fact that it is new; one step beyond who we were, somewhere we thought we could not possibly be. The pleasure and the importance of art is perhaps that move up the meta organization of our understanding, to a more general space that gives us a different, if not a better insight into the world.

There is nothing new about this confluence of problematics. Art as combinatory, love, divine madness, knowledge, and writing are at the heart of Plato's *Phaedrus*. Socrates cites Midas's epitaph, spoken by a bronze Eliza, a kind of rigid chatbot:

> Bronze maiden am I and on Midas' mound I lie.
> As long as water flows and tall trees bloom,
> Right here fixed fast on the tearful tomb,
> I shall announce to all who pass near: Midas is dead and buried here.
> (264e; cited in Carson 1986: 134)

Socrates's point seems to be that combinatory, like Midas's gold, is without meaning:

> I suppose you notice that it makes no difference which line is read first or which is read last. (264e; cited in Carson 1986: 135)

Art lies elsewhere than in combinatory, and yet art is fundamentally combination, as its etymology suggests. It lies somewhere in the vast domain of post-play. Socrates contrasts uncreative potential and creative virtuality; true knowledge and sophistry; love and convention. Artful discourse must have a beginning and an end. It must go somewhere, and that where is up. Like eros, it is a winged thing (Carson 1986).

Plato's multifaceted *Phaedrus* gives us a very ancient and general definition of RP:

> Definition 5: RP is the study of art through the foil of mechanical art.

Note

1   My thanks go to Greg Lessard and Michael Levison for technical assistance with *Vinci* as well as their explanations of its formalism.

REFERENCES FOR FURTHER READING

ACL (Association for Computational Linguistics) (2002). *Natural Language Software Registry.* At <http://registry.dfki.de/>.

A.L.I.C.E AI Foundation (2002). *A.L.I.C.E. AI Foundation.* At <http://alice.sunlitsurf.com/>.

Aarseth, Epsen J. (1997). *Cybertext: Perspectives in Ergodic Literature.* Baltimore: Johns Hopkins University Press.

Anis, J. (1995). La Génération de textes littéraires : cas particulier de la génération de textes ou discipline à part? [Generation of literary texts: a particular example of text generation or a separate field?]. In *Littérature et informatique,* ed. A. Vuillemin and M. Lenoble (pp. 33–48). Arras: Artois Presses Université.

Balpe, Jean-Pierre and Bernard Magné (eds.) (1991). *L'Imagination informatique de la littérature* [Literature's computerized imagination]. Saint-Denis: Presses Universitaires de Vincennes.

Butt, Miriam, Tracey Holloway King, María-Eugenia Niño, and Frédérique Segond (1989). *A Grammar Writer's Cookbook.* Stanford, CA: CSLI Publications.

Calder, Jo (2002). *The Scottish Natural Language Generation Homepage.* At <http://www.cogsci.ed.ac.uk/~jo/Gen/snlg/nlg.html>.

Carson, Anne (1986). *Eros the Bittersweet.* Princeton, NJ: Princeton University Press.

Coelho, Helder, José Carlos Cotta, and Luís Moniz Pereira (1982). *How to Solve It with Prolog,* 3rd edn. Lisbon: Ministério Da habiacao e Obras Públicas.

Danlos, Laurence (1987). *The Linguistic Basis of Text Generation,* tr. Dominique Debize and Colin Henderson. Cambridge: Cambridge University Press. (Original work published 1985.)

Fournel, Paul (1986). Computer and the Writer: The Centre Pompidou Experiment. In *Oulipo: A Primer of Potential Literature,* ed. and tr. W. F. Motte (pp. 140–2). Lincoln and London: University of Nebraska Press.

Gazdar, Gerald and Chris Mellish (1989). *Natural Language Processing in PROLOG.* New York: Addison-Wesley Publishing.

Gibson, William (1986). *Count Zero.* New York: Ace Books.

Jurafsky, Daniel and James H. Martin (2000). *Speech and Language Processing.* Upper Saddle River, NJ: Prentice Hall.

Klein, Sheldon, J. F. Aeschlimann, M. A. Appelbaum, D. F. Balsiger, E. J. Curtis, M. Foster, S. D. Kalish, S. J. Kamin, Y.-D. Lee, L. A. Price, and D. F. Salsieder (1977). Modelling Propp and Lévi-Strauss in a Meta-symbolic Simulation System. In *Patterns in Oral Literature,* ed. H. Jason and D. Segal (pp. 141–222). The Hague: Mouton.

Kurzweil, Ray (2002). The Age of Intelligent Machines: "A (Kind of) Turing Test." At <http://www.kurzweilcyberart.com/poetry/rkcp_akindofturingtest.php3>.

Lessard, Greg and Michael Levison (2002). *Vinci Laboratory.* At <http://www.cs.queensu.ca/CompLing/>.

Lévy, Pierre (1998). *Qu'est-ce que le virtuel?* [What is the virtual?]. Paris: La Découverte and Syros.

Motte, Warren (1995). *Playtexts: Ludics in Contemporary Literature.* Lincoln: University of Nebraska Press.

Queneau, Raymond (1973). *Cent mille milliards de poèmes* [One hundred trillion poems]. Paris: Gallimard.

Rastier, François, Marc Cavazza, and Anne Abeillé (1994). *Sémantique pour l'analyse* [Semantic for analysis]. Paris: Masson.

Reiter, Ehud (2002). *KPML*. At <http://www.fb10.uni-bremen.de/anglistik/langpro/kpml/READ-ME.html>.

Reiter, Ehud, and Robert Dale (2000). *Building Natural Language Generation Systems*. Cambridge: Cambridge University Press.

Shannon_Team (2002). *The Shannonizer*. At <http://www.nightgarden.com/shannon.htm>.

SIGGEN (2002). *ACL Special Interest Group on Generation*. At <http://www.dynamicmultimedia.com.au/siggen/>.

Winder, Bill (1994). Le Robo-poète: littérature et critique à l'ère électronique [The robo-poet: literature and criticism in the electronic era]. In *Littérature, Informatique, Lecture*, ed. A. Vuillemin and M. Lenoble (pp. 187–213). Limoges: Presses Universitaires de Limoges.

Winograd, Terry (1990). Thinking Machines: Can There Be? Are We? In *The Foundations of Artificial Intelligence*, ed. D. Patridge and Y. Wilks (pp. 167–89). Cambridge: Cambridge University Press.

Zholkovsky, Alexander (1984). *Themes and Texts*. Ithaca and London: Cornell University Press.

PART IV
Production, Dissemination, Archiving

31

Designing Sustainable Projects and Publications

Daniel V. Pitti

Introduction

Designing complex, sustainable digital humanities projects and publications requires familiarity with both the research subject and available technologies. It is essential that the scholar have a clear and explicit understanding of his intellectual objectives and the resources to be used in achieving them. At the same time, the scholar must have sufficient comprehension of available technologies, in order to judge their suitability for representing and exploiting the resources in a manner that best serves his intellectual objectives. Given the dual expertise required, scholars frequently find it necessary to collaborate with technologists in the design and implementation processes, who bring different understandings, experience, and expertise to the work. Collaboration in and of itself may present challenges, since most humanists generally work alone and share the research's results, not the process.

Collaborative design involves iterative analysis and definition, frequently accompanied by prototype implementations that test the accuracy and validity of the analysis. While computers enable sophisticated data processing and manipulation to produce desired results, the scholar must analyze, define, and represent the data in detail. Each data component and each relation between data components needs to be identified, and, when represented in the computer, named and circumscribed. Data must not simply be entered into a computer, but be accompanied by additional data that identify the data components. This decomposition is necessary to instruct the computer, through programs or applications, to process the data to achieve the objectives, a process of locating, identifying, and manipulating the data.

The data need not be endlessly analyzed and decomposed. It is only necessary to identify the data components and relations deemed essential to achieving desired results. To determine what is essential in reaching the objectives, it is necessary also to understand the objectives in detail and subject them to a rigorous analysis, defining and making explicit each important function. Analysis of the objectives informs analysis of the data, determining what data and features of the data will be required to meet the objectives, and thus what features will need to be identified and explicitly represented. Conversely, analysis of the data will inform analysis of the objectives.

Analyzing objectives relies on identifying and defining the intended user community (or communities) and the uses. Are the intended users peers, sharing the same or similar research interests? Are they students, or perhaps the interested public? If the users are students, then at what level: K-12, K-16, 9–12, or 13–16? Perhaps they are a very focused group, such as high school literature or history classes? For the intended user community, is the project primarily intended to facilitate research, scholarly communication of research, reference, pedagogy, or perhaps a combination of one or more of these? The answers to these questions will assist in determining the functions that will be most likely to serve the perceived needs and at the appropriate level or levels.

As important as users are, those responsible for creation and maintenance of the project must also be considered. In fact, they may be considered another class of users, as distinct from the so-called end users. Before a project begins to produce and publish data content, the project must have an infrastructure that will support its production and publishing. Someone – project manager, researcher, lead design person – needs to specify the steps or workflow and methods involved in the complex tasks of identifying, documenting, and digitizing artifacts; creating original digital resources; and the control and management of both the assets created and the methods used. The design must incorporate the creator's requirements. Control, management, and production methods are easily overlooked if the designer focuses exclusively on the publication and end user. Asset management does not present a particular problem in the early stages of a project, when there are only a handful of objects to track. As the number of files increases, though, it becomes increasingly difficult to keep track of file names, addresses and versions.

Focusing on achieving particular short-term results may also lead to neglecting consideration of the durability or persistence of the content and its publication. Ongoing changes in computer technology present long-term challenges. Changes in both applica- tions and the data notations with which they work will require replacing one version of an application with another, or with an entirely different application, and will eventually require migrating the data from one notation to another. Generally these changes do not have a major impact in the first four or five years of a project, and thus may not seem significant to projects that are intended to be completed within three or four years. Most researchers and creators, though, will want their work to be available for at least a few years after completion. If a project has or will have a publisher, the publisher will certainly want it to remain viable as long as it has a market. The cultural heritage community, important participants in scholarly communication, may judge a publication to have cultural value for future generations. Archivists, librarians, and museum curators, in collaboration with technologists, have been struggling seriously since at least the 1980s to develop methods for ensuring long-term access to digital information. Though many critical challenges remain, there is broad consensus that consistent and well-documented use of computer and intellectual standards is essential.

Economy must also be considered. There are the obvious up-front costs of computer hardware and software, plus maintenance costs as these break or become obsolete. Human resources are also an important economic factor. Human resources must be devoted to the design, prototyping, and, ultimately, implementation. Once implemented, more resources are needed to maintain a project's infrastructure. Data production and maintenance also require human resources. Data needs to be identified, collected, and analyzed; created, and maintained in machine-readable form; and reviewed for accuracy and consistency. Realizing complex, detailed objectives requires complex, detailed implementations, production methods, and, frequently, a high degree of data differentiation. As a general rule, the more detailed and complex a project becomes, the more time it will take to design, implement, populate with data, and maintain. Thus every objective comes with costs, and the costs frequently have to be weighed against the importance of the objective. Some objectives, while worthwhile, may simply be too expensive.

Design is a complex exercise: given this complexity, the design process is iterative, and each iteration leads progressively to a coherent, integrated system. It is quite impossible to simultaneously consider all factors. Both the whole and the parts must be considered in turn, and each from several perspectives. Consideration of each in turn leads to reconsideration of the others, with ongoing modifications and adjustments. Prototyping of various parts to test economic, intellectual, and technological feasibility is important. It is quite common to find an apparent solution to a particular problem while considering one or two factors but to have it fail when other factors are added, requiring it to be modified or even abandoned. Good design, then, requires a great deal of persistence and patience.

Disciplinary Perspective and Objects of Interest

Humanists study human artifacts, attempting to understand, from a particular perspective and within a specific context, what it means to be human. The term artifact is used here in the broadest sense: an artifact is any object created by humans. Artifacts may be primary objects of interest or serve as evidence of human activities, events, and intentions. Archivists make a useful distinction between an object intentionally created, as an end in itself, and an object that is a by-product of human activities, the object typically functioning instrumentally as a means or tool. Novels, poems, textbooks, paintings, films, sculptures, and symphonies are created as ends in themselves. Court records, birth certificates, memoranda, sales receipts, deeds, and correspondence facilitate or function as a means to other objectives, or as evidence or a record of particular actions taken. After serving their intended purpose, instrumental artifacts primarily function as evidence. Artifacts that are ends in themselves may of course also function as evidence. A novel, for example, may be viewed as a literary object, with particular aesthetic and intellectual qualities, or a source of evidence for language usage or for identifying important cultural values in a particular historical context. Many disciplines share an interest in the same or similar objects or have similar assumptions and methods. Linguists and students of literature may share an interest in written texts, perhaps even literary texts, but differ substantially in what characteristics of texts are of interest or considered significant. Socio-cultural historical studies, while differing widely in the phenomena studied, will nevertheless employ similar methods, with the shared objective of a historical understanding.

In order to apply computer technology to humanities research, it is necessary to represent in machine-readable form the artifacts or objects of primary or evidentiary interest in the research, as well as secondary information used in the description, analysis, and interpretation of the objects. The representations must reflect the disciplinary perspective and methods of the researcher, and facilitate the analytic and communication objectives of the project. In addition to perspective and intended uses, the method of representation will depend upon the nature of the artifact to be represented. As modes of human communication, pictorial materials, printed texts, mathematical formulae, tabular data, sound, film, sculptures, buildings, and maps, to name a few possible artifact types, all have distinct observable characteristics or features, and representations will generally isolate and emphasize those deemed essential to the research.

All information in computers exists in a coded form that enables it to be mechanically read and processed by the computer. Such codes are ultimately based on a binary system. Combinations of fixed sequences of 0s and 1s are used to create more complex representations, such as picture elements or pixels, sound samples, and alphabetic and numeric characters. Each of these is then combined to create more complex representations. For example, an array of pixels is used to form a picture, a sequence of alphabetic and numeric characters a text, and a sequence of sound samples a song. The codes so developed are used to represent both data and the programs that instruct the computer in reading and processing the data. There are a variety of ways of creating machine-readable texts. Text can be entered or transcribed from a keyboard. Some printed textual materials can be scanned and then rendered into machine-readable form using optical character recognition (OCR) software, although many texts, particularly in manuscript form, exceed the capability of current OCR technology. Either way, creating a sequence of machine-readable characters does not take advantage of major technological advances made in the representation and manipulation of written language and mathematics.

Written language and mathematics are composed of character data, marks, or graphs. Characters include ideographs (such as Chinese characters) and phonographs (as in the Latin alphabet), as well as Arabic numbers and other logograms. The discrete codes used in writing are mapped or reduced to machine-readable codes when represented in computers. Unicode (defined in ISO/IEC 10646) represents the most extensive attempt to map the known repertoire of characters used by humans to machine-readable codes. While written language (text) and mathematics are not the only types of information represented in computers, text constitutes an essential component of all humanities projects. Many projects will use one or more historical texts, the literary works of an author or group of related authors, a national constitution, or a philosophical work as the principal subject. For other projects, particular texts and records may not be the object of study, but texts may still be used for information about individuals, families, and organizations; intellectual, artistic, political, or other cultural movements; events; and other socio-cultural phenomena. Projects employ text to describe and document resources and to communicate the results of analysis and research. Further, text is used to identify, describe, control, and provide access to the digital assets collected in any project, and is essential in describing, effecting, and controlling interrelations between entities and the digital assets used to represent them. Comparing, identifying, describing, and documenting such interrelations are essential components of all humanities research.

The power and complexity of computer processing of textual data require complex representation of the text. A simple sequence of characters is of limited utility. In order to take full advantage of computing, textual data must be decomposed into their logical components, with each component identified or named, and its boundaries explicitly or implicitly marked. This decomposition and identification is necessary because sophisticated, accurate, and reliable processing of text is only possible when the computer can be unambiguously instructed to identify and isolate characters and strings of characters and to perform specified operations on them. There are a variety of specialized applications available for recording and performing mathematical operations on numerical data. There are also a variety of applications available for recording and processing textual data, though most do not have characteristics and features that make them appropriate for sustainable, intellectually complex humanities research.

Database and markup technologies represent the predominant technologies available for textual information. Though they differ significantly, they have several essential characteristics and features in common. Both exist in widely supported standard forms. Open, community-based and widely embraced standards offer reasonable assurance that the represented information will be durable and portable. Database and markup technologies are either based on or will accept standard character encodings (ASCII or, increasingly, Unicode). Both technologies enable an explicit separation of the logical components of information from the operations that are applied to them. This separation is effected by means of two essential features. First, each requires user-assigned names for designating and delimiting the logical components of textual objects. While there are some constraints, given the available character repertoire, the number of possible names is unlimited. Second, each supports the logical interrelating and structuring of the data components.

Though each of these technologies involves naming and structurally interrelating textual entities and components, each does so using distinctly different methods, and exploits the data in different ways. Deciding which technology to use will require analyzing the nature of the information to be represented and identifying those operations you would like to perform on it. With both technologies, the naming and structuring requires anticipating the operations. Each of these technologies is optimized to perform a set of well-defined operations. Though there is some overlap in functionality, the two technologies are best described as complementary rather than competitive. Information best represented in databases is characterized as "data-centric," and information best represented in markup technologies is characterized as "document-centric." Steve DeRose, in a paper delivered in 1995 at a conference devoted to discussing the encoding of archival finding aids, made much the same distinction, though he used the terms "document" and "form" to distinguish the two information types (see Steve DeRose, "Navigation, Access, and Control Using Structured Information," in *The American Archivist* (Chicago: Society of American Archivists), 60,3, Summer 1997, pp. 298–309).

Information collected on many kinds of forms is data-centric. Job applications are a familiar example. Name, birth date, street address, city, country or state, postal codes, education, skills, previous employment, date application completed, name or description of a position sought, references, and so on, are easily mapped into a database and easily retrieved in a variety of ways. Medical and student records, and census data are other common examples of data-centric information. These familiar examples have the following characteristics in common:

- Regular number of components or fields in each discrete information unit.
- Order of the components or fields is generally not significant.
- Each information component is restricted to data. That is, it has no embedded delimiters, other than the formal constraints of data typing (for example, a date may be constrained to a sequence of eight Arabic numbers, in the order year–month–day).
- Highly regularized structure, possibly with a fixed, though shallow, hierarchy.
- Relations between discrete information units have a fixed number of types (though the number of occurrences of each type may or may not be constrained).
- Processing of data-centric information (such as accurate recall and relevance retrieval, sorting, value comparison, and mathematical computation) is highly dependent on controlled values and thus highly dependent on machine-enforced data typing, authority files, and a high degree of formality, accuracy, and consistency in data creation and maintenance.

Common types of databases are hierarchical, network, relational, and object-oriented. Today, relational databases are by far the most prevalent. Structured Query Language (SQL), an ISO standard first codified in 1986 and substantially revised in 1992 and again in 1999, is the major standard for relational databases. While compliance with the standard is somewhat irregular, most relational databases comply sufficiently to ensure the portability and durability of data across applications. There are only a few viable implementations of object-oriented databases, though the technology has contributed conceptual and functional models that influenced the 1999 revision of SQL. SQL is both a Data Definition Language (DDL) and a Data Manipulation Language (DML). As a DDL, it allows users to define and name tables of data, and to interrelate the tables. Such definitions are frequently called database schemas. Tables have rows and columns. Within the context of databases, rows are commonly called records, and columns called fields in the records. Each column or field is assigned a name, typically a descriptive term indicating the type of data to be contained in it. The DML facilitates updating and maintaining the data, as well as sophisticated querying and manipulating of data and data relations.

Most historical or traditional documents and records are too irregular for direct representation in databases. Data in databases are rigorously structured and systematic and most historical documents and records simply are not. Nevertheless, some documents and records will be reducible to database structures, having characteristics approximating those listed above. Many traditional government, education, and business records may lend themselves to representation in databases, as will many ledgers and accounting books. But a doctoral dissertation, while a record, and generally quite regularized in structure, lacks other features of data that it would have to have to fit comfortably in a database architecture – for example, the order of the text components matters very much, and if they are rearranged arbitrarily, the argument will be rendered incoherent.

While database technology may be inappropriate for representing most historical documents and records, it is very appropriate technology for recording analytic descriptions of artifacts and in systematically describing abstract and concrete phenomena based on analysis of evidence found in artifacts. Analytic descriptive surrogates will be useful in a wide variety of projects. Archaeologists, for example, may be working with thousands of objects. Cataloguing these objects involves systematically recording a vast array of details, frequently including highly articulated classification schemes and controlled vocabularies. Database technology will almost always be the most appropriate and effective tool for collecting, classifying, comparing, and evaluating artifacts in one or many media.

Database technology is generally an appropriate and effective tool for documenting and interrelating records concerning people, events, places, movements, artifacts, or themes. Socio-cultural historical projects in particular may find databases useful in documenting and interrelating social and cultural phenomena. While we can digitize most if not all artifacts, many concrete and abstract phenomena are not susceptible to direct digitization. For example, any project that involves identifying a large number of people, organizations, or families will need to represent them using descriptive surrogates. A picture of a person, when available, might be very important, but textual identification and description will be necessary. In turn, if an essential part of the research involves describing and relating people to one another, to artifacts created by them or that provide documentary evidence of them, to events, to intellectual movements, and so on, then database technology will frequently be the most effective tool. Individuals, artifacts, places, events, intellectual movements, can each be identified and described (including chronological data where appropriate). Each recorded description can be associated with related descriptions. When populated, such databases enable users to locate individual entities, abstract as well as concrete, and to see and navigate relations between entities. If the database is designed and configured with sufficient descriptive and classificatory detail, many complex analytic queries will be possible, queries that reveal intellectual relations between unique entities, but also between categories or classes of entities based on shared characteristics.

Textbooks, novels, poems, collections of poetry, newspapers, journals, and journal articles are all examples of document-centric data. These familiar objects have in common the following characteristics:

- Irregular number of parts or pieces. Documents, even documents of a particular type, do not all have the same number of textual divisions (parts, chapters, sections, and so on), paragraphs, tables, lists, and so on.
- Serial order is significant. It matters whether this chapter follows that chapter, and whether this paragraph follows that paragraph. If the order is not maintained, then intelligibility and sense break down.
- Semi-regular structure and unbounded hierarchy.
- Arbitrary intermixing of text and markup, or what is technically called mixed content.
- Arbitrary number of interrelations (or references) within and among documents and other information types, and generally the types of relations are unconstrained or only loosely constrained.

Extensible Markup Language (XML), first codified in 1998 by the World Wide Web Consortium (W3C), is the predominant markup technologies standard. XML is a direct descendant of Standard Generalized Markup Language (SGML), first codified in 1986 by the International Standards Organization (ISO). While the relationship between XML and SGML is quite complex, XML may be viewed as "normalized" SGML, retaining the essential functionality of SGML, while eliminating those features of SGML that were problematic for computer programmers.

XML is a descriptive or declarative approach to encoding textual information in computers. XML does not provide an off-the-shelf tagset that one can simply take home and apply to a letter, novel, article, or poem. Instead, it is a standard grammar for expressing a set of rules according to which a class of documents will be marked up. XML provides conventions for naming the logical components of documents, and a syntax and metalanguage for defining and expressing the logical structure and relations among the components. Using these conventions, individuals or members of a community sharing objectives with respect to a particular type of document can work together to encode those documents.

One means of expressing analytic models written in compliance with formal XML requirements is the document type definition, or DTD. For example, the Association of American Publishers has developed four DTDs for books, journals, journal articles, and mathematical formulae. After thorough revision, this standard has been released as an ANSI/NISO/ISO standard, 12083. A consortium of software developers and producers has developed a DTD for computer manuals and documentation called DocBook. The Text Encoding Initiative (TEI) has developed a complex suite of DTDs for the representation of literary and linguistic materials. Archivists have developed a DTD for archival description or finding aids called encoded archival description (EAD). A large number of government, education and research, business, industry, and other institutions and professions are currently developing DTDs for shared document types. DTDs shared and followed by a community can themselves become standards. The ANSI/NISO/ISO 12083, DocBook, TEI, and EAD DTDs are all examples of standards.

The standard DTDs listed above have two common features. First, they are developed and promulgated by broad communities. For example, TEI was developed by humanists representing a wide variety of disciplines and interests. The development process (which is ongoing) requires negotiation and consensus-building. Second, each DTD is authoritatively documented, with semantics and structure defined and described in detail. Such documentation helps make the language public rather than private, open rather than closed, standard rather than proprietary, and thereby promotes communication. These two features – consensus and documentation – are essential characteristics of standards, but they are not sufficient in and of themselves to make standards successful (i.e., make them widely understood and applied within an acceptable range of uniformity).

The distinction between document-centric and data-centric information, while useful, is also frequently problematic. It is a useful distinction because it highlights the strengths of markup languages and databases, although it does not reflect information reality, as such. Frequently any given instance of information is not purely one or the other, but a mixture of both. Predominantly data-centric information may have some components or features that are document-centric, and vice-versa. The distinction is of more than theoretical interest, as each information type is best represented using a different technology, and each technology is optimized to perform a specific set of well-defined functions and either does not perform other functions, or performs them less than optimally. When deciding the best method, it is unfortunately still necessary to weigh what is more and less important in your information and to make trade-offs.

In addition to text representation. XML is increasingly used in realizing other functional objectives. Since the advent of XML in 1998, many database developers have embraced XML syntax as a data-transport syntax, that is, for passing information in machine-to-machine and machine-to-human communication, XML is also increasingly being used to develop standards for declarative processing of information. Rendering and querying are probably the two primary operations performed on XML-encoded textual documents. We want to be able to transform encoded documents into human-readable form, on computer screens, and on paper. We also want to be able to query individual documents and collections of documents. There are currently several related standards for rendering and querying XML documents that have been approved or are under development: Extensible Stylesheet Language – Transformation (XSLT), Extensible Stylesheet Language – Formatting Objects (XSLFO), and XQuery. These declarative standards are significant because they ensure not only the durability of encoded texts, but also the durability of the experienced presentation.

Users and Uses

Developing XML and database encoding schemes, as we have seen, involves consideration of the scholarly perspective, the nature and content of the information to be represented, and its intended use. For example, if we have a collection of texts by several authors, and we want users to be able to locate and identify all texts by a given author, then we must explicitly identify and delimit the author of each text. In the same way, all intended uses must be identified, and appropriate names and structures must be incorporated into the encoding schemes and into the encoded data. In a sense, then, XML and database encoding schemes represent the perspective and understanding of their designers, and each DTD or schema is an implied argument about the nature of the material under examination and the ways in which we can use it.

Specifying an intended use requires identifying and defining users and user communities. The researcher is an obvious user. In fact, the researcher might be the only user, if the intention is to facilitate collection and analysis of data, with analytic results and interpretation published separately. Such an approach, though, deprives readers of access to the resources and methods used, and there is an emerging consensus that one of the great benefits of computers and networks is that they allow us to expose our evidence and our methods to evaluation and use by others. If that is considered desirable, design must then take other users into consideration. As a general rule, the narrower and more specific the intended audience, the easier it will be to identify and define the uses of the data. If the intended audience is more broadly defined, it is useful to classify the users and uses according to educational and intellectual levels and abilities. While there may be overlap in functional requirements at a broad level, there will generally be significant differences in the complexity and detail of the apparatus made available to users.

We can divide user functions or operations into three types: querying, rendering, and navigation. This division is simply an analytic convenience. The categories are interrelated and interdependent, and some functions may involve combinations of other functions. Querying, simply characterized, involves users submitting words, phrases, dates, and the like, to be matched against data, with matched data or links to matched data returned, typically in an ordered list, to the user. Browsing is a type of querying, though the author of the research collection predetermines the query and thus the list of results returned. Rendering is the process by which machine-readable information is transformed into human-readable information. All information represented in computers, whether text, graphic, pictorial, or sound, must be rendered. Some rendering is straightforward, with a direct relation between the machine-readable data and its human-readable representation. Navigational apparatus are roughly analogous to the title page, table of contents, and other information provided in the preliminaries of a book. They inform the user of the title of the research collection, its intellectual content, scope, and organization, and provide paths or a means to access and traverse sub-collections and individual texts, graphics, pictures, videos, or sound files. The navigational apparatus will frequently employ both text and graphics, with each selectively linked to other navigational apparatus or directly to available items in the collection. Much like the design of the representation of digital artifacts, and necessarily related to it, designing the navigational apparatus requires a detailed analysis of each navigational function and steps to ensure that the underlying representation of the data will support it.

Determining and defining the querying, rendering, and navigational functions to be provided to users should not be an exclusively abstract or imaginative exercise. Many designers of publicly accessible information employ user studies to inform and guide the design process. Aesthetics play an important role in communication. Much of the traditional role of publishers involves the aesthetic design of publications. The "look and feel" of digital publications is no less important. While content is undoubtedly more important than form, the effective communication of content is undermined when aesthetics are not taken sufficiently into consideration. Researchers may wish to enlist the assistance of professional designers. While formal, professionally designed studies may be beyond the means of most researchers, some attempt at gathering information from users should be made. Interface design should not be deferred to the end of the design process. Creating prototypes and mockups of the interface, including designing the visual and textual apparatus to be used in querying, rendering, and navigating the collection and its parts, will inform the analysis of the artifacts and related objects to be digitally collected, and the encoding systems used in representing them.

Creating and Maintaining Collections

Creating, maintaining, managing, and publishing a digital research collection requires an infrastructure to ensure that the ongoing process is efficient, reliable, and controlled. Building a digital collection involves a large number of interrelated activities. Using a variety of traditional and digital finding aids, researchers must discover and locate primary and secondary resources in private collections and in public and private archives, museums, and libraries. Intellectual property rights must be negotiated. The researcher must visit the repository and digitally capture the resource, or arrange for the resource to be digitally captured by the repository, or, when possible, arrange to borrow the resource for digital capture. After each resource is digitally captured, the capture file or files may be edited to improve quality and fidelity. One or more derivative files may also be created. Digital derivatives may be simply alternative versions. For example, smaller image files may be derived from larger image files through sampling or compression to facilitate efficient Internet transmission or to serve different uses. Derivatives also may involve alternative representational technologies that enhance the utility or functionality of the information, for example, an XML-encoded text rather than bitmap images of original print materials. Creation of enhanced derivatives may constitute the primary research activity, and typically will involve extended analysis and editing of successive versions of files. Finally, complex relations within and between files and file components may be identified and explicitly recorded or encoded, and must be managed and controlled to ensure their persistence. All of these activities will require documentation and management that in turn will require recording detailed information.

The detailed information needed to intellectually and physically manage individual files and collections of interrelated files can be divided into four principal and interrelated categories: descriptive, administrative, file, and relations or structural data.

These categories represent the prevailing library model for recording management and control data, commonly called metadata, and they have been formalized in the Metadata Encoding and Transmission Standard (METS). Each of these four areas addresses specific kinds of management and control data. Each is also dependent on the others. Only when they are related or linked to one another will they provide an effective means of intellectual, legal, and physical control over collections of digital materials. These sorts of data are primarily data-centric, and thus best represented using database technology.

Descriptive data function as an intellectual surrogate for an object. Descriptive information is needed to identify the intellectual objects used in building as well as objects digitally represented in a research collection. Documenting and keeping track of the sources and evidence used in creating a research project is as important in digital research as it is in traditional research. For example, if particular sources are used to create a database that describes individuals and organizations, those sources need to be documented even though they may not be directly accessible in the collection. Typically, descriptive information includes author, title, and publisher information and may also contain subject information. When existing traditional media are digitized, it is necessary to describe both the original and its digital representation. While there may be overlapping information, the two objects are distinct manifestations of the same work. Traditional media will generally be held in both public repositories and private collections. This is particularly important for unique materials, such as manuscripts and archival records, but also important for copies, such as published books, as copies are in fact unique, even if only in subtle ways. The repositories and collections, even the private collection of the researcher, that hold the resources need to be recorded and related to the description of each resource used or digitized. When interrelated with administrative, file, and relations data, descriptive data serves the dual role of documenting the intellectual content, and attesting to the provenance and thus the authenticity of the sources and their digital derivatives.

When linked to related descriptive and file data, administrative data enable several essential activities:

- managing the agents, methods, and technology involved in creating digital files;
- ensuring the integrity of those digital files;
- tracking their intellectual relation to the sources from which they are derived;
- managing the negotiation of rights for use;
- controlling access based on negotiated agreements.

A wide variety of hardware and software exists for capturing traditional media, and the environmental conditions and context under which capture takes place varies. Digital capture always results in some loss of information, even if it enhances access and analytic uses. An image of a page from a book, for example, will not capture the tactile features of the page. Hardware and software used in capture differ in quality. Each may also, in time, suffer degradation of performance. Hardware and software also continue to develop and improve. The environmental conditions that affect capture may also vary. For example, differences in lighting will influence the quality of photographs, ambient noise will influence sound recording. The knowledge and skill of the technician will also affect the results. Direct capture devices for image, sound, and video have a variety of options available that will affect both the quality and depth of information captured.

Following capture, versions may be directly derived from the capture file or files, or alternative forms may be created using different representational methods. Versions of files are directly derived from the capture file, and represent the same kind of information (such as pixels or sound samples) but employ different underlying representations that facilitate different uses of the information. Tag Image File Format (TIFF), for example, is currently considered the most lossless capture format for pictorial or image data, but they are generally quite large. JPEG (Joint Photographic Experts Group), a compression technology, is generally used for creating smaller files that are more efficiently transmitted over the Internet. Such compression results in a loss of information, and thus impacts the image's intellectual content and its relation to the capture file and the original image. Other kinds of capture involve human judgment and intervention, as the underlying representations are fundamentally different. A bitmap page image differs fundamentally from an XML encoding of the text on the page, since the former is a pixel representation and the latter a character-based encoding. While OCR software can be used to convert pixel representations of characters to character representations, manual correction of recognition errors is still necessary. Accurate encoding of a text's components requires judgment and manual intervention, even if some encoding is susceptible to machine-assisted processing. The agents, methods, and technology used in deriving versions and alternative forms of data need to be recorded and related to each file in order to provide the information necessary to evaluate the authenticity and integrity of the derived data.

Intellectual property law or contract law will protect many of the resources collected and published in a digital humanities research project. Use of these materials will require negotiating with the property owners, and subsequently controlling and managing access based on agreements. Currently there are several competing initiatives to develop standards for digital rights management, and it is too early to determine which if any will satisfy international laws and be widely embraced by users and developers. A successful standard will lead to the availability of software that will enable and monitor access, including fee-based access and fair use. It is essential for both legal and moral reasons that researchers providing access to protected resources negotiate use of such materials, record in detail the substance of agreements, and enforce, to the extent possible, any agreed-upon restrictions. It is equally important, however, that researchers assert fair use when it is appropriate to do so: fair use, like a right of way, is a right established in practice and excessive self-policing will eventually undermine that right. The Stanford University Library's site on copyright and fair use is a good place to look for guidance on when it is appropriate to assert this right (see <http://fairuse.stanford.edu> for more information).

File data enable management and control of the files used to store digital data. When linked to related descriptive data, the intellectual content of files can be identified, and when linked to administrative data, the authenticity, integrity, and quality of the files can be evaluated, and access to copyright-protected materials can be controlled. It is quite easy to overlook the need to describe and control files early on in projects. It is easy to simply create *ad hoc* file names and directory structures to address their management and control. As projects develop, however, the number of files increases and the use of *ad hoc* file names and directory structures begins to break down. It becomes difficult to remember file names, what exactly each file name designates, and where in the directory structure files will be located.

On the other hand, it is quite common to create complex, semantically overburdened file names when using file names and directories to manage files. Such file names will typically attempt, in abbreviated form, to designate two or more of the following: source repository, identity of the object represented in a descriptive word, creator (of the original, the digital file, or both), version, date, and digital format. If the naming rules are not carefully documented, such faceted naming schemes generally collapse quite quickly, and even when well documented, are rarely effective as the number of files increases. Such information should be recorded in descriptive and administrative data linked to the address of the storage location of the file. A complete address will include the address of the server, the directory, and the file name. The name and structure of the directory and file name should be simple, and easily extensible as a collection grows.

There are a wide variety of possible approaches to naming and addressing files. Completely arbitrary naming and addressing schemes are infinitely extensible, though it is possible to design simple, extensible schemes that provide some basic and useful clues for those managing the files. For example, most projects will collect representations of many artifacts from many repositories. Each artifact may be captured in one or more digital files, with one or more derivative files created from each capture file. In such scenarios, it is important to create records for each repository or collection source. Linked to each of these repository records will be records describing each source artifact. In turn, each artifact record will be linked to one or more records describing capture files, with each capture record potentially linked to one or more records describing derivative files. Given this scenario, a reasonable file-naming scheme might include an abbreviated identifier for the repository, followed by three numbers separated by periods identifying the artifact, the capture, and the derivative. Following file-naming convention, a suffix designating the notation or format of the file is appended to the end. Ideally, the numbers reflect the order of acquisition or capture. For example, the first artifact digitally acquired from the Library of Congress might have the base name "loc.0001," with "loc" being an abbreviated identifier for "Library of Congress." The second digital file capture of this artifact would have the base name "loc.0001.02" and the fourth derivative of the original capture "loc.0001.02.04." A suffix would then be added to the base to complete the file name. For example, if the capture file were in the TIFF notation and the derivative in the JPEG notation, then the file names would be "loc.0001.02.tif" and "loc.0001.02.04.jpg." Full identification of any file can be achieved by querying the database for the file name. The directory structure might simply consist of a series of folders for each repository.

The file-naming scheme in this example is relatively simple, sustainable, and despite the weak semantics, very useful, even without querying the database. All files derived from artifacts in the same repository will be collocated when sorted, and all related versions of a file will also be collocated. In addition, the order in which artifacts are identified and collected will be reflected in the sorting order of each repository. The example provided here is not intended to be normative. Varying patterns of collecting, the nature of the artifacts collected, and other factors might lead to alternative and more appropriate schemes. The important lesson, though, is that database technology is ideally suited to management and control of intellectual and digital assets, and clever naming schemes and directory structures are not. Naming schemes should be semantically and structurally simple, with linked database records carrying the burden of detailed descriptive and administrative data.

Interrelating information is important as both an intellectual and a management activity. Interrelating intellectual objects within and between files requires creating explicit machine-readable data that allow automated correlation or collocation of related resources. For our purposes, there are two types of relations: intrinsic and extrinsic. Intrinsic relation data support is a feature of the character-based database and markup technologies. Database technology enables the creation, maintenance, and use of relations between records or tables *within a particular database*. XML technology enables the creation, maintenance, and use of relations between components *within a particular encoded document*. Care must be taken in ensuring that the feature is properly employed to ensure the integrity of the relations.

Extrinsic relations are external to databases and XML-encoded documents. Relations between one database and another, between a database and XML documents, between XML documents, between XML documents and files in other notations or encodings, and relations between image or sound files and other image or sound files are all types of extrinsic relations. Extrinsic relations are not currently well supported by standards and standard-based software. There are a large number of loosely connected or independent initiatives to address the standardization of extrinsic relations. Extrinsic relations thus present particular challenges in the design of digital research collections. Especially difficult are relations between resources in the collection under the control of the researcher, and resources under the control of others.

In the absence of standard methods for recording and managing extrinsic relations, it is necessary to design *ad hoc* methods. Given the complexity of managing relations, it is difficult to provide specific guidance. Both database and markup technologies provide some support for extrinsic relations, but this support must be augmented to provide reasonable control of relations. Some databases support direct storage of Binary Large Objects (BLOBs). Despite the term, BLOBs may include not only binary data, such as image and sound files, but also complex character data such as XML documents, vector graphics, and computer programs. While not standardized, XML Catalog, a standard for mapping the extrinsic relations of XML documents, provides some support. XML catalogues, though, primarily represent a method for communicating data about relations and offer no direct support for managing them effectively. Database technology is reasonably effective in managing the relations data communicated in XML catalogues. XQuery offers a standardized but indirect way of articulating extrinsic relations, though it is not intended as a means of controlling them or ensuring referential integrity. According to the World Wide Web Consortium, XQuery is "designed to be a language in which queries are concise and easily understood. It is also flexible enough to query a broad spectrum of XML information sources, including both databases and documents" (see <http://www.w3.org/TR/xquery/#id-introduction>). However, at this point none of these approaches will be completely reliable and effective without care and vigilance on the part of the human editors and data managers.

Conclusion: Collaboration

In the late twentieth and early twenty-first centuries, the most significant impact of information technology may be increased collaboration. Collaboration, when successful, offers many intellectual, professional, and social benefits. A group of scholars working together can create research collections more intellectually complex and comprehensive than is possible for an individual working alone. Complementary and even competing disciplinary perspectives and specialties will support broader and richer analysis and understanding. Collaboration will enable greater productivity. Collaboration between humanists and technologists may lead to more profound understandings and more incisive tools than either would develop by working alone. The explicitness and logical rigor required to represent and use digital information exposes to criticism many of the traditional disciplinary assumptions, and often leads to a deeper understanding of our methods and the subjects to which they are applied.

Despite these benefits, collaboration, whether with fellow humanists or technologists, also presents unfamiliar challenges, which require careful attention and time – often more time than is anticipated at the beginning. The most fundamental challenge of collaboration is balancing individual interests and shared objectives. Collaborators need to discuss, negotiate, and clearly document the research and publication objectives, a process that will require cooperation and compromise. Collaborators also need to recognize individual differences in aptitude for digital technology, and differences in expertise, methodology, and emphasis. Individual responsibilities, obligations, and production goals need to be negotiated and documented, and should reflect expertise and aptitude. Intellectual and social compatibility, trust, and mutual respect are essential characteristics of successful collaboration. Individual professional and intellectual needs and goals must also be recognized. The nature of the academic culture of recognition and rewards requires that individual scholars be productive and that the scholarship be of high quality. Individual contributions need to be clearly documented, in order to provide reliable evidence for reviewers. Depending upon the nature of the collaboration, individual contributions may be intermingled, and without careful project design it may be difficult or impossible to reliably indicate who is responsible for what. Such documentation is essential, for example, in the statements of responsibility incorporated into the descriptive data correlated with digital objects, and in bylines of digital objects, where this is possible.

In collaborative projects, standards and guidelines or manuals will need to be augmented with training. Left alone, different people will interpret and apply guidelines
differently. With respect to character-based technologies, in particular text encoding and
database entry, but including geographic information systems (GIS), computer-assisted
design (CAD), and many graphic systems, data entry and encoding will also involve
analysis and interpretation of source materials. Because human judgment is involved, it
will be impossible to entirely eliminate differences and to achieve absolute, complete
intellectual and technological consistency. Happily, absolute consistency is rarely necessary – it is generally only necessary to have absolute consistency in those data components
that are directly involved in automated processing. An acceptable range of consistency can
generally be achieved with training. Typically such training, as in all education, will
require both instruction and an initial period of intensive, thorough review, evaluation,
and revision. After intellectual and technological quality reaches an acceptable level,
periodic review will ensure that the level is sustained.

Given the amount of communication involved, it is generally easier to collaborate when
all or most of the participants work in the same location. One of the most attractive
benefits of the Internet, though, is the ability to communicate with anyone else on the
Internet, regardless of where they are connected, and to work remotely in the creation and
maintenance of shared resources. As with all other aspects of designing a research
collection, care must be taken to provide an infrastructure to support communication
and shared editing of the database. It is advisable to set up an e-mail list for project
communication (using software such as Mailman, Majordomo, or Listserv), and to archive
the correspondence it distributes (software such as Hypermail can automatically produce a
web-accessible version of this archive). An e-mail list will facilitate broadcasting messages
to a group. Archiving the messages will serve the purpose of preserving discussions,
negotiations, decisions, and other transactions that document the creation and maintenance of the collection. Among other things, such an archive will serve the important
function of providing documentary evidence for reviewers of individual participation and
contributions. Shared editing also needs to be managed, typically by a database, to control
and manage workflow, tracking additions, changes, and deletions. As attractive and useful
as remote collaboration can be, it frequently is still necessary to meet periodically in
person for discussions, negotiations, and training.

Collaboration with technologists may also present its own challenges. Although
technologists who elect to participate in digital humanities projects may themselves
have some background in the humanities, it will more often be the case that technologists
have little training in humanities disciplines. Humanities methods, perspectives, and
values may be strange to them, and unfamiliar terminology may hinder communication.
Carefully negotiated and apparently shared understandings will frequently be illusory,
requiring further discussion and renegotiation. Close and successful collaboration will
require goodwill and persistence, and will rely on developing a shared language and an
enduring mutual understanding.

Depending upon the size and constitution of a collaborative group, it may be necessary
to formally address issues of administration and supervision. A small number of peers who
are comfortable working with one another may rely only on informal discussion and
consensus. A project driven by one scholar who enlists graduate assistants will implicitly
be led and managed by that scholar. Larger groups, involving scholars of various ranks and

prestige and perhaps also graduate assistants, may require formal designation of a leader. Even when a particular individual is in charge, a project manager or administrative assistant may be beneficial, to tend to coordination and monitoring deadlines and the like.

Finally, collaboration depends on sustainable project design. It is relatively easy for one person to work, in the short run, in an idiosyncratic framework of his or her own design: it is more difficult for two people to do this, and it becomes increasingly difficult the more people are involved, and the longer the project continues. If a project is collaborative, and if it is to succeed, it will require the attributes of standardization, documentation, and thoughtful, iterative design that have been recommended throughout this chapter, in different contexts.

32

Conversion of Primary Sources

Marilyn Deegan and Simon Tanner

Material Types

The primary source materials for humanists come in many data forms, and the digital capture of that data needs to be carefully considered in relation to its formats and the materials that form the substrates upon which it is carried. It is difficult to list these comprehensively, but it is true to say that anything that can be photographed can be digitized, and that some materials can be photographed or digitized with more fidelity than others. This is an interesting point, as many digitization projects aim to present some kind of "true" representation of the original, and some materials can get closer to this goal than others.

The materials of interest to humanists are likely to include the following, and there are probably many more examples that could be given. However, this list covers a sufficiently broad area as to encompass most of the problems that might arise in digitization.

Documents

This category covers a huge variety of materials, from all epochs of history, and includes both manuscript and printed artifacts. Manuscripts can be from all periods, in any language, and written on a huge variety of surfaces: paper, parchment, birch bark, papyrus, lead tablets, wood, stone, etc. They will almost certainly have script or character set issues, and so may require special software for display or analysis. They may be music manuscripts, which will have issues of notation and representation of a whole range of special characters; or a series of personal letters, which being loose-leafed will pose their own organizational problems. Manuscripts may be composite in that they will have a number of different (often unrelated) texts in them, and there may be difficulties with bindings. They may be very large or very small – which will have implications for scanning mechanisms and resolutions. With handwritten texts, there can be no automated recognition of characters (although some interesting work is now being done in this area by the developers of palm computers and tablet PC computers – we need to wait to see if the work being done on handwriting recognition for data input feeds into the recognition of scripts on manuscript materials of the past), and they may also have visual images or illuminated letters. The documents that humanists might want to digitize also include printed works from the last 500 years, which come in a huge variety: books, journals, newspapers, posters, letters, typescript, gray literature, musical scores, ephemera, advertisements, and many other printed sources. Earlier materials and incunabula will have many of the same problems as manuscripts, and they may be written on paper or parchment. With printed materials, there can be a wide range of font and typesetting issues, and there is often illustrative content to deal with as well. Printed materials will also come in a huge range of sizes, from posters to postage stamps.

Visual materials

These may be on many different kinds of substrates: canvas, paper, glass, film, fabric, etc., and for humanists are likely to include manuscript images, paintings, drawings, many different types of photographs (film negatives, glass plate negatives, slides, prints), stained glass, fabrics, maps, architectural drawings, etc.

Three-dimensional objects and artifacts

With present technologies, it is not possible to create a "true" facsimile of such objects, but there are now three-dimensional modeling techniques that can give good representations of three-dimensional materials. These are likely to include the whole range of museum objects, sculpture, architecture, buildings, archaeological artifacts.

Time-based media

There is increasing interest in the digitization of film, video, and sound, and indeed there have been large advances in the techniques available to produce time-based media in born-digital form in the commercial world, and also to digitize analogue originals. The *Star Wars* movies are a good example of the historical transition from analogue to digital. The first three movies were filmed totally in analogue and then later digitally remastered; then all the films were made available on DVD. Finally, the last film to be made, *Attack of the Clones*, was totally filmed in the digital medium.

The conversion of three-dimensional objects and of time-based media is more problematic than that of text or still images. It draws upon newer technologies, the standards are not as well supported, and the file sizes produced are very large. The hardware and software to manipulate such materials is also generally more costly.

The Nature of Digital Data

If the nature of humanities data is very complex, the nature of digital data in their underlying form is seemingly very simple: all digital data, from whatever original they derive, have the same underlying structure, that of the "bit" or the *bi*nary digi*t*. A bit is an electronic impulse that can be represented by two states, "on" or "off," also written as "1" or "0." A "byte" consists of 8 bits, and 1 byte represents 1 alphanumeric character. A 10-letter word, for example, would be 10 bytes. Bits and bytes are linked together in chains of millions of electronic impulses; this is known as the "bit stream." A "kilobyte" is 1,024 bytes, and a "megabyte" 1,024 kilobytes. Digital images are represented by "pixels" or picture elements – dots on the computer screen or printed on paper. Pixels can carry a range of values, but at the simplest level, one pixel equals one bit, and is represented in binary form as "black" (off) or "white" (on). Images captured at this level are "bi-tonal" – pure black and white. Images can also be represented as 8-bit images, which have 256 shades of either gray or color and 24-bit images, which have millions of colors – more than the eye can distinguish. The number of bits chosen to represent each pixel is known as the "bit depth," and devices capable of displaying and printing images of higher bit depths than this (36 or 48 bits) are now emerging.

Bit depth is the number of bits per pixel, "resolution" is the number of pixels (or printed dots) per inch, known as ppi or dpi. The higher the resolution, the higher the density of a digital image. The resolution of most computer screens is generally in the range of 75 to 150 pixels per inch. This is adequate for display purposes (unless the image needs to be enlarged on-screen to show fine detail), but visual art or photographic content displayed at this resolution is inadequate for printing (especially in color), though images of black and white printed text or line art are often acceptable. High-density images of originals (manuscripts, photographs, etc.) need to be captured in the range 300–600 ppi for print quality output. Note that this will depend on the size of the original materials: 35 mm slides or microfilm originals will need to be captured at much higher resolutions, and scanners are now available offering resolutions of up to 4,000 dpi for such materials. These issues are discussed further below.

Almost any kind of information can be represented in these seemingly simple structures, as patterns of the most intricate complexity can be built up. Most primary sources as outlined above are capable of digital representation, and when digital they are susceptible to manipulation, interrogation, transmission, and cross-linking in ways that are beyond the capacity of analogue media. Creating an electronic photocopy of a plain page of text is not a complex technical process with modern equipment, but being able to then automatically recognize all the alphanumeric characters it contains, plus the structural layout and metadata elements, is a highly sophisticated operation. Alphanumeric symbols are the easiest objects to represent in digital form, and digital text has been around for as long as there have been computers.

As will be clear from what is outlined above, there are diverse source materials in the humanities and, using a variety of techniques, they are all amenable to digital capture. Nowadays there are many different approaches that can be taken to capture such artifacts, dependent upon (a) the materials themselves; (b) the reasons for capturing them; (c) the technical and financial resources available to the project; and (d) the potential uses and users. One point that should be emphasized is that digital capture, especially capture of materials with significant image content, is a skilled process that is best entrusted to professionals if high-quality archive images are required. However, for the production of medium- or lower-quality materials for Web delivery or for use in teaching, and for learning about the issues and processes attendant upon digital capture, scholars and students may find it valuable to experiment with the range of medium-cost, good-quality capture devices now available commercially.

There is rarely only one method for the capture of original source materials, and so careful planning and assessment of all the cost, quality, conservation, usage, and access needs for the resultant product needs to be done in order to decide which of several options should be chosen. It is vital when making these decisions that provision is made for the long-term survivability of the materials as well as for immediate project needs: the costs of sustaining a digital resource are usually greater than those of creating it (and are very difficult to estimate) so good planning is essential if the investments made in digital conversion are to be profitable. (See chapters 31 and 37, this volume, for more information on project design and long-term preservation of digital materials.) However, when working with sources held by cultural institutions, the range of digitization options may be limited by what that institution is willing to provide: rarely will an institution allow outsiders to work with its holdings to create digital surrogates, especially of rare, unique, or fragile materials. Many now offer digitization services as adjuncts or alternatives to their photographic services, at varying costs, and projects will need to order digital files as they would formerly have ordered photographs. See Tanner and Deegan (2002) for a detailed survey of such services in the UK and Europe.

The Advantages and Disadvantages of Digital Conversion

Digital conversion, done properly, is a difficult, time-consuming and costly business, and some of the properties of digital objects outlined above can be prove to be disadvantageous to the presentation and survivability of cultural materials – the resultant digital object, for instance, is evanescent and mutable in a way that the analogue original isn't. It can disappear in a flash if a hard drive crashes or a CD is corrupt; it can be changed without trace with an ease that forgers can only dream about. However, the digitization of resources opens up new modes of use for humanists, enables a much wider potential audience, and gives a renewed means of viewing our cultural heritage. These advantages may outweigh the difficulties and disadvantages, provided the project is well thought out and well managed – and this applies however large or small the project might be. The advantages of digitization for humanists include:

- the ability to republish out-of-print materials
- rapid access to materials held remotely
- potential to display materials which are in inaccessible formats, for instance, large volumes or maps
- "virtual reunification" – allowing dispersed collections to be brought together
- the ability to enhance digital images in terms of size, sharpness, color contrast, noise reduction, etc.
- the potential for integration into teaching materials
- enhanced searchability, including full text
- integration of different media (images, sounds, video etc.)
- the potential for presenting a critical mass of materials for analysis or comparison.

Any individual, group or institution considering digitization of primary sources will need to evaluate potential digitization projects using criteria such as these. They will also need to assess the actual and potential user base, and consider whether this will change when materials are made available in digital form. Fragile originals which are kept under very restricted access conditions may have huge appeal to a wide audience when made available in a form which does not damage the originals. A good example of this is the suffrage banners collection at the Women's Library (formerly known as the Fawcett Library). This is a unique collection of large-sized women's suffrage banners, many of which are woven from a variety of materials – cotton and velvet, for instance, often with appliqué lettering – which are now in a fragile state. The sheer size of the banners and their fragility means that viewing the original is heavily restricted, but digitization of the banners has opened up the potential for much wider access for scholarly use, adding a vital dimension to what is known about suffrage marches in the UK at the beginning of the twentieth century (see <http://ahds.ac.uk/suffrage.htm>).

An important question that should be asked at the beginning of any digitization project, concerns exactly what it is that the digitization is aiming to capture. Is the aim to produce a full facsimile of the original that when printed out could stand in for the original? Some projects have started with that aim, and then found that a huge ancillary benefit was gained by also having the digital file for online access and manipulation. The Digital Image Archive of Medieval Music (DIAMM) project, for instance, had as its original goal the capture of a specific corpus of fifteenth-century British polyphony fragments for printed facsimile publication in volumes such as the Early English Church Music (EECM) series. However, early studies showed that there was much to be gained from obtaining high-resolution digital images in preference to slides or prints. This was not only because of the evidence for growing exploitation of digital resources at that time (1997), but also because many of these fragments were badly damaged and digital restoration offered opportunities not possible with conventional photography. The project therefore decided to capture manuscript images in the best quality possible using high-end digital imaging equipment, set up according to the most rigorous professional standards; to archive the images in an uncompressed form; to enhance and reprocess the images in order to wring every possible piece of information from them; to preserve all these images – archive and derivative – for the long term. That has proved to be an excellent strategy for the project, especially as the image enhancement techniques have revealed hitherto unknown pieces of music on fragments that had been scraped down and overwritten with text: digitization has not just enhanced existing humanities sources, it has allowed the discovery of new ones (see <www.diamm.ac.uk>).

Digital techniques can also allow a user experience of unique textual materials that is simply not possible with the objects themselves. Good-quality images can be integrated with other media for a more complete user experience. In 2001, the British Library produced a high-quality digital facsimile of the fifteenth-century Sherborne Missal that is on display in its galleries on the largest touch screen in the UK. The unique feature of this resource is that the pages can be turned by hand, and it is possible to zoom in at any point on the page at the touch of a finger on the screen. High-quality sound reproduction accompanies the images, allowing users to hear the religious offices which make up the text being sung by a monastic choir. This is now available on CD-ROM, and such facsimiles of other unique objects are now being produced by the British Library. See <www.bl.uk/collections/treasures/missal.html>.

The Cornell Brittle Books project also started with the aim of recreating analogue originals: books printed on acid paper were crumbling away, and the goal was to replace these with print surrogates on non-acid paper. Much experimentation with microfilm and digitization techniques in the course of this project has produced results which have helped to set the benchmarks and standards for the conversion of print materials to digital formats all around the world. See Chapman et al. (1999) for further details.

Another aim of digital conversion might be to capture the *content* of a source without necessarily capturing its *form*. So an edition of the work of a literary author might be rekeyed and re-edited in electronic form without particular reference to the visual characteristics of an existing print or manuscript version. Or, if the aim is to add searchability to a written source while preserving the visual form, text might be converted to electronic form and then attached to the image.

With a visual source such as a fine art object or early manuscript, what level of information is needed? The intellectual content or the physical detail of brushstrokes, canvas grain, the pores of the skin of the animal used to make the parchment, scratched glosses? Is some kind of analysis or reconstruction the aim? The physics department at the University of Bologna has developed a digital x-ray system for the analysis of paintings (Rossi et al. 2000) and the Beowulf Project, a collaboration between the British Library and the University of Kentucky, has used advanced imaging techniques for the recovery of letters and fragments obscured by clumsy repair techniques, and demonstrated the use of computer imaging to restore virtually the hidden letters to their place in the manuscript. See <www.bl.uk/collections/treasures/beowulf.html>.

With three-dimensional objects, no true representation of three-dimensional space can be achieved within the two-dimensional confines of a computer screen, but some excellent results are being achieved using three-dimensional modeling and virtual reality techniques. The Virtual Harlem project, for instance, has produced a reconstruction of Harlem, New York, during the time of the Harlem Renaissance in the 1920s, using modeling and VR immersion techniques. (See <www.evl.uic.edu/cavern/harlem/> and Carter 1999.) The Cistercians in Yorkshire project is creating imaginative reconstructions of Cistercian abbeys as they might have been in the Middle Ages, using three-dimensional modeling and detailed historical research. (See <http://cistercians.shef.ac.uk/>.)

Methods of Digital Capture

Text

Humanists have been capturing, analyzing, and presenting textual data in digital form for as long as there have been computers capable of processing alphanumeric symbols. Thankfully, long gone are the days when pioneers such as Busa and Kenny laboriously entered text on punchcards for processing on mainframe machines – now it is an everyday matter for scholars and students to sit in the library transcribing text straight into a laptop or palmtop computer, and the advent of tablet PC computers could make this even easier and more straightforward. Gone, too, are the days when every individual or project invented codes, systems, or symbols of their own to identify special features, and when any character that could not be represented in ASCII had to be recoded in some arcane form. Now the work of standards bodies such as the Text Encoding Initiative (TEI, <www.tei-c. org>), the World Wide Web Consortium (W3C, <www.w3c.org>) and the Dublin Core Metadata Initiative (DCMI, <http://dublincore.org/>) has provided standards and schemas for the markup of textual features and for the addition of metadata to non-textual materials that renders them reusable, interoperable, and exchangable. The work done to develop the Unicode standard, too, means that there is a standard way of encoding characters for most of the languages of the world so that they too are interoperable and exchangable (<http://www.unicode.org/unicode/standard/WhatIsUnicode.html>).

In considering the different features of electronic text, and the methods of their capture, it is important to make the distinction between machine-readable electronic text and machine-viewable electronic text. A bitmap of a page, for instance, is machine-displayable, and can show all the features of the original of which it is a representation. But it is not susceptible to any processing or editing, so though it is human-readable, it is not machine-readable. In machine-readable text, every individual entity, as well as the formatting instructions and other codes, is represented separately and is therefore amenable to manipulation. Most electronic texts are closer to one of these two forms than the other, although there are some systems emerging which process text in such a way as to have the elements (and advantages) of both. These are discussed further below.

For the scholar working intensively on an individual text, there is probably no substitute for transcribing the text directly on to the computer and adding appropriate tagging and metadata according to a standardized framework. The great benefit of the work done by the standards bodies discussed above is that the schemas proposed by them are extensible: they can be adapted to the needs of individual scholars, sources and projects. Such rekeying can be done using almost any standard word processor or text editor, though there are specialist packages like XMetaL which allow the easy production and validation of text marked up in XML (Extensible Markup Language).

Many scholars and students, empowered by improvements in the technology, are engaging in larger collaborative projects which require more substantial amounts of text to be captured. There are now some very large projects such as the Early English Books Online Text Creation Partnership (EEBO TCP, <www.lib.umich.edu/eebo/>), which is creating accurately keyboarded and tagged editions of up to 25,000 volumes from the EEBO corpus of 125,000 volumes of English texts from between 1473 and 1800, which has been microfilmed and digitized by ProQuest. The tagged editions will be linked to the image files. For projects like these, specialist bureaux provide rekeying and tagging services at acceptable costs with assured levels of accuracy (up to 99.995 percent). This accuracy is achieved through double or triple rekeying: two or three operators key the same text, then software is used to compare them with each other. Any differences are highlighted and then they can be corrected manually. This is much faster, less prone to subjective or linguistic errors, and therefore cheaper than proofreading and correction. There will always be a need for quality control of text produced by any method, but most specialist bureaux give an excellent, accurate, reliable service: the competition is fierce in this business, which has driven costs down and quality up. For an example of a project that effectively used the double rekeying method see the Old Bailey Court Proceedings, 1674 to 1834 (<www.oldbaileyonline.org/>).

Optical character recognition

The capture of text by rekeying either by an individual or by a specialist bureau is undertaken either because very high levels of accuracy are needed for textual analysis or for publication, or because the originals are not susceptible to any automated processes, which is often the case with older materials such as the EEBO corpus discussed above. While this level of accuracy is sometimes desirable, it comes at a high cost. Where modern, high-quality printed originals exist, it may be possible to capture text using optical character recognition (OCR) methods, which can give a relatively accurate result. Accuracy can then be improved using a variety of automated and manual methods: passing the text through spellcheckers with specialist dictionaries and thesauri, and manual proofing. Research is currently being done to improve OCR packages and to enable them to recognize page structures and even add tagging: the European Union-funded METAe Project (the Metadata Engine Project) is developing automatic processes for the recognition of complex textual structures, including text divisions such as chapters, sub-chapters, page numbers, headlines, footnotes, graphs, caption lines, etc. See <http://meta-e.uibk.ac.at/>. Olive Software's Active Paper Archive can also recognize complex page structures from the most difficult of texts: newspapers. This is described more fully below. OCR techniques were originally developed to provide texts for the blind. OCR engines can operate on a wide range of character sets and fonts, though they have problems with non-alphabetic character sets because of the large number of symbols, and also with cursive scripts such as Arabic. Software can be "trained" on new texts and unfamiliar characters so that accuracy improves over time and across larger volumes of data. Though this requires human intervention in the early stages, the improvement in accuracy over large volumes of data is worth the initial effort.

Though OCR can give excellent results if (a) the originals are modern and in good condition and (b) there is good quality control, projects must consider carefully the costs and benefits of deciding between a rekeying approach and OCR. Human time is always the most costly part of any operation, and it can prove to be more time-consuming and costly to correct OCR (even when it seems relatively accurate) than to go for bureau rekeying with guaranteed accuracy. It is worth bearing in mind that what seem like accurate results (between 95 and 99 percent, for instance) would mean that there would be between 1 and 5 incorrect characters per 100 characters. Assuming there are on average 5 characters per word then a 1 percent character error rate equates to a word error rate of 1 in 20 or higher.

OCR with fuzzy matching

OCR, as suggested above, is an imperfect method of text capture which can require a great deal of post-processing if accurate text is to be produced. In an ideal world, one would always aim to produce electronic text to the highest possible standards of accuracy; indeed, for some projects and purposes, accurate text to the highest level attainable is essential, and worth what it can cost in terms of time and financial outlay. However, for other purposes, speed of capture and volume are more important than quality and so some means has to be found to overcome the problems of inaccurate OCR. What needs to be taken into account is the *reason* a text is to be captured digitally and made available. If the text has important structural features which need to be encoded in the digital version, and these cannot be captured automatically, or if a definitive edition is to be produced in either print or electronic form from the captured text, then high levels of accuracy are paramount. If, however, retrieval of the information contained within large volumes of text is the desired result, then it may be possible to work with the raw OCR output from scanners, without post-processing. A number of text retrieval products are now available which allow searches to be performed on inaccurate text using "fuzzy matching" techniques. However, at the moment, fuzzy searching will only work with suitable linguistic and contextual dictionaries, and therefore is pretty much limited to the English language. Other languages with small populations of speakers are poorly represented, as are pre-1900 linguistic features.

Hybrid solutions: page images with underlying searchable text

An increasing number of projects and institutions are choosing to deliver textual content in digital form through a range of hybrid solutions. The user is presented with a facsimile image of the original for printing and viewing, and attached to each page of the work is a searchable text file. This text file can be produced by rekeying, as in the EEBO project described above, or by OCR with or without correction. Decisions about the method of production of the underlying text will depend on the condition of the originals and the level of accuracy of retrieval required. With the EEBO project, the materials date from the fifteenth to the eighteenth centuries, and they have been scanned from microfilm, so OCR is not a viable option. The anticipated uses, too, envisage detailed linguistic research, which means that retrieval of individual words or phrases will be needed by users. The highest possible level of accuracy is therefore a requirement for this project.

The Forced Migration Online (FMO) project based at the Refugee Studies Centre, University of Oxford, is taking a different approach. FMO is a portal to a whole range of materials and organizations concerned with the study of the phenomenon of forced migration worldwide, with content contributed by an international group of partners. One key component of FMO is a digital library of gray literature and of journals in the field. The digital library is produced by attaching text files of uncorrected OCR to page images: the OCR text is used for searching and is hidden from the user; the page images are for viewing and printing. What is important to users of FMO is documents or parts of documents dealing with key topics, rather than that they can retrieve individual instances of words or phrases. This type of solution can deliver very large volumes of material at significantly lower cost than rekeying, but the trade-offs in some loss of accuracy have to be understood and accepted. Some of the OCR inaccuracies can be mitigated by using fuzzy search algorithms, but this can give rise to problems of over-retrieval. FMO (<www.forcedmigration.org>) uses Olive Software's Active Paper Archive, a product which offers automatic zoning and characterization of complex documents, as well as OCR and complex search and retrieval using fuzzy matching. See Deegan (2002) and <http://www.oclc.org/digitalpreservation/digitizing/newspaper/>.

One document type that responds well to hybrid solutions is newspapers, which are high-volume, low-value (generally), mixed media, and usually large in size. Newspaper digitization is being undertaken by a number of companies, adopting different capture strategies and business models. ProQuest are using a rekeying solution to capture full text from a number of historic newspapers, and are selling access to these through their portal, *History Online* (<http://historyonline.chadwyck.co.uk>). These newspapers include *The Times*, the *New York Times* and the *Wall Street Journal*. A number of Canadian newspapers are digitizing page images and offering searchability using the Cold North Wind software program (<http://www.coldnorthwind.com/>); and the TIDEN project, a large collaboration of Scandinavian libraries, is capturing content using advanced OCR and delivering page images with searchability at the page level using a powerful commercial search engine, Convera's RetrievalWare (<http://tiden.kb.se/>). OCLC (the Online Computer Library Center) has an historic newspaper digitization service which provides an end-to-end solution: the input is microfilm or TIFF images, the output a fully searchable archive with each individual item (article, image, advertisement) separated and marked up in XML. Searches may be carried out on articles, elements within articles (title, byline, text), and image captions. OCLC also uses Olive Software's Active Paper Archive.

Images

As we suggest above, humanists deal with a very large range of image-based materials, and there will be different strategies for capture that could be employed, according to potential usage and cost factors. Many humanists, too, may be considering digital images as primary source materials rather than as secondary surrogates: increasingly photographers are turning from film to digital, and artists are creating digital art works from scratch. Many digital images needed by humanists are taken from items outside their control: objects that are held in cultural institutions. These institutions have their own facilities for creating images which scholars and students will need to use. If they don't have such facilities, analogue surrogates (usually photographic) can be ordered and digitization done from the surrogate. The costs charged by institutions vary a great deal (see Tanner and Deegan 2002). Sometimes this depends on whether a reproduction fee is being charged. Institutions may offer a bewildering choice of digital and analogue surrogate formats with a concomitant complexity of costs. A thorough understanding of the materials, the digitization technologies and the implications of any technical choices, the metadata that need to be added to render the images useful and usable (which is something that will almost certainly be added by the scholar or student), and what the potential cost factors might be are all essential for humanists embarking on digital projects, whether they will be doing their own capture or not. Understanding of the materials is taken as a given here, so this section will concentrate upon technical issues.

Technical issues in image capture

Most image materials to be captured by humanists will need a high level of fidelity to the original. This means that capture should be at an appropriate resolution, relative to the format and size of the original, and at an appropriate bit depth. As outlined above, resolution is the measure of information density in an electronic image and is usually measured in dots per inch (dpi) or pixels per inch (ppi). The more dots per inch there are, the denser the image information provided. This can lead to high levels of detail being captured at higher resolutions. The definition of "high" resolution is based upon factors such as original media size, the nature of the information, and the eventual use. Therefore 600 dpi would be considered high-resolution for a photographic print, but would be considered low-resolution for a 35 mm slide. Careful consideration must be given to the amount of information content required over the eventual file size. It must be remembered that resolution is *always* a factor of two things: (1) the size of the original and (2) the number of dots or pixels. Resolution is expressed in different ways according to what particular part of the digital process is being discussed: hardware capabilities, absolute value of the digital image, capture of analogue original, or printed output. Hardware capabilities are referred to differently as well: resolution calculated for a flatbed scanner, which has a fixed relationship with originals (because they are placed on a fixed platen and the scanner passes over them at a fixed distance) is expressed in dpi. With digital cameras, which have a variable dpi in relation to the originals, given that they can be moved closer or further away, resolution is expressed in absolute terms, either by their x and y dimensions (12,000 × 12,000, say, for the highest-quality professional digital cameras) or by the total number of pixels (4 million, for instance, for a good-quality, compact camera). The digital image itself is best expressed in absolute terms: if expressed in dpi, the size of the original always needs to be known to be meaningful.

The current choices of hardware for digital capture include flatbed scanners, which are used for reflective and transmissive materials. These can currently deliver up to 5,000 dpi, but can cost tens of thousands of dollars, so most projects can realistically only afford scanners in the high-end range of 2,400 to 3,000 dpi. Bespoke 35 mm film scanners, which are used for transmissive materials such as slides and film negatives, can deliver up to 4,000 dpi. Drum scanners may also be considered as they can deliver much higher relative resolutions and quality, but they are generally not used in this context as the process is destructive to the original photographic transparency and the unit cost of creation is higher. Digital cameras can be used for any kind of material, but are generally recommended for those materials not suitable for scanning with flatbed or film scanners: tightly bound books or manuscripts, art images, three-dimensional objects such as sculpture or architecture. Digital cameras are becoming popular as replacements for conventional film cameras in the domestic and professional markets, and so there is now a huge choice. High-end cameras for purchase by image studios cost tens of thousands of dollars, but such have been the recent advances in the technologies that superb results can be gained from cameras costing much less than this – when capturing images from smaller originals, even some of the compact cameras can deliver archive-quality scans. However, they need to be set up professionally, and professional stands and lighting must be used.

For color scanning, the current recommendation for bit depth is that high-quality originals be captured at 24 bit, which renders more than 16 million colors – more than the human eye can distinguish, and enough to give photorealistic output when printed. For black and white materials with tone, 8 bits per pixel is recommended, which gives 256 levels of gray, enough to give photorealistic printed output.

The kinds of images humanists will need for most purposes are likely to be of the highest possible quality for two reasons. First, humanists will generally need fine levels of detail in the images, and, secondly, the images will in many cases have been taken from rare or unique originals, which might also be very fragile. Digital capture, wherever possible, should be done once only, and a digital surrogate captured that will satisfy all anticipated present and future uses. This surrogate is known as the "digital master" and should be kept under preservation conditions. (See chapter 37, this volume.) Any manipulations or post-processing should be carried out on copies of this master image. The digital master will probably be a very large file: the highest-quality digital cameras (12,000 × 12,000 pixels) produce files of up to 350 Mb, which means that it is not possible to store more than one on a regular CD-ROM disk. A 35 mm color transparency captured at 2,700 dpi (the norm for most slide scanners) in 24-bit color would give a file size of 25 Mb, which means that around 22 images could be stored on one CD-ROM. The file format generally used for digital masters is the TIFF (Tagged Image File Format), a *de facto* standard for digital imaging. There are many other file formats available, but TIFF can be recommended as the safest choice for the long term. The "Tagged" in the title means that various types of information can be stored in a file header of the TIFF files.

The actual methods of operation of scanning equipment vary, and it is not the intention of this chapter to give details of such methodologies. There are a number of books which give general advice, and hardware manufacturers have training manuals and online help. Anyone who wishes to learn digital capture techniques in detail is advised to seek out professional training through their own institution, or from one of the specialist organizations offering courses: some of these are listed in the bibliography at the end of this chapter.

Compression and derivatives

It is possible to reduce file sizes of digital images using compression techniques, though this is often not recommended for the digital masters. Compression comes in two forms: "lossless," meaning that there is no loss of data through the process, and "lossy," meaning that data is lost, and can never be recovered. There are two lossless compression techniques that are often used for TIFF master files, and which can be recommended here – the LZW compression algorithm for materials with color content, and the CCITT Group 4 format for materials with 1-bit, black and white content.

Derivative images from digital masters are usually created using lossy compression methods, which can give much greater reduction in file sizes than lossless compression for color and greyscale images. Lossy compression is acceptable for many uses of the images, especially for Web or CD-ROM delivery purposes. However, excessive compression can cause problems in the viewable images, creating artifacts such as pixelation, dotted or stepped lines, regularly repeated patterns, moiré, halos, etc. For the scholar seeking the highest level of fidelity to the originals, this is likely to be unacceptable, and so experimentation will be needed to give the best compromise between file size and visual quality. The main format for derivative images for delivery to the web or on CD-ROM is currently JPEG. This is a lossy compression format that can offer considerable reduction in file sizes if the highest levels of compression are used, but this comes at the cost of some compromise of quality. However, it can give color thumbnail images of only around 7 KB and screen resolution images of around 60 KB – a considerable benefit if bandwidth is an issue.

Audio and video capture

As technology has advanced since the 1990s, more and more humanists are becoming interested in the capture of time-based media. Media studies is an important and growing area, and historians of the modern period too derive great benefit from having digital access to time-based primary sources such as news reports, film, etc. Literary scholars also benefit greatly from access to plays, and to filmed versions of literary works.

In principle the conversion of audio or video from an analogue medium to a digital data file is simple, it is in the detail that complexity occurs. The biggest problem caused in the digital capture of video and audio is the resultant file sizes:

> There is no other way to say it. Video takes up a lot of everything; bandwidth, storage space, time, and money. We might like to think that all things digital are preferable to all things analog but the brutal truth is that while analog formats like video might not be exact or precise they are remarkably efficient when it comes to storing and transmitting vast amounts of information. (Wright 2001a)

> Raw, uncompressed video is about 21 MB/sec. (Wright 2001b)

There are suppliers that can convert audio and video, and many scholars will want to outsource such work. However, an understanding of the processes is of great importance.

The first stage in the capture process is to have the original video or audio in a format that is convertible to digital formats. There are over thirty types of film and video stock and many types of audio formats that the original content may be recorded upon. Most humanists, however, should only need to concern themselves with a limited number of formats, including:

- VHS or Betamax video
- mini-DV for digital video cameras
- DAT tape for audio
- cassette tape for audio
- CD-ROM for audio

The equipment needed to capture video and audio includes:

- video player capable of high-quality playback of VHS and mini-DV tapes
- hi-fi audio player capable of high-quality playback of DAT and cassette tapes
- small TV for review and location of video clips
- high-quality speakers and/or headphones for review and location of audio clips

Once the suitable video or audio clip has been identified on the original via a playback device, this has to be connected to the capture device for rendering in a digital video (DV) or digital audio (DA) format upon a computer system. This is normally achieved by connecting input/output leads from the playback device to an integrated digital capture card in the computer or via connection to a device known as a "breakout box." The breakout box merely allows for more types of input/output leads to be used in connecting to and from the playback device. Whatever the method of connection used, there must be a capture card resident in the machine to allow for digital data capture from the playback device. Usually, a separate capture card is recommended for video and for audio: although all video capture cards will accept audio input, the quality required for pure audio capture is such that a bespoke capture card for this purpose is recommended; indeed, it is probably best to plan the capture of audio and video on separate PCs – each card requires its own Input/Output range, Interrupt Request number and its own software to control the capture. These are temperamental and tend to want to occupy the same I/O range, interrupts and memory spaces, leading to system conflicts and reliability problems. This of course adds to cost if a project is planning to capture both audio and video.

The benefit of having a capture card is that it introduces render-free, real-time digital video editing, DV and analogue input/output, and this is usually augmented with direct output for DVD, and it also provides Internet streaming capabilities, along with a suite of digital video production tools. Render-free real-time capture and editing is important because capture and editing can then happen without the long waits (which can be many minutes) associated with software packages for rendering and editing. The capture from video or audio will be to DV or DA, usually at a compression rate of around 5 : 1 which gives 2.5–3.5 MB/sec. This capture is to a high standard even though there is compression built into the process. It is also too large for display and use on the Internet and so further compression and file format changes are required once edited into a suitable form for delivery.

Editing of Captured Content

The editing of the content captured is done via software tools known as non-linear editing suites. These allow the content to be manipulated, edited, spliced, and otherwise changed to facilitate the production of suitable content for the prospective end user. The ability to do this in real time is essential to the speed and accuracy of the eventual output. Also, the editing suite should have suitable compressors for output to Web formats and Internet streaming.

Compressors for the Web

When viewing video or listening to audio on the Web the content has to go through a process of *c*ompression and *de-c*ompression (CODEC). There is initial compression at the production end using a suitable CODEC (e.g., Sorenson, Qdesign) to gain the desired file size, frames per second, transmission rate, and quality. This content may then be saved in a file format suitable for the architecture of the delivery network and expected user environment – possibly QuickTime, Windows Media or Real. The user then uses viewer software to decompress the content and view/hear the content.

Compression is a difficult balancing act between gaining the smallest file size and retaining suitable quality. In video, compression works by taking a reference frame that contains all the information available and then subsequent frames are represented as changes from the reference frame. The number of frames between the reference frames is a defining factor in the compression and quality – the fewer reference frames the more compressed the file but the lower quality the images are likely to be. However, if the number of reference frames is increased to improve visual quality then the file size will also rise. As the nature of the content in video can differ radically, this compression process has to be done on a case by case basis. A video of a "talking head" type interview will require fewer reference frames than, say, sports content because the amount of change from frame to frame is less in the "talking head" example. Thus higher compression is possible for some content than for others if aiming for the same visual quality – there is no "one size fits all" equation in audio and video compression.

It is generally assumed with images that the main cost will be in the initial capture and that creating surrogates for end-user viewing on the Internet will be quick and cheap. In the video sphere this paradigm is turned on its head, with the initial capture usually cheaper than the creation of the compressed surrogate for end-user viewing as a direct consequence of the increased amount of human intervention needed to make a good-quality Internet version at low bandwidth.

Metadata

Given that humanists will almost certainly be capturing primary source data at a high quality and with long-term survival as a key goal, it is important that this data be documented properly so that curators and users of the future understand what it is that they are dealing with. Metadata is one of the critical components of digital resource conversion and use, and is needed at all stages in the creation and management of the resource. Any creator of digital objects should take as much care in the creation of the metadata as they do in the creation of the data itself – time and effort expended at the creation stage recording good-quality metadata is likely to save users much grief, and to result in a well-formed digital object which will survive for the long term.

It is vitally important that projects and individuals give a great deal of thought to this documentation of data right from the start. Having archive-quality digital master files is useless if the filenames mean nothing to anyone but the creator, and there is no indication of date of creation, file format, type of compression, etc. Such information is known as technical or administrative metadata. Descriptive metadata refers to the attributes of the object being described and can be extensive: attributes such as: "title," "creator," "subject," "date," "keywords," "abstract," etc. In fact, many of the things that would be catalogued in a traditional cataloguing system. If materials are being captured by professional studios or bureaux, then some administrative and technical metadata will probably be added at source. Or it may be possible to request or supply project-specific metadata. Descriptive metadata can only be added by experts who understand the nature of the source materials, and it is an intellectually challenging task in itself to produce good descriptive metadata.

Conclusion

Understanding the capture processes for primary source materials is essential for humanists intending to engage in digital projects, even if they are never going to carry out conversion activities directly. Knowing the implications of the various decisions that have to be taken in any project is of vital importance for short- and long-term costs as well as for the long-term survivability of the materials to which time, care, and funds have been devoted. The references below cover most aspects of conversion for most types of humanities sources, and there are also many websites with bibliographies and reports on digital conversion methods. The technologies and methods change constantly, but the underlying principles outlined here should endure.

References for Further Reading

Publications

Baca, M. (ed.) (1998). Introduction to Metadata, Pathways to Digital Information. Los Angeles, CA: Getty Research Institute.

Carter, B. (1999). From Imagination to Reality: Using Immersion Technology in an African American Literature Course. *Literary and Linguistic Computing* 14: 55–65.

Chapman, S., P. Conway, and A. R. Kenney (1999). Digital Imaging and Preservation Microfilm: The Future of the Hybrid Approach for the Preservation of Brittle Books. *RLG DigiNews*. Available at <www.rlg.org/preserv/diginews/diginews3-1.html>.

Davies, A. and P. Fennessey (2001). *Digital Imaging for Photographers*. London: Focal Press.

Deegan, M., E. Steinvel, and E. King (2002). Digitizing Historic Newspapers: Progress and Prospects. *RLG DigiNews*. Available at <http://www.rlg.org/preserv/diginews/diginews6-4.html#feature2>.

Deegan, M. and S. Tanner (2002). *Digital Futures: Strategies for the Information Age*. London: Library Association Publishing.

Feeney, M. (ed.) (1999). *Digital Culture: Maximising the Nation's Investment*. London: National Preservation Office.

Getz, M. (1997). Evaluating Digital Strategies for Storing and Retrieving Scholarly Information. In S. H. Lee (ed.), *Economics of Digital Information: Collection, Storage and Delivery*. Binghamton, NY: Haworth Press.

Gould, S. and R. Ebdon (1999). *IFLA/UNESCO Survey on Digitisation and Preservation*. IFLA Offices for UAP and International Lending Available at <www.unesco.org/webworld/mdm/survey_index_en.html>.

Hazen, D., J. Horrell, and J. Merrill-Oldham (1998). Selecting Research Collections for Digitization CLIR. Available at <www.clir.org/pubs/reports/hazen/pub74.html>.

Kenney, A. R. and O. Y. Rieger (eds.) (2000). *Moving Theory into Practice: Digital Imaging for Libraries and Archives*. Mountain View, CA: Research Libraries Group.

Klijn, E. and Y. de Lusenet (2000). *In the Picture: Preservation and Digitisation of European Photographic Collections*. Amsterdam: Koninklijke Bibliotheek.

Lacey, J. (2002). *The Complete Guide to Digital Imaging*. London: Thames and Hudson.

Lagoze, C. and S. Payette (2000). Metadata: Principles, Practices and Challenges. In A. R. Kenney and O. Y. Rieger (eds.), *Moving Theory into Practice: Digital Imaging for Libraries and Archives* (pp. 84–100). Mountain View, CA: Research Libraries Group.

Lawrence, G. W., et al. (2000). Risk Management of Digital Information: A File Format Investigation. Council on Library and Information Resources. Available at <www.clir.org.pubs/reports/reports.html>.

Parry, D. (1998). *Virtually New: Creating the Digital Collection*. London: Library and Information Commission.

Robinson, P. (1993). *The Digitization of Primary Textual Sources*. London: Office for Humanities Communication Publications, 3, King's College, London.

Rossi, M., F. Casali, A. Bacchilega, and D. Romani (2000). An Experimental X-ray Digital Detector for Investigation of Paintings. 15th World Conference on NonDestructive Testing, Rome, 15–21 October.

Smith, A. (1999). Why Digitize? CLIR. Available at <http://www.clir.org/pubs/abstract/pub80.html>.

Tanner, S. and M. Deegan (2002). Exploring Charging Models for Digital Cultural Heritage. Available at <http://heds.herts.ac.uk>.

Watkinson, J. (2001). *Introduction to Digital Video*. London: Focal Press.

Wright, G. (2001a). *Building a Digital Video Capture System*. Part I, Tom's Hardware Guide. Available at <www.tomshardware.com/video/20010524/>.

Wright, G. (2001b). *Building a Digital Video Capture System*. Part II, Tom's Hardware Guide. Available at <www.tomshardware.com/video/20010801/>.

Courses

School for Scanning, North East Documentation Center, <www.nedcc.org>.

Cornell University Library, Department of Preservation and Conservation, <www.library.cornell.edu/preservation/workshop/index.html>.

SEPIA (Safeguarding European Photographic Images for Access), project training courses, <www.knaw.nl/ecpa/sepia/training.html>.

33

Text Tools

John Bradley

One should not be surprised that a central interest of computing humanists is tools to manipulate text. For this community, the purpose of digitizing text is to allow the text to be manipulated for scholarly purposes, and text tools provide the mechanisms to support this. Some of the scholarly potential of digitizing a text has been recognized from the earliest days of computing. Father Roberto Busa's work on the *Index Thomisticus* (which began in the 1940s) involved the indexing of the writings of Thomas Aquinas, and arose out of work for his doctoral thesis when he discovered that he needed to systematically examine the uses of the preposition *in*. Busa reports that because of this he imagined using "some sort of machinery" that would make it possible. Later, but still relatively early in the history of humanities computing, the writings of John B. Smith recognized some of the special significance of text in digitized form (see a relatively late piece entitled "Computer Criticism," Smith 1989). Indeed, even though computing tools for manipulating text have been with us for many years, we are still in the early stages of understanding the full significance of working with texts electronically.

At one time an important text tool that one would have described in an article such as this would have been the word processor. Today, however, the word processor has become ubiquitous both inside and outside the academy and it is no longer necessary to describe its benefits or categorize its applications. Today many people believe that the World Wide Web can be at the center of computing for humanists, and much discussion has focused on the significance of presenting materials on the WWW for a worldwide audience. Although some of the tools I will describe here could greatly facilitate the preparation of materials for the WWW, I will not be writing very much about HTML or the significance of using it. Instead, this article will focus on tools that can manipulate texts in ways that might usefully support the development of scholarship on those texts rather than merely prepare and present them.

Some of the tools described here have been developed specifically to support humanities scholarship. The intellectual origins of many in this group flow directly from the word-oriented work of Father Busa and other early researchers, and these ones tend to be mainly designed to support a certain kind of word- or wordform-oriented inquiry. Another important group of tools described later were not developed by humanists and have a broad range of applications in general computing, although they have proven themselves to be powerful tools when applied to scholarly tasks. The chapter finishes with a brief description of TuStep – a system developed by Wilhelm Ott that is potentially useful in a range of applications within and outside the humanities, but was developed with a humanities focus.

Not surprisingly, given their very different origins, the two groups present very different challenges to the humanities researcher who is beginning to use them. The first group of tools, generally designed to support text analysis, are relatively straightforward to understand once one is operating within a tightly defined problem domain. The general-purpose tools, however, are not so easily categorized, and can perform a very broad range of tasks on a text. Because they are not focused on a specific problem domain, as the "Text Analysis" tools are, they contain very abstract components, and the difficulty for the beginner is to understand whether, and then how, these abstract elements can be applied to any particular problem.

Those who begin with the tools that are specially developed for textual analysis or critical work often find that they wish to do something that goes beyond what their software does – for example, apply a statistical program to some materials that the software has given them. Often the form of the data generated by their first program is different from that needed by the second program. As we will see, one of the important tasks of the general-purpose tools described later in this chapter is to provide ways to bridge these gaps.

Tools to Support Text Analysis

Paradoxically, the task of writing general-purpose software is highly specialized; it is also both costly and difficult. Perhaps for this reason most humanities computing software available "off the shelf" (with the exception of TuStep) performs a relatively simple set of functions. Of those pieces of software that do exist, many are designed to assist with text analysis.

Wordform-oriented tools

Most of this section describes software that supports the analysis of texts through wordforms, and relies on the KWIC (Key Word In Context) and related displays. These tools are the most accessible for new users, and often are taught to students. See, for example, Hawthorne's (1994) article for examples of student uses of TACT. An ancestor of many of the currently available wordform-oriented programs is the Oxford Concordance Program (OCP), with which they share a number of concepts.

All the "wordform" programs described in this section provide a relatively limited set of operations. Nonetheless, there are reports of them being useful in a broad range of text-research activities, including:

- language teaching and learning;
- literary research;
- linguistic research, including corpus linguistics, translation and language engineering, supported at least at a relatively basic level (although see the next paragraph);
- lexicography; and
- content analysis in many disciplines including those from both the humanities and the social sciences.

As the category suggests, they all operate on wordforms and to work they must be able to automatically collect the wordforms from the provided texts. Most of the programs described here are thus oriented towards alphabetic languages, and allow one to identify both the characters that are acting as letters in the target language, and to identify characters that may appear in a word but are not letters (such as a hyphen).

At the center of most of these programs is the word list – a list of all wordforms that occur in the processed text, generally shown with a count of how many times that wordform occurred and usually sorted in alphabetical order or by frequency, with the most frequently occurring forms listed first. In most programs, users can ask to view information about a wordform by selecting it from this list, e.g., "show me all occurrences of the word 'avuncular.'" In some programs one types in a query to select the words one wants to view. Wildcard schemes in queries can support word stemming, e.g., "show me all occurrences of the word beginning 'system,'" and some allow for the wildcard to appear in other places than the end, thereby allowing for queries such as "show me all occurrences of words ending in 'ing.'" Some pieces of software allow for selection based around the occurrence close together of one or more wordforms. An example of *selection by phrase* would be "show me where the phrase 'the * moon' occurs" (where "*" means any word). A *collocation* selection query would allow one to ask "show me where the words 'moon' and 'gold' appear close together."

After you have selected wordforms of interest the programs are ready to show results. All the tools offer a KWIC display format – similar to that shown below – where we see occurrences of the word "sceptic" in David Hume's *Dialogues Concerning Natural Religion*.

sceptic (11)

[1,47]	abstractions. In vain would the	**sceptic** make a distinction
[1,48]	to science, even no speculative	**sceptic**, pretends to entertain
[1,49]	and philosophy, that Atheist and	**Sceptic** are almost synonymous.
[1,49]	by which the most determined	**sceptic** must allow himself to
[2,60]	of my faculties? You might cry out	**sceptic** and railer, as much as
[3,65]	profession of every reasonable	**sceptic** is only to reject
[8,97]	prepare a compleat triumph for the	**Sceptic**; who tells them, that
[11,121]	to judge on such a subject. I am	**Sceptic** enough to allow, that
[12,130]	absolutely insolvable. No	**Sceptic** denies that we lie
[12,130]	merit that name, is, that the	**Sceptic**, from habit, caprice,
[12,139]	To be a philosophical	**Sceptic** is, in a man of

A viewer uses the KWIC display to see what the context of the word says about how it is used in the particular text.

The KWIC display shown above also indicates where in the text the word occurs: the first of the two numbers in square brackets is the number of the dialogue, and the second is a page number in a standard edition. This information comes from textual markup. Markup can often provide useful information about the text's structure, and some software allows the markup to be identified and used in several ways:

(a) As shown in the KWIC display above, it can be used to indicate where a particular word occurrence occurs in the text – e.g., "*paragraph* 6 of *chapter* 2", or "spoken by *Hamlet.*"

(b) It can be used to select wordform occurrences that might be of interest – e.g., "tell me all the places where *Hamlet* speaks of a color."

(c) It can be used to define a collocation range – e.g., "show me all the words that occur in the same *sentence* as a color-word."

(d) It can be used as the basis for a distribution – "show me how a word is used by each *speaker.*"

(e) It can be used to delimit text to be ignored for concording – e.g., "do not include text found in the *prologue* in your index."

Although working with markup is clearly useful, support for XML/SGML markup is poor in current wordform programs. None of the wordform-oriented software described here can make good use of the full expressive power of TEI (the Text Encoding Initiative) XML markup, and some cannot even properly recognize the appearance of markup in a text document so that they can at least ignore it. A couple of the programs recognize a rather more simple form of markup – called COCOA markup after the piece of concordance software (COCOA, for *c*ount and *c*oncordance generation on the Atlas) for which it was first designed. A typical COCOA tag might look like this: "<S Hamlet>." The angle brackets announce the presence of a COCOA tag, and the tag's content is divided into two parts. The first part (here, an "S") announces the kind of thing being identified – "S" presumably stands for "speaker." The second part announces that starting with the spot in the text where the tag has appeared, the Speaker is "Hamlet." Although perhaps at first glance the COCOA tagging scheme might remind one a little of XML or SGML markup, it is technically quite different, and is structurally largely incompatible with texts marked up in XML/SGML.

Some wordform software offers other kinds of displays for results. A distribution graph, for example, could show graphically how the word use was distributed through the text, and might allow the user to see areas in the text where usage was concentrated. Some programs provide displays that focus on words that appear near to a selected word. TACT's *collocation display*, for example, is a list of all wordforms that occur near to selected words, ordered so that those with proportionally the most of their occurrences near the selected words (and therefore perhaps associated with the selected word itself) appear near the top of the list.

Some of the programs allow for some degree of manual lemmatization of wordforms – the grouping together of different forms that constitute a single word into a single group, although none of the wordform-oriented tools include software to do this task automatically. Stemming with wildcards can help to lemmatize many words in languages where the initial word stems can be used to select possible related wordforms. Several programs, including *Concordance*, *WordSmith Tools*, and *TACT*, allow one to store a list of wordforms that belong in a single lemma in a separate file and automatically apply these against a text. A group of words for the verb "to be" in English would contain the various wordforms that make it up: "am, are, is, be, was, were," etc. By applying this list the software would group these various wordforms under a single heading: "to be." Of course, the task of doing a proper lemmatization is often more complex than this. For one thing, one must separate homographs (a single wordform that might have several different meanings, such as "lead" in English). To allow the machine to do this task automatically would require it to understand the use of each word occurrence in its particular context – something outside the capabilities of any of the software reviewed here. TACT, however, allows the user to review the groups created by the simple wordform selection process and individually exclude wordform occurrences – thereby allowing the separation of homographs to be carried out manually, although at the cost of a significant amount of work.

The following paragraphs outline some of the important characteristics of the pieces of wordform-oriented software that are available today. (Only software readily available at the time of writing will be discussed – thus software such as OCP or WordCruncher, important and influential as they were in their day, are not described.) There are many differences in detail that might make one tool better suited to a task at hand than another. If you choose and use only one, you may need to direct your investigations to suit the program's strengths – a case of the tool directing the work rather than the other way around.

Concordance 3.0 is a Windows-based program written by R. J. S. Watt, who is Senior Lecturer in English at the University of Dundee. An evaluation copy (30 days) of the software is available at <http://www.rjcw.freeserve.co.uk>, with information about current prices. As the name suggests, the program focuses on providing a good KWIC Concordance generation and display engine. The user loads a text, selects words from the resultant word list (displayed on the left) and immediately sees a KWIC display on the right. The program supports some degree of lemmatization, and makes limited use of COCOA-like tags. I found its Windows interface quite easy to use. Concordance has been used with languages written in a range of alphabets. Furthermore, Professor Marjoie Chann, Ohio State University, reports success in using Concordance 3.0 even with Chinese, Japanese, and Korean texts on Windows 2000/XP. See <http://deall.ohio-state.edu/chan.9/conc/concordance.htm> for details.

Concordance 3.0 has the ability to transform its concordance into what becomes a large number of interconnected HTML pages that together could be made available on the WWW – a "Web Concordance." The resulting web pages present the full KWIC concordance, with links between the headwords in one frame, and the KWIC contexts in another. In the sample text that I tried (0.127 MB in size, containing about 23,300 words) the resulting concordance website was 7.86 MB, and contained 204 interlinked HTML documents.

MonoConc and *ParaConc* is software developed by Michael Barlow at the Department of Linguistics, Rice University. See <http://www.ruf.rice.edu/~barlow/mono.html>, and *A Guide to MonoConc* written by Barlow at <http://www.ruf.rice.edu/~barlow/mc.html>. MonoConc is sold by the Athelstan company (Houston, Texas). With MonoConc you enter a search string to select words and it then generates a KWIC concordance. The search query language supports various kinds of wildcards, so that, for example, "speak*" will select all words beginning with "speak." There is also a query specification language (similar to *regular expressions*) that provides a more sophisticated pattern-matching capability. MonoConc also provides a way of sorting the KWIC display by preceding or following words – an option that causes similar phrases involving the selected word to be more evident. Like other programs described here, MonoConc can also generate some wordform frequency lists. ParaConc provides similar functions when one is working with parallel texts in more than one language.

TACT is a suite of programs developed first by John Bradley and Lidio Presutti, and then somewhat further developed by Ian Lancashire and Mike Stairs, at the University of Toronto. The software was developed in the late 1980s and early 1990s and presents a DOS, rather than Windows, interface. It is still used, in spite of this limitation, by a significant user community. The software is available free from <http://www.chass.utoronto.ca:8080/cch/tact.html> – however, there is no manual for it available from that site. Instead, a user's guide – containing both the suite of programs and a selection of electronic texts on CD-ROM – can be purchased from the Modern Language Association (MLA).

Although TACT's DOS-based interface is difficult to learn for users familiar with Windows, TACT remains popular with some users because it presents a relatively broad range of functions within the general wordform-oriented context described above, including the most sophisticated support for textual markup and word collocation of any of the programs described here. TACT works immediately with texts from the standard western European languages, and can be extended to work with other languages based on the Roman alphabet, and with classical Greek, although how to do this is unfortunately poorly documented. Compared to other programs described here, TACT is limited in the size of texts it can handle. Although users have reported working successfully with texts as large as the Bible, that is roughly TACT's upper limit. New users will find the system difficult at the beginning because of the DOS interface, the need to purchase the User's Guide to receive any written help, and the lack of technical support. TACTweb (http://tactweb.humanities.mcmaster.ca/) allows TACT's textbases to be searched by queries over the WWW.

WordSmith Tools Version 3.0 is a suite of programs developed by Mike Scott (Department of English Language and Literature, University of Liverpool) and now distributed by the Oxford University Press. A version may be downloaded for evaluation from <http://www.oup.co.uk/> or the author's website at <http://www.liv.ac.uk/~ms2928/>. Word-Smith Tools consists of six programs, one of which is a *Controller* component – used to invoke the others – and several others provide facilities for the basic text editing of large text files, and will not be described further here. Most users will begin by pointing the *WordList* component at one or more text documents to generate a word list. From there the user can select some words to form the basis for KWIC concordance, displayed in the *Concord* component. An unusual feature of WordSmith Tools is its *KeyWords* component. This allows the word list generated by your text to be compared with a control word list (for example, a word list generated from the *British National Corpus* is available over the WWW for this purpose), and the words that occur proportionally more frequently in your text than in the control text are emphasized in the resulting display.

Although WordSmith Tools has only limited facilities to handle text with markup, it provides a richer set of functions to support statistical analysis than the other programs mentioned here. WordSmith Tools are Windows-based, but the modular nature of the program, where the word list, concordance, and keyword functions are packaged in different, albeit linked, components, made the software slightly more difficult for me to master than some of the other programs mentioned here.

Readers of this chapter may have noted that all the software mentioned so far runs on the IBM PC and/or Windows. Users of the Apple Macintosh have a smaller number of programs to choose from. The *AnyText* search engine, marketed by Linguist's Software, is described as "a HyperCard®-based Full Proximity Boolean Search Engine and Index Generator that allows you to create concordances and do FAST word searches on ordinary text files in English, Greek and Russian languages." The software was originally designed to work with Biblical text, and it can be purchased by itself, or with one or more versions of the Bible included (at a higher cost). More information is available at <http://www.linguistsoftware.com/atse.htm> – but it should be noted that HyperCard itself is no longer supported in the current generation of Macintosh operating systems (OS X). D. W. Rand's *Concorder* Version 3.1 is available free of charge, although a printed manual is sold by *Les Publications CRM* of the Université de Montréal, Canada. More information about *Concorder* can be found at <http://omega.crm.umontreal.ca/~rand/CC_an.html>.

Several sets of tools developed for linguistics-oriented research support more sophisticated word-oriented research. See, for example, the GATE system developed at the University of Sheffield's Natural Language Processing Group at <http://gate.ac.uk>, or TIPSTER, developed with the support of various agencies in the USA (http://www.itl.nist.gov/iaui/894.02/related_projects/tipster/). As powerful as these environments generally are, they have been developed in a technical culture that is largely foreign to the humanities, and they require both extensive knowledge of linguistics and computing environments such as Unix to operate. They are not discussed further in this chapter.

Qualitative analysis

Software developed for qualitative analysis within the social sciences provides a very different view of how computers can assist with the analysis of texts. Here the focus is on software that allows the user to explicitly label and organize thematic categories that they discover while reading the text. Three widely used pieces of software that work in this way are *Nud*ist*, *NVivo* (both from QSR International: <http://www.qsr.com.au/>) and *Atlas.ti* from Scientific Software Development, Berlin (<http://www.atlasti.de/intro.shtml>). An interesting review of text analysis software that comes from this social sciences perspective is provided in the book *A Review of Software for Text Analysis* (Alexa and Zuell 1999). An article describing the use of these tools for research can be found in Kelle (1997).

Text collation

The use of computers to support the collation of textual variants is almost as old as the wordform work described earlier in this chapter. Although the early belief that collation was largely a mechanical task has been shown to be false, much useful work has been done in this area, nonetheless. Perhaps the best known tool available to support collation is Peter Robinson's *Collate* program for the Macintosh. You can read more about it at *Getting Started with Collate 2*, from <http://www.cta.emu.ac.uk/projects/collate/res.html>.

Wilhelm Ott's *TuStep* system has components in it that are specifically designed to support collation and the broader task of the preparation of a critical edition. See the further discussion about *TuStep* later in this chapter.

A Text Tool for XML: XSLT

Up to now we have focused primarily on tools specifically developed to support certain kinds of research in the humanities. If your work is focused on these particular tasks, then you may find many of your needs met by these tools. However, for many of us, the work we do with a text is not so tightly focused, and these tools will rarely be sufficient to support all the work we wish to do.

In this section we will describe a set of tools built on XSLT that are available to work with XML markup. The Text Encoding Initiative (TEI) has made it evident that many of the things in a text that are of interest to textual scholars can be usefully identified with SGML or XML markup. However, once these things *are* marked up this is rarely the end of the story – after all, one puts the markup in so that one can do further work with it later. These days one often wants to publish such materials on the WWW and, of course, the resulting website would contain the base text in HTML. Often, however, the markup can provide the source for various supporting index documents that provide a set of alternative entry points into the text itself. The automatic generation of such indices and of the original text in HTML is well supported by XSLT.

XSLT stands for "Extensible Stylesheet Language: Transformations" (compare with *XML*: "Extensible Markup Language"). It is one of a pair of standards that are named *XSL* (Extensible Stylesheet Language). The second part of XSL, *XSLFO* – "Extensible Stylesheet Language: Formatting Objects" – provides a language describing how a text should be laid out for display – usually for the printed page. The XSLT language is developed by the World Wide Web Consortium (W3C: <http://www.w3c.org>), a group of individuals and corporations who have taken on the task of maintaining and developing standards for the World Wide Web.

The emphasis in XSLT is on transformation, and today the principal use of XSLT is the transformation of an XML document into HTML for presentation on the WWW. The virtues of using a form of XML more complex and specifically adapted than HTML as the initial markup scheme for a text have been extensively described elsewhere in this book, and I will not repeat them here. However, if one is to present material on the

WWW then (at least today) one needs to present the material in HTML, and an approach that consistently transforms any well-formed XML into HTML is very valuable. Often a single tag in XML needs to be transformed into a set, sometimes a complex set, of HTML tags. In XSLT one describes this transformation once, in what is called in XSLT a *template*. An XSLT processor can then apply the specification given in the template to all places in the original text where it fits. Normally the transformation process requires the specification of many different templates. Thus, one groups the set of templates one needs in a single document, called an XSLT stylesheet.

Here is a simple example that will give a little of the flavor of XSLT. Suppose the original text is marked up in TEI (the example, slightly modified to be in XML rather than SGML, is from section 6.3.2.2. "Emphatic Words and Phrases" of the TEI P3 guidelines):

```
What it all comes to is this,</q> he said.
<q><emph rend="italic">What does Christopher
Robin do in the morning nowadays?</emph></q>
```

For presentation in HTML, the *q* element needs to be transformed so that the contained text is surrounded by quote marks. The *emph* element, when the *rend* attribute is set to "italic," needs to be transformed into HTML's *I* element. The following two templates, which would, of course, be included with many others in a complete XSLT stylesheet, would accomplish this:

```
<xsl:template match="q">
"<xsl:apply-templates/>"
</xsl:template>
<xsl:template match="emph[@rend='italic']">
<I><xsl:apply-templates/></I>
</xsl:template>
```

XSLT is itself written in XML. In this excerpt we see two XSLT *template* elements. Each has a *match* attribute which specifies where the particular transformation contained therein should be applied. The match attribute for the first template element simply asserts that this template is applicable for all *q* elements in the input text. The match attribute in the second template asserts that it is applicable to all *emph* elements which have their rend attribute set to *italic*. The content of each template element describes what should be generated as output from the transformation process. In both template elements you can see the *apply-templates* element which, in effect, says "place the matched element's content here while also applying their templates as appropriate." In the first template, then, the content is simply surrounded by quote marks. In the second template, the content is surrounded by HTML's *I* element. If these transformation templates were applied to the text above, then, the resulting output would be:

```
"What it all comes to is this," he said.
"<I>What does Christopher
Robin do in the morning nowadays?</I>"
```

Although this example gives a little bit of the flavor of what XSLT can do, by itself it barely hints at the kinds of transformations that can be expressed in XSLT. With an XSLT stylesheet, for example, it is possible to specify a transformation that reorganizes and duplicates the content of some elements so that, say, each section heading in an input document appears in two places in the output – once as heading for its respective section, but also at the front of the document as an element in a table of contents. Material can also be sorted and grouped in different ways (although grouping is rather complex to express in the XSLT version 1). It is possible, for example, to write a transformation stylesheet that scans an XML document looking for references to people that have been tagged using TEI's "name" tag: (e.g., from TEI P3 guidelines section 6.4.1, slightly modified):

> <name type="person" reg="de la Mare, Walter">Walter de la Mare</name> was born at <name type="place">Charlton</name>, in <name type="county">Kent</name>, in 1873.

XSLT can be used to select all material in name tags and generate an index from them. All the references to "de la Mare, Walter" and to the places "Charlton" and "Kent" could be grouped together under their respective headwords, and links could be generated below each heading to take the user from the index to the spots in the text where the references were found.

Examples so far have emphasized the use of XSLT to generate output in HTML for making material available on the WWW. However, XSLT is designed to produce output in other XML formats as well as HTML. As XML becomes the scheme of choice for feeding data to many programs, it is likely that XSLT will be used more and more to transform one type of XML markup into another. For example, suppose you had a text with all the words tagged, and you wished to perform a statistical calculation based, say, on the number of occurrences of the wordforms in different chapters, one could write a (complex) stylesheet that would locate the words, count up the number of occurrences of each wordform in each chapter, and generate a document containing this information. If the statistical analysis program accepted data of this kind in XML then your stylesheet could write out its results in the XML format your statistical program wanted.

Learning XSLT is difficult, particularly if you wish to take advantage of its more advanced features. Jeni Tennison's Book *Beginning XSLT* (Tennison 2002) provides a thorough introduction to many features of XSLT and is understandable to the non-programmer, although one does have to put up with examples drawn from the processing of television program listings! Michael Kay's *XSLT: Programmer's Reference* (Kay 2001) is, as the name suggests, a complete, in-depth review of XSLT and the software that supports it, and is aimed at a rather technical audience. A search on Google for "XSLT Tutorials" will find many online tutorials. A number of learning resources are also listed at <http://www.xslt.com/resources_tutorials.htm>.

There are several XSLT transformation tools available, and all the ones described here are free.

Microsoft's *MSXML* (XML Core Services) contains an XSLT processor for Windows and is incorporated inside the company's *Internet Explorer* (IE) browser. If you send IE an XML document with an XSLT stylesheet, it will transform the XML within the browser and present the display as if the resulting HTML document had been sent instead. Microsoft was much involved in the development of XSLT, and until Internet Explorer 6, the processor provided was not compatible with the now-standard version of XSLT. Hence, be sure that you are using the latest version. Information about MSXML, and a download package to set it up on your Windows machine can be found at <http://msdn.microsoft.com/xml>.

There are several XSLT processors available that run separately from a browser. To use one of them you would give your XML document and XSLT stylesheet to it, and it would save results of the transformation into a file on your hard disk. HTML files generated this way would then be made available using any web server, and by transforming the documents in HTML before serving them, you allow any web browser to view them. The two most widely used XSLT processors are SAXON and XALAN. Both these XSLT processors are most readily run on a Windows machine from the DOS prompt. You will need to be familiar with the basics of a DOS window in order to be able to use these processors effectively.

Michael Kay's SAXON processor (<http://saxon.sourceforge.net/>) is considered to be very highly conformant with the XSLT standard. Saxon versions up to 6.5.2 have been packaged in an "Instant Saxon" format that runs readily on many Windows machines, and is relatively easy to set up and use. It is packaged in a ZIP file on the Saxon website, and setting it up involves only unzipping the two files it contains into an appropriate directory on your computer. Once I had unzipped the Saxon program from the ZIP file I was immediately able to use it with a Hamlet text and stylesheet by starting a DOS/Command window and typing the command:

```
saxon hamlet.xml hamlet.xsl >hamlet.htm
```

(which asked SAXON to read an XML document in *hamlet.xml*, and an XSLT stylesheet in *hamlet.xsl* and to generate as output a file *hamlet.htm*). The ZIP file contains an HTML document that describes how to invoke the Saxon program in some detail. A version of SAXON is also available which operates with the support of Sun's Java system. If you are familiar with Java, you might find it as easy to use this version instead.

XALAN, from the Apache Software Foundation, is another widely used XSLT processor. It comes in two versions. One version, implemented in Java, can be found at <http://xml.apache.org/xalan-j/index.html>, and requires you to also set up Sun's Java system on your computer. The second version (at <http://xml.apache.org/xalan-c/index.html>) does not require Java, but seems to be a less complete implementation of XSLT.

Macintosh OS X users who are able to set up Java on their machines in the background Unix environment that underpins OS X will be able to use XALAN or SAXON on their machines.

Perl and TuStep: General Purpose Text Manipulation

In the first section of this chapter we described tools designed to support particular kinds of text-oriented tasks. The section on XML introduced tools that are potentially much more general-purpose. In this section we come to the tools that could be applied the most broadly, and we will be describing two "toolkit environments" that at first may seem quite different: *Perl* and *TuStep*. By the end of the chapter we will have shown some of the ways in which they are also similar.

Perl

Perl was created by Larry Wall in 1987 to respond to a need to be able to perform complex administrative-oriented text processing and report generation of data on Unix systems. Perl was so successful that it soon became the tool of choice for getting all sorts of things done in the Unix environment, and it eventually spread from the Unix world to many other computing environments. It has become (in Andrew Johnson's words) "*the* tool to use for filling gaps everywhere." Perl is good at reading, processing, transforming and writing plain text. If you have ASCII data that come out of one program in one format, and you want to feed them into another program that requires a slightly different format, then Perl might allow you to quickly develop the transformation you need in a matter of minutes. We will introduce Perl here, but other languages such as *Python* can do similar work.

Perl is a programming language, and as such shares some of its characteristics with other programming languages – including a syntactical structure that is broadly similar to several important ones. Thus, those who are familiar with other widely used languages such as Java or C will start off already knowing something of how to write Perl programs. This means that for many computing professionals, Perl is "easy to learn." However, if you do not have a programming background, you will find that you will not be able to draw in the years of training and experience that allow Perl to be "easy to learn" for this community. Instead, initially you are likely to find learning to program in Perl slow-going. Make friends with a programmer!

Filling of gaps – Perl's strength – often involves the creation of small pieces of throwaway software specifically tailored for a task at hand. When one knows how to write Perl, one can often throw a little program together to do something simple in a matter of minutes. The price for this informal nature of the language is sometimes paid in performance – the program might take longer to run than a carefully written program to do the same task in C would take – however, the C program to do the same job might take a day to write.

To help introduce Perl, I will describe a bit of the Perl programming I did for Willard McCarty's *Onomasticon of Ovid's Metamorphoses*. In this project, McCarty has marked up some aspects of personification in the *Metamorphoses* by a tagging scheme of his own invention. Here is an example from his text:

```
<<13.040>>optima num sumat, quia sumere noluit ulla :
{on/ Achilles : [arma] optima}
{on/ Ulixes : [arma] optima[Achilles]}
{v/ Ulixes : sumo(v103)}
{v/ Ulixes : sumo(v501)}
{v/ Ulixes : nolo(v21) sumere}
{on/ Ulixes : [arma] ulla}
```

These seven lines represent one line from book 13 of the *Metamorphoses*. The first line, above, is the actual Latin text of Ovid's poem. The remaining six lines represent the tagging that McCarty has added. Most of the lines of poetry, like this one, have a number of tags attached to them. Each tag is surrounded by brace brackets "{" and "}", and the contents are divided into three parts. The first part (in the first tag "on") categorizes the kind of personification – here the individual is personified by being given a person-like attribute. Tags beginning with "v" represent personification through a verb. The second part (here "Achilles") identifies the person/god being talked about, and the third part (here "{arma} optima") links the tag to words in the text. Tags can be more complex, but this is sufficient for our purposes here.

One obvious way to transform this text and make the tagging very useful would be to turn it inside out – producing indices based around the tags, producing something that looks like this (here showing a fragment from the index of Attributes):

ARMA
¶Acharnan* & Amphoteros* ~ *nec 9.432;*
¶Achelous | anguis ~ *aliena 9.76;*
¶Achilles ~ *12.621, 13.94, 97, 97, 254, 380; ~ haec 13,180; ~ illa 13.158; ~ ista 13.101;*
~ *neganda mihi{Aiax¹} 13.35; ~ optima 13.40; ~ proposita 13.150; ~ quae non intellegi-*
t{Aiax¹} 13.295; ~ quae nunc quoque ferre laboro{Ulixes} 13.285; ~ tua 13.130; ~ viri fortis
13.121, 383;
¶Acrisius ~ *4.609;*
¶Aeneas ~ *victricia nati{Venus} 14.573;*
. . .

You can see the reference to Achilles *arma optima* from line 13.40 in the second line of the Arma/Achilles entry. The indices were represented as a set of linked HTML pages, with references to the poem acting as links. One can use the indices to first get an overview of the kind of attributes that appear across the entire text, and can then use the index to review all the occurrences in the poem.

Writing the Perl code to transform this tagged text into these indices was, of course, significantly more than a 10-minute job, and it is beyond the space we have here to begin to analyze the processing in any detail. However, a small example of Perl coding will give you the flavor of what working with Perl is like.

An important component of Perl is its regular expression processor. Regular expressions provide a way to express relatively complex patterns to select and pull apart text for further processing. The expression:

```
{.*/ .*? : .*}
```

uses the regular expression operator sequence ".*?"and ".*" to specify "any sequence of characters." This pattern matches the form of all the tags in McCarty's text: a "{" followed by any sequence of characters, followed by a "/", followed by any sequence of characters, followed by a ":", followed by any sequence of characters and ending with a "}".

If we put parentheses around the "any sequence of characters" in this expression, then Perl will make available for further processing the component of each specific text string that matched the pattern. Thus, the sequence:

```
{(.*?)/ (.*?) : (.*)}
```

if applied against the sequence "{on/ Achilles : [arma] optima}" would have Perl identify "on" as the first part, "Achilles" as the second part, and "[arma] optima" as the third part, and make those subcomponents available to the rest of the program for further processing. Here is the same regular expression as it might be used in a bit of Perl code:

```
while(<INPUT>){
chomp($txt = $_);
if($txt =~ m|{(.*?)/ (.*?) : (.*)}|){
$code = $1; $name = $2; $text = $3;
[...]
}
}
```

The example has been slightly simplified from what was actually used. Even then one can see the formal nature of the Perl language, and perhaps get a sense of the challenge it presents for non-programmers to learn. The first line says "fetch a new line of input from the input file and do the following chunk of Perl code (enclosed in '{}'s) for each line." The second line says "assign the line of input you read in the first line to $txt, and chop off any ending newline character that you find." The third line says "if the string of characters in $txt matches the given pattern (you can see the pattern we described above embedded in this line), do the lines enclosed below within '{}'s." The fourth line asks Perl to save the first bit of the matched regular expression in $code, the second bit in $name, and the third bit in $text. The code would continue with instructions that made Perl do something useful with the chunks of the tag in $code, $name, and $text.

During my analysis of the task of transforming the tagged text into a set of linked indices, it became evident that the process to generate the separate indices was largely the same for each index, albeit using different data by selecting different tags from the tagged text. Thus, it became clear that the entire processing could be written as a small set of separate modular programs that could be directed to each appropriate tagset in turn. We chose, then, to apply Perl to the task of transforming the marked-up text into indices (expressed as collections of HTML pages) by applying a modular approach – breaking the transformation tasks into a number of smaller steps, writing Perl code for each one of the bits. Then, by combining them together in the correct order, the entire task would be performed.

For example, a small program we called *text2htm.pl* transformed the text and tags into a set of HTML documents. A small module was also written (called *tagproc.pl*) that extracted data from the tags and stored them in a large table-like structure which would be used, and added to, by the other processing Perl programs that worked on the material. These two programs only needed to be run once. A set of three Perl scripts then did the bulk of the work of transforming the tabular data derived from the tags into a particular index presentation (divided into a number of separate HTML pages) you see above. Two further scripts were also used during the generation of each index to create two kinds of navigational aids for the index. Thus, after the first two programs were run, the other five could be used in sequence for each of the three indices that were to be generated.

When the Perl scripts were ready, it was a simple matter to record the sequence in which they should run and what data they should process in a small DOS batch file.

When this has been done the process of transforming the entire text with its thousands of tags into the integrated collection of several thousand HTML pages could then be performed by typing only one command. When the batch file was invoked, it was then a matter of simply waiting for the couple of minutes while the computer worked its way through the batch file and Perl scripts to generate the completed version.

The writing of the Perl scripts to work over the material was not a trivial matter. However, because they could be packaged up and invoked in such a simple manner, they allowed McCarty to quickly generate a new version of the reference website for his materials as often as he liked.

Getting started with Perl

Perl is free software. It was originally developed for Unix systems and is nowadays provided as a built-in tool in systems like Linux. The ActiveState company (http:// www.activestate.com) has produced the most popular (free) version of Perl for Windows machines. Versions of Perl have been available on the Macintosh for several years (see, for example, MacPerl), although until OS X (which is Unix-based), they were generally incomplete implementations.

Development of Perl is, these days, a worldwide phenomenon. There is not only continued work to enhance and further develop the basic Perl language, but there is a substantial number of developers who develop Perl modules that allow the Perl programmer to do tasks other than simply process text files. The DBI module, for example, provides a standard way to allow a Perl script to connect to and extract data from a relational database. There is a set of XML modules that allow XML files to be manipulated in Perl programs. Indeed, among the thousands of modules now available it is possible to find one that will help you apply Perl to almost any kind of computer data now available, including material available over the Internet. The CPAN website (<http://www.cpan.org/>) is the usual place to go for information about all the modules that people have written. For Windows Perl users, the ActiveState company maintains a set of these modules specially packaged up for use on Windows, and allows you to download any of them and set them up for free, simply by invoking their "ppm" program and asking for them by name.

Perl, like any full-function programming language, is difficult for non-programmers to learn, and most books and online tutorials that purport to provide an "easy" introduction to Perl are, in fact, written for the programmer audience. Andrew L. Johnson's book *Elements of Programming with Perl* (Johnson 2000), however, provides an introduction to Perl programming for non-programmers, and is recommended for this purpose.

TuStep

Willhelm Ott's *TuStep* (Tübingen System of Text Processing Programs) system has a long history. The software that developed into TuStep was begun in 1966, and the first version of TuStep that was made available under that name appeared in 1978. It is still in use today – extensively at Tübingen and in other centers in Germany, and in a number of other places in the world – for the manipulation of texts for all sorts of scholarly purposes. TuStep consists of a set of 45 commands that operate in an environment containing a text editor and a macro program. Ott describes the task domain for his system as "textdata processing," and describes what he means by this in the introduction to the English version of the TuStep manual:

> These basic operations of textdata processing (and the corresponding TUSTEP programs) encompass functions that can be generally characterized as follows: *Collation* of different text versions; *correcting* not only in the interactive Editor mode, but also with the use of prepared (or automatically generated) correction instructions; *breakdown* of text into user-defined elements (z. B. semantic patterns); *sorting* text elements or lengthy units of text according to a number of different alphabets and other criteria; *Generating an index* by compiling sorted text-elements; *Processing* textdata according to user-defined selective criteria, replacing, moving, enhancing, concluding and comparing text, calculating numerical values contained in the text (e.g. calender dates) or those which can be determined from the text (e.g. the number of words in a sentence), and output in various formats, including those required by other operating systems (e.g. SPSS for statistical evaluation). (1993: 8)

TuStep, then, consists of a large number of rather abstract processes that can be instructed to perform a large number of individual operations on a set of text files. The processes are designed to be combined together in a sequence to perform a large number of useful tasks. The sequence of operations can then be stored in a command file and subsequently reapplied at any time. One of TuStep's components is a high-quality typesetting program which is controlled by a command language that can be generated by other elements of the system, and which is capable of producing letterpress-quality printing – indeed a significant use of TuStep is in the preparation of printed critical editions. In the same way that a set of woodworking tools can, in the hands of a skilled craftsperson, produce beautiful results, TuStep's tools can be applied to text to produce beautiful printed editions. Of course, it is only after years of practice that the woodworker can produce a beautiful bookcase using the basic carpentry tools such as a saw, plane, chisel, etc. In the same way, one has to learn how to take the similarly abstract tools provided by TuStep and combine them to generate the best product that they are capable of producing.

We mentioned earlier that TuStep modules are meant to be combined into a sequence of operations. To generate an index of McCarty's *Onomasticon* material described earlier using TuStep, one would first invoke its PINDEX program to extract the materials that are meant to make up the index – putting the result into an intermediate file. Then one would sort the resulting intermediate file and use the result of that to feed into another program called GINDEX to transform the properly ordered file into a hierarchical index-like structure. Next one could take the hierarchically structured entries and write instructions that would transform them into a series of typesetting codes that could drive the typesetting program.

TuStep modules often incorporate a large number of separate functions within a single program. Parameters are provided to tell the PINDEX program how to recognize material in the input text file that belongs in the index, and how to assign the pieces that are found into a multilevel index. Instructions to TuStep programs are given in a notational scheme that is especially developed for the program. For example, the following lines would be stored in a file and passed to the PINDEX program to tell it how to extract the tags from McCarty's *Onomasticon* texts:

ea | = |:|
ee |}|_| = |
ena |/|
ene |}|
enk |#f+|

The letters at the front of each line specify parameters that the PINDEX program is to use. The "ea" line specifies that an index entry from the text file begins after a ":." The "ee" line indiciates that the text for an index entry ends before either a "}" or a "_." The "ena" and "ene" lines identify characters that delimit supplementary text that belong with the collected index entry. The "enk" line specifies that the text after the index entry should be in bold.

TuStep is a very versatile system, but learning how to use the software components to do the things you want is not easy. TuStep can be inexpensively purchased from the University of Tübingen. Most of the documentation for TuStep is in German. There is a version of the TuStep reference manual in English, but it cannot really be used to learn the program in the first place. There is a tutorial on TuStep, in German, called *Lernbuch TUSTEP*, and there are training courses each March and September in Tübingen that will help you get started. There is a brief introduction to TuStep, its concepts, and its facilities in Ott (2000). There is also further information on the TuStep website at <http://www.uni-tuebingen.de/zdv/tustep/tustep_eng.html>.

TuStep and Perl compared

Both TuStep and Perl can be used to do almost any kind of manipulation of a text in electronic form. Perl is a general-purpose programming language and can also perform any kind of transformation that you can ask a computer to do on a text file, although the task of learning how to use it is large – especially for non-programmers. TuStep is especially developed for performing tasks of interest to scholars working with texts, although it will still take real work to learn how to use it. TuStep also comes with a high-quality typesetting program which is capable of professional-quality typesetting – something Perl does not have (although, of course, Perl could be used to generate texts to feed into other typesetting systems such as TeX). For non-programmers, then, both TuStep and Perl have steep and long learning curves. Since TuStep is specifically designed for scholarly work, it does contain some helpful features – such as strategies that are built in for the proper sorting of text in many languages – that make specifying processing easier. However, on the other hand, there is a great deal of material available about how to program in Perl, and it is possible to hire a programmer who already knows Perl to do work for you.

Conclusion

The reader will, by this point, have hopefully seen that the range of text tools described here can support a very wide range of scholarly activities on texts, and in the limited space available here it is possible to only hint at the full potential of these tools. Susan Hockey's book *Electronic Texts in the Humanities* (Hockey 2000), while not explicitly about text tools, does describe many different projects and suggests the range of things that a set of tools like the ones described here can accomplish.

Certainly, XSLT, Perl, and TuStep are complex and powerful systems. Certain kinds of useful results can be achieved with a modest amount of work, but learning to use any of them both efficiently and to their full potential will commit the learner to a process that could take years to complete. Often reviews of software for the humanities talk about "user friendliness." Are these tools "user-friendly?" If you mean, "are they immediately usable," then the answer is "no." However, are a good set of carpentry tools user-friendly? They are if you are skilled in their use. In a similar way, these tools can do significant work on texts, but all of them require a significant amount of skill to make use of them.

BIBLIOGRAPHY

ActivePerl (2002). ActiveState Corp. At <http://www.activestate.com/Products/ActivePerl/>.

Alexa, Melina and Cornelia Zuell (1999). *A Review of Software for Text Analysis*. Mannheim: ZUMA.

Barlow, Michael (1995). A Guide to MonoConc. At <http://www.ruf.rice.edu/~barlow/mc.html>.

Clark, James (ed.) (1999). XSL Transformations (XSLT): Version 1.0. W3C. Accessed November 16, 1999. At <http://www.w3.org/TR/xslt>.

Concordance. Accessed November 10, 2002. At <http://www.rjcw.freeserve.co.uk/>.

Hawthorne, Mark (1994). The Computer in Literary Analysis: Using TACT with Students. *Computers and the Humanities* 28: 19–27.

Hockey, Susan (2000). *Electronic Texts in the Humanities*. Oxford: Oxford University Press.

Johnson, Andrew L. (2000). *Elements of Programming with Perl*. Greenwich, CT: Manning Publications.

Kay, Michael (2001). *XSLT: Programmer's Reference*. Birmingham, UK: WROX Press.

——(2002). SAXON: The XSLT Processor. Accessed August 28, 2002. At <http://saxon.sourceforge.net/>.

Kelle, U. (1997). Theory-building in Qualitative Research and Computer Programs for the Management of Textual Data. *Sociological Research Online* 2,2. At <http://www.socresonline.org.uk/socresonline/2/2/1.html>.

Lancashire, Ian, et al. (1996). *Using TACT with Electronic Texts*. New York: Modern Languages Association of America.

Microsoft MSDN: XML. Microsoft. At <http://msdn.microsoft.com/xml>.

Ott, W. (2000). Strategies and Tools for Textual Scholarship: the Tübingen System of Text Processing Programs (TUSTEP). *Literary and Linguistic Computing* 15,1: 93–108.

Robinson, Peter (2000). Collate Software: Resources. Accessed March 2, 2000. At <http://www.cta.dmu.ac.uk/projects/collate/res.html>.

Scott, M. (2002). Mike Scott's Web: WordSmith Tools. Accessed July 16, 2002. At <http://www.liv.ac.uk/~ms2928/>.

Smith, J. B. (1989). Computer Criticism. In Rosanne G. Potter (ed.), *Literary Computing and Literary Criticism: Theoretical and Practical Essays on Theme and Rhetoric* (pp. 13–44). Philadelphia: University of Pennsylvania Press.

Tennison, Jeni (2002). *Beginning XSLT*. Birmingham, UK: WROX Press.

TUebingen System of TExt processing Programs: TuStep. Accessed October 22, 2002. At <http://www.uni-tuebingen.de/zdv/tustep/tustep_eng.html>.

Wall, Larry, et al. (1996). *Programming Perl*. Sebastopol, CA: O'Reilly and Associates.

Wooldridge, T. Russon (ed.) (1991). *A TACT Exemplar*. Toronto: CCH, University of Toronto.

34

"So the Colors Cover the Wires": Interface, Aesthetics, and Usability

Matthew G. Kirschenbaum

Introduction: A Glass Darkly

The idea of interface, and related concepts such as design and usability, are some of the most vexed in contemporary computing. Definitions of interface typically invoke the image of a "surface" or a "boundary" where two or more "systems," "devices," or "entities" come into "contact" or "interact." Though these terms encourage spatial interpretation, most interfaces also embody temporal, haptic, and cognitive elements. The steering wheel of a car, the control panel of a VCR, and the handle of a door are all examples of everyday interfaces that exhibit these dimensions. In the context of computers and computing, the word "interface" is often used interchangeably with "graphical user interface," or GUI, most frequently encountered as a desktop windows environment. The command line prompt is perhaps the best-known alternative to the GUI, but there are a plethora of others, including screen readers, motion trackers, tangible user interfaces (TUIs, breathtakingly rendered in the 2002 film *Minority Report*), and immersive or augmented computing environments. In the humanities, meanwhile, it is increasingly common to encounter the idea that a book or a page is a kind of interface, a response to the understanding that the conventions of manuscript and print culture are no less techno-logically determined than those of the digital world. At least one observer, Steven Johnson, has defined our present historical moment as an "interface culture," a term he wields to embrace not only the ubiquity of computers and electronic devices but also the way in which interface has come to function as a kind of trope or cultural organizing principle – what the industrial novel was to the nineteenth century or television to the suburban American 1950s are his examples.

As much as it is talked about, however, interface can at times seem little loved. Usability guru Donald A. Norman writes: "The real problem with interface is that it is an interface. Interfaces get in the way. I don't want to focus my energies on interface. I want to focus on the job" (2002: 210). Nicholas Negroponte holds that the "secret" of interface design is to "make it go away" (1995: 93). To further complicate matters, interface is often, in practice, a highly recursive phenomenon. Take the experience of a user sitting at her computer and browsing the Web, perhaps accessing content at a digital humanities site. The site's internal design imposes one layer of interface between the user and the content, and the web browser – its buttons and menus and frames – immediately imposes another. The user's desktop environment and operating system then impose a third layer of interface. The ergonomics of the situation (we'll assume our user is working with a keyboard and mouse, looking at a screen positioned the recommended 18 inches away) create still another layer of interface, a layer which becomes apparent when one considers alternatives such as accessing the same content with a PDA or a wearable device, or in a room-based virtual reality setting like a CAVE. Importantly, each of these "layers," as I have been calling them, exhibits the potential for interaction with one another as well as with the user. The desktop environment governs the behavior of the browser software, whose features and functions in turn directly affect many aspects of the user's interaction with the site's internal design and content.

While everything I have just been rehearsing is familiar enough in computer science circles, particularly the domain known as human–computer interaction (HCI, also sometimes identified as human–computer interface), aspects of this narrative may seem problematic to readers trained in humanities disciplines. It would not be hard to find someone willing to argue that my entire scenario is the product of yet another unacknowledged interface, a kind of common cultural gateway whose socially constructed ideologies govern our expectations with regard to technology, representation, and access to information. Moreover, in the scenario sketched above, my distinction between different layers of interface and something I casually called "content" is one that runs counter to decades of work in literary and cultural criticism, where form and content are almost instinctively understood as inextricable from one another. Thus, the weight of established wisdom in a field like interface design rests on a fundamental disconnect with the prevailing intellectual assumptions of most humanists – that an "interface," whether the windows and icons of a website or the placement of a poem on a page, can somehow be ontologically decoupled from whatever "content" it happens to embody. This is precisely the point at which Brenda Laurel begins her dissent in *Computers as Theatre*, her influential critique of mainstream interface theory:

> Usually we think about interactive computing in terms of two things: an application and an interface. In the reigning view, these two things are conceptually distinct: An application provides specific functionality for specific goals, and an interface represents that functionality to people. The interface is the thing that we communicate with – the thing we "talk" to – the thing that mediates between us and the inner workings of the machine. The interface is typically designed last, after the application is thoroughly conceived and perhaps even implemented; it is attached to a preexisting bundle of "functionality" to serve as its contact surface. (Laurel 1991: xv)

Laurel is writing to challenge this prevailing viewpoint. Yet the truth is that, from a developer's perspective, the interface is often not only conceptually distinct, but also *computationally* distinct. As John M. Carroll points out, it wasn't until the comparatively recent advent of languages like Visual Basic that it even became practical to program both a user interface and an application's underlying functionality with the same code (Carroll 2002: xxxii). Like the history of hand-press printing, which teaches us that paper-making, typesetting, etching or engraving, and bookbinding came to encompass very different domains of labor and technical expertise (rarely housed under the same roof), resource development in the digital world is typically highly segmented and compartmentalized.

Interfaces are mostly discussed in mundane and utilitarian terms, but computing lore contains its share of instances where poor interface design has had lethal and catastrophic results. One notorious episode involved the Therac-25, a machine employed for cancer radiation therapy in the mid-1980s, whose cumbersome software interface contributed to several patient deaths from overexposure. Likewise, the small-plane accident that killed singer-songwriter John Denver has been attributed to a poorly designed cockpit interface, specifically the placement of a fuel switch. While the stakes in digital humanities research are (happily) other than life and death, interface is nonetheless an indispensable component of any project.

Indeed, interface presents a number of interesting and unique problems for the digital humanist. Understandably driven by pragmatic and utilitarian needs, the interface is also where representation and its attendant ideologies are most conspicuous to our critical eyes. Ostensibly wedded to the ideal of user-friendliness, the interface is also where we deploy our most creative features and imaginative flourishes. Too often put together as the final phase of a project under a tight deadline and an even tighter budget, the interface becomes the first and in most respects the exclusive experience of the project for its end users. Seemingly the most creative or intuitive stage of the development process, the interface is also potentially the most empirical, subject to the rigorous quantitative usability testing pioneered by HCI. This chapter makes no attempt to offer a comprehensive survey of the vast professional literature on interface and usability, nor does it seek to serve as a design primer or guide to best practices. (Readers interested in those topics should consult the chapter's suggestions for further reading.) Instead, in the pages that follow I seek to develop some broader frameworks for thinking about the major challenges that interface poses for both theorists and developers in the digital humanities.

Ways of Seeing

Computers compute, of course, but computers today, from most users' points of view, are not so much engines of computation as *venues* for *representation*. The first use of CRT displays as output devices in the 1950s irretrievably situated computers within a complex cultural genealogy of screens, a genealogy which also includes video, television, cinema, photography, and indeed, as Lev Manovich and others have argued, the full lineage of visual aesthetics in the West since the advent of perspective. This context is important because it allows interface design to take its place alongside the other representational forms that have inhabited our many varieties of screens, frames, and windows. Moreover, although a graphical user interface built around the familiar desktop and windows metaphor currently constitutes the normative interface experience for the vast majority of users, it is worth remembering that this particular graphical environment, and the representational practices it encourages, is historically quite specific.

From one perspective, our interface and display technologies have remained remarkably stable and consistent over the past thirty years. Though the Alto, built at Xerox PARC in 1973, is widely regarded as the first computer to implement a functional graphical user interface, the more important date is probably 1968, when Stanford's Douglas Engelbart demonstrated an operational GUI to a standing-room-only audience in San Francisco. Steven Johnson articulates the importance of Engelbart's presentation, which included a feature recognizable as "windows," this way:

> [H]istorians a hundred years from now will probably accord it the same weight and significance we now bestow on Ben Franklin's kite-flying experiments or Alexander Graham Bell's accidental phone conversation with Watson. Engelbart's thirty-minute demo was our first public glimpse of information-space, and we are still living in its shadow. (Johnson 1997: 11)

By "information-space," Johnson means the abrupt transformation of the screen from a simple and subordinate output device to a bounded representational system possessed of its own ontological integrity and legitimacy, a transformation that depends partly on the heightened visual acuity a graphical interface demands, but ultimately on the combined concepts of interactivity and direct manipulation. Engelbart's demo included the first public use of a mouse, and the sight of its pointer sweeping across the screen instantly collapsed the stark input/output rhythms of batch-process and command-line computing into a single, continuous sweep of user activity. Just as important, however, was the spectacle of Engelbart dividing his screen into distinct regions, heterogeneous in content but spatially adjoining, a feat demonstrated most dramatically by a window with a live audio and video feed to a colleague in Menlo Park, California. The computer – or more specifically, the screen – had clearly become a much more complex representational space, an *information* space whose surface owed as much to modernist collage as it did to brute force calculation. A crucial refinement came several years later when a team at Xerox PARC, led by Alan Kay (and including many of Engelbart's former Stanford colleagues), arrived at the realization that windows could actually *overlap*, thereby immediately imbuing the screen with the third dimension we take for granted today. As Johnson suggests, "The whole idea of imagining a computer as an environment, a virtual world, comes out of this seemingly modest innovation" (1997: 47).

While Engelbart's 1968 demo is the most venerable touchstone for contemporary human–computer interaction, there are other origin stories that bear repeating. Ivan Sutherland, for example, working on a PhD thesis at MIT in 1963, introduced Sketchpad, a system that allowed users to draw lines on a screen in real time with what we would today recognize as a light pen. Sketchpad is significant because it reminds us that the current hegemony of mouse and keyboard was not always in place, and indeed, there are indications that alternative input devices like light pens – which fundamentally alter the nature of one's bodily interaction with a computer – may once again displace the mouse (see this chapter's "Coda" section, below). Sketchpad is also significant in another context, the history of computer graphics (without which there would be no graphical user interfaces). Nicholas Negroponte comments:

The achievement was of such magnitude and breadth that it took some of us a decade to understand and appreciate all of its contributions. Sketchpad introduced many new concepts: dynamic graphics, visual simulation, constraint reduction, pen tracking, and a virtually infinite coordinate system, just to name a few. Sketchpad was the big bang of computer graphics. (1995: 103)

Sketchpad was a vector system, meaning that the lines and shapes drawn by the user were mathematical formulas (vectors) that could be reproduced at will on-screen. Vector images provide another important context for understanding the significance of Englebart's work because the latter led directly to Xerox PARC's refinement of bitmapping as an alternative to Sketchpad and the era's prevailing vector displays. A "bitmap," as many readers will know, is a grid or matrix of pixels ("picture elements"), which, not unlike a Seurat painting or a photographic halftone, yield a coherent visual image through the optical interpretation of the aggregate composition. Bitmapped displays are what permit the gorgeous, high-quality facsimile images that we see in many of today's digital humanities projects, but their significance is much greater. (Note that bitmap displays, which are also known as raster displays, can refer to individual image files in formats such as JPEG, TIFF, or GIF, as well as to an entire screen display; there is also a proprietary image format known as "Bitmap," or BMP, which is not to be confused with bitmapping as a general concept.) If vector images were the graphical inheritance of the computer's mathematical roots, bitmapped images were the visual realization of Turing's ideal of the universal machine: bitmaps enabled the computer screen to function as a representational surface capable of emulating *other* representational surfaces. Through bitmapping, the computer screen was transformed into a second-order or "meta" representational venue. This transformation quickly gave rise to intensive research on photorealistic rendering techniques in computer graphics as well as (eventually) the advent of hardware devices like scanners and digital cameras – which enable the computer screen to operate in the photographic tradition. (JPEG compression algorithms, it is worth noting, were introduced precisely to provide an image format that lent itself to reproducing photographic images.)

William M. Ivins, in *Prints and Visual Communication* (1953), his landmark survey of print-making technologies in the West, argues eloquently for the importance of photography and what he terms "exactly repeatable visual statements" in enabling the dissemination of scientific knowledge. Bitmapping, I would argue, endows the computer screen with much those same qualities and capabilities, and although Manovich is right to point to the origins of computer graphics in the vector images of Cold War radar displays, the visual authority of computers as we know it today clearly owes more to the advent of bitmapping. Taken together, however, Sutherland and Englelbart laid the foundations for contemporary computer graphics and today's graphical user interface through their competing paradigms of vector and bitmap displays; competing not in a strict commercial sense, but in offering alternative visions of the computer as a representational medium and as an information space.

Unlike bitmap or raster graphics, vector graphics are not well suited to representing continuous tone (especially photographic) images. Consequently, they may seem of little use in the digital humanities, where much of our work consists in providing high-quality facsimile renderings of documents, artwork, and other artifacts of cultural heritage.

However, because vector graphics exist as a kind of mathematical abstraction, with no one-to-one mapping to an external referent, they are scalable and modular in ways that raster graphics are not. Today the most popular vehicle for vector graphics is the animation tool Flash, which, characterized by its colorful, dynamic displays, is rapidly colonizing large segments of the Web; indeed, there are those who believe that at the level of interface design the Web itself will eventually be made over as an animated Flash-based environment, with static HTML (more likely, XML) documents existing as subsidiary, special-purpose content. Interestingly for our purposes, Flash is also capable of supporting embedded bitmapped images, suggesting that the representational field I described earlier has receded by one full order of magnitude and that vector graphics are now the true heir to Turing's universalism. (On the other hand, it remains true that all general-purpose screen displays, whether LCD or CRT, are rendered as bitmaps.)

To build a Flash animation, the designer creates a so-called "movie" consisting of a series of timed, sequenced, or triggered events. For some this may suggest that the Web is evolving into a medium that owes more to television than to the now-familiar (and comfortably humanistic) conceit of the "page." I would cast the argument differently. If, as Jerome McGann has repeatedly said, computers lend themselves to representing books because they exist on a different material plane, then vector images, whose mathematical construction allows them to operate in registers unavailable to raster images, may offer the opportunity for a similar re-conception of our current information spaces. Whereas Alan Kay's overlapping windows added a third dimension to our interfaces, event-based vector graphics may, I believe, give rise to more playful and pliable information *places*: interfaces that occupy a material middle ground between the bitmapped data objects they enfold and the bitmapped surface of the screen.

If all of that sounds hopelessly speculative and abstract, there are nonetheless some tantalizing glimpses to be had from the digital art world. Tomoko Takahashi's *Word Perhect* [*sic*], for instance, a Flash-based parody of a typical word processing interface: users encounter what appears to be a hand-drawn cartoon GUI, roughly limned in black ink on a white background. Typing generates crude, seemingly handwritten, less-than-perfect characters on the screen. Takahashi's word processor is fully functional, but the interface yields an inversion of the typical user-friendly experience, one that serves to underscore the distinctive materialities of both print and electronic textuality. Clicking the Mail icon produces the following set of instructions, which appear as a scrap of notepaper "taped" to the screen: "print the document. put into an envelope or ssomething similair [*sic*] which can contain the document. Go to post office and weigh it and buy stamps..." and so on, for another hundred words, including further typos and blemishes. Jason Nelson, another Flash artist, in a piece entitled *the last machine with moving parts*, deploys the color picker interface familiar to users of image processing and paint programs to control the sequence of events in an animated word poem. As the reader moves the picker over the color palette, arrangements of words are pulled in and out of the visual field. "So the colors / cover the wires," reads this text at one point – and so the brilliant disguises of Nelson and Takahashi's localized parodies of interface culture cover (and discover) the hardwired histories of our information spaces.

The Artist of the Beautiful

Mary Shelley's 1818 novel *Frankenstein* is often invoked in discussions of computing for its meditation on the dualistic nature of science and technology, and has long been read as a parable of the promise and the peril of the Promethean flame. Yet *Frankenstein* is also, importantly, a novel of aesthetics. The anonymous creature at the center of the text ("Frankenstein's monster") is described repeatedly as a "wretch," "a thing such as even Dante could not have conceived" (Shelley 1992: 57). In fact, the creature's visage is so hideous that apart from Victor (his creator), the only person who can stand to conduct an extended conversation with him is a blind man.

It might be tempting to adopt *Frankenstein* for my own ends and make Shelley's creature into a figure for the graphical user interfaces of the current day and age; wretched and hideous are qualifiers we can debate, but there is no doubt that most of our desktop views are oddly unlovely, dull and listless information spaces that, as has been pointed out many times, hew to the conspicuously corporate metaphor of the office. But I would like to turn instead to another, less well-known text in the *Frankenstein* tradition: Nathaniel Hawthorne's (1844) short story, "The Artist of the Beautiful." It is the tale of one Owen Warland, a watchmaker with an exquisitely refined aesthetic sensibility who, bored with crafting mechanisms in the service of "old blind Father Time," eventually succeeds in his experiments to "spiritualize machinery," imbuing a tiny, mechanical butterfly with the living breath of his artist's imagination:

> He produced, as he spoke, what seemed a jewel box. . . . This case of ebony the artist opened, and bade Annie place her fingers on its edge. She did so, but almost screamed as a butterfly fluttered forth, and, alighting on her finger's tip, sat waving the ample magnificence of its purple and gold-speckled wings, as if in prelude to a flight. It is impossible to express by words the glory, the splendor, the delicate gorgeousness which were softened into the beauty of this object. Nature's ideal butterfly was here realized in all its perfection; not in the pattern of such faded insects as flit among earthly flowers, but of those which hover across the meads of paradise for child-angels and the spirits of departed infants to disport themselves with. The rich down was visible upon its wings; the lustre of its eyes seemed instinct with spirit. The firelight glimmered around this wonder – the candles gleamed upon it; but it glistened apparently by its own radiance, and illuminated the finger and outstretched hand on which it rested with a white gleam like that of precious stones. (Hawthorne 1948: 235–6)

Unlike Shelley's *Frankenstein*, however, there is some ambiguity as to the true nature of Warland's creation – whether it is indeed a living creature or a delicate clockwork automaton. "But is it alive?" the onlookers in the story ask repeatedly. Warland refuses to answer definitively: "'Wherefore ask who created it, so it be beautiful?' . . . 'it may well be said to possess life, for it has absorbed my own being into itself; and in the secret of that butterfly, and in its beauty, – which is not merely outward, but deep as its whole system, – is represented the intellect, the imagination, the sensibility, the soul of an Artist of the Beautiful!'" (1948: 237).

As in *Frankenstein*, "The Artist of the Beautiful" is structured by the classic binaries of nature and culture, animate spirit and technological artifice; but it is also a story about form versus function, art for art's sake colliding with honest industry and labor. Warland's chief rival and antagonist is Robert Danforth, the village blacksmith, whose response to the butterfly is to exclaim, "There is more real use in one downright blow of my sledge hammer than in the whole five years' labor that our friend Owen has wasted on this butterfly" (1948: 238). These are the same binaries that have structured debate in interface and design since Apple introduced the Macintosh; it is not hard to hear the echo of Danforth's sledgehammer in the firm finger striking the Return key at the end of the command line, or to see Warland's labored handicraft reflected in the incessant mouse manipulations of the GUI. What role, then, should aesthetics have in interface design? How do we balance the competing demands of truth and beauty? For while most software and websites have pragmatic or functional ends, an interface such as Apple's OS X – with its zooming windows, gossamer transparencies, and luscious drop shadows – encourages us to cultivate an aesthetic sensibility even in the most mundane corners of the desktop.

Yale computer scientist David Gelernter has written at length on the subject of aesthetics in software design:

> Most computer technologists don't like to discuss it, but the importance of beauty is a consistent (if sometimes inconspicuous) thread in the software literature. Beauty is more important in computing than anywhere else in technology.... Beauty is important in engineering terms because software is so complicated.... Beauty is our most reliable guide to achieving software's ultimate goal: to break free of the computer, to break free conceptually.... But as we throw off the limits, what guides us? How do we know where to head? Beauty is the best guide we have. (Gelernter 1998: 22–3)

Gelernter, who often comes across as an unreconstructed Platonist in his writing, goes on to speak of "deep beauty," his term for an idealized integration of form and function that bears a striking resemblance to Owen Warland's statement (above) that the beauty he apprehends is "not merely outward, but deep as its whole system." Gelernter also quotes approvingly Ted Nelson's dictum that "the integration of software cannot be achieved by committee.... It must be controlled by dictatorial artists" (1998: 22). Historically, however, human–computer interaction has its origins not in the poet's eye in a fine frenzy rolling, but rather in the quantitative usability testing of the sort pioneered by Ben Shneiderman and his colleagues in the 1970s. (Shneiderman himself, interestingly, has just recently put forward the Renaissance artist/technologist Leonardo da Vinci as the inspirational muse for his vision of a user-oriented "new computing.") I propose to begin addressing the aesthetics of interface by narrowing the field to look closely at two projects, both from the realm of text analysis, and each of which, it seems to me, exhibits a "beautiful" user interface.

The first is a prototype tool called Eye-ConTact. Conceived and implemented by Geoffrey Rockwell and John Bradley in explicit relation to its predecessor TACT, Eye-ConTact is perhaps not beautiful in the superficial sense of being (especially) pleasing to look at; nonetheless, I believe the program well instantiates Gelernter's "deep beauty" in its stated approach to textual analysis. Rockwell describes its operations this way:

> Eye-Contact deals with the problem of recording the logic of an exploration by encouraging the user to lay out the fundamental steps in a visual environment. The user creates the logic

by dragging out icons and "connecting the dots." This has the advantage of acting as both a record of the flow of choices made and a synoptic description of that flow, which should make the research easier to grasp. (Rockwell, website)

Note then that Eye-ConTact requires the user to make explicit procedural choices which are then recorded and represented in an evolving graphical construction of each specific analytical operation. The software, in other words, serves to model a series of ongoing hermeneutical events (by contrast, TACT lacks the means to log a record of a user's operations with a text). Eye-ConTact is also a realization of what Bruce Tognazzini, who has had a distinguished career at Apple, celebrates as a *visible* (as opposed to a merely graphical) interface: "A visible interface is a complete environment in which users can work comfortably, always aware of where they are, where they are going, and what objects are available to them along the way" (Tognazzini 1992: xiii). Still another way of thinking about Eye-ConTact is as an example of what happens when an application adopts as central that which is peripheral in most other tools, in this case the History feature – an approach that offers the basis for some interesting experiments in software design (see also in this regard Matthew Fuller's essay on his Web Stalker browser). Eye-ConTact clearly illustrates the way in which a particular tool, rather than seeking to hide its user interface, can instead use that interface as an active – indeed essential – component of the intellectual activity it aims to support: "not merely outward, but deep as its whole system."

My second example is even more contemporary. In April 2002, information designer and digital artist W. Bradford Paley debuted a web-based tool called TextArc. Drawing upon publicly available electronic texts in the online collections of Project Gutenberg, TextArc produces intricate visualizations of novels and other literary works. Every word of the original text is rendered on-screen, both in a one-pixel font that reprints the entire work line by line clockwise around the perimeter of the display, and then again in a larger font, a cloud of words with those appearing most frequently clustered brightly in the center. Paley describes the result as "[s]ome funny combination of an index, concordance, and summary." Clicking on a word highlights all of its appearances within the visualized text as well as generating rays or spokes connecting them so that a user can study whatever patterns may emerge. The visualization is also dynamically linked to a clear reading text of the work and a keyword-in-context concordance, and together these tools offer a powerful package for textual investigation. What is most striking about TextArc, however, is not its analytical engine, but rather its gorgeous, luminescent fields of display that seem to subordinate traditional hermeneutics to more stochastic modes of knowledge representation. The visualizations have a marked aesthetic dimension, asserting their integrity on a purely visual register independent of any functional use to which they might be put. Paley understood this from the start, and indeed supports TextArc (which is free) in part by selling hard copies of its output, each offset-printed and ready for framing on high-quality paper.

TextArc has received a great deal of positive press, including mainstream coverage in the *New York Times*; yet the basic functionality it provides – word frequency counts, distribution patterns, and keyword-in-context displays – has long been available with other tools. The platform-independent Oxford Concordance Program, which was capable of generating word lists, indices, and concordances for text analysis, first appeared in 1981, followed by desktop software such as WordCruncher (1985) and TACT (1988). Yet all of these programs, as well as more recent packages like WordSmith Tools, deploy stark, ascetic interfaces very different from the illuminated constellations of a TextArc visualization.

Undoubtedly that contrast has much to do with the tools and development environments available to the authors of those earlier packages, as well as limited time and limited resources. These factors cannot be overstated: in one software project with which I was involved we spent eleven months of a one-year development period on the underlying architecture – which performed flawlessly – but mere days on the final user interface (all but unusable). Then the money ran out. Such problems are endemic to any institutional setting. But the digital humanities have also not yet begun (or else only just begun – see chapter 29, this volume) to initiate a serious conversation about its relationship to visual design, aesthetics, and, yes, even beauty. And just as Owen Warland's gilded creation fed the skepticism of Robert Danforth and the other artisans of his village, so too do conspicuous graphical displays often engender mistrust in contemporary academic settings – as though, like the traditional library carrel, our electronic surroundings have to be sensually impoverished in order to be intellectually viable. Visually suggestive interfaces are often derided as "slick," or "eye candy," or gratuitously "cool," or else – in an interesting bit of synaesthesia – too cluttered with "bells and whistles."

To understand what is at issue here we might return to Donald A. Norman's contention, quoted in the opening section: "The real problem with interface is that it is an interface. Interfaces get in the way. I don't want to focus my energies on interface. I want to focus on the job" (2002: 210). Interestingly, despite this fierce disavowal of interface, in their original typographic presentation Norman's words are printed in boldface, for emphasis. Pausing for a moment, we can enumerate many typographical conventions for cueing a reader: not just the weight, but also the size and face of the type, its justification, margins, and so forth. Not to mention more diffuse bibliographical features including paper, binding, illustrations, and even the size, shape, and heft of the codex. As scholars such as Johanna Drucker and Jerome McGann (among others) have long argued, these extra-linguistic elements cannot be written off as merely expendable or extraneous to "the text itself." They are, indeed, the working vocabulary of a particular graphical user interface that has become transparent to us only through long familiarity. All of us know how to *read* a modern newspaper or magazine in terms of its visual and typographic layout as well as its journalistic content. The debate over transparency in interface design that Donald Norman and Brenda Laurel (and more recently Matthew Fuller, Jay David Bolter and Diane Gromala) have all participated in thus mirrors the debate in the literary and textual studies community over the nature of a book's "contact surface," those physical and material features widely seen as incidental to the production of textual meaning. In both communities, the ideal of transparency is now being called into question and replaced with a broader awareness of how the visual (and aural, or tactile and olfactory) elements on page or screen function as integral aspects of the information experience, rather than as afterthoughts to some "pre-existing bundle of functionality."

Some may object that the language I have been using ("integral aspects of the information experience," "deep beauty," "deep as the whole system"), in addition to fostering a curious kind of New Critical organicism – for Cleanth Brooks, a poem was, famously, a well-wrought urn – is also militated against by actual information design practices, which frequently make a virtue of the deliberate and explicit segregation of form and function. We see this in markup languages such as SGML and XML, when data tagged with a descriptive schema are then rendered with external stylesheets. Or if not stylesheets then so-called "skins," which allow different visual themes to be swapped in and out of a web page or desktop application. With the appropriate skins a generic MP3 application can be dressed to look like a jukebox or a crystal radio or in a thousand other guises. Likewise, a site called the CSS Zen Garden offers a striking demonstration of the power of stylesheets to represent the "same" underlying content in a dazzling array of different configurations. Moreover, as noted earlier, interface is recursive: thus we can use stylesheets to skin our data, skins to thematize our browsers and applications, and desktop themes to stylize our information spaces. Do we not then see interface and application cleaving apart in precisely the ways Laurel and Gelernter speak against?

The truth is that the variability introduced by such effects is literally and deliberately only skin-deep. Standards compliance and validated code are essential. At the Zen Garden site, valid XHTML and CSS "cleave" in the other sense of that Janus-word: they work together as an integrated whole fused by the centripetal force of an open, community-based standards environment. Littering this "road to enlightenment," notes the site's designer, are the "dark and dreary" relics of the past: "browser-specific tags, incompatible [Document Object Models], and broken CSS support." The visual effects that play across the shimmering surface of a site such as the Zen Garden are now practical precisely because the Web design community has come to an understanding (as expressed by its standards and tools) that clearly regards a well-wrought information space as a deeply integrated system, not just a series of on-screen effects. Compare this to the state of affairs captured in David Siegel's old essay "Severe Tire Damage on the Information Superhighway," advertised as "an open letter to Netscape Communications and the WWW community," which details the baroque array of spoofs, tricks, workarounds, fixes, and kludges that characterized professional Web design circa 1996.

If there is a lesson here for the digital humanities it is simply this: just as interface cannot – finally – be decoupled from functionality, neither can aesthetics be decoupled from interface. Nor does talk of beauty always have to resort to mystification. I ultimately prefer the poet and critic Lisa Samuels to either Gelernter's neo-Platonism or Hawthorne's transcendentalism: "[W]e think that those parts of beauty which resist the translation back to knowledge are uselessly private and uncommunicative. In fact, they are what beauty 'knows': that knowledge is also – perhaps most importantly – what we do not yet know.... Beauty is therefore endlessly talk-inspiring, predictive rather than descriptive, dynamic rather than settled, infinitely serious and useful." The important new wave of software studies (led by Manovich, Fuller, Bolter and Gromala, and others), which cultivates granular, material readings of the inevitable cultural and ideological biases encoded by particular applications and interfaces, offers one way to offset the potential risks of unvarnished aestheticism, and this literature should be watched – many of its contributors are also practicing digital artists. In the meantime, in the digital humanities, where we deal with the rich and varied legacy of cultural heritage, we ought to think about what it means to be artists of the beautiful ourselves. As we will see in the next section, however, being an artist isn't always easy.

The Blake Archive for Humans

"The Blake Archive for Humans" is the title of a page that collects William Blake resources on the Web. It is authored and maintained by an amateur enthusiast who links together a wide range of material. As visitors quickly learn, however, the page defines itself in part through explicit contrast to the Blake Archive for "non-humans": that is, the *William Blake Archive* (WBA), an extensive scholarly text- and image-encoding project that has been freely available online since 1995, with funding and support from the Getty Grant Program, the National Endowment for the Humanities, the Library of Congress, and the Institute for Advanced Technology in the Humanities at the University of Virginia. As of this writing the *Archive* contains SGML-encoded electronic facsimile editions of some 49 separate copies of all 19 of Blake's illuminated books, as well as a growing selection of paintings, drawings, separate plates, engravings, and manuscript materials. The *Blake Archive* has also won the Modern Language Association's 2002–3 prize for a Distinguished Scholarly Edition, the first time this award has been given to an electronic project.

What could possibly be wrong with any of that? The author of the "Blake Archive for Humans" site expresses his objections this way:

> Their site may be complete and accurate, but it is not particularly easy to use, and it's chock-full of all the ridiculous trappings of the scholarly profession. While such things certainly have their place, they can also interfere with the appreciation of the actual work itself. On the other hand, this site is the only place you're going to find this many of the illuminated books in forms you can actually read.... And it, too is a work in progress, so it will only be getting better; especially when we all have broadband connections.

I will say at the outset that I am not a disinterested party, having been affiliated with the *William Blake Archive* since 1997, first as its project manager and now as a consultant. If, however, as Blake claimed, "opposition is true friendship," then the opinions expressed above offer a friendlier-than-usual occasion for examining aspects of the WBA's interface – and the development and design process that produced it – in some detail as this chapter's central case study in usability. For the phrase "the Blake Archive for humans" can't help but raise the damning specter of divided loyalties, the suggestion that the *Blake Archive*, with its admittedly formidable layouts of menus and button panels and search tables, may ultimately be more suited to a machine's vision than the human eye. And there is a certain truth to that, since the evolution of the *Archive* has been marked by constant trade-offs between the (perceived) needs of our (human) users and certain non-negotiable demands of our adopted technologies. This divide between humans and machines is the crux of applied human–computer interaction, and is nowhere more visible than at the level of the user interface.

The notion that the WBA is "not particularly easy to use" and "chock-full" of "scholarly trappings" in fact typifies a certain range of responses we have received over the years. On the one hand, while we are happy to have users from many different constituencies, the site's primary mission has always been expressly conceived as scholarly research. To a certain point we make no apologies for that, since we emphatically believe there is place for serious humanities scholarship – presented in all its customary "completeness and accuracy" – on the Web. On the other hand, however, the comments I quoted above clearly speak to a real, felt frustration that the most comprehensive online resource on its subject should sometimes prove awkward for the non-specialist to navigate and use. Don't we understand (I hear these users saying) that what really matters here is *Blake*, and access to "the actual work itself?" Sometimes a particular feature of the site, which may appear intrusive to lay users (one of those aforementioned bells and whistles), is indeed there for more specialized audiences; for example, the ImageSizer applet, which allows scholars to display Blake's work on-screen at its true physical dimensions. This slippage between scholarly complexity and bad design is suggestive, however, and deserving of further study – many years ago, in the pages of the *New York Times Review of Books*, Lewis Mumford and Edmund Wilson famously railed against the user interfaces they found in the edited texts of the Center for Editions of American Authors, with their "barbed wire" thickets of scholarly apparatus. I suspect something of that same dynamic is at work here, and the challenge would seem to lie in distinguishing legitimate intellectual complexity from what is merely a poorly executed design.

But that is perhaps easier said than done. The interface users encounter when they come to the *Archive* on the Web today is known to us behind the scenes as "WBA 2.0." In 2000–1 we undertook a major overhaul that introduced several new features into the *Archive* and also remedied certain design flaws that had been noted by users and reviewers.

As Stuart Curran wrote in his review of the 1.0 version of the site (figure 34.1), the then-current design was "luckily malleable and [could] be altered to accommodate altering circumstances." The revised design we see in WBA 2.0 (figure 34.2) clearly has been altered in a number of ways, and there is not space here to discuss all of them. A modest interface element, such as the arrow icons that are visible just beneath the pull-down menus toward the bottom of the screen, serves well to illustrate the nature of the revision process. The problem was that users who wished to view the images of a work in sequence were forced to scroll down the page to examine the image and perhaps work with the transcription, enlargement, or other associated features, and then scroll back up again to where the "Previous" and "Next" links were located. Moreover, the long vertical profile of the page meant that its top and bottom halves could not both be kept on-screen at the same time. This turned out to be particularly awkward in classroom settings, where the instructor was forced to do much scrolling upwards and downwards in order present students with a sequential series of images. The arrows situated in the lower portion of the screen now alleviate that extraneous scrolling, a simple design solution to a more or less straightforward usability problem.

The generous screen-space around the facsimile image of Blake's work (which contributes significantly to the page's vertical dimensions) is partly the result of the display area for our ImageSizer applet, but it is also a product of the site's aesthetic values. From the outset, the WBA was conceived as an image-based resource, with the "actual work itself" (to borrow our friendly critic's phrase) visibly central to the user's active eye, and buttons, links, and apparatus positioned either above or below. While the earlier version of the site relied on a tables layout for its presentation of this apparatus, WBA 2.0 employs pull-down menus. The pull-downs offer an efficient way to condense a number of different user options, but there was considerable internal debate among the project team as to whether or not they were the right solution. I reproduce below an abridged version of a long and

Figure 34.1 WBA 1.0: The *William Blake Archive* (1997–2001)

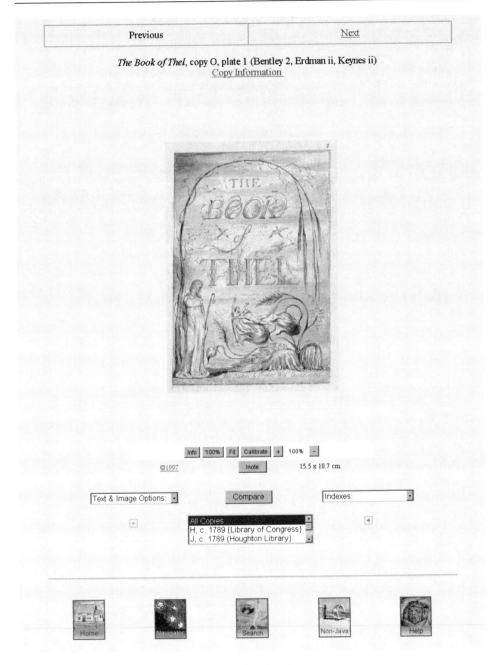

Figure 34.2   WBA 2.0: *William Blake Archive* (2001 to the present)

thoughtful piece of e-mail from Morris Eaves, one of the WBA's three general editors (Eaves, e-mail to blake-proj Discussion List, "WBA 2.0." July 11, 2000), not only because it captures well the flavor of those internal discussions, but also because it illustrates the way in which humanities scholars are nowadays thrust into the role of interface designer –

an impromptu role that some are quite comfortable in assuming, while others find it altogether unnatural. Eaves is clearly in the former category:

> I'm pretty sure I've read the whole discussion of the WBA 2.0 interface from start to finish. I know that time is short – but one of the nicest things about these digital confections is that they can be changed. . . . Here are a few personal reactions to the options that have been presented and discussed: . . .
>
> For me at least, there's a small chasm between form and function here. We all want the page to look good, and we all want it to respond readily and efficiently to the user's needs. . . . The way to make it look the best, probably, is to put everything on the page except the image behind a digital curtain and hide it from users until they want to do something – then they can open the curtain, rummage through those ugly old technical contents (previous/next, comparisons, enlargements, indexes, etc.) to find what they want, and close the curtain again to recreate the pretty image on a nice, paperlike background. . . .
>
> On the other hand, the way to make the page function the best is probably to pull down the curtain, arrange all the tools neatly, and label them clearly, so that the user always has everything needful right at hand. Commercial kitchens usually have open shelves and overhead racks; home kitchens usually have doors on the cabinets and tools in drawers that close.
>
> One of our problems is that our user's toolbox is so large – much larger than the toolbox of a book-reader. So we have a lot more to label, organize, and (maybe) hide until needed. . . . It's worth remembering how hard it is for us to look at this stuff without insider's prejudice – after all, we've been using Imagesizer and Inote and several of the other functions available in those lower areas of the page for a very long time now, so we constitute the least confusable set of users on earth. But I think it's very hard to imagine other users – and I don't mean dumb users, I mean very smart, alert, expert Blakean users – who wouldn't welcome some visual help in organizing that formidable display of tools and information below the image.
>
> PS: Final confession about *my* kitchen: Georgia and I have two big commercial overhead racks full of hanging stuff, but then, at her insistence, we also have doors on our cabinets and drawers that close. I may be showing my hand when I say that I've never been completely happy about those doors on the cabinets – we built open shelves in our Albuquerque kitchen and I always loved them. The Rochester kitchen compromise must have something to do with living together for 100 years.

As it happens, we arrived at a similar compromise (in much less time) for WBA 2.0, the doors variously put on and left off different interface elements. And as both Curran and Eaves note, "digital confections" like the WBA can always be changed – at least in theory. But in practice, as I suggested in my introduction, the interface tends to come very late in a project's development cycle (Eaves's recognition above that "time is short" is a reference to the fact that our lead programmer was about to be reassigned to another project). Most digital humanities scholarship is produced incrementally, in layers; at least for large-scale projects like the WBA, housed within particular institutional ecosystems, those layers tend to be more sedentary than we like to admit. The truth is that WBA 2.0 is unlikely to change much in its interface until the site's next major incarnation as WBA 3.0.

There is also another consideration, beyond the exigencies of project management. The conventional wisdom, reinforced by commercial marketing campaigns like Microsoft's

"Where Do You Want to Go Today?" and AT&T's "You Will," is that computers can do just about anything we want them to do. As programmers and developers know, however, there are always limitations that come with particular hardware and software environments, and those limitations render the computer an eminently material medium, this materiality not so different in its way from the characteristic marks and traces left by Blake's brushes and burins. Both versions of the WBA, for example, rely upon Inso's DynaWeb software to provide the stylesheets needed to display our SGML-encoded electronic editions in a conventional web browser. We have, in the process, customized the appearance and behavior of the DynaWeb environment to such an extent that it may be unrecognizable from its out-of-the-box implementation. But while DynaWeb has been an enormous boon to the Archive, making possible (among much else) powerful search functions, its idiosyncratic architecture clearly imposes constraints that manifest themselves at the level of the site's interface. In the case of the navigation arrows that I discussed above, for example, some readers may have wondered why we opted for icons on the bottom half of the page but retained the textual "Previous/Next" links up top. The answer is that (for reasons too esoteric to detail) the DynaWeb environment could not be made to accommodate the graphical image files of the icons in the top portion of the screen. Curran, likewise, notes the strong hierarchical nature of the WBA: "the user must descend four levels to get to the texts of the individual illuminated works.... This notion of penetrating to an inner sanctum is, of course, antithetical to Blake." We have attempted to rectify this in WBA 2.0 through the addition of Comparison and Navigator features, but the broader point is that this particular order of things is largely an artifact of the DynaWeb architecture, which was originally intended to support not Blake's illuminated visions but, rather, large volumes of text organized in top–down hierarchical structures. The technologies we work with at the WBA thus constantly make their presence felt, visibly and palpably pushing back against the interface we attempt to enfold around them. This situation is particularly acute in the digital humanities, where necessity often dictates that we adopt and adapt tools and technologies that were originally developed for other needs and audiences. If, as I suggested earlier, interface design is a dialectic between the competing demands of human and machine, then the art and science of usability lies in striking a balance between the two.

The *William Blake Archive* is – emphatically – for humans. But humans are not homogeneous, and different users will have different needs. While it will be impossible to please everybody all of the time, a design team must at least ensure that it is meeting the needs of its most important user communities most of the time. We believe we can now make this claim. Following the example of the large portals, more and more sites on the Web are also trending towards user-customizable interfaces, and this is a potential long-term solution for a project like the WBA. But it is a solution that, like all others, will have to be tempered by the non-virtual realities of staffing and development time, software and data standards, and project funding.

Coda: Magic Carpet Ride

The basic conventions of the desktop windows GUI have not evolved much since their popular inception with the Apple Macintosh in 1984. Until recently, however, our display hardware had not changed very greatly either (despite higher resolutions and the universal shift from monochrome to color). But if, as I insisted earlier, the addition of a glass pane in the 1950s irrevocably situated the computer within the sphere of visual representation, then everywhere today there are signs that computers may be on the verge of another broad-based shift in the tangible construction of their information spaces. The rise of featherweight laptops, tablet computers, PDAs, and wearable devices, on the one hand, and wall-sized or room-based projection and display systems, on the other, is even now wrenching apart the Procrustean setup of the desktop workstation, which has forced users to accept what hindsight will reveal to be an almost unbearably constricted and contorted relationship with our machines (while the ongoing pandemic of carpal tunnel syndrome and other repetitive strain injuries offer more immediate and irrefutable bodily evidence). In this same climate, HCI research has also convincingly demonstrated that the conventions of the desktop GUI do not scale well to either larger displays, such as one might find with wall-sized projections, or to smaller displays, such as one now finds on a PDA.

What, then, does the future hold? Of one thing I am sure: the typewriter and the television set will not enjoy their conceptual monopoly over our computing machinery for much longer. My own ideal system might look and feel something like this. I think of it as a magic carpet: a rectangle of thin, flexible, waterproof plastic, perhaps 3×4 feet, which I carry about rolled up under my arm (or folded in a bag). I can lay it out on any tabletop or flat surface, or else unfold only a corner of it, like newspaper readers on a train. The plastic sheet is actually an LCD screen, with an embedded wireless uplink to the Web. Applications, both local and remote, appear on its surface like the tiles of a mosaic. I move them about physically, dragging, shrinking, or enlarging them with my hands, pushing and pulling them through the information space. Text entry is primarily by voice recognition. The keyboard, when needed, is a holographic projection coupled to a motion tracker. Data are stored on a solid state memory stick I keep on my keychain, or else uploaded directly to secure network servers.

All of this may sound like over-indulgent science fiction – "Hamlet on the holodeck," to borrow a phrase from Janet Murray. But in fact, most of the elements listed here – wireless networking, voice recognition, keychain data storage, touch-screen and tangible user interfaces – are already in common use. And the rest – the motion trackers, paper-thin LCDs, and holographic input devices – are all already at or past the initial development stage. The "magic" carpet is actually just an extrapolation of real-world research that is ongoing at places like the Tangible Media Group (and elsewhere) in the Media Lab at MIT, the Interactivity Lab at Stanford, the Metaverse Lab at the University of Kentucky, the GVU Center at Georgia Tech, and the Human–Computer Interaction Lab at the University of Maryland. While the fortunes of any one individual technology will invariably prove volatile, even a quick scan of these sites leaves no question that the next decade of research in interface, usability, and HCI will take us for quite a ride. One of the major challenges for the digital humanities in the coming decade will therefore be designing *for* interfaces (and designing interfaces themselves) outside of the 13- to 21-inch comfort zone of the desktop box.

Works Cited or Suggestions for Further Reading

The Blake Archive for Humans. Accessed November 15, 2002. At <http://www.squibix.net/blake/>.

Bolter, J. D. and D. Gromala (2003). *Windows and Mirrors: Design, Digital Art, and the Myth of Transparency.* Cambridge, MA: MIT Press.

Carroll, J. M. (2002). *Human-Computer Interaction in the New Millennium.* Boston: Addison-Wesley.

Cooper, A. (1995). *About Face: The Essentials of User Interface Design.* Hoboken, NJ: John Wiley.

CSS Zen Garden: The Beauty of CSS Design. Accessed December 30, 2003. At <http://www.csszengarden.com/>.

Curran, S. (1999). Review of the *William Blake Archive. TEXT* 12: 216–19.

Drucker, J. (1994). *The Visible Word: Experimental Typography and Modern Art, 1909–1923.* Chicago: University of Chicago Press.

Fuller, M. (2003). *Behind the Blip: Essays on the Culture of Software.* Brooklyn, NY: Autonomedia.

Gelernter, D. (1998). *Machine Beauty: Elegance and the Heart of Technology.* New York: Basic Books.

GVU Center, Georgia Tech. Accessed May 16, 2003. At <http://www.cc.gatech.edu/gvu/>.

Hawthorne, N. (1948). *The Portable Hawthorne,* ed. M. Cowley. NewYork: Penguin Books.

Human–Computer Interaction Lab, University of Maryland. Accessed May 16, 2003. At <http://www.cs.umd.edu/hcil>.

Ivins, W. M. (1953). *Prints and Visual Communication.* Cambridge, MA: MIT Press.

Johnson, S. (1997). *Interface Culture: How New Technology Transforms the Way We Create and Communicate.* San Francisco: HarperEdge.

Laurel, B. (1991). *Computers as Theatre.* Reading, MA: Addison-Wesley.

Manovich, L. (2001). *The Language of New Media.* Cambridge, MA: MIT Press.

McGann, J. (1993). *Black Riders: The Visible Language of Modernism.* Princeton, NJ: Princeton University Press.

Metaverse Lab, University of Kentucky. Accessed November 15, 2002. At <http://www.metaverselab.org/>.

Negroponte, N. (1995). *Being Digital.* New York: Knopf.

Nelson, J. (2000). *The Last Machine with Moving Parts.* Accessed May 14, 2003. At <http://www.heliozoa.com/ending3.html>.

Nielsen, J. (2000). *Designing Web Usability: The Practice of Simplicity.* Indianapolis: New Riders Publishing.

Norman, D. A. (1990). Why Interfaces Don't Work. In B. Laurel (ed.), *The Art of Human–Computer Interface Design* (pp. 209–19). Reading, MA: Addison Wesley.

——(2002). *The Design of Everyday Things.* New York: Basic Books.

Paley, B. *TextArc.* Accessed November 15, 2002. At <http://www.textarc.org>.

Raskin, J. (2000). *The Humane Interface: New Directions for Designing Interactive Systems.* Boston: Addison-Wesley.

Rockwell, G. Eye-ConTact: Towards a New Design for Text-Analysis Tools. *Computers and the Humanities Working Papers.* November 15, 2002. At <http://www.chass.utoronto.ca/epc/chwp/rockwell/index.html>.

Samuels, L. (1997). Poetry and the Problem of Beauty. *Modern Language Studies* 27, 2. At <http://epc.buffalo.edu/authors/samuels/beauty.html>.

Shelley, M. (1992). *Frankenstein,* ed. M. Hindle. London: Penguin Classics.

Shneiderman, B. (1998). *Designing the User Interface: Strategies for Effective Human–Computer Interaction.* Reading, MA: Addison-Wesley.

——(2002). *Leonardo's Laptop: Human Needs and the New Computing Technologies.* Cambridge, MA: MIT Press.

Siegel, D. (1995–6). Severe Tire Damage on the Information Superhighway. At <http://www.dsiegel.com/damage/index.html>.

Stephenson, N. (1999). *In the Beginning Was the Command Line*. New York: Avon.

Takahashi, T. *Word Perhect*. Accessed May 14, 2003. At <http://www.e-2.org/commissions _wordperhect.html>.

Tangible Media Group, MIT Media Lab. Accessed May 16, 2003. At <http://tangible.media.mit.edu/>.

Tognazzini, B. (1992). *Tog on Interface*. Reading, MA: Addison-Wesley.

William Blake Archive. Eds. M. Eaves, R. N. Essick, and J. Viscomi. Accessed November 15, 2002. At <http://www.blakearchive.org>.

35

Intermediation and its Malcontents: Validating Professionalism in the Age of Raw Dissemination

Michael Jensen

Over the last few years it has become clear that digital publishing is far more than just making a digital version of paper available online. Rather, we are (finally) beginning to view networked e-content as a new form of publication in its own right, with its own strengths and weaknesses, its own imperatives, its own necessary logics. What I hope to do in the next few thousands of words is to explore the issues of networked publishing from a nonprofit publisher's perspective, having been involved in computers and digital publishing within the nonprofit publishing world since the late 1980s.

I'll make a case, I hope, for encouraging a broader engagement between the many sectors within scholarly communication (publishers, scholars, libraries, technologists, editors, collaborators) by dint of common fundamental mission, audiences, and funding sources. Further, I hope to survey some of the themes that are important to consider as networked publishing matures from its infancy, matters of significance to anyone considering the issues raised by digital publications in the new century. Finally, I hope to address the value of professionalism in the digital publishing arena.

The Nonprofit's Metamission

At an Online Computer Library Center (OCLC) conference in the late 1990s, the new President of the University of Arizona, Peter. W. Likins, made an intellectually compelling distinction that I've tried to promote ever since:

> A for-profit's mission is to create as much value for its stockholders as possible, within the constraints of society. The non-profit's mission is to create as much value for society as possible, within the constraints of its money.

The academic and educational communication sectors have much in common, which ought to be driving many of the trends in online communication. How do we take advantage of this moment of unparalleled interconnectivity to "create as much value for society as possible," given the cultural constraints on our money? Do we maintain the same structures as before? Do the new capabilities militate for a revolution?

Networked publishing is going through its toddler phase, it seems to me – stumbly, never quite balanced, uncertain of its size and abilities, and amazed and delighted by itself. One key to toddlerhood is an utter ignorance of one's own ability to be ignorant. To counter that, let me first outline what I think are some of the constraints and capabilities of the current system – from the perspective of a nonprofit publisher.

The Current System

University presses, scholarly societies, academic publishers, and other nonprofit publishers currently perform a set of societal and scholarly roles, as well as performing a set of practical roles.

The societal and scholarly roles include identifying promising (and often nascent) scholarly research, encouraging the development of scholarly work, and enhancing the accessibility, readability, and comprehensibility of that work. In the context of scholarly communications in general, these publishers validate scholarly material, integrate and coordinate scholarship in discipline-specific collections, and (not least) provide authority for humanities and social sciences scholarship for tenure and promotion. They are also frequently publishers of what are called "midlist" publications – works which may sell between 500 and 5,000 copies, indicating a small (if committed) audience. It also can be the scholarly publisher's job both to provide a promotional context for a work, and to put the works into the largest context within the discipline or the field.

Everything Old is New Again

For an author, scholar, or scholarly publisher in the twenty-first century, the seemingly obvious approach to the new capabilities – and the seeming imperative – is to perform all these roles in the "e-arena." It's becoming ever more clear that this seeming simplicity is anything but simple. Let me lay out some of the complexities before moving on.

In the world of print publishing, there is a truism: that "journals publishing can't be done small" – that developing the skill-set and software for maintaining and applying individual subscription mechanisms is so costly that you need at least six or eight journals to share the costs. Otherwise, the publishing requirements and concomitant costs cannot be amortized across enough projects to make it affordable. Because of this principle, among the 120 university presses, only a handful have journals programs. "Stay with your strengths," says conventional wisdom.

That truism applies to technology as well. When the implications of the revolutionary changes of the last few years are taken into account, it becomes evident that entirely new systems have to be created to handle the realities of the New Publishing. It's not as if the set of problems a publisher must face is only transformed into a new set of problems when you factor in networked publishing. Rather, the diversity of problems – and the diversity of skills necessary to address them – blossoms. Entirely new problems, unconnected to anything from the print world, must be confronted.

A print publisher must deal with physical returns of books from bookstores, while strategizing about how much content to give away on the Press website. A print publisher must determine print run sizes (because most books are still generally more economic to print in quantities of 600 at a time than they are to "print on demand" – at least as of January 2004), while deciding whether to include a CD in the book and adding $10 to the retail price. A print *and* digital publisher must not only produce product, record-keep, and generate monthly reports on the order fulfillment of paper books (an inventory-based system), but may also need to produce, record-keep, and generate monthly reports on inventoryless material (e-books), and may need to do so on potential-inventory material (print-on-demand), and may even need to produce, record-keep, and the rest on subscription-based access methodologies. This is not a decision like "paper or plastic." It's rather "cash or coins or check card or credit card or check or voucher or foodstamps or green-stamps or goldstamps or barter." It's not only "transformed," it's metamorphosed.

The electronic enterprises themselves hold danger: it is painfully easy to choose the wrong preferred technology for an audience or discipline by misunderstanding their readiness for new technology or misreading their desire for alternative presentation modes. Or choose the wrong technology for material by force-fitting new tools on old content, or locking older accommodations to print restrictions into new presentations. Or choose the wrong technology for a changing environment and by so doing lock the content into a non-adaptive format. Or spend the publication budget on cutting-edge cul-de-sac software, or confuse "cool" with "valuable," or conflate readers with purchasers, or audience with customer, such as by presuming that by developing a site aimed at students to promote one's texts, one can entice the libraries serving those markets to purchase what their readers are acquiring for free. Or depend overly much on the novelty value of e-publishing, and believe that simply by building it, you will attract business. Any single one of these threatens to either beggar the publisher or compromise the project, and shouts "Danger!" to most publishers.

Those who have deep and broad knowledge of the processes of publication – publishing professionals – are vital in many ways. Who better than a professional publisher to help navigate these dangerous waters?

Appropriate Presentational Models

Every living reader today has grown up in a world in which paper dominated the informationscape in terms of authority, validity, and value. The primary models of argumentation and presentation in scientific and scholarly discourse are still predominantly linear, partly because of the nature of exposition and presentation in a linear-publishing, paper-based world.

This makes it likely that a large proportion of the output of scholars and specialists can be expected, whether consciously or unconsciously, to mimic the modalities of linear expression. Does that mean that most publications are served best by paper? Perhaps – though the answer to that question depends on many factors. Some material is ideal for online publication (reference works, huge resource bases, highly interconnected and changing material, multimedia collections), though there may be no simple cost-recovery system that can be implemented effectively for such publications. Other material may not be well suited to digital publication – novels, traditional monographs, linear argumentation of thesis/promotion/conclusion, poetry, art (still), typographically challenging material, etc.

Different media serve different content types more or less effectively; it's important to recognize what a medium is best suited for. A million JPGs couldn't tell the story of *Moby Dick* like the words do; a million words can't thrill like the Ninth Symphony. We are just discovering the potential of networked presentation, but shouldn't be seduced into thinking that Javascript or Flash is the inevitable best (or only eventual) means of communication.

Appropriate Cost-recovery Models

Just as there are media appropriate for particular communications, there are economic models appropriate for particular media, content, and audience.

"Cost recovery is destiny," and an organization's mission should dictate cost-recovery models. For nonprofit publishers with whom dissemination is the priority, new models are more easily implementable than with nonprofit publishers for whom fiscal stability is the prime directive. For associations, cost-recovery models are different than for corporately owned publishers. Fiction publishers have different uses of the medium than reference publishers do.

Distinguishing between the possible publishing choices is complicated. To make the best choices, one must understand appropriate (even available) technologies, appropriate cost recovery and maintenance plans, and what the appropriate media (and cost recovery mechanisms) are for the particular audience.

What model will work best with your project? Institutional subscription? Print-ready PDF for a fee? Print-on-demand? Time-based access? Free old material, charged new? Free new material, charged archive? Making these choices ain't easy.

"Free" Publishing

I once realized that a project I was directing was spending more on developing access-restriction mechanisms (for subscription-only access) than it was on developing deeper-exploration mechanisms. Over 60 percent of our development dollars were being spent *on keeping people from reading our material*. That seemed silly, and helped convince me that I should be a bit more open to alternative models for scholarly and academic publishing.

At the National Academies Press, we make more than 3,000 reports of the National Academy of Sciences, the Institute of Medicine, and the National Academy of Engineering freely available to any browser, hoping to encourage browsers to purchase what we consider to be an "optimal version" – the print book, or multi-page PDF. We recognize that nearly all of our publications are designed for print reading (being predominantly linear exposition of how the best science may inform issues of public policy), and so see the online versions as only a minor "threat" to traditional print sales. That's one model of "free" publishing – using the Web to promote the content, while selling the container.

In the new networked environment, there are many mechanisms of nearly "outlay-free publishing" – though it's worth discriminating outlay-free publishing from the mythical "cost-free" publishing. With enough volunteer labor, or hierarchical control, or browbeating, or passion, today virtually anything can be made available "for free" via online presentation. The work may not be best served by this model, but it is a viable means of presentation.

The Web makes such raw dissemination possible, and it's an exciting prospect. Today, we're still in the wonderful volunteerism phase, where individual labors of love and institutional experimentation into electronic publishing are going on. My worry is that volunteerism is reaching its limits as the true complexities of online publishing begin to demand cost-recovery mechanisms for sustenance.

Like many other volunteer efforts, e-projects have proven hard to sustain. Countless worthwhile volunteer projects have died when a central figure moves on, or when the project reaches that first grand plateau (after which the real work begins), or when the grant funding for the "e-project" is two years gone.

Promoting a Sustainable Scholarly Information Infrastructure

Especially in an online world where disintermediation is at play, it's my contention that there is still a need for some kinds of intermediation – for publishers to be involved in the "making public the fruits of scholarly research" (as Daniel Quoit Gilman, first director of the oldest University Press in the country, Johns Hopkins, so famously said). I'd further contend that it generally makes more sense for our culture to support nonprofit, networked publishing through its institutional mechanisms (university presses, association publishing, NGO publishing, and the like) than to either relinquish it to the commercial sector, or to presume that volunteerism will enable educated discourse and debate based on a rich, robust set of resources disseminated online.

To accomplish that, it's important to have cultural cost-recovery systems that support the right processes – that promote experimentation, expand dissemination and access, yet prevent disruption. Without an appropriate means of supporting the institutional acquisition, digitization, and presentation of significant resources, real dangers accrue, the likes of which I've personally witnessed.

The "Publishing Revolution" in Eastern Europe

I saw the results of those dangers first-hand, in another place and time. During the period 1990 to 1995, during and after the fall of the Soviet Union, I was involved in a sequence of educational endeavors helping publishers in Estonia, Latvia, Lithuania, Poland, Hungary, and Czechoslovakia adapt to new technologies, understand how nonprofit publishing worked in a free-market capitalist system, and helping university presses adapt to the new realities of technology.

By far the deepest experience I had was in Czechoslovakia, before it split into two countries. Throughout this period I worked with publishers and scholars, frequently visiting Prague and other towns, and watching as the totalitarian socialist model – which had strengths as well as significant weaknesses – was replaced by systems constructed by amateur capitalists who had at best a naive understanding of the nature of capitalism. This created a publishing system with significant weaknesses, as well as (perhaps) a few strengths, especially in arenas like public-value, scholarly, and educational publishing.

The Soviet model of scholarly publishing was tremendously inefficient. Every university published its own material for its own students: introductory biology coursebooks, collections of essays, lecture notes, monographs, specific research, all were printed and bound at the professor's behest. There was heavy subvention from the universities, which were (in turn) heavily subvened by the state. There was virtually no economic feedback in this system of scholarly publishing, because there were virtually no cost-recovery mechanisms at all, apart from a token fee of the equivalent of about 25 cents or so per "scripta," as the class publications were called. Hardbacks cost the equivalent of a pack of Czech cigarettes.

Editorial selection hardly entered into the matter at the "university publishing" level. Every year, a few works from university publishing were designated as worthy of being published in hardback, usually in order to give their universities a medium of exchange for publications from the outside, non-Soviet world (librarians still remember the awkward near-barter system between Soviet institutions and Western ones).

Often these hardbacks were lavishly produced, but there was rarely any relationship between "list price" and publication costs. The system separated all indirect costs to the point of immeasurability, by massive bureaucracy, and in fact discouraged any cost-containment systems based on merit or audience. Instead, decisions were based mostly on "old-boy" status. An important professor, for example, could insist on having 50,000 copies of his book on the anatomy and aerodynamics of bat wings printed (in Czech, without translation); this was to his advantage because his personal royalty was based (by the Soviet diktat) on number of pages printed, rather than number of copies sold.

Other state-run publishing houses also published scholarly work in philosophy, science, metaphysics, etc.; they had more freedom of choice of what to publish than university presses, but their work was also heavily subsidized, and prices and print runs were often at the whim of "important" people. Nonetheless, publishing was considered a social value, and publishers operated in that way.

When the Soviet Union collapsed, there were countless warehouses with hundreds of thousands of copies of the writings of Stalin which nobody would buy, even at the minuscule prices charged in the Soviet days, much less in the post-Soviet economic crises. And those warehouses also contained about 49,800 copies of that book on the aerodynamics of the bat wing. In Czech.

But that same socially supported, exceedingly expensive publishing industry produced a broad variety of valuable, diverse, and very inexpensive books, which deeply affected the habits of the Czech culture. New books came out every Wednesday, and book sales bloomed like flowers in a field – every square had bookstores, every tram stop had a cardtable with someone selling books.

When I first spent time in Prague, just after the November 1989 revolution, I saw everyone – and I mean the butcher and the hardhat and the professor alike – reading books. On the trams, the metro, the streetcorners, and lining up to pay a few crowns for new titles, the citizenry read books – not True Romance, or escapist potboilers but, rather, philosophy, history, science, metaphysics. The inefficient system of subvention had created a highly literate, exceedingly well-read populace, who read for fun, and read in depth, all the time.

When the revolution set in fully, suddenly universities, whose subventions were being completely reconsidered by new governments, were telling their "presses" that they had to become self-sufficient in two years, and many were told they had to start giving money back to their universities – that is, make a profit – in the third year (much like several major US university presses have been asked recently to do). For most of the Czech university policy-makers, their recipe for capitalism was: add a pinch of slogan-level ideas picked up from reruns of *Dallas*, blend with the flour of the Voice of America, add a dash of Hayek, and finally spice with an understanding gleaned from dinner-table conversations.

The resulting policies gave little consideration to the realities of publishing costs and cost recovery; had no understanding of the infrastructure needs of the industry (like distribution, and warehousing, not to mention computers, databases, editorial experience, knowledge); had no understanding of the place of scholarly publishing in the educational system; and no recognition that in a revolutionary economy, nobody would have spare money to make discretionary purchases.

Three years after the revolution, the prices for books were often ten to fifty times what they were in 1990. The publishers who were managing to survive did so by subsidizing their continuing translations of Derrida and Roethke with pornography. During that period, bookstores closed down everywhere. Publishers closed down across the country. Citizens stopped reading every day. By 1995, nobody was reading metaphysics on the tram. A quarter of the university presses I knew of were closed, well over half of the bookstores I knew of in Prague were closed, and the scholars I'd befriended were telling me that they couldn't get anything published any more – there were fewer outlets than ever.

This transformation was a sad thing to watch, especially when I'd been so delighted by the intense literacy I'd seen initially. The culture turned to free or cheap content (television, newspapers, advertising, radio, Walkmen) rather than to the new – and more complex – ideas contained in books. Promotion and branding became the watchwords of the day, rather than subtlety of analysis or clarity of presentation.

Let me be clear that I think that neither model was fully right: the absurd redundancies and inefficiencies of the Soviet system were far too costly for me to support. However, the result was frequently a marvelously high level of intellectual discourse. Regardless, the follow-on quasi-capitalist system was far too brutal, and had consequences that they are still feeling in the Czech Republic to this day: far fewer high-level publications in their own language, far fewer high-quality scholarly publications in general (a significant problem in a small language group), and cultural costs that are hard to quantify but easy to identify as causing a kind of intellectual hunger.

What this has to do with the current revolution of digital presentation should be self-evident, though the parallels are somewhat indirect. We must recognize that we are in a revolutionary period, and we must be careful not to damage the valuable qualities of the current system based on inexperienced premises – that is, based on a naive understanding of the coming state of scholarly communication, which is based on a few visionaries' description of what is "inevitable." As users and creators of scholarly communication, we must carefully assess what qualities we want to maintain from the current system, and be sure that we create evolutionary pressures that encourage a "scholarly communication biosystem" which serves scholarship well.

My fear is that without some care, we may undercut (if not destroy) the valuable characteristics of our current nonprofit publishing system by revolutionizing it without understanding it. That is, if we revolutionize ourselves out of the ability to effectively support a nonprofit industry disseminating public value, we will have done more harm than good.

The Value of Publishers

Currently, scholarly publishers – specialists in the selection, preparation, presentation, and dissemination of scholarly material – are a valuable and necessary part of scholarly communication. There are some who are still under the false impression that in the new environment, publishers aren't necessary, just as there are others under the false impression that libraries are soon to be moot, or that universities are outmoded institutions.

In our "disintermediated world" there is some truth to all of those points. Every intermediary is potentially erasable by the direct producer-to-end-user contact made possible by the existence of the Internet.

It's true, for example, that some professors could teach students directly, without a university's intervention, or with only one big university's accreditation (and conceivably only a handful of professors); similarly, scholars could spend the time producing the complicated presentational structures required for effective online publication, without the need for a publisher. Universities could conceivably contract with mega-information providers for just-in-time provision of scholarly content using contractual agents, re-placing the need for an active library.

But I maintain that having specialists do what they do best is the most efficient model in general, and that intermediaries, though not required, will tailor the intermediation for particular audiences, and will identify and produce material preferable to non-selected, non-edited, non-vetted, non-enhanced material. None of the intermediaries I mentioned – the universities, the scholarly community, the scholarly publishers – will become moot in our lifetime, if for no other reason than the inertia of the credentialing culture combined with the inertia of presentation systems.

Enough Naive to Go Around

For well over a decade I've watched members of the computer scientist community and the librarian community naively discuss publishing as either a networked-database problem or as a distribution and classification problem, and conclude that they each can do the job of publishing better than the existing publishing institutions.

And while some very interesting and valuable projects have come out of both communities (SPARC, the physics preprint server, UVA's Etext Center, etc.), many of the rest were diversions of resources that I believe might have been more usefully applied to supporting and expanding the scholarly world's existing strengths in the scholarly/academic publishing arena. The shortcomings in the perspectives of the various interest groups are worth noting:

- Librarians too often think of scholarly content as primarily something to purchase, categorize, metatag, and archive (and provide to patrons), independent of the content's quality or utility.
- Technologists too often see the world of scholarly content as a superlarge reference set, crying out for full-text indexing and automated interconnections. "It's really just a bunch of XML content types," you can almost hear them muttering.
- Publishers – even nonprofit publishers – too often see the world of scholarly content as primarily composed of products, each requiring a self-sustaining business model to be deemed "successful." Unless a publication is self-supporting, it's suspect.
- And status-conferring enterprises (like tenure committees) seem to see innovative work engaging digital tools in the service of scholarship as being "interesting exercises" akin to, say, generating palindromic verse, or writing a novel without an "o" in it.

The humanities/social sciences scholar generally sees his/her work as an abstract and tremendously personal effort to illuminate something previously hidden. S/he sees technology simultaneously as a hindrance to, a boon to, an obvious precondition for, and utterly inconsequential to, his/her work. Scholarly communication is all of these, and even more. There are other players in the game of scholarly publishing: intermediaries, agents, public information officers, sycophants, supporting scholars and scholarship, student engagement, pedagogical application, external validation, etc. Each has its own interests and agendas, and sees the world through its own interest-lens.

The question scholarly publishing should be answering is "how can we most appropriately support the creation and presentation of intellectually interesting material, maximize its communicative and pedagogical effectiveness, ensure its stability and continual engagement with the growing information universe, and enhance the reputations and careers of its creators and sustainers?" If that question is asked, we are likely to answer it.

Without a mission driven by that question, the evolutionary result will be driven by the interests of the enterprises initiating the publication: library, scholar, nonprofit press, academic departments, associations – or, if the publication is initiated in the commercial sector, by the potential for profit.

Mission-driven Publishing

The projects with sustainable futures, it seems to me, are those which are joint partnerships between stakeholders – such as scholar/publisher enterprises, publisher/library, scholar/technologist, association/publisher, association/scholar/publisher, etc. Hybrid vigor is a wonderful thing, and makes for hearty crops.

The History Cooperative (<http://www.historycooperative.org>), for example, is a joint project between the two major historical associations (the American Historical Association and the Organization of American Historians) and the University of Illinois Press, with technology participation from the National Academies Press. These groups form the executive core of a project enabling the integrated networked publication of History journals, on terms established by the executive body. Currently consisting of nine journals and growing, the two-year-old project is increasing its specialized tools, its interdisciplinary value, and its pedagogical utility. More importantly, it has helped these groups understand each other in a collegial environment of shared goals.

The National Academies Press is another example (<http://www.nap.edu>) – a publisher "run by its authors" in the sense that it is a dual-mission-driven publisher, expected to maximize dissemination of the 180 reports annually produced by the Academies, and sustain itself through print sales. This expert/publisher/technologist project has resulted in 3,000+ reports being browsed by 7 million visitors for free in 2002. Every page is accessible for free, yet tens of thousands of book orders annually support the enterprise.

Project Muse (<http://muse.jhu.edu>), a joint publisher/library/journal project, uses institutional subscription to make itself available online. Within subscribed organizations, free unlimited browsing of over 100 journals is enabled.

CIAO, the Columbia International Affairs Online (<http://www.ciaonet.org>), is a joint publisher/technologist/library project, providing a resource pertaining to International Affairs that combines formal, informal, primary, secondary, and "gray" literature together in a coherent, institutional-subscription-based context.

The University of Virginia Press's Electronic Imprint (<http://www.ei.virginia.edu/>) is leveraging the strengths of its University's electronic-publishing capabilities (IATH, the E-text Center, the Press), to craft sustainability models for significant electronic publishing projects. The Press's institutional skill (and ability) in processing income enables that craftsmanship, which may end up maintaining and growing important works of scholarship.

These and other examples of multiple institutions recognizing their common goals give strength to the hope that coordination is possible among the various stakeholders in the scholarly publishing arena.

The Big C

If the nonprofit stakeholders can coordinate, even slowly and gently, to achieve that mission to "support the creation and presentation of intellectually interesting material, maximize its communicative and pedagogical effectiveness, ensure its stability and continual engagement with the growing information universe, and enhance the reputations and careers of its creators and sustainers," then perhaps their shared interests will become clearer in confronting the Big C of educational and scholarly publishing: Copyright.

"The Big C" usually means Cancer, and in this context is intended to, since the principles of copyright are currently metastasizing in ways unhealthy for our culture. The principles of author's rights have been shanghaied for the benefit of the vested interests of copyright-holders: publishers, museums, rights-holders, and other potential parasites.

I'm generally disgusted by the intellectual and academic boat-anchor represented by intellectual property law in the newly networked world. So far, copyright law has done more to preclude full intellectual analysis of our digital condition than anything else in society. As an author, I certainly am glad to assert rights to my own work, but the blade honed to cut paper doesn't necessarily cut wood well, nor styrofoam, nor tin. That is, intellectual property law differentiates quite poorly between use types, which means that I can't glancingly allude (even transclusively) to someone else's work without risking lawsuits; I can't sample Snoop Dogg's samples without that risk; without risking legal action, I can't quote my own words (that is, if I've contractually signed away rights to those words). I certainly cannot harvest the video footage of CNN or the articles of the *New York Times* and the *Washington Post*, and then use that footage in a multimedia monograph, analyzing Bush's strategies for forcing a war attitude toward Iraq in the two pre-election months of 2002 – *even if it does not threaten CNN's or the* Times's *or the* Post's *cost-recovery mechanisms.*

Intellectual property restrictions, compounded by the attitudes of publishers, technologists, librarians, and academic bureaucracies, have left many writers and scholars dispirited. To acquire tenure, the scholar must have work published in print. To do that, great labor is required on many counts, but developing rich Webliographies is not one of them. Integrating intellectual-property-controlled material into one's own work is dangerous, unless it's done in the "dead" form of print.

In light of these barriers to full intellectual analysis of our own cultural and social condition, it's clear to me that something needs to change. Since the 1990s, nonprofit publishers have been kneecapping themselves, by routinely siding with the for-profit publishers on intellectual property and copyright issues, instead of working to develop more culture-friendly standards and practices by engaging more fully and flexibly with the authors, scholars, societies, associations, libraries, and academic institutions upon which nonprofit publishing depends.

By making these choices (often passively, by making no choice), the nonprofit publishers have allowed themselves to be tarred with the same brush that is painting the commercial publishers, who are seen as parasites feeding off the authors, rather than as participants in the process of scholarly communication. In this way the nonprofit publishing sector is impeding its own ability to be recognized as a resource; instead, it has allowed the meme that "all publishers are the same" to prevail. From my perspective, nonprofit publishers – academic, nonprofit, scholarly publishers – are very different from commercial publishers.

The Needful Intermediary

The naive belief that publishers are a needless intermediary permeates a great deal of the intellectual culture, mostly because so many publishers can be seen to be parasitic freeriders. Most truly aren't, I believe – we may be parasites, but it's hard work doing it. The value of the dissemination a good publisher can provide is rarely understood, and the ways in which nonprofit, academic publishers can assist the pursuit of knowledge have been poorly presented.

Remember the Likins quotation from earlier – "a for-profit's mission is to create as much value for its stockholders as possible, within the constraints of society." Commercial publishers are by definition trying to make money. But the nonprofit publishing world is by definition about something different, even if it's forced to confront the constraints of budgets and risk. In Likins's words, the goal is to "create as much value for society as possible, within the constraints of its money." That's what the National Academies Press tries to do for its institution – which itself is trying to create as much value for society as possible. We are part service, part business, part entrepreneur, part inventor, and an interesting model to explore.

As the publisher for the National Academies (the National Academy of Sciences, the National Academy of Engineering, the Institute of Medicine, and the National Research Council), we produce an actual physical entity – a book. Print is far from dead. In fact, it is our belief that for at least the next decade, without such an artifact, a National Academies publication would be perceived as something akin to a long, very erudite memo. We produce something that is a pleasure to read, thereby providing the prestige of a real book, an item that can be purchased and possessed, seen in bookstores, promoted in the world, and read in an office, a plane, a bathroom, or a tram.

The Press makes every page of its publications browsable online, and is almost certainly the most open book publisher in the world. We had almost 9 million visitors in 2003; reading almost 53 million report pages. That dissemination allows the recommendations of the reports to be communicated throughout the world to anyone wanting to read them.

The Press also disseminates and promulgates the works of the National Academies through traditional means. A colleague recently sent an e-mail to me and said, "I ran into an NAP title at Powell's yesterday. It was in the Agriculture section and had a picture of a field on the cover." That small impact – of being found serendipitously while performing concrete topical searches – is easy to underestimate, *when the goal is to provide value for society.* In contrast, that impact is meaningless – in fact not desired – for a commercial publisher.

The Press's business model provides an economic incentive at the institutional level for "push" marketing – catalogues, direct mail, e-mail marketing, targeted contacts of all kinds. Without a business underlying the enterprise, it's hard to justify the expense of, for example, space ads in a particular journal.

The Press also provides an economic brake for political influence from "big swagger-ers." Without a business underpinning, there is little to prevent the influence of a loud institutional voice from directing limited resources to his/her own pet project – like translating a Czech bat wing book. Similar waste is just as easy to generate via other "bad publishing decisions": bad online Webwork, insistence on "multimedia" or interactivity or animation for no communicative reason, poor design of a print component, insistence on four-color everywhere, dismal titling, and on and on.

We provide a business reason for good judgment, which can save huge amounts of money. A "print-on-demand" (POD) book may have a fixed unit cost – say $6 per unit – regardless of the print run. A unit cost for an offset print run can be as little as $1.50 per unit. The advantages of POD are certain, within certain constraints; the financial benefit of good judgment (predicting demand sufficiently to decide between traditional offset and POD) is not encouraged by a POD-only model. Without a business-based motivator, routine internal expedience will be the intrinsically rewarded model.

We also provide a business reason to generate "pull" – to enhance the search value and search visibility of National Academies texts within the context of the world's search engines. Without professional attention at that level, there would at best be spotty "search engine optimization" by those within the institution with the funds and staff to do so. There would be no systematic, institution-wide strategy to continuously strengthen the online visibility of all Academies reports.

Finally, we provide a business motivator that can justify underwriting the development of publishing enhancements. Since 1999, the NAP has underwritten the development of "special collections" software, the development of novel search and information discovery projects, and much more. These sorts of tools are justified because, on our website, they do a better job of engaging the value of our unique resources to readers. We want to promote that value, because any researcher might be the one visitor in two hundred who might decide to buy the book.

The Press is far from perfect, but it's a successful model of alternative modes of publishing, responding to the unique needs of its parent institution and authors, and to the media requirements of its primary audiences.

Conclusions

If there are four things I hope the reader takes away from this article, they are the following. First, the depiction of the collapse of a vibrant state of public literacy in Prague between 1990 and 1995, in which too-sudden changes in the economics of publishing resulted in the loss of cultural and societal habits that encouraged educational engagement. Naïve revolutionaries are usually the most dangerous. To editorialize, it's important to recognize that revolutions can too often end up in dictatorships of one kind or another. In this digital revolution, we in the USA are running the risk of ceding (by passive acceptance) the rights to the intellectual property of the public, nonprofit, and educational sectors to commercial interests, whose metric of value is commercial, not societal.

Next, I hope I made clear the need to acknowledge the limits of volunteerism, and to see that some projects require a foundation beyond the passionate involvement of a few people; that cost-recovery models can dictate the possibilities. A cost-recovery model can enable or inhibit more development, may encourage or discourage dissemination and access, or may allow gymnastics on the high wire, rather than simply forcing a static balance on the tightrope of survival.

I hope I made the point for a broader engagement between the many sectors within scholarly communication (publishers, scholars, libraries, technologists, editors, collaborators), and made a convincing argument that because of our common fundamental mission, audiences, and funding sources, we should be collaborating more with each other, and making accommodations for each other more often.

Finally, I hope that the underlying theme of publishing as a set of choices, with which professional help is useful, was clear. There are ever more potential traps that every publishing project of scope and depth must now recognize and elude. Choosing appropriate partners – outside institutions, intermediaries, disseminators – can make the difference between a project of scholarly/academic/educational significance and a publishing novelty.

Networked publishing will begin to mature in the next decade. I hope that we can work to ensure that it matures within a rich community of support and engagement, and that the public sector finds ways to add value to society through a robust culture of publishing.

36

The Past, Present, and Future of Digital Libraries

Howard Besser

Digital libraries will be critical to future humanities scholarship. Not only will they provide access to a host of source materials that humanists need in order to do their work, but these libraries will also enable new forms of research that were difficult or impossible to undertake before. This chapter gives a history of digital libraries. It pays particular attention to how they have thus far failed to incorporate several key elements of conventional libraries, and discusses current and future digital library developments that are likely to provide these missing elements. Developments of concern to humanists (such as preservation, the linking of collections to one another, and standards) are discussed in detail.

Why are Digital Libraries Important to Humanists?

Historically, libraries have been critical to humanities scholarship. Libraries provide access to original works, to correspondence and other commentary that helps contextualize those works, and to previous humanities commentaries.

As we enter the twenty-first century, digital libraries appear to be as critical to humanities scholarship as brick-and-mortar libraries were to scholarship in previous centuries. Not only do digital libraries provide access to original source material, contextualization, and commentaries, but they also provide a set of additional resources and service (many of them closely matching humanities trends that emerged in the late twentieth century).

Digital libraries allow scholars to engage in a host of activities that were difficult or impossible to do before. Libraries, archives, and museums have been gathering together high-quality digital surrogates of original source material from many different repositories so that they appear to be a single repository to users (for example, see the

Online Archive of California <http://www.oac.cdlib.org>) or Artstor (<http://www.artstor.org>). Researchers can now consult online facsimiles of rare works residing in a host of different institutions without having to visit each one. Students now have the opportunity to explore facsimiles of rare works and correspondence. Researchers who engage in lexical analysis now have the opportunity to count word/phrase occurrences or do syntactical analysis not just on a single work, but across a whole body of works. Digital libraries permit instructors and repository managers to reflect multiple interpretations of works, authors, or ideas alongside each other – a realization of decentered critical authority, one of the tenets of postmodernism.

But it would be a mistake to see digital libraries as primarily providing ways to access material more quickly or more easily, without having to visit a repository across the country. Though the promise of digital technology in almost any field has been to let one do the same things one did before but better and faster, the more fundamental result has often been the capability of doing entirely new things. It is very possible that digital libraries will enable future humanities scholars to engage in new activities that we haven't yet envisioned.

What is a Library?

Traditionally, libraries have been more than just collections. They have components (including service to a clientele, stewardship over a collection, sustainability, and the ability to find material that exists outside that collection) and they uphold ethical traditions (including free speech, privacy, and equal access). In the last decade of the twentieth century, both technological changes and reduced funding for the public sector led to significant changes in libraries. For the first time in history it became possible to divorce the physical aspects of a library from the (digital) access and services that a library provides. This has led to much discussion of the past and possible future role of libraries, and some speculation as to whether they have a future. In her discussion of why conventional libraries will not disappear simply because we develop online collections, Christine Borgman states that the conventional library's role is to "select, collect, organize, preserve, conserve, and provide access to information in many media, to many communities of users." I have argued, elsewhere, that the four core characteristics of a public library are: that it is a physical place, that is, a focus spot for continuous educational development, that it has a mission to serve the underserved, and that it is a guarantor of public access to information (Besser 1998).

Almost all conventional libraries have a strong service component. All but the smallest libraries tend to have a substantial "public service" unit. Library schools teach about service (from "public service" courses to "reference interviews"). And the public in general regard librarians as helpful people who can meet their information needs. Many libraries also deliver information to multiple clienteles. They are very good at using the same collection to serve many different groups of users, each group incorporating different modalities of learning and interacting, different levels of knowledge of a certain subject, etc. Public libraries serve people of all ages and professions, from those barely able to read, to high school students, to college students, to professors, to blue-collar workers. Academic libraries serve undergraduates who may know very little in a particular field, faculty who may be specialists in that field, and non-native English speakers who may understand detailed concepts in a particular domain, but have difficulty grasping the language in which those concepts are expressed.

Most libraries also incorporate the component of stewardship over a collection. For some libraries, this is primarily a matter of reshelving and circulation control. But for most libraries, this includes a serious preservation function over at least a portion of their collection. For research libraries and special collections, preservation is a significant portion of their core responsibilities, but even school, public, and special libraries are usually responsible for maintaining a core collection of local records and works over long periods of time.

Libraries are organizations that last for long periods of time. Though occasionally a library does "go out of business," in general, libraries are social entities that have a great deal of stability. Though services may occasionally change slightly, people rely on their libraries to provide a sustainable set of services. And when services do change, there is usually a lengthy period when input is solicited from those who might be affected by those changes.

Another key component of libraries is that each library offers the service of providing information that is not physically housed within that library. Libraries see themselves as part of a networked world of libraries that work together to deliver information to an individual (who may deal directly only with his or her own library). Tools such as union catalogues and services such as inter-library loan have produced a sort of interoperable library network that was used to search for and deliver material from afar long before the advent of the World Wide Web.

Libraries also have strong ethical traditions. These include fervent protection of readers' privacy, equal access to information, diversity of information, serving the underserved, etc. (see resolutions of the American Library Association – American Library Association 1995). Librarians also serve as public guardians over information, advocating for these ethical values.

The library tradition of privacy protection is very strong. Librarians have risked serving jail time rather than turn over whole sets of patron borrowing records. Libraries in the USA have even designed their circulation systems to only save aggregate borrowing statistics; they do not save individual statistics that could subsequently be data-mined to determine what an individual had borrowed.

Librarians believe strongly in equal access to information. Librarians traditionally see themselves as providing information to those who cannot afford to pay for that information on the open market. And the American Library Association even mounted a court challenge to the Communications Decency Act because it prevented library users from accessing information that they could access from venues outside the library. Librarians have been in the forefront of the struggle against the privatizing of US government information on the grounds that those steps would limit the access of people who could not afford to pay for it.

Librarians also work to ensure diversity of information. Libraries purposely collect material from a wide variety of perspectives. Collection development policies often stress collection diversity. And librarians pride themselves on being able to offer patrons a rich and diverse set of information.

Librarians are key public advocates for these ethical values. As guardians of information, they try to make sure that its richness, context, and value do not get lost.

As more and more information is available in digital form, a common misperception is that a large body of online materials constitutes a "digital library." But a library is much more than an online collection of materials. Libraries (either digital or brick-and-mortar) have both services and ethical traditions that are a critical part of the functions they serve. The digital collections we build will not truly be digital libraries until they incorporate a significant number of these services and ethical traditions.

Brief Digital Library History

The first major acknowledgment of the importance of digital libraries came in a 1994 announcement that $24.4 million of US federal funds would be dispersed among six universities for "digital library" research (NSF 1994). This funding came through a joint initiative of the National Science Foundation (NSF), the Department of Defense Advanced Research Projects Agency (ARPA), and the National Aeronautics and Space Administration (NASA). The projects were at Carnegie Mellon University, the University of California-Berkeley, the University of Michigan, the University of Illinois, the University of California-Santa Barbara, and Stanford University.

These six well-funded projects helped set in motion the popular definition of a "digital library." These projects were computer science experiments, primarily in the areas of architecture and information retrieval. According to an editorial in *D-Lib Magazine*, "Rightly or wrongly, the DLI-1 grants were frequently criticized as exercises in pure research, with few practical applications" (Hirtle 1999).

Though these projects were exciting attempts to experiment with digital collections, in no sense of the word did they resemble libraries. They had little or no service components, no custodianship over collections, no sustainability, no base of users, and no ethical traditions. We will call this the "experimental" stage of digital library development (see table 36.1). Because efforts during this experimental stage were the first to receive such

Table 36.1 *Stages of digital library development*

Stage	Date	Sponsor	What
I *Experimental*	1994	NSF/ARPA/NASA	Experiments on collections of digital materials
II *Developing*	1998/99	NSF/ARPA/NASA, DLF/CLIR	Begin to consider custodianship, sustainability, user communities
III *Mature*	?	Funded through normal channels?	Real sustainable interoperable digital libraries

widespread acknowledgment under the term "digital library," they established a popular understanding of that term that has persisted for many years.

By 1996, social scientists who had previously worked with conventional libraries began trying to broaden the term "digital libraries" (Bishop and Star 1996; Borgman et al. 1996). But the real breakthrough came in late 1998 when the US federal government issued their highly funded DL-2 awards (Griffin 1999) to projects that contained some elements of traditional library service, such as custodianship, sustainability, and relationship to a community of users. Also around that time, administrators of conventional libraries began building serious digital components.

As librarians and social scientists became more involved in these digital projects, efforts moved away from computer science experiments into projects that were more operational. We shall call this the "developing" stage of digital libraries. By the late 1990s, particularly under the influence of the US Digital Library Federation, projects began to address traditional library components such as stewardship over a collection and interoperability between collections. But even though digital library developers have made great progress on issues such as real interoperability and digital preservation, these are far from being solved in a robust operational environment. In order to enter the "mature" stage where we can really call these new entities "digital libraries," they will need to make much more progress in moving conventional library components, such as sustainability and interoperability, into the digital realm. And developers need to begin to seriously address how they can move library ethical traditions (such as free speech, privacy, and equal access) into the digital realm as well. The remainder of this chapter examines important efforts to move us in those directions.

Moving to a More User-centered Architecture

Both the early computer science experiments in digital libraries and the earlier initial efforts to build online public access catalogues (OPACs) followed a model similar to that in figure 36.1. Under this model, a user needed to interact with each digital repository independently, to learn the syntax supported by each digital repository, and to have installed on his or her own computer the applications software needed to view the types of digital objects supported by each digital repository.

So, in order for a user to search Repository A, s/he would need to first adjust to Repository A's specialized user interface, then learn the search syntax supported by this repository. (For example, NOTIS-based OPACs required search syntax like *A=Besser, Howard*, while Inovative-based OPACs required search syntax like *FIND PN Besser, Howard*.) Once the search was completed, s/he could retrieve the appropriate digital objects, but would not necessarily be able to view them. Each repository would only support a limited number of encoding formats, and would require that the user have specific software installed on their personal computer (such as viewers for Microsoft Word 98, SGML, Adobe Acrobat, TIFF, PNG, JPEG, or specialized software distributed by that repository) in order to view the digital object. Thus users might search and find relevant works, but not be able to view them.

The user would then have to repeat this process with Repository B, C, D, etc., and each of these repositories might have required a different syntax and different set of viewers.

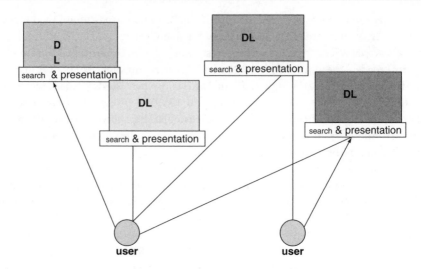

Figure 36.1   "Traditional" digital collection model

Once the user had searched several different repositories, he or she still could not examine all retrieved objects together. There was no way of merging sets. And because different repositories supported different viewing software, any attempt to examine objects from several repositories would likely require going back and forth between several different applications software used for display.

Obviously the model in figure 36.1 was not very user-friendly. Users don't want to learn several search syntaxes, they don't want to install a variety of viewing applications, and they want to make a single query that accesses a variety of different repositories. Users want to access an interoperable information world, where a set of separate repositories looks to them like a single information portal. A more user-friendly model is outlined in figure 36.2. Under this model, a user makes a single query that propagates across multiple repositories. The user must only learn one search syntax.

The user doesn't need to have a large number of software applications installed for viewing, and retrieved sets of digital objects may be looked at together on the user's workstation. The model in figure 36.2 envisions a world of interoperable digital repositories, and is a model we need to strive for.

Over the years, developers have made some significant progress towards the figure 36.2 model, particularly in the area of OPACs. Web browsers have provided a common "look-and-feel" between different repository user interfaces. The Z39.50 protocols have allowed users to employ a single, familiar search syntax, even when the repository's native search syntax appears foreign. Z39.50 has also promised to let user queries propagate to different repositories. But when one leaves the world of OPACs and enters the world of digital repositories, much work still needs to be done to achieve real interoperability. Most of this work involves creation and adoption of a wide variety of standards: from standards for the various types of metadata (administrative, structural, identification, longevity), to ways of making those metadata visible to external systems (harvesting), to common architectures that will support interoperability (open archives).

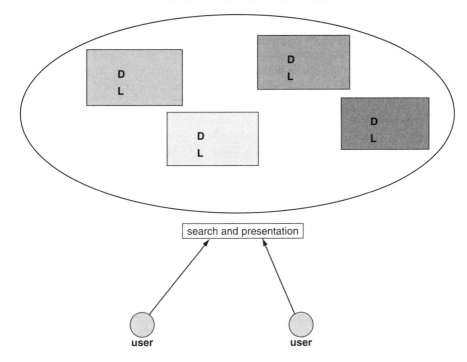

Figure 36.2

General processes and stages of technological development

The automation of any type of conventional process often follows a series of pragmatic steps as well as a series of conceptual stages.

Pragmatic implementation steps usually begin by using technology to experiment with new methods of performing some function, followed by building operational systems, followed by building interoperable operational systems. And at the later stages of this, developers begin trying to make these systems useful for users. We have seen this pattern (experimental systems to operational systems to interoperable systems to useful systems) repeated in the development of OPACs, Indexing and Abstracting services, and image retrieval. The automation of each of these has begun with experiments, followed by implementations that envisioned closed operational systems (with known bodies of users who need to learn particular user interfaces and syntaxes to interact with the system), followed by implementations that allowed the user to more easily interact with multiple systems (and sometimes to even search across various systems). Today's "digital libraries" are not much beyond the early experimental stage, and need a lot more work to make them truly interoperable and user-centered.

The conceptual steps typically include first trying to replicate core activities that functioned in the analogue environment, then attempting to replicate some (but not all) of the non-core analogue functions, then (after using the systems for some time) discovering and implementing new functions that did not exist within the previous analogue environment. Only with this final step do we actually realize the new functional environment enabled by the new technology. So, for example, word processors were initially built as typewriters with storage mechanisms, but over time grew to incorporate functions such as spell-checking and revision-tracking, and eventually enabled very different functions (such as desktop publishing). Our early efforts at creating MARC records began as ways to automate the production of catalogue cards, then moved to the creation of bibliographic utilities and their union catalogues, then to OPACs. Functionally, our OPACs began as mere replicas of card catalogues, then added Boolean searching, then title-word searching capabilities, and now are poised to allow users to propagate distributed searches across a series of OPACs. Today's digital collections are not much past the initial stage where we are replicating the collections of content and cataloguing that existed in analogue form, and just beginning to add minor functions. In the future we can expect our digital libraries to incorporate a variety of functions that employ the new technological environments in ways we can hardly imagine today.

The Importance of Standards

In moving from dispersed digital collections to interoperable digital libraries, the most important activity developers need to focus on is *standards*. This includes standards and protocols for open archives and metadata harvesting. But most important is the wide variety of metadata standards needed. The most extensive metadata activities have focused on discovery metadata (such as the Dublin Core), but metadata also include a wide variety of other functions: structural metadata are used for turning the pages of a digital book, administrative metadata are used to ensure that all the individual pages of a digital book are kept together over time, computer-based image retrieval systems employ metadata to help users search for similar colors, shapes, and textures, etc. Developers need to widely employ descriptive metadata for consistent description, discovery metadata for finding works, administrative metadata for viewing and maintaining works, structural metadata for navigation through an individual work, identification metadata to determine that one has accessed the proper version of a work, and terms and conditions metadata for compliance with use constraints.

Having consensus over metadata and other standards is important for a variety of reasons. Administrative and longevity metadata are needed to manage digital files over time, to make sure all the necessary files are kept together, and to help view these files when today's application software becomes unusable. Because of the mutability of digital works, developers need standards to ensure the veracity of a work, and to help assure users that a particular work has not been altered, and is indeed the version of the work that it purports to be. And developers need a variety of types of metadata and standards to allow various digital collections to interoperate, and to help users feel that they can search across groups of collections. One side benefit of reaching consensus over metadata that will be recorded in a consistent manner is that vendors will have an economic incentive to re-tool applications to incorporate this metadata (because they can spread their costs over a wide variety of institutions who will want to employ these standards).

The various metadata types

Libraries have had agreements on metadata standards for many decades. The Anglo-American Cataloguing Rules defined a set of *descriptive* metadata for bibliographic (and later, other) works, and the MARC format gave us a syntax for transporting those bibliographic records. Likewise, Library of Congress Subject Headings and Sears Subject Headings have for many years provided us with *discovery* metadata to help users find relevant material. In the last quarter of the twentieth century, other types of discovery metadata emerged to serve specialized fields, including the Art and Architecture Thesaurus (AAT) and the Medical Subject Headings (MeSH). Though both AAT and MeSH envisioned use in an online environment, both were developed in an era when indexing and cataloguing records might sit on a computer, but the works they referred to would not. And both were developed at a point in time when the merging of records from these specialized fields with records for more general works was unlikely to take place on a widespread basis.

The rapid acceptance of the World Wide Web led a number of us to consider how one might allow users to search across a variety of online records and resources, particularly when some of those resources received extensive cataloguing, while others received little or none. This led to the March 1995 meeting that defined the Dublin Core as a type of *discovery* metadata that would allow users to search across a wide variety of resources including both highly catalogued (often legacy) material, and material (much of it new and in electronic form) that was assigned only a minimal amount of metadata. We envisioned the Dublin Core as a kind of unifying set of metadata that would permit discovery across all types of digital records and resources. Library cataloguing records or museum collection management records could be "dumbed down" to look like Dublin Core (DC) records, while DC records for resources like an individual's research paper might either be easy enough for the individual to create, or might even be automatically generated by the individual's word processor. The not-yet-realized promise of the Dublin Core (see next section on Harvesting) was to provide discovery-level interoperability across all types of online indexes and resources, from the highly-catalogued OPACs to the websites and webpages of individuals and organizations. And because the Dublin Core has been in existence for approximately seven years (and has recently been designated as NISO Standard Z39.85), it is more developed and better known than any of the other types of metadata created for electronic resources.

Though the Dublin Core was developed as a form of digital metadata to be applied to works in both digital and non-digital form, a variety of other metadata types have more recently been developed specifically for collections of works in digital form. Below we will briefly discuss efforts to define structural metadata, administrative metadata, identification metadata (particularly for images), and longevity metadata. All these metadata types are critical for moving from a set of independent digital collections to real interoperable digital libraries. Hence they all incorporate functions likely to lead either to increased interoperability, or to the fuller and more robust services that characterize a library rather than a collection.

Structural metadata recognize that, for many works in digital form, it is not enough merely to display the work; users may need to navigate through the work. Structural metadata recognize that users expect certain "behaviors" from a work. For example, imagine a book that is composed of hundreds of digital files, each one the scan of a single book page. Structural metadata are needed for users to perform the normal behaviors they might expect from a book. Users will expect to be able to view the table of contents, then jump to a particular chapter. As they read through that chapter, they will expect to turn the page, and occasionally go back to re-read the previous page. When they come to a citation, they will want to jump to the bibliography to read the citation, then jump back. And when they come to a footnote marker, they may want to jump to where they can read the footnote contents, then jump back. These are all just normal behaviors we expect from any type of book, but these behaviors all require structural metadata. Without them, the book would just be a series of individual scanned pages, and users would have a great deal of difficulty trying to even put the pages in the correct order, let alone read the book. Structural metadata have a role in any kind of material that would benefit from internal navigation (including diaries and journals).

Administrative metadata maintain the information necessary in order to keep a digital work accessible over time. In the case of a digitized book, the administrative metadata would note all the individual files needed to assemble the book, where the files were located, and what file formats and applications software would be necessary in order to view the book or its individual pages. Administrative metadata become particularly important when moving files to a new server, or engaging in activities related to digital longevity such as refreshing or migration.

Instead of employing open standards for structural and administrative metadata, many individuals and organizations choose to encode their documents within commercial products such as Adobe Acrobat. Although this is highly convenient (particularly given the proliferation of Acrobat readers), it could be a dangerous practice for libraries and similar repositories. Commercial products are proprietary, and focus on immediate convenience rather than long-term access. Hence, there is no guarantee of continued compatibility or future access to works encoded in earlier versions of commercial software. In order to cope with long-term preservation and access issues, as well as to provide a higher level of structural functionality, in 1997 a group of US libraries began the Making of America II Project to define structural and administrative metadata standards for library special collection material (Hurley et al. 1999). These standards were further refined within the Technology Architecture and Standards Committee of the California Digital Library (CDL 2001a), and have since been renamed the Metadata Encoding and Transmission Standards (METS). METS was adopted by the US Digital Library Federation and is now maintained by the US Library of Congress (<http://www.loc.gov/standards/mets/>). The Research Libraries Group recently announced plans to lead the METS development effort.

Identification metadata attempt to address the proliferation of different versions and editions of digital works. In the print world, the publishing cycle usually both enforced an editorial process and created time lags between the issuance of variant works. But for a highly mutable digital work, those processes and time lags are often eliminated, and variants of the work are created quickly and with very little thought about their impact on what we used to call bibliographic control. In addition, the networked digital environment itself leads information distributors to provide a variety of different forms of a given work (HTML, Postscript, Acrobat, XML, and Microsoft Word forms of documents to support different user capabilities and needs; thumbnail, medium-sized, and large images to support image browsing, viewing, and study).

To illustrate the identification metadata problem, let us turn to figure 36.3, an illustration of variant forms of images. The original object (a sheep) is shown in the upper left corner. There are four photographs of the original object, taken from three different angles. Two of the photographs (A and D) are taken from the same angle, but photograph D has captured a fly on the side of the sheep. The images to the right of photograph D are variant forms of that photograph after image processing was done to remove the fly from the side of the sheep, while the images below photograph D show variant forms that include the fly. Spread throughout the figure are variant forms including different-sized images (thumbnail to high-resolution), different compression ratios (including both lossy and lossless), and different file encoding formats (PICT, TIFF, JFIF). Certain users may only want particular resolutions or compression ratios (e.g., a serious researcher may require an uncompressed high-resolution image). All the images illustrated in this figure share a base set of metadata that refer to the initial object of origin (the sheep), and adapting Leazer's idea of Bibliographic Families (Leazer and Smiraglia 1999), we can say that all the images in this illustration form an "Image Family" which shares a common set of metadata. Each image instantiation in the family also inherits metadata from its parents, and knowledge about that inheritance can often be critical to someone viewing a particular instantiation (for example, someone using one of the lower-right corner instantiations to study wool characteristics should be able to ascertain that image processing was done on a parent or grandparent of this image [to remove the fly], and that this image processing might affect the matting of the wool). Thus, it is critical that any image inherits important metadata from its lineage, or that systems at least provide ways that a researcher can trace upwards in lineage to discover metadata that might affect their use of the work. A first step in this direction is in the US National Information Standards Organization efforts at creating a Technical Imaging Metadata Standard that incorporates "change history" and "source data" (NISO 2002). But our community has much more work to do in order to provide the type of identification of variant forms that users (particularly researchers) have come to expect from libraries of analogue materials. And we still need to come to grips with the problem of how to preserve dynamic documents – documents that are essentially alive, and changing on a daily basis.

As digital library developers construct large collections of material in digital form, we need to consider how digital works will provoke changes in long-standing practices that have grown up around analogue works. Elsewhere this author has outlined how electronic art will likely provoke changes in conservation and preservation practices (Besser 2001a) and how the growing body of moving image material in digital form is beginning to reshape the role of film archives and archivists (Besser 2001b). But at a very pragmatic level, all repositories of digital works need to worry about the persistence of those works over time. *Longevity* metadata are necessary in order to keep digital material over long periods of time. While saving bits may be fairly straightforward, saving digital works is not. Digital works are very fragile, and pro-active steps need to be taken in order to make sure that they persist over time (for more on this subject, see the Digital Longevity website maintained by this author at <http://sunsite.berkeley.edu/Longevity>). Else-where, I have outlined five key factors that pose digital longevity challenges (the Viewing

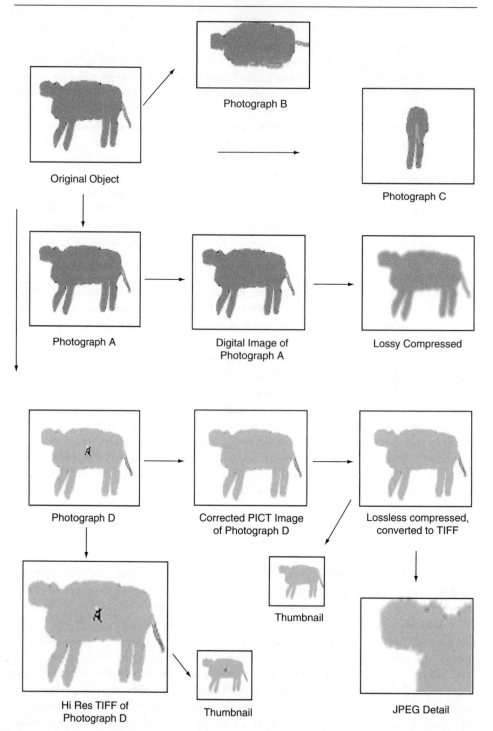

Figure 36.3 Image families

Problem, the Scrambling Problem, the Interrelation Problem, the Custodial Problem, and the Translation Problem), and have suggested that community consensus over metadata can be a key factor in helping digital works persist over time (Besser 2000). Recently, the major US bibliographic utilities have begun serious efforts to reach consensus on preservation metadata for digital works (OCLC/RLG 2001a, 2001b). Widespread adoption of this type of standard will make the challenge of digital persistence much more tractable. And late in 2001 the Library of Congress, with the help of the Council on Library and Information Resources, began a planning process for a National Digital Information Infrastructure and Preservation Program (see <http://www.digitalpreservation.gov/ndiipp/>). Widespread support for the emerging metadata standards mentioned here will greatly improve interoperability between collections and the sustainability of those collections over time. This will help us move away from isolated experiments with digital collections towards sustainable digital libraries.

Metadata philosophies and harvesting: Warwick vs. MARC

Though agreement on a variety of metadata standards is a necessary prerequisite for interoperable digital collections, implementation of interoperability also requires a set of architectures and a common approach to making that metadata available to other collections, middleware, and end users. In this section we will discuss two philosophical approaches to metadata, as well as methods for sharing metadata with applications and individuals outside the designer's home collection.

Libraries have traditionally employed the MARC/AACR2 philosophical approach to metadata. This approach employs a single overarching schema to cover all types of works and all groups of users. As new types of works arise, new fields are added to the MARC/AACR2 framework, or rules for existing fields are changed to accommodate these new works. And as communities emerge with new metadata needs, these are also incorporated into the existing schema. The MARC/AACR2 philosophy maintains that one big schema should serve all user needs for all types of works. Critics of this approach point out that the schema has become so overly complex that only highly trained specialists (library cataloguers) are able to assign metadata using it, and that the system is too slow to adapt to emerging types of works. They also claim that groups of users often have sets of metadata needs that the controllers of MARC/AACR2 are unwilling to accommodate.

In recent years, a rival philosophy has emerged from within the Dublin Core community. This philosophy, based upon the Warwick Framework, relies upon interlocking containers and packages of metadata, each maintained by a particular community. According to this philosophy, each community can support the packages of metadata it needs for its own particular uses, while still interoperating with the metadata packages from other communities. Under this philosophy, the Dublin Core serves as a unifying set of metadata to allow discovery across all communities. And even within the Dublin Core (DC), certain communities can employ qualifiers that meet their own detailed needs, while still providing useful metadata to other communities. (For example, the library community could use qualifiers to reflect the nuances of differences between main title, alternate title, transliterated title, and translated title, while other communities could find any of these as part of a search under unqualified title.) This philosophy supports metadata packages that are modular, overlapping, extensible, and community-based.

Advocates believe that they will aid commonality between communities while still providing full functionality within each community. This approach is designed for a networked set of communities to interrelate to one another.

No matter which philosophical approach one follows, any collection faces the pragmatic issue of how to make their metadata available to other collections and external searching software. The traditional library model was to export MARC records to a bibliographic utility (like OCLC or RLIN) and to have all external users search through that utility. While this works fine for MARC-based records, increasingly users want to search across a much wider base of information from a world not circumscribed by bibliographic records (such as web pages and sites, PDF documents, images, databases, etc.). Therefore, most digital collections are beginning to consider how to export reduced records into a space where they can be picked up by Internet search engines. For records following the MARC/AACR2 approach, this means extracting simple records (probably in DC format) from complex MARC records, and exporting these. For both the Warwick and the MARC/AACR2 approaches, this means developing methods for metadata harvesting that allow the appropriate exported records to be found by Internet search engines. A number of projects are currently under way to test metadata harvesting.

Best practices

Along with standards and architectures, community agreement on best practices is another important ingredient in helping make collections of digital materials more interoperable and sustainable. Best practices ensure that content and metadata from different collections will meet minimum standards for preservation purposes, and that users can expect a baseline quality level.

A key best practice principle is that any digital project needs to consider users, potential users, uses, and actual characteristics of the collections (Besser and Trant 1995). This means that decision-making both on digital conversion of analogue material and on metadata assignment needs to be carefully planned at the start of a digital project. The pioneering best practices for digital conversion developed by the Technology Architecture and Standards Committee of the California Digital Library (CDL 2001b) introduced important concepts designed to aid in the longevity and sustainability of digital collections. These concepts included differentiating between masters and derivatives, inclusion of greyscale targets and rulers in the scan, using objective measurements to determine scanner settings (rather than matching the image on a nearby monitor to the original object), storing in common formats, and avoiding compression (particularly lossy compression). This document also suggested that collections strive to capture as much metadata as is reasonably possible (including metadata about the scanning process itself). The relationship of best practices for scanning to the longevity of digital works is more fully explained in the Digital Library Federation's draft benchmarks for digital reproductions (DLF 2001).

The Making of America II Project (Hurley et al. 1999) introduced the idea that metadata could begin in fairly raw form, and, over time, move toward being seared and eventually cooked. This notion of incrementally upgrading metadata appears to have assuaged the fears of some groups that metadata schemes like METS were too overblown and complicated for them to undertake. In effect, this notion appears to have increased the adoption level of more complicated metadata schemes.

Other standards issues

A number of other standards issues need to be addressed in order to bring interoperability and other conventional library services to our emerging digital libraries. These include open archives, metadata harvesting, persistent identification, helping users find the appropriate copy, and user authentication.

Metadata stored in local systems are often not viewable by external applications or users that may be trying to discover local resources. This seriously inhibits interoperability, and the ability of a user to search multiple collections. The Open Archives Initiative (<http://www.openarchives.org/>) is tackling this problem by developing and testing interoperability protocols that will allow applications to harvest metadata, even those residing in deep archives. The success of a project like this is critical to providing users with the type of access outlined in figure 36.2. In addition, this project's focus on e-print archives should provide users with a diverse body of content free of onerous constraints.

Persistent naming is still an important issue for building real digital libraries. Though the World Wide Web has brought us increased access to works, Web architecture has violated traditional library practices of providing relative location information for a work by instead providing a precise location address. Failures in the Web's precise location-addressing system (the URL) produce the most common error message that Web users encounter: 404 – File Not Found. Most of these error messages result from normal maintenance of a website (renaming higher-order folders or directories, re-organizing file locations). Librarians would never consider telling a user that to find the book they're seeking they must go to the third tier of the stacks, in the eighth row, the fifth bookcase, the third shelf, and grab the seventh book from the left; they know that once someone removes the third book from the left, the entire system of locating will break down. Yet, this is the type of system that URLs are based upon. In recent years there has been much work done on indirect naming (in the form of PURLS, URNs, and handles). But to replicate the power that libraries have developed, we need truly persistent naming. This means more than just the indication of a location for a particular work. Sophisticated persistent naming would include the ability to designate a work by its name, and to distinguish between various instantiations of that work and their physical locations. Just as conventional libraries are able to handle versions and editions and direct users to particular copies of these, our digital libraries will need to use identification metadata to direct users to an appropriate instantiation of the work they are seeking.

Ever since the advent of indexing and abstracting services, conventional libraries have had to face the problem of answering a user's query with a list of works, some of which may not be readily available. Conventional libraries have striven to educate users that some sources are not physically present in the library, and they have also developed both interlibrary loan and document delivery services to help get material to users in a timely fashion. But the recent proliferation of licensed full-text electronic resources has greatly complicated this problem. For a variety of reasons, it may be very difficult to match a user with an appropriate document they are licensed to use: certain users may be covered by a given license while others are not; the same document may be provided by several aggregators under different licenses; much of the online content is physically stored by the licensor (content provider) rather than by the licensee (library). Recent standardization efforts have begun to address part of this problem; the US National Information Standards Organization has formed the OpenURL Standard Committee AX (<http://www.niso.org/ commitax.html>) to allow a query to carry context-sensitive information. This will help a library authenticate their licensees to a remote content site. But there are still many more problems to solve in getting users appropriate copies (particularly when content licenses are complex and overlapping).

Still another critically important standards and protocols area that is under development is that of authentication of users. With more and more licensed content being physically stored by content providers, those providers want assurances that users accessing the content are indeed covered by valid licenses to do so. Yet conventional methods of user authentication (such as password or IP addressing) would allow content providers to track what an individual reads, and develop complex profiles of user habits. Legal scholars have warned of the dangers this poses (Cohen 1996), and it flies in the face of the important library ethical tradition of privacy. Work has begun on a project that lets an institution authenticate users to a resource provider without revealing individual identities. It still remains to be seen whether the Shibboleth project (<http://middleware.internet2.edu/shibboleth/>) will be acceptable to resource providers, yet still provide the privacy and anonymity that libraries have traditionally assured users. Success becomes more questionable in the wake of the September 11, 2001, US building destructions, as the US federal government has increased the pressure to eliminate anonymous library access (ALA et al. 2001).

The Next Stage: Moving from Isolated Digital Collections to Interoperable Digital Libraries

Conventional libraries have both functional components and ethical traditions. The digital collections currently under construction will not truly be "digital libraries" until they incorporate a significant number of the components of conventional libraries, and adhere to many of the important ethical traditions and values of libraries. And though our digital collections have made significant progress in these areas in the past seven years, they still have a long way to go.

For the component of interoperability, projects such as open archives, metadata harvesting, and structural and administrative metadata hold great promise. For the component of stewardship over collections, digital preservation projects have finally begun, but it will be some time before we will be able to say with confidence that we can preserve the portion of our culture that is in digital form. Additionally, developers have only recently begun to grapple with the issue of economic sustainability for digital libraries (CLIR 2001). For other components such as service to clientele, they have barely scratched the surface in one important area where conventional libraries perform very well – delivering information to different groups of users (by age level, knowledge base, particular need, etc.) in ways appropriate to each group. The California Digital Library and the UCLA/ Pacific Bell Initiative for 21st Century Literacies have recently completed a project to explore this problem (<http://www.newliteracies.gseis.ucla.edu/design/>).

Those constructing digital collections have spent less energy trying to build library ethical traditions into our systems, and in many cases have relied on those outside the *digital* library community (such as the American Library Association filing lawsuits on privacy and free speech, or the Internet Engineering Task Force developing protocols to preserve privacy) to work on upholding library ethical traditions such as free speech, privacy, and equal access. But as Lawrence Lessig has made clear, the choices we make in the architecture and design of our systems will limit the social choices we can make around use of those systems in the future (Lessig 1999). For example, some of our online public-access circulation systems purposely saved only aggregate user data so that no one in the future could attempt to track individual reading habits. While recent projects such as Shibboleth are trying to design library ethical traditions into the technological infrastructure, the digital libraries we're building still have not addressed many of our important library ethical traditions.

As designers build digital collections they will also need to uphold library ethical traditions of equal access and diversity of information. Both of these are threatened by the commercialization of intellectual property. As we see the increased commodification of information and consolidation of the content industry into fewer and fewer hands, less and less creative work enters the public domain and more requires payment to view (Besser 2002a). Commodification and consolidation also bring with them a concentration on "best-seller" works and a limiting of diversity of works (Besser 1995, 1998). The builders of digital collections need to go beyond content that is popular and become aggressive about collecting content that reflects wide diversity; instead of using the now-familiar opportunistic approach to converting content to digital form, they will need to develop carefully planned digital collection development policies. Developers will find that they need to closely collaborate with others both to leverage resources, and to ensure that the efforts of different organizations together look like virtual digital libraries to our users. Developers and scholars also need to be involved in these efforts, to ensure that a broad range of content eventually leaves the marketplace and enters the public domain. We need to involve ourselves in struggles such as the American Library Association's current effort to build a coalition to protect the "information commons" in cyberspace.

Digital library developers also will find that they need to maintain the role of the library as guardian over individuals' rights to access a rich variety of information, and to see that information within its context. They will need to continue to be vigilant about making sure that other forms of "equal access to information" extend to the new digital world. They would also do well to extend the "library bill of rights" into cyberspace, and they will find themselves having to struggle to keep the digital world from increasing the distance between "haves" and "have-nots."

Finally, in the move towards constructing digital libraries, we need to remember that libraries are not merely collections of works. They have both services and ethical traditions and values that are a critical part of their functions. Libraries interoperate with each other to serve the information needs of a variety of different user groups today, and expect to sustain themselves and their collections so that they can serve users 100 years from now. They defend their users' rights to access content, and to do so with some degree of privacy or anonymity. The digital collections being built will not truly be digital libraries until they incorporate a significant number of these services and ethical traditions.

ACKNOWLEDGMENTS

Extensive portions of this chapter were previously published in the online journal *First Monday* as "The Next Stage: Moving from Isolated Digital Collections to Interoperable Digital Libraries" (Besser 2002c) and in the Victorian Association for Library Automation's *E-Volving Information Futures* 2002 conference proceedings (Besser 2002a). This chapter also involves a synthesis of a number of different talks and workshops the author delivered between 1996 and 2002, and he wishes to thank the many individuals who offered critical comments or encouragement after those presentations.

REFERENCES

American Library Association (1995). American Library Association Code of Ethics adopted by the ALA Council on June 28, 1995. At <http://www.ala.org/alaorg/oif/ethics.html>.

American Library Association et al. (ALA) (2001). Library Community Statement on Proposed Anti-Terrorism Measures (October 2). At <http://www.ala.org/washoff/>.

Besser, Howard (1995). From Internet to Information Superhighway. In James Brook and Iain A. Boal (eds.), *Resisting the Virtual Life: The Culture and Politics of Information* (pp. 59–70). San Francisco: City Lights.

——(1997). The Changing Role of Photographic Collections with the Advent of Digitization. In Katherine Jones-Garmil (ed.), *The Wired Museum* (pp. 115–27). Washington: American Association of Museums.

——(1998). The Shape of the 21st Century Library. In Milton Wolf et al. (eds.), *Information Imagineering: Meeting at the Interface* (pp. 133–46). Chicago: American Library Association.

——(2000). Digital Longevity. In Maxine K. Sitts (ed.), *Handbook for Digital Projects: A Management Tool for Preservation and Access* (pp. 155–66). Andover, MA: Northeast Document Conservation Center.

——(2001a). Longevity of Electronic Art. In David Bearman and Franca Garzotto (eds.), *ICHIM 01 International Cultural Heritage Informatics Meeting: Cultural Heritage and Technologies in the Third Millennium*, vol. 1: *Full Papers. Proceedings of the September 3–7, 2001, Milan Meeting* (pp. 263–75). Milan: Politecnico di Milano.

——(2001b). Digital Preservation of Moving Image Material. *The Moving Image* (Fall): 39–55.

——(2002a). Moving from Isolated Digital Collections to Interoperable Digital Libraries. In Victorian Association for Library Automation's *E-Volving Information Futures. Proceedings of the 11th Biennial Conference, 6-8 February, 2002, Melbourne*, vol. 2 (pp. 707–25).

——(2002b). Commodification of Culture Harms Creators. Information Commons website by American Library Association. At <http://www.infocommons.org>. <http:///gseis.ucla.edu/~howard/Copyright/ala-commons.html>.

——(2002c). The Next Stage: Moving from Isolated Digital Collections to Interoperable Digital Libraries. *First Monday* 7,6 (June). At <http://www.firstmonday.org/issues/issue7_6/besser/>.

——(website). Digital Longevity. At <http://sunsite.berkeley.edu/Longevity/>.

Besser, Howard and Jennifer Trant (1995). *Introduction to Imaging: Issues in Constructing an Image Database.* Santa Monica: Getty Art History Information Program.

Bishop, Ann and Susan Leigh Star (1996). Social Informatics for Digital Library Use and Infrastructure. In Martha Williams (ed.), *Annual Review of Information Science and Technology 31* (pp. 301–401). Medford, NJ: Information Today.

Borgman, Christine (1997). Now that We Have Digital Collections, Why Do We Need Libraries? In Candy Schwartz and Mark Rorvig (eds.), *ASIS '97: Proceedings of the 60th ASIS Annual Meeting*, vol. 34. Medford, NJ: Information Today.

Borgman, Christine, et al. (1996). Social Aspects of Digital Libraries, Final Report to the National Science Foundation. *Digital Libraries Initiative.* At <http://dli.grainger.uiuc.edu/national.htm>.

California Digital Library (CDL) (2001a). Technology Architecture and Standards Committee (May 18), California Digital Library Digital Object Standard: Metadata, Content and Encoding. *California Digital Library.* At <http://www.cdlib.org/about/publications/>.

——(2001b). Best Practices for Image Capture. California Digital Library (February). At <http://www.cdlib.org/about/publications/>.

CLIR (2001). Building and Sustaining Digital Collections: Models for Libraries and Museums (August). Council on Library and Information Resources (CLIR). At <http://www.clir.org/pubs/reports/pub100/pub100.pdf>.

Cohen, Julie (1996). A Right to Read Anonymously: A Closer Look at "Copyright Management" in Cyberspace. *Connecticut Law Review* 28: 981–1039.

Digital Library Federation (DLF) (2001). Draft Benchmark for Digital Reproductions of Printed Books and Serial Publications (July). At <http://www.diglib.org/standards/draftbmark.htm>.

Digital Preservation and Archive Committee (DPAC) (2001). *Draft Final Report* (October 8).

Griffin, Stephen M. (1999). Digital Libraries Initiative – Phase 2: Fiscal Year 1999 Awards, *D-Lib Magazine* 5,7–8 (July/August). At <http://www.dlib.org/dlib/july99/07griffin.html>.

Hirtle, Peter (1999). A New Generation of Digital Library Research. Editorial. *D-Lib Magazine* 5,7–8 (July/August). At <http://www.dlib.org/dlib/july99/07editorial.html>.

Hurley, Bernard, John Price-Wilkin, Merrillee Proffitt, and Howard Besser (1999). The Making of America II Testbed Project: A Digital Library Service Model. *Council on Library and Information Resources.* Digital Library Federation (December). At <http://sunsite.berkeley.edu/moa2/wp-v2.html>.

Leazer, Gregory and Richard Smiraglia (1999). Bibliographic Families in the Library Catalogue: A Qualitative Analysis and Grounded Theory. *Library Resources and Technical Services* 43,4 (October).

Lessig, Lawrence (1999). *Code and Other Laws of Cyberspace.* New York: Basic Books.

McClure, Charles et al. (1987). *Planning and Role Setting for Public Libraries* (figure 11). Chicago: American Library Association.

National Information Standards Organization (NISO) (2002). Standards Committee AU. Data Dictionary – Technical Metadata for Digital Still Images (June 1). At <http://www.niso.org/standards/resources/Z39_37_trial_use.pdf>.

National Science Foundation (NSF) (1994). NSF Announces Awards for Digital Libraries Research; $24.4 Million to Fund Advanced Research and Technology Development by Teams from Universities, Industries and Other Institutions (September). At <http://elib.cs.berkeley.edu:80/admin/proposal/nsf-press-release.html>.

OCLC/RLG Working Group on Preservation Metadata (2001a). Preservation Metadata for Digital Objects: A Review of the State of the Art (January 31). At <http://www.oclc.org/digitalpreservation/presmeta_wp.pdf>.

OCLC/RLG Working Group on Preservation Metadata (2001b). A Recommendation for Content Information (October). At <http://www.oclc.org/research/pmwg/contentinformation.pdf>.

37

Preservation

Abby Smith

What is Preservation and Why Does it Matter?

The purpose of preserving cultural and intellectual resources is to make their use possible at some unknown future time. A complete and reliable record of the past is important for many reasons, not the least of which is to provide an audit trail of the actions, thoughts, deeds, and misdeeds of those who have gone before us. For the humanities – a field of open-ended inquiry into the nature of humankind and especially of the culture it creates – access to the recorded information and knowledge of the past is absolutely crucial, as both its many subjects of inquiry and its methodologies rely heavily on retrospective as well as on current resources. Preservation is a uniquely important public good that underpins the health and well-being of humanistic research and teaching.

Preservation is also vitally important for the growth of an intellectual field and the professional development of its practitioners. Advances in a field require that there be ease of communication between its practitioners and that the barriers to research and publishing be as low as possible within a system that values peer review and widespread sharing and vetting of ideas. Digital technologies have radically lowered the barriers of communication between colleagues, and between teachers and students. Before e-mail, it was not easy to keep current with one's colleagues in distant locations; and before listservs and search engines it was hard to learn about the work others were doing or to hunt down interesting leads in fields related to one's own. Those who aspire to make a mark in the humanities may be attracted to new technologies to advance their research agenda, but those who also aspire to make a career in the humanities now feel hampered by the barriers to electronic publishing, peer review, and reward for work in advanced humanities computing. The common perception that digital creations are not permanent is among the chief obstacles to the widespread adoption of digital publishing, and few scholars are rewarded and promoted for their work in this area.

In research-oriented institutions such as libraries, archives, and historical societies, primary and secondary sources should be maintained in a state that allows – if not encourages – use, and therefore the concept of "fitness for use" is the primary principle that guides preservation decisions, actions, and investments. (This is in contrast to museums, which seldom loan objects to patrons or make them available for people to touch and manipulate.) Of course, fitness for use also entails describing or cataloguing an item, ensuring that it is easily found in storage and retrieved for use, and securing the object from mishandling, accidental damage, or theft (Price and Smith 2000). Imagine a run of journals that contains information a researcher wants to consult: the researcher must be able to know what the title is (it is often found in a catalogue record in a database) and where it is held. He or she must be able to call the journals up from their location, whether on site, in remote storage, or through inter-library loan or document delivery. Finally, the researcher must find the journals to be the actual title and dates requested, with no pages missing in each volume and no volume missing from the run, for them to be of use.

In the digital realm, the ability to know about, locate and retrieve, and then verify (or reasonably assume) that a digital object is authentic, complete, and undistorted is as crucial to "fitness for use" or preservation as it is for analogue objects – the manuscripts and maps, posters and prints, books and journals, or other genres of information that are captured in continuous waves, as opposed to discrete bits, and then recorded onto physical media for access (see chapter 32, this volume).

The general approach to preserving analogue and digital information is exactly the same – to reduce risk of information loss to an acceptable level – but the strategies used to insure against loss are quite different. In the analogue realm, information is recorded on to and retrieved from a physical medium, such as paper, cassette tapes, parchment, film, and so forth. But as paper turns brittle, cassette tapes break, or film fades, information is lost. Therefore, the most common strategy for preserving the information recorded onto these media is to ensure the physical integrity of the medium, or carrier. The primary technical challenges to analogue preservation involve stabilizing, conserving, or protecting the material integrity of recorded information. Physical objects, such as books and magnetic tapes, inevitably age and degrade, and both environmental stresses such as excess heat or humidity, and the stresses of use tend to accelerate that loss. Reducing stress to the object, either by providing optimal storage conditions or by restricting use of the object in one way or another (including providing a copy or surrogate to the researcher rather than the original object), are the most common means to preserve fragile materials. Inevitably, preservation involves a trade-off of benefits between current and future users, because every use of the object risks some loss of information, some deterioration of the physical artifact, some compromise to authenticity, or some risk to the data integrity.

In the digital realm, there are significant trade-offs between preservation and access as well, but for entirely different reasons. In this realm information is immaterial, and the bit stream is not fixed on to a stable physical object but must be created ("instantiated" or "rendered") each time it is used. The trade-offs made between long-term preservation and current ease of access stem not from so-called data dependencies on physical media *per se*, but rather from data dependencies on hardware, software, and, to a lesser degree, on the physical carrier as well.

What is archiving?

The concept of digital preservation is widely discussed among professional communities, including librarians, archivists, computer scientists, and engineers, but for most people, preservation is not a common or commonly understood term. "Archiving," though, is widely used by computer users. To non-professionals, including many scholars and researchers unfamiliar with the technical aspects of librarianship and archival theory, digital archiving means storing non-current materials some place "offline" so that they can be used again. But the terms "archiving," "preservation," and "storage" have meaningful technical distinctions – as meaningful as the difference between "brain" and "mind" to a neuroscientist. To avoid confusion, and to articulate the special technical needs of managing digital information as compared with analogue, many professionals are now using the term "persistence" to mean long-term access – preservation by another name. The terms "preservation," "long-term access," and "persistence" will be used interchangeably here.

Technical Challenges to Digital Preservation and Why They Matter

The goal of digital preservation is to ensure that digital information – be it textual, numeric, audio, visual, or geospatial – be accessible to a future user in an authentic and complete form. Digital objects are made of bit streams of 0s and 1s arranged in a logical order that can be rendered onto an interface (usually a screen) through computer hardware and software. The persistence of both the bit stream and the logical order for rendering is essential for long-term access to digital objects.

As described by computer scientists and engineers, the two salient challenges to digital preservation are:

- physical preservation: how to maintain the integrity of the bits, the 0s and 1s that reside on a storage medium such as a CD or hard drive; and
- logical preservation: how to maintain the integrity of the logical ordering of the object, that code that makes the bits "renderable" into digital objects.

In the broader preservation community outside the sphere of computer science, these challenges are more often spoken of as:

- media degradation: how to ensure that the bits survive intact and that the magnetic tape or disk or drive on which they are stored do not degrade, demagnetize, or otherwise result in data loss (this type of loss is also referred to as "bit rot"); and
- hardware/software dependencies: how to ensure that data can be rendered or read in the future when the software they were written in and/or the hardware on which they were designed to run are obsolete and no longer supported at the point of use.

Because of these technical dependencies, digital objects are by nature very fragile, often more at risk of data loss and even sudden death than information recorded on brittle paper or nitrate film stock.

And from these overarching technical dependencies devolve nearly all other factors that put digital data at high risk of corruption, degradation, and loss – the legal, social, intellectual, and financial factors that will determine whether or not we are able to build an infrastructure that will support preservation of these valuable but fragile cultural and intellectual resources into the future. It may well be that humanities scholars, teachers, and students are most immediately affected by the copyright restrictions, economic barriers, and intellectual challenges to working with digital information, but it will be difficult to gain leverage over any of these problems without a basic understanding of the ultimate technical problems from which all these proximate problems arise. Without appreciating the technical barriers to preservation and all the crucial dependencies they entail, humanists will not be able to create or use digital objects that are authentic, reliable, and of value into the future. So a bit more detail is in order.

Media degradation: Magnetic tape, a primary storage medium for digital as well as analogue information, is very vulnerable to physical deterioration, usually in the form of separation of the signal (the encoded information itself) from the substrate (the tape on which the thin layer of bits reside). Tapes need to be "exercised" (wound and rewound) to maintain even tension and to ensure that the signal is not separating. Tapes also need to be reformatted from time to time, though rates of deterioration are surprisingly variable (as little as five years in some cases) and so the only sure way to know tapes are sound is by frequent and labor-intensive examinations. CDs are also known to suffer from physical degradation, also in annoyingly unpredictable ways and time frames. (Preservationists have to rely on predictable rates of loss if they are to develop preservation strategies that go beyond hand-crafted solutions for single-item treatments. Given the scale of digital information that deserves preservation, all preservation strategies will ultimately need to be automated in whole or in part to be effective.) Information stored on hard drives is generally less prone to media degradation. But these media have not been in use long enough for there to be meaningful data about how they have performed over the decades. Finally, a storage medium may itself be physically intact and still carry information, or signal, that has suffered degradation – tape that has been demagnetized is such an example.

Hardware/software obsolescence: Data can be perfectly intact physically on a storage medium and yet be unreadable because the hardware and software – the playback machine and the code in which the data are written – are obsolete. We know a good deal about hardware obsolescence and its perils already from the numerous defunct playback machines that "old" audio and visual resources required, such as Beta video equipment, 16 mm home movie projectors, and numerous proprietary dictation machines. The problem of software obsolescence may be newer, but it is chiefly the proliferation of software codes, and their rapid supersession by the next release, that makes this computer software concern intractable. In the case of software, which comprises the operating system, the application, and the format, there are multiple layers that each require attending to when preservation strategies, such as those listed below, are developed.

There are currently four strategies under various phases of research, development, and deployment for addressing the problems of media degradation and hardware/software obsolescence (Greenstein and Smith 2002).

- *Migration*. Digital information is transferred, or rewritten, from one hardware/software configuration to a more current one over time as the old formats are superseded by new ones. Often, a digital repository where data are stored will reformat or "normalize" data going into the repository; that is, the repository will put the data into a standard format that can be reliably managed over time. As necessary and cost-effective as this process may be in the long run, it can be expensive and time-consuming. In addition, digital files translated into another format will lose some information with each successive reformatting (loss similar to that of translations from one language to another), ranging from formatting or presentation information to potentially more serious forms of loss. Migration works best for simple data formats and does not work well at all for multimedia objects. It is the technique most commonly deployed today and it shows considerable reliability with ASCII text and some numeric databases of the sort that financial institutions use.

- *Emulation*. Emulation aims to preserve the look and feel of a digital object, that is, to preserve the functionality of the software as well as the information content of the object. It requires that information about the encoding and hardware environments be fully documented and stored with the object itself so that it can be emulated or essentially recreated on successive generations of hardware/software (though, of course, if that information is itself digital, further problems of accessibility to that information must also be anticipated). Emulation for preservation is currently only in the research phase. People are able to emulate retrospectively recently deceased genres of digital objects – such as certain computer games – but not prospectively for objects to be read on unknown machines and software programs in the distant future. Many in the field doubt that proprietary software makers will ever allow their software code to accompany objects, as stipulated by emulation, and indeed some in the software industry say that documentation is never complete enough to allow for the kind of emulation 100 or 200 years out that would satisfy a preservation demand (Rothenberg 1999; Bearman 1999; Holdsworth and Wheatley 2000). Perhaps more to the point, software programs that are several decades or centuries old may well be no more accessible to contemporary users than medieval manuscripts are accessible to present-day readers who have not been trained to read medieval Latin in a variety of idiosyncratic hands. Nonetheless, emulation remains a tantalizing notion that continues to attract research dollars.
- *Persistent object preservation*. A relatively new approach being tested by the National Archives and Records Administration for electronic records such as e-mails, persistent object preservation (POP) "entails explicitly declaring the properties (e.g., content, structure, context, presentation) of the original digital information that ensure its persistence" (Greenstein and Smith 2002). It envisions wrapping a digital object with the information necessary to recreate it on current software (not the original software envisioned by emulation). This strategy has been successfully tested in its research phase and the Archives is now developing an implementation program for it. At present it seems most promising for digital information objects such as official records and other highly structured genres that do not require extensive normalization, or changing it to bring it into a common preservation norm upon deposit into the repository. Ironically, this approach is conceptually related to the efforts of some digital artists, creating very idiosyncratic and "un-normalizable" digital creations, who are making declarations at the time of creation on how to recreate the art at some time in the future. They do so by specifying which features of the hardware and

software environment are intrinsic and authentic, and which are fungible and need not be preserved (such things as screen resolution, processing speed, and so forth, that can affect the look and feel of the digital art work) (Thibodeau 2002; Mayfield 2002).

- *Technology preservation.* This strategy addresses future problems of obsolescence by preserving the digital object together with the hardware, operating system, and program of the original. While many will agree that, for all sorts of reasons, someone somewhere should be collecting and preserving all generations of hardware and software in digital information technology, it is hard to imagine this approach as much more than a technology museum attempting production-level work, doomed to an uncertain future. It is unlikely to be scalable as an everyday solution for accessing information on orphaned platforms, but it is highly likely that something like a museum of old technology, with plentiful documentation about the original hardware and software, will be important for future digital archaeology and data mining. Currently, digital archaeologists are able, with often considerable effort, to rescue data from degraded tapes and corrupted (or erased) hard drives. With some attention now to capturing extensive information about successive generations of hardware and software, future computer engineers should be able to get some information off the old machines.

The preservation and access trade-offs for digital information are similar to those for analogue. To make an informed decision about how to preserve a embrittled book whose pages are crumbling or spine is broken, for example, one must weigh the relative merits of aggressive and expensive conservation treatment to preserve the book as an artifact, versus the less expensive option of reformatting the book's content onto microfilm or scanning it, losing most of the information integral to the artifact as physical object in the process. One always needs to identify the chief values of a given resource to decide between a number of preservation options. In this case, the question would be whether one values the artifactual or the informational content more highly. This consideration would apply equally in the digital realm: some of the technologies described above will be cheaper, more easily automated, and in that sense more scalable over time than others. Migration appears to be suitable for simpler formats in which the look and feel matters less and in which loss of information at the margins is an acceptable risk. The other approaches have not been tested yet in large scale over several decades, but the more options we have for ensuring persistence, the likelier we are to make informed decisions about what we save and how. There is no silver bullet for preserving digital information, and that may turn out to be good news in the long run.

Crucial Dependencies and Their Implications for the Humanities

Preservation by benign neglect has proven an amazingly robust strategy over time, at least for print-on-paper. One can passively manage a large portion of library collections fairly cheaply. One can put a well-catalogued book on a shelf in good storage conditions and expect to be able to retrieve it in 100 years in fine shape for use if no one has called it from the shelf. But neglect in the digital realm is never benign. Neglect of digital data is a death sentence. A digital object needs to be optimized for preservation at the time of its creation (and often again at the time of its deposit into a repository), and then it must be conscientiously managed over time if it is to stand a chance of being used in the future.

The need for standard file formats and metadata and the role of data creators

All the technical strategies outlined above are crucially dependent on standard file formats and metadata schemas for the creation and persistence of digital objects. File formats that are proprietary are often identified as being especially at risk, because they are in principle dependent on support from an enterprise that may go out of business. Even a format so widely used that it is a *de facto* standard, such as Adobe Systems, Inc.'s portable document format (PDF), is treated with great caution by those responsible for persistence. The owner of a such a *de facto* standard has no legal obligation to release its source code or any other proprietary information in the event that it goes bankrupt or decides to stop supporting the format for one reason or another (such as creating a better and more lucrative file format).

Commercial interests are not always in conflict with preservation interests, but when they are, commercial interests must prevail if the commerce is to survive. For that reason, the effort to develop and promote adoption of non-proprietary software, especially so-called open source code, is very strong among preservationists. (Open source, as opposed to proprietary, can be supported by non-commercial as well as commercial users.) But to the extent that commercial services are often in a better position to support innovation and development efforts, the preservation community must embrace both commercial and non-commercial formats. While preservationists can declare which standards and formats they would like to see used, dictating to the marketplace, or ignoring it altogether, is not a promising solution to this problem. One way to ensure that important but potentially vulnerable proprietary file formats are protected if they are orphaned is for leading institutions with a preservation mandate – national libraries, large research institutions, or government archives – to develop so-called fail-safe agreements with software makers that allow the code for the format to go into receivership or be deeded over to a trusted third party. (For more on file formats, see chapter 32, this volume.)

Metadata schemas – approaches to describing information assets for access, retrieval, preservation, or internal management – is another area in which there is a delicate balance between what is required for ease of access (and of creation) and what is required to ensure persistence. Extensive efforts have been made by librarians, archivists, and scholars to develop sophisticated markup schemes that are preservation-friendly, such as the Text Encoding Initiative (TEI) *Guidelines*, which were first expressed in SGML, or Encoded Archival Description, which, like the current instantiation of the TEI, is written in XML, and open for all communities, commercial and non-commercial alike. The barriers to using these schemas can be high, however, and many authors and creators who understand the importance of creating good metadata nevertheless find these schema too complicated or time-consuming to use consistently. It can be frustrating to find out that there are best practices for the creation of preservable digital objects, but that those practices are prohibitively labor-intensive for most practitioners.

The more normalized and standard a digital object is, the easier it is for a digital repository to take it in (a process curiously called "ingest"), to manage it over time, and to provide the objects back to users in their original form. Indeed, most repositories under development in libraries and archives declare that they will assume responsibility for persistence only if the objects they receive are in certain file formats accompanied by certain metadata. This is in sharp contrast to the more straightforward world of books, photographs, or maps, where one can preserve the artifact without having to catalogue it first. Boxes of unsorted and undescribed sources can languish for years before being discovered, and once described or catalogued, they can have a productive life as a resource. Although fully searchable text could, in theory, be retrieved without much metadata in the future, it is hard to imagine how a complex or multimedia digital object that goes into storage of any kind could ever survive, let alone be discovered and used, if it were not accompanied by good metadata. This creates very large up-front costs for digital preservation, both in time and money, and it is not yet clear who is obligated to assume those costs.

For non-standard or unsupported formats and metadata schemas, digital repositories might simply promise that they will deliver back the bits as they were received (that is, provide physical preservation) but will make no such promises about the legibility of the files (that is, not guarantee logical preservation). Though developed in good faith, these policies can be frustrating to creators of complex digital objects, or to those who are not used to or interested in investing their own time in preparing their work for permanent retention. This is what publishers and libraries have traditionally done, after all. Some ask why should it be different now.

There is no question that a digital object's file format and metadata schema greatly affect its persistence and how it will be made available in the future. This crucial dependency of digital information on format and markup begs the question of who should pay for file preparation and what economic model will support this expensive enterprise. Who are the stakeholders in digital preservation, and what are their roles in this new information landscape? There is now an interesting negotiation under way between data creators and distributors on the one hand, and libraries on the other, about who will bear the costs of ingest. Various institutions of higher learning that are stepping up to the challenge of digital preservation are working out a variety of local models that bear watching closely (see below, the section on solutions and current activities).

Need for early preservation action and the role of copyright

Regardless of the outcome, it seems clear that those who create intellectual property in digital form need to be more informed about what is at risk if they ignore longevity issues *at the time of creation*. This means that scholars should be attending to the information resources crucial to their fields by developing and adopting the document standards vital for their research and teaching, with the advice of preservationists and computer scientists where appropriate. The examples of computing-intensive sciences such as genomics that have developed professional tracks in informatics might prove fruitful for humanists as more and more computing power is applied to humanistic inquiry and pedagogy. Such a function would not be entirely new to the humanities; in the nineteenth century, a large number of eminent scholars became heads of libraries and archives in an age when a scholar was the information specialist *par excellence*.

One of the crucial differences between the information needs of scientists and those of humanists is that the latter tend to use a great variety of sources that are created outside the academy and that are largely protected by copyright. Indeed, there is probably no type of information created or recorded by human beings that could not be of value for humanities research at some time, and little of it may be under the direct control of the researchers who most value it for its research potential. The chief concern about copyright that impinges directly on preservation is the length of copyright protection that current legislation extends to the rights holders – essentially, the life of the creator plus 70 years (or more) (Copyright Office, website). Why that matters to preservation goes back to the legal regime that allows libraries and archives to preserve materials that are protected by copyright. Institutions with a preservation mission receive or buy information – books, journals, manuscripts, maps – to which they may have no intellectual rights. But rights over the physical objects themselves do transfer, and the law allows those institutions to copy the information in those artifacts for the purposes of preservation.

This transfer of property rights to collecting institutions breaks down with the new market in digital information. Publishers and distributors of digital information very seldom sell their wares. They license them. This means that libraries no longer own the journals, databases, and other digital intellectual property to which they provide access, and they have no incentive to preserve information that they essentially rent. Because publishers are not in the business of securing and preserving information "in perpetuity," as the phrase goes, there is potentially a wealth of valuable digital resources that no institution is claiming to preserve in this new information landscape. Some libraries, concerned about the potentially catastrophic loss of primary sources and scholarly litera- ture, have successfully negotiated "preservation clauses" in their licensing agreements, stipulating that publishers give them physical copies (usually CDs) of the digital data if they cease licensing it, so that they can have perpetual access to what they paid for. While CDs are good for current access needs, few libraries consider them to be archival media. Some commercial and non-commercial publishers of academic literature have forged experimental agreements with libraries, ensuring that in the event of a business failure, the digital files of the publisher will go to the library.

It is natural that a bibliocentric culture such as the academy has moved first on the issue of what scholars themselves publish. The greater threat to the historical record, however, is not to the secondary literature on which publishers and libraries are chiefly focused. The exponential growth of visual resources and sound recordings in the past 150 years has produced a wealth of primary source materials in audiovisual formats to which humanists will demand access in the future. It is likely that most of these resources, from performing arts to moving image, photographs, music, radio and television broadcasting, geospatial objects, and more, are created for the marketplace and are under copyright protection (Lyman and Varian 2000).

Efforts have barely begun to negotiate with the major media companies and their trade associations to make film and television studios, recording companies, news photo services, digital cartographers, and others aware of their implied mandate to preserve their corporate digital assets for the greater good of a common cultural heritage. As long as those cultural and intellectual resources are under the control of enterprises that do not know about and take up their preservation mandate, there is a serious risk of major losses for the future, analogous to the fate of films in the first 50 years of their existence. More than 80 percent of silent films made in the United States and 50 percent made before 1950 are lost, presumably for ever. Viewing film as "commercial product," the studios had no interest in retaining them after their productive life, and libraries and archives had no interest in acquiring them on behalf of researchers. It is critical that humanists start today to identify the digital resources that may be of great value now or in the future so that they can be captured and preserved before their date of expiration arrives.

Need to define the values of the digital object and the role of the humanist

Among the greatest values of digital information technologies for scholars and students is the ability of digital information to transform the very nature of inquiry. Not bound to discrete physical artifacts, digital information is available anywhere at any time (dependent on connectivity). Through computing applications that most computer users will never understand in fine grain, digital objects can be easily manipulated, combined, erased, and cloned, all without leaving the physical traces of tape, erasure marks and whiteouts, the tell-tale shadow of the photocopied version, and other subtle physical clues that apprise us of the authenticity and provenance, or origin, of the photograph or map we hold in our hands.

Inquiring minds who need to rely on the sources they use to be authentic – for something to be what it purports to be – are faced with special concerns in the digital realm, and considerable work is being done in this area to advance our trust in digital sources and to develop digital information literacy among users (Bearman and Trant 1998; CLIR 2000). Where this issue of the malleability of digital information most affects humanistic research and preservation, beyond the crucial issue of authenticity, is that of fixity and stability. While the genius of digital objects is their ability to be modified for different purposes, there are many reasons why information must be fixed and stable at some point to be reliable in the context of research and interpretation. For example, to the extent that research and interpretation builds on previous works, both primary and secondary, it is important for the underlying sources of an interpretation or scientific experiment or observation to be accessible to users in the form in which it was cited by the creator. It would be useless to have an article proposing a new interpretation of the Salem witch trials rely on diary sources that are not accessible to others to investigate and verify. But when writers cite as their primary sources web-based materials and the reader can find only a dead link, that is, in effect, the same thing.

To the extent that the pursuit of knowledge in any field builds upon the work of others, the chain of reference and ease of linking to reference sources are crucial. Whose responsibility is it to maintain the persistence of links in an author's article or a student's essay? Somehow, we expect the question of persistence to be taken care of by some vital but invisible infrastructure, not unlike the water that comes out of the tap when we turn the knob. Clearly, that infrastructure does not yet exist. But even if it did, there are still nagging issues about persistence that scholars and researchers need to resolve, such as the one known as "versioning," or deciding which iteration of a dynamic and changing resource should be captured and curated for preservation. This is a familiar problem to those who work in broadcast media, and digital humanists can profit greatly from the sophisticated thinking that has gone on in audiovisual archives for generations.

The problem of persistent linking to sources has larger implications for the growth of the humanities as a part of academic life, and for the support of emerging trends in scholarship and teaching. Until publishing a journal article, a computer model, or a musical analysis in digital form is seem as persistent and therefore a potentially long-lasting contribution to the chain of knowledge creation and use, few people will be attracted to work for reward and tenure in these media, no matter how superior the media may be for the research into and expression of an idea.

Solutions and Current Activities

There has been considerable activity in both the basic research communities (chiefly among computer scientists and information scientists) and at individual institutions (chiefly libraries and federal agencies) to address many of the critical technical issues of building and sustaining digital repositories for long-term management and persistence. The private sector, while clearly a leading innovator in information technologies, both in the development of hardware and software and in the management of digital assets such as television, film, and recorded sound, has not played a leading public role in the development of digital preservation systems. That is primarily because the time horizons of the preservation community and of the commercial sectors are radically different. Most data storage systems in the private sector aim for retention of data for no more than five to ten years (the latter not being a number that a data storage business will commit to). The time horizon of preservation for libraries, archives, and research institutions must include many generations of inquiring humans, not just the next two generations of hardware or software upgrades.

Because digital preservation is so complex and expensive, it is unlikely that digital repositories will spring up in the thousands of institutions that have traditionally served as preservation centers for books. Nor should they. In a networked environment in which one does not need access to a physical object to have access to information, the relationship between ownership (and physical custody) of information and access to it will be transformed. Within the research and nonprofit communities, it is likely that the system of digital preservation repositories, or digital archives, will be distributed among a few major actors that work on behalf of a large universe of users. They will be, in other words, part of the so-called public goods information economy that research and teaching have traditionally relied upon for core services such as preservation and collection building.

Among the major actors in digital archives will be academic disciplines whose digital information assets are crucial to the field as a whole. Examples include organizations such as the Inter-university Consortium for Political and Social Research (ICPSR), which manages social science datasets, and the Human Genome Data Bank, which preserves genetic data. Both are supported directly by the disciplines themselves and through federal grants. The data in these archives are not necessarily complex, but they are highly structured and the depositors are responsible for preparing the data for deposit. JSTOR, a non-commercial service that preserves and provides access to digital versions of key scholarly journals, is another model of a preservation enterprise designed to meet the needs of researchers. It is run on behalf of researchers and financially supported by libraries through subscriptions. (Its start-up costs were provided by a private foundation.)

Some large research university libraries, such as the University of California, Harvard University, Massachusetts Institute of Technology, and Stanford University, are beginning to develop and deploy digital repositories that will be responsible for some circumscribed portion of the digital output of their faculties. Another digital library leader, Cornell, has recently taken under its wing the disciplinary pre-print archive developed to serve the high-energy physics community and its need for rapid dissemination of information among the small but geographically far-flung members of that field. In the sciences, there are several interesting models of digital information being created, curated, and preserved by members of the discipline, among which arXiv.org is surely the best known. This model appears difficult to emulate in the humanities because arts and humanities disciplines do not create shared information resources that are then used by many different research teams. Nevertheless, where redundant collections, such as journals and slide libraries, exist across many campuses, subscription-based services are being developed to provide access to and preserve those resources through digital surrogates. Examples include JSTOR, AMICO, and ARTstor, now under development. The economies of scale can be achieved only if the libraries and museums that subscribe to these services believe that the provider will persistently manage the digital surrogates and that they are therefore able to dispose of extra copies of journals or slides.

Learned societies may be a logical locus of digital archives, as they are trusted third parties within a field and widely supported by members of the communities they serve. But they are not, as a rule, well positioned to undertake the serious capital expenditures that repository services require. That seems to be the reason why these subscription-based preservation and access services have appeared in the marketplace.

The Library of Congress (LC), which is the seat of the Copyright Office and receives for inclusion in its collections one or more copies of all works deposited for copyright protection, is beginning to grapple with the implications of digital deposits and what they mean for the growth of the Library's collections. (At present, with close to 120 million items in its collections, it is several times larger than other humanities collections in the United States.) LC is developing a strategy to build a national infrastructure for the preservation of digital heritage that would leverage the existing and future preservation activities across the nation (and around the globe) to ensure that the greatest number of people can have persistent rights-protected access to that heritage. The National Archives is also working to acquire and preserve the digital output of the federal government, though this will entail an expenditure of public resources for preservation that is unprecedented in a nation that prides itself on its accountability to its people.

The final word about major actors in preservation belongs to the small group of visionary private collectors that have fueled the growth of great humanities collections for centuries. The outstanding exemplar of the digital collector is Brewster Kahle, who has designed and built the Internet Archive, which captures and preserves a large number of publicly available sites. While the visible and publicly available Web that the Internet Archive harvests is a small portion of the total Web (Lyman 2002), the Archive has massive amounts of culturally rich material. Kahle maintains the Archive as a preservation repository – that is its explicit mission – and in that sense his enterprise is a beguiling peek into the future of collecting in the digital realm.

Selection for Preservation

While much work remains to ensure that digital objects of high cultural and research value persist into the future, many experts are cautiously optimistic that, with enough funding and will, technical issues will be addressed and acceptable solutions will be found. The issue that continues to daunt the most thoughtful among those engaged in preservation strategies is selection: how to determine what, of the massive amount of information available, should be captured and stored and managed over time.

In theory, there is nothing created by the hands of mankind that is not of potential research value for humanities scholars, even the humblest scrap of data – tax records, laundry lists, porn sites, personal websites, weblogs, and so forth. Technology optimists who believe that it will be possible to "save everything" through automated procedures have advocated doing so. Some teenager is out there today, they point out, who will be president of the United States in 30 years, and she no doubt already has her own website. If we save all websites we are bound to save hers. If completeness of the historical record is a value that society should support, then saving everything that can be saved appears to be the safest policy to minimize the risk of information loss.

There may well be compelling social reasons to capture everything from the Web and save it forever – if it were possible and if there were no legal and privacy issues. (Most of the Web, the so-called Deep Web, is not publicly available, and many copyright experts tend to think that all non-federal sites are copyright-protected.) Certainly, everything created by public officials in the course of doing their business belongs in the public record, in complete and undistorted form. Further, there are the huge and expensive stores of data about our world – from census data to the petabytes of data sent back to Earth from orbiting satellites – that may prove invaluable in future scientific problem solving. On the other hand, humanists have traditionally valued the enduring quality of an information object as much as the quantity of raw data it may yield. There is reason to think that humanists in the future will be equally interested in the depth of information in a source as they are in the sheer quantity of it. Indeed, some historians working in the modern period already deplore the promiscuity of paper-based record making and keeping in contemporary life.

But the digital revolution has scarcely begun, and the humanities have been slower to adopt the technology and test its potential for transforming the nature of inquiry than have other disciplines that rely more heavily on quantitative information. Some fields – history is a good example – have gone through periods when quantitative analysis has been widely used, but this was before the advent of computing power on today's scale. If and when humanists discover the ways that computers can truly change the work of research and teaching, then we can expect to see the growth of large and commonly used databases that will demand heavy investments in time and money and that will, therefore, beg the question of persistence.

We will not be able in the future to rely on traditional assessments of value for determining what deserves preservation. In the digital realm, there will be no uniqueness, no scarcity, no category of "rare." There will remain only the signal categories of evidential value, aesthetic value, and associational value, the very criteria that are, by their subject-ivity, best assessed by scholar experts. The role of humanists in building and preserving collections of high research value will become as important as it was in the Renaissance or the nineteenth century. Unlike those eras, however, when scholars could understand the value of sources as they have revealed themselves over time, there is no distinction between collecting "just in case" something proves later to be valuable, and "just in time" for someone to use now. Scholars cannot leave it to later generations to collect materials created today. They must assume a more active role in the stewardship of research collections than they have played since the nineteenth century or, indeed, ever.

Digital Preservation as a Strategy for Preserving Non-digital Collections

There seems little doubt that materials that are "born digital" need to be preserved in digital form. Yet another reason why ensuring the persistence of digital information is crucial to the future of humanities scholarship and teaching is that a huge body of very fragile analogue materials demands digital reformatting for preservation. Most moving image and recorded sound sources exist on media that are fragile, such as nitrate film, audio tapes, or lacquer disks, and they all require reformatting on to fresher media to remain accessible for use. Copying analogue information to another analogue format results in significant loss of signal within a generation or two (imagine copying a video of a television program over and over), so most experts believe that reformatting onto digital media is the safest strategy. Digital reformatting does not result in significant (in most cases in *any*) loss of information.

For those who prize access to the original source materials for research and teaching, the original artifact is irreplaceable. For a large number of other uses, an excellent surrogate or access copy is fine. Digital technology can enhance the preservation of artifacts by providing superlative surrogates of original sources while at the same time protecting the artifact from overuse. (See chapter 32, this volume.)

All this means that, as creators and consumers of digital information, humanists are vitally interested in digital preservation, both for digital resources and for the abundance of valuable but physically fragile analogue collections that must rely on digitization. Given the extraordinary evanescence of digital information, it is crucial now for them to engage the copyright issues, to develop the economic models for building and sustaining the core infrastructure that will support persistent access, and, most proximate to their daily lives, to ensure that students and practitioners of the humanities are appropriately trained and equipped to conduct research, write up results for dissemination, and enable a new generation of students to engage in the open-ended inquiry into culture that is at the core of the humanistic enterprise.

ACKNOWLEDGMENTS

The author thanks Amy Friedlander, Kathlin Smith, and David Rumsey for their invaluable help.

REFERENCES

Bearman, David (1999). Reality and Chimeras in the Preservation of Electronic Records. *D-Lib Magazine* 5,4. At <http://www.dlib.org/dlib/april99/bearman/04bearman.html>.

Bearman, David and Jennifer Trant (1998). Authenticity of Digital Resources: Towards a Statement of Requirements in the Research Process. *D-Lib Magazine* (June). At <http://www.dlib.org/dlib/june98/06bearman.html>.

Copyright Office. Circulars 15 and 15a. Accessed April 27, 2004. At <http://www.loc.gov/copyright/circs/circ15.pdf> (CLIR) <http://www.loc.gov/copyright/circs/circ15a.pdf>.

Council on Library and Information Resources; (2000). *Authenticity in a Digital Environment*. Washington, DC: Council on Library and Information Resources. At <http://www.clir.org/pubs/reports/pub92/contents.html>.

Greenstein, Daniel and Abby Smith (2002). Digital Preservation in the United States: Survey of Current Research, Practice, and Common Understandings. At <http://www.digitalpreservation.gov>.

Holdsworth, David and Paul Wheatley (2000). Emulation, Preservation and Abstraction. CAMiLEON Project, University of Leeds. At <http://129.11.152.25/CAMiLEON/dh/ep5.html>.

Lyman, Peter (2002). Archiving the World Wide Web. In *Building a National Strategy for Digital Preservation: Issues in Digital Media Archiving*. Washington, DC: Council on Library and Information Resources and the Library of Congress. At <http://www.clir.org/pubs/reports/pub106/contents.html>; and <http://www.digitalpreservation.gov/ndiipp/repor/repor_back_web.html>.

Lyman, Peter, and Hal R. Varian (2000). How Much Information? At <http://www.sims.berkeley.edu/how-much-info>.

Mayfield, Kedra (2002). How to Preserve Digital Art. *Wired* (July 23). At <http://www.wired.com/news/culture/0,1284,53712,00.html>.

Price, Laura and Abby Smith (2000). *Managing Cultural Assets from a Business Perspective*. Washington, DC: Council on Library and Information Resources. At <http://www.clir.org/pubs/reports/pub90/contents.html>.

Rothenberg, Jeff (1999). *Avoiding Technological Quicksand: Finding a Viable Technical Foundation for Digital Preservation*. Washington, DC: Council on Library and Information Resources. At <http://www.clir.org/pubs/reports/pub77/contents.html>.

Thibodeau, Kenneth (2002). Overview of Technological Approaches to Digital Preservation and Challenges in Coming Years. In *The State of Digital Preservation: An International Perspective. Conference Proceedings. Documentation Abstracts, Inc., Institutes for Information Science Washington, DC, April 24–25, 2002.* Washington, DC: Council on Library and Information Resources. At <http://www.clir.org/pubs/reports/pub107/contents.html>.

Websites of Organizations and Projects Noted

Art Museum Image Consortium (AMICO). <www.amico.org>.

ARTstor. <http://www.mellon.org/programs/otheractivities/ARTstor/ARTstor.htm>.

ArXiv.org. <www.arXiv.org>.

Internet Archive. <www.archive.org>.

Inter-university Consortium for Political and Social Research (ICPSR). <www.icpsr.umich.edu>.

JSTOR. <www.jstor.org>.

Library of Congress. The National Digital Information and Infrastructure Preservation Program of the Library of Congress is available at <http://www.digitalpreservation.gov>.

National Archives and Record Administration (NARA). Electronic records Archives. <http://www.archives.gov/electronic_records_archives>.

For Further Reading

On the technical, social, organizational, and legal issues related to digital preservation, the best source continues to be *Preserving Digital Information: Report of the Task Force on Archiving of Digital Information* (Washington, DC, and Mountain View, CA: Commission of Preservation and Access and the Research Libraries Group, Inc.). Available at <http://www.rlg.org/ArchTF>.

Digital preservation is undergoing rapid development, and few publications remain current for long. To keep abreast of developments in digital preservation, see the following list, which themselves regularly digest or cite the latest information on the subject and present the leading research of interest to humanists on the subject:

D-Lib Magazine. <http://www.dlib.org>.
Council on Library and Information Resources (CLIR). <www.clir.org>.
Digital Library Federation (DLF). <www.diglib.org>.
National Science Foundation (NSF), Digital Libraries Initiative (DLI). <http://www.dli2.nsf.gov>.
National Library of Australia, Preserving Access to Digital Information (PADI). <www.nla.gov.au/padi/format/case.html>.

Index

Page references in *italics* refer to illustrations

creation of 3-D mock-ups of filmic spaces, 387

and databases, 393–5

development of software for searching images, 95

"Digital Hitchcock" project, 386–7

and DVDs, 392–4

feminist and gender theory, 384

history of, 383–4

pioneering work, 386–8

and point-of-view (POV) module, 389

and programming, 386

publication of *Film, Form and Culture* project, 389–90, 391–2

tools available to execute design and usability, 386

and World Wide Web, 385, 389

Finch, Alison, 242

first-person shooters (FPS), games, 425–6, 429

Fish, Stanley, 203, 277–8, 279, 373

"fixed format" scheme, 6

Flanagan, George, 157

Flanders, Julia, 250

Flash, 114, 528, 546

flatbed scanners, 498

Fogel, Robert and Engerman, Stanley, *Time on the Cross*, 57–8, 60, 61, 377

folksong, 104

Forced Migration Online (FMO) project, 496

Ford, John, 282

Fortier, Paul, 93, 369

Foucault, Michel, 283

fragile originals, digitization of, 492

Franklin, R.W., 310, 311, 312, 316

French New Wave, 383

Friedlander, Larry, 122, 124

Frye, Northrop, 261

Funerall Elegie for William Peter, 282

Furbank. N. and Owens, W.R., 283, 285, 286–7

fuzzy matching, 496

Galison, Peter, 263, 264

Games, 453; *see also* computer games

Gary, Romain, 285

GATE system, 298, 511

Geertz, Clifford, 255

Gelernter, David, 530

GenCode project, 225–6, 227

Generalized Markup Language *see* GML

generative aesthetics, 434, 437–40

genre, 214

geographic information system *see* GIS

Gershenfeld, Neil, 127

Gertrude Stein Repertory Theater (GSRT), 128

Getty Art History Information Program, 16

Gibson, William

Count Zero, 465–6

Neuromancer, 115

Gilder, George, 117

GIS (geographic information system), 53, 355, 368, 376

and archaeologists, 23–4, 26

historical, 66

GML (Generalized Markup Language), 221, 226, 313

Golden Books, 391–2

Golder, Robert, 123

Goldfarb, Charles, 221, 222, 226

Goodman, Nelson, 257, 259

Google, 74

grammar, 79–80

robotic poetics, 457–65

Graph View Software, 375

graphic design, 441

graphical user interface (GUI), 368, 375, 523, 525, 526, 527, 539

Graphical/Auditional Dimension, 213–14

graphics, 526–7

and archaeologists, 23–4

and art history, 34–7

first computers with capabilities for, 113

Graphics Communications Association (GCA), 221, 225

GenCode project, 225–6, 227

Greenblatt, Stephen, 319

Greenstein, Daniel *A Historian's Guide to Computing*, 60–1

Grenville, Kate, 254

Griffith in Context, 387

Gromala, Diane, 127

GUI *see* graphical user interface

Guidelines for Electronic Editions, 308

Guidelines for Scholarly Editing, 310

Gutman, Herbert, 57–8

Hacking, Ian, 265

Hamlet on the Ramparts, 350

Hanauer, D., 373

handwriting recognition, 489

hard disk drives (HDD), 149–50, 151

hardware obsolescence, 579

Hardwick, Elizabeth, 399

Hart, Michael, 244, 245

Harvard Classics Department, 48–53

Harvard University Press, 310, 312

modeling, 254–65
  and analogy, 259
  background, 255–7
  and computational tractability, 256, 258
  definition, 255
  and diagram, 261–2
  distinction between "model" and "idea," 256–7
  and experiment, 264–5
  of and for, 255, 260
  and manipulability, 256–7, 258
  and mapping, 262–3
  philological analysis of related terms, 258–65
  and representation, 259–61
  and simulation, 263–4
  Temporal, 433–4, 442–6
  and thematic research collections, 355–6
  as tool of research, 256
modems, 150, 151
Modern Language Association (MLA), 319
  Committee on Scholarly Editions, 308, 315
  Guidelines for Electronic Editions, 308
  Guidelines for Scholarly Editing, 310
Mohler, Frank, 123–4
MonoConc, 510
Monuments and Dust, 354
Moore, Gordon E., 50
Morgan, Augustus de, 5
Morgan, Mary S., 264
morpho-syntactic annotation *see* part-of-speech
  tagging
morphology, 79, 213
Morton, Andrew, 5
Mosaic, 13, 38
Mosteller, F., 5
motherboard, 147, 148
motion capture technology, 124
Mouthrop, Stuart, 245
MP3, 97, 99, 116
MPEG, 115
MSXML, 514–15
Mullaly, Edward, 122
Multilevel Annotation, Tools Engineering
  (MATE) project, 298
multimedia, 108–18
  academic issues in study of, 116–17
  definition, 108–10
  history of, 112–16
  and interactivity, 110
  theories and histories of, 117
  types of, 111–12
MULTITEXT project, 298
multivariant narratives, 415–29

  chunking and directed linking, 418–19
  and *The Impermanence Agent*, 428
  variable discourse, 419–22
  and variable plot, 423–7
  variable point of view, 422–3
Mulvey, Laura, 384
Mumford, Lewis *Technics and Civilization*, 152,
  153, 154,155
Murray, Janet H., 117, 418
Muse, 397, 400, 404, 406
MuseData, 101
Museum Computer Network, 39
museums, 22, 41, 348, 577
music, 97–105, 127
  computer applications, 103–4
  and databases, 100–2
  Digital Image Archive of Medieval Music
    (DIAMM), 104, 492
  information retrieval, 105
  and Internet, 97–8
  MIDI and MP3, 99
  notation software, 97, 98
  and optical music recognition (OMR), 97, 98–9
Music Index, 100
Musical Instrument Data Interchange (MIDI), 99
Musical Instrument digital interface (MIDI), 115,
  127
musicians, electronic, 127
Mutual Information (MI) score, 302
Myst (computer game), 111, 114

naming of files *see* file- naming scheme
Napster, 97, 390
narratives
  definition, 417
  effect of invention of writing and printing
    press, 415
  properties of digital media as most relevant to,
    416–17
  see also multivariant narratives
National Academies Press, 546, 552, 554–5
National Archaeological Database of US public
  archaeological sites, 23
National Archives and Records Administration,
  580, 587
National Endowment for the Humanities, 50,
  232, 392
National Information Standards Organization
  (US), 567, 572
National Institute of Health, 50
National Science Digital Library (NSDL), 55
National Science Foundation (NSF), 50, 560